HANDBOOK OF ADOLESCENT LITERACY RESEARCH

HANDBOOK
OF ADOLESCENT
LITERACY RESEARCH

Edited by

LEILA CHRISTENBURY
RANDY BOMER
PETER SMAGORINSKY

THE GUILFORD PRESS
New York   London

© 2009 The Guilford Press
A Division of Guilford Publications, Inc.
72 Spring Street, New York, NY 10012
www.guilford.com

Printed in the United States of America

This book is printed on acid-free paper.

Last digit is print number: 9 8 7 6 5 4 3 2 1

Library of Congress Cataloging-in-Publication Data

Handbook of adolescent literacy research / edited by Leila Christenbury,
Randy Bomer, Peter Smagorinsky.
    p. cm.
  Includes bibliographical references and index.
  ISBN 978-1-59385-829-2 (hardcover : alk. paper)   1. Reading (Middle school)—
Handbooks, manuals, etc.   2. Reading (Secondary)—Handbooks, manuals, etc.
3. Literacy—Handbooks, manuals, etc.   I. Christenbury, Leila.   II. Bomer, Randy.
III. Smagorinsky, Peter.
  LB1632.H363 2009
  428.4071'2—dc22
                                                2008018309

About the Editors

Leila Christenbury, EdD, is Professor of English Education at Virginia Commonwealth University (VCU), Richmond. She is a past president of the National Council of Teachers of English (NCTE), a former editor of *English Journal*, and the author or coauthor of 10 books, including *Writing on Demand: Best Practices and Strategies for Success* and *Making the Journey: Being and Becoming a Teacher of English Language Arts* (now in its third edition). Her book *Retracing the Journey: Teaching and Learning in an American High School* is the 2008 recipient of both the Conference on English Education James N. Britton Award and the NCTE David H. Russell Award for Distinguished Research in the Teaching of English. Dr. Christenbury is a former member of the Steering Committee of the National Assessment of Educational Progress, and is the 1997 national recipient of the Rewey Belle Inglis Award for Outstanding Woman in English Education, as well as the 2000 recipient of VCU's University Award of Excellence. Most recently, she received the Distinguished Service Award from the NCTE. Dr. Christenbury is a frequent speaker on issues of English teaching and learning and has been featured and quoted on CNN and in the *New York Times, USA Today, Washington Post, Chicago Tribune, Baltimore Sun*, and *U.S. News & World Report*.

Randy Bomer, PhD, teaches in the Language and Literacy Studies Program in the College of Education at the University of Texas at Austin, where he also directs the Heart of Texas Writing Project. Formerly a middle and high school teacher, he has consulted with urban school districts across the United States. Dr. Bomer is the author of *Time for Meaning: Crafting Literate Lives in Middle and High School* and *For a Better World: Reading and Writing for Social Action*, and has written articles in *Teachers College Record, Research in the Teaching of English, English Education, Language Arts, Journal of Adolescent and Adult Literacy, Journal of Early Childhood Literacy*, and the *National Reading Conference Yearbook*, among other publications. He is a former president of the National Council of Teachers of English.

Peter Smagorinsky, PhD, teaches in the Department of Language and Literacy Education in the College of Education at the University of Georgia. He has published articles in the *American Journal of Education; Journal of Literacy Research; Mind, Culture, and Activity; Reading Research Quarterly; Research in the Teaching of English; Review of Educational Research; Written Communication*; and other journals, along with 14 books. Dr. Smagorinsky is past chair of the National Council of Teachers of English (NCTE) Standing Committee on Research, NCTE Assembly for Research, and the University of Oklahoma Research Council; past president of the National Conference on Research in Language and Literacy; past fellow and chair of the NCTE Research Foundation, and past coeditor of *Research in the Teaching of English*; he currently chairs the NCTE Research Forum. He is the 1999 recipient of the American Educational Research Association's Raymond B. Cattell Early Career Award for Programmatic Research, the Janet Emig Award from NCTE's Conference on English Education, the Association of Teacher Educators Distinguished Research in Teacher Education Award, and the University of Georgia Graduate School Outstanding Mentoring Award in Humanities and Fine and Applied Arts.

Contributors

Donna E. Alvermann, Department of Language and Literacy Education, University of Georgia, Athens, Georgia

Sana Ansari, College of Education, University of Illinois–Chicago, Chicago, Illinois

Arnetha F. Ball, School of Education, Stanford University, Stanford, California

Richard Beach, Department of Curriculum and Instruction, University of Minnesota–Twin Cities, Minneapolis, Minnesota

Anne Beaufort, Department of Interdisciplinary Arts and Sciences, University of Washington–Tacoma, Tacoma, Washington

Mary Jiron Belgarde, Department of Language, Literacy, and Sociocultural Studies, University of New Mexico, Albuquerque, New Mexico

Rebecca W. Black, Department of Education, University of California–Irvine, Irvine, California

Randy Bomer, Department of Curriculum and Instruction, University of Texas at Austin, Austin, Texas

David L. Bruce, Department of Learning and Instruction, University at Buffalo, The State University of New York, Buffalo, New York

Robert Burroughs, Department of Teacher Education, University of Cincinnati, Cincinnati, Ohio

Leila Christenbury, Department of Teaching and Learning, Virginia Commonwealth University, Richmond, Virginia

Jamal Cooks, College of Education, San Francisco State University, San Francisco, California

Antillana del Valle, Department of Curriculum and Instruction, University of Minnesota–Twin Cities, Minneapolis, Minnesota

María E. Fránquiz, Department of Curriculum and Instruction, University of Texas at Austin, Austin, Texas

Danling Fu, School of Teaching and Learning, College of Education, University of Florida, Gainesville, Florida

Jennifer M. Graff, Department of Language and Literacy Education, University of Georgia, Athens, Georgia

Cynthia Greenleaf, Strategic Literacy Initiative, WestEd, Oakland, California

Barbara J. Guzzetti, Department of Curriculum and Instruction, Arizona State University, Tempe, Arizona

Angela Hampton, Department of Curriculum and Instruction, University of Texas at Austin, Austin, Texas

Linda Harklau, Department of Language and Literacy Education, University of Georgia, Athens, Georgia

Holly Hungerford-Kresser, Department of Curriculum and Instruction, University of Texas at Arlington, Arlington, Texas

Sam M. Intrator, Department of Education and Child Study, Smith College, Northampton, Massachusetts

Larry R. Johannessen, Department of English, Northern Illinois University, DeKalb, Illinois

Jung Kim, College of Education, University of Illinois–Chicago, Chicago, Illinois

Robert Kunzman, School of Education, Indiana University, Bloomington, Indiana

Judith A. Langer, Department of Educational Theory and Practice, University at Albany, Albany, New York

Cynthia Lewis, Department of Curriculum and Instruction, University of Minnesota–Twin Cities, Minneapolis, Minnesota

Richard K. LoRé, Department of Liberal Arts, Southwestern Indian Polytechnic Institute, Albuquerque, New Mexico

Allan Luke, Faculty of Education, Queensland University of Technology, Brisbane, Queensland, Australia

Yolanda J. Majors, College of Education, University of Illinois–Chicago, Chicago, Illinois

James Marshall, Department of Language and Literacy Education, University of Georgia, Athens, Georgia

Carmen M. Martínez-Roldán, Department of Curriculum and Instruction, Arizona State University, Tempe, Arizona

Wayne Martino, Faculty of Education, University of Western Ontario, Ontario, Canada

Thomas M. McCann, Elmhurst Community Unit School District 205, Elmhurst, Illinois

Richard Meyer, Department of Language, Literacy, and Sociocultural Studies, University of New Mexico, Albuquerque, New Mexico

David O'Brien, Department of Curriculum and Instruction, University of Minnesota–Twin Cities, Minneapolis, Minnesota

Rachel Pinnow, Department of Language and Literacy Education, University of Georgia, Athens, Georgia

Joan A. Rhodes, Department of Teaching and Learning, Virginia Commonwealth University, Richmond, Virginia

Valerie J. Robnolt, Department of Teaching and Learning, Virginia Commonwealth University, Richmond, Virginia

Ruth Schoenbach, Strategic Literacy Initiative, WestEd, Oakland, California

Peter Smagorinsky, Department of Language and Literacy Education, University of Georgia, Athens, Georgia

Michael W. Smith, Department of Curriculum, Instruction, and Technology in Education, Temple University, Philadelphia, Pennsylvania

Constance Steinkuehler, Department of Curriculum and Instruction, University of Wisconsin–Madison, Madison, Wisconsin

Roger Stewart, Department of Literacy, Boise State University, Boise, Idaho

Jeffrey D. Wilhelm, Department of English, Boise State University, Boise, Idaho

Annette Woods, Faculty of Education, Queensland University of Technology, Brisbane, Queensland, Australia

Jo Worthy, Department of Curriculum and Instruction, University of Texas at Austin, Austin, Texas

Kathleen Blake Yancey, Department of English, Florida State University, Tallahassee, Florida

Michelle Zoss, Department of Middle–Secondary Education and Instructional Technology, Georgia State University, Atlanta, Georgia

Contents

Part I

OVERVIEW

CHAPTER 1

Introduction

LEILA CHRISTENBURY
RANDY BOMER
PETER SMAGORINSKY

When we three first conceptualized this *Handbook*, we spent some time talking about how we hoped this book would be immediately useful and make a substantial contribution to our current understanding of adolescents, the research that has been conducted, and that which is still needed regarding young people's literacy practices. We also looked at the current political and educational landscape and discussed how this *Handbook* might extend to a broader audience and have a wider mission. In an early memo to the almost 50 authors and coauthors who had been invited and who had agreed to write for the *Handbook*, we noted:

A range of factors contributes to the exigency of this volume. A number of current policy discussions in the United States have focused on adolescents, literacy, and schooling: the American Diploma Project; the Striving Readers programs proposed by the president, funded by Congress, and granted through the U.S. Department of Education; the desire in some quarters to bring the provisions of No Child Left Behind into high schools; studies by the National Endowment for the Arts that claim adolescents rarely read; the activity of fairly recently founded nonprofit organizations such as the Alliance for Excellent Education and the National Adolescent Literacy Coalition. These

developing conversations have whipped up a desire for quick answers sometimes and thoughtful evidence at other times, but they have certainly caused questions about adolescents and their literate lives to be asked with more urgency than has typically been the case. Interestingly, these events all occur at a moment when research into adolescent literacy has developed significantly over the past few decades—perhaps not into full maturity, but at least approaching a kind of adolescence. It seems that the time might be ripe to attempt to pull together the status of the field, to name where we have come and to look down the road as far as we can see from here.

Looking down the metaphorical road, we see a number of things. Although you, our readers, will certainly find within this volume a variety of voices and ideas, we also want you, along with those involved in the underlying policy and educational context, to notice that in this *Handbook* is a deliberate attempt to contextualize: In almost every chapter you will see a consistent thread of argument that neither *adolescent, literacy,* nor *research* is a simple, unified, unproblematic term. Each depends on particular kinds of contexts: Adolescent identity emerges in the culture in which young people's development takes place; literacy practices are afforded and constrained by what is available in their settings; and research is a cultural practice that reflects local goals and practices. Thus Part II of this *Handbook* recognizes that school is one important setting for literacy, one in which many readers will have special interest, perhaps the reason that most people come to this book in the first place. Part III, however, sets beside school other important contexts for literacy among adolescents, environments that circumscribe a much larger space for learning, knowing, and performing literacy. In Part IV, we see *adolescent* as referring to many different kinds of people—male; female; gay, lesbian, bisexual, transgendered, and queer (GLBTQ); African American; immigrant; Latina/o; Native American; and others—whose differences must be acknowledged and respected, not just because it is ethically right to do so but because it is analytically and empirically necessary.

That said, in this Introduction, we would like to set out our terms and our three areas of focus within this *Handbook of Adolescent Literacy Research*—that is, what we mean by the *adolescent,* how we define the field of *literacy,* and how we assess the limitations of *research.*

WHO IS THE ADOLESCENT?

Adolescence as a concept has a relatively short history. It became widely accepted as an idea and widely used as a term only in the late 19th and early 20th centuries and was buttressed in the United States and other Western countries by changes in child labor laws and in expectations of schooling (Kett, 1977; Modell & Goodman, 1990; Tyack, 1990). Adolescence is thus a modern—and even postmodern—concept that acknowledges the unique space between childhood and full adulthood. Although the ancients, Plato and Aristotle, certainly appreciated the significance of adolescence, particularly in the development of reasoning abilities, modern understanding has firmly moved away from the belief that adolescence is not so much a difficult and unpleasant transition, a stormy and stressful way station to adulthood (Hall, 1904), but is a legitimate and vital stage of human development that deserves our attention and our respect. Thus, adolescence is not typically characterized by

behavior disorders or even extremes (Lesko, 2001; Offer & Schonert-Reichl, 1992; Steinberg, 2001; Strauch, 2003), although that stereotype certainly persists in segments of popular culture and can be rightly critiqued as both myth and fiction (Vadeboncoeur & Stevens, 2005). (For a look at U.S. adolescence through the lens of cultural history, see Jon Savage's [2007] *Teenage.*) In addition, as every reader of this text also knows, adolescence is highly variable among cultures. Thus, being an adolescent—its roles, its responsibilities, its expectations, even its duration—is in Baghdad and Bahrain, Calcutta and Cairo, Melbourne and Miami very different in scope and content, not only in terms of culture but also, within that culture, in terms of economics, gender, sexual orientation, ethnicity, and other crucial factors.

That said, this volume addresses the postindustrial, postmodern Western world adolescent (see both Alvermann [Chapter 2] and Intrator & Kunzman [Chapter 3] in this volume for further exploration). Adolescence is not just a chronological time, often reduced to the span of the teen years, 13–19, with some leeway on either side, most commonly extended as 11–20. Adolescence is also not simply a developmental stage, with its centerpiece as puberty and one of its major psychological tasks independence from adults, particularly individuation from parents. It is also not a temporal zone of sorts after childhood and before adulthood. And, looking at the individual, adolescents are not all the same, nor do they share identical characteristics. Adolescence and adolescents are, as Lesko (2001) notes, characterized by nothing more than their complexity:

> Youth are simultaneously young and old, learning and learned, working and in school. This idea of time (that is, of past, present, and future) as holding seemingly opposing identities *simultaneously* is, I believe, a necessary dimension of a retheorizing of adolescence. (p. 197)

And this retheorizing is an ongoing event. Hersch (1999) spent 3 years with eight adolescents and tries, in *A Tribe Apart,* to capture the issues regarding young people. Hersch sees these youth as indeed *apart* but also as those who are connected and even wish to be more connected. Hersch urges adults not simply to study but also to listen to young people, and she insists that adolescents actually need more—not fewer—adults in their lives and need to have a positive relationship with them:

> It is a popular notion that adolescents careen out of control, are hypnotized by peer pressure or manipulated by demons for six years or so, and then if they don't get messed up or hurt or killed, they become sensible adults. That's ridiculous. . . . The turbulence of adolescence today comes not so much from rebellion as from the loss of communication between adults and kids, and from the lack of realistic, honest understanding of what the kids' world really looks like. (p. 365)

An adolescent's world has always had its own rules and boundaries and, particularly in this age of texting and instant messaging, is characterized by its own language, both as a traditional defense against outsiders (i.e., adults) and as a group identity-sharing. The latter is something in which most adolescents have historically engaged although the shape of it is varied in different generations. Today's adolescent, though, faces some challenges that were not part of previous generations: earlier physical maturation and later economic (and possibly emotional) independence. In today's schools, adolescents are the most tested group of young people in history, in most middle-class households the most regulated and scheduled, and a group that, as a whole, faces some real insecurity regarding societal stability, expectations, and pressures. For adolescent immigrants, people of color, and those in poverty, the playing field remains uneven. The same is true for teen girls and GLBTQ teens, and some even maintain that for adolescent males the climate is no longer welcoming (e.g., Sommers, 2000).

The challenges abound as do the proposed solutions. Yet, as Alvermann (Chapter 2, this volume) notes, in order to be effective as educators, we need to view adolescents not as individuals in crisis, and not in deficit, but as those who have a true "degree of agency" and whose expertise is something we can use and foster. Intrator and Kunzman (Chapter 3, this volume) make a case for a true dialogic relationship between adolescents and adults. Certainly in her return to high school

teaching, Christenbury (2007) found that even apparently straightforward classroom disputes regarding school curriculum were often characterized by her adolescent students as the adult teacher's failure to *listen*.

Adolescents in the first decade of the 21st century are somewhat definable although not, it appears, defined as accurately or thoughtfully as needed. The acceptance of them, both in and outside school contexts, as experts and authorities remains unfinished business. Reverting to stereotype, myth, and fiction, many adults—policymakers and educators included—would prefer to relegate young people to the status of adults-in-training who have not quite mastered their roles. One of their major roles, of course, is the practice of literacy, a topic to which we now turn.

HOW DO WE DEFINE LITERACY?

Time was when people were deemed literate when they could indicate their signature with an "X" (Reay, 1991). In today's world, literacy comprises so many competencies that even getting a grip on the construct can be a slippery process. In this section we attempt to review how notions of what it means to be literate have changed over time, and how people conceive of being literate early in the 21st century.

Dictionary definitions can help establish at least a populist sense of word meanings, if not those argued to fine points by researchers and theorists. Our *Merriam-Webster's 11th Collegiate Dictionary* (2003) defines *literacy* as "the quality or state of being literate," tracing the origins of the term to 1883. *Literate*, we then learn, comes from the 15th century and evolved from "Middle English *literat*, from Latin *litteratus*, marked with letters, *literate*, from *litterae*, letters, literature." From its origins in a term that references the written word, *literate* then more broadly came to refer to people who are "able to read and write." More recently, the term has come to indicate "having knowledge or competence," such as being computer literate, media literate, workplace literate, or being skilled in some other realm; ultimately, these proficiencies have spawned such terms as *computacy, mediacy,* and other neologisms. From this set of definitions, literacy's origins are clearly in the realm of letters, yet have evolved to refer to competencies of any kind. Although most people would agree that literacy concerns letters in some regard, others dispute any effort to expand the term's meaning to include fluency with other symbol systems or mediators.

Even within these broad perspectives, there is disagreement. For instance, it is not clear how to determine whether or not someone can "read." President Bill Clinton helped to accelerate the current emphasis on testing when he said during his 1997 State of the Union Address that "we must do more . . . to make sure every child can read well by the end of the third grade," a belief that framed the Reading Excellence Act (*www.ed.gov/ inits/FY99/1-read.html*). Among other things, this Act promised to "provide professional development for teachers based on the best research and practice." Yet reading specialists have profound differences on what constitutes the "best research and practice," leading to the highly contentious and divisive Reading Wars (see Allington & Woodside-Jiron, 1999) over both federal funding and the stature and wealth that follow from a federal endorsement. Given that researchers cannot agree on which evidence suggests that a person can read, which research approaches most usefully identify this ability, and which instruction is most likely to produce it, even the most conservative definition of literacy—the ability to read and/or produce letters—does not provide consensus among those whose careers are devoted to understanding the process people go through in learning to be fluent with written expression.

Historically, literacy has been determined in different ways. Resnick and Resnick (1977) describe an evolution consisting of four stages in which the definition of literacy has involved different types and levels of performance. First, the *signature* stage simply involved the ability to sign one's name. Next, the *recitation* stage required one to demonstrate an ability to read or recite from memory selected passages, without necessarily understanding the words (more on "understanding" to follow). The *comprehension* stage followed, requiring both the reading or recitation and a literal understanding of the passage. Next (in the 1970s) came the *analysis* stage, which considered a literate reading one in which the reader engages with an unfamiliar text, both comprehending it and taking a critical stance.

This notion of reading's evolution is interesting for several reasons. First, it is concerned solely with reading; writing is not required beyond the ability to write one's signature. As Kintgen, Kroll, and Rose (1988) have pointed out, reading and writing have not always both been considered properties of a literate performance. They provide the example of the 14th-century raconteur Geoffrey Chaucer, who told his stories but relied on others to write them down in an era when writing was the province of a few select scribes. One could count back an additional 2,200 years to make the same observation about the Greek poet Homer. Writing, note Kintgen et al. (1988), has not always been valued, and has even been distrusted and scorned by such luminaries as Plato, who opposed writing because it reduced the demands on memory and so, he believed, weakened the mind.

Second, Resnick and Resnick's (1977) account requires, at the most sophisticated stages, "comprehension" of what one reads. Yet it has proven quite difficult to operationally define what is involved in the comprehension of written speech. For the most part, this ability has been measured by students' ability to answer multiple-choice questions that have been devised by researchers or assessment specialists in response to a given passage. We find this narrow means of determining comprehension to be problematic for many reasons. Primarily, it assumes that the questions are uniquely capable of producing information about what students do and do not understand about what they have read. Yet as many researchers working from a transactional perspective have demonstrated, students may find meaning in their reading that is quite different from what a test designer, teacher, or researcher might consider to be important (e.g., Siegel, 1984; Smagorinsky & Coppock, 1994, 1995). This meaning often comes through a student's compathy with literary characters' emotions and experiences, something not available through multiple-choice questions posed by someone else, because of the constructive, interrelational nature of the meaning that emerges through reading and response.

Finally, each of these conceptions is what Street (1995) has called an *autonomous* view of literacy, that is, one that takes literacy out of its social and cultural context and views it as a discrete skill. As an autonomous skill rather than cultural practice, literacy can be measured through the sorts of tests that we find so troublesome and that still constitute the basis of reading assessment in the United States. As a cultural practice, literacy becomes intertwined with a host of other variables that require fine-grained, small-sample research of the sort that is impossible to test through large-scale assessments. Therefore, literacy in its autonomous conception is reductive, eliminating attention to the contexts, intertexts, intercontexts, and other factors that are implicated in readers' efforts to become engaged in their reading.

Since Kintgen et al. (1988) produced their collection of foundational readings, another major shift has occurred in literacy research, that corresponding to the dictionary's definition involving "having knowledge or competence" in relation to a field, technology, or other mediator. One conceivably could trace this conception of reading a nonverbal text to the 6th century, when Pope Gregory the Great proposed that the scriptures be depicted on the walls of churches for the education of the largely unlettered Christian masses. In the French city of Arras in 1025, religious leaders revived this idea, believing that it might enable "illiterate people to learn what books cannot teach them" (Gies & Gies, 1994, p. 130). During the Middle Ages sculpture was the most esteemed artistic medium because it could be appreciated and understood by both aristocrats and uneducated peasants. Because the Cathedral of Notre Dame depicted the biblical narrative in sculpture and other art forms so that it could be "read" by the masses, the church was variously known as the Sermon in Stone and the Bible of the Poor.

Many centuries later, this belief in the efficacy of the nonverbal text was revived again. Perhaps this movement began in the 1950s with the work of Yuri Lotman (1974, 1977),

founder of the Tartu-Moscow Semiotic School in Estonia. Adopted in the 1980s by Suhor (1984), Harste, Woodward, and Burke (1984), Street (1984), Blonsky (1985), and others, a semiotic perspective on literacy is based on the notion that every human construction is a text that is composed of signs and therefore has potential for providing a meaning to be constructed by its readers. This notion of semiotics has influenced researchers interested in textuality, reading, writing, educational achievement, and other facets of learning that are oriented to understanding how people communicate through texts, written or not.

This work has been pursued by many researchers and teachers, including Witte (1992), Gallas (1994), Smagorinsky (1995, 2001), the New London Group (1996), Whitin (1996), and Cope and Kalantzis (2000), all of whom argue that textuality should not be limited to alphabetic texts. This body of work has spawned such terms as *multiliteracies* (the New London Group, 1996) and *multimodality* (Kress & van Leeuwen, 2001), which people produce through such processes as *design* (the New London Group, 1996) and *composition* (Smagorinsky, 1995), terms that suggest a broader set of practices than simply *writing*.

In addition to expanding the cultural tool kit (Wertsch, 1991) available for constructing texts, this work has taken on an ideological, cultural, and economic perspective that is lacking from conventional notions of literacy. Gee (1990) argues that literacy is not limited to words but comprises the full set of attributes and attitudes that one brings to a social interaction. Literacy is thus ideological in that it represents a stance in relation to the world. The New London Group (1996) argues that educators must view literacy in the context of global change, particularly that involving technology that produces images, sounds, icons with particular spatial relations, and other sign systems along with language to produce texts with meaning potential. Producing and making sense of these signs requires a sophisticated approach to "reading" that is typically ignored in school, a problem that both alienates students from their studies and widens the chasm of economic potential for students who do not have access to technology at home. Finally, all of these considerations require attention to culture and the ways in which different cultures organize social practices and the means through which social practices involve communication.

This review suggests the importance of Scribner and Cole's (1981) insight that literacy is a social and cultural practice, that is,

> a recurrent, goal-directed sequence of activities using a particular technology and particular systems of knowledge . . . [a set of] socially developed and patterned ways of using technology and knowledge to accomplish tasks. . . . [Literacy consists of] a set of socially organized practices which make use of a symbol system and a technology for producing and disseminating it. Literacy is not simply knowing how to read and write a particular script but applying this knowledge for specific purposes in specific contexts of use. The nature of these practices, including, of course, their technological aspects, will determine the kinds of skills ("consequences") associated with literacy. (p. 236)

Scribner and Cole's (1981) definition orchestrates many of the ideas we have reviewed into a useful conception of literacy. From their account and from the history of literacy, we can only conclude that the meaning of literacy is local and situated; as Kintgen et al. (1988) argue, "literacy must be defined in relation to a particular society or culture" (p. xiv). To Heath (1983), a culture's organization of its social life suggests different purposes for literacy and different stances toward literate practices. The fundamentalist Christians in her study, for instance, came to regard the written word of the Bible as literal and unquestionable, resulting in difficulties in school when children were given ambiguous texts to read and discuss.

Although signing an X to represent a signature might have been acceptable for adults a century ago, in today's U. S. schools this ability would not be sufficient for a first-grade student in ordinary school lessons. The degree to which a person is considered literate, then, is not static, but is a judgment based on the local standards that follow from the ways in which particular cultures construe the purpose of using texts for communication and expression. How and why others then read those texts is a topic taken up in detail by the contributors to this book.

WHAT ARE THE LIMITATIONS OF RESEARCH?

Literacy researchers working within the multiple, complex, and generous understanding of literacy we have described must develop a conceptualization of "research" that is appropriate to the "literacy" they investigate. If literacy is not bounded by correct oral pronunciation of printed words, or by comprehension of printed text, then a researcher attempting to study literacy through methods that capture or measure only those phenomena circumscribes literacy into a smaller space than is appropriate. For if literacy consists of drawing purposefully from varied semiotic resources, and if it occurs in connection with others and in the context of settings, cultures, political relations, identities, and histories, then there is more to examine than the improvement of a statistical sample on a set of predetermined test items.

Like perhaps most educational researchers, we editors value a wide range of methodologies and traditions in inquiry, and we see a plurality of approaches as offering multiple angles on common questions and problems. Across the contributions to this *Handbook,* we see discussions of many different approaches to adolescent literacy research. There is, however, a special value attached to studies that describe systematically the sorts of things that go on when literacy is occurring *in situ*—whether the location is in school, in an after-school program, on the Internet, in homes and communities, or among peer groups. That valuing of context seems to make sense. If you want to study adolescent literacy, you have to go find it and look at its conditions and how it works.

Such an approach to practices of generating knowledge about literacy corresponds to our conception of literacy as "a set of socially organized practices which make use of a symbol system and a technology for producing and disseminating it" (Scribner & Cole, 1981, p. 236). Among many researchers, this understanding of literacy has contributed to a preference for analyzing descriptions of people doing things together around various kinds of texts. In the research methods that produce such descriptions, one keeps the social context within the picture frame in order to keep looking at a recognizable and legitimate representation of the phenomenon. The commitment to doing so has led to the adoption and development of a wide variety of methods for data collection and analysis. As in most other disciplines, research in adolescent literacy may be historical, philosophical, or theoretical and may not involve data collected from the synchronous practices of human beings. Among the studies that do gather empirical evidence from human participants, researchers employ such techniques as interviews, think-aloud protocols, collection of student writing, participant journals, and ethnographic methods with varying degrees of participation. They collect these data from classrooms, after-school activities, community centers, homes, online spaces, informal youth groupings, and other settings in which literacy occurs without the researcher setting it up. Frames for analyzing these data range from those based on information processing to semiotics to critical theory to space–time chronotopes, among many others. These kinds of data and analysis allow literacy to be taken not only as a psychological skill, but as an event in the social and material world, as something that needs to be located and observed in order to be understood. Moreover, situated literacy typically involves the sort of open-ended, problem-framing thinking that is usually absent from standardized assessments.

An approach to research that respects adolescent literacy as a real-world phenomenon observable in settings not created for research permits something else as well. It allows researchers to view adolescent literacy through the eyes of the people who participate in it. Many of the researchers who have contributed to this book are particularly concerned with how adolescent literacy looks from the point of view of the people we call adolescents. This insider, or emic, perspective is essential to validity in qualitative research. If a study of "adolescent literacy" looks only at activities that are not meaningful or recognizable to the adolescents investigated, then there is a set of problems with the study's validity and therefore its applicability to the lives and experiences of the people it is presumably designed to help. Furthermore, such a study is likely to find false deficits—that adolescents have some deficiency in their literacy that, if one looked in the setting where the adolescent

was already pursuing literacy, would be evident. To take an emic point of view, then, is to make it possible to counter the fallacies that inhere in a deficit perspective (Valencia, 1997). Much of the research reviewed in this *Handbook* provides evidence that adolescents are, in fact, sophisticated, motivated, purposeful users of literacy, contrary to the deficit assumptions of many observers. When one takes on an understanding of literacy as situated, multimodal, and purposeful social action, the approach to research must be capable of accounting for that kind of complexity as it emerges, rather than cordoning it off in advance.

Discussing the nature of logic in scientific inquiry and the ways it may go wrong, Kaplan (1964) invoked the old joke about the drunkard's search for his lost key. Rather than looking where he dropped it, he looks under a lamppost, because there the light is better. For many in the field of adolescent literacy research, looking for the key involves locating settings of adolescent literacy and then using investigatory approaches that permit the study to capture what happens there. Contrast that outlook with one that commits first to a set of research procedures considered scientific and an expectation that adolescent literacy will appear when bidden within a research study, instructional treatment, or test administration. The light may be good under such conditions, but that does not make such contexts the only places to search for the key.

Jervis (1993) tells us that people in government are particularly susceptible to the drunkard's search. He writes, "Without being able to specify exactly how much effort would be optimal, it seems like people seize on easier ways of processing and calculating information than they would if they were fully aware of what they are doing" (p. 338). As an extension of the federal education initiatives we referred to in our discussion of literacy, the U.S. Congress in 2002 passed the Education Sciences Reform Act (*www.ed.gov/policy/rschstat/leg/PL107-279. pdf*), which created the Institute for Education Sciences and its What Works Clearinghouse. This law and the ways it has been interpreted have privileged a different approach to research, one that has valorized—and, in fact, legislated—a notion of "scientific research," which seeks to arrive at interventions that will produce gains in test scores for all students in any context, so that national education policy can proceed with the certainty that money spent will result in predictable, desired results on a national scale. In order to gain this level of certainty in the relations between cause and effect in teaching and learning, powerful voices in education policy have advocated for the application of a "gold standard" that they argue is used in medical-pharmaceutical research, the randomized trial, to be applied to questions about education. Often such methods are viewed as especially important for research that attempts to explain or address the differences in test scores between middle-class White students and the rest of the population. Many chapters in this book discuss the complexity of this so-called "achievement gap" and shed some light on reasons why isolating a single cause–effect chain in test performance might be a futile quest. After engaging with those chapters, readers may even wonder why the term "gap" is so often employed in the singular, when there are so many differences among so many different groups of young people with different cultures, histories, and societal locations.

The full brunt of the pressure for "scientific research" has landed upon reading in the primary grades in elementary school, not adolescent literacy (or the writing of any age), though Alvermann (Chapter 2, this volume) describes the swell of interest in Washington for bringing the same framework to a "crisis" of adolescent achievement, school completion, and the rigor of high school. Policymakers assert that they want to improve schools, to make the outcome of schooling more predictable, and to bring success to all students, especially those whom schools have failed historically. Any and all of these motives have fueled what Dewey (1929) called "the quest for certainty," which some believe will be satisfied by experimental research with standardized tests as measures.

The U.S. federal government's encouragement, through funding and attention, of one form of research does not, in fact, amount to censorship of other forms. Many of the studies reviewed in this book testify to the continued vitality of not only other methods of inquiry, but also inventiveness in the field of literacy education in devising new means of

gathering evidence of phenomena and applying analytic procedures to data. And governing bodies must prioritize and certainly do not need to fund every kind of study. The national conversation around the federal policy, however, has built a sense in the profession as a whole—among many foundation officers, university deans and presidents, and state and local school administrators, and within some professional organizations and journals—that education research is of high quality when it produces certainty about particular ways of teaching all students, when it randomizes subjects, when it standardizes and broadcasts treatments to large numbers, when its analysis employs statistical tools. These methods may come to be considered to be the most illuminating—the most like a lamppost. For many of the contributors to this volume, the actual key may still be missing, even when such methods seem useful. Although the chapters herein may employ, say, the results of an administration of the National Assessment for Educational Progress, a nationally distributed, standardized test, they still, without exception, also draw upon studies that involve direct observation of classrooms, communities, and individuals actually doing something with literacy.

Ultimately, these different perspectives on research arise from differing intentions about the uses to which research might be put. Creating policy governing reading instruction for young children, the U.S. federal government has been fond of the phrase "scientifically based reading instruction," which has been used often enough to gain its own acronym, SBRI. The explicit claim of this phrase is that what teachers do with their individual students should be based on research findings. The notion that particular teaching actions can be proven effective is perhaps understandably seductive when millions are being spent on the purchase of reading programs. But numbers of teachers, like many other practitioners, including those in medicine, make decisions not about statistical samples but about individual students and classes, on the basis of a wide variety of commitments, some of which concern science but others of which are philosophical, moral, political, and aesthetic.

We editors, along with, we expect, most of the authors of the chapters that follow, want to argue that the goal of research in education is not directly to tell teachers and schools what to do, or to provide findings that prove in advance the correctness of a teaching method. Most of the researchers writing in these chapters think of teachers as thoughtfully adaptive decision makers, who may benefit from understandings that research produces as they take up a wide range of considerations in responding to the particular students from particular backgrounds with particular histories in their particular schools in particular communities. Understandings of how students engage with literacy when they are involved in activities outside school have sometimes produced insights into the conditions under which adolescents may be active, motivated, and thoughtful users of literacy.

From such understandings, teachers and schools may be able to construct environments that position students to be similarly competent in academic work. In addition, observations of classrooms and schools that are especially successful at supporting adolescent literacy have produced principles that may be taken up in widely varying ways in other settings. Therefore, the degree of expectation that research will produce definitive cause–effect relationships that control the future actions of schools and teachers versus a grounded understanding that may help to orient free decision making (along with teachers' other commitments) is a significant difference in expectations about the purpose and use of research findings.

This *Handbook*, then, may not provide many finalizing, authoritative statements like "the research says X," which once and for all settle an argument for the speaker of those words about a course of educational action. However, readers will, we think, be better equipped to examine the tangled and tense decisions that face educators charged with supporting adolescents' literacy. They will have more to think about, more to be curious about, more to learn from the adolescents facing them. We read this research and find that it is generative, that it opens up new and future-oriented thinking, rather than closing down curricular possibilities to proven methods.

The authors of the chapters that follow draw upon and participate in varied research communities and traditions—from

linguistics to English, composition to media studies, cultural studies to psychology of reading, aesthetics to critical theory. That range helps to account for the diversity in approach, genre, and voice that one encounters reading through these entries. In selecting authors, we chose people we knew had themselves done quality work in the area, who we had reason to believe were knowledgeable about the research literature on the topic. Our directions to authors did not limit the sorts of research they should consider, but only stated that they should be clear about what they mean by *research, literacy,* and *adolescence*. The range of methodologies they represent, then, is the range they found in their reviews of the literature. Despite the wealth in this field, many chapters include observations that empirical research on particular topics is scant and not of consistently high quality. For young scholars working on adolescent literacy, there is still much to be done. Indeed, at times it seems as if almost everything is yet to be done.

CONCLUSION

So we welcome you, our readers, to the *Handbook of Adolescent Literacy Research.* To return to the memo we sent our 50 contributors early in the project, we were thinking of you from the very beginning:

We imagine this book, then, being read by some of the people in policy, research, and funding conversations. But even more of our readers will be people who are interested in those conversations and affected by them: teachers, teacher educators, and scholars with a special interest in adolescent literacy. We would like to think that this volume would be useful in graduate courses about adolescent literacy. The understandings of students and readers may become, through transactions with this text, more organized, informed, and complicated, so that they may participate in local, state, and national conversations with more strength and wisdom.

Thus, despite the political context, the book is not mainly a policy book. We envision it feeding the insight and imagination of practitioners and researchers—raising new inquiry questions, proposing new avenues of research, provoking the development of new curricular ideas and pedagogical practices on the basis of what has come to be understood through systematic inquiry already undertaken and published.

And imagination and courage are needed. One of the challenging—even distressing—aspects of writing and editing this volume has been the recurring theme of the need for real social justice in education so that all our adolescents are truly served. It is also clear from many of these chapters that not only is more research needed in adolescent literacy, but, sadly, that we are not implementing in the schools and our communities what researchers, including those who study their own practice, have found and also what merits further implementation and investigation. We are not, in sum, serving our adolescents well enough, and it is not easy to explain why: If you believe the scholars in this book, there is a consistent gap between what we know and what we are doing, and it is not acceptable. There is much work to be done, and we can, if we have the will, begin it now.

REFERENCES

Allington, R. L., & Woodside-Jiron, H. (1999). The politics of literacy teaching: How "research" shaped educational policy. *Educational Researcher, 28*(8), 4–13.

Blonsky, M. (Ed.). (1985). *On signs.* Baltimore: Johns Hopkins University Press.

Christenbury, L. (2007). *Retracing the journey: Teaching and learning in an American high school.* New York: Teachers College Press.

Cope, B., & Kalantzis, M. (Eds.). (2000). *Multiliteracies: Literacy learning and the design of social futures.* New York: Routledge.

Dewey, J. (1929). *The quest for certainty: A study of the relation of knowledge and action.* New York: Minton Balch.

Gallas, K. (1994). *The languages of learning: How children talk, write, dance, draw, and sing their understanding of the world.* New York: Teachers College Press.

Gee, J. P. (1990). *Social linguistics and literacies: Ideology in discourses.* New York: Falmer.

Gies, F., & Gies, J. (1994). *Cathedral, forge, and waterwheel: Technology and invention in the Middle Ages.* New York: HarperCollins.

Hall, G. S. (1904). *Adolescence: Its psychology and its relation to physiology, anthropology, sociology, sex, crime , religion, and education* (Vols. I & II). Englewood Cliffs, NJ: Prentice-Hall.

Harste, J. C., Woodward, V. A., & Burke, C. L. (1984). *Language stories and literacy lessons.* Portsmouth, NH: Heinemann.

Heath, S. B. (1983). *Ways with words: Language, life, and work in communities and classrooms.* New York: Cambridge University Press.

Hersch, P. (1999). *A tribe apart: A journey into the heart of American adolescence.* New York: Random House.

Jervis, R. (1993). The drunkard's search. In S. Iyengar & W. J. McGuire (Eds.), *Explorations in political psychology* (pp. 338–360). Durham, NC: Duke University Press.

Kaplan, A. (1964). *The conduct of inquiry: Methodology for behavioral science.* San Francisco: Chandler.

Kett, J. F. (1977). *Rites of passage: Adolescence in America, 1790 to the present.* New York: Basic Books.

Kintgen, E. R., Kroll, B. M., & Rose, M. (1988). Introduction. In E. R. Kintgen, B. M. Kroll, & M. Rose (Eds.), *Perspectives on literacy* (pp. xi–xix). Carbondale, IL: Southern Illinois University Press.

Kress, G., & van Leeuwen, T. (2001). *Multimodal discourse.* London: Edward Arnold.

Lesko, N. (2001). *Act your age!: A cultural construction of adolescence.* New York: Falmer.

Lotman, Y. M. (1974). The sign mechanism of culture. *Semiotica, 12,* 301–305.

Lotman, Y. M. (1977). *The structure of the artistic text* (G. Lenhoff & R. Vroon, Trans.). Ann Arbor: University of Michigan, Department of Slavic Languages and Literatures.

Merriam-Webster. (2003). *Merriam-Webster's 11th collegiate dictionary* (Electronic ed.). Springfield, MA: Author.

Modell, J., & Goodman, M. (1990). Historical perspectives. In S. S. Feldman & G. Elliott (Eds.), *At the threshold: The developing adolescent* (pp. 93–122). Cambridge, MA: Harvard University Press.

The New London Group. (1996). A pedagogy of multiliteracies: Designing social futures. *Harvard Educational Review, 66,* 60–92.

Offer, D., & Schonert-Reichl, K. A. (1992). Debunking the myths of adolescence: Findings from recent research. *Journal of the American Academy of Child and Adolescent Psychiatry, 31,* 1003–1014.

Reay, B. (1991). The context and meaning of popular literacy: Some evidence from nineteenth-century rural England. *Past and Present, 131*(1), 89–129.

Resnick, D. P., & Resnick, L. B. (1977). The nature of literacy: A historical explanation. *Harvard Educational Review, 47,* 370–385.

Savage, J. (2007). *Teenage: The creation of youth culture.* New York: Viking.

Scribner, S., & Cole, M. (1981). *The psychology of literacy.* Cambridge, MA: Harvard University Press.

Siegel, M. G. (1984). *Reading as signification.* Unpublished doctoral dissertation, Indiana University, Bloomington.

Smagorinsky, P. (1995). Constructing meaning in the disciplines: Reconceptualizing writing across the curriculum as composing across the curriculum. *American Journal of Education, 103,* 160–184.

Smagorinsky, P. (2001). If meaning is constructed, what is it made from? Toward a cultural theory of reading. *Review of Educational Research, 71,* 133–169.

Smagorinsky, P., & Coppock, J. (1994). Cultural tools and the classroom context: An exploration of an alternative response to literature. *Written Communication, 11,* 283–310.

Smagorinsky, P., & Coppock, J. (1995). The reader, the text, the context: An exploration of a choreographed response to literature. *Journal of Reading Behavior, 27,* 271–298.

Sommers, C. H. (2000). *The war against boys: How misguided feminism is harming our young men.* New York: Simon & Schuster.

Steinberg, L. (2001, March). We know some things: Parent–adolescent relations in retrospect and prospect. *Journal of Research on Adolescence, 11,* 1–19.

Strauch, B. (2003). *The primal teen: What the new discoveries about the teenage brain tell us about our kids.* New York: Doubleday.

Street, B. V. (1984). *Literacy in theory and practice.* New York: Cambridge University Press.

Street, B. V. (1995). *Social literacies: Critical approaches to literacy in development, ethnography, and education.* New York: Longman.

Suhor, C. (1984). Towards a semiotics-based curriculum. *Journal of Curriculum Studies, 16,* 247–257.

Tyack, D. B. (1990). *The one best system: A history of American urban education.* Cambridge, MA: Harvard University Press.

Vadeboncoeur, J. A., & Stevens, L. P. (Eds). (2005). *Re/constructing "the adolescent."* New York: Peter Lang.

Valencia, R. (Ed.). (1997). *The evolution of deficit thinking: Educational thought and practice.* New York: Falmer.

Wertsch, J. V. (1991). *Voices of the mind: A sociocultural approach to mediated action.* Cambridge, MA: Harvard University Press.

Whitin, P. (1996). *Sketching stories, stretching minds: Responding visually to literature.* Portsmouth, NH: Heinemann.

Witte, S. (1992). Context, text, intertext: Toward a constructivist semiotic of writing. *Written Communication, 9,* 237–308.

CHAPTER 2

Sociocultural Constructions of Adolescence and Young People's Literacies

DONNA E. ALVERMANN

This chapter begins by highlighting some unexamined assumptions about adolescence and an adolescent literacy achievement gap that allegedly, if not closed, will lead to dire consequences for those youth who are on the "wrong" side of the divide. After a brief tracing of the epistemological and structural constraints through which literacy historically has been enacted and regulated, attention is drawn to the ways in which certain sociocultural constructions of adolescence produce sites for opening up new ways of thinking about contemporary youth and what counts as literacy. One such possibility is that in a digital world where privileging the linguistic mode for communicating shows signs of loosening, educators, researchers, and policymakers will do well to consider the implications of this turn for reaching and teaching the very adolescents who are at the center of their attention.

Perhaps it would not be too much of an overstatement to claim that *adolescents* and *adolescent literacy* are terms that most educators, literacy researchers, and policymakers in the United States today would have little trouble defining or reaching consensus on in terms of their importance to the national workforce. Media headlines that call attention to a literacy achievement "gap" among this country's youth and the singling out of secondary schools that fail to make adequate yearly progress (AYP) are but two indicators of the so-called slippage in young people's literacy performance and its purported drain on the economy—an argument that has been around at least since the release of the report *A Nation at Risk: The Imperative for Educational Reform* (National

Commission on Excellence in Education, 1983), though not without critique (see, for example, Guthrie & Springer, 2004).

But the current state of affairs has garnered more than the media's attention: Congress, too, has taken note. In the space of 2 months during the spring of 2007, the Striving Readers Act was introduced in both the Senate and the House chambers by a group of bipartisan legislators intent on providing "grants to every state for reading and comprehension programs to meet the needs of students in grades four through twelve" (Alliance for Excellent Education, 2007, n. p.). Preceding this move to legislate on behalf of a certain segment of the country's youth who were deemed "struggling" readers (now renamed "striving"), no fewer than eight major reports on adolescent literacy were released in the last 2 years by groups such as the National Governors Association, the National Association of Secondary School Principals, the National Association of State Boards of Education, and the National School Boards Association (for a complete listing see Beers, Probst, & Rief, 2007, p. 14). In an unprecedented move in the spring of 2007, the International Reading Association (IRA) published a special report authored entirely by policymakers and leaders of advocacy groups committed to closing the literacy achievement gap among adolescents. This report, *Multiple Dimensions of Achievement: Defining, Identifying, and Addressing "the Gap,"* was later entered into IRA's archival journal, *Reading Research Quarterly* (New Directions in Research, 2007).

Judging from the level and magnitude of interest in the literacy achievement gap, a reasonable assumption might be that there is some consensus in the field regarding the degree to which there is a problem and the characteristics of those who are at the center of it. Moreover, it might be assumed that once formalized, a legislated approach to closing the gap would be sufficiently broad to meet the needs of students who are struggling for different reasons, including but not limited to inadequate reading skills, a definition of school literacy that is out of sync with their everyday lives, less than optimal instructional conditions, and socioeconomic factors beyond their control.

Rather than leave such assumptions unexamined, I propose to step back and take a closer look at the characterizations of *adolescence* itself—for unless that period of time in young people's lives is scrutinized to reveal at least some of its various constructions, one runs the risk of prescribing solutions for a subpopulation that may or may not fit any of its members particularly well. In fact, such solutions may preempt the very need for further discussion about what counts as literacy and who does the counting, a point to which I later return. But first I concentrate on foregrounding the importance of "knowing" adolescents and their literacies through examining the social and cultural contexts of adolescence. I begin by tracing the epistemological and structural constraints through which literacy histori-

cally has been enacted and regulated. I then use what can be learned from that tracing to analyze various social and cultural constructions of adolescence in an effort to better understand who adolescents are and how their literacy needs might be met.

FROM LITERACY TO LITERACIES: A NECESSARY TRACING

A sweep of human history over the past 50,000 years reveals that "it was not until the last 150 years, and primarily in the twentieth century, that universal education—that is, literacy for everyone—became a goal of most nations" (Collins & Blot, 2003, p. 2). Concurrent with this call for universal education was the privileging of written language over the spoken word and a retreat from valuing oral communication as an equally valid indicator of human intellect and creativity. Yet, according to Collins and Blot (2003), one of the most creative periods in human history occurred roughly between 8000 and 3500 B.C. with the advent of agriculture, the domestication of animals, and increased technical resourcefulness in observing, classifying, and communicating. Instruction in reading and writing, which was initially reserved for the elites of society and for individuals entrusted with preserving sacred practices, gradually became synonymous with schooled literacy, especially as the structure of Western institutions spread and arguments for a narrowly defined view of literacy—one that presumably would bring economic and social benefits to the properly instructed—took hold. It is to this model of literacy and a competing one that I now turn.

Two Dominant and Competing Models of Literacy

Helping to shape the form of literacy instruction as we know it today have been two dominant and competing models of literacy: the autonomous and the ideological (Street, 1984, 1995). The autonomous model, which is prevalent in schools in the United States, views reading and writing as neutral processes that are largely explained by individual variations in cognitive and physiological functioning. It is a view that assumes a universal set of reading and writing skills for decoding and encoding printed text. Its persistence is notable, especially in light of Heath's (1983) influential research that demonstrated that it is how children are socialized into different literacies (their different "ways with words" and whether those ways match the school's approach to literacy instruction) that matters. Reading and writing are anything but neutral processes when considered within Heath's findings.

In a critique of the autonomous model of literacy, Brian Street, professor and chair of Language in Education at King's College, London University, drew from anthropological field work on literacy in Iran during the 1970s to question the assumption of reading and writing as neutral processes, thereby laying the groundwork for his ideological model. Street (1995), who has had a long-standing commitment to linking the cultural dimension of language and literacy to contemporary practices in education, explains the autonomous model this way:

> A great deal of the thinking about literacy . . . has assumed that literacy with a big "L" and single "y" [is] a single autonomous thing [with] consequences for personal and social development. . . . One of the reasons for referring to this position as an autonomous model of literacy is that it represents itself as though it is not a position located ideologically at all, as though it is just natural. One of the reasons why I want to call the counterposition ideological is precisely in order to signal that we are not simply talking here about technical features of the written process or the oral process. What we are talking about are competing models and assumptions about reading and writing processes, which are always embedded in power relations. (pp. 132–133)

A point worth underscoring is that viewing literacy as ideologically embedded does not require giving up on the cognitive aspects of reading and writing, nor on the technical skills associated with the autonomous model. Rather, according to Street (1995), the ideological model subsumes the autonomous model and simultaneously incorporates an array of social and cultural ways of knowing that can account for seemingly absent but always present power structures. As used here, *power* refers not to something that is seized and held onto by a person seeking to suppress the rights of others, but rather to something that circulates and speaks through silences as well as utterances (Foucault (1994/1997). Power relations are everywhere—in the way we use words, images, sounds, gestures, beliefs, clothing, and so on to identify ourselves as particular types of people who will be recognized by others like us. These *Discourses*, to use Gee's (1990) convention for naming socially recognized ways of being in the world, enjoy what Lesko (2001) has described as "an aura of naturalness or inevitability to them" (p. 15). Applied to adolescence, such Discourses produce certain expectations of youth across social sites and practices, including reading and writing (Heath, 1983; Scribner & Cole, 1981; Vadeboncoeur & Stevens, 2005).

The New Literacies

In the year 2000, five years after Street's (1995) critique of the autonomous model of literacy and within a decade of Gee's (1990) seminal publication, *Social Linguistics and Literacies: Ideology in Discourses*, the New London Group published its treatise on multiliteracies. This work drew attention to the need for a multiplicity and integration of communication modes (e.g., linguistic, visual, oral, sound, and kinesthetic) in the context of a culturally diverse world grown significantly more attached to new communication technologies, though multiliteracies need not involve digital technologies (Lankshear & Knobel, 2006). Typically, the term *multiliteracies* denotes more than "mere literacy" (Cope & Kalantzis, 2000, p. 5), which remains language- and print-centered.

Through a series of events, then, the notion of literacy with a big "L" and single "y" began to give way to the plural form, *literacies.* Soon other related terms emerged and quickly entered the lexicons of most literacy researchers and a few classroom teachers, but rarely those of policymakers. In particular, terms such as *multiple literacies, situated literacies, digital literacies,* and the *New Literacy Studies* (NLS; Gee, 1996) became commonplace and part of a burgeoning research literature that focused on reconceptualizing the literacies in adolescents' lives (Alvermann & McLean, 2007; Alvermann, Hinchman, Moore, Phelps, & Waff, 2006;

Lankshear & Knobel, 2006). Of central interest in this literature is the range of theories available for framing and reframing research in the areas of NLS and multimodalities (see, for example, Lewis, Enciso, & Moje, 2007).

A theory that is particularly germane to any discussion of the NLS is the social semiotic theory of multimodality, which guides the work of Kress and his colleagues (Kress, 1997; Kress & Van Leeuwen, 1996; Lemke, 1989) and is concerned primarily with communication in its widest sense—visual, oral, gestural, linguistic, musical, kinesthetic, and digital. It is a theory that attempts to explain how people play a central role in making meaning—how they use various resources (signs) that are available to them in representing through different modes what they wish to communicate to others. For example, consider the different modes one might choose to represent a car: It could be its sleekness and shine, or perhaps its speed, the sound it makes when accelerating, or maybe its gas consumption. Choices made in representing "car," then, would indicate what is salient about "car" for a particular individual. Such choices would also indicate the person's perception of his or her audience's interests and needs. In other words, through the representations people make of the resources available to them, it is possible to infer what *matters* to them (Jewitt & Kress, 2003, p. 12). Inferences of this kind have particular relevance in the study of adolescents and their literacy needs.

A Challenge to Studying Literacies in Local Contexts

With the advent of New Literacy Studies and adequate theories for framing research that could account for individual preferences in multimodal meaning making, scholars in the field of literacy education turned their attention increasingly toward studying people's literacy practices at the local level. But it was this preoccupation with local contexts, Brandt and Clinton (2002) argued, that was leading to methodological biases in research and conceptual impasses in theory building. In a much cited article titled "Limits of the Local: Expanding Perspectives on Literacy as a Social Practice," Brandt and Clinton (2002) claimed that critics of the autonomous model of literacy had

gone too far. Specifically, they argued that by focusing attention almost exclusively on individual agency in reading and writing practices at the local level, proponents of the ideological model all but ignored the material consequences associated with literacy at a more global level.

To address the imbalance, Brandt and Clinton drew on the work of Latour (1993) in recommending that researchers design studies in which literacy was treated not simply as an outcome of local practices but rather as "a thing"—an actor, a participant in those practices. Specifically, Brandt and Clinton (2002) illustrated through real-life examples why it was necessary to remain alert to the possibility that decisions made in distant places can constrain people's literacy practices in local contexts. In striking this cautionary note, they were advocating for a perspective that acknowledges the following: "Where anyone is observed reading and writing something, it is well worth asking who else is getting something out of it; often that somebody will not be at the scene" (p. 347). This more complicated notion of literacy is used in analyzing the discourse of adolescence in the next section of this chapter.

Before going there, however, it is instructive to note Street's (2003) response to Brandt and Clinton's (2002) critique. In his foreword to Collins and Blot's (2003) book, *Literacy and Literacies: Texts, Power, and Identity,* Street acknowledged that there were indeed limits to the local. Couching his remarks in a time when policymakers in the United States and Great Britain were enacting into law increasingly narrowed definitions of literacy and ever more stringent accountability measures—Street (2003) wrote:

> Policymakers . . . bringing the "light" of literacy to the "darkness" of the "illiterate," and educationalists . . . similarly arguing for the economic and social benefits of a narrowly defined and disciplined "literacy" can simply argue that all of those counter-examples of the complexity and meanings of literacy in people's everyday lives are not relevant to their agenda. Local, everyday, home literacies are seen within that frame as failed attempts at the real thing, as inferior versions of the "literacy" demanded by the economy, by educational institutions, by the politics of centralizing and homogenizing tendencies. (pp. xi–xii)

Although these remarks might appear on first inspection to signal a retreat from the NLS, they were anything but that. In an effort to address the limits of the local, Street was building a case for staying the course while making a strategic correction along the way. That correction, he argued, would need "to lift the account of local literacies towards a more general, theoretically comparative set of terms whilst not losing the specificity that NLS has brought to the field" (Street, 2003, p. xii). Specifically, Street proposed that the NLS take up as a major focus Collins and Blot's (2003) question, "What is a text?" He reasoned that this question, in addition to acknowledging Kress and Van Leeuwen's (1996) earlier argument for the need to study texts in all their many representations, offered a way to account for intersecting issues of texts, power, and identity in a way that the NLS's emphasis on the local had too often neglected. Building further on this corrective course for the NLS, Street, in his keynote address to the National Reading Conference in 2005, argued for considering how Kress and his colleagues' work in multimodalities complements the work in NLS, and vice versa. An extension of that argument can be seen in his coauthored foreword with Kress to *Travel Notes from the New Literacy Studies*:

> [While] both approaches look at broadly the same field, from each of the two positions the field has a distinctive look: one that tries to understand what people acting together are doing [NLS], the other that tries to understand about the tools with which the same people do what they are doing [multimodalities]. (Kress & Street, 2006, p. ix)

With this bridging of the NLS and multimodalites in mind, I end my tracing of the epistemological and structural frameworks through which U.S. educators, researchers, and policymakers have come to "know" literacy. It is but one of several available tracings, because by deliberately concentrating on the sociocultural underpinnings of literacy, I have downplayed other aspects of reading and writing that are primarily physical and cognitive in orientation. Narrowing the scope, however, allows reflection on possible intersections between evolving notions of literacy and adolescence as they are con-

structed in contemporary times. This reflection, in turn, leads to the following set of questions as a starting point for analyzing adolescence from a sociocultural perspective:

- How do the evolving views of literacy inform what Lesko (2001) calls the "discourse of adolescence"?
- What if adolescence and the struggling adolescent reader are fictions?
- Why might adolescence be a site for opening up new possibilities involving youth and their multiliteracies?

CONSTRUCTIONS OF ADOLESCENCE: A SOCIAL AND CULTURAL ANALYSIS

Scholars who view the concept and images of adolescence as being socially and culturally constructed point to certain historical, societal, economic, and political conditions that seek to normalize and regulate youth. In particular, they critique largely unexamined assumptions about "the modern, scientific adolescent" (Lesko, 2001, p. 13), whose construction is steeped in psychological and developmental theories dating back to the turn of the 20th century (Hall, 1904). By relegating young people to marginalized positions on the periphery of adulthood, the discourse (or system of reasoning) about youth in the United States offers but a limited set of options for engaging with society and literacy learning in particular (Vadeboncoeur & Stevens, 2005). In an effort to work toward alternate ways of seeing and talking about adolescents and their literacies in postmodern times, I use the three questions mentioned earlier to examine Lesko's (2001) and Vadeboncoeur and Stevens' (2005) critiques of the discourse of adolescence.

Evolving Views of Literacy and the Discourse of Adolescence

In *Act Your Age! A Cultural Construction of Adolescence*, Lesko (2001) argued that a monolithic view of youth prevails in the United States. It is a long-standing view with roots in developmental psychology and sociology that conceptualizes adolescents as being supposedly all the same and essentially different from adults. As a categorical term for marking the space and time of being an adolescent—that is, someone who is a not-yet adult (Amit-Talai & Wulff, 1995)—*adolescence* comes under criticism on at least two fronts. First, there is the issue of biological determinism and its claim that adolescents are trapped within bodies destined to fall prey to the so-called physical, sexual, and emotional "excesses" of youth (Hall, 1904). Critics of this claim, aside from Lesko (e.g., Aitken, 2001; Wyn & White, 1997), dispute a literature based in developmental psychology that is replete with accounts of adolescence as a period in young people's lives when turmoil is thought to consume most of youth's waking moments. A second critique of adolescence as an isolatable category separating young people from adults draws on a perspective that points to the centrality of people's use of language to socially construct negotiated understandings about their lived experiences and the experiences of others. Although this perspective offers warranted interpretations of various race, class, and gender differences among adolescents, it fails to address the underlying assumption that adolescents as a group are basically the same owing to developmental, age-driven factors.

Consequently, Lesko (2001), in her critique of this assumed sameness, turned to research on sociohistorically informed practices to better understand how age categorization is achieved by adults and adolescents in interaction over time. Her work and that of others (e.g., Cintron, 1991; Hagood, Stevens, & Reinking, 2002) has produced understandings of generational interdependency that move the conversation about sameness and hierarchical positioning to a new level. Thinking of young people not as lacking in adult knowledge and experience but as knowing things that have relevance for them and their particular situations argues for exploring how all of us, adults and youth alike, act provisionally at times, given particular circumstances and within particular discourses (Morgan, 1997). It also argues for viewing adolescents as having at least some degree of agency within a larger collective of social practices (Connell, 1995; Finders, 1997; Mac an Ghaill, 1994; Marsh & Stolle, 2006).

Undoubtedly, the potential for young people to exercise such agency over their own reading and writing practices was at least theoretically enabled by Street's (1995) assertion of an ideological model of literacy more than a decade ago. Shortly thereafter, literacy researchers, no longer constrained by the autonomous model, began to broaden their definitions of literacy and to question the transparency and stability of a number of other dominant discourses pertaining to youth. As a result of this move, findings from contemporary research on young people's multiliteracies have revealed some underlying issues of power that complicate the very notion of *adolescence*—a term Appleman (2001) once described as "a kind of purgatory between childhood and adulthood" (p. 1). In brief, this research, whether reported in books (Alvermann, 2002; Rogers & Schofield, 2005; Wilder & Dressman, 2006), in refereed print journals (Chandler-Olcott & Mahar, 2003; Guzzetti & Gamboa, 2004; Moje, 2000), or in e-journals (Cammack, 2005; Stalwick, 2007), challenges certain assumptions about communicative competence and what counts (or should count) as valued literacy practices among people of all ages, and among youth in particular.

Although these challenges produced new knowledge that has been taken up and discussed at length in the international research community, they are for all practical purposes ignored at the school and policy level in the United States. With a monolithic view of youth and a narrowly defined sense of literacy in place, it is not surprising that, with few exceptions (e.g., Leander, 2007; Miller & Borowicz, 2006), classroom teachers have been reluctant to incorporate various aspects of the new literacies into their instruction, even on a trial basis, and especially in districts where high-stakes testing and AYP are the *sine qua non* (No Child Left Behind Act, 2001; Zuckerbrod, 2007).

In sum, the potential for research on multiliteracies and the NLS to inform the discourse of adolescence, and ultimately adolescent literacy instruction, remains largely unfulfilled in the United States, though this country is not unique in that regard. For example, Luke (2002), in reflecting on what he had observed in Australia as a result of his meetings with the Queensland Department of Education about the specification and assessment of core curriculum outcomes, wrote, "New literacies, new technologies, and multiliteracies did not even merit a mention, aside from a passing comment that the new technology syllabus had some 'good outcomes statements' " (p. 186). Finding this ironical in the face of what he perceived was a shared commitment among most modern governments to reshape education systems for better positioning in a global economy, Luke (2002) went on to add:

> The imperative to engage with new literacies is not a particularly radical move. At the same time, the wall between these debates and government and bureaucrat boardroom debates of literacy policy is, well, a wall, and a pretty stolid one at that. (p. 188)

What If Adolescence and the Struggling Adolescent Reader Are Fictions?

Asking a question such as the one in the section heading could be considered tantamount to blasphemy, not only in political circles but among literacy educators as well. Why ask it? Perhaps William Ayers (2005) in his introduction to Re/Constructing "the Adolescent" answers that question best when he writes: "[This book] can help us crack open the common sense assumptions that sit heavy on the body of adolescence. . . . Puberty is a fact; everything surrounding that fact is fiction. We construct the myths, and just like that, the myths construct us" (p. ix). The claim that adolescence is fraught with socially constructed fictions of youth is a theme that the editors of that book, Vadeboncoeur and Stevens (2005), have highlighted in their chapters on how discourses of naturalization, restriction, and commodification create spaces for young people to take up, modify, or resist certain fictions. One of those discourses, naturalization, bears closer scrutiny here.

By avoiding simplistic celebrations of youth culture, chapter authors in Re/Constructing "the Adolescent" succeed in illustrating how the "naturally developing" adolescent does not exist outside the discourse of adolescence that produced this fiction in the first place. For example, Finders (2005), drawing on data from a year-long ethnography in which she served as the language arts

teacher in a transitional middle school for youthful offenders, used Davies's (1993) work on subjectivity and discourse to examine schooling as it was experienced by unsuccessful middle school students. Her description of a discourse of adolescence (naturalization) that dictates how "normal" juvenile offenders must display resistant and sexualized behaviors illustrates its pervasiveness.

Note, for instance, the "naturalizing" language of Angel, a 15-year-old European American mother of a 2-year-old, who was one of the participants in Finders's study: "You know, we did a lot of things to prove we were the way we were. We were *juvenile delinquents*. And so we gotta be worse" (Finders, 2005, p. 98). In another data clip—one that included self-introductions by Angel and two of her classmates on the occasion of a visitor to the alternative school—there is evidence of a gendered and sexualized version of the naturalizing discourse associated with juvenile delinquency:

> Ricky: I'm Ricky. I've been here since the beginning of the year. I got arrested for paraphernalia and driving without a license.
> Wayne: Wayne. I'm in eighth grade. I threw a punch at Ferguson [middle school principal].
> Angel: Uh. [Appearing to wake up] Oh I'm tired. I was out all night with my boyfriend if you know what I mean. I didn't get any sleep. Ha. You know what I mean. (p. 105)

A major insight that Finders drew from this study was the difficulty of crossing discursive boundaries—her own as a teacher steeped in critical pedagogy, and the "naturalized" discourse of juvenile offenders, where one had to be "bad" to live up to peers' and teachers' expectations. Although space limitations prevent sharing Finders' instructional intervention in detail, suffice it to say that she attempted to help students see how young people, and in particular, juvenile offenders, were represented in the texts they read. Although Angel was a competent reader in the sense that she could decode rapidly enough to comprehend the texts Finders put before her, the critical literacy intervention did not work particularly well for Angel. Reflecting on this finding, Finders wrote:

After teaching language arts at TLC for one year, I would argue that our first move is to disrupt the dominant discourses that position some students as non-competent members of the classroom. Angel, for example, was a highly competent reader and writer. Yet the discourse of female sexuality prevented even me from viewing her as competent. Clearly, Angel did not neatly fit my category of the middle school literacy learner; nor did I fit her categories either. She constructed me as someone who, as she said, "You have no clue, do you, Peg? You don't understand anything about me. You think that reading some book is going to make some big difference. You think you are better than me. You think I'm a little slut, don't you?"

She was right. Even in this chapter, I hear myself casting her behaviors as deviant, in need of remediation or control. Maybe I am guilty of allowing one discourse to speak for another, still trapped in my discursive readings of her actions. Perhaps her enacted sexuality is not, as I have argued from a middle-class, middle-aged discursive position, an attempt to maintain her position as "being bad." (p. 120)

In some ways, this illustration of category maintenance in the face of competing discourses is a reminder of Brandt and Clinton's (2002) cautionary note regarding the limits of the local when studying literacy as a social practice. In Finders's study, one might argue that Literacy (with a big "L" and single "y") was indeed "a thing"—an actor, a participant in the discourses of both the middle-class, middle-aged teacher and the juvenile offender, Angel. Although agency was alive and well in each of the performers (the "local literates"), what transpired was not a solo performance, but rather a case of Literacy asserting itself from afar.

Findings from a Detroit-based community ethnography (Moje & van Helden, 2005) that spanned 4 years and deconstructed what it means to be young, of Latina heritage, and a user of popular cultural texts, provide further support for Vadeboncoeur and Stevens's (2005) thesis that the "naturally developing" adolescent is a fiction who does not exist outside particular assumptions about particular youth living in particular times. In this ethnography, four young Latinas who identified themselves at various points in the study as Mexican, Chicana, Tejana, Mexicana, and Mexican American demonstrated that their uses of popular cul-

ture and popular cultural texts could not be reduced to any one fiction of how a "naturally developing" Latina responded to a media-saturated world in which there were choices to be made, albeit within a larger discourse that had marketing to youth as its central tenet.

Because both examples might be construed as nothing more than a simple nod to cultural relativism, I think it is useful here to draw attention to Clifford Geertz's (1984) frequently cited lecture on "Anti Anti-Relativism." In that lecture printed in the *American Anthropologist*, Geertz (1984) characterized cultural relativism as a condition deemed inescapable and reviled more for the unfounded dread it evoked than for its actual existence. Claiming that "pasteurized knowledge" (p. 263) is hardly a substitute for escaping the clutches of cultural relativism, Geertz went on to add: "Whatever cultural relativism may be or originally have been (and there is not one of its critics in a hundred who has got that right), it serves these days largely as a specter to scare us away from certain ways of thinking and toward others" (p. 263). The two examples drawn from Vadeboncoeur and Stevens's (2005) edited book on *Re/Constructing "the Adolescent,"* although certainly not "pasteurized knowledge" in Geertz's sense of the term, point to, along with a discourse of multiliteracies, new ways of thinking about adolescence.

Adolescence as a Site for Exploring New Possibilities in Youth's Multiliteracies

One could make the case that a discussion focused on exploring new possibilities is almost certain to lead to yet another fictionalization of adolescence. Perhaps so, but with Geertz's (1984) challenge freshly in mind to pursue certain ways of thinking that others might discourage, I begin with an example from Leander's (2007) research into adolescents' capacity for multitasking during the regular school day in classrooms where traditional text reading butted up against the demands of instant messaging, blogging, web browsing, chatting, and other online activities not remotely associated with school learning (e.g., shopping, gaming, and downloading music). It seems an apt beginning for exploring adolescence as a discursive site for opening up new possibilities involving youth and their multiliteracies. It also offers a way of thinking about text that I want to follow up on later.

In the wireless classrooms that provided Leander (2007) entry into a multitasking youth culture that typically exists on the outskirts of school-sanctioned learning environments, adolescents were observed participating in a range of self-selected activities, only some of which were related to the teacher's intended instructional goals. What is particularly noteworthy about this set of findings is that the young people Leander interviewed claimed to be able to attend to regular classroom activities at the same time that they were tracking an object of interest through cyberspace—sometimes, several objects of interest at once. Perhaps of even greater note were data suggesting that on-task students did not have an edge on their multitasking peers when it came to participation levels in regularly scheduled whole-group activities, such as class discussion. The multitaskers were particularly adept at "doing school" while surfing the web to relieve what they claimed was boredom with the pacing and content of the school's curriculum. Commenting on these findings, Lankshear and Knobel (2007) countered a common misconception about multitaskers' attention spans:

> This is not to imply that people operating from a [cyberspatial] mindset cannot and do not compartmentalize time and space and/or dedicate long stretches of time within a particular space to a single task or purpose—for clearly they do. It is, however, to say that a lot of contemporary literacy activity *is* conceived and undertaken "on the fly" and simultaneously with other practices. New literacies spaces are often fluid, continuous and open. Online and offline lives and "literacyscapes" (Leander, 2003) merge and augment. (p. 15)

A cyberspatial mindset does not assume that schools are the same learning spaces as they were even two decades ago, and it's not only because new communication technologies are more easily acquired than ever before. Instead, as Lankshear and Knobel (2007) explain, a new ethos exists in a discourse of adolescence that is in sync with a cyberspatial mindset. It is at sites like those in which Leander and his colleagues (Leander & Lovvorn, 2006) conduct their research—ones in which multitasking is almost ubiquitous—that adolescents experience how authority and expertise are distributed across age, race, class, and gender lines, to name but a few of the "old-school" identity markers that continue to serve some youth well, and others not so well. The new ethos does not ration literacy "success," as is the case in the older scarcity paradigm where high-stakes tests are typically renormed once the pass rate rises to an unacceptable level. Nor does it sanction the dominance of the book over other forms of text, such as fan fiction, manga, zines, anime, and online gaming in which multiple players perform certain roles in keeping with a particular game's storyline.

In this new textual realm, literacy practices that require collaboration and participation in disseminating knowledge deemed valuable to a particular affinity group (Gee, 2000–2001) are but some of the factors that index achievement and communicative competence. Others include the opportunity for dialogue, the gratification that comes with virtually immediate feedback, and the lure of a real community in which writers can see how many people visit their sites and ostensibly read their writing (Black, 2006). As Lankshear and Knobel (2007) have pointed out, however, there are still norms for publishing one's work in cyberspace, but they are "less fixed ... and less controlled by 'centralized' authorities and experts" (p. 14). And the texts to which such norms apply are also less likely to assume that all readers will respond in similar fashion, much less depend on monomodal representations of meaning.

The idea that writers produce texts that provide what Smagorinsky (2001) called "a meaning potential realized by different readers in different ways" (p. 142) has largely superseded an earlier notion that meaning inheres in the text, or what Olson (1977) meant by the autonomous text. Although the concept of the autonomous text has largely disappeared, the autonomous model of literacy has not. Any adolescent who has sat for a high-stakes reading test knows full well where the meaning resides, assuming of course that he or she is test savvy and not prone to taking chances that could lead to failure by reading critically. Nor could the hypothesized adolescent expect to demonstrate proficiency in reading on the National Assessment of Educational Progress (NAEP) by means other than print (National Assessment Governing Board, 2007). Yet, in 2009, the date set for the next Program for International Student Assessment (PISA) survey of 15-year-olds' ability to analyze, reason, and communicate effectively about what they read, the assessment will involve reading electronic texts (Organization for Economic Co-Operation and Development, 2007)—a stark contrast to NAEP's 2009 Reading Framework that assesses only students' ability to read traditional print texts. Moreover, findings from longitudinal research on youth's digital literacies, such as a 10-year study of the *Apple Classroom of Tomorrow,* demonstrate that adolescents engaged in project-based learning using multimedia platforms, when compared with peers without the same opportunities, have "clear advantages related to achievement, identity, strategies and tools for learning, problem-solving, discovering and communicating" (Tierney, in press).

To return to the question that guided this section—why might adolescence be a site for opening up new possibilities involving youth and their multiliteracies?—I want to answer, somewhat glibly, because it is already a contested space filled with contradictory constructions of who adolescents are and what they're about. At least some of those constructions (e.g., Lesko's, 2001, and Vadeboncoeur and Stevens's, 2005) argue strongly for considering the social and cultural contexts in which adolescents are produced, at times choose to reproduce themselves, but not infrequently resist or negotiate their way through. Moreover, sociocultural constructions of adolescence would appear supportive of multiliteracies as a viable alternative to (though not necessarily a replacement of) the autonomous model of literacy. The latter, with its emphasis on a neutral and universal set of reading and writing skills for decoding and encoding written text, is a view of literacy that discourages discussions of the very power relations that sustain its hold on literacy instruction in the United States. Although looking to adolescents and their multiliteracies as potential change agents in the doing, redoing, and undoing of schooled literacy (Alvermann & Eakle,

2007) may be but yet another fiction in the already crowded discourse of adolescence, it is one that resonates well with the award-winning Nigerian author Chinua Achebe's thoughts on the truth of fiction. In paraphrasing Achebe (1988), Vadeboncoeur (2005) wrote, "Perhaps the penultimate judgment on human kind is not whether we acquiesce to a fiction, but rather what kind of fiction will persuade us to comply" (p. 6).

IMPLICATIONS FOR EDUCATORS, RESEARCHERS, AND POLICYMAKERS

A dilemma exists, or is it an irony? More to the point, does it matter which of the two terms gets used? From the perspective of Mark Dressman (cited in Alvermann, 1998), it does. In Dressman's words:

> I think this distinction is an important one, because to characterize a situation as a dilemma is to call out in the next moment for a solution, whereas to name a situation as ironic is to ask us to live with it for a while, and to see what comes of it. The search for solutions to dilemmas and those solutions' deployment, regardless of how decent or noble our intentions may be, necessarily also calls for an end to debate about the nature of a dilemma itself, for a shutting down of discussion and for ignoring or filling in any contradictions or gaps in our logic in the name of Taking Action. (p. 354)

I am persuaded. Thus, an irony exists, and it is this: Despite calls for opening up the category of literacy, for viewing it more broadly within the social and cultural contexts of adolescence, the fact remains that in a world ideologically divided and growing arguably more digital by the nanosecond,

> the literacy field has tended to maintain a tradition of theorizing literacy and studying texts in a fashion which is singular and separated from the growing fabric of digital literacies with which most of us most of the time engage as our primary sources. Further, the field has tended to focus upon the individual(s) versus group(s) as the meaning makers. (Tierney, in press)

The focus on individual rather than group meaning making is indeed difficult to account for if one views literacy as a social practice. Even more perplexing is how to reconcile such a focus with Smagorinsky's (2001) call to move toward a cultural theory of reading, and more specifically, a reconceptualization of engaged reading. Like Lensmire (1994), Smagorinsky viewed engagement as being inclusive of readers and writers transacting with texts, but much more than that. If youth are to participate fully in a community's literacy practices, they argued, then it stands to reason that their voices must be heard in the classroom. In a nutshell, "Students' engagement with texts ... requires engagement with each other, thereby establishing an environment of mutual care and concern" (Smagorinsky, 2001, p. 161).

A concern of mine from the start has been youth who do not see themselves as capable and engaged readers and writers, who for whatever reason may be labeled as low achievers, even "contributors" to the literacy achievement gap. Some of these young people, like Angel, may be able to decode and comprehend their assignments relatively well, but their engagement with literacy and those around them is limited in an untold number of ways. Because many adolescents growing up in a digital world will find their own reasons for becoming literate—reasons that go beyond reading and writing to acquire academic knowledge—it is important that teachers create opportunities for them to engage actively in meaningful subject matter learning that both extends and elaborates on the literacy practices they already possess and value. Some researchers have begun to look more closely at the literacy skills and practices that youth could potentially bring to academic learning if they were encouraged to do so in ways that matter to them. For example, O'Brien (2003) found that when engaging a group of so-called struggling high school readers in the production of multimodal texts using a popular culture genre they admired, their perceptions of themselves changed from "struggling" to competent. This finding was later instrumental in directing his attention to how concepts such as *ability, effort,* and *task* play out differently in a traditional print classroom and a media literacy lab.

As illustrated elsewhere (Alvermann & McLean, 2007) but worth repeating here, the kind of literacy learning that O'Brien

(2003) enabled in the youth with whom he worked presents its own set of challenges. Indeed, becoming adept at orchestrating complex learning opportunities is but one skill classroom teachers will need in a world that is fast becoming so information-driven that students with access to the same resources as teachers often know as much if not more than their teachers about particular topics and subject areas of study (Leu, Kinzer, Coiro, & Cammack, 2004). That reality, especially when considered in light of the increased availability of multimodal texts, makes the present disconnect between the literacy field's mindset and a world dependent on digital literacies even more ironic. Yet within our field, as demonstrated by any number of currently influential position papers, books, reports, and instructional guides on literacy teaching and learning (e. g., Deshler, Palincsar, Biancarosa, & Nair, 2007; Harvey & Housman, 2004; Heller & Greenleaf, 2007), there is little or no attention being paid to the impact that reading and interpreting images and other representational modes beyond traditional print are having on youth and society at large. I offer this observation not as a critique but rather in the spirit of Heim (cited in Lankshear & Knobel, 2003), whose views, on first reading, startled but intrigued me:

> [The] word now shares Web space with the image, and text appears inextricably tied to pictures. The pictures are dynamic, animated, and continually updated. The unprecedented speed and ease of digital production mounts photographs, movies, and video on the Web. Cyberspace becomes visualized data, and meaning arrives in spatial as well as in verbal expressions. (p. 170)

Although this shift in attention from the word to the image, from the book to the screen might be viewed as a portent of print literacy's demise, that is not my argument here; nor was it Hull and Nelson's (2005) conclusion as a result of studying young people's involvement with multimodal learning. In what they admit is a radical claim still to be worked out, Hull and Nelson offer the possibility that "multimodality can afford, not just a new way to make meaning, but a different kind of meaning" (p. 225). They acknowledge, however, the possibility that new technologies could engender literacy practices that are not necessarily in print's best interests. Lewis and Fabos (2005) pointed to a similar possibility after reflecting on findings from their study of young people's instant messaging practices. However, as Lewis and Fabos were quick to add, if we fret about the loss of print literacy as we think we once knew it, then we risk shortchanging the very youth whose voices and literate lives, present and future, we wish to champion.

The work of these researchers calls to mind that until now the student voice has been largely absent from this chapter. Indeed, the arguments made here have been couched within an academic discourse deemed relevant to, and supportive of, the irony that Tierney's (in press) observation evoked in me. Although such absence of student voice was intentional to avoid unnecessary overlap with other chapters in this book, the case still needs to be made, if ever so briefly, that adolescents are active producers of texts. They have demonstrated many times over their ability to make use of whatever resources are readily available, whether in classrooms (e.g., Hinchman & Chandler-Olcott, 2006; Moje, Dillon, & O'Brien, 2000) or in the deregulated spaces of after-school media clubs, on museum trips, or in youth activist groups (Alvermann & Eakle, 2007; Guzzetti & Gamboa, 2004; Humphrey, 2006), to perform what Thomas (2008) refers to as a literate citizenship in cyberspace. Thus, it's not as if young people, including struggling readers, aren't reading, writing, and using literacy to accomplish things that have relevance for them. In point of fact, a recent Pew Internet study documented that adolescents are using their digital literacies to read and write themselves into the highly multimodal world in which they live (Lenhart, Madden, & Hitlin, 2005). According to this study, close to 9 out of 10 young people ages 12–19 in the United States are wired; this represents roughly 21 million youth who use daily some aspect of the Internet in their lives.

Given this brand of activism, know-how, and the increasingly blurred boundaries that once separated school, home, and community, why is it digital literacies continue to be viewed as part and parcel of the larger sociocultural practices that must remain outside the classroom door? Elsewhere I have argued (Alvermann & Eakle, 2007) that to reify distinctions between in-school and out-of-school literacies (Hull & Schultz, 2001) serves mainly to divorce those literacies from the very spaces that give them meaning and make them worth pursuing. It also limits what teachers, researchers, and policymakers can learn from students' experiences, at least to the extent that students are willing to share their perceptions of those experiences. Listening to and observing youth as they communicate their familiarity with multiple kinds of texts across space, place, and time can provide valuable insights into how to approach both instruction and research—insights that might otherwise be lost or taken for granted in the rush to categorize literacy practices as either in-school or out-of-school, adolescents as either struggling or competent, and thereby either worthy of our attention or not. Irony or dilemma, what matters most is that we understand "how conceptions of adolescence play a 'conserving' role" (Lesko, 2001, p. 190) in what we can ever hope to know about youth and their literacies.

REFERENCES

Achebe, C. (1988). The truth of fiction. *Hope and impediments: Selected essays 1965–1987.* Oxford, UK: Heinemann.

Aitken, S. C. (2001). *Geographies of young people: The morally contested spaces of identity.* New York: Routledge.

Alliance for Excellent Education. (2007). Legislative update: Bill S.958 and H.R. 2289. Retrieved June 16, 2007, from *www.all4ed.org/legislative/Striving Readers_Summary.pdf.*

Alvermann, D. E. (1998). Imagining the possibilities. In D. E. Alvermann, K. A. Hinchman, D. W. Moore, S. F. Phelps, & D. R. Waff (Eds.), *Reconceptualizing the literacies in adolescents' lives* (pp. 353–372). Mahwah, NJ: Erlbaum.

Alvermann, D. E. (Ed.). (2002). *Adolescents and literacies in a digital world.* New York: Peter Lang.

Alvermann, D. E., & Eakle, A. J. (2007). Dissolving learning boundaries: The doing, redoing, and undoing of school. In D. Thiessen & A. Cook-Sather (Eds.), *International handbook of student experience in elementary and secondary school* (pp. 143–166). Dordrecht, the Netherlands: Springer.

Alvermann, D. E., Hinchman, K. A., Moore, D. W., Phelps, S. F., & Waff, D. R. (2006). *Reconceptual-*

izing the literacies in adolescents' lives (2nd ed.). Mahwah, NJ: Erlbaum.

Alvermann, D. E., & McLean, C. A. (2007). The nature of literacies. In L. Rush, A. J. Eakle, & A. Berger (Eds.), *Secondary school reading and writing: What research reveals for classroom practices* (pp. 1–20). Urbana, IL National Council of Teachers of English.

Amit-Talai, V., & Wulff, H. (Eds.). (1995). *Youth cultures: A cross-cultural perspective.* New York: Routledge.

Appleman, D. (2001, April). *Unintended betrayal: Dilemmas of representation and power in research with youth.* Paper presented at the meeting of the American Educational Research Association, Seattle.

Ayers, W. (2005). Introduction. In J. A. Vadeboncoeur & L. P. Stevens (Eds.), *Re/constructing "the adolescent"* (pp. ix–xi). New York: Peter Lang.

Beers, K., Probst, R. E., & Rief, L. (Eds.). (2007). *Adolescent literacy: Turning promise into practice.* Portsmouth, NH: Heinemann.

Black, R. W. (2006). Language, culture, and identity in online fanfiction. *E-learning, 3*(2), 170–184.

Brandt, D., & Clinton, K. (2002). Limits of the local: Expanding perspectives on literacy as a social practice. *Journal of Literacy Research, 34,* 337–356.

Cammack, D. (2005). No straight line: Wrinkling binaries in literacy and technology research. *E-Learning, 2*(2), 153–168. Retrieved June 24, 2007, from *www.wwwords.co.uk/pdf/viewpdf.asp?j=elea&vol=2&issue=2&year=2005&article=5_Cammack_ELEA_2_2_web&id=97.81.111.239.*

Chandler-Olcott, K., & Mahar, D. (2003). Tech-savviness meets multiliteracies: An exploration of adolescent girls' technology-mediated literacy practices. *Reading Research Quarterly, 38,* 356–385.

Cintron, R. (1991). Reading and writing graffiti: A reading. *Quarterly Newsletter of the Laboratory of Comparative Human Cognition, 13,* 21–24.

Collins, J., & Blot, R. K. (2003). *Literacy and literacies: Texts, power, and identity.* New York: Cambridge University Press.

Connell, R. W. (1995). *Masculinities.* Berkeley and Los Angeles: University of California Press.

Cope, B., & Kalantzis, M. (2000). *Multiliteracies: Literacy learning and the design of social futures.* New York: Routledge.

Davies, B. (1993). *Shards of glass.* Cresskill, NJ: Hampton Press.

Deshler, D. D., Palincsar, A. S., Biancarosa, G., & Nair, M. (2007). *Informed choices for struggling adolescent readers: A research-based guide to instructional programs and practices.* Newark, DE: International Reading Association.

Finders, M. (1997). *Just girls: Hidden literacies and life in junior high.* New York: Teachers College Press.

Finders, M. (2005). "Gotta be worse": Literacy, schooling, and adolescent youth offenders. In J. A. Vadeboncoeur & L. P. Stevens (Eds.), *Re/constructing "the adolescent": Sign, symbol, and body* (pp. 97–122). New York: Peter Lang.

Foucault, M. (1997). *Ethics: Subjectivity and truth.* (P. Rabinow, Ed.; R. Hurley et al., Trans.). New York: New Press. (Original work published 1994).

Gee, J. P. (1990). *Social linguistics and literacies: Ideology in discourse.* New York: Falmer.

Gee, J. P. (1996). *Social linguistics and literacies: Ideology in discourse.* (2nd ed.). London: Taylor & Francis.

Gee, J. P. (2000–2001). Identity as an analytic lens for research in education. *Review of Research in Education, 25,* 99–125.

Geertz, C. (1984). Distinguished lecture: Anti anti-relativism. *American Anthropologist, 86,* 263–278.

Guthrie, J. W., & Springer, M. G. (2004). A Nation at Risk revisited: Did "wrong" reasoning result in "right" results? At what cost? *Peabody Journal of Education, 79*(1), 7–35.

Guzzetti, B. J., & Gamboa, M. (2004). Zines for social justice: Adolescent girls writing on their own. *Reading Research Quarterly, 39,* 408–436.

Hagood, M. C., Stevens, L. P., & Reinking, D. (2002). What do *they* have to teach *us?* Talkin' 'cross generations! In D. E. Alvermann (Ed.), *Adolescents and literacies in a digital world* (pp. 68–83). New York: Peter Lang.

Hall, G. S. (1904). *Adolescence: Its psychology and its relation to psychology, anthropology, sociology, sex, crime, religion, and education.* New York: Appleton-Century-Crofts.

Harvey, J., & Housman, N. (2004). *Crisis or possibility? Conversations about the American high school.* Washington, DC: National High School Alliance.

Heath, S. B. (1983). *Ways with words: Language, life, and work in communities and classrooms.* New York: Cambridge University Press.

Heller, R., & Greenleaf, C. (2007). *Literacy instruction in the content areas: Getting to the core of middle and high school improvement.* Washington, DC: Alliance for Excellent Education and Carnegie Corporation of New York.

Hinchman, K. A., & Chandler-Olcott, K. (2006). Literacies through youth's eyes: Lessons in representation and hybridity. In D. E. Alvermann, K. A. Hinchman, D. W. Moore, S. F. Phelps, & D. R. Waff (Eds.), *Reconceptualizing the literacies in adolescents' lives* (2nd ed., pp. 231–251). Mahwah, NJ: Erlbaum.

Hull, G., & Nelson, M. E. (2005). Locating the semiotic power of multimodality. *Written Communication, 22,* 224–261.

Hull, G., & Schultz, K. (2001). Literacy and learning out of school: A review of theory and research. *Review of Educational Research, 71,* 575–611.

Humphrey, S. (2006). Getting the reader on side—Exploring adolescent online political discourse. *E-Learning, 3,* 143–157.

Jewitt, C., & Kress, G. (Eds.). (2003). *Multimodal literacy.* New York: Peter Lang.

Kress, G. (1997). *Before writing: Rethinking the pathways to literacy.* London: Routledge.

Kress, G., & Street, B. V. (2006). Foreword. In K. Pahl

& J. Rowsell (Eds.), *Travel notes from the new literacy studies: Instances of practice* (pp. vii–x). Clevedon, UK: Multilingual Matters.

Kress, G., & Van Leeuwen, T. (1996). *Reading images: The grammar of visual design.* New York: Routledge.

Lankshear, C., & Knobel, M. (2003). *New literacies: Changing knowledge and classroom learning.* Buckingham, UK: Open University Press.

Lankshear, C., & Knobel, M. (2006). *New literacies: Everyday practices and classroom learning* (2nd ed.). Berkshire, UK: McGraw-Hill/Open University Press.

Lankshear, C., & Knobel, M. (2007). Sampling the "new" in new literacies. In M. Knobel & C. Lankshear (Eds.), *A new literacies sampler* (pp. 1–24). New York: Peter Lang.

Latour, B. (1993). *We have never been modern.* Cambridge, MA: Harvard University Press.

Leander, K. M. (2003). Writing travelers' tales on new literacyscapes. *Reading Research Quarterly, 38,* 392–397.

Leander, K. M. (2007). "You won't be needing your laptops today": Wired bodies in the wireless classroom. In M. Knobel & C. Lankshear (Eds.), *A new literacies sampler* (pp. 25–48). New York: Peter Lang.

Leander, K. M., & Lovvorn, J. (2006). Literacy networks: Following the circulation of texts, bodies, and objects in the schooling and online gaming of one youth. *Cognition and Instruction, 24,* 291–340.

Lemke, J. (1989). Social semiotics: A new model for literacy education. In D. Bloome (Ed.), *Classrooms and literacy* (pp. 289–309). Norwood, NJ: Ablex.

Lenhart, A., Madden, M., & Hitlin, P. (2005). *Youth are leading the transition to a fully wired and mobile nation.* Pew Internet and American Life Project.

Lensmire, T. J. (1994). *When children write: Critical revisions of the writing workshop.* New York: Teachers College Press.

Lesko, N. (2001). *Act your age! A cultural construction of adolescence.* New York: Falmer.

Leu, D. J., Jr., Kinzer, C. K., Coiro, J. L., & Cammack, D. W. (2004). Toward a theory of new literacies emerging from the Internet and other information and communication technologies. In R. B. Ruddell & N. J. Unrau (Eds.), *Theoretical models and processes of reading* (5th ed., pp. 1570–1613). Newark, DE: International Reading Association.

Lewis, C., Enciso, P., & Moje, E. B. (2007). *Reframing sociocultural research on literacy: Identity, agency, and power.* Mahwah, NJ: Erlbaum.

Lewis, C., & Fabos, B. (2005). Instant messaging, literacies, and social identity. *Reading Research Quarterly, 40,* 470–501.

Luke, A. (2002). What happens to literacies old and new when they're turned into policy. In D. E. Alvermann (Ed.), *Adolescents and literacies in a digital world* (pp. 186–203). New York: Peter Lang.

Mac an Ghaill, M. (1994). *The making of men: Masculinities, sexualities, and schooling.* Buckingham, UK: Open University Press.

Marsh, J. P., & Stolle, E. (2006). Re/constructing identities: A tale of two adolescents. In D. E. Alvermann, K. A. Hinchman, D. W. Moore, S. F. Phelps, & D. R. Waff (Eds.), *Reconceptualizing the literacies in adolescents' lives* (2nd ed., pp. 47–63). Mahwah, NJ: Erlbaum.

Miller, S. M., & Borowicz, S. (2006). *Why multimodal literacies? Designing digital bridges to 21st century teaching and learning.* Buffalo, NY: GSE Publications & SUNY Press.

Moje, E. B. (2000). "To be part of the story": The literacy practices of gangsta adolescents. *Teachers College Record, 102,* 651–690.

Moje, E. B., Dillon, D. R., & O'Brien, D. G. (2000). Reexamining the role of learner, text, and context in secondary literacy. *Journal of Educational Research, 93,* 165–180.

Moje, E. B., & van Helden, C. (2005). Doing popular culture: Troubling discourses about youth. In J. A. Vadeboncoeur & L. P. Stevens (Eds.), *Re/constructing "the adolescent": Sign, symbol, and body* (pp. 211–247). New York: Peter Lang.

Morgan, W. (1997). *Critical literacy in the classroom.* London: Routledge.

National Assessment Governing Board. (2007). *Reading framework for the 2009 National Assessment of Educational Progress* (Prepublication ed.). Washington, DC: American Institutes for Research. Retrieved June 27, 2007, from *www.nagb.org/frameworks/ reading_fw_03_07_prepub_edition.doc.*

National Commission on Excellence in Education. (1983). *A nation at risk: The imperative for educational reform.* Washington, DC: U.S. Department of Education.

New Directions in Research. (2007). Multiple dimensions of achievement: Defining, identifying, and addressing "the gap." *Reading Research Quarterly, 42,* 406–407.

New London Group. (2000). A pedagogy of multiliteracies. In B. Cope & M. Kalantzis (Eds.), *Multiliteracies: Literacy learning and the design of social futures* (pp. 9–37). London: Routledge.

No Child Left Behind Act of 2001. PL 107-110, 115 Stat.1425, 20 U.S.C. 6301 *et. seq.*

O'Brien, D. (2003, March). Juxtaposing traditional and intermedial literacies to redefine the competence of struggling adolescents. *Reading Online, 6*(7). Retrieved June 26, 2007, from *www.readingonline.org/ newliteracies/lit_index.asp?HREF=obrien2/.*

Olson, D. R. (1977). From utterance to text: The bias of language in speech and writing. *Harvard Educational Review, 47,* 257–281.

Organization for Economic Co-Operation and Development (OECD). (2007). *PISA: The OECD Programme for International Student Assessment* (p. 16). Retrieved May 29, 2007, from *www.pisa.oecd.org/ dataoecd/51/27/37474503.pdf.*

Rogers, T., & Schofield, A. (2005). Things thicker than words. Portraits of multiple literacies in an alternative secondary program. In J. Anderson, M. Kendrick, T. Rogers, & S. Smythe, (Eds.), *Portraits of literacy across families, communities and schools: Tensions and intersections* (pp. 205–220). Mahwah, NJ: Erlbaum.

Scribner, S., & Cole, M. (1981). *The psychology of literacy.* Cambridge, MA: Harvard University Press.

Smagorinsky, P. (2001). If meaning is constructed, what is it made from? Toward a cultural theory of reading. *Review of Educational Research, 71,* 133–169.

Stalwick, A. (2007). Constructing masculinity: How three grade eight boys explore the boundaries of masculinity through writing toward a bio-cultural theory of reading and learning. *Language and Literacy: A Canadian Educational E-Journal, 9*(1). Retrieved June 24, 2007, from *www.langandlit.ualberta.ca/Spring2007/Stalwick.htm.*

Street, B. V. (1984). *Literacy in theory and practice.* New York: Cambridge University Press.

Street, B. V. (1995). *Social literacies: Critical approaches to literacy in development, ethnography and education.* London: Longman.

Street, B. V. (2003). Foreword. In J. Collins & R. K. Blot, *Literacy and literacies: Texts, power, and identity* (pp. xi–xv). Cambridge, UK: Cambridge University Press.

Thomas, A. (2008). Community, culture, and citizenship in cyberspace. In J. Coiro, M. Knobel, C. Lankshear, & D. J. Leu (Eds.), *Handbook of research on new literacies* (pp. 671–697). New York: Erlbaum.

Tierney, R. (in press). The agency and artistry of meaning makers within and across digital spaces. In S. E. Israel & G. G. Duffy (Eds.), *Handbook of research on reading comprehension.* Mahwah, NJ: Erlbaum.

Vadeboncoeur, J. A. (2005). Naturalised, restricted, packaged, and sold: Reifying the fictions of "adolescent" and "adolescence." In J. A. Vadeboncoeur & L. P. Stevens (Eds.), *Re/constructing "the adolescent"* (pp. 1–24). New York: Peter Lang.

Vadeboncoeur, J. A., & Stevens, L. P. (Eds.). (2005). *Re/constructing "the adolescent."* New York: Peter Lang.

Wilder, P., & Dressman, M. (2006). New literacies, enduring challenges? The influence of capital on adolescent readers' Internet practices. In D. E. Alvermann, K. A. Hinchman, D. W. Moore, S. F. Phelps, & D. R. Waff (Eds.), *Reconceptualizing the literacies in adolescents' lives* (2nd ed., pp. 205–229). Mahwah, NJ: Erlbaum.

Wyn, J., & White, R. (1997). *Rethinking youth.* London: Sage.

Zuckerbrod, N. (2007, June 20). 2,300 schools: 'No Child' overhaul. Retrieved June 22, 2007, from *www.time.com/time/printout/0,8816,1635267,00.html.*

CHAPTER 3

Who Are Adolescents Today?

Youth Voices and What They Tell Us

SAM M. INTRATOR
ROBERT KUNZMAN

This chapter begins with a brief demographic portrait of American adolescents followed by some empirical insights into how teenagers spend their time. The primary focus is on how youth narrate and describe their own experiences of adolescence: how youth give voice to their subjective realities, and in particular, how they experience school. This "youth voice portrait" helps to reveal how adolescents represent the experience of schooling and literacy development from the inside. The orientation of these studies is grounded in a belief that youth are self-conscious, observant, critical consumers of educational experience. They have sophisticated capacities of discernment and a unique perspective on what happens in school and classrooms. The chapter presents what we can learn from listening to the voices of youth narrate their experiences of schooling. Researchers have found that youth are largely excluded from the discourse around schooling; adolescents possess a consumerist orientation toward engagement; literacy emerges from an ecology of relationships; youth yearn for opportunities to explore and express their distinctive voices; opportunities to refine and develop these voices should be a central goal of education; and this education, this potential transformation, is not limited to formal school settings. Although the experience of adolescence varies according to the sociocultural environment, researchers do agree that the experience includes transition, voyage, and a series of passages or psychosocial tasks to be accomplished. These psychosocial tasks are both psychological, in that they refer to an individual's sense of self, and influence an individual's social relationships with peers, families, and institutions. Educators, we conclude, should help students develop and refine authentic and powerful tools of analysis and self-expression.

Who are American adolescents today? The answer to this question depends greatly on who answers it. Social commentators and some teachers decry a loss of manners and moral fiber. Blue ribbon panels question American adolescents' capacity to compete in a global economy. Marketers see them as their emerging target audience. A critical and often overlooked perspective on the question, however, comes from adolescents themselves (Cook-Sather, 2002; Erickson & Shultz, 1992; Pope, 2001). This chapter seeks to convey an understanding about adolescents in the classroom context by presenting a review of research studies that reveal youth's perspectives on their experiences with the curriculum and, in particular, the literacy curriculum.

Before we turn to their voices, however, we offer a brief sketch of what others say about adolescents. The 2000 census revealed a population of just over 40 million adolescents ages 10–19, and the projected rate of increase through 2010 is only a third as rapid as the general population increase. Already, however, the adolescent population is significantly more racially/ethnically diverse than the U.S. population as a whole; this diversity will continue to increase, with a 2020 estimate of approximately 56% White (non-Hispanic), 23% Hispanic, 14% Black, 6% Asian/Pacific Islander, and 1% American Indian/Alaskan Native (United States Census Bureau, 2004).

As recent controversies over census categories themselves indicate, this diversity is increasingly difficult to measure by single-race categories. At least some research suggests, however, that adolescents navigate this imprecision perhaps more easily than adults, recognizing the blurring of racial/ethnic boundaries while still employing standard single-race categories when grappling with social injustice engendered by those very categories (Pollock, 2005).

The etymology of *adolescence* is derived from the Latin *adolescere*, which suggests a growing toward adulthood. Adolescence is a series of transitions that involve the emergence of cognitive capacities for more abstract and advanced thought, and the transition into new institutions and social structures results in dramatic and fundamental change for the individual. Although the experience of adolescence varies according to the sociocultural environment, researchers do agree that the period can be understood through metaphors that suggest a phase of transition, voyage, series of passages, or psychosocial tasks to be accomplished. These psychosocial tasks are both psychological, in that they refer to an individual's sense of self, and social relating to an individual's relationships with peers, families, and institutions. The intensity of these psychosocial transitions is profound as youth strive to negotiate a series of developmental projects (Erikson, 1968; Simpson, 2001; Steinberg, 2005). Buechner (1993)

puts it succinctly: "Being not quite a child and not quite a grown-up either is hard work, and they look it. Living in two worlds at once is no picnic" (p. 2).

A perennial question surrounding adolescent development (even well before such a concept or developmental stage was identified) has considered how different or unique the adolescent experience really is "today." Upon emerging from adolescence, are individuals somehow given a furtive "memory wipe" that hamstrings their ability to truly understand the experiences and perspectives of those years? And even if they could remember with perfect clarity, would the time and context of their experiences prove helpful in this new age, this new world?

Marketers would certainly have society believe that (without their interpretive assistance, of course) the world of adolescence is both dynamic and deeply mysterious, and they are continually trumpeting teens' cultural impact and economic clout. And although it's true that today's teenagers have more discretionary income than previous generations (breathless marketing reports cite anywhere from $110 to $175 billion or more in teen spending in 2003), this affluence hardly qualifies them as "savvy" consumers. Gladwell's (1997) exploration of the "coolhunters" employed by market researchers to anticipate the next big trend seems as much about figuring out how to tell teens what *should be* important to them as about genuinely listening. While we certainly think it is important to recognize the perpetual evolution of youth experience and culture, we are skeptical that marketers are the most dependable interpreters. "The American invention of youth culture," as one analyst puts it, capitalizes on and manipulates youth experience at least as much as it genuinely reflects it (Hine, 1999). Listening to youth voices is certainly vital, but educators' purposes and processes should be radically different from those of the coolhunters of Madison Avenue.

As this chapter ultimately contends, the growing research on "youth voice" suggests to us that the relationships between teachers and their adolescent students must be *dialogical* in nature, a cultivation of listening and learning by both adults and teens. Take, for example, the realm of technology. Adolescents today seem at home with technology in ways unfamiliar to older generations, multitasking through life with an array of iPods, cell phones, laptops, and whatever else has appeared on the scene between the writing of this chapter and its publication. And yet countless classroom teachers have endured reading their students' research papers clogged with uncritical "cutting and pasting" of dubious websites and undocumented information. Becoming *literate* in technology means teachers and students must approach the task with a willingness to explore together, recognizing the skills and insights each one brings to the interaction.

In addition to debates about just how different "adolescents today" are from those of yesteryear, disagreement exists about the popular image of adolescence as an inevitable time of stress and rebellion. Recent brain research suggests that adolescence involves a period of brain development second only to the first years of life, and much of this development involves decision making and higher-order thinking (Strauch, 2003). Although the biological and chemical changes that occur during such development are certainly significant, some researchers maintain that these factors need not result in the emotional upheaval that conventional wisdom often associates with the teenage years (Steinberg, 2005; Strauch, 2003).

Regardless, it seems clear that our schools struggle to engage adolescents in the formal curriculum. Although learning and succeeding in school require *active engagement,* a term used to describe the degree to which students are psychologically and emotionally connected to what is transpiring in their classrooms, data from a wide range of studies focused on reporting youth perspective suggest that students are generally bored and disengaged in school (Csikszentmihalyi & Larson, 1984; Center for Evaluation and Education Policy, 2006; Intrator, 2003; Pope, 2001). Steinberg's (2005) 3-year study of nine schools and 20,000 students from diverse educational settings found that fewer than half of the students reported taking school or their studies seriously; this finding was consistent across socioeconomic strata. As Steinberg concludes, whether students are "surrounded by suburban affluence or urban poverty, students' commitment to school is at an all-time low" (p. 13).

The studies we review invited students from a range of educational settings and social contexts to reflect on their curricular experiences. It is important to note that although the consequences of disengagement have implications for all students, the National Research Council Institute of Medicine (2003) asserts that the toll of disengagement has particularly dire implications for students who come from disadvantaged backgrounds or from high-need schools:

> When students from advantaged backgrounds become disengaged, they may learn less than they could, but they usually get by or they get second chances; most eventually graduate and move on to other opportunities. In contrast, when students from disadvantaged backgrounds in high-poverty, urban high schools become disengaged, they are less likely to graduate and consequently face severely limited opportunities. (p. 1)

Being bored, it appears, costs more to those who can afford it least.

When adolescents critique their academic experiences as boring and disconnected from their lives, their feelings can be understood as a catch basin for other, more nuanced critiques that speak to the consequences of being sorted, tracked, and labeled by the system. Perhaps most starkly visible when students are identified as "basic" or "remedial," the stratification process suggests a singular or at least a limited view of value that tells the majority of kids, "You're not special"—at least not in any way to feel good about. Cotton (1989) argues that such categorizations can be difficult to shake and do not allow for what seems perhaps *most clear* about adolescent development and experience: the incredible variation within. Most observers can recognize the vast differences in priorities, experiences, and perspectives between a 13-year-old and a 17-year-old, but such diversity often exists between two 13-year-olds as well. What's more, consistency of perspective and behavior cannot even be assumed within the same adolescent, a phenomenon that sometimes takes more patience to understand than even the most well-meaning adult can muster.

A common theme throughout much of the research literature as well as the anecdotal observations of longtime educators, however, is the deep (albeit not always expressed) need of adolescents for adults in their lives who genuinely care about them as individuals. Hersch (1998) reveals the experiences of many teenagers as isolated from and unsupervised by adults. The "rush" of connection and attention provided by virtual environments such as MySpace or instant messaging seems testament to the desperate desire for getting noticed felt by many adolescents. While certainly the role and influence of peers grows tremendously during the teenage years, the need and desire (however sublimated) for adult role models and support does not evaporate—but too often, it seems, the opportunities for such relationships do. Clark (2004) contends that the greatest challenge of adolescents today is abandonment: Teens are desperate for adults who are about them and for them.

Caring for and supporting adolescents requires more than well-intentioned gathering of information about them. Yazzie-Mintz (2007) directs the High School Survey of School Engagement (HSSSE; Center for Evaluation and Education Policy, 2006), which is a multiple-choice, fill-in-the-bubbles survey instrument. Yazzie-Mintz also provides space for students to add narrative comments at the end to supplement their answers. A frequent response, he has found, is as follows: "These surveys are pointless because you guys will do nothing even if there is a problem" (Yazzie-Mintz, 2007, p. 10). Although surveys such as HSSSE provide important large-scale data, the need to listen to adolescent voices, expressed in their own idioms and with sensitivity to context, remains vitally important if adults are to help make schools places that matter to adolescents.

YOUTH VOICE AND THE EXPERIENCED CURRICULUM

In a study that attempted to understand what students from three comprehensive English schools serving a diverse and predominately working-class population had to say to educators about school life, Rudduck, Chaplain, and Wallace (1996) contend that

young people are seldom consulted about their schooling. Typically they are seen as merely its passive beneficiaries. Little attention is paid to

their experience; their critiques are rarely sought, let alone acted on. Yet, as insiders, intimately familiar with every detail of school practice, pupils represent a valuable resource, and potentially, an agency for positive change. (p. 66)

What is particularly missing from the research is student perspective on teaching strategies (Cook-Sather, 2002; Cothran & Kulinna, 2006; Flutter, 2006; Flutter & Rudduck, 2004; Shultz & Cook-Sather, 2001; Walford & Massey, 1998). Cothran and Kulinna (2006) characterize this absence as a critical oversight because current conceptualizations of student learning focus on the influential, constructivist nature of student cognition and the meaning that students assign to their experiences. Adolescents are accustomed to making choices or adopting a consumerist orientation toward experiences. In light of this tendency, it is important to understand the youth perspective and reaction to a range of teaching strategies and approaches.

Even when student voice *is* solicited for research or school improvement initiatives, the rarest form of study involves exploration of a student's immediate experience. Most studies that explore student experience rely on retrospective interviewing or survey techniques to reconstruct student attitudes about a past event. A particularly useful example of this approach is the HSSSE. In 2004 the Center for Evaluation and Education Policy at Indiana University launched HSSSE, a short survey designed to be administered by high schools to lend insight into student engagement with educational activities. Since 2004, the survey has been administered to 300,000 students across 29 states. The most recent survey reveals some disturbing signs of disengagement by many students. For instance, nearly one-third report that they spent *no* time in school-sponsored activities. In addition, respondents spent relatively little time preparing for class. More than 40% spent 1 hour or less *per week* on written homework, and 55% reported spending more than an hour *per week* on reading or studying for class. Only 17% devoted more than 5 hours per week to written homework, and a mere 9% spent at least that much time reading or studying for class. The

2004 survey also points to the importance of student participation in the educational process: Students who strongly agreed (16%) that they have a voice in making classroom decisions were far more likely to indicate that

- They are supported and respected by teachers (81% compared to 25%).
- What they learn at school is useful (73% to 23%).
- They feel safe at school (69% to 25%).
- They work harder than they expected to work in school (59% to 26%).
- They take pride in their schoolwork (86% to 34%).
- They place a high value on learning (90% to 36%).

Although this study and those like it provide useful insight into student perception, the directed nature of the questioning (HSSSE, for example, is a multiple-choice survey) and the frequent time lag between students' specific experiences and the inquiry into the events blunts the adolescents' ability to convey the nuanced attributes of their experiences.

In sum, researchers know relatively little about the social, emotional, and cognitive experiences students have in the classroom setting (Erickson & Shultz, 1992; Pope, 2001). Curiously, research has revealed substantially more about how students experience other settings in schools. Such studies present student perspectives on a broad range of questions, such as how peer groups interact (Eckert, 1989); how the school environment and milieu shape the nature of student experience (Cusick, 1973; Fine, 1991; Henry, 1965; Hollingshead, 1949; Peshkin, 1986, 1991, 1994, 2001; Powell, Cohen, & Farrar, 1985); how powerful social and cultural forces shape the transition from school to work (Hodkinson, Sparkes, & Hodkinson, 1996; Willis, 1977); and how cultural and political forces operate on the lives of high school dropouts (Fine, 1991; Olsen, 1997). These studies provide perspectives on the experience of schooling; however, the studies only tangentially explore the students' subjective experience on the nature, nuances, and dynamics of everyday classroom life.

Although educational events hinge on the intricate dance performed among teacher, student, and subject matter, very little is known and understood about how teachers and students experience daily classroom situations (Kamberelis, 1995). Langer and Allington (1992) argue that although researchers have made strides in understanding the processes of subject matter instruction, they have neglected important contextual factors. Langer and Allington exhort researchers to focus on the complexities of classroom life, the multiple contexts experienced by students, and the practiced rather than the planned curriculum. Shuell (1996) argues that teaching and learning have typically been studied as separate entities and that the complexities of the teaching–learning exchange have been ignored. Doyle (1992) observes that the study of teaching and curriculum must be "grounded much more deeply than it has been in the events that students and teachers jointly construct in classroom settings" (p. 509). Kamberelis (1995) argues that researchers must direct their efforts toward "new ways of looking at and interpreting the vicissitudes and opportunities of classroom life" (p. 149).

Curriculum is a powerful word in our educational discourse (Burroughs & Smagorinsky, Chapter 12, this volume). It's a broad term that connotes a variety of meanings, from some as general as "what schools in this country should teach" to others as narrow as a "specific educational activity planned for a particular student at a particular point in time" (Eisner, 1994, p. 25). In considering the question, "Who are adolescents today?" we have chosen to focus on an especially neglected and particularly vital issue: how adolescents make sense of their in-the-classroom literacy experiences. We call this dynamic the operationalized or experienced curriculum because its focus is on the unique events that unfold in a classroom and places the adolescent's subjective interpretation of those experiences at the center of study. Our effort is to understand adolescents' perspectives on teaching, learning, and literacy through research that attempts to showcase their words, impressions, judgments, and reflections. In short, we are concerned with the stories that youth tell themselves about the character of education they experience within the activities experienced in the classroom.

CONCEPTUAL ROOTS
OF YOUTH VOICE RESEARCH

The framework guiding our examination of
the experienced curriculum is rooted in a
philosophical premise offered by John
Dewey. Dewey (1938) tries to sort through
the competing arguments between what he
terms progressive and traditional education. He acknowledges many of the structural complexities of the progressive movement and its "uncertainties" (p. 25) but
reiterates a claim made in his earlier work
that there is "one permanent frame of reference," which is the "organic connection
between education and personal experience." He then goes on to claim that when
considering schools and learning, "everything depends upon the *quality* of the experience had" (p. 27; emphasis in the original). Here, then, lies the heart of youth
voice research and the focus of this chapter: How do students experience the classroom curriculum?

More specifically, Dewey's conception of
experience enables educators to appreciate
the importance of trying to make sense of
what he calls the transaction between the
student and the environing conditions. For
Dewey (1938), the first principle of experience is that it happens as an unceasing
"moving force" (p. 38). Experience occurs
continuously and subsumes everything from
the instinctive fluttering of a baby's eyelashes to the fastidious brushstrokes of an
artist. Edman (1939) concludes that experience is "irretrievably there," and it is in
"primordial flux" (p. 12). In *Experience and
Nature*, Dewey (1929) describes the envel-
oping stretch of experience:

> Like its congeners, life and history, it includes,
> *what* men do and suffer, *what* they strive for,
> love, believe, and endure, and also *how* men
> act and are acted upon, the ways in which they
> do and suffer, desire and enjoy, see, believe,
> imagine—in short, process of *experiencing*.
> "Experience" denotes the planted field, the
> sowed seeds, the reaped harvests, the changes
> of night and day, spring and autumn, wet and
> dry, heat and cold, that are observed, feared,
> longed for; it also denotes the one who plants
> and reaps, who works and rejoices, hopes,
> fears, plans, invokes magic or chemistry to aid
> him, who is downcast or triumphant. (p. 66;
> emphasis in the original)

In this quote, Dewey (1929) leaves nothing out of his inventory. Experience is all-
inclusive, which means that "life goes on
between and among things of which the organism is but one" (p. 282). Experience
happens whether or not the individual se-
cures meaning from the experience or not.
The fact that experience happens separately
from the grasping of experience is a critical
one in understanding Dewey's system of
experience. Usually, when people use the
verb *experience*, they highlight the fact that
they "experienced something." Likewise,
when they use it as a noun to suggest a
compelling episode, they say, "Now, *that*
was an experience." Both cases represent
the most common conception of experience
and are indicative of what Dewey criticizes
as "selective emphasis" and the "philo-
sophic fallacy" (p. 29). The fallacy locates
experience primarily within the person and
limits it to "a very personal and private af-
fair" (Jackson, 1998, p. 3). Dewey's (1929)
version of experience embraces more than
the mental state; it encompasses what was
experienced as well as the experiencer's
psychological state:

> The thing essential to bear in mind is that liv-
> ing as an empirical affair is not something
> which goes on below the skin-surface of an or-
> ganism: it is always an inclusive affair involv-
> ing connection, interaction of what is within
> the organic body and what lies outside in space
> and time, and with higher organisms far out-
> side. (p. 282)

The emphasis on the interaction between
organism and environment leads to Dewey's
(1934) second cardinal principle of experience: Experience is not an internal process,
but a transaction.

> The first great consideration is that life goes on
> in an environment; not merely *in* it but because
> of it, through interaction with it. No creature
> lives merely under its skin; its subcutaneous or-
> gans are means of connection with what lies
> beyond its bodily frame. . . . The career and
> destiny of a living being are bound up with its
> interchanges with its environment. (p. 35; em-
> phasis in the original)

Transaction is the process that encompasses all that passes between an organism
and its surroundings. Therefore, individuals

are not merely organisms who breathe air, but organisms together with air being breathed. The phrase *together with air* highlights this central principle of Dewey's (1934) system of experience: "An experience is a product, one might almost say a byproduct of continuous and cumulative interaction of an organic self with the world" (p. 220).

Our capacity to secure meaning from these transactions is a cognitive achievement and in many ways represents the pivotal focus of this chapter. Youth experience many things in the context of the activities in which they participate in the classroom. Much of what happens whirls by them and is never processed in a way that yields learning or, as Dewey (1934) would describe it, "educative experience" (p. 25). Understanding those experiences that result in students securing meaning would appear to be fundamental, according to Dewey's framework, because it is within experience that learning about self and the world takes place. Dewey offers a way of understanding that, although schools have an intended curriculum that involves aims, aspirations, and the materials generated to enact those objectives, these planned agendas cannot be understood and appreciated in isolation. Rather, educators must consider their relationship to the experienced curriculum—those understandings, impressions, and judgments secured by students from the series of events that transpire in the classroom.

THE EMERGENCE OF STUDENT VOICE RESEARCH

Despite the tremendous influence of Dewey's ideas on American education, there is little evidence that educators have ever systematically explored the character of student experience. Until Erickson and Shultz (1992), no comprehensive handbook of curriculum or literacy devoted a chapter to the subjective experience of students in the classroom. Erickson and Shultz (1992) observe, "Neither in conceptual work, nor in empirical research, nor in the conventional wisdom and the discourse of practice does the subjective experience of students as they are engaged in learning figure in any central way." They conclude that

in sum, virtually no research has been done that places student experience at the center of attention. We do not see student interest and their known and unknown own fears. We do not see the mutual influence of students and teachers or see what the student or the teacher thinks or cares about during the course of that mutual influence. . . . Rarely is the perspective of the student herself explored. Classroom research typically does not ask what the student is up to, nor does it take the critical stance toward its own categories and assumptions so as to question whether "failing" or "mastering" or being "unmotivated" or "misconceiving" adequately captures what the student might be about in daily classroom encounters with the curriculum. (pp. 467–468)

Erickson and Shultz (1992) mobilized a small number of researchers to pursue research agendas that attempt to put student experience at the center of educational discourse. Researchers such as Pope (2001) use Erickson and Shultz's chapter as a substantive warrant to frame the characterization of the educational problem they seek to explore. Pope writes,

As I reviewed the literature on adolescents and secondary schools, I noticed a peculiar gap in the research in this area. I found a wide range of studies on adolescent behavior in schools, studies that addressed academic achievement, study habits, classroom discipline, peer culture, and youth dropout rates. However, I did not find many studies that addressed the educational experience in the school from the adolescents' points of view. The few studies that I found that relied on the youths' perspectives examined mostly the social aspects of schooling, such as life in the hallways and parking lots, instead of the students' classroom experiences and the character of their intellectual engagement—topics that lie at the very heart of the mission of the school. It seems ironic that we require young people to attend high school, and yet we know relatively little about what they think of the place. (p. xiii)

As Pope (2001) describes, her work is an effort to hear youth perspective for the purposes of understanding students' classroom experiences. Her research is tightly focused on listening to youth give voice to their experience in the classroom and narrate the degree to which they are engaged with academic experiences. This inquiry focus represents one strand of youth voice research. We briefly describe the other three strands before returning to dwell on those studies that probe how youth experience their academic context and, in particular, what youth have to say about their literacy experiences in the classroom.

Youth Voice on School Organization, School Policies, and School Reform

There has been a broad range of studies that focus on qualities of school structure. The intent of these studies is to provide adult leadership with an inside perspective on what works and what does not work. For example, in Wilson and Corbett's (2001) study of 247 students from five of Philadelphia's poorest and lowest-scoring middle schools, they articulate the rationale guiding this strand of youth voice research: "If substantial reforms to improve what and how much students learn actually occur in schools, then students' descriptions of their classroom experiences should reflect those changes. Reform, in other words, should become noticeable in what students say about school" (p. 1).

This orientation toward the promotion of youth voice suggests that efforts to include youth in the decision-making process promote more effective school reform. Fletcher (2004) argues that

> listening to students plays an important role in education reform, in that it provides a necessary foundation from which education leaders can develop informed opinions and take practical action for school change. These leaders face multiple pressures and are often faced with making decisions "on-the-spot." By understanding what students think, experience, feel, and know, these types of decisions can be better informed. (p. 8)

Youth Voice on Participating in the Civic Process of Education

An expanding set of studies has focused on what students learn through participating in processes that value the voice of students as contributing members of intergenerational communities. For example, Mitra (2004) focuses on how youth involved in a school change initiative composed of youth and adults expanded their "youth development outcomes," including their capacity to critique their environment, as well as expanding their skills in problem solving, facilitation, and public speaking. Although these skills identified by Mitra clearly relate to a range of literacy outcomes that adults aspire to cultivate in students, the youth voice experience here was located in a cocurricular setting rather than the classroom.

Youth Voice on the Relationship among Community, Culture, and Schooling

Several studies—including numerous books—have attempted to listen in on the inner working of youth culture. These projects put youth perspective at the center of the narrative, and while they often focus on school-related topics, they do so as part of a larger narrative. One example is that of Hersch (1998), who spent 3 years with a group of eight suburban youth as they moved through the variety of contexts in their lives. In her narrative, she privileges youth voice by structuring the text so that youth speak for themselves about what matters to them and how they negotiate the moral, sexual, ethical, and relational challenges of their lives. Although schools and curricular issues do receive attention, they are a secondary emphasis in the study.

Youth Voice on Teaching and Learning

The focus of these studies is on how youth narrate their experiences with teaching, learning, and the conditions of learning in their classrooms. Intrator's (2003) study of a comprehensive high school in a small urban community describes the collective orientation and aspiration of this strand of youth voice research:

> I remember one day sitting with a group of teachers and picking up the magazine section of the *New York Times*. There was a picture of a family sitting at a table. Accompanying the picture was a short article that described what the individuals were thinking and feeling in the moment the photograph was taken. I turned to the teachers and asked, "How often would you like to be able to do this during class?" We chuckled because every teacher with whom I've ever worked, from the most grizzled veteran to the most idealistic novice, has de-

scribed the feeling of looking at their students and wondering, "What is in their heads?" Answering this question is the heart of this work. I wanted to understand not just what students were thinking and feeling when they were in our classrooms, but I wanted to then use what I learned to determine which specific conditions are present when teenagers find inspiration in their academics. (p. 8)

Similarly, in describing her research goals, Pope (2001) notes, "I wanted to find out what was going on inside their heads as they sat in my classroom each day. What did they make of their school experiences? Which educational endeavors, if any, were meaningful and valuable to them?" (p. xii). Flutter and Rudduck (2004), whose work with the Consulting Pupils about Teaching and Learning Project has been a force in the youth voice movement, frame the purpose of their work as inviting reflection on the following questions that pertain to the learning process:

- How do you learn best?
- What helps you to learn?
- What gets in the way of your learning?
- Why do you find it more difficult to learn certain things?
- Do you learn better through particular styles of teaching?
- What encourages you to work harder at your learning?
- How do you know if you have succeeded in learning something? (p. 4)

WHAT DO YOUTH HAVE TO SAY ABOUT THEIR CURRICULAR EXPERIENCES?

Boring, Boring, Boring

In light of the questions framed by Flutter and Rudduck (2004), what do researchers learn about teaching and learning when they ask youth? First and foremost, they hear from students that the secondary curriculum is boring. Although it hardly takes focused youth voice research to unearth such claims from students, the breadth and depth of such sentiment should not be underestimated, and educators continue to downplay it at the cost of adolescent engagement and growth. The pervasiveness of student testimony describing boredom and disengagement with school-related tasks is alarming, because learning depends on active engage-

ment (National Research Council Institute of Medicine, 2003).

This central theme of the studies examining student perspective on classroom life is captured powerfully by Goodlad (1984). After collecting data on more than 1,000 classrooms, Goodlad surmises that although schooling is marked by grandiose, humane rhetoric and lofty aspirations, there is a huge gap between such promulgations and what is experienced by students in classrooms. He finds in the classrooms a "flat, neutral emotional ambiance [where] . . . boredom is a disease of epidemic proportion" (p. 9). The theme of ubiquitous lethargy prevails throughout the literature on student experience.

Cusick's (1973) study of a comprehensive high school where he inserted himself as a student and participant observer finds that students were relegated to the role of passive listeners in the classroom situation and that student group life, rather than classroom experiences, is the dominant interest of the student. Although Cusick acknowledges that occasionally in music class or a ceramics class there would be evidence of collective student engagement, most time spent in school was devoid of significant experience:

The time spent actively engaged with some teacher over a matter of cognitive importance may not exceed twenty minutes a period for five periods a day. That is a high estimate. I would say that if an average student spent an hour to one and a half hours a day in school involved in subject matter, that was a good day. (p. 56)

A consistent theme in Cusick's work is that in any given class, only a minority of students actively participate. When he finds evidence of collective attention, he links it not to academic matters but to procedural and maintenance elements necessary for success in the school organization. Teacher-initiated, academic issues have little effect on students. His analysis is careful not to indict the actors for the vapid environment he describes. The villain is the organization that has shaped students' experience by denying their involvement in basic educational processes and relegated them "to the position of watchers, waiters, order-followers, and passive-receptacles for the depositing of disconnected bits of information" (p. 222).

Powell et al.'s (1985) study of high schools seeks to understand the central images and metaphors through which the people inside schools comprehend their experience of schooling. Their focus is on themes, not particulars; however, what the authors learn from observation and interviews helps illuminate important features of student experience in the classroom. The findings of this study are organized around the central theme stated in the first sentence of the book: "If Americans want to understand their high schools at work, they should imagine them as shopping malls" (p. 8). The law of the mall is "consumer choice" (p. 309). The researchers describe and explain everyday classroom life through the theme of "treaties" (see pp. 66–118). They find that although students and teachers articulate a vast range of purposes, intentions, goals, and expectations of the classroom, there is very little tension or "banging heads" (p. 67). Instead, teachers and students develop ways of accommodating each other: "They arrange deals or treaties that promote mutual goals or that keep the peace" (p. 68). These tacit arrangements accommodate the differences and are usually not even explicit to the students and teachers. The impact of these treaties is that they legislate a mandate against intensity in the classroom experience. They make the ironic point that intensity is the mantra of extracurricular activities such as sports, but it is a rarely talked-about or thought-about feature of classroom life. In a compelling vignette, the researchers present a segment of Mr. Snyder's sophomore English class reading Ralph Waldo Emerson. This short passage describes a classroom where teachers and students construct a treaty whereby "mutual intensity" is an expectation. A student responds to the researchers by saying that Mr. Snyder "digs at you until you finally come out with it" (p. 97). The researchers use Mr. Snyder as a countervailing example of a rare teacher who induces intensity, in opposition to other teachers whose classrooms are devoid of passion and energy.

Csikszentmihalyi and Larson's (1984) study of conflict and growth in adolescence provides a perspective on adolescent student experience in the classroom. In short, in their study of teenagers drawn from a diverse community bordering Chicago, they find

bleak, abysmal patterns of activation, cognitive engagement, and intrinsic motivation:

> Compared to other contexts in their lives, time in class is associated with lower-than-average states on nearly every self-report dimension. Most notably, students report feeling sad, irritable and bored; concentration is difficult; they feel self-conscious and strongly wish they were doing something else. . . . The founders of the American high school undoubtedly envisioned rows of attentive students happily absorbing lesson after lesson. One hundred years later the reality is far from this vision. Even in a very good high school, such as the one studied here, students are neither attentive nor happy, and are probably absorbing only a fraction of the information being presented. (p. 206)

Furthermore, classes that are usually considered the linchpin subjects of the school curriculum (English, math, science) rate as the least stimulating.

Disengagement is manifested in a number of ways, ranging from apathetic effort on the part of students, to disrespect of the classroom space, to the most visible indication of disengagement: dropping out. In fact, in a recent study of high school dropouts (Bridgeland, Dilulio, & Morrison, 2006), intense focus group research and interview methods find that youth identified uninteresting classes as the single most critical factor in their decision to drop out. Again and again, participants recount how high school was "boring, nothing I was interested in," or "it was boring . . . the teacher just stood in front of the room and just talked and didn't really like involve you." A female from Baltimore said, "There wasn't any learning going on," and another complained, "They make you take classes in school that you're never going to use in life." Many felt that even their teachers were not engaged in the classes and that they "only care about getting through their day, too" (p. 25).

More than anything else voiced by students throughout the research, boredom in the classroom infects the experienced curriculum. Only by listening carefully to the qualities and causes of this disengagement can educators consider how the intended curriculum—and more important, its dialogical implementation—needs to change. But responding to what students don't care about will not suffice; teachers also need to listen more carefully to youth about what *does* matter to them in the classroom context and understand the broader contextual forces that shape their attitude and disposition toward school. Smagorinsky (2001; Smagorinsky & O'Donnell-Allen, 1998) theorizes that engagement and disengagement of individual students cannot be understood without considering students' individual social worlds as well as their prior experiences and relationships with the school culture. Smagorinsky's studies on classroom literacy practices emphasize that teachers face great challenges in constructing classroom environments conducive to engaging diverse students in meaningful transactions with text. Although teachers can develop engaging literacy activities that would seemingly invite student interaction, Smagorinsky (2001) found that "even the most conducive context can be resisted by students whose goals do not include having rich transactions with texts or becoming engaged with school" (p. 162).

Relationships Matter

Students describe wanting affirmation, acceptance, and support from the adults who work with them in the classroom setting. Students yearn for positive relationships with their teachers. In interpreting the responses of students in their study of urban students, Wilson and Corbett (2001) conclude that students evaluate teachers on the basis of how caring they perceive a particular teacher to be. They define caring as "acting in the best interests of others" and suggest that students intuitively understand which teachers demonstrate their caring by holding students to high standards and by "refusing to allow them [students] to fail" (p. 89). Wilson and Corbett's (2001) interview study with middle school age students from poor urban contexts concludes that "it was the quality of the relationships in the classrooms that determined the educational value of the setting" (p. 122).

There exists substantial research showing that perceptions of positive teacher–student relationship and feelings of school belonging relate positively to increased academic motivation and achievement (Goodenow, 1993; Roeser, Midgley, & Urdan, 1996; Scales, 1996). Scholars also theorize that support

may be particularly important to the healthy and positive development of adolescents because of the intensity of the physical, emotional, social, spiritual, and intellectual changes they are undergoing (Scales, Leffert, & Lerner, 1999; Starkman, Scales, & Roberts, 1999). These findings are echoed by other research pointing to the often critical need for nonparental adults to take a sustained interest in teenagers' lives; as adolescents undergo transitions of social definition (including an emerging sense of autonomy and changes in interpersonal, political, economic, and legal status), they simultaneously undergo significant transformations in family relationships. These transformations are complex, but studies do suggest that many adolescent–parent relationships experience an increase in conflict and a decrease in closeness (Steinberg, 2005). Csikszentmihalyi and Larson's (1984) study of how teenagers spend their time concludes that they are seldom in the company of adults. In fact, their research suggests that youth spend only 5% of their time interacting with parents. Furthermore, this proportion of time is not evenly distributed across both parents, as they find that the average teenager spends only about ½ hour per week interacting exclusively with his or her father.

Across the studies we reviewed, youth express the perception that adults who can engage them in supportive and affirmative relationships matter in how they experience the curriculum. Mitra's (2004) study of a Bay Area high school predominately composed of first-generation immigrants and described as a "school serving families who rarely have a voice in schools in the United States" (p. 3) concludes that the connection to a caring adult proved to be the most important developmental influence for students. Nieto's (1994) interview study of academically successful students, employing a broad range of students who reflect a variety of racial and ethnic backgrounds, found that students continually identify key qualities of a teacher's character as important, characteristics such as being interesting, creative, and caring. Certo, Cauley, and Chafin's (2003) interview study of 33 students from seven diverse comprehensive high schools in Richmond, Virginia, also highlights how students identify the importance of caring teachers; what's more, they found that:

the most common descriptor of a teacher who cares ... was one who listens. These teachers could read student moods, "cared about what grade you got," and offered appropriate guidance and direction. ... Caring teachers listened to students' ideas about classroom rules or about classroom projects, letting them have some input. (p. 714)

One of the most compelling studies of youth voice was done by Cushman (2003). Her project involved recruiting 40 students from New York City, Providence, Rhode Island, and the San Francisco Bay Area to serve as research assistants on a project devoted to reflecting on the quality of teaching and learning they experienced in their schools. Her method included engaging the students in focus groups, informal discussions, and debate, and asking for a range of writings focused on how youth experience school. One of the chief findings corroborates the pivotal role youth attribute to connections and genuine relationships between students and teachers. Cushman (2003) describes how her original structure of the book intended to break down her findings across each of the key academic disciplines. "But as the torrent of student voices mounted with each work session, we realized the mistake of that assumption. Our groups offered surprisingly little critique of curriculum and assessment. They focused more on the relationships that made learning possible" (p. xii).

WHAT CAN STUDENT VOICE CONTRIBUTE TO LITERACY EFFORTS?

Although students' voices make clear their frequent classroom boredom and their need for significant relationships, student voice research can inform literacy efforts as well. Two primary themes emerge: Focus more on classroom dialogue and focus on connectedness. These emphases should be understood in the broader context of this chapter: Who are today's adolescents and what do they advise educators to do in order to optimize their school experience? Flutter and Rudduck (2004) describe this process as "pupil consultation" in that

consultation is defined as "the action of taking counsel together; deliberation or conference"

... [which] suggests that the parties involved in the consultation process have been invited to contribute because they have relevant and important views and information to share. Pupil consultation, therefore, rests on the principle that pupils can bring something worthwhile to discussions about schooling. (p. 5)

Focus More on Classroom Dialogue

Students describe wanting classrooms that promote substantive classroom dialogue; they express a clear predilection for teachers who possess skills of facilitation and whose approach to teaching views text and writing as conducive to creating the "context for conversation" (Intrator, 2003, p. 116). Cushman's (2003) youth report that they are most motivated when a passionate teacher asks questions about issues and listens deeply to students reflect on their understandings on paper and through conversation. In a Public Agenda (1997) telephone survey of 1,000 high school age youth, 67% claim that they would learn a lot more if teachers used hands-on projects and class discussion, as compared with 14% who believe they would learn more if their teachers lectured.

Other youth explain that not only do they want more dialogue, but they yearn for classroom conversation that explores questions of central purpose and meaning in their lives. In her analysis of secondary classrooms at three schools (a suburban public school, a diverse Catholic urban school, and a suburban Jewish school), Simon (2001) concludes that "although moral and existential issues arise frequently, they are most often shut down immediately" (p. 53). In a ninth-grade English class studying Elie Weisel's *Night*, she observed a student raise the honest and profound question, "How is it possible for anyone to believe in God after the Holocaust?" (p. 223). The teacher acknowledged the importance of the question—and then suggested the student ask his clergyperson.

Simon (2001) also points out that not only do students come to view school as disconnected from what matters most to them, they also miss out on rich opportunities for intellectual development. Students are willing to do the hard work of critical thinking when the issues are important to them, when they find the content relevant to their own experiences or desires to learn. Simon relates the story of a student who asked a teacher repeatedly about whether "the blue blood is bad blood" in the midst of a science lecture. It turns out this student had sickle cell anemia, and thus an interest in the material beyond the next exam. The teacher's brief, rote responses demonstrated no recognition that academic content might, in Simon's words, "actually touch them [the students], help them, give them power to understand and to act" (pp. 229–230).

Simon (2001) acknowledges the challenges of rethinking curricula to make "room for students' selves" (p. 164), but the voices of students make clear the need and desire for such a transformation. She notes, however, the surprising paucity of research aimed at understanding what truly engages students by actually putting their voices at the center of scholarly inquiry. This theme of needing to process feelings and ideas occupies a central place in student voice research. Cushman (2003) summarizes her students' perspectives:

> Ask us to share our reactions to what we read and write. Help us think about print as another way of talking back and forth about ourselves and our lives. Everybody sees written-down things in different ways depending on our own life experiences, and we can learn from each other. Treat all our responses as important, whether or not we like something to agree with the experts. (p. 116)

Focus on Connectedness

Students describe rarely having a sense of being connected to the big picture associated with their academic work (Pope, 2001; Rudduck et al., 1996) or to the subject matter in a way that draws on their preexisting understandings, interests, culture, and real-world experiences. They experience the school day as a series of disconnected classes with little coherence or overarching narrative and describe feeling almost no pleasure in their learning. Students articulate this disconnect in two distinctively different ways. First, they detail a general sense that the curriculum does not relate to who they are, and second, they detail how the grind of school renders them unable to derive any intrinsic interest in classroom learning.

Many of the studies that focus on representing the perspectives and experiences of traditionally underrepresented minorities highlight a perception by students that their particular identities are typically absent from the curriculum. For example, Sleeter and Grant (1991) find in a study of a desegregated junior high school that *none* of the class content relates to the students' lives. Nieto's (1994) study of diverse high-achieving young people suggests that curricula linked to students' background and experiences are missing in many schools, and in particular for those students whose native language is not English. Nieto also finds that students respond positively when a teacher creates informal opportunities for students to draw on their heritage and identity. For example, she highlights how appreciative a Vietnamese student was when the teacher let him speak Vietnamese with other students during the class. Phelan, Yu, and Davidson's (1994) study of 55 ethnically and academically diverse youth in four urban desegregated high schools describes how students who perceive themselves as outsiders needing to navigate across different worlds/borders composed of social class, ethnicity, and race often find themselves adrift or having to "deny fundamental aspects of their personal and ethnic identities" in order to "fit in" (p. 442).

Other students explain that the only connection to the curriculum they feel is in pursuit of high grades, test scores, and building college résumés. Pope (2001) describes what she learned shadowing five motivated and successful students through a high-performing suburban high school for more than a year. The students she writes about worked hard, were honored for their academic and civic achievement, and appeared to represent "model students," yet Pope concludes that these students were not genuinely engaged in school but instead had learned to "do school": to manipulate the system to get good grades. One of the students in her study said, "This school turns students into robots . . . just going page by page, doing the work, doing the routine" (p. 154). Comments such as these led Pope to conclude that students found school to be "a system that appeared to show little support for intellectual engagement and passion. They studied the material, read the textbooks, and completed the assignments, for the most part, not because the subjects genuinely interested them. Students often memorized facts and figures without stopping to ask what they meant or why they were asked to learn the facts in the first place" (p. 155).

One of the strengths of student voice research, of course, is that it not only helps identify such problems, but provides youth an opportunity to express alternatives. In response to this classroom culture of disconnectedness, students offer a range of suggestions, including a focus on higher-order thinking, the need for choices and flexibility, and opportunities for meaningful public expression of their ideas.

Focus on Higher-Order Thinking

Phelan, Davidson, and Yu's (1998) study showed that students valued teachers who demanded higher-order conceptual thinking. One student reported, "You ask him a question and he . . . gives you the clues, and then you have to figure it out yourself. . . . I like that, because he makes you think" (p. 132). Students in Intrator's (2003) study appreciated the English teacher because he "taught with questions, not with answers" (p. 144). Wilson and Corbett (2001) describe how students who engaged routinely with a curriculum focused on the iterative and complex nature of the writing process found writing to be a "frequent, creative and constructive act" (p. 101).

Give Us Choices and Build in Flexibility

The students in Cushman's (2003) study entreat teachers to provide choice, when possible, regarding reading and writing topics. The National Research Council Institute of Medicine's (2003) report on school engagement points out that students need opportunity to create their own meaningful connections to school, a process that can be cultivated by giving choices so that students can create bridges between their personal interests and situations and the curriculum. In a study of a single student's composing process in a course on interior design, Smagorinsky, Zoss, and Reed (2006) note an exchange at the end of one of the class sessions:

> STUDENT: It's time for the bell.
> DEE: Really? (p. 325)

The authors describe this exchange as suggestive of an engrossment that demonstrates deep engagement in the act of composition. They suggest that this immersive focus can be attributed to task-related factors and teaching that were not present in Dee's core academic classes. The work the student did in designing her project is described by the researchers as flexible, open-ended within the parameters of a general design task, collaborative, and informed by continual feedback from peers and audiences. As the researchers note, the qualities of the project resemble in character those pedagogical design features identified as key to successful writing programs.

Promote Opportunities for Students to Go Public with Their Work in Meaningful Ways

As one of Cushman's (2003) students writes, "If you care enough to make it public, we care more about what we say and how we say it" (p. 120). Pope's (2001) students describe how doing work that brings them into contact with the outside community makes the academic work feel more real. Olsen's (1997) ethnography of recently arrived immigrant students in an urban high school describes how the students she studied relished the opportunity to reach out beyond the context of their own self-contained classrooms and share their experiences and learning. One of the students in Intrator's (2003) study similarly described his goal to write and perform for audiences beyond his teacher. He said, "'School really matters when I believe that what's happening might actually mean something to me beyond just merely doing what I'm supposed to do'" (p. 130).

WEAVING TOGETHER STUDENT VOICE AND TEACHER WISDOM

In sum, the collective voices of the students implore educators to listen to their critique of schooling. Educators' response to their concerns, of course, requires much more than simply turning schools and classrooms over to students. A central theme that emerges from an exploration of "who are adolescents today?"—using both traditional research inquiry as well as student voice methods—is the ongoing importance of adults in their lives. What students seek—and what they need to grow as learners and people—is a *dialogical* encounter with adults. For classroom teachers, this process means not only a literal talking back and forth, but also drawing upon their own professional wisdom and experience to connect what students already care about with the important growth and learning they need.

For researchers and teacher educators, developing habits of practice and methodologies that engage youth in systematic conversation about who they are, what they experience in their schooling, and how their future aspirations are being shaped by those institutional forces in their life is a worthy project. As Cook-Sather (2002) contends:

> We need to embrace more fully the work of authorizing students' perspectives in conversations about schooling and reform—to move toward trust, dialogue, and change in education. Because of who they are, what they know, and how they are positioned, students must be recognized as having knowledge essential to the development of sound educational policies and practices. (p. 12)

In order to understand adolescents today or in any era, adults must be willing to provide time and space to listen to what kids have to tell them.

REFERENCES

Bridgeland, J., Dilulio Jr., J., & Morrison, K. (2006, March). *The silent epidemic: Perspectives of high school dropouts.* Washington DC: Bill and Melinda Gates Foundation.

Buechner, F. (1993). *Whistling in the dark: A doubter's dictionary.* San Francisco: Harper.

Center for Evaluation and Education Policy. (2006). High school survey of student engagement. Retrieved June 9, 2007, from *ceep.indiana.edu/hssse/pdf/HSSSE_2006_Report.pdf.*

Certo, J. L., Cauley, K. M., & Chafin, C. (2003). Students' perspectives on their high school experience. *Adolescence, 38*(152), 705–724.

Clark, C. (2004). *Hurt: Inside the world of today's teenagers.* Grand Rapids, MI: Baker Academic.

Cook-Sather, A. (2002). Authorizing students' perspectives: Toward trust, dialogue, and change in education. *Educational Researcher, 31*(4), 3–14.

Cothran, D. J., & Kulinna, P. H. (2006). Students' per-spectives on direct, peer, and inquiry teaching strategies. *Journal of Teaching in Physical Education, 25,* 166–181.

Cotton, K. (1989). *Expectations and student outcomes.* Portland, OR: Northwest Regional Educational Laboratory.

Csikszentmihalyi, M., & Larson, R. (1984). *Being adolescent: Conflict and growth in the teenage years.* New York: Basic Books.

Cushman, K. (2003). *Fires in the bathroom: Advice for teachers from high school students.* New York: New Press.

Cusick, P. (1973). *Inside high school.* Toronto: Holt, Rinehart & Wilson.

Dewey, J. (1929). *Experience and nature.* New York: Norton.

Dewey, J. (1934). *Art as experience.* New York: Perigree Books.

Dewey, J. (1938). *Experience and education.* New York: Macmillan.

Doyle, W. (1992). Curriculum and pedagogy. In P. W. Jackson (Ed.), *Handbook of research on curriculum* (pp. 486–516). New York: Macmillan.

Eckert, P. (1989). *Jocks and burnouts: Social categories and identity in the high school.* New York: Teachers College Press.

Edman, I. (1939). *Arts and the man.* New York: Norton.

Eisner, E. (1994). *The educational imagination: On the design and evaluation of school programs* (3rd ed.). New York: Macmillan.

Erikson, E. (1968). *Identity, youth and crisis.* New York: Norton.

Erickson, F., & Shultz, J. (1992). Students' experience of the curriculum. In P. W. Jackson (Ed.), *Handbook of research on curriculum* (pp. 465–485). New York: Macmillan.

Fine, M. (1991). *Framing dropouts: Notes on the politics of an urban public high school.* Albany, NY: SUNY Press.

Fletcher, A. (2004). *Meaningful student involvement: Research guide.* Olympia, WA: SoundOut!. Retrieved June 9, 2007, from *www.soundout.org/MSIResearch. pdf.*

Flutter, J. (2006). This place could help you learn: Student participation in creating better school environments. *Educational Review, 58*(2), 183–193.

Flutter, J., & Rudduck, J. (2004). *Consulting pupils: What's in it for schools?* New York: Falmer.

Gladwell, M. (1997, March 17). The coolhunt. *New Yorker,* 78–88.

Goodenow, C. (1993). Classroom belonging among early adolescent students: Relationships to motivation and achievement. *Journal of Early Adolescence, 13*(1), 21–43.

Goodlad, J. (1984). *A place called school: Prospects for the future.* New York: McGraw-Hill.

Henry, J. (1965). Golden rule days: American schoolrooms. In J. Henry (Ed.), *Culture against man* (pp. 283–321). New York: Vintage.

Hersch, P. (1998). *A tribe apart: A journey into the*

heart of American adolescence. New York: Fawcett Columbine.

Hine, T. (1999). The rise and decline of the teenager. *American Heritage, 50*(5). Retrieved June 9, 2007, from *www.americanheritage.com/articles/magazine/ah/1999/5/1999_5_70.shtml.*

Hodkinson, P., Sparkes, A. C., & Hodkinson, H. (1996). *Triumphs and tears: Young people, markets and the transition from school to work.* London: David Fulton.

Hollingshead, A. B. (1949). *Elmtown's youth: The impact of social classes on adolescents.* New York: Wiley.

Intrator, S. M. (2003). *Tuned in and fired up: How teaching can inspire real learning in the classroom.* New Haven, CT: Yale University Press.

Jackson, P. W. (1998). *John Dewey and the lessons of art.* New Haven, CT: Yale University Press.

Kamberelis, G. (1995). Performing classroom community: A dramatic palimpsest of answerability. In D. Leu, C. Kinzer, & K. Hinchman (Eds.), *Literacies for the 21st century: 44th yearbook of the National Reading Conference* (pp. 148–160). Chicago: National Reading Conference.

Langer, J. A., & Allington, R. L. (1992). Curriculum research in writing and reading. In P. Jackson (Ed.), *Handbook of research on curriculum* (pp. 687–725). New York: Macmillan.

Mitra, D. L. (2004). The significance of students: Can increasing student voice in schools lead to gains in youth development? *Teachers College Record, 106*(4), 651–688.

National Research Council Institute of Medicine. (2003). *Engaging schools: Fostering high school students' motivation to learn.* Washington, DC: National Academies Press.

Nieto, S. (1994). Lessons from students on creating a chance to dream. *Harvard Educational Review, 64,* 392.

Olsen, L. (1997). *Made in America: Immigrant students in our public schools.* New York: New Press.

Peshkin, A. (1986). *God's choice: The total world of a fundamentalist Christian school.* Chicago: University of Chicago Press.

Peshkin, A. (1991). *The color of strangers, the color of friends: The play of ethnicity in school and community.* Chicago: University of Chicago Press.

Peshkin, A. (1994). *Growing up American: Schooling and the survival of community.* Prospect Heights, IL: Waveland Press.

Peshkin, A. (2001). *Permissible advantage?: The moral consequences of elite schooling.* Mahwah, NJ: Erlbaum.

Phelan, P., Davidson, A. L., & Yu, H. C. (1998). *Adolescents' worlds: Negotiating family, peers, and school.* New York: Teachers College Press.

Phelan, P., Yu, H. C., & Davidson, A. L. (1994). Navigating the psychosocial pressures of adolescence: The voices and experiences of high school youth. *American Educational Research Journal, 31,* 415–447.

Pollock, M. (2005). Race bending: "Mixed" youth practicing strategic racialization in California. In S. Maira & E. Soep (Eds.), *Youthscapes: The popular, the national, the global* (pp. 43–63). Philadelphia: University of Pennsylvania Press.

Pope, D. C. (2001). *"Doing school": How we are creating a generation of stressed out, materialistic, and miseducated students.* New Haven, CT: Yale University Press.

Powell, A., Cohen, D., & Farrar, T. (1985). *The shopping mall high school: Winners and losers in the educational marketplace.* New York: Houghton Mifflin.

Public Agenda. (1997). *Getting by: What American teenagers really think about their schools.* New York: Author.

Roeser, R., Midgley, C., & Urdan, T. (1996). Perceptions of the school psychological environment and early adolescents' psychological and behavioral functioning in school: The mediating roles of goals and belonging. *Journal of Educational Psychology, 88,* 408–422.

Rudduck, J., Chaplain, R., & Wallace, G. (Eds.). (1996). *School improvement: What can pupils tell us?* London: David Fulton.

Scales, P. (1996). *Boxed in and bored: How middle schools continue to fail young adolescents—and what good middle schools do right.* Minneapolis: Search Institute.

Scales, P., Leffert, N., & Lerner, R. M. (1999). *Developmental assets: A synthesis of the scientific research on adolescent development.* Minneapolis: Search Institute.

Shuell, T. J. (1996). Teaching and learning in the classroom context. In D. Berliner & R. Calfee (Eds.), *Handbook of educational psychology* (pp. 725–764). New York: Macmillan.

Shultz, J. J., & Cook-Sather, A. (2001). *In our own words: Students' perspectives on school.* Lanham, MD: Rowman & Littlefield.

Simon, K. G. (2001). *Moral questions in the classroom: How to get kids to think deeply about real life and their schoolwork.* New Haven, CT: Yale University Press.

Simpson, R. (2001). *Raising teens: A synthesis of research and a foundation for action.* Boston: Center for Health Communication, Harvard School of Public Health.

Sleeter, C. E., & Grant, C. (1991). Mapping terrains of power: Student cultural knowledge vs. classroom knowledge. In C. E. Sleeter (Ed.), *Empowerment through multicultural education* (pp. 49–67). Albany, NY: SUNY Press.

Smagorinsky, P. (2001). If meaning is constructed, what is it made from? Toward a cultural theory of reading. *Review of Educational Research, 71,* 133–169.

Smagorinsky, P., & O'Donnell-Allen, C. (1998). The depth and dynamics of context: Tracing the sources and channels of engagement and disengagement in students' response to literature. *Journal of Literacy Research, 30,* 515–559.

Smagorinsky, P., Zoss, M., & Reed, P. M. (2006) Residential interior design as complex composition: A case study of a high school senior's composing process. *Written Communication, 23,* 295–330.

Starkman, N., Scales, P., & Roberts, C. (1999). *Great places to learn: How asset-building schools help students succeed.* Minneapolis: Search Institute.

Steinberg, L. D. (2005). *Adolescence* (7th ed.). Boston: McGraw-Hill.

Strauch, B. (2003). *The primal teen: What the new discoveries about the teenage brain tell us about our kids.* New York: Doubleday.

United States Census Bureau. (2004). *U.S. interim projections by age, sex, race, and Hispanic origin,* Washington, DC. Retrieved June 9, 2007, from *www.census.gov/ipc/www/usinterimproj/.*

Walford, G., & Massey, A. (1998). *Children learning in context.* Stamford, CT: JAI Press.

Willis, P. (1977). *Learning to labour.* Westmead, UK: Saxon.

Wilson, B. L., & Corbett, H. D. (2001). *Listening to urban kids: School reform and the teachers they want.* Albany, NY: SUNY Press.

Yazzie-Mintz, E. (2007). *Voices of students on engagement: A report on the 2006 high school survey of student engagement.* Bloomington, IN: Center for Evaluation and Education Policy.

Part II

LITERACY IN SCHOOL

POLICY MATTERS: Excerpt from *Reading at Risk*[1]

Reading at Risk provides an invaluable snapshot of the role of literature in the lives of Americans. It comes at a critical time, when electronic media are becoming the dominant influence in young people's worlds. *Reading at Risk* adds new and distressing information to the discussion. It contains solid evidence of the declining importance of literature to our populace. Literature reading is fading as a meaningful activity, especially among younger people. If one believes that active and engaged readers lead richer intellectual lives than non-readers and that a well-read citizenry is essential to a vibrant democracy, the decline of literary reading calls for serious action.

COUNTERPOINT

Research reviewed by Bruce (Chapter 19), Black and Steinkuehler (Chapter 18), and Zoss (Chapter 13) may raise questions about whether emphasizing the reading of literary novels warrants the kind of crisis rhetoric adopted here.

As Burroughs and Smagorinsky (Chapter 12) argue, the role of literature in the English curriculum has always been central, and so one wonders why schooling thus far seems not to have produced a populace that is committed to literary reading.

When one considers demographic trends and associated changing literacies reported in Fu and Graff (Chapter 26), Harklau and Pinnow (Chapter 9), and Martínez-Roldán and Fránquiz (Chapter 21), one notices that, for example, the word *Spanish* does not appear in *Reading at Risk*. The significance of a multilingual population is not addressed in the report or in most policy reports about literacy. How might a report on the nation's reading habits look if it included people who are reading in other languages?

—L. C., R. B., and P. S.

POLICY MATTERS: Excerpt from *Why the Crisis in Adolescent Literacy Demands a National Response*[2]

Over the past four decades, Congress has directed substantial resources toward improving young children's literacy skills, and that investment has grown significantly in recent years.

---

[1]Excerpt from National Endowment for the Arts. (2004). *Reading at risk: A survey of literary reading in America.* Research division report #46. Washington, DC: Author. Available at *www.nea.gov/news/news04/ReadingAtRisk. html.*

[2]Excerpt from Alliance for Excellent Education. (2006, June). *Why the crisis in adolescent literacy demands a national response* (pp. 1–2). Washington, DC: Author. Available at *www.all4ed.org/publications/StrivingBrief3_numbers_02.pdf.*

Through initiatives such as Title I of the Elementary and Secondary Education Act (better known as the No Child Left Behind Act), Reading First, and Head Start, the federal government has spent billions of dollars promoting vital research and improved reading instruction in the home, in preschool settings, and during the first few years of elementary school. As long as millions of young readers continue to struggle, this work should remain a high priority.

But it can't be the only priority.

America's adolescents face a literacy crisis every bit as alarming as the one confronting younger children. Millions of middle and high school students lack the reading and writing skills they need to succeed in college, compete in the workforce, or even understand their daily newspaper. However, while Congress has demonstrated a real commitment to improve reading instruction in grades K–3, it has made relatively trivial investments (mainly through the new Striving Readers program) in the literacy skills of students in grades 4–12.

Today, according to the National Assessment of Educational Progress (also known as "the nation's report card"), more than two thirds of all eighth graders read below grade level, and half of these students are so far behind that they drop off the scale entirely, scoring below what the U.S. Department of Education defines as its most basic level. Students in this group read at the equivalent of two or more grades below their proficient peers. Moreover, while fourth grade reading scores have risen for several years, reflecting the nation's investment in early reading instruction, eighth and twelfth grade scores have remained flat since the 1970s.

In total, more than six million of America's middle and high school students are struggling readers. Many of them are likely to drop out—it seems no coincidence that the dropout rate closely mirrors the percentage of students reading at "below basic" levels—and of those who go on to receive their diplomas, many will remain unprepared and unlikely to succeed in college or at work. Struggling adolescent readers may be able to sound out the words they see on a page or to comprehend simple texts, but most have difficulty understanding substantive reading assignments, following complicated directions, drawing conclusions, or thinking critically about what they read, whatever the subject.

Educators are now beginning to recognize that the teaching of reading and writing cannot end at third grade; they must provide intensive, high-quality literacy instruction throughout the K–12 curriculum. Not only must educators teach decoding skills to middle and high school students who still struggle with the very basics of reading, but they must help all students to go beyond those basics. They must teach students reading comprehension strategies, vocabulary, writing, and other forms of communication, or millions of adolescents will lose whatever momentum they may have gained as a result of improvements in early reading instruction.

COUNTERPOINT

While looking at adolescents from within school walls has alarmed some policymakers, research such as that reviewed by Alvermann (Chapter 2), Black and Steinkuehler (Chapter 18), Bruce (Chapter 19), and Lewis and del Valle (Chapter 20) suggests that adolescents' literacy is complex, deep, engaged, and advanced when viewed from outside school.

Beaufort (Chapter 16) demonstrates that the literacies required by the workplace are complex, social, and flexible and that they are highly specific to particular contexts. Will it be effective to control, regiment, and standardize adolescent literacy in preparing students for the contemporary world of work?

O'Brien, Stewart, and Beach (Chapter 6) challenge what they view as a common but simplistic notion of proficiency in reading, and the research they review calls for a more multifaceted view.

—L. C., R. B., and P. S.

CHAPTER 4

Contexts for Adolescent Literacy

JUDITH A. LANGER

This chapter focuses on school contexts for literacy. Adolescents need a safe and stimulating environment to explore ideas and take risks with literacy, so the environments of middle and high schools are critically important. During adolescence, schools can help students find their voices and learn the skills they need to hone their ideas and reasoning abilities as well as to further develop their self-images and tastes. This chapter describes "literate thinking" and why this conception can develop visions of successful school contexts for adolescent literacy beyond simply focusing on acts of reading and writing. At school, it requires educators to look to the classroom, program, school, and school–community relations—all contexts that deeply affect learning. Calling on studies of adolescent literacy based on a sociocognitive view, the chapter focuses on aspects of school environments where students do better than in other schools with similar students. Several findings relate to the overall school environment, showing how positive schools provide layers of supportive contexts, such as *Personal Contexts,* in which individual and shared identities are displayed; *Networking Contexts,* in which each participant is supported in relation to each other participant; *Management Contexts,* in which the power of running the school is shared; and *School Support Contexts* that keep students from getting lost. Several other findings relate specifically to the teaching and learning environment in a school, including *Professional Contexts,* in which adults in a building keep up with knowledge in their fields; *Programmatic Contexts,* which include the teams, departments, grade levels, groups, and other committees working on the curricular program; and *Classroom Contexts* that are both learning communities as well as social ones. Improving adolescent literacy demands a consideration of the contextual features described as more focused vectors for examination and direction.

Despite the array of research on adolescent literacy evident in this *Handbook,* there has often been a greater focus on what to teach than on the contexts and approaches that might be age appropriate. This chapter cuts a broad swath, culling information from a range of related areas, to guide educators in conceptualizing and creating the most effective environments in the support of adolescent literacy.

Adolescence is an era of tremendous personal and cognitive growth with some similarities to, but also differences from, the years before and after. New skills and strategies are needed to do well as the school years progress and student needs, interests, and abilities shift. As Luke and Elkins (1998) and Csikszentmihalyi and Larson (1984) point out, adolescent literacy is about complex social relationships between adolescents and their rich symbolic and discursive lives. Adolescents want the security of known people and routines in their lives, even as they are reaching out to the unknown world for new role models and ideas they can try on as they explore the possible selves they might become. In their search, they look to the people they meet both indirectly and directly (e.g., movies, media, books, observations, discussions) for inspiration—however transitory or influential these might be. Some adolescents encounter identity conflicts associated with academic achievement and class, culture, or gender boundaries, complicated by their understanding of what is significant and what it takes to be competent (Davidson, 1996; Everhart, 1983; Fine, 1989; Gilyard, 1991; Miron & Lauria, 1998; Rose, 1990; Sarris, 1993). To travel this winding course of growing up, adolescents need both a personally safe and a cognitively stimulating environment where they can explore ideas and take risks. This is why middle and high schools play such a critically important role in life development. Middle and high schools can help them become thinkers and learners who are reasoned and self-aware, as well as competent. By acting as "safe houses" (Pratt, 1991) where students can feel they are accepted as they are and where they can be shielded from the personal and social tensions they may experience in their various communities outside, schools can be supportive contexts where adolescents have the trust to explore and find themselves and their possible places in the world.

Despite the fact that some students are learning quite well and others are "beating the odds" (Langer, 2001a), the overall literacy record based on test results in United States schools raises questions. The Alliance for Excellent Education (2006) reports that approximately 1.2 million high school students fail to graduate each year and that only 70% of students who enter eighth grade actually graduate from high school. In the 2002 National Assessment of Educational Progress (NAEP) in reading, 26% of eighth graders and 28% of twelfth graders who took the exam scored in the lowest category ("below basic"), and only 2% of eighth graders and 4% of twelfth graders scored in the highest category ("advanced"). Further, only 31% of the eighth-grade and 34% of

the twelfth-grade students tested scored "at or above proficient."

NAEP writing results are similar. In the 2002 assessment of writing, 16% of eighth graders and 27% of twelfth graders scored "below basic," and only 2% of both eighth and twelfth graders scored at the "advanced" level. Thirty percent of eighth graders and 22% of twelfth graders scored "at or above proficient."

Although a fuller picture using more than one indicator of students' literacy abilities is critical for decision making, the NAEP results point to a real and pervasive problem, one that, despite small ups and downs, has remained relatively persistent since NAEP was authorized by Congress in 1969 to take the pulse of students' school development. What does this mean for the field of adolescent literacy, and what can we do?

It is easy to take aim at the tests (see, e.g., Fair Test, n.d.), charging that they are culturally biased, tap only a subset of the academic knowledge and skills students learn and perform at school, and leave no room for the multiliteracy tools that students communicate with and gain meaning from outside school (Hull & Zacher, 2004; Langer, 1985, 1987b); Marshall (Chapter 8) and Intrator & Kunzman (Chapter 3), this volume; Moje et al., 2004; Moll, Amanti, Neff, & Gonzalez, 1992; Oakes, 1985; Wraga, 1999). However, it is also easy to feel that even given these failings of standardized assessments, a consistent message from the test results points to a need for improvement—in the ways in which curriculum and instruction are conceived and taught and in how they are tested (Darling-Hammond, 1991, 2004; Darling-Hammond, Ancess, & Falk, 1995; Garcia, 1991; Langer, 2004; Solano-Flores & Trumbull, 2003; Spillane & Jennings, 1997; Wilson, Peterson, Ball, & Cohen, 1996).

LITERATE THINKING

From my perspective, substantive changes in instruction and assessment will not occur without substantive changes in our notions of literacy. Because literacy is generally taken to connote only reading and writing, I have found it more useful to focus on what I call "literate thinking" (Langer 1987a, 2005a, 2005b). This concept extends beyond the acts of reading and writing themselves to also include what the mind thinks about and does when people gain knowledge, reason with it, and communicate about it in a variety of contexts. There are some common abilities that are called upon when we read, write, think, and speak—when we use the various signs, languages, and dialects that bring and convey meaning (Danesi, 1994; Kress et al., 2005; Morris, 1971; Sebeok, 1977; Sebeok & Danesi, 2000; Peirce, 1992). From this perspective, literacy can be thought of as the ability to think like a literate person, to call upon the kinds of reasoning abilities people generally use when they read and write (such as the ability to reflect on text and its meanings) even when reading and writing are not involved, such as watching a TV program or sports event (Langer, 1985, 1987a). It involves the use of signs, the ability to gain meaning from them, and the ability to understand and control them. Sign systems such as films, music, dance, websites, multimodal constructions and performances (see Alvermann, Chapter 2, and Black & Steinkuehler, Chapter 18, this volume) pervade our society. But the text, whatever its presentational form, must be meaningful to be a sign, and it is the environment in which the sign lives that gives it meaning (Bakhtin, 1986). Reading and writing are also systems of signs, and although strategies involved in meaning-building and meaning-communicating across this wide array of signs are different, there also are similarities across them all, which are at the heart of literate thinking.

For example, if you listen to people leaving a movie theater, often you hear them talking not merely about what they liked or disliked but about things that surprised them and why; some give examples, and others disagree and give counterexamples. They engage in literate thinking. Such literate acts also take place when people search the Web for information about a purchase they would like to make, or write a report using photos, graphics, other visual objects, and sound as the format for a multimodal research report.

I believe this conception of literate thinking can take us much farther in developing new visions of successful school contexts for adolescent literacy than simply focusing on acts of reading and writing. Flood, Lapp, Heath, and Langer (in press), for example, discuss ways in which media and the range of communicative arts such as film, music, images, dance, websites, multimodal constructions, and performance involve literacy-related behaviors that are central to success in today's society (see also Alvermann, Chapter 2, and Zoss, Chapter 13, this volume; and Black & Steinkuehler, Chapter 18, this volume). Literate thinking assumes individual, cultural, and group differences and leaves room for teachers to invite students to use what they understand and have experienced as a starting place for learning. It expects differing perspectives and gives students a place to try ideas out, to manipulate what they think, and to use language in ways that help them refine and rethink. It moves students to become analytic about the content at hand as they gain skills and knowledge to relate to new content and learning. Thus, literate thinking is literacy with a bigger-than-traditional context.

I have been studying various aspects of adolescent literacy learning and instruction for the past 30 years and at this time am particularly interested in the kinds of school contexts that are supportive of adolescent literacy growth. This is because I believe literacy is essentially a social enterprise in which social behaviors move cognition and affect both what and how things get learned (Langer, 1987a, 2005b; see also Bloome, 1986; Fairclough, 1992; Gee, 1999; Greenleaf, Schoenbach, Cziko, & Mueller, 2001; Wenger, 1998). Literacy grows from the social environments in which participants are regularly a part, including school. Each adolescent is a complex individual who belongs to a number of cultures that may be identified by any number of qualities, such as shared beliefs and dress, as well as ways of communicating and behaving. The home can be considered one such culture, the neighborhood another. The place of worship, groups of friends, and school are potential others. Some of these cultures may overlap, and adolescents often try out new ones and leave some older ones. What counts as *smart* and *doing well* often differs from group to group. An extended notion of literacy needs to take these multiple cultures into account, and literacy education needs to leave room for individuals' experiences to be used in the course of gaining academic literacies (Langer, 1995).

School life involves tensions and conflicts between individual and group experience. Adolescents spend a great amount of time at school, and schools are not neutral contexts. Peterson (2002) developed labels of "positive" versus "toxic" to describe school cultures, because schools differ in the degree to which they emanate messages that make adolescents feel welcome as school members, or function as Pratt's (1991) safe havens. The task before us, as I see it, is to envision the kinds of secondary schools where most students want to attend, like to participate, and learn well. This task requires us to look not only at, but also beyond, instruction—to the classroom, program, school, and school/community relations—all contexts that deeply affect learning.

SCHOOLS THAT WORK WELL

What are school environments like in places where students do better than in other schools with similar students? What can we learn about school contexts that make a difference in student literacy? The rest of this chapter explores possible answers to these questions and calls on a number of recent studies in which I have been engaged at the Center on English Learning and Achievement (CELA).

In my 5-year Beating the Odds research project (see Langer, 2000, 2001a, 2001b, 2002, 2004, 2005b), I studied professional, programmatic, classroom, and neighborhood communities and their roles in the educational picture of 25 schools, 44 teachers, 88 classes, and more than 2,000 students in four states. Because I was interested in understanding features of "schools that worked," I paired schools with comparable demographics, one higher and one lower performing, based on their reputations as well as their high-stakes test scores (see Langer, 2002, for more details). Each teacher, school, and situation was studied for 2 years each, so my research team and I had ample time to examine how patterns within these communities played themselves out and affected students over time. We visited the schools for 5 weeks each year, seeing students arrive at school and leave, observing classes and meetings of all sorts, and spending time in each community.

From these studies, we learned that middle and high schools where students do better on high-stakes tests, as well as in their course work, than those in other schools with similar demographics, have significantly different school cultures than their counterparts. Because schools were compared only to schools with similar characteristics, it was possible to identify, for example, the more effective versus the more typical schools with high percentages of students in poverty or from racially and culturally diverse backgrounds, as well as the more effective and more typical suburban, middle-class schools. Overall, however, there were some substantial features that were common to all the more effective schools regardless of demographics, and it was these that differentiated them from the schools that were more typical. For the rest of this chapter, the terms *more effective* and *more typical* are used to describe various contextual features found in the well-regarded and higher-performing schools and those schools that performed more like others of their type. Examples are drawn from my Beating the Odds and Effective Literacy Instruction studies to provide a coherent overview of the various contexts that shape effective adolescent literacy instruction.

First, the social as well as instructional messages students receive from the moment they step onto school property are undeniably different in the two types of schools. The more effective schools are the more inviting ones, day after day after day. In addition to being educational centers, they are caring community centers, communities where everyone involved (teachers, administrators, secretaries, related teaching staff, cleaners and drivers, other helpers, and students as well as parents) are members. And, as is usual in caring communities (Noddings, 1984; Langer, 2000), everyone is recognized, acknowledged, and in some sense, watched over—both educationally and personally. People work together, and everyone counts; from the moment you enter the school, there is a palpable sense of caring. The school motto, stated or not, is that everyone *can* learn and that it is the joint responsibility of community members to see that everyone *does*.

Successful teaching and learning take place within caring communities. Administrators go the extra mile by showing kindness to teachers in a host of large and small ways, and teachers do the same for students. The professionals stop problems before they start and also serve as role models. For example, in one more effective middle school in a poor community with a large Spanish-speaking population, a teacher who was himself a native speaker of Spanish said, "Kids need to be comfortable. They need to see me as a resource, and I hope that's what's happening—not only that they see me as an authoritative figure, that they see me as a mentor, as a role model. When I walk out in the hall they can say, 'Well, . . . he's my teacher. He's what I would like to be when I grow up' " (see Langer, 2002, for more examples).

In more effective schools a sense of caring pervades both the school culture and the teaching and learning culture. Let us look at each separately, first the school culture and then the teaching and learning culture, to understand the various contexts within each culture that contribute to their success in more effective schools.

SCHOOL CULTURE

Personal Context

More effective schools are humane, they have a social present and past history, and show it. Although all schools have what Kress and his colleagues (2005) call a semiotic sense, a meaning-laden way of presenting themselves, their messages can vary widely. In a semiotic sense, the school building makes a personal statement that can be more or less welcoming, however unintended this may be. The building and the physical images of the people inside are outward signs of a school's attitude toward students, education, and learning, as well as its relationship to the world outside school. More effective schools send an undeniable message of welcome. We can see a welcome in the entrance doors holding messages of greeting, in the walls adorned with photographs and student work, and in people's welcoming body language. As you enter a school, the sights and sounds, as well as the faces, bodies, and voices, tell you whether the school is a welcoming place for its parents, teachers,

community members, and students. A glance at the walls and display cases can introduce you to the members of the community—who and what it is interested in, who and what it values.

In the halls, public rooms, and classrooms of the more effective schools, you may see photos of past classes, present school and class activities, announcements of school events, related school and community news and reminders, student work, and lots of student art and photos. In more effective schools, students can see themselves as well as their friends, relatives and neighbors everywhere. They know they belong. The teachers and other faculty and staff members, whose faces and work are evident, also know they belong.

Each day when students arrive, the principal and other school staff meet them at the door, welcoming them with a smile and words of greeting. Their teachers meet them at the open classroom doors to greet them and exchange words of welcome. They often comment or inquire about family, friends, or outside interests. Teachers and students ask each other how they are doing and make small talk. They show an interest in one another. When parents and visitors arrive, there are signs of greeting on the walls and useful directions pointing newcomers to the school office or other destinations. When doors are not or cannot be open, someone is waiting inside to greet visitors with a smile and available help—whatever the community. The feeling is one of welcome. The classroom doors are also generally open, and when a door is not or cannot be open, there is a glass window in the door that invites one to peek inside and see the activity. Visits are welcome. Facial expressions are open. As a result of this home–school connection, adolescents find school a safe place, a bridge between their known and unknown worlds. It becomes a place where they can try out whatever new ideas, opinions, or self-presentations they are ready for. And someone caring is nearby to listen, help, or simply be there when needed.

Compare this with the closed feeling you get from some other schools, the less effective ones. At these schools, often no one meets students at the door; they find their way into the buildings and classrooms on their own (Langer, 2004, Ch. 7). Aides are assigned to monitor the entrance and halls, primarily to stop unruly behavior and maintain decorum, not to greet. When students enter their classrooms, they sit and wait for the room to fill and the door to be closed. Kind words and questions of interest are rare. At best, it is *down to business*. At worst, the mood is adversarial, especially in the least effective schools. For adolescents, such schools often become alien territories rather than safe houses. Although individual wonderfully effective teachers may work in these schools, they are not the norm. Wonderful teachers can be a joy to remember, but they are the exceptions; more suffused and connected experiences across the years are needed to make a difference in student attitude and learning (Langer 2002, 2004). In less effective schools, students are rarely known as individuals or understood as people, and finding themselves within school walls becomes a difficult and sometimes uncomfortable venture, one far more distant and less supportive than in the more effective schools with students just like them.

Networking Contexts

More effective schools are organized around a wide range of networking contexts: school (administration and teachers) with parents and students; school (administration and teachers) with community; faculty with faculty; and faculty with administration and with students, to name some. Beyond the work tasks and necessary interactions within each network, each has a variety of subnetworks as well as viable links to the other networks. Each of these networks engages in communication and feedback, so no one is out of the loop. Reeves (2006) calls these nodes, hubs, and superhubs (see also Barabasi, 2003). The node is the individual, the hub is a node with connections to other hubs, and a superhub is a network to which numerous other nodes and hubs are connected. They foster communication and distribute knowledge across the participants, who can build bridges (Reeves, 2006). More effective schools can be identified by the existence of hubs and bridges. The communication system is not hierarchical but nonlinear and highly interactive, and as result of this structure, it affirms everyone's value as an integral part of the school community: its parents and teachers (all its employees), community members, and its students.

Management Contexts

The personal inclusion felt in more effective schools as a result of hubs and bridges creates a school–community bond beyond the usual parent–teacher conferences, help on school trips, and fund-raising. Parents and community members are seen as resources in the students' education, and used as such. They are considered as having "funds of knowledge" (Moje et al., 2004; Moll, Amanti, Neff, & Gonzalez, 1992). Bringing local knowledge out of the community and into the school validates what parents as well as schools know, fosters ties to the community, and at the same time creates a sense of connectedness and affirmation for students. For example, teachers identify parents and community members with abilities, jobs, or hobbies that can be related to instruction or students' future plans, and the teachers invite them to share their expertise at school. In addition, members of the school community approach local businesses and industries for varying degrees of educational involvement.

One middle school in Florida invites parents who run small businesses to explain the math they use in their work and to help the students solve some of their work problems. In a New York school district, parents with computer expertise are brought in to interact with students and teachers about software, helping them gain both new knowledge and practice. A high school in Texas that is close to a small airport where many parents work has created an optional aviation magnet program for students of all abilities, where students can learn related skills and knowledge, from airport maintenance to aviation, within an academic environment that combines these with math, science, history, and literacy. Similarly, a high school in Florida has created a mathematics academy as well as a construction academy, both also within academic programs for college- or job-bound students. Here, students work with local stockbrokers, architects, and construction firms (some of whom are parents and most of whom are community members) as they learn beyond the basics of academic knowledge. To help them become comfortable in a college environment, students at a combined middle and high school in Los Angeles take some of their regular classes at the University of California, Los Angeles (UCLA), while they and their parents receive counseling about their present work, including expectations, work habits, study skills, and socialization. In all cases, home–school connections are recognized and strengthened, and students can develop interests and see opportunities for themselves. (For more information about these schools and more, at both middle and high school levels, see Langer, 2002.)

In the most effective schools (those that are higher performing and also have good reputations), parents, community members, and students also participate in school management. Even in the poorest communities where parents hold two jobs and students work after school, the schools reach out to include parents and students. Parents have room to serve on decision-making committees and to be involved in other ways to voice ideas and to be heard. The schools make time for them and make allowances for their schedules. There is a true interaction about shared problems and shared dreams. Disagreements are confronted and worked out before they escalate. Students, too, are on committees and have a voice, and their comments are taken seriously to inform decision making. One school district in New York, for example, has a long-standing, districtwide school-based management system, individual school building cabinets, and working groups of parents, community members, and students at each school. These committees have teeth; although administrators are committee members, they never serve as chair.

Thus, in more effective schools, there is room for students to be part of the community at the very time they may also be trying also to move beyond. They have emotional support and a sense of efficacy locally, and their participation in school management also helps them to hone management skills: planning, decision making, and anticipating consequences—all related to literate reasoning behaviors as well as life.

School Support Contexts

In the more effective schools, there is a substantial student support network to keep individual students from getting lost. Parents and community members are kept informed of school activities and of changes in school programs, offerings, and routines. Parents are involved in their children's course planning and are kept up-to-date about their progress, abilities, and difficulties. Although the door is always open for parents to discuss their child's school experiences, a support group of counseling services and parent education courses are also available with help for such parenting issues as anger, crisis, sobriety, and drug treatment and management. These schools believe students' nonacademic needs affect both attitude and academic performance, and they try to help students and their families with such concerns (Langer, 2004).

Beyond this, more effective schools are also proactive. At their weekly team meetings, teachers discuss not only their curriculum and teaching approaches, but also how their students are doing. A student whose behavior, attendance, or work habits seem to be changing is discussed by the group of teachers that student takes courses with. Students are identified early, in the hope that a potentially escalating problem can be averted. In one middle school in New York that is divided into smaller *houses* to ensure each student is known, the house principal, guidance counselor, and special education teacher meet weekly with each team of teachers. That way, everyone remains informed about student needs and work as the year progresses. Parents are called in for team meetings sooner rather than later, and together with the student, work on helpful next steps. Progress and well-being are monitored, and everyone, including the student, has a voice, from early on, in defining and addressing problems. The school offers group meetings and counseling services on such education-related topics as homework, test preparation, school expectations, and state requirements. The school opens courses to parents and students together, as well as to the community as a whole, including classes on many levels of computer and digital camera use, as well as on topics students and parents request—from growing flowers to losing weight to keeping a checkbook.

All these activities are about students and involve students. There is a pervasive sense of caring, community, and trust.

These permeate the environment and are merged into the semiotic sense of welcome and well-being that more effective schools convey. They create the safe houses for learning and growth that parents want and adolescents need. Yet less effective schools, in comparison to the higher-performing schools that are otherwise like them, offer none of this. They say parents are too busy and that students don't care or can't do better. They say they try their best but do not engage in the kinds of active support efforts their better-performing peer schools do. (For more about school culture, see Fullan, 1991; Langer, 2002, 2004; Lieberman, 1992; Little & McLaughlin 1993; Peterson, 2002.)

TEACHING AND LEARNING CULTURE

Just as students, their parents, and community members have personal experiences with more effective schools in ways that are so very comfortable and compelling, so too do teachers and administrators. The ways in which educators work together to understand student and school needs, grow professionally, fine-tune programs, and offer engaging and effective instruction bring into view another vector in the more effective school's semiotic presentation of self. We can "read" this aspect of a school by looking at its professional, programmatic, and classroom contexts.

Professional Context

As discussed earlier, the effective school building offers a semiotic message of welcome, and so too does it offer a message of professional competence and concern, whatever student community it serves. Teachers, administrators, and related staff members are deeply involved in keeping up with the knowledge in their fields, in program offerings as they relate to their students' learning, and in ways to make that learning happen well and happily. You can see this professional semiotic at work as you walk through the hallways. Educators are meeting in groups to discuss curriculum or something they have seen, heard, or read that is relevant to teaching and learning. In the faculty lounge, you can hear discussions about lessons that went well, and those that didn't, what the teacher will do differently, and other ideas about lessons to come. You also see teachers reaching out to offer more and more engaging activities and discussing how to fine-tune them. You see them reflecting on the curriculum and changes they think need to be made. They share and help each other. They work together informally as well as formally.

More effective schools are marked by profoundly well-working professional communities. Teachers and administrators pool their knowledge, work together, and learn together to help them better understand their students' needs and to be responsive to the bigger picture of societal demands and changing times. They try to stay current with their fields, with their students, and with society. And they work collaboratively to leverage their knowledge for the benefit of the school. One way they do this is by meeting regularly to discuss the academic programs, what the teachers and administrators are doing, and how the students are doing. They never lose sight of who their students are and the special planning it takes for all students to do better. Thoughtful and enriched classroom experiences that engage their students in the ideas of the course work and help them gain new skills and knowledge is the goal. How to make it work for their students is their challenge. They believe all students can become more highly literate and that it is their professional responsibility to make it happen. Their students' successes are theirs, and their students' failures are theirs. They work as a team toward ongoing success—which to them is actualized when students like school and do well. They aim for both.

They know professional learning is at the core of a school's growth. Therefore, administrators and teachers encourage their colleagues to belong to professional groups, attend conferences, read professional literature, visit other schools, take workshops and courses, and also to give them. They are expected to be active members in their professional communities. They know that the richest professional knowledge is gained through participation in a combination of these activities. But they know too that school growth does not stop with the learning experiences of an individual professional. This knowledge needs to be shared, discussed, and debated in terms of their school and their students. For example, one school district in New York has a deep undercurrent of professional enthusiasm. It values professional involvement and encourages teachers and administrators to work and grow together. Administrators provide time for meetings and working groups, and individual schools plan schedules with these in mind. These administrators also spend money on invited consultants the staff members feel would be helpful (rather than deciding on staff development apart from teachers), and they encourage teachers to participate in professional organizations, take time off to visit other schools, attend workshops, or give workshop sessions themselves. They know the payoff comes when the teachers return and share their experiences so as to offer the larger faculty, through their informal as well as formal networks, a fresh look at themselves and at their own schools and students. All the more effective schools had similar professional qualities, whatever their demographics. (For more about professional contexts, see Fullan, 1991; Hargreaves, 2003; Langer, 2002, 2005b; Lieberman, 1992; Little & McLaughlin, 1993; Grossman, Wineburg, & Woolworth, 1998.)

Programmatic Contexts

As part of their "hubs and bridges" organizational approach, more effective schools have a number of professional networks, all working simultaneously: instructional teams, academic departments, grade-level meetings, curriculum development groups, self-study committees, and other collaborative structures. Some of these groups work across grade levels and subject areas and some do not. Because teachers and administrators are members of more than one group, they cross lines; together they ensure a greater communication of ideas and directions. When they are not meeting face-to-face, they share articles, e-mails, and comments. In more effective schools, professional ideas are in the air all the time. When they work and share together, the educators in a school develop a common understanding over time—of what their students need and how best to help them learn. Over time, they also develop a

shared philosophy of education, with a related way of looking at their students and their needs, as well as at instructional goals and approaches that are appropriate for their students. They find their thought-through way of responding to changes in their fields, to societal demands, to changing school populations, and to changing times (Langer, 2002).

These staff members also know that their job as educators is never done. As a professional community, they are always at some part of a looking-in and looking-out cycle, assessing the effectiveness of what they are doing, exploring possibilities for improvement, experimenting with change—and when it works, making it happen. Students are very much part of such activities. They are sought after for feedback as well as suggestions for change. Their ideas are taken seriously. Community-minded schools have students on governance committees. In addition, teachers often canvas their classes for feedback about teaching approaches, activities, and materials—all with instructional improvement and finding ways to more fully engage their students as their goal.

Professional communities of this sort inevitably lead to changes in both how the teachers teach and what they teach; in their instructional approaches as well as in the broader curricular programs. They come to realize that beyond the contributions of individual wonderful teachers, students benefit most when they experience a connected and coherent program over time. It is when all teachers have a sense of who the students are and how they are doing, as well as what has come before and what students will learn later (ideally both within and across subject areas), that they can make content and experiential connections overt to students. For example, a teacher might say, "I know last year you learned about characterization and plot in mythology. I know you studied myths from a number of countries. Let's discuss what you learned. . . . Now we're going to discuss the same things— characterization and plot—but this time in relation to epics. What do you think an epic is?" This kind of connection seems so simple, but it is rarely done in most schools. Yet it makes a significant difference to students who have learned to treat each school year as a separate body of knowledge, instead of realizing they have some useful background knowledge to which they can connect their new course work.

However, it is almost impossible for a teacher to help students make these connections unless there is a planning and sharing of the curriculum, a hub. In more effective schools teachers discuss what they are teaching at the moment and how, and share what worked and what needs to be picked up in the future—often by the next year's teacher. They look for connections across content, approaches, and grades, and they use this knowledge to help their students make links across time and experience. They discuss students' reactions to the content—what was difficult and what was easy, what was engaging and what was not—and plan ways in which problems might be ameliorated, not only during the year by a particular teacher, but also across years—before and after.

My studies have shown that whoever they are and however they have been doing at school, students enjoy becoming engaged with ideas they can question, challenge, discuss, and use to form their own interpretations (Langer 1995, 1997, 2001a, 2001b). Too often programmatic work such as the kind I have described is seen as being apart from students, but in the most effective schools, it never is. In more effective schools, whatever the student body, teachers search for ways to make the curriculum inviting and engaging, even enticing for their students, while also ensuring the coherence and connectedness that will result in the greatest cumulative and comprehensive learning. (For more on programmatic contexts, see Fullan, 1991; Langer, 2001a, 2001b, 2005a; McLaughlin & Talbert, 1993; Peterson, McCarthy, & Elmore 1996; Siskin, 1994.)

Classroom Contexts

Like whole schools, classrooms have their own semiotics, and these can be more effective, less effective, or somewhere in between (see Kress et al., 2005). More effective classrooms visually show you who the students are, even when the room is empty. You see the products of student activity everywhere: photographs, writing, art, and projects of all sorts. If you look closely, you can see the students' thinking—about the content. It is

evident in the papers on the wall. Read them and you will see. In more effective schools you can hear the students' written ideas and their learners' voices. You can also tell whether the students were intellectually engaged in an activity and in the content. You can read the class and who its members are. One middle school class in New York tells it all. There are photographs of students at work and examples of a variety of their papers from across the semester on the walls. Sometimes students are asked to look at their older papers for ideas about the new—to make cognitive connections. Because there never is enough room for student work, the teacher took over the ceiling. Strings were fastened across the ceiling at many anchor points, and illustrated papers were hung on them with clothespins. You see the students' names as well as their work, and they greet visitors as well as students each day of the year.

When the students are in class, you can again hear their voices, even when you are not listening carefully to what they are saying. The social semiotic is often one of oral engagement, of real discussion about the ideas at hand, with enthusiasm. Students' ideas are front and center as they debate with each other and return to the text. Teachers help and teach, but are not the only voices. In addition to offering needed information and explanations, they guide students in where to find the material or evidence they need, help them inspect it, question it, and refine it. You can hear their students' cognitive engagement, whether they are working as a whole class, in groups, in pairs, or alone. They are on task and love it. As the bell rings and the students begin leaving class, their discussions continue. These are class contexts where students are hooked—even the lowest performing and most troubled of them. What a difference from less effective schools with a very different semiotic, where we see students' books stacked on their desks, arms folded on their books, and their heads resting on their arms—eyes half closed or fast asleep.

Critical and Creative Learning Context

If you listen to classroom talk, to what teachers and students say to one another, you can get a semiotic map of thought and interaction. It is from this view of the classroom that you can get a sense of how the students are dealing with the content, the help they receive, and what they are learning. In more effective schools you see that discussion is dialogic (Nystrand, 1997). Students talk with one another, and the focus is sharply on the content.

That is, students are truly interacting with one another: sharing ideas, questioning, agreeing or disagreeing with, or adding to, each other's ideas. They are picking up on what others have said and using it to communicate with the group as a way to try out and shape their own ideas. In each case they tell why, and thus need to inspect what they and others have said. They learn to become critical. Their teachers have helped them learn how to locate and give evidence and to test it out as they test their ideas. They engage in highly literate conversations, ones that are thoughtful and thought provoking—where the course content is learned and refined by examining the ideas, what they mean, how they connect with other things the students know—where they learn to analyze and to be critical as they gain the power to make their ideas grow (Applebee, Langer, Nystrand, & Gamoran, 2003). They learn to be thinkers and learners as they are also learning the content.

In effective schools, during their conversations, students engage in envisionment building; their understandings are poised to change and grow as they develop and refine ideas through reading, writing, media activities, drama, discussion, and other class activities (Langer, 1990, 1995; Fillmore, 1982). In envisionment-building classrooms, it is assumed that ideas change and grow over time as one reads, writes, hears, and thinks. Therefore, teachers try to help students engage in "meaning in motion," questioning ideas, leaving them open to new refinements and connections as they are in the act of gaining fuller understandings. In more effective classrooms, teachers do this in a number of ways.

First, they treat their students as lifelong envisionment builders. Teachers assume that by the time students have become adolescents, they have spent much of their lives building envisionments in their efforts to make sense of themselves and the world. They also have past experiences with literacy and can make some connections with the content—given the chance. In the effective classroom context where teachers understand this, they invite students to further develop their understandings about the content and provide room for students to take ownership for their developing ideas. Activities abound. Students read, write, discuss—they gain ideas and do research using paper, media, and people as sources. They work with the teacher, in small groups, and in the whole class. They get feedback all the time in each of these groups (Adler & Rougle, 2005; Bomer, 1995). They look for help because they know that they are envisionment builders and their ideas are forming. Instead of copying, they think, question, challenge, revise, refine, and grow.

Because they need to keep open minds, teachers treat questions as part of the learning experience. When students ask questions, the teacher takes it to mean they are trying to go beyond what they presently understand, and helps them to do so in a way that accepts the students' knowledge as well as their efforts to go beyond. Students are encouraged to raise such issues as "I'm not sure about … ", "What if? …", "It surprised me when …", "I really didn't understand why …". Questions and comments such as these are discussion starters that can serve to help all students revisit the material in new ways and to build beyond their initial understandings. This is very different from what happens in the less effective class, where teachers treat questions as evidence that a student has not learned well, didn't read the text or failed to do the homework. As a result, in less effective classes, students do not ask questions; they keep them to themselves, shutting off a critical part of the learning process.

In more effective classroom contexts teachers also treat class meetings as a time for students to further develop their understandings, rather than as a time to review what they might have missed. These teachers believe that, through questions and discussions, students can work through their misunderstandings and move beyond. The focus is forward, to what the students are working toward, rather than behind, on what they didn't get. Through such discussion, students also have an opportunity to explore multiple perspectives, those of other students, their teachers, and the more widely accepted understandings in the field or parts of society. Thus, as their growing ideas are encouraged and as they are supplied with a context in which to try them out, students also have models of content and thought to inspect and learn from—and with which respectfully to disagree. And they know why they agree or disagree. For example, stories or social studies events can be revisited from a number of the participants' perspectives, from the perspective of history, culture, and tradition, as well as from the perspective of class, gender, and power. Through this sort of perspective taking, students can ask *what if* questions and explore possibilities. They can agree, disagree, defend, challenge, and ponder well-explained ideas, some that might extend or change their own views, others that they might disregard, and still others that they might hold as interesting alternatives to their own.

These more effective classrooms are intellectual playing grounds for the development of whole people who can engage in both critical and creative thinking (Langer, 1990, 1995). In some of my work, I refer to critical thinking as "point of reference" thinking. This is the type of thinking you do when you know the topic or point of the quest, but need to gain more information to understand it more fully or to reach the destination. Point of reference thinking offers an informational goal that can be built toward. Another type of thinking I call "exploring horizons of possibilities." In this case, neither the topic nor the point is wholly understood; thus, students need to ask questions about understandings they have at the moment because these lead them to also consider possibilities about the whole (the point or topic or theme). In both cases students and teachers need to seek, find, and refine many ideas. Connections need to be made and checked out—but the kinds of thinking and what is thought about differ. Point of reference thinking involves more critical thinking strategies, whereas exploring horizons of possibilities involves more creative thinking strategies. The content students think about during point of reference thinking is more readily available for direct close inspection, but exploring horizons of possibilities, by its very nature, involves a more open-ended and broader search. Both modes of thinking are part of sharp and highly literate thought in all disciplines and in life. In more effective classes both happen in reading literary and informational texts, in all subjects. The two are a function of how the mind works as it is creating meaning, based on the student's purpose and available knowledge. Often one mode of thinking plays louder than the other and for a longer time during a particular activity, but then the thinker changes modes as new ideas or problems come to mind that the prior mode could not readily make sense of or solve. Each is used when it is more facilitative to the thinker's purpose. Thus, the two modes complement each other, as they enrich the kinds of thinking, as well as actual understandings and solutions, that occur.

But students often have many more opportunities to learn and practice critical rather than creative thinking in their course work, where the focus is on reading for a particular goal (e.g., the causes of the French and Indian War, the behavior of the digestive system, or the mythical allusions in a sonnet). These are all important in content learning, but creative thinking is an additional dimension. This is what happens in the more effective schools, where students are encouraged to ask an array of open-ended questions, to explore possibilities in a variety of ways, and are given the materials and experiences that help them do this. They engage in activities that help them question their present understandings and see how new possibilities might move them to reshape their understandings of the war, the digestive system, or the sonnet. More effective classrooms, in all subject areas, provide an instructional environment that invites richer and more varied thinking within and across the two modes. To ensure this environment, teachers make available a variety of knowledge sources, including a range of paper, media, human, and other potentially useful knowledge-bearing sources to stimulate students' thinking and understanding of the topics they are studying and their relations to big issues within the particular discipline and in life (Applebee, 1996). They also support students' engagement in both critical and creative thinking about the content and help students learn to judge when one approach is more helpful or appropriate than the other; together, critical and creative thinking permit a wider range of ideas to be considered and a deeper range of under-standings to develop. In more effective class-rooms, close inspection, analysis, discovery, and invention all have a place. Such class-rooms are stimulating places of learning.

Classroom Community Contexts

The last aspect of the classroom context that I discuss here is the affect in the classroom. In more effective schools, classrooms indeed become working, living, and thriving class-room communities. The participants know each other as people and as learners. Al-though critical and creative envisionments are built in these contexts, they are also so-cial contexts for real interaction. Students reach out to one another, they help one an-other, they challenge one another, and they correct one another. They are not antago-nists, but colleagues; there is a sense of be-longing they feel in which their interactions and learning (about self as well as content) are an important and beneficial outgrowth. They may not be friends outside school, but within the class they are important to one another. They learn to hear one another and understand that how each individual reads the social situation, as well as course con-tent, is bound up in that person's past expe-riences—social, personal, and educational. Because they listen to each other, they learn that each student has something new and worthwhile to give to, as well as to take from, the group. Without realizing it, as a group, they help each other develop and change—personally and educationally. In more effective schools such as the ones I have been describing, even the teachers change. With each new group of students come new individuals to learn to work with, new ideas and knowledge to think about, and new activities. The teachers' responsive-ness to the individuality of each group con-tributes to the development of the class com-munity. It is coconstructed.

For example, in describing her teaching approach, a teacher in New York said to me, "In one sense, every year the material I teach is the same but the students are different. But it isn't really that way. Both are really new. Although there is a body of knowledge I want each group to learn, I need to go about it differently each year, because of who they are and what they know and what they've studied and how they've been taught. So, in a way, it's all new each year. I don't use all the same materials each year, but if I do, I use them in different ways. And I don't use exactly the same activities each year, but when I do, I don't necessarily use them in the same ways. Some stay the same but I de-cide based on the class. Even when the mate-rials and activities are the same, the students react to them in different ways, so I have to handle the lessons differently. My goal is to get them thinking about the material and to get them working together as a group, what-ever it takes." (For more information about classroom contexts, see the chapters in Part II of this volume, as well as Adler & Rougle, 2005; Bomer, 1995; Greenleaf et al., 2001; Guthrie & Alvermann, 1998; Moje & Hinch-man, 2004.)

Less effective classrooms are a far cry from what this teacher described. Students often work alone and have less opportunity to get to know one another as learners. Teachers often focus more on the material to be covered than on the students who need to learn it and how to help them feel connected to the class and to the content. Lessons from year to year are often the same. A veteran teacher in a Texas school, attempting to be helpful to a new teacher, went to her cup-board and lifted out two very large piles of papers. She said, "Here are my lesson plans and class work for the course. They start here, and this (pointing) is the end of the year. I've been using them for years and they're great, so you just need to follow them." The students in this class were a community of a different sort. Instead of getting to know each other and getting to grow together, they worked together to fig-ure out the teacher and what she wanted, as a way to get through the class. They wan-dered into class, worked separately or in pairs, figuring out the answers they thought their teacher wanted. Both this classroom and the aforementioned effective classrooms were communities, yet the ethos of each com-munity was as different as the ways the stu-dents interacted with and about the content.

DISCUSSION

I have explored several contexts for literacy in this chapter as a way to emphasize the many semiotic vectors that are at play within a school—semiotic because there are sights, sounds, and artifacts that resound with messages throughout the school: in the yard, entryways, halls, offices, meeting rooms, and classrooms. What messages do they convey, more or less effectively? Even the telephones and computers are meaning laden. Are they objects for easy communication and sharing, or are they not?

Each context I have described can be considered a semiotic vector through which to view literacy education, what is facilitating and what is limiting it. Some are broader contexts and some more particular. Some focus on the school, some on the professionals, some on the programs, and some on the classrooms. When you look closely, with a zoom lens, more can be said about each context, and contexts-within-contexts can be pulled out to be examined. For example, if you look carefully at the variety of the more effective school contexts I have discussed, you can get an indication of their attitudes regarding diversity, student behavior, or tolerance. But to understand the features influencing each school's effectiveness better, we would need to pull each out within several contexts for closer examination.

I trust I have written enough for the reader to guess how the contexts discussed in this chapter might differ in more or less effective settings, and why. However, it would be enlightening to look closely at both kinds of settings. Both more and less effective schools are contexts that need to be examined more fully both by teachers who are working in classrooms on a day-to-day basis and by researchers who want to understand them in ways that can drive pedagogy, decision making, and substantive changes at the secondary level.

As stated earlier in this chapter, my studies have indicated that what I have described as the more effective schools are also the more successful schools (Langer, 2002). Students in these schools and classes do better both in their course work at school and on their high-stakes tests than students who are in other schools with students from similar socioeconomic backgrounds. Are there schools that are somewhere in between what I have described as more effective and more typical? In a sense, there are. Some schools have some aspects of both types. How well do

they do? Not terribly well. My research indicates that students in more effective schools have, on average, higher test scores and better course performance than students in schools that do not have all the features of effective schools. It takes all of the more effective contexts I have described to make a shift in school culture, class culture, and student performance. All these more effective features need to be in place to make a difference; a few features do not suffice to make a school an effective context for adolescent literacy. Together, these multiple, overlapping contexts reflect one pedagogical vision of how good schools work for everyone. They have at their root the understanding that humane and thinking communities, based on respect for difference, love of learning, and a goal of agency through knowledge and literate thinking, support student learning. They want to graduate literate learners for life, and student learning in more effective schools indicates that this can happen.

REFERENCES

Adler, M., & Rougle, E. (2005). *Building literacy through classroom discussion.* New York: Scholastic.

Alliance for Excellent Education (2006, July 10). Who's Counted? Who's Counting? *Straight As, 6*(14), 1.

Applebee, A. (1996). *Curriculum as conversation: Transforming traditions of teaching and learning.* Chicago: University of Chicago Press.

Applebee, A., Langer, J., Nystrand, M., & Gamoran, A. (2003). Discussion-based approaches to developing understanding: Instruction and achievement in middle and high school English. *American Educational Research Journal, 40,* 685–730.

Bakhtin, M. M. (1986). *Speech genres and other late essays* (C. Emerson & M. Holquist, Eds., V. W. McGee, Trans.). Austin, TX: University of Texas Press.

Barabasi, A. (2003). *Linked: How everything is connected to everything else and what it means.* New York: Plume Books.

Bloome, D. (1986). Reading as a social process in a middle school classroom. In D. Bloome (Ed.), *Literacy and schooling* (pp. 123–149). Norwood, NJ: Ablex.

Bomer, R. (1995). *Time for meaning: Crafting literate lives in middle and high school.* Portsmouth, NH: Heinemann.

Csikszentmihalyi, M., & Larson, R. (1984). *Being adolescent: Conflict and growth in the teenage years.* New York: Basic Books.

Danesi, M. (1994). *Messages and meanings: An intro duction to semiotics.* Toronto: Canadian Scholars Press.

Darling-Hammond, L. (1991). The implications of testing policy for educational quality and equality. *Phi Delta Kappan, 73,* 220–225.

Darling-Hammond, L. (2004). Standards, accountability and school reform. *Teachers College Record, 106,* 1047–1085.

Darling-Hammond, L., Ancess, J., & Falk, B. (1995). *Authentic assessment in action: Studies of schools and students at work.* New York: Teachers College Press.

Davidson, A. L. (1996). *Making and molding identity in schools: Student narratives on race, gender and academic engagement.* Albany, NY: SUNY Press.

Everhart, R. B. (1983). *Reading, writing and resistance: Adolescence and labor in a junior high school.* Boston: Routledge and Kegan Paul.

Fairclough, N. (1992). *Discourse and social change.* Malden, MA: Blackwell.

Fair Test (n.d.). Cambridge, MA: National Center for Fair and Open Testing. Retrieved July 31, 2007, from *www.fairtest.org.*

Fillmore, C. J. (1982). Ideal readers and real readers. In D. Tannen (Ed.), *Analyzing discourse: Text and talk. Proceedings of the 32nd Georgetown University Round Table Conference* (pp. 248–270). Washington, DC: Georgetown University Press.

Fine, M. (1989). Silencing and nurturing voice in an improbable context: Urban adolescence in a public school. In H. Giroux & P. McLaren (Eds.), *Critical pedagogy, the state and cultural struggle* (pp. 152–173). Albany, NY: SUNY Press.

Flood, J., Lapp, D., Heath, S. B., & Langer, J. A. (in press). The communicative, visual and performative arts: Core components of literacy education. In Y. Goodman & J. Hoffman (Eds.), *Changing literacies for changing times.* New York: Routledge.

Fullan, M. (1991). *The meaning of educational change* (2nd ed.). New York: Teachers College Press.

Garcia, G. E. (1991). Factors influencing the English reading test performance of Spanish speaking Hispanic children. *Reading Research Quarterly, 25,* 371–392.

Gee, J. P. (1999). *An introduction to discourse analysis: Theory and method.* New York: Routledge.

Gilyard, K. (1991). *Voices of the self.* Detroit: Wayne State University Press.

Greenleaf, C., Schoenbach, R., Cziko, C., & Mueller, F. (2001). Apprenticing adolescent readers to academic literacy. *Harvard Education Review, 71,* 79–129.

Grossman, P. L., Wineburg, S. S., & Woolworth, S. (2001). Toward a theory of teacher community. *Teachers College Record, 103,* 942–1012.

Guthrie, J., & Alvermann, D. (1998). *Engaged reading: Processes, practices, and policy implications.* New York: Teachers College Press.

Hargreaves, A. (2003). *Teaching in the knowledge society: Education in the age of insecurity.* New York: Teachers College Press.

Hull, G., & Zacher, J. (2004). What is after school worth? Developing literacy and identity out of school. *Voices in Urban Education, 3,* 36–44.

Kress, G., Jewitt, C., Franks, A., Hardcastle, J., Jones K., & Bourne, J. (2005). *English in urban classrooms: A multicultural perspective on teaching and learning.* New York: Falmer.

Langer, J. A. (1985). Examining background knowledge and text comprehension. *Reading Research Quarterly, 14,* 468–481.

Langer, J. A. (1987a). A sociocognitive perspective on literacy learning. In J. Langer (Ed.), *Language, literacy and culture: Issues of society and schooling* (pp. 1–20). Norwood, NJ: Ablex.

Langer, J. A. (1987b). The construction of meaning and the assessment of comprehension: An analysis of reader performance in standardized test items. In R. Freedle (Ed.), *Cognitive and linguistic analyses of standardized test performance* (pp. 225–244). Norwood, NJ: Ablex.

Langer, J. A. (1990). The process of understanding: Reading for literary and informational purposes. *Research in the Teaching of English, 24,* 229–260.

Langer, J. A. (1995). *Envisioning literature: Literary understanding and literature instruction.* New York: Teachers College Press.

Langer. J. A. (1997). Literacy through literature. *Journal of Adolescent and Adult Literacy, 40,* 606–615.

Langer, J. A. (2000). Excellence in English in middle and high school: How teachers' professional lives support student achievement. *American Educational Research Journal, 37,* 397–439.

Langer, J. A. (2001a). Beating the odds: Teaching middle and high school students to read and write well. *American Educational Research Journal, 38,* 837–880.

Langer, J. A. (2001b). Succeeding against the odds. *English Journal, 91,* 37–42.

Langer, J. A. (2002). *Effective literacy instruction: Building successful reading and writing programs.* Urbana, IL: National Council of Teachers of English.

Langer, J. A. (2004). *Getting to excellent: How to create better schools.* New York: Teachers College Press.

Langer, J. A. (2005a). Developing the literate mind. Center on English Learning and Achievement. New York: University at Albany. Retrieved July 30, 2007, from *cela.albany.edu/researcher/langer/IRA_Develop.pdf.*

Langer, J. A. (2005b). The literate mind in school and life. In A. Kulinen (Ed.), *Literacy in mother tongue* (pp. 94–112). Helsinki: University of Turku Press.

Lieberman, A. (1992). The meaning of scholarly activity and the building of community. *Educational Researcher, 21,* 5–12.

Little, J. W., & McLaughlin, M. (Eds.). (1993). *Teachers' work: Individuals, colleagues, and contexts.* New York: Teachers College Press.

Luke, A., & Elkins, J. (1998). Reinventing literacy in "New Times." *Journal of Adolescent and Adult Literacy, 42,* 4–7.

McLaughlin, M., & Talbert, E. (1993). *Contexts that matter for teaching and learning.* Palo Alto, CA:

Stanford University Center for Research in the Context of Secondary School Teaching.

Miron, L. F., & Lauria, M. (1998). Student voice as agency: Resistance and accommodation in inner-city schools. *Anthropology and Education Quarterly, 29,* 189–213.

Moje, E. B., Ciechanowski, K. M., Kramer, K., Ellis, L., Carrillo, R., & Collazo, T. (2004). Working toward third space in content literacy: An examination of everyday funds of knowledge and discourse. *Reading Research Quarterly, 39,* 38–70.

Moje, E., & Hinchman, K. (2004). Culturally responsive practices for youth literacy learning. In T. Jetton & J. A. Dole (Eds.), *Adolescent literacy research and practice* (pp. 321–350). New York: Guilford Press.

Moll, L., Amanti, C., Neff, D., & Gonzalez, N. (1992). Funds of knowledge for teaching. *Theory into Practice, 31,* 132–141.

Morris, C. W. (1971). *Writing on the general theory of signs.* The Hague: Mouton.

National Assessment of Educational Progress, Reading. (2002). U.S. Department of Education, Institute of Education Sciences, National Center for Education Statistics. (2003). *The Nation's Report Card: Reading 2002* (ED Pubs No. NCES 2003-521). Washington, DC: Author.

Noddings, N. (1984). *Caring: A feminine approach to ethics and moral education.* Berkeley: University of California Press.

Nystrand, M. (with Gamoran, A., Kachur, R., & Prendergast, C.). (1997). *Opening dialogue: Understanding the dynamics of language and learning in the English classroom.* New York: Teachers College Press.

Oakes, J. (1985). *Keeping track: How schools structure inequality.* New Haven: Yale University Press.

Peirce, C. S. (1992). *The essential Peirce: Selected philosophical writings, Vol. 1, 1867–1893.* N. Houser & C. Kloesel (Eds.). Bloomington: Indiana University Press.

Peterson, K. (2002). Changing school culture. *Journal of Staff Development, 23,* 3.

Peterson, P. L., McCarthy, S. J., & Elmore, R. F. (1996). Learning from school restructuring. *American Educational Research Journal, 33,* 119–154.

Pratt, M. L. (1991). Arts of the contact zone. *Profession 91,* 33–40.

Reeves, D. B. (2006). Of hubs, bridges and networks. *Educational Leadership, 63,* 32–37.

Rose, M. (1990). *Lives on the boundary.* New York: Free Press.

Sarris, G. (1993). Keeping Slug Woman alive. In J. Boyarin (Ed.), *The ethnography of reading* (pp. 238–269). Berkeley: University of California Press.

Sebeok, T. A. (Ed.). (1977). *A perfusion of signs.* Bloomington: Indiana University Press.

Sebeok, T. A., & Danesi, M. (2000). *The forms of meaning: Modeling systems theory and semiotic analysis.* Berlin: Mouton de Gruyter.

Siskin, L. S. (1994). *Realms of knowledge: Academic departments in secondary schools.* New York: Falmer.

Solano-Flores, G., & Trumbull, E. (2003). Examining language in context: The need for new research and practice paradigms in the testing of English-language learners. *Educational Researcher, 32,* 3–13.

Spillane, J., & Jennings, N. (1997). Aligned instructional policy and ambitious pedagogy: Exploring instructional reform from the classroom perspective. *Teachers College Record, 98,* 449–481.

Wenger, E. (1998). *Communities of practice: Learning, meaning and identity.* New York: Cambridge University Press.

Wilson, S. M., Peterson, P. L., Ball, D. L., & Cohen, D. K. (1996). Learning by all. *Phi Delta Kappan, 77,* 468–476.

Wraga, W. (1999). The educational and political implications of curriculum alignment and standards-based reform. *Journal of Curriculum and Supervision, 15*(1), 4–25.

CHAPTER 5

Adolescents Who Struggle with Literacy

LARRY R. JOHANNESSEN
THOMAS M. MCCANN

In this chapter, we refer to *literacy* as a lifelong continuum of experiences with the processing, interpretation, and production of texts of all sorts. We consider the factors that influence the struggles that some adolescents experience in accomplishing the kind of literacy tasks that are valued in schools and that influence social and economic mobility. Whereas discussions of literacy struggles typically address pedagogical issues as the primary factors to influence development, our review of the research literature emphasizes that hope for struggling adolescent literacy learners derives from the interplay of three domains: (1) the establishment of supportive and trusting relationships between teachers and learners; (2) the cultivation of partnerships among families, their communities, and the schools; and (3) the refinement of teaching practices that connect with the lives of learners in a culturally and socially responsive way.

Any discussion of adolescents who struggle with literacy invites definitions of *literacy* and of *struggling adolescents*. In the climate of assessment and accountability engendered by the passage of the No Child Left Behind Act (NCLB), school leaders who disaggregate achievement test data see time and again that, as a group, the learners for whom English is a second language and learners from low-income homes are the adolescents who appear to be struggling with literacy. As noted by Smith and Wilhelm (Chapter 23, this volume), one could also add adolescent males as another pertinent— and vulnerable—subgroup. Of course, in an NCLB context, literacy is defined in large part by how learners perform on standardized assessments of reading.

From our perspective, literacy is not a static level of language achievement that separates the *literate* from the *illiterate*. Instead, *literacy* refers to a lifelong continuum of experiences with the processing, interpretation, and production of texts of all sorts. Other commentators in this volume (see, e.g., Langer, Chapter 4, Schoenbach & Greenleaf, Chapter 7, Marshall, Chapter 8, and Rhodes & Robnolt, Chapter 11) explore the many contexts, facets, and complexities of literacy. For our purposes in this chapter, though, we consider the factors that influence the struggles that some adolescents experience in accomplishing the literacy tasks that are valued in schools and that influence social and economic mobility.

Gee (1989) provides a frame for thinking

about literacy that is germane to the discussion. He notes that as an individual emerges as a literate person, he or she develops a primary discourse and is immersed in a discourse community. Gee insists that one's identity is inextricably bound to one's discourse, and he notes the challenges confronting a learner who attempts to move in and out of different discourse communities. From this perspective, an obvious source of the struggle for many adolescents is that their primary discourse does not match readily with the literacy activities sponsored by schools and inherent in many academic assessments. At the same time, Delpit (1996) and Lee (2005) offer encouragement to educators to help all students to develop a positive sense of self and to recognize their potential to navigate through the discourses that dominate schools and their assessments.

As we discuss the ongoing concern for adolescents who struggle with literacy, we focus primarily on reading and writing. Although most suggestions regarding intervention for struggling learners typically address pedagogical issues as the primary factors to influence development, we recognize from our review of the related literature that the potential for struggling adolescent literacy learners derives from the interplay of three domains: (1) the establishment of supportive and trusting relationships between teachers and learners; (2) the cultivation of partnerships among families, their communities, and the schools; and (3) the refinement of teaching practices that connect with the lives of learners in a culturally responsive way.

TEACHING PRACTICES IN READING

Johannessen (2004) points out that the traditional approach to dealing with low-achieving or struggling students is through compensatory education; however, he maintains that this widely accepted prescription for teaching such students has largely failed. He points out that this prescription has attempted to remedy students' reading deficiencies by promoting a discreet skills approach to instruction; in other words, educators believed that the most effective way to reach these most reluctant students was through a heavy emphasis on basic

skills. The implication of this approach is that "lower track" students lack the skills they need to have meaningful transactions with literary texts. Johannessen (2004) maintains that a more productive approach to teaching struggling students is based on cognitive views of learning that focus on problem-solving learning tasks. Indeed, a number of researchers raise questions about the basics approach and suggest that a more productive approach to teaching struggling adolescent readers is based on cognitive views of learning. This view challenges the value of direct instruction that focuses on basic skills. Two prominent educators and psychologists who advocate such views of learning, and are critical of the basics approach to teaching struggling or at-risk adolescent readers, are Means and Knapp (1991). They argue that a summary of critiques of standard approaches to teaching academic skills to at-risk students offered by a prominent group of national experts in reading, writing, and mathematics education found that such approaches tend to:

1. underestimate what students are capable of doing; 2. postpone more challenging and interesting work for too long—in many cases, forever; 3. and deprive students of a meaningful or motivating context for learning or for employing the skills that are taught. (pp. 283–284)

Furthermore, Applebee (1989) argues that such basic approaches to learning tend to "focus on the mechanics of language and low-level recall at the expense of the reading and discussion of literature" (p. 35). Cognitive approaches offer hope for struggling adolescent literacy learners because they derive their strength from the interplay of three domains discussed above.

THE IMPORTANCE OF CLASSROOM DISCOURSE

Applebee (1996), Nystrand and Gamoran (1991), Nystrand (1997), and Nystrand (2006) maintain that classroom discourse has a powerful impact on shaping literacy skills as a result of how it establishes classroom epistemology. They maintain that what counts as knowledge and understanding in the classroom is largely shaped by the questions teachers ask, how they respond to their students, and how they structure small-group and other instructional activities. As they argue, recitation and other monologic practices in teaching reading comprehension are largely ineffective, especially when compared with discussion and instructional conversation, because meaning is realized only in the process of active, responsive understanding. In other words, this research suggests that teaching practices that are based on discussion and instructional conversation may have a powerful effect on reading comprehension in part because these practices engender supportive and trusting relationships between teachers and learners. Nystrand, Wu, Gamoran, Zeiser, and Long (2003) found that the effects of using authentic, open-ended questions and uptake, a discussion strategy that involves turning a student response into a statement or a question in order to encourage further elaboration, were even more pronounced for struggling readers, negating the potentially negative effects of tracking, socioeconomic status (SES), race, and ethnicity. In a review of research on classroom discourse and reading comprehension, Nystrand (2006) argues that "this finding clarifies the critical importance of high-quality classroom discourse in English language arts instruction" (p. 403). We add that it also makes clear the importance of quality classroom discourse for creating and sustaining supportive and trusting relationships between teachers and students.

The research also indicates that struggling readers need teaching practices that connect with their lives in culturally responsive ways. Nystrand (2006) and Nystrand et al. (2003) examined more than 200 eighth- and ninth-grade English and social studies classrooms in 25 midwestern middle and high schools and found that using authentic teacher questions and uptake by teachers suppressed potentially negative effects of variables such as track, SES, race, and ethnicity on instruction and learning. It appears that using authentic questions and uptake may help students connect reading to their lives out of school.

Langer (2001) even goes so far as to make the case that schools should make dialogue with students the central medium for teaching and learning. In a large-scale study conducted by the National Research Center on English Learning and Achievement, Langer (2001 and Chapter 4, this volume) examined 25 schools in four states, 44 teachers, and 88 classes over a 2-year period each. The study focused on English language arts programs in schools that have a large proportion of poor-performing at-risk students. The study examined performances among schools that were demographically comparable. In other words, the study looked at schools that beat the odds, and the results found six features that permeated those schools:

(1) Skills and knowledge are taught in a variety of types of lessons;
(2) tests are analyzed "to inform curriculum and instruction";
(3) the school curriculum and instruction encouraged connections "across content and structure to ensure coherence";
(4) the curriculum and instruction emphasized "strategies for critical thinking and doing";
(5) the school and/or curriculum and instruction encouraged "generative learning"; and
(6) "classrooms are organized to foster collaboration and shared cognition." (Langer, 2001, p. 876)

What is most striking is that Langer maintained that it is the "whole cloth" environment that included all of these features that enabled students to internalize the knowledge, strategies, and skills to use on their own in and out of school. Langer (2001) maintained that making dialogue with students the central medium for teaching and learning may be one key way to bring about the complete environment of all of these features. For example, she described one practice observed in her study in which the teacher, or a more experienced peer, models a powerful thinking strategy for students by leading the class through a discussion aimed at interpreting a difficult text passage before asking students to try it on their own. This kind of modeling scaffolds the strategy for students as they learn how to use it. Indeed, much of the research discussed in this chapter might be linked to one or more of the six features that Langer identified in her study that characterize schools that performed far beyond expectations.

Another effective strategy that Langer

(2001) observed and that places dialogue with students at the center of classroom instruction is reciprocal teaching. According to Palincsar (1986) and Palincsar and Brown (1984, 1989), the goal of reciprocal teaching is to help students think deeply about what they read. In a series of studies, the researchers, working in small groups, taught struggling readers four strategies: summarizing, asking a question, clarifying, and predicting. These are strategies that skilled readers apply almost automatically, but poor readers seldom apply, or perhaps do not know how to apply. To use the strategies effectively, poorer readers need direct instruction, modeling, and practice in actual reading situations.

First, the teacher presents these strategies, usually focusing on one strategy each day. The teacher carefully explains and models each strategy and encourages students to practice. Next, the teacher and the students read a short passage silently. Then the teacher again provides a model by summarizing, questioning, clarifying, and predicting, on the basis of the reading. The next step is that everyone reads another passage, and the students gradually begin to assume the teacher's role. Often the students' first attempts are halting and incorrect; but the teacher gives clues, guidance, encouragement, support in doing parts of the task, and models (scaffolds) to help the students master these strategies. The final goal is for students to learn to apply these strategies independently as they read so they can make sense of the text. A key element of reciprocal teaching is dialogue.

After many years of working with at-risk students in inner city alternative and charter high schools, Stern (1992, 1995), offers an approach that echoes some of the ideas expressed by Langer (2001), Palincsar (1986), and Palincsar and Brown (1984, 1989). Stern asserts that at-risk students need a balance of structure and spontaneity. She designed and taught a series of instructional units that contained a number of interesting features, such as a focus on comprehension and interpretive and/or critical thinking strategies, a mixture of conventional and unconventional works, connection to the lives of students outside school through addressing "everyday topics, artifacts and materials that serve as the critical bridge between school and life," and dialogue through co-development of the units with students and numerous discussion activities, including oral presentations (1992, p. 53). Stern maintains that her work taught her that instruction for struggling students must treat their lives, "their realities," as a positive source for planning instruction rather than a liability that must be overcome. The curriculum, she argues, should reflect student experience, and larger goals and topics within courses should fit the students both academically and socially and, most important of all, "must be determined with them" (1992, p. 55). Finally, she asserts that instruction should involve students at all levels, including planning, teaching, and assessment.

Alvermann (2001) suggests that effective literacy instruction for adolescents must address the multiple literacies that young adolescents possess. According to this view, school-related literacy often favors print-based literacies over other types of competencies such as adolescents' ability to interact effectively with technologies. Alvermann believes that effective literacy instruction for adolescent learners must address self-efficacy and engagement in reading. Instruction also needs to help students perform their academic reading and writing tasks. Further, Alvermann calls for culturally responsive reading instruction for adolescents who struggle, as well as instruction that teaches students to read critically. Finally, effective instruction for all adolescents should foster the use of participatory approaches to reading such as readers workshops, book clubs, or discussion groups, as opposed to teacher-led reading formats. Alvermann (2001) suggests that instruction for struggling adolescents is appropriate when it "taps into struggling readers' funds of knowledge, encourages them to use their textbooks and other sources of information, and supports such usage through strategy instruction" (p. 15).

Guthrie and Davis (2003) concur with Alvermann and suggest teaching practices for middle school reading instruction that encourage engagement with reading. First, reading instructional practices need to emphasize strategies for the effective comprehension of texts. Explicit strategy instruction should include modeling of strategies, teacher support in the use of newly learned strategies, and contexts that allow students time to practice strategies independently. Like Stern (1992, 1995), Guthrie and Davis (2003) further assert that reading instruction must include what they refer to as real-world interactions or occasions to interact with a variety of texts in authentic ways. Finally, much like Stern, these researchers would allow adolescents some voice and choice in topics to explore through their reading, as well as contexts that encourage interaction with their peers and support those students who struggle, thereby enhancing the likelihood of engagement even further.

GIRLS AND BOYS WHO STRUGGLE WITH READING

Struggling adolescent girls may benefit from classroom instruction that emphasizes different kinds of interaction or dialogue along with critical thinking and comprehension strategies. DeBlase (2003) spent 6 months studying eighth-grade girls. The researcher interviewed 11 girls in order to gain understandings and insights into their perceptions about the literature they read, the contexts in which they participated in reading and thinking about texts, and their thinking regarding their reading experiences. The girls represented a variety of racial and ethnic backgrounds, and most came from economically challenging backgrounds. DeBlase found that the girls in her study related more readily to characters in their reading who shared life experiences similar to their own.

The girls in DeBlase's (2003) study experienced conflicts between the texts they read and their popular cultural models of female behavior; the behavior of their female popular cultural models often clashed with the female behavior represented in their classroom reading assignments. DeBlase's findings led her to recommend that one way to help adolescent girls move away from stereotypical female representations in texts is through the teaching of critical reading strategies in order to arm them with the ability to question the traditional ways of being female and allowing girls to "question and problematize the authority of text" (p. 634). She recommends a variety of interactive reading arrangements in the classroom such as discussion

groups and opportunities to read and discuss multiple texts that offer depictions of females in real-life situations where girls can see themselves and other women they know.

Gender and its relationship to the literacy of adolescent boys has received its share of concern in the literature as well. In a study involving 49 middle and high school boys, Smith and Wilhelm (2002) sought to better understand adolescent boys' poor performance and subsequent declines in reading performance on a variety of measures, as compared with the performance of girls of the same age. Smith and Wilhelm used interview data of boys' literate activities in and out of school to conclude that the boys in their study often turned away from reading activities in school because they found it difficult to perform well on most of the reading tasks they were asked to do in school. The boys in their study tended to gravitate toward and become engaged in activities that would make them feel more competent, such as photography, sports, or mountain biking. The results of this study indicate that adolescent boys feel that school texts are too difficult, that they are often asked to read unfamiliar genres, that they therefore feel unsuccessful, and that they routinely feel unsupported by teachers in their reading classrooms. Smith and Wilhelm concluded that boys, indeed all students, benefit from activities that pique their interest in the texts they are asked to read as well as supportive contexts, such as assistance from capable peers and other expert readers, in order for them to gain a sense of accomplishment in reading. The data from their study indicates that because of the ways in which boys encounter reading in school they often dislike and reject it. What can schools do to reverse this disturbing situation? Smith and Wilhelm argue it is very important that reading programs provide instruction that involves dialogue as a major component of teaching and learning.

Extending the scope of their recommendations from their 2002 study, Smith and Wilhelm (2006) argue further that schools need to connect outside-of-school literacy to school purposes and encourage students to continue to grow as readers and writers. They maintain that boys' and girls' engagement is crucial in literacy learning. They provide a variety of high-interest prereading or "frontloading" activities and show teachers how to create units of instruction that will engage struggling readers in learning strategies crucial to comprehension and interpretation of literature.

"LEARNING-CENTERED" INSTRUCTION

In a similar manner, Wilhelm, Baker, and Dube (2001) note that students' reading skills do not grow automatically to meet the demands of reading challenging texts in middle and high school. Struggling readers, especially, need assistance in learning how to read, not just what to read. Wilhelm et al. question the value of what they term "student-centered" and "teacher-centered" instruction and offer in its place a "learning-centered" approach to reading. Their "learner-centered" approach places a premium on "scaffolding" instruction, providing numerous kinds of "frontloading exercises." Many of these activities involve drama, as well as "quick-writes," opinionnaire, scenario, and role-playing activities that are designed to engage students and prepare them for complex reading tasks. Wilhelm et al. place an emphasis on learning how to learn and making students active participants in their own education, thus becoming part of a classroom community of learners. Many of their sample activities tap into students' own experiences outside school, and they argue that an inquiry approach, one that makes problem solving and critical thinking key features of instruction, is crucial to helping students learn how to learn. The authors indicate that their students have pursued projects that inquired into the role of sports in American culture and social justice issues in their school, town, and nation, and attempted to define the nature of good romantic relationships, among many other issues. Another feature of their approach is that interaction in the classroom, with high levels of student talk, is an essential feature of instruction that makes reading processes visible and available to students. Modeling by the teacher and more experienced peers and practice in different contexts with a variety of strategies are key elements of their approach to helping students learn comprehension and interpretive strategies that they will

use in the English classroom and in their lives as well.

In a long-term study of six adolescent readers, Wilhelm (1997) examined engaged and struggling readers. He found that using drama and visual art is a powerful way to encourage less proficient readers to participate more fully in literacy activities and experiences. Participatory activities such as role playing or dramatic reenactments of scenes from stories can offer struggling readers multiple opportunities to interact with texts in active ways. In addition, participatory activities may foster engagement and build confidence and competence in less proficient readers. This study reinforces the findings of Wilhelm et al.'s (2001) work because both focus on the kinds of instruction that encourages a high level of student engagement.

PREPARING STUDENTS FOR ENRICHED READING

Wilhelm et al.'s (2001) "frontloading exercises" provide one approach to prereading or introductory activities that can scaffold reading skills and strategies for struggling readers. Smagorinsky, McCann, and Kern (1987) and Smagorinsky (1993) offer a variety of activities designed to engage students in thinking strategies that are key to comprehending and interpreting literature. These activities prepare students for reading and interpreting complex texts, and Smagorinsky et al. (1987) also offer activities that can connect reading to writing.

Johannessen (2004) focuses specifically on a scenario-based prereading activity for struggling readers. McCann (1996) focuses on a simulation activity to prepare students for reading and writing about complex literature. Johannessen (2004) and McCann (1996) recommend that the use of these activities to initiate the reading of classroom texts, which is similar to Smith and Wilhelm's (2002) recommendations, relies on inquiry units to read and study literature. Similarly, Tatum (2005) uses a comprehensive framework of literacy teaching to help Black adolescent struggling readers. In addition, Kahn, Walter, and Johannessen (1984) offer a comparable approach with an emphasis on activities, including prereading activities, that encourage comprehension and interpretation of literature and writing about literature in a classroom context that emphasizes critical thinking and discussion. Using a similar approach specifically focused on struggling readers, Hamel and Smith (1998) examine the impact of an inquiry-based unit on two lower-track secondary English classrooms. The study examines the extent to which direct instruction of specific interpretive strategies would promote critical engagement with literature. The study reveals that students took a questioning stance toward literary texts, read between the lines, and made personal connections. In addition, the authors report that placing interpretive strategies at the center of the curriculum frees the teacher from endorsing a particular interpretation and helps redistribute literary authority in the classroom. Although the students in the study were capable of complex interactions with literature, the key ingredients included focused practice in a collaborative setting with specific criteria so that they could experience the rich transactions that literature can provide.

It is interesting to note that Smith and Wilhelm's (2002) model, which focuses on effective instructional practices for boys from a variety of cultural backgrounds, shares key components of Tatum's (2005) model for responsive literacy teaching, as based on his work with African American boys. Furthermore, careful examination of such practices suggests that such approaches would benefit all students who struggle with reading. Indeed, all of these approaches extend the notion of what struggling readers need in terms of instruction and offer increased opportunities for growth in self-concept and engagement, as well as mastery of skills and strategies for reading in the classroom and beyond.

These approaches share common features that focus on complex meaningful questions and problems so that students' reading and writing can be in the service of genuine inquiry, and they embed basic skills instruction in the context of more global tasks by including reading comprehension and composing skills in introductory reading and writing activities or instruction. Furthermore, they make connections to students' out-of-school experiences and cultures, and they model critical thinking strategies for stu-

dents and utilize various types of discussions to help students figure out a difficult reading passage before they are asked to make interpretations on their own. These approaches also provide scaffolding to enable students to accomplish complex reading tasks, encourage students to use multiple approaches, and involve students in describing their answers aloud to the class so that all students hear different ways to solve problems. Most important, these approaches make dialogue with students the centerpiece of teaching and learning, and they use strategies that will help students internalize the questions that good readers ask when they read literature.

RESEARCH ON THE TEACHING OF WRITING

In considering how to support struggling adolescents as they develop writing skills, it is reasonable to turn first to the research about effective approaches to the teaching writing generally. The teaching of writing is a complicated business, but Hillocks (1984, 1986, 1995, 2005) provides the reader of the research with a useful framework for assessing a large body of literature and offers accessible language for categorizing treatments and talking about the data. Hillocks (1984, 1986) classifies treatments under four *modes* of instruction: *presentational, environmental, individualized,* and *natural process. Presentational* instruction features teacher lecture and large-group discussion led by the teacher. A presentational mode of instruction is comparable to what Goodlad (1984) describes as a "frontal" style of teaching in most classrooms. In contrast, an *environmental* approach engages students in problem-centered activities that allow for high levels of student interaction. For writing instruction, students would, for example, work with each other in examining a body of data and work out processes that are appropriate to a particular writing task. In his meta-analysis comparison of the four modes of instruction for writing, Hillocks (1984, 1986) reports that instruction in the environmental mode resulted in greater mean effect sizes than instruction in the presentational, natural process, or individualized mode. These results indicate that instruction in the environmental mode can hold great promise for improving students' writing skills.

In addition to comparing four modes of instruction, Hillocks groups experimental treatment studies by *focus* of instruction: *grammar/mechanics, models, sentence combining, scales, inquiry,* and *free writing.* A comparison of the relative effects of the six foci of instruction suggests that instruction that focuses on the practice of *inquiry* can have the greatest effect in developing students' writing.

Hillocks (1986) discusses at some length Troyka's (1974) study that focused on the effects on writing quality that were produced through the use of simulation role-playing activities. Hillocks reports that the overall experimental/control effect size for the Troyka study was 1.69 standard deviations. This effect was so large that it represented an outlier and could not be included in the meta-analysis. The experimental treatment in the Troyka study had these features:

1. The students worked toward solving a particular policy question.
2. The teachers provided students with relevant data that they could use in their analysis.
3. The students recognized a specific context for addressing the policy question.
4. The students worked with particular strategies for making sense of the data and addressing the problem.
5. The activities relied on purposeful peer interaction.

The results from the Troyka study and from others in the Hillocks meta-analysis suggest that an *inquiry* approach, in which students interact with each other in the process of analyzing data and responding to particular policy questions, can be an effective way to teach writing.

Hillocks, Kahn, and Johannessen (1983) report that students who had been engaged in extended discussions about problem-based scenarios developed related composing strategies for writing extended definitions. Under the experimental condition, the students work in small groups to discuss the scenarios. The students make judgments about the appropriateness of the actions of the characters in the scenarios. Through discussion, the students engage in the processes for defining. They offer criterion statements and explain why they think they are appropriate. In the discussion, group members challenge the speaker to defend the statements. It is common for students to offer other scenarios that test the validity of each other's observations. Students learn defining strategies by engaging in the defining process with peers: stating defining criteria, offering examples to illustrate the general ideas, and explaining the connection between the general assertions and the examples.

The essential element in the Troyka (1974) study was the use of role-playing simulations to teach students to use a variety of strategies to analyze and compose. Simulations like those used in the Troyka study have these features in common:

1. A carefully constructed simulation immerses a student in an environment that has much in common with his or her own world.
2. Each participant usually has a clearly defined role and functions according to the rules of the environment.
3. Students attempt solutions to a problem with which they are familiar or that has a connection to their lives.
4. Students have data available to help them complete their tasks.
5. Students interact with each other—to plan, to negotiate, to argue, to resolve. These interactions engage students in thinking about issues and allow them to rehearse their approach to ideas before writing.
6. The simulation, especially if there is some sort of game component, provides motivation for subsequent reading and writing.

The approaches to the teaching of writing that have the greatest positive effect on learners in general offer the greatest promise for supporting learners who struggle with literacy learning. The examples above are two among many possibilities for engaging struggling learners in an inquiry process that can support their development as writers. In each case, students focus their attention on a specific problem: In one case, they attempt to define a standard; in other cases they defend a policy through logical argument. The students interact with each other so that they direct their discussion through each other rather than filter it through the teacher. The students engage in processes appropriate to the writing tasks: They define, they explain, they illustrate, and they argue. These activities have features that Langer (2001) associates with English language arts programs that "beat the odds": that is, programs whose participants far outperform their cohort groups in measures of literacy.

Several authorities offer further illustrations of approaches to teaching writing in an environmental mode. Hillocks (1975, 1979) shows how to promote careful observation as a tool for descriptive and narrative writing. Smith (1984) explains ways to help students overcome their apprehension of writing. Johannessen, Kahn, and Walter (1982) offer a design for sequencing lessons to teach writing in an environmental mode. Kahn et al. (1984) offer approaches for writing about literature. Smagorinsky et al. (1987) offer thinking strategies to prepare students to write and to connect their writing to their reading. Hafertepe and McCann (1995) take apart common writing tasks and suggest ways to help students to solve problems and collect the data necessary for completing their compositions. Smith and Wilhelm (2006) and McCann, Johannessen, Kahn, Smagorinsky, and Smith (2005) suggest a variety of ways of engaging students in processes of writing. There is a common thread among these practitioners: They introduce students to relevant thinking strategies as they are needed for the writing task; they plan for a great deal of student interaction; and they provide students with the means to access the data they will need for the substance of their writing. For learners who struggle with literacy learning, inserting detailed elaboration within a boilerplate organizational model makes less sense than helping them to develop a repertoire of composing strategies to use with the substantive knowledge relevant to each task.

The research underscores the promise of taking an environmental approach that focuses on inquiry. Composition textbooks do not provide the blueprint for creating an environmental classroom, and the teacher is left to invent the inquiry-based lessons that invite students to work with each other. The sources discussed above provide examples of useful activities. The individual teacher can adapt or invent new activities to help students develop their writing skills during a relatively short period of time.

RESEARCH ON TEACHING WRITING TO LANGUAGE-MINORITY LEARNERS

The research on the teaching of writing provides guidance in designing writing instruction for the general school population. For the English language learner (ELL), the process of learning to write well may be a long and arduous one. Multilingualism is, of course, a valuable resource, and educators should take care not to categorize all ELLs as academically struggling. However, with school curriculum structured as it is, many ELLs do face challenges in navigating new discourse communities. Typically, the nonnative speaker can take years to learn the complexity of new lexical and syntactic structures in a second language (Leki, 1992, 2000; Samway, 2006). The teacher should reflect on his or her role in the long-term process of development. It is not realistic to expect to see the same pace of growth that one would see in native speakers as a result of a relatively brief period of instruction in writing, even though in the current climate of accountability, assessment practices presume that language-minority learners can develop literacy proficiencies rapidly, even at a pace more rapid than that of the native speaker and writer of the language.

Many of the practices that are effective for native speakers of English (L1) are also appropriate for ELL students, as long as one keeps in mind that the rates of development for ELL students and L1 students will not be the same. Language development is complex, and there are nuances of language proficiency. Part of a teacher's assessment of students' readiness for contending with a particular writing task is the recognition that the students' demonstrated proficiency in the social language of the halls and cafeteria does not mean mastery of the cognitive academic language proficiency that most academic writing demands. Although it is not possible here to address the challenge in all its complexity, we can operate safely under two assumptions:

1. Language-minority students, including long-term language learners, have greater difficulty than their middle-class, English-speaking peers in composing texts in English, because they have less developed *cognitive academic language proficiency* (CALP). According to Cummins (1981), CALP refers to the communicative skills necessary to comprehend and use "academic" language to complete cognitively demanding decontextualized learning tasks. In other words, students who may have never been in English as a Second Language (ESL) or bilingual classes in school and speak English fluently in social settings, can still have great difficulty in producing the kind of texts required in conventional academic writing.

2. As a general rule, all students are responsive to teachers and schools that set reasonably high standards and convey an expectation that they can achieve, regardless of their language or cultural background. McGee (2003) reports that schools that make a difference in achievement set consistently high standards, expect students to achieve, and provide the necessary support to help them to achieve.

Padron, Waxman, and Rivera (2003) review the research on effective practices for teaching language-minority learners, especially for Hispanic learners. They conclude that effective instructional practices have the following features: They (1) rely on cooperative learning structures, (2) are culturally responsive, (3) engage students in extended instructional conversations, (4) are cognitively guided, and (5) provide a technologically enriched environment.

Students benefit from working collaboratively with peers. The cooperative learning structures and activities must be carefully planned so that the work is truly collaborative and not parallel work in groups. Group work certainly cannot mean that one person does the work and the rest copy it. Cooperative effort means that tasks must be completed through the sharing of materials and responsibilities. The teacher will need to direct the position of the groups and the appropriate manner of functioning within each group. There must be an overtly expressed standard for functioning in collaboration.

One must be cautious not to generalize from one culture to another. For example, although Hispanic learners might thrive with cooperative learning, students from other cultures might feel uncomfortable and resist working in such structures. One's understanding of the values and predispositions of a culture should guide the choice of learning activities and structures.

Culturally responsive teaching means that teachers know the students: their academic knowledge, their individual traits, their talents, limitations, interests, and concerns. As a basic principle of learning, teachers need to connect new knowledge to what students already have stored in memory. Language-minority learners find instruction especially appealing if it connects with their lives, with their immediate concerns, and with the issues in their community. Teachers also need to be sensitive to the values within families and the obligations that sometimes challenge academic work.

The process of getting to know students through informal and formal methods can help teachers to build rapport and serve teachers in planning strategically for instruction. ELL students benefit from having opportunities to write about topics they value and know much about.

Freeman, Freeman, and Mercuri (2002, 2003) offer similar considerations for approaching instruction in a culturally responsive way. Furthermore, Kaplan (1966, 1987) invites teachers to reflect on the possibility that learners who enter schools from a variety of countries and cultures may not think in the dominant sequential way that most U.S. schools seem to privilege. Kaplan (1966) suggests that a "contrastive analysis of rhetoric" can offer teachers clues as to whether learners approach problems in a sequential, circular, zigzag, or other pattern. Although Kaplan (1987) pulls back a bit from his earlier generalizations about specific rhetorical patterns, he maintains that "the point is that scholars looking at other languages have perceived significant differences between languages in their rhetorical structure, even if, in all fairness, they have not agreed on the nature of the differences" (p. 10). The safe approach is not to assume that the dominant structures and modes of thinking that seem rational to most native speakers of English will necessarily seem rational to the newcomers to U.S. schools.

Cognitively guided instruction emphasizes the development of procedural knowledge (e.g., reading, writing, critical thinking, problem solving) as opposed to the simple recall of declarative knowledge alone (e.g., the memorization of dates, vocabulary, "facts," etc.). The development of procedural knowledge means that the learner can transfer the learning to other occasions. In regard to the teaching of writing, the emphasis is on helping learners to take command of the processes of composing, elevating the importance to *teaching procedures* rather than familiarizing learners with a particular *form* (Hillocks, 2005). The procedures for planning, generating, and refining a text can transfer to many new occasions.

Cognitively guided instruction also means that there is a meta-cognitive component to teaching and learning, in that the learner can monitor understanding and make adjustments to self-correct. Writing instruction that builds in distinct stages for reflection, revision, and editing is an example of cognitively guided instruction because it involves the learner in making judgments about the work in comparison to a recognized standard.

Applebee (1996) recommends envisioning the curriculum as conversation. The idea is to engage students in purposeful conversations or authentic discussions about issues and concepts that are essential to a discipline but connect with students' lives. One can imagine the importance of participating in extended dialogue for language-minority learners and students from low-income homes, who are required to have cognitive academic language proficiency in order to produce extended academic writing. In short, the more one practices extensively in the use of academic language, the more one is likely to develop proficiency. Providing structures and opportunities for all students to engage in extended dialogues signals the expectation that all learners will meet challenging academic standards.

Seldom can teachers control the amount and quality of the instructional technology available to learners. Typically, however, there is a broad gap in the access to technology when one compares new arrivals or students from low-income families and others who are middle-class native speakers of English. If schools have technology that supports the planning, researching, composing, revising, and editing of texts, then teachers of ELL students and students from low-income homes should seek to have their students access the technology.

GENERAL RULES

The teaching of writing to ELL or other language-minority students is a complex endeavor, requiring patience and careful planning. Several sources (Freeman, Freeman, & Mercuri, 2002, 2003; Hill & Flynn, 2006; Padron et al., 2003; Samway, 2006) offer suggestions and models to help teachers design instruction for ELL students. To simplify, however, here are a few general rules:

• At first, emphasize *fluency* rather than correctness. Students need to be at ease in their attempts to produce texts, without the inhibitions of self-conscious error avoidance. Once students can begin to produce compositions with some fluency, then they have texts to work with in order to revise and refine.

• Expect development over the long term. No teacher is going to influence overnight gains in writing quality. Realize that the ELLs begin school years behind L1 peers who have already become familiar with a sizable working vocabulary in English. Similarly, students from communities where the primary discourse is distinct from the discourse of the academic community need to know how to make the conscious shift into the language that is appropriate in a given context. The mastery of a broad vocabulary and familiarity with "standard" English syntax will take years. Each teacher's work with a student is one step in a lifelong process, and the development of writing proficiencies takes an especially long time.

• Familiarize the students with instructional processes (e.g., writing conferences, peer review, etc.) and technical language that might be unfamiliar to them from past school experiences. Although many teachers teach writing as a process that includes prewriting activities, drafting, revising, and editing, the language used to identify the stages and the process itself may be unfamiliar to the ELL student and other language-minority learners.

• Capitalize on the cultural and social interests and knowledge of the learners. Any student has a wealth of knowledge and experience from which to draw when composing. Teachers need to learn what their students know and what interests them. The learners should have opportunities to write about subjects they know about and care about.

• In the composing process, build in stages that allow for extended, purposeful peer interaction. All students, including ELL students, need opportunities to engage in extended discourse, including times when they simply listen to the more proficient English speakers as they use academic language. Over time, the ELL students will make attempts to talk the way the L1 peers talk and then transfer that talk into writing.

• Provide oral and written feedback that supports positive efforts and growth and does not subject the learner to public criticism. Like most other writers, ELL students want to have support for the things they are doing well and gentle guidance in improving those things they are still learning.

• Reassure and encourage ELL students to ask for help. ELL students may not readily ask for assistance. In some cultures, asking for help suggests that the teacher has not done a good job of teaching. A student may resist "disgracing" the teacher by admitting that he or she does not understand the teacher's instruction.

In the end, researchers such as Rose (1989), Gilyard (1991), Au (1993), and Villanueva (1993) point to the importance of respecting students' language and mining the rich reserve of knowledge that all learners can bring to the various writing tasks they encounter in schools. In this sense, teaching writing in a "culturally responsive" way requires that the teacher make the efforts necessary to understand the issues that are critical to the learners, to their families, and to their communities. Au (1993) emphasizes the importance of affirming for learners and their families that their home languages and literacy practices have value, even though they may be different from the literacies often most privileged in the schools.

MAKING A DIFFERENCE

Researchers and some teachers know quite a bit about some of the best ways to teach

reading and writing to adolescents who struggle. We have come a long way from the days of compensatory education. As Johannessen (2004) asserts, this widely accepted prescription sought to remedy students' deficiencies by teaching "the basics" through skills-based instruction, which has the effect of numbing young minds and is "demeaning and boring for students and teachers alike" (p. 639). Although Langer (2001) and others show exemplary teachers and teaching practices, as Hillocks (2006) asserts, "most teachers appear to know little about the teaching of writing beyond the most general knowledge" (p. 74), and, as Snow and Biancarosa (2003) note, instructional approaches like reciprocal teaching are underutilized by teachers. Furthermore, as Williams (2006) suggests, the underuse of effective instructional practices for reading must be addressed through improved teacher education and professional development. She asserts that teacher education programs can promote more responsive teaching in reading instruction by introducing preservice teachers to models of instruction that focus on participatory approaches rather than more traditional teacher-centered models of teaching.

Although we certainly seem to have a way to go in preparing English/language arts teachers to meet the challenges of struggling readers and writers, the research presented here provides a map for what we need to do. The research points to the need to establish supportive and trusting relationships between teachers and learners, cultivate partnerships among families, their communities, and the schools, and utilize and improve teaching practices that connect with the lives of learners in a culturally responsive way. At the heart of all the approaches and strategies presented in this review is the idea that instead of focusing on the mechanics of language and accumulating facts and information, all of those concerned with educating struggling students need to work toward providing instruction that will enable non-academic, struggling students to learn how to learn. As Smith and Wilhelm (2002) argue, this "learning-centered" approach

aims to capitalize on the expertise that students bring with them to class, and to teach them what we know as more experienced readers and writers so they can become more expert in ways of reading, writing, and thinking that are valued in the classroom and workplace. (pp. 192–193)

Furthermore, the research presented in this review suggests that we need to create a new kind of classroom, a classroom that is inquiry driven and is not driven by teacher-centered instruction. In *Pedagogy of the Oppressed*, Paulo Freire (1970) writes about the change that occurs in a discussion-based classroom:

The teacher is no longer merely the-one-who-teaches, but one who is himself taught in dialogue with the students, who in turn while being taught also teaches. They become jointly responsible for a process in which all grow. (p. 67)

Our review of the literature about learners who struggle with literacy underscores the important role of frequent student interaction that creates a community of learners that promotes literacy learning and advances social justice.

REFERENCES

Alvermann, D. (2001). *What really matters for struggling readers: Designing research-based programs.* New York: Longman.

Applebee, A. N. (1989). *The teaching of literature in programs with reputations for excellence in English* (Tech. Rep. No. 1.1). Albany: University of Albany, State University of New York, Center for the Learning and Teaching of Literature.

Applebee, A. N. (1996). *The curriculum as conversation: Transforming traditions of teaching and learning.* Chicago: University of Chicago Press.

Au, K. (1993). *Literacy instruction in multicultural settings.* Belmont, CA: Wadsworth/Thomson Learning.

Cummins, J. (1981). The role of primary language development in promoting educational success for language minority students. In California State Department of Education (Ed.), *Schooling and language minority students: A theoretical framework.* Los Angeles: Evaluation, Dissemination and Assessment Center, California State University, Los Angeles.

DeBlase, G. (2003). Acknowledging agency while accommodating romance: Girls negotiating meaning in literacy transactions. *Journal of Adolescent and Adult Literacy, 46,* 624–635.

Delpit, L. (1996). *Other people's children: Cultural conflict in the classroom.* New York: New Press.

Freeman, Y., Freeman, D., & Mercuri, S. (2002). *Closing the achievement gap: How to reach limited-formal-schooling and long-term English learners.* Portsmouth, NH: Heinemann.

Freeman, Y., Freeman, D., & Mercuri, S. (2003, Winter). Helping middle and high school age English language learners achieve academic success. *National Association of Bilingual Education Journal of Research and Practice, 1,* 110–122.

Freire, P. (1970). *Pedagogy of the oppressed.* (M. B. Ramos, Trans). New York: Herder.

Gee, J. P. (1989). Literacy, discourse, and linguistics: An introduction. *Journal of Education, 171,* 5–17.

Gilyard, K. (1991). *Voices of the self: A study of language competence.* Detroit: Wayne State University Press.

Goodlad, J. I. (1984). *A place called school: Prospects for the future.* New York: McGraw-Hill.

Guthrie, J., & Davis, M. H. (2003). Motivating struggling readers in middle school through an engagement model of classroom practice. *Reading and Writing Quarterly, 91,* 59–85.

Hafertepe, M., & McCann, T. M. (1995, Spring). Anatomy of a writing activity. *Illinois English Bulletin, 82,* 15–28.

Hamel, F. L., & Smith, M. W. (1998). You can't play if you don't know the rules: Interpretive conventions and the teaching of literature to students in lower-track classes. *Reading and Writing Quarterly, 14,* 355–377.

Hill, J. D., & Flynn, K. M. (2006). *Classroom instruction that works with English language learners.* Alexandria, VA: Association for Supervision and Curriculum Development.

Hillocks, G., Jr. (1979). The effects of observational activities on student writing. *Research in the Teaching of English, 13,* 23–35.

Hillocks, G., Jr. (1984). What works in teaching composition: A meta-analysis of experimental treatment studies. *American Journal of Education, 93,* 133–170.

Hillocks, G., Jr. (1986). *Research on written composition: New directions for teaching.* Urbana, IL: ERIC/NCRE.

Hillocks, G., Jr. (1995). *Teaching writing as reflective practice.* New York: Teachers College Press.

Hillocks, G., Jr. (2005). The focus on form vs. content in teaching writing. *Research in the Teaching of English, 40,* 238–248.

Hillocks, G., Jr. (1975). *Observing and writing.* Urbana, IL: National Council of Teachers of English.

Hillocks, G., Jr. (2006). Middle and high school composition. In P. Smagorinsky (Ed.), *Research on composition: Multiple perspectives on two decades of change* (pp. 48–77). New York: Teachers College Press.

Hillocks, G., Jr., Kahn, E., & Johannessen, L. (1983). Teaching defining strategies as a mode of inquiry. *Research in the Teaching of English, 17,* 275–284.

Johannessen, L. (2004). Helping "struggling" students achieve success. *Journal of Adolescent and Adult Literacy, 47,* 638–647.

Johannessen, L., Kahn, E., & Walter, C. (1982). *Designing and sequencing prewriting activities*. Urbana, IL: National Council of Teachers of English.

Kahn, E., Walter, C., & Johannessen, L. (1984). *Writing about literature*. Urbana, IL: National Council of Teachers of English.

Kaplan, R. B. (1966). Cultural thought patterns in inter-cultural education. *Language Learning: A Journal of Applied Linguistics, 16*, 1–20.

Kaplan, R. B. (1987). Cultural thought patterns revisited. In U. Connor & R. B. Kaplan (Eds.), *Writing across languages: Analysis of L₂ text* (pp. 9–21). Reading, MA: Addison-Wesley.

Langer, J. A. (2001). Beating the odds: Teaching middle and high school students to read and write well. *American Educational Research Journal, 38*, 837–880.

Lee, C. D. (2005). Cultural modeling in the Hillocks tradition. In T. M. McCann, L. R. Johannessen, E. Kahn, P. Smagorinsky, & M. E. Smith (Eds.), *Reflective teaching, reflective learning: How to develop critically engaged readers, writers, and speakers* (pp. 166–177). Portsmouth, NH: Heinemann.

Leki, I. (1992). *Understanding ESL writers: A guide for teachers*. Portsmouth, NH: Heinemann.

Leki, I. (2000). Writing, literacy and applied linguistics. *Annual Review of Applied Linguistics, 20*, 99–115.

McCann, T. M. (1996). A pioneer simulation for writing and for the study of literature. *English Journal, 85*(3), 62–67.

McCann, T. M., Johannessen, L. R., Kahn, E., Smagorinsky, P., & Smith, M. W. (Eds.). (2005). *Reflective teaching, reflective learning: How to develop critically engaged readers, writers, and speakers*. Portsmouth, NH: Heinemann.

McGee, G. W. (2003). *Closing the achievement gap: Lessons from Illinois' "Golden Spike" high-poverty high-performing schools*. Paper presented at the fall conference of the Illinois Association for Supervision and Curriculum Development, Naperville, IL.

Means, B., & Knapp, M. S. (1991). Cognitive approaches to teaching advanced skills to educationally disadvantaged students. *Phi Delta Kappan, 73*, 282–289.

Nystrand, M. (with Gamoran, A., Kachur, R., & Prendergast, C.). (1997). *Opening dialogue: Understanding the dynamics of language and learning in the English classroom*. New York: Teachers College Press.

Nystrand, M. (2006). Research on the role of classroom discourse as it affects reading comprehension. *Research in the Teaching of English, 40*, 392–412.

Nystrand, M., & Gamoran, A. (1991). Instructional discourse, student engagement, and literature achievement. *Research in the Teaching of English, 25*, 261–290.

Nystrand, M., Wu, L., Gamoran, A., Zeiser, S., & Long, D. (2003, March–April). Questions in time: Investigating the structure and dynamics of unfolding classroom discourse. *Discourse Processes, 35*, 135–196.

Padron, Y. N., Waxman, H. C., & Rivera, H. H. (2003, Spring). Educating Hispanic students: Obstacles and avenues to improved academic achievement. *ERS Spectrum, 21*(2), 27–39.

Palincsar, A. S. (1986). The role of dialogue in providing scaffolded instruction. In J. Levin & M. Presle (Eds.), *Educational Psychologist, 21* [Special issue on learning strategies], 73–98.

Palincsar, A. S., & Brown, A. L. (1984). Reciprocal teaching of comprehension-fostering and monitoring activities. *Cognition and Instruction, 1*, 117–175.

Palincsar, A. S., & Brown, A. L. (1989). Classroom dialogues to promote self-regulated comprehension. In J. Brophy (Ed.), *Advances in research on teaching* (Vol. 1, pp. 35–67). Greenwich, CT: JAI Press.

Rose, M. (1989). *Lives on the boundary: A moving account of the struggles and achievements of America's educationally underprepared*. New York: Penguin Books.

Samway, K. D. (2006). *When English language learners write: Connecting research to practice, K–8*. Portsmouth, NH: Heinemann.

Smagorinsky, P. (1993). Preparing students for enriched reading: Creating a scaffold for literary understanding. In G. E. Newell & R. K. Durst (Eds.), *Exploring texts: The role of discussion and writing in the teaching and learning of literature* (pp. 153–174). Norwood, MA: Christopher-Gordon.

Smagorinsky, P., McCann, T., & Kern, S. (1987). *Explorations: Introductory activities for literature and composition, 7–12*. Urbana, IL: National Council of Teachers of English.

Smith, M. W. (1984). *Reducing writing apprehension*. Urbana, IL: National Council of Teachers of English.

Smith, M. W., & Wilhelm, J. (2002). *"Reading don't fix no Chevys": Literature in the lives of young men*. Portsmouth, NH: Heinemann.

Smith, M. W., & Wilhelm, J. (2006). *Going with the flow: How to engage boys (and girls) in their literacy learning*. Portsmouth, NH: Heinemann.

Snow, C. A., & Biancarosa, G. (2003). Adolescent literacy and the achievement gap: Where do we go from here? *Adolescent Literacy Funders meeting report*. New York: Carnegie Corporation. Retrieved October 5, 2006, from *www.all4ed.org/resources/Carnegie AdolescentLiteracyReport*.

Stern, D. (1992). Structure and spontaneity: Teaching with the student at risk. *English Journal, 81*(6), 49–55.

Stern, D. (1995). *Teaching English so it matters: Creating curriculum for and with high school students*. Thousand Oaks, CA: Corwin Press.

Tatum, A. W. (2005). *Teaching reading to Black adolescent males: Closing the achievement gap*. Portland, ME: Stenhouse.

Troyka, L. Q. (1974). *A study of the effect of simulation-gaming on expository prose competence of college remedial English composition students*. Unpublished doctoral dissertation, New York University (ERIC Document Reproduction Service No. ED 090 541).

Villanueva, V. (1993). *Bootstraps: From an American academic of color.* Urbana, IL: National Council of Teachers of English.

Wilhelm, J. D. (1997). *"You gotta BE the book": Teaching engaged and reflective reading with adolescents.* New York: Teachers College Press.

Wilhelm, J. D., Baker, T. N., & Dube, J. (2001). *Strategic reading: Guiding students to lifelong literacy, 6–12.* Portsmouth, NH: Heinemann.

Williams, M. C. (2006). *Understanding middle school readers who struggle with reading.* Unpublished doctoral dissertation, Northern Illinois University, DeKalb.

CHAPTER 6

Proficient Reading in School

Traditional Paradigms and New Textual Landscapes

DAVID O'BRIEN

ROGER STEWART

RICHARD BEACH

The predominant view of proficient reading in the 21st century is based on a technocratic rationality driven by skills and standards movements and high-stakes tests that focus on low-level learning outcomes. This view is obsolete, given the sophisticated demands placed on readers in schools, in communities, and in the global economy and mediasphere. In this chapter, we discuss the challenge of fusing in-school and out-of-school literacies in ways that help adolescents develop the critical skills needed to be informed consumers and producers of texts in the digital age. We provide a broader definition of proficiency along with consequences for schooling via three foci: (1) proficient reading as situated practice, (2) proficient reading as engagement in digital literacies, and (3) proficient reading as critical literacy. Recognizing reading as a socially mediated practice underscores an important distinction between reading as a set of practices to participate in activities and the technocratic, autonomous notion of reading as sets of specific skills and test performances dominating schools today. Proficient reading online or in other digital platforms redefines left-to-right and top-to-bottom processing, and web pages with widely dispersed links draw readers to increasingly specialized content or take them farther from their original intent. An expanded definition of adolescent literacy can be realized in secondary classrooms only if educators, policymakers, and parents reshape their interest in adolescent reading. The critical reading of texts of all types should figure more prominently in school. Proficiency must be fostered and measured under conditions in which adolescents are deeply engaged with diverse texts, and the measurement of proficiency under such conditions should include the new demands placed on readers as a consequence of the digital age.

In the field of reading, *proficiency* is typically defined in terms of efficiency of processing, specifically the coordination of reading subcomponents such as decoding and rapid word recognition skills and the effective use of phonemic, orthographic, lexical, syntactic, and semantic systems. From the predominant view, proficient or "skilled" readers are defined as people who efficiently and automatically use skills and strategies, capitalizing on strong subcomponent processes and compensating for weaker ones to comprehend what they read (Pressley, 2006; Stanovich, 1980). In short, proficient readers automatically negotiate a complex system of interwoven subcomponents. We do not deny the importance and utility of such a definition of proficient reading, but we argue in this chapter that the predominant subcomponent definition is too narrow and thus fails to take into account the full complexity of the reading process and its highly situated nature. We further assert that in order to gauge adolescent reading performance accurately and fully, broader definitions of reading proficiency are needed, along with accompanying assessments.

The predominant subcomponent notion of proficient reading is largely measured through performance on large-scale assessments that do an inadequate job of tapping an expanded conception of the complexity and situated nature of reading. The tests too often focus only on students' ability to recognize and synthesize the main idea and details of a restricted set of "textoids" (Hunt, 1993): short passages selected not because they are engaging but because of their bland neutrality and freedom from bias that might favor a particular reader's background knowledge. Even though test makers have made considerable progress in controlling for cultural bias, or in using passages that may have broad general appeal with minimal bias, test passages are still too often about topics familiar to middle-class students instead of topics related to working-class students' funds of knowledge (Gonzalez, Moll, & Amanti, 2005).

Such simplistic measures of proficient reading, derived from equally simplistic definitions, fail to take into account that adolescents read particular texts for specific reasons, related to the completion of certain tasks; that they approach these texts with various stances, motivations, and expectations; and that they harbor a range of perceptions about themselves as readers before, during, and after tackling a particular text. A consequence of this complex textual and reading landscape is that adolescent readers may at times choose to read texts that exceed their levels of competency owing to their commitment to a particular topic, resulting in a stance of persevering and trying hard to comprehend an engaging text. At other times students may fail to read texts at

or below their competency because of lack of interest and motivation. This more ecological approach to conceiving of reading proficiency accounts for its strongly situated nature, revealing the limitations of current subcomponent definitions and narrow large-scale assessments.

The assessments also have significant implications for how readers are classified and how they see themselves. The popular discourse about readers is that they are proficient, or that they have attained *basic, proficient,* or *advanced* levels of performance on tests (these levels are discussed in detail later). Too often this discourse turns into an either/or scenario—whether they read competently or are *struggling readers.* This bifurcation reflects a simplistic definition of reading proficiency that may cause educators to overlook the reading proficiency spectrum and its highly contextualized nature. Educators don't dissect proficient reading into its finer points because proficient readers are expected to be successful in school, and few educators worry about them. Struggling readers, however, are lumped together as students who "struggle to read at grade level" (Biancarosa & Snow, 2006, p. 3) or read below *basic level* (Kamil, 2003) and are often routed into intervention programs with the focus of bringing them "up to grade level." But "proficient" readers are not always proficient and "struggling" readers do not always struggle. Proficient readers encounter texts that—because of their lack of interest, motivation, or background knowledge or because of the complexity or quality of the text—cause them to struggle. Furthermore, struggling readers encounter texts that they can read successfully because of high interest, motivation, background knowledge, or the qualities of the text in relation to their approach to reading. As noted, reading is highly situated, and bifurcating students into proficient and struggling camps based on performance on large-scale assessments oversimplifies a complex issue.

In making this claim, we are not denying the existence of significant reading difficulties that some struggling readers manifest. These students often can't or won't read traditional academic texts. Most struggling adolescent readers, identified by performance on tests, have been behind in reading since primary grades, have not been brought up to grade level in their academic histories, and are likely to be struggling when they graduate from high school. What is more, struggling readers not only lack the skills and strategies that proficient readers enjoy, they are increasingly disengaged from reading and develop low perceptions about their abilities. They are unlikely to choose to read because they are not good at it and feel incompetent at it (O'Brien, 2006); and because they avoid it, they lack the practice that could make them more proficient. They thus fall farther behind as their more competent peers get better and better, reflecting what Stanovich (1986) has termed the *Matthew effect* in reading. By middle school and especially high school, years of Matthew effect have rendered these kids too tired, disengaged, and lacking in self-esteem to want to become proficient. These are significant concerns that an expanded definition of proficiency will help to better frame and address.

What is needed is a more multifaceted definition of adolescent reading proficiency that reflects the wide range of reading practices and events adolescents participate in, or should be *able* to participate in. But given the pressures to prepare students to pass the reading tests that are part of adequate yearly progress (AYP) levels mandated by the No Child Left Behind Act (2001), districts and schools often develop highly compartmentalized curricula correlated with sets of standards or adopt "quick fix" programs and instructional methods. These approaches emphasize the kind of reading assessed by tests rather than the kinds of reading adolescents need in order to successfully engage with the range of texts and purposes for reading they encounter in and out of school. Street's (1984) notions of *autonomous and ideological literacies* help frame this tension. Street emphasizes that literacies are *plural* because there are as many types of reading as there are situations—events, activities, and tasks in which versions of reading are enacted. The autonomous notion of literacies, in this case, reading, is that there are skills and strategies that can be carefully articulated, sequenced, and taught, which are directly connected to the social and economic benefits of schooling. If students acquire these skills and strategies, they enable themselves to succeed in school and ultimately to attain academic and life goals. Acquisition of and eventual proficiency at reading are not connected to any particular situation, and skills and strategies are assumed to automatically generalize to a range of situations. Scopes and sequences, standards, and tests have roots in this notion.

By contrast, ideological literacies are particular to institutions, are socially and culturally situated, and are always connected to political and ideological significance. Ideological literacies have significance at the individual and institutional levels. Rather than being tied to predetermined trajectories of skills and strategies leading toward fixed outcomes, they are articulated and practiced to accomplish specific things that allow people to engage in certain practices as part of certain events. To bend Street's (1984) notions a bit, a proficient reader defined through an autonomous reading lens will have mastered the skills and strategies in the sequence, as evidenced by performance on tests. Conversely, a proficient reader defined through an ideological reading lens has the ability to engage in a range of reading practices, socially and culturally situated in various institutions and events. These practices enable the reader to successfully work with people, get jobs done, and participate in activities such as reading a novel for a book club, reading a website to acquire information about a political candidate, or reading a description of a historical event as part of visiting a park in which that event occurred.

PREDOMINANT VIEWS OF READING PROFICIENCY

This chapter provides an expanded definition for proficient reading that goes beyond autonomous notions. Ideally, as readers critique our expanded definition and its consequences for classrooms, they will reflect on the following questions:

1. Are secondary students provided the depth and breadth of literacy instruction and experience necessary for them to successfully navigate a text-based world that is increasingly sophisticated, complex, and diverse?
2. Do assessments account for the full range of youth's literacy competencies?

But before we explore the expanded definition, we turn to a more detailed discussion of the current, common definition of proficient reading.

Proficiency Defined by Tests

The predominant view of reading is sustained by the current preoccupation with accountability, most evident in large-scale assessments and standards. Although all states have high-stakes assessments to gauge AYP, perhaps the most important test is the national-level assessment, the National Assessment of Educational Progress (NAEP). Its importance stems from the fact that many of its design features and performance-level definitions influence state assessment designs. The NAEP defines proficiency in a hierarchical series of levels.

In the NAEP 2007 Report Card for eighth grade, the following levels of proficiency are given:

1. *Basic level,* in which students must "demonstrate a literal understanding of what they read and be able to make some interpretations. When reading text appropriate to eighth grade, they should be able to identify specific aspects of the text that reflect overall meaning, extend the ideas in the text by making simple inferences, recognize and relate interpretations and connections among ideas in the text to personal experience, and draw conclusions based on the text."

2. *Proficient level,* in which they "show an overall understanding of the text, including inferential as well as literal information. When reading text appropriate to eighth grade, they should be able to extend the ideas in the text by making clear inferences from it, by drawing conclusions, and by making connections to their own experiences—including other reading experiences. Proficient eighth-graders should be able to identify some of the devices authors use in composing text."

3. *Advanced level,* in which students can "describe the more abstract themes and ideas of the overall text. When reading text appropriate to eighth grade, they should be able to analyze both meaning and form and support their analyses explicitly with examples from the text; they should be able to extend text information by relating it to their experiences and to world events. At this level, student responses should be thorough, thoughtful, and extensive." (National Center for Educational Statistics at *nces.ed.gov/nationsreportcard/pdf/main2007/2007496.pdf*; Lee, Grigg, & Donahue, 2007)

Even given the limitations of the autonomous definition of reading proficiency embodied in large-scale assessments, the NAEP description of advanced-level reading should be one component of *proficiency* exhibited by most readers at the secondary level. Most readers should be able to evaluate texts critically; interpret their meaning within and across genres, including print and digital media; and make connections between their textual worlds and lived worlds. Achieve, Inc. (2005) published a report on its website, *Achieve.org,* analyzing the NAEP 2005 reading data state-by-state and noted that states do not agree on what reading proficiency means—at least in terms of cut scores for AYP. But it was clear in its analysis that the trend for states is to define *proficient* reading in a manner similar to the way NAEP defines *basic* level reading.

On the basis of this analysis, even with this meager standard of what proficient reading means, only nine states reported that 80% of their readers were proficient or above. Hence, if states define proficient reading as the basic level, to be a proficient reader at the state level means that students can synthesize the gist of what they read and draw some inferences, but students typically cannot extend ideas beyond the text, draw conclusions based on the text and their experiences in the world, or critically evaluate an author's purpose and perspectives. We assert that most adolescents should be able to read critically, at least as it is defined by the test, unless of course they exhibit specific etiologies that classify them as struggling readers—for example, learning disabilities, specific neurobiological issues such as dyslexia, or developmental lag or lower-level cognitive language functioning producing so-called "garden variety" poor reading (Stanovich, 1988).

But we need to qualify our apparent advocacy that the NAEP advanced level should become a minimum standard. The NAEP is a large-scale measure, and we critiqued such measures above, pointing out their significant flaws and limitations. The NAEP is no exception. Although it employs a significant number of constructed response items and the test is well designed, it is still a narrow measure of reading proficiency, given the wide range of purposes and contexts in which people read a variety of texts. Like all large-scale assessments, it has the potential to narrow curriculum and instruction that operate from a narrow base of what reading is and what reading proficiency looks like. Stake (2007) argues that

> as NAEP styles its items, so do other test makers, and teachers are increasingly drawn to teach accordingly. As it identifies its topics, teachers adjust and conform, a little more resistant to the voice of conscience saying teach more deeply and more personally into the subject matter. The curriculum narrows and discourages diversity of learning. Teachers are hired and teachers are trained increasingly in response to state standards, state testing, state-approved textbooks, and other standardizing influences such as NAEP. (p. 17)

Authors of the NAEP 2009 Reading Framework (National Assessment Governing Board, 2004) state that the next version of the assessment will improve upon the range and depth of comprehension assessed on both literary and information texts.

Even if the advanced level on the NAEP is used as a minimum, the standard remains set at a minimally acceptable level of performance on a restricted set of test items rather than the wide range of practices adolescents would be expected to engage in regularly in school if they were expected to understand the full range of texts they encounter. Large-scale assessments need to place readers in a variety of authentic reading situations where their interest, motivation, and background knowledge can be systematically varied so that the students' full range of reading ability can be assessed. Think of such an assessment as being like a treadmill test for a cardiovascular workup. Just as the incline and speed of the treadmill are adjusted to vary the load on the heart, a truly authentic reading assessment that paralleled an expanded definition of reading proficiency would adjust variables to test the reader's mettle under different conditions. Nevertheless, the NAEP is a good initial metric against which to measure progress toward more proficient adolescent reading on the basis of an expanded definition.

Proficiency Defined by Leveling Readers and Texts

Because of renewed interest in assessing texts with readability measures and assigning grade equivalents to students' reading performances via tests and reading inventories, proficiency is increasingly tied to matching readers to certain text levels. O'Brien, Beach, and Scharber (2007) found that when struggling readers in an "intervention" class were interviewed about their perceptions of themselves as readers—specifically, whether they thought they had improved in the class—about a third of the respondents referred to Lexiles, a measure associated with the Lexile Framework® for Reading (Metametrics, 2007) to gauge their reading proficiency. The students made statements such as, "I moved up 60 Lexiles," or "I am at Lexile 550." This form of response is compelling because Lexiles, used as a popular leveling tool, are computations of text difficulty similar to traditional readability analyses. They are based on semantic difficulty (frequency with which words in passages occur in typical running text) and syntactic complexity (sentence length), not reader proficiency. Nevertheless, the Lexile measures are offered as measures of both text difficulty and reader level. The measure tells how well a given student reads on the basis of his or her ability to read texts classified in the Lexile system. Lexiles are useful measures, with the limitations of other measures of readability, but their usefulness has been overextended by some publishers and educators.

Whereas proficiency defined by tests shows how well readers can understand the gist of the "textoids," readability measures level readers by matching a reader's ability to read a text with that text's location in a hierarchy of text difficulty. This approach assumes that a text has its own level of difficulty apart from the stance, competencies, and expectations that a reader has for it. Nystrand (1986) has critiqued this belief in the *autonomous text,* arguing instead that "difficulty" is as much a function of what readers bring to texts as the characteristics of the text itself. A second problem with this approach is that these matches are based on limited semantic and syntactic measures of text difficulty. Within the leveling perspective, reader proficiency is defined as one's ability to read a particular text with a difficulty level assigned (e.g., independent level or range matched to a grade level). Hence, a fifth-grade reader is a person reading up to grade level—one who can read texts leveled at fifth grade or at a range specified for fifth graders.

Yet a fourth grader who can read at grade equivalent 6.2 may be a better reader than some other fourth graders (depending on what being in fourth grade and being a fourth-grade reader means in a particular school) but wouldn't be given sixth-grade texts to read because of content that may be inappropriate for fourth graders. Lexile ranges and other readability measures are matched to grade equivalents, measures that everyone feels comfortable with and even demands in reporting because school is organized by grades. Grade equivalents, however, still reveal very little. Grade equivalents are not standard scores; rather, a grade equivalent is generated by using the median raw score for persons who happen to be in a given grade. That is, when people who are in fourth grade take a test, the raw score that falls in the middle of their distribution is associated with the grade equivalent—say 4.0. And raw scores do not increase at a uniform rate across various skill areas.

In short, grade equivalents tell little about a person's reading proficiency, and text levels tell little about what makes a text accessible. *Accessibility* includes readability, but it also includes a host of other factors such as text structure, style, appealing features, interest level, and motivation. And it is heavily influenced by a reader's stance toward the topic or the author. Accessibility, undoubtedly, is more difficult to assess, but it provides a much better indication of whether a reader and a text are matched.

Commercial publishers and specific intervention programs have adopted readability measures such as Lexiles and Degrees of Reading Power (DRP; Touchstone Applied Science and Associates, TASA, 2006) to gauge the difficulty of texts (Fry, 2002; Hiebert, 2002) and to sort into grade levels textbooks, classroom libraries, intervention programs, and school libraries. This interest in leveling has resulted in huge online databases of leveled texts and automated online systems for leveling texts that are not yet in the databases. David O'Brien's teacher preparation students bring texts to class to level as part of a class discussion of readability and other leveling tools. The last time they did this, one student entered samples of texts written by Kurt Vonnegut and the measures gauged them at fourth-grade level; another person applied a readability measure that rated a tenth-grade biology text far into college level.

In the rigid adherence to seeming scientific precision and credibility, educators accept without critique the text levels derived from readability formulas, all the while denying that these formulas are limited in their conceptions of what text difficulty is and therefore in their accuracy at leveling texts. Educators tend to see only those texts that readability formulas level appropriately and fail to see the many texts that are inaccurately leveled. Perhaps Vonnegut does write at a fourth-grade level when only sentence length and vocabulary difficulty are considered, but the content is far from a fourth-grade level. And handing a college-level biology textbook to high school sophomores may or may not be the travesty that it appears, because the text may score at a high level due to the heavy load of technical vocabulary it contains.

It is possible that the text is well written and the technical vocabulary is fully explained and illustrated so that sophomores are quite capable of reading it, especially if they find the subject engaging. But the field writes off as anomalies such exceptions as Vonnegut or the biology textbook and continues giving students leveling tests and visiting the Lexile and DRP websites to see where a particular text falls in the hierarchy of difficulty. Educators may level all the texts and students around them without seriously considering what they are doing and the consequences, both positive and negative, that can come from it. Students are matched to "level-appropriate" texts regardless of other crucial factors such as interest, motivation, and purpose. Clearly, however, young readers who are interested in reading *Harry Potter* can successfully engage with the texts in spite of readability levels that place the texts beyond their reading levels.

In the previous sections we discussed how reading proficiency is currently defined and provided preliminary ideas for how that definition should change. We now turn to a more detailed discussion of what a new definition of proficiency looks like.

NEW CONTEXTS FOR BROADENING THE DEFINITION OF PROFICIENCY IN SCHOOL READING

There are new and exciting material and theoretical contexts within which secondary education can operate. These new contexts, such as greater access to a diversity of texts and new theories of reader response, create the opportunity for a radically revised secondary school experience for students that better reflects an expanded definition of reading proficiency. A discussion of these contexts follows.

Beyond Textbooks to the Internet and the Popular Trade

Not all proficient adolescent readers *choose* to read assigned reading in school, and many of them develop elaborate ways to succeed without engaging in school texts (O'Brien et al., 2007). For example, one of our participants in a 3-year study of middle school "struggling readers," Sandy, was an avid reader and producer of manga texts. She was able to interpret complex meanings of manga stories, an ability that transferred to her writing of complex plots. However, she had little interest in traditional school texts, was therefore not doing well in school, and was referred to an intervention setting for help. Thus, an expanded definition of reading proficiency must look beyond traditional school classrooms, defined largely by single textbooks, to a rich landscape of varied literate practices constituting various ways of reading texts. Beyond the constraints of textbooks and typical school assignments are proficient readers, defined not by performance on tests but by their engagement with a wide range of texts read for a range of purposes to accomplish things they need to do or to engage in sets of practices that are important in their lives.

Students develop negative attitudes toward reading from elementary to middle grades (Ivey & Broaddus, 2001; McKenna, Kear, & Ellsworth, 1995), and this negative mindset continues into high school (O'Brien, 1998). These individuals are commonly referred to as *reluctant readers,* despite the range of literate practices they engage in outside of school in their personal lives (Moje, 2000; O'Brien, 1998; Smith & Wilhelm, 2002). The term *aliteracy* (Mikulecky, 1978) is also applied to them—meaning that even though they can read well enough, they choose not to read the texts on the shelves of school libraries or assigned in class. The complexity of this phenomenon needs to be incorporated into an expanded definition of reading proficiency. Educators can no longer label a student as reluctant or aliterate since, like reading itself, reluctance and aliteracy are situated phenomena. The amount and breadth of reading that adolescents do outside school are substantial (Ivey & Broaddus, 2001), and much of it represents the reading of digital texts, including web pages and text messages (Lenhart & Madden, 2005; Lenhart, Rainie, & Lewis, 2001). Eighty-seven percent of 12- to 17-year-olds use the Internet, and the number of teenagers using the Internet increased by 24% from 2001 to 2005 (Lenhart & Madden, 2005). Fifty-seven percent of adolescents who use the Internet can be considered content creators; that is, they create web pages, blogs, or other web-based forms of expression (Lenhart & Madden, 2005).

Furthermore, teens are active users of public libraries and have been so for quite some time. Research in the mid-1990s revealed that about one in four people who walk through the doors of public libraries are between the ages of 12 and 18 (Heaviside, Farris, Dunn, & Fry, 1995). Current research continues to show teenagers regularly frequenting public libraries (De Rosa et al., 2005). There has also been an explosion in the publishing of children's and young adult fiction and nonfiction over the past decade. The number of juvenile titles of all types published per year between 1993 and 2004 has gone from 7,755 to 21,161 (Bowker, 2005). A lot of this growth is coming from the children's literature market, but young adult fiction and nonfiction have also increased dramatically over the decade. Thus, there is evidence that adolescents are reading extensively outside school, so when adolescent readers manifest reluctance or aliteracy, the specific situations and circumstances wherein it occurs must be carefully articulated and catalogued.

Reading on the Internet is a crucial part of an expanded definition of proficient reading, although it is not yet clear what that complex proficiency entails. It is clear from research in this relatively new field of inquiry, however, that adolescents vary in their proficiences in complex, online reading tasks (Coiro, 2003, 2005). And developing this new online proficiency is not as simple as importing digital literacies into classrooms by co-opting for classroom purposes the texts that adolescents consume and create on the Internet. The texts that adolescents read and create on the Internet are often personal (Black & Steinkuehler, Chapter 18, this volume; Kress, 2003). Co-opting such texts for classroom use may represent an invasion of privacy because students may find it uncomfortable or even offensive if such texts are brought into public school classrooms and talked about in traditional academic ways. Adolescents might be embarrassed to discuss these texts in face-to-face public forums, and the consequence may be that adolescents retreat deeper into the Internet to have their private conversations.

The opposite could also happen, however, and students might enjoy having some of their Internet texts exposed in classroom forums. For Internet texts students want to share, teachers will have an immediately relevant curriculum resource just a few mouse clicks away; but if students are reluctant to "give up" their texts, then teachers will have to be more creative and find surrogate texts to help them expand the text base in their classrooms. Either way, Internet texts, and the reading proficiencies required to access them, will increasingly continue to move into classrooms, potentially providing more ways to engage readers.

Although we highlight the Internet in our expanded definition of reading proficiency, it is only one way to broaden the text base in secondary classrooms. The explosion in publishing fiction and nonfiction trade books is another. But this explosion raises the obvious question: Why do single textbooks predominate in secondary schools even though a call for diversifying the range of texts in public school classrooms spans decades (e.g., Gray, 1948)? We attribute some of this stagnation to the predominant autonomous view of reading—reading means completing academic tasks that involve efficiently extracting information from textbooks and interpreting texts in school-sanctioned ways. It is also an economic issue—single textbooks are a better buy per topic than multiple texts—and a facet of the technical rationality of schools—single textbooks provide a way to control content and to map curricula onto standards for accountability systems.

Whatever the reasons, this single-textbook focus requires neither extensive reading nor critical evaluation of texts. What is more, the textbook topics are often treated in politically correct and bland ways so as not to offend any particular constituent group (Ravitch, 2003). And the rapidly increasing volume of information included, even after the sanitization, in areas such as sciences and social studies requires textbooks that are thicker and thicker to cover all of the topics that teachers want. But the large number of topics covered in thicker textbooks, in tandem with the standards movement, means that few topics will be covered in depth. In turn, few students want to read these books, and, as noted, this type of reading actually contributes to more negative attitudes toward reading. An expanded definition of proficient reading must include an expanded text base and practices such as reading across multiple texts on a topic to see different slants on the information, to see different depths and quality of coverage of the information, and to arrive at an informed synthesis of the information.

If adolescent readers are to read more and read more critically, then schools will have to change. Choice, voice, and time will have to become the norm instead of the exception (Stewart, Paradis, Ross, & Lewis, 1996). Students will have to be given choice among trade books and textbooks in all subject areas. Some may choose textbooks, but many will not. Thus, large numbers of fiction and nonfiction trade books will have to be readily available to teachers and their students, along with Internet access, so that choice is a reality in classrooms. In addition, students will have to be engaged in deep and meaningful conversations about their reading with both their teachers and their peers, as well as with those outside the school walls.

And students will need time within the school day to read. Some will always have the time and inclination to read assignments outside of school, but many will not.

Thus far we have talked about the material contexts that are available and necessary for an expanded definition of reading proficiency to be enacted in secondary classrooms. These contexts include Internet resources and hard copy texts in addition to the traditional single textbook that dominates classrooms. We now turn to concerns that are less material but just as tangible and important to our expanded definition. These are the social and political contexts in which adolescents read.

An Ecology of Proficient Reading as Situated Practice

Reading, like other literate enactments, occurs within an ecology of practice. Proficient readers don't simply extract meaning from a text, and meaning does not simply reside in the text. It also resides in readers' social participation in purpose-driven activities (Hunt, 2000). From a sociocultural, activity-theory perspective, the meaning of, and therefore the understanding of, texts is driven by readers' participation in purpose-driven activities (Beach, 2000; Smagorinsky, 2001). A member of a book club reads the novel, *Beloved,* with the idea of sharing her knowledge about slavery with her book club members. And the purposes driving readers' participation in these activities motivate them to engage in reading for social reasons, reading that contributes to their success in these activities. As we noted above, students operating under the dominant definition of proficient reading participate in instructional activities that are driven by the purpose of improving reading skills primarily to pass tests or complete school assignments. Students who see no value in doing well on high-stakes assessments or don't value traditional academic pursuits are neither motivated nor engaged, because they perceive little social purpose tied to simply passing the test or completing assignments. Conversely, when students are engaged in reading to participate in activities in which they value the purposes driving those activities, they are motivated to read well.

Proficient readers, from a situated practice perspective, are already motivated to read, because they are able to contextualize their reading in terms of participation in activities. To continue to engage them and increase their proficiency, it is important to devise activities that foster social practices related to reading and producing texts. These facets of engaged learning suggest the need to shift the focus of reading instruction from simply teaching "reading" for its own sake to teaching reading within the context of purposeful activities that serve to help students frame their interpretations of texts.

Acquiring Literacy and Social Practices

In participating in activities in a community of practice, proficient readers learn to employ certain literacy and social practices valued within that community of practice related to reading and producing texts (Ivey & Fisher, 2005; Simpson, Stahl, & Francis, 2004). For instance, members of a fantasy football league acquire the practice of reading for statistics in the newspaper and Web sports pages so that they can be perceived as knowledgeable members of their league. Because students want to be perceived as valued members of their peer communities, there are social motives for acquiring ways of reading essential to establishing membership in these communities or "affinity groups" (Gee, 2008; Guthrie, 2004). By being known as someone who "knows his stats," a student acquires status in a community or group as a person who gains knowledge from reading the sports pages.

Teachers foster the development of literacy by promoting participation in communities of practice in which reading is an inherent part of participation. To illustrate: In a study of reading practices in a culinary arts high school class for special education students, the researcher found that both the teacher, Mr. Demetrie, and the students in the class were engaged in extensive reading associated with practices valued in learning to cook (Darvin, 2006). The students read and wrote a variety of texts, both print and computer based, in their classroom: cooking reference books, Mr. Demetrie's notes about those books, handouts, assignment sheets, journals, procedure sheets, conversion charts, and other charts. Reading for information was the dominant form in the culinary arts class, and students read primarily to locate information relevant to cooking a certain dish. In preparing a dish, students contextualized their purpose for reading a recipe, notes, handouts, or measurement conversion charts in order to prepare that dish successfully. The students were also acquiring certain literacy and social practices important to becoming cooks—for example, the practice of copying recipes on cards to create recipe files for future use. They also read texts consistent with specific purposes for completing particular tasks. For instance, when students baked gingerbread and then constructed gingerbread houses, they did background reading about housing design to determine how to create their houses and about the melting processes of candied decorations for their houses.

An example of the important distinction between reading to participate in activities and reading to perform on standardized tests is that students engaged in reading in the culinary arts class were not consciously aware of being involved in improving their proficiency in reading; rather, they perceived reading as part of learning practices specific to certain activities. Unfortunately, on the basis of interviews with a large number of vocational teachers in the school, Darvin (2006) found that the teachers still assumed that "real reading" was compatible with autonomous perceptions—that is, that reading should include traditionally labeled skills activities such as summarizing or committing texts to memory to complete certain narrow tasks. Reading in school was not viewed as situated practice, and vocational teachers did not perceive their own reading or instruction related to using texts as having the same status as reading instruction in language arts/reading classes.

Reading Texts in Different Genres

Proficient readers also learn that certain types or genres of texts serve to achieve certain purposes in certain activities. Proficient readers who want to write stories draw on their knowledge of literary genres to write mystery, romance, comedy, horror, or character portraits. In the culinary arts class, students were also learning about how genre features of texts were related to specific literacy and social practices (Pappas & Pette-

grew, 1998). For example, they learned to read recipes as lists of ingredients as a necessary first step in initially selecting and measuring the ingredients necessary for cooking a dish. Students also contrasted different sections of recipes, such as cake recipes that contained separate sections on filling, icing, and cake preparation.

Different text genres involve different ways of reading and so require different sets of practices. This differentiation challenges the generic notion of "reading ability" associated with test scores used to identify students as "proficient" or "struggling" readers. Tests themselves include a narrow range of genres of texts accompanied by constrained tasks. To illustrate: Comprehension tests generally include expository texts, sometimes "ecologically" suspect in that they are constructed to include more detail, and require limited literacy practices—typically selecting a gist statement from different multiple-choice items. The generic notion of reading ability as a set of autonomous skills fails to account for the wide variation in the kinds of practices associated with reading different genre texts in school, and particularly with the genres students engage in outside school. In our research with early adolescent students, we find that they draw on knowledge of narrative genres in video games when reading and writing stories (O'Brien et al., 2007).

Proficient readers also engage in practices associated with "typified rhetorical strategies" (Bawarshi, 2003; Coe, Lingard, & Teslenko, 2002). That is, they understand that certain social genres demand sets of strategies that contextualize the reading of texts associated with participation in these activities. For example, students engaged in college admissions activities write application letters and participate in interviews, assuming that they need enough understanding of a college to which they are applying to characterize how they would be a good "fit" as students in that college. They may read materials from a particular college to extract and synthesize relevant information about the college to include in their letters or interviews. Similarly, as part of engaging in job interviews for after-school employment, students know that in order to do well in an interview, they need to demonstrate an understanding of the job, something shaped by their reading of a job posting.

Learning to Read Online Identities and Social Agendas

The newest facet of proficient reading involves the ability to read online texts such as chat sites, websites, blogs, or wikis on multiple levels. And, in addition to reading the "content" of these digital texts, students read the identities being constructed and the social agendas being adopted by other participants. One of the major shifts with the Internet is toward active use of what Richardson (2006) describes as the "Read/Write" Web 2.0, in which students not only read texts, but also write them using such venues as blogs, wikis, and MySpace. In the early days of the shift from print text to the Web, students often passively read the Web as an information source. They have now shifted from the reader stance to a writer stance and use the Web to actively share their writing (Richardson, 2006). At the same time, given the differences between digital and print text conventions, students draw on their experience in reading online digital texts to know how to write digital texts.

Given the temptation of wandering aimlessly from site to site, it is important that teachers help students clarify their purposes for searching the Web. A study of students' navigation of hypertext (McNabb, Thurber, Dibuz, McDermott, & Lee, 2005) cites the example of two students reading the same official site about cyclist Lance Armstrong to write about influence of lifestyle on one's health. One student clicked on different links only to discover information about buying bikes, because she was planning to buy a new bike, and gained little from the Lance Armstrong site. In contrast, another student knew that he needed to acquire information about Armstrong's fight against cancer, so he knew which link—the one to "The Lance Armstrong Foundation"—would provide him with that information. However, because he found information only about other people's survivor stories and not Armstrong's, he then realized that he needed to go to Google and insert the categories "lifestyle," "health," and "Lance Armstrong." Because this student was continually monitoring the results of his search, he realized the need to seek out information on Google.

Reading and writing digital texts requires a different set of practices than the left-to-right, linear processing of print. In the textual migration from the page to the screen, students learn to scan the screen for visual cues, icons, location on the page, and function to determine what item to click on, according to what is considered most relevant to the information they are seeking. This navigation requires that they have some sense of the importance of certain cues over others on the basis of what is most relevant to achieving their purposes for reading (Kress, 2003). Reading proficiency on the Web is an evolving construct, but it clearly extends the notion of cognitive processing based on linear text to much more sophisticated multimediating (Lankshear & Knobel, 2003) in which electronic print, images, icons, and links to more media provide both information and distraction, often equally engaging, with multiple options for selecting links to converge on topics or diverge into aimless pleasure. In this world an emerging definition of a proficient reader is a person with both prowess in following purpose and the development of a cyborg brain (Beach & O'Brien, 2008) matched to the mediasphere. Teachers need to help students clarify their purposes for searches within the context of their activity, while at the same time letting students formulate their own purposes. If students are clicking on links in a random order without a clear sense of purpose or self-monitoring, then teachers can model selecting appropriate links and categories based on a sense of purpose.

EXAMPLES OF READING AS SOCIAL AND CULTURAL PRACTICES OPERATING IN SOCIAL WORLDS AND SPACES

Thus far we have compared and contrasted the current definition of reading proficiency and the policies and practices that support it with a new more ecologically valid definition. We now turn to a more focused discussion of how these principles might look when applied to the specific context of English literature classrooms.

A key component of reading proficiency is the ability to take a stance to read critically and deeply. This ability goes to the heart of our definition of proficient reading, for if adolescents lack the ability to read critically or choose not to read critically, then they will be unable to rationally deliberate about issues of justice and resource allocation in a democratic society. Rational deliberation is both an internal and an external process. Citizens in a democracy need to think through issues in logical ways and then move into the public sphere to discuss and debate those issues in order to work toward equitable solutions to social and political problems. Gutmann (1999) argues that fostering critical thinking should be a primary purpose of American public education: "Children must learn not just to behave in accordance with authority but to think critically about authority if they are to live up to the democratic ideal of sharing political sovereignty as citizens" (p. 51). Reading instruction for proficient readers therefore not only needs to provide students with rich venues for debating issues but should also foster their awareness of the social, political, historical, and cultural forces shaping those issues. We believe that literature is an excellent example of such a venue. We now turn to a discussion of how traditional response to literature pedagogy will need to change in order to create this rich venue.

Literary Anthropology: Expanded Horizons of Literature Study

Character study is often the central focus in literature studies in secondary schools, and too often students are required to explain characters' actions only within limited conceptions of a book's context. We believe that students need to contextualize character actions in terms of larger conflicting sociohistorical and cultural norms operating in text worlds so that they learn to engage in critiques of the institutional forces shaping characters. This situating requires that students learn to contextualize characters' actions as shaped by institutional and historical forces operating in the world of the text. For example, institutional forces of class differences operate in the world of *The Great Gatsby* (Fitzgerald, 1991). Inferring these in-

stitutional forces involves identifying race, class, and gender Discourses as ways of knowing or thinking (Gee, 2008). Students, then, can draw on Discourses of class difference to understand better the institutional forces operating in Gatsby's world of the 1920s—the differences between Daisy and Tom's "old-money" inherited wealth versus Gatsby's "new-money" acquired wealth. These insights may then be extended into modern-day societies, including our own, where class differences remain.

In our expanded conception of literature study, rather than responding in terms of simply empathizing or identifying with characters and texts consistent with traditional reader-response pedagogy, students construct meaning on the basis of how readers, texts, and contexts are mediated by ideologies of difference through engaging in what Sumara (2002) describes as "literary anthropology" (p. 238) (cf. Galda & Beach, 2001; Schweickart & Flynn, 2004; Smagorinsky, 2001). In responding to literature using a literary anthropology lens, students engage in critically reflecting on characters' experiences in different social and political worlds, which force them to grapple with the dialogic tensions constituted by conflicting cultural perspectives (Beach, Thein, & Parks, 2007). As Hicks (1996) notes, "reading involves a set of cultural practices, as integrally embedded within webs of relationships as any other social act of being and knowing" (p. 221).

From this experience, students begin to recognize how institutional and historical forces shape characters' behaviors (Beach, Appleman, Hynds, & Wilhelm, 2006). Thus, in responding to multicultural literature, readers experience the influence of institutional racism and discourses of White privilege on characters' beliefs and actions. As students experience how some characters in multicultural literature grow in awareness of how they are shaped by these institutional and historical forces while other characters remain less aware, a rich substrate forms for critical discussions. Discussions then subsequently become the foundations for a range of activities and assignments that help students reflect on the influences these forces have on their own lives and where they and those around them fall on the awareness continuum.

Examining Dialogic Tensions in Text Worlds

Proficient readers also learn to examine dialogic tensions (Bakhtin, 1981) related to characters' negotiations of the competing demands of these different institutional forces. As Bakhtin (1981) argues, characters are continually "double-voicing" different discourses that reflect these rival allegiances. These competing voices in a text create what Bakhtin described as heteroglossia—the competing tensions in characters' voices and language use within a novel, including the narrator's or author's voice. Thus, when Gatsby comments about Daisy that "'her voice was full of money'" (Fitzgerald, 1991, p. 144), he is recognizing how the language constituting her identity reflects a discourse of inherited wealth as distinct from his own newly acquired wealth. This quote is also "double-voicing" Fitzgerald's perspective on the corrupting forces of a class-based, capitalist system.

A Model for Expanded Character Study

Responding to Discourses of Gender, Class, and Race in Events, Spaces, and Institutions/History

How do teachers help students go beyond explaining characters' actions within specific events in a story to interpreting those actions as being shaped by broader norms and discourses operating within larger institutional/historical forces and within internal and external spaces? To accomplish these ends, students can create a chart with three different sections for events, spaces, and institutional/historical forces to map visually the influences of space and institutional/historical forces on specific events in a text, as illustrated below:

Events

|

Spaces

|

Institutional/Historical Forces

At the top of the chart, they create a circle that depicts a specific event, such as Nora's rejection of her husband in Ibsen's (1999) *A Doll's House,* along with inferences about specific traits, beliefs, and agendas. Then, in the middle of the chart, students can draw circles representing the different gendered spaces inhabited by Nora—her home space versus other spaces in which she experiences a sense of agency—and then draw lines between the aspects of spaces and events. Next, at the bottom of the chart, students can include descriptions of the patriarchic institutional/historical forces shaping both the event and the spaces, drawing other lines between these descriptions and the event/spaces.

To further illustrate this process, we discuss some activities for teaching "Womanhood," by Catherine Anderson (2000), from her collection *The Work of Hands*[1]. In this poem a 15-year-old female works in a rug factory:

She slides over
the hot upholstery
of her mother's car,
this schoolgirl of fifteen
who loves humming & swaying
with the radio.
Her entry into womanhood
will be like all the other girls'—
a cigarette and a joke,
as she strides up with the rest
to a brick factory
where she'll sew rag rugs
from textile strips of kelly green,
bright red, aqua.

When she enters,
and the millgate closes,
final as a slap,
there'll be silence.
She'll see fifteen high windows
cemented over to cut out light.
Inside, a constant, deafening noise
and warm air smelling of oil,
the shifts continuing on . . .
All day she'll guide cloth along a line
of whirring needles, her arms & shoulders
rocking back & forth
with the machines—
200 porch size rugs behind her
before she can stop

---

[1] Copyright 2000 by Catherine Anderson. Reprinted from *The Work of Hands,* with the permission of Perugia Press, Florence, Massachusetts.

to reach up, like her mother,
and pick the lint
out of her hair.

In contextualizing the event of a girl sitting in the car listening to songs on the radio, a student may infer that the girl is perhaps imagining herself in an alternative, romantic world beyond her current world. However, once she is in the factory, she is engaged in the same ritualized, redundant pattern of work that her mother experienced, suggesting that she is probably stuck in the same pattern as her mother. Students may then contrast the space outside the factory in which the workers share jokes and cigarettes, a space of human interaction, with the dark, prison-like space inside the factory. In doing so, students explore the differences between spaces that afford alternative possibilities and variation and spaces that limit these possibilities and variations. Students may then contextualize these events and spaces in terms of the institutional and historical forces related to largely working-class women of different generations working in nonunion factories with poor working conditions for low wages.

Although what we provide here is quite brief, it may give readers a glimpse at what literature studies might look like if English classrooms become venues for the development of proficient readers within our expanded definition. All of these critical response activities are designed to help students go beyond simply interpreting texts to analyzing texts critically, analysis that can then be applied to thinking critically about their own lives and the lives of others.

NEW TEXTUAL LANDSCAPES: REALIZING THE POTENTIAL OF PROFICIENT READERS IN SCHOOL

Here we synthesize key points from this chapter and make focused recommendations to show how an expanded definition of reading proficiency can come about in secondary schools. Our suggestions critique current practices and provide directions for the future.

Taking Reading Seriously

Educators need to require reading as an integral part of any curricula and set their sights on teaching beyond textbooks, tests, and standards if they are to achieve advanced-level NAEP performance as a minimum for all students. The out-of-school reading landscape is rich and varied, and many adolescents read often and deeply. However, school textbooks and titles from the literary canon that are read by an entire class in lockstep fashion continue to dominate, just as they have for decades (National Education Association, 2002). We know that textbooks are viewed by students as almost universally boring and superficial (Ravitch, 2003; Thomas B. Fordham Institute, 2004). Thus, an important step in reading being taken more seriously is to expand the text base. This extension can serve as an open invitation to students to read more and for teachers to take reading more seriously as a component of their curricula. If teachers provide more choice and relevance in reading material and the activities they ask students to undertake to process and respond to those materials, students will read more and improve in doing so.

Redefining the Institution of School as a Critical Space

The institution of the school sets up a climate that militates against an expanded definition of reading proficiency. When students read a restricted range of texts for quite narrow purposes, reading often becomes boring drudgery. The national profile of reading in the NAEP Reading Report Cards reflects the increasing distaste adolescent readers have for reading in school at the same time it shows how little students are challenged to read critically to meet personally relevant goals. The trend of flat national-level performance on reading assessments that spans decades is not due to students who just can't improve and are not motivated to read. It is due to the fact that we do not demand more critical reading of texts for purposes and activities that students find important. The challenge is to resist pressures to focus solely on autonomous notions of reading in the misguided belief that such an approach will magically produce higher test scores.

Instead, the profession needs to work toward more sophisticated and challenging curriculum, instruction, and assessments that reflect a broader definition of reading proficiency. But classroom educators and their leaders should not be left to do this work alone. It is imperative that reading and literacy researchers begin and then sustain a sophisticated, wide-ranging research and development program to develop, initiate, and evaluate these new approaches. If researchers and scholars, including teacher researchers, assert that more sophisticated curriculum, instruction, and assessments are needed, then they need to help do the sustained hard work necessary to develop these approaches and thoroughly test them for efficacy. Education scholars and their practitioner colleagues in secondary classrooms need to produce conclusive evidence one way or the other of the efficacy of their pronouncements (Stewart, 2006). Consequently, a coordinated research agenda needs to be developed that thoroughly explores our assertion that a more sophisticated and challenging curriculum produces more proficient adolescent readers.

The Complexity of the Current Landscape

In research dating back to the 1970s and 1980s in content literacy, a key question was this: *What is the role of the text?* The perspective that we and many of our colleagues took was simplistic compared to the complexity of the current landscape, but it is still important. What do teachers do with the text? Is it present in class? Do they hold it, refer to it, talk about how they are reading it and model and think through reading it with students? If teachers take texts seriously, model how they read them, provide students opportunities to read and monitor their understanding, and have students share reading strategies with one another, do more students become proficient; that is, do they read with greater engagement, purpose, and strategic awareness? These are all important questions to this day, but we have others that need to be added of equal importance. *What* are the texts and *where* are texts? and *How are texts and textual worlds connected*

to one another in time and space? Students encounter a range of text genres, or subgenres, every day, represented by print, images, audio tracks, or combinations of these. They easily access them, read them for various purposes, write them, and construct meaning intertextually and intermedially. What they want are more opportunities to use these texts in school to engage in activities and to learn things they deem important. In short, educators need to look realistically at students' levels of engagement in reading in school. If they are not engaged, they are not building proficiency. Reading proficiency, as situated practice, means that students are reading because they are intrinsically motivated as they read to learn things and complete activities. They are enjoying the experience of reading because it is useful, and they feel competent and persevere at it because they have strategies for reading various types of texts and they know which strategies to use and when (Guthrie, 2004; Wigfield, 2004). Given this definition of engaged reading, most reading in school falls short of its criteria.

CONCLUSIONS

In recent work O'Brien (2006) discusses the ramifications in moving from print-centric to media-centric notions of literate competence. This discussion applies to Kress's (2003) notion of moving from the page to the screen and Beach and O'Brien's (2008) strategies involved in interpreting and producing popular culture texts. Students now engage in multimediating (Doneman, 1997; Lankshear & Knobel, 2003). In addition to old paradigm competences of processing print, students who are proficient in the new literacies must know how and when to engage intertextual/ hypertextual constructions of texts as extensions of each other. That is, the texts they read and write exist across media space. We are not sure what the evolving competencies are. But as they read and write media texts, students are developing proficiencies in interrogating texts' meaning by transporting texts from their original context into another context. For example, print text from *Harry Potter and the Chamber of Secrets* by J. K. Rowling (1999) has found its way into the video game of the same title. Students who have watched the movie, read the book, and played the video game write stories that draw from all three. Teachers need to provide ongoing support in offering opportunities in school for students to read critically the multimodal intermedial texts that they read outside of school.

Jenkins (2006) explores the collision of old and new media. Media, including text, are losing their distinctive features and functions. Digitization has provided a means for the same content to take on multimodal forms. Media are both tools and protocols of cultural practices, which represent a range of social, economic, and material relationships (Gitelman, 2006). In the case of reading proficiency, defined almost exclusively as competency with print, students are working with the convergence of media outside school at the same time they exist within school environments that exclude most media other than print. Their proficiency, more broadly defined, could be markedly improved if schools participated more in the media convergence and used it to help students learn in school. The other important issue, even if educators accept the perennial prominence of print, is that reading proficiency of students in school should be defined more in terms of advanced competencies rather than basic levels. The bar for proficiency is set too low because schools feel pressure to show achievement to avoid failing the AYP benchmarks rather than challenging students to read as well as they could.

Finally, as long as proficiency is defined according to the autonomous notion that there is a certain scope and sequence of skills that operates independently of specific social and cultural practices in which the skills are applied to achieve relevant ends, students' horizons are limited. If educators instead work on reading as a set of social and cultural practices, situated within lessons designed to engage students, the horizon is almost limitless.

REFERENCES

Achieve Inc. (2005). *NAEP 2005 results: State vs. Nation*. Washington, DC: Author. Retrieved February 27, 2007, from *www.achieve.org/node/482*.

Anderson, C. (2004). Womanhood. *The work of hands*. Florence, MA: Perugia Press.

Bakhtin, M. M. (1981). *The dialogic imagination: Four essays by M. M. Bakhtin* (M. Holquist, Ed.; C. Emerson & M. Holquist, Trans.). Austin: University of Texas Press.

Bawarshi, A. (2003). *Genre and the invention of the writer: Reconsidering the place of invention in composition*. Logan: Utah State University Press.

Beach, R. (2000). Reading and responding at the level of activity. *Journal of Literacy Research, 32,* 237–251.

Beach, R., Appleman, D., Hynds, S., & Wilhelm, J. (2006). *Teaching literature to adolescents*. Mahwah, NJ: Erlbaum.

Beach, R., & O'Brien, D. (2008). Teaching popular-culture texts in the classroom. In J. Corio, M. Knobel, C. Lankshear, & D. J. Leu (Eds.), *Handbook of research on new literacies* (pp. 775–804). Mahwah, NJ: Erlbaum.

Beach, R., Thein, A., & Parks, D. (2007). *High school students' competing social worlds: Negotiating identities and allegiances through responding to multicultural literature*. New York: Routledge.

Biancarosa, G., & Snow, C. E. (2006). *Reading Next: A vision for action and research in middle and high school literacy: A report to Carnegie Corporation of New York* (2nd ed.). Washington, DC: Alliance for Excellent Education.

Bowker, R. R. (2005, May). *U.S. book production reaches new high of 195,000 titles in 2004; fiction soars*. Retrieved August 27, 2007, from Bowker website at *www.bowker.com/press/bowker/2005_0126_bowker.htm*.

Coe, R. M., Lingard, L., & Teslenko, T. (Eds.). (2002). *The rhetoric and ideology of genre: Strategies for stability and change*. Cresskill, NJ: Hampton.

Coiro, J. (2003). Reading comprehension on the Internet: Expanding our understanding of reading comprehension to encompass new literacies. *Reading Online*. (Reprinted from *Reading Teacher, 56,* 458–464) [OnlineSerial]. Retrieved April 17, 2007, from *www.readingonline.org/electronic/elec_index.asp?HREF=/electronic/rt/2-03_Column/index.html*.

Coiro, J. (2005). Making sense of online text. *Educational Leadership, 63,* 30–35.

Darvin, J. (2006). "On reading recipes and racing forms": The literacy practices and perceptions of vocational educators. *Journal of Adolescent and Adult Literacy, 50,* 10–18.

De Rosa, C., Cantrell, J., Cellentani, D., Hawk, J., Jenkins, L., & Wilson, A. (2005). *Perceptions of libraries and information resources: A report to the OCLC membership*. Dublin, OH: OCLC Online Computer Library Center.

Doneman, M. (1997). Multimediating. In C. Lankshear, C. Bigum, & C. Durant (Eds.), *Digital rhetorics: Literacies and technologies in education: Current practices and future directions* (Vol. 3, pp. 131–148). Brisbane: QUT/DEETYA.

Fitzgerald, F. S. (1991). *The great Gatsby*. New York: Cambridge University Press.

Fry, E. (2002). Readability vs. leveling. *Reading Teacher,* 56, 286–291.

Galda, L., & Beach, R. (2001). Theory and research into practice: Response to literature. *Reading Research Quarterly,* 36, 64–73.

Gee, J. P. (2008). *Social linguistics and literacies: Ideology in discourses* (3rd ed.). New York: Routledge.

Gitelman, L. (2006). *Always already new: Media, history, and the data of culture.* Cambridge, MA: MIT Press.

Gonzalez, N., Moll, L. C., & Amanti, C. (Eds.). (2005). *Funds of knowledge: Theorizing practices in households and classrooms.* Mahwah, NJ: Erlbaum.

Gray, W. S. (1948). Nature and scope of a sound reading program. In N. B. Henry (Ed.), *Reading in the high school and college: 47th yearbook of the National Society for the Study of Education* (pp. 46–68). Chicago: University of Chicago Press.

Guthrie, J. T. (2004). Teaching for literacy engagement. *Journal of Literacy Research,* 36, 1–29.

Gutmann, A. (1999). *Democratic education.* Princeton, NJ: Princeton University Press.

Heaviside, S., Farris, E., Dunn, C., & Fry, R. (1995, August). *Services and resources for children and young adults in public libraries.* Retrieved October 4, 2006, from the National Center for Education Statistics website at *nces.ed.gov/surveys/frss/publications/95357/.*

Hicks, D. (1996). Contextual inquiries: A discourse-oriented study of classroom learning. In D. Hicks (Ed.), *Discourse, learning, and schooling* (pp. 104–144). New York: Cambridge University Press.

Hiebert, E. H. (2002). Standards, assessment, and text difficulty. In A. E. Farstrup & S. J. Samuels (Eds.), *What research has to say about reading instruction* (3rd ed., pp. 337–369). Newark, DE: International Reading Association.

Hunt, R. A. (1993). Texts, textoids and utterances: Writing and reading for meaning, in and out of classrooms. In S. B. Straw & D. Bogdan (Eds.), *Constructive reading: Teaching beyond communication* (pp. 113–129). Portsmouth, NH: Heinemann.

Hunt, R. A. (2000). Reading reader, reading readers. *Reader,* 43, 47–51.

Ibsen, H. (1999). *A doll's house.* Chicago: Ivan R. Dee.

Ivey, G. S., & Broaddus, K. (2001). "Just plain reading": A survey of what makes students want to read in middle school classrooms. *Reading Research Quarterly,* 36, 350–377.

Ivey, G. S., & Fisher, D. (2005). Learning from what doesn't work. *Educational Leadership,* 63(2), 8–14.

Jenkins, H. (2006). *Convergence culture: Where old and new media collide.* New York: New York University Press.

Kamil, M. L. (2003). *Reading for the 21st century.* Washington, DC: Alliance for Excellent Education.

Kress, G. (2003). *Literacy in the new media age.* New York: Routledge.

Lankshear, C., & Knobel, M. (2003). *New literacies, changing knowledge, and classroom learning.* Buckingham, UK: Open University Press.

Lee, J., Grigg, W., & Donahue, P. (2007). *The nation's report card: Reading 2007* (NCES 2007-496). Washington, DC: National Center for Education Statistics, Institute of Education Sciences, U.S. Department of Education.

Lenhart, A., & Madden, M. (2005, November 2). *Teen content creators and consumers.* Retrieved October 4, 2006, from Pew Internet and American Life Project website at *www.pewInternet.org/PPF/r/166/report_display.asp.*

Lenhart, A., Rainie, L., & Lewis, O. (2001, June 20). *Teenage life online: The rise of the instant-message generation and the Internet's impact on friendships and family relationships.* Retrieved October 4, 2006, from Pew Internet and American Life Project website at *www.pewInternet.org/PPF/r/36/report_display.asp.*

McKenna, M. C., Kear, D. J., & Ellsworth, R. A. (1995). Children's attitude toward reading: A national survey. *Reading Research Quarterly,* 30, 934–955.

McNabb, M. L., Thurber, B. B., Dibuz, B. V., McDermott, P., & Lee, C. A. (2005). *Literacy learning in networked classrooms: Using the Internet with middle-level students.* Newark, DE: International Reading Association.

Metametrics. (2007). The Lexile Framework for Reading. Retrieved February 1, 2008, from *http://www.metametricsinc.com/TheLexileFrameworkforReading.pdf.*

Mikulecky, L. (1978, May). *Aliteracy and the changing view of reading goals.* Paper presented at the annual meeting of the International Reading Association, Houston (ED 157 052).

Moje, E. B. (2000). *"All the stories that we have": Adolescents' insights about literacy and learning in secondary schools.* Newark, DE: International Reading Association.

National Assessment Governing Board. (2004). Resolution on the NAEP 2009 Reading Framework. Retrieved February 1, 2008, from *www.nagb.org/release/resolution_09.html.*

National Education Association. (2002). NEA/AAP survey finds nationwide textbook shortages, teachers don't have enough books to assign homework. Retrieved February 1, 2008, from *www.nea.org/nr/nr021008.html.*

No Child Left Behind Act. (2001). P.L. 107-110.

Nystrand, M. (1986). *The structure of written communication.* Orlando, FL: Academic Press.

O'Brien, D. G. (1998). Multiple literacies in a high school program for "at-risk" adolescents. In D. E. Alvermann (Ed.), *Reconceptualizing the literacies in adolescents' lives* (pp. 27–49). Mahwah, NJ: Erlbaum.

O'Brien, D. G. (2006). "Struggling" adolescents' engagement in multimediating: Countering the institutional construction of incompetence. In D. E. Alvermann, K. A. Hinchman, D. W. Moore, S. F. Phelps, & D. R. Waff

(Eds.), *Reconceptualizing the literacies in adolescents' lives* (pp. 29–46). Mahwah, NJ: Erlbaum.

O'Brien, D. G., Beach, R., & Scharber, C. (2007). "Struggling" middle schoolers: Engagement and literate competence in a reading-writing intervention class. *Reading Psychology, 28*(1), 51–73.

Pappas, C. C., & Pettegrew, B. S. (1998). The role of genre in the psycholinguistic guessing game of reading. *Language Arts, 75,* 36–44.

Pressley, M. (2006). *Reading instruction that works* (3rd ed.). New York: Guilford Press.

Ravitch, D. (2003). *The language police: How pressure groups restrict what students learn.* New York: Knopf.

Richardson, W. (2006). *Blogs, wikis, podcasts and other powerful Web tools for the classroom.* Thousand Oaks, CA: Corwin Press.

Rowling, J. K. (1999). *Harry Potter and the chamber of secrets.* New York: Scholastic.

Schweickart, P. P., & Flynn, E. A. (Eds.). (2004). *Reading sites: Social differences and reader response.* New York: Modern Language Association.

Simpson, M. L., Stahl, N. A., & Francis, M. A. (2004). Reading and learning strategies: Recommendations for the 21st century. *Journal of Developmental Education, 28,* 2–6, 8–14.

Smagorinsky, P. (2001). If meaning is constructed, what is it made from? Toward a cultural theory of reading. *Review of Educational Research, 71,* 133–169.

Smith, M. W., & Wilhelm, J. D. (2002). "*Reading don't fix no Chevys*": Literacy in the lives of young men. Portsmouth, NH: Heinemann.

Stake, R. E. (2007, February 4). NAEP, report cards and education: A review essay. *Education Review, 10*(1), 1–22. Retrieved February 8, 2007, from *http: edrev.asu.edu/essays/v10n1index.html.*

Stanovich, K. E. (1980). Toward an interactive-compensatory model of individual differences in the de-

velopment of reading fluency. *Reading Research Quarterly, 16,* 32–71.

Stanovich, K. E. (1986). Matthew effects in reading: Some consequences of individual differences in the acquisition of literacy. *Reading Research Quarterly, 21,* 360–406.

Stanovich, K. E. (1988). Explaining the differences between the dyslexic and the garden variety poor reader: The phonological core variable-difference model. *Journal of Learning Disabilities, 21,* 590–612.

Stewart, R. A. (2006). Literacy research in the era of increasing centralized control of United States public schooling. *Journal of Literacy Research, 37,* 529–540.

Stewart, R. A., Paradis, E. E., Ross, B., & Lewis, M. J. (1996). Student voices: What works best in literature-based developmental reading. *Journal of Adolescent and Adult Literacy, 39,* 468–478.

Street, B. (1984). *Literacy in theory and practice.* New York: Cambridge University Press.

Sumara, D. J. (2002). *Why reading literature in school still matters: Imagination, interpretation, insight.* Mahwah, NJ: Erlbaum.

Thomas B. Fordham Institute. (2004, September). *The mad, mad world of textbook adoption.* Retrieved October 4, 2006, from *www.edexcellence.net/foundation/publication/publication.cfm?id=335.*

Touchstone Applied Science and Associates (TASA) Inc. (2006). *Degrees of reading power program.* Brewster, NY: Author. Retrieved March 9, 2007, from *www.tasaliteracy.com.*

Wigfield, A. (2004). Motivation for reading during the early adolescent years. In D. S. Strickland & D. E. Alvermann (Eds.), *Bridging the literacy achievement gap in grades 4–12* (pp. 56–69). New York: Teachers College Press.

CHAPTER 7

Fostering Adolescents' Engaged Academic Literacy

RUTH SCHOENBACH
CYNTHIA GREENLEAF

This chapter provides evidence that educators can have a significant impact on students' academic engagement and achievement by fostering adolescent students' development in four interrelated areas: (1) dispositions for engagement in academic tasks; (2) disciplinary knowledge; (3) capacities for problem solving with texts; and (4) shifts in learner identity. We discuss research supporting *engaged academic literacy* as a model for school-based literacy that contrasts in pedagogy and purpose with a more traditional conception of academic literacy. The model presented in this chapter builds on recent conceptions of reading and writing as literacy practice and adds support for an apprenticeship model that develops affective aspects of interaction with texts. The importance of students' active engagement in literacy tasks is central and is seen here as a quality that teachers can foster and actively support. Given our assumption that academic literacy practices are shaped by the conventions and discourses of the disciplines, we discuss some of the relevant literature on discipline-specific literacy, focusing on science and history. These discussions of discipline-specific learning are then illustrated through snapshots of two classrooms from our research studies—a high school Introduction to Chemistry classroom and a high school U.S. History classroom. We conclude with a brief discussion of ideas for fostering the kind of engaged academic literacy portrayed in these classroom snapshots, as opposed to the superficial version of academic literacy described in the introduction to the chapter.

> . . . *it wasn't like it was spread all over the place, like you had to read it. It was just like, if the "red square question" was here, you knew it was somewhere around that area right there. And you could just look for the answer and copy it down and you got full credit for it. So you didn't have to read. It was something that you could like slide by without them knowing. I don't know if they cared or not, but that's the way everybody did it. You see the "red square question" and you sort of calculate where it's around, you find the answer, and you write it down, and that's it.*
> —Rosa, a ninth-grade student, describing her experiences reading history

The learning opportunities students experience shape the literacy capacities they develop; these opportunities also shape students' conceptions of the academic disciplines in which these capacities are used (Greenleaf, Schoenbach, Cziko, & Mueller, 2001). The tasks teachers ask students to do as they work with subject area texts also powerfully influence students' beliefs about their capacities and identities as learners (National Research Council, 2004). If we want students to be able to think and read critically, to write and talk knowledgeably about historical, scientific, mathematical, or literary topics, we need to provide richer learning opportunities than those "red square questions" Rosa describes above. In this chapter, we argue that in order for students to become increasingly independent, capable, and critical in their thinking, reading, writing, and speaking in varied disciplinary domains and the complex literacy tasks of daily life, they need learning opportunities that help them develop the following dispositions, skills, and capacities:

1. Dispositions for engagement in academic tasks.
2. Text-based problem-solving capacities.
3. Discipline-based literacy practices.
4. Resilient learner identities.

Research reviewed in many recent reports on adolescent literacy indicates that the majority of middle and high school students—including most who go to college (ACT, 2006)—are not prepared for higher-level comprehension, critical reading, writing, and speaking skills required in high school and beyond (e.g. Snow & Biancarosa, 2005). Although there are disagreements about the severity of the problem (Berliner & Biddle, 1995), few would argue that secondary educators are doing an adequate job helping students develop required levels of literacy.

These recent reports and the growing policy attention surrounding them reflect increased awareness of the need to help a large majority of students attain more sophisticated literacy levels. But rather than supporting educators to move in the direction of creating learning environments in which more students can achieve higher literacy capacities, current prevailing policies create the opposite effect. The vast majority of high-stakes tests currently in use across the United States simply do not promote this kind of learning (Hillocks, 2002). Instead, many teachers and administrators face tremendous pressure pushing them to promote the kind of rote learning—the search for the kind of "red square question" mentioned above—that has long characterized teaching in U.S. secondary schools (Cuban, 1989).

In this chapter we present an alternative way of supporting adolescents' content-area learning at the secondary level: building what we call *engaged academic literacy*. The perspective and ways of teaching we present come from a deep reservoir of work on literacy that has been developed by scholars and practitioners working in varied and interrelated areas, including cognitive science and sociocultural learning theory; psychological research on motivation, engagement, achievement, and identity; and sociology and anthropology focused on the practices of communities such as historians and engineers.

Our view of academic literacy as active, engaged, and empowering is grounded in recent conceptions of reading and writing as literacy practice (e.g. Scribner & Cole, 1981; Street, 1995). Literacy is understood as a social, cultural, and cognitive activity shaped by particular communities and by the particular situations and contexts in which reading and writing occur. Academic disciplines, in this conception, are understood as socially constructed, evolving, and open to interaction with other disciplines. Reading researchers who focus on content-area literacy have called for a shift toward a social practices conception of the subject areas (Bean, 2000), and toward explicitly teaching academic literacies in ways that make apparent, and support the development of, valued reasoning practices in the subject areas (Greenleaf et al., 2001). Thus, scholars helping to reframe the way we think about academic literacy emphasize the importance of helping students learn discipline-specific literacy practices as well as more general literacy strategies (Moje, Dillon, & O'Brien, 2000).

In addition to the work on specific literacy practices of varied disciplines, there are studies of youth literacy in out-of-school settings demonstrating the capacity of young people to engage deeply in reading, writing, and communicating through textual, visual, and other means (Alvermann, 2002). These studies point to important resources for adolescent learning that are largely unrecognized and underutilized in academic classrooms. And while voluminous studies have aimed to describe situated literacies, instructional models—methods that secondary school teachers can actually use in instruction—that draw from these newer conceptions are just beginning to be developed and used in the field (e.g., Ford & Forman, 2006; Greenleaf, Hale, Charney-Sirott, & Schoenbach, 2007; Langer, 2001; McConachie et al., 2006).

We use the phrase *engaged academic literacy* to refer to the kinds of learning environments in which students work actively with one another, with teachers, and independently, to understand challenging texts in ways that have meaning for them and that build on their knowledge, experience, creativity, and questions. We use this phrase to emphasize that academic literacy is not merely "the basic reading and writing skills taught in a conventional literacy medium . . . during elementary and middle school years" (Holbrook & Koenig, 2000, p. 265) applied to learning information from expository texts. By adding the word *engaged,* we mean to distinguish between the skilled but rote and unsophisticated kind of academic literacy that many "successful" students master, and the more analytic, critical, and discipline-specific ways of making meaning emblematic of engaged learners. Also crucial to our view of academic literacy is that students develop their own reasons to become more interested and competent in using discipline-based literacy practices.

In the following sections, we discuss the four types of learning opportunities we argue are essential for fostering students' academic literacy development. We ground this discussion in examples from two classroom cases. One is an introductory chemistry classroom in an urban high school in which 40% of students scored below the 10th percentile on a standardized reading test. The other is an honors U.S. history classroom in a rural high school serving many students from migrant worker families. We conclude with a brief discussion of what we believe helps to foster the engaged academic literacy demonstrated in both of these classrooms.

LEARNING OPPORTUNITIES THAT FOSTER ADOLESCENTS' ENGAGED ACADEMIC LITERACY

We view the kind of engaged academic literacy learning described below as best supported through what has been called an apprenticeship model of learning (Rogoff, 1990). When teachers apprentice students in the literacy practices of their disciplines, they make explicit the tacit reasoning processes, strategies, and discourse rules that shape successful readers' and writers' work (Brown, Collins, & Newman, 1989; Lee, 1995; Osborne, 2002). As apprentices, students need plentiful opportunities to use these strategies with authentic texts and to discuss their ideas and experiences with others (see RAND Reading Study Group, 2002, for a review of this research).

Developing Dispositions for Engagement in Academic Tasks

Teachers who establish successful literacy apprenticeships for adolescents are attentive to affective and identity issues as well as to cognitive and knowledge issues. They create learning opportunities that help students develop dispositions for engagement in academic tasks, text-based problem-solving capacities, discipline-based literacy practices, and resilient learner identities. We describe these in general terms and then refer to them within the context of Will Brown's introductory chemistry class.

Students' willingness to make mistakes as part of learning is closely tied to their beliefs about whether intellectual ability is fixed or (at least partially) the result of effort (Dweck & Molden, 2005). For many students, the sense of a fixed identity ("I'm not a reader," "I'm not a good student," or "I just don't have that kind of mind") is a powerful barrier to learning. The heightened self-consciousness and sensitivity to peer group perceptions of students in middle school and high school can make this especially difficult.

To marshal and focus the effort required for academic work, most adolescents need support for developing key dispositions for approaching and engaging in challenging tasks. These include general dispositions to be interested and critical learners—having, for example, characteristics such as curiosity, tolerance for ambiguity, and the expectation that one should be constructing understanding rather than passively carrying out prescribed procedures (Yore, 2004). Such dispositions also include maintaining confidence in their own abilities and in the value of persistence, even while struggling through challenging text—for example, through motivating self-talk (National Research Council, 2004). Many adolescents who struggle with academic reading have misconceptions of what reading is, seeing it as a magical process in which comprehension just happens for successful readers (Greenleaf et al., 2001). For such students, developing the disposition of feeling in control of their reading, or having a sense of agency in their reading and learning, is crucial.

In addition, students often need support to develop dispositions to read, write, and think critically and to learn to do so with reference to evidence as required in particular disciplines. Support for the disposition to approach unfamiliar text with a *code-breaking stance* in which they have analytic skills for using strategies is especially important for students classified as struggling readers.

Introducing students to the idea that texts are not repositories of received wisdom, but documents constructed by particular authors in particular contexts for particular purposes, can empower them to begin to read more critically. Support for students to develop general dispositions toward engagement in learning must be complemented by varied practices for extending and elaborating students' capacity to do in-depth intellectual work. These include helping them develop stamina for reading and writing for increasing lengths of time, as well as sustaining interest in and participating productively in meaningful discussions.

In the classroom introduced below, we illustrate some of the ways in which a chemistry teacher in an Oakland, California, public high school provides support for his students as they develop these kinds of dispositions and intellectual habits.

Introduction to Chemistry:
Developing Dispositions for
Engagement in Academic Tasks

It is the first day of the school year in teacher Will Brown's Oakland high school class, Introduction to Chemistry. Forty percent of the students have scored below the 10th percentile on the state's standardized reading test. Students are taking the course as a graduation requirement.

The computer monitor in the front of the classroom reads:

Welcome to Introduction to Chemistry

Please take your assigned seat. See seating chart on front table.

Preamble #1: *Write 1/3 page and keep.*

What do you know or think about mixtures and solutions?

What do you want to learn about mixtures and solutions?

As students find their way to nine round tables labeled with team names such as Carbon Cavaliers, Kinetic Kids, Solubility Stars, and Periodic Pros, Will explains, "We start every day with a 'preamble,' about a third of the page each. We do a lot of things in the preambles that you won't want to miss. This is something you'll want to put back in your binder." As students begin to write, Will tells them, "Leave some space and when you hear good ideas from your peers, you can fill them in." A few minutes later, Will invites volunteers to share their responses to the preamble questions.

Before hearing from students, Will introduces norms for classroom discourse. "Let's all turn so we can see the person who's talking. And I'm going to go to the side of the room, to help train you to talk to the class. Everyone here needs to hear what you're saying to be part of that learning process." As three students share what they know or think about mixtures and solutions, Will acknowledges, validates, paraphrases, frames, and elaborates students' contributions in ways that demonstrate his undivided attention and respect for student thinking.

Erika, an English learner from the Sudan, offers, "I think it's something that you can make or something like that. I don't really know."

"So we can *make* solutions? That's a good thing to know about," Will responds. "We can, and we *will* make them—very generally or very particularly."

The preamble discussion leads to a hands-on investigation and observation of mixtures and solutions, with students immediately immersed in active science inquiry and sense making. Most of the students in this classroom did not initially see themselves as people who were capable of understanding science. They were not particularly interested in learning science—chemistry in this case. From day one, however, Will puts these young people in the role of science learners, naming small groups with chemical terms, inviting them to become interested in mixtures and solutions and to bring their thinking and experiences into the room, and making them responsible for listening to and learning from each other. He builds routines that support their risk taking, sets thoughtful expectations for classroom discourse, and models and supports collaboration in a learning community. From the first day of class, he treats them as capable students, eager and able to "do science." Further, he designs lessons to engage students' interests, leverage their preference for social interaction toward academic ends, and draw on their knowledge and experience.

Developing Text-Based Problem-Solving Capacities

Reading is a process of solving problems to make meaning of texts (Pressley, 1998). Over the past several decades, a great deal of research has demonstrated that integrating the explicit teaching of comprehension, text structure, and word-level strategies into compelling sense-making activities with texts increases student reading achievement (Pearson, 1996). Researchers argue that for the reading and reasoning processes of academic disciplines to become part of the repertoires of a broader population of students, teachers need to engage a much broader range of students in complex academic literacy tasks, at the same time providing the explicit teaching and support necessary for students to perform the tasks successfully (Delpit, 1995). Accordingly, recent national reading research reports, including those of the National Reading Panel (National Institute of Child Health and Human Development, NICHD, 2000) and the RAND Reading Study Group (2002), have called for more classroom instruction time devoted to key cognitive strategies, such as questioning, clarifying, summarizing, and predicting.

Explicit instruction in such strategies—as when teachers continually model and demonstrate as well as talk about what they are doing—is critical to students' gaining the necessary metacognitive awareness and control to determine which strategies to use how, depending on the content and difficulty of the text (e.g., Bransford, Brown, & Cocking, 1999). When readers learn strategies in the context of in-depth content learning, they are more likely to understand the strategies as purposeful tools that they can and will use flexibly to support their understanding of new texts (Guthrie, 2004).

Introduction to Chemistry:
Developing Text-Based
Problem-Solving Capacities

Midway through the academic year, Will Brown's students are immersed in a unit on acids and bases, which involves an extended investigation of the properties of acids and bases by determining the pH of 12 household chemicals. Over several days, class activity moves fluidly between hands-on inquiry, exploration with laboratory materials, and inquiry structured by science texts. In a 5-minute video of Will's Introduction to Chemistry classroom, these low-achieving students work with *multiple texts*, concentrating intently on reading, taking notes, and working through the lab. This short video clip and accompanying text can be viewed at *www.wested.org/cs/sli/print/docs/922.*

Students have completed one laboratory investigation when Will introduces the article "Chemical Reactivity: Acids and Bases" and tells students how he will help them build their capacity for handling the challenges of reading chemistry. "This reading is structured in a very particular way," Will explains, "I'm going to . . . do some modeling of the reading, then we're going to sort of practice it individually, and then together, and then more and more it's going to move to you taking more and more responsibility for the practice."

Will demonstrates his own thinking processes as he reads a section of the text, stopping to highlight the work he is doing to: (1) clarify any confusing words or ideas, (2) ask questions that come to mind about the science, and (3) summarize as he reads to capture the gist of what he read before moving on. He asks students to practice these three thinking processes as they read, working individually and with their small groups. Students read the first section of the article using *Talking to the Text,* a metacognitive reading strategy that is a routine in this class.

When Will invites students to share any difficulties they are having with the text, Erika complains that the reading is boring. In response, Will initiates a whole-class conversation about what makes reading boring. Among the answers Erika and her classmates offer is that the text doesn't make sense. Because Erika's lack of interest in the reading stems from her failure to make sense of the text, Will encourages her to return to the text, writing questions and comments in the margin to identify places where she needs the help of the class, and then to work with classmates to clarify confusions. As Erika and her classmates share their confusions, understandings, and reading processes, her evident stamina for solving reading comprehension problems increases.

Jeffrey offers something the text made him wonder: "I had a question on where it said, 'A fundamental property of acids and bases is that an acid and a base always react to "neutralize" one another.' Why do they neutralize one another?" As he shares his curiosity with the class, Will records this question on the board at the front of the room.

Durrell points the class to the place in the text that prompted his question: "It said, 'One excellent way to tell whether an acid–base reaction has occurred is to use an indicator in the reaction mixture.' Is there more, what's the other ways? Are there more than one way?" In effect, Durrell has modeled using signal words in the text ("one way") to anticipate what he may learn through the unit ("other ways"). As Will writes this question on the board, he comments, "We're going to explore some of the answers to it, so I'm not going to respond right now."

Monae contributes a question focused on the chemistry of acids and bases: "It says that it indicates whether a substance is an acid or a base depending on what color change it produces in the dye. Like how do you know what colors are acids and which are bases?" Monae's question about the text foreshadows the continuing work of the lab exploration. Will is delighted to have this connection made for him: "Ah! Acid and base colors. That's one of the big issues of this lab!" Students' questions remain on the board as a record of their thinking and of the questions that will animate their further work in the unit.

As new reading opportunities arose in the classroom, Will modeled his own sensemaking processes by thinking aloud as he worked to understand a reading or chemistry problem. By making his own reading and reasoning processes—the confusions, clarifications, and connections—visible, Will demonstrated mental engagement and problem solving as the hidden work of comprehension. His willingness to show his students how he actually *works* to comprehend texts helped students realize that it is strategic effort and not magic that is involved in comprehension. To support students' development as science readers, Will provided ongoing opportunities and made students responsible to reflect on their own thinking and learning through a small number of metacognitive literacy routines such as Talking to the Text, double-entry reading logs, K-W-L activities (Ogle, 1986), and *Team Reads,* his own adaptation of Reciprocal Teaching (Palinscar & Brown, 1989). Through repeated cycles of reading and exploring and talk, Will's students practiced reading comprehension strategies and gained stamina for challenging reading along with a growing understanding of the chemistry content.

Developing Discipline-Based Literacy Practices

Literacy practices and the language used in school texts become increasingly specialized throughout the school career, reflecting the broader activities that characterize the academic disciplines (Borasi & Seigel, 2000; Lemke, 1990; Wineburg, 1991, 2001). Canonical knowledge, reasoning processes, interpretive practices, ways of engaging, reasoning processes, the terrain of ideas, activities, literacy tasks, texts, and genres—all vary across and within disciplinary traditions.

As students encounter more sophisticated disciplinary texts and tasks, they need support to learn more discipline-specific strategies. When teachers see their own invisible mental processes as they encounter challenging texts in their disciplines, and when they bring students into a community of learners where student thinking is made visible and available for discussion, students are significantly empowered to work with academic texts (Greenleaf & Schoenbach, 2004).

What Is Specific to Academic Literacy in Science?

To learn science is to learn not only a body of scientific knowledge but also ways of participating in scientific exploration and reasoning. Access to the scientific community and the ability to carry out or evaluate the outcomes of science inquiry rely on sophisticated literacy skills—the ability to make sense of scientific terminology, to interpret arrays of data, to comprehend scientific texts, to use and interpret models and illustrations, and to read and write scientific explanations (Osborne, 2002). Several research studies have also shown the reciprocal effect of science inquiry on developing students' reading skills and comprehension (Baker, 1991). Yet many science teachers are not certain how to integrate science reading experiences with hands-on investigations and are keenly aware of students' difficulty in comprehending science texts. As a result, in recent years there has been a widespread reduction of reading in secondary science classrooms, precisely as policymakers are raising alarms about the reading proficiencies of adolescents (Rycik & Irvin, 2001).

Introduction to Chemistry: Developing Discipline-Based Literacy Practices

As the students in the Introduction to Chemistry class work through the acids and bases unit, they not only gain stamina for bringing problem-solving strategies to bear on reading complex texts, but they also receive abundant support in thinking scientifically as they read and carry out their hands-on investigations. Will provides a three-page handout describing the exploration tasks that students are to carry out. In order to help them actively make sense of their work, take an inquiring stance, and extend their inquiry into an investigation they design, he prompts them with questions such as the following:

"Do you see a pattern in the two groups' acid–basic properties?"

"Predict the pH trend you might observe as you add NaOH to the vinegar. What information guided your prediction (best guesses are okay here!)?"

"As a team, review your data. For each task, discuss and answer both of the following questions: What interesting observations, trends, or patterns do you find? How might you interpret or explain the observations, trends, or patterns you see?"

"What did you learn through this lab? What else do you want to learn about acids and bases? What experiment would you like to try?"

Students begin the unit working in teams to generate two lists to share with the class: things they already know about acids and bases—"an acid–base idea inventory"—and questions showing what they would like to learn about acids and bases. Will also assigns the first 15 pages of the textbook chapter on acids and bases as homework. Students construct reading logs as they work through the assigned pages in the textbook, noting excerpts and ideas from the text in the left column of a T-chart and recording their thoughts, interpretations, confusions, and questions in the right column. Will collects and responds to these reading logs, focusing his attention on the right column in order to find student questions that he can make salient, prompt students into thinking more deeply about the text and the science, celebrate students' insights, and make note of students' growing stamina and effort in learning.

In the laboratory, teams experience the drama of acid and base chemistry firsthand. They make pH meters and then confer with peers as they read and follow the directions for using them and recording their results. They use T-charts for recording "observations, data, calculations, and answers" and "thoughts, reflections, and questions." As a metacognitive tool, the T-chart glides from textbook to laboratory exploration and back, making student thinking and reasoning processes visible and leaving a record of the observations and explanations students construct as they work.

Working through the ancillary text, "Chemical Reactivity," students alternate between reading a small section of the text individually and discussing it with their three teammates. In both the individual reading and small-group conversations, students continue to monitor their reading and thinking processes and practice the three cognitive strategies Will has modeled: clarifying, questioning, and summarizing. As they work, Will moves through the class, listening to their discussions and helping them learn to carry out Team Reads, his version of Reciprocal Teaching that is guided by role cards that ask individuals to be the "clarifying coach," the "questioning coach," or the "summarizing coach." Will moves the class in and out of cycles, modeling these coaching roles as students' work in their teams. The questions students have generated move them back into investigations, guided now by their own thinking, inquiries, and need for clarification.

The texts of the science world and of Will's chemistry classroom are clearly multiple and varied, ranging from traditional, encyclopedic textbooks to trade journals and science reports, numerical equations, visual and physical models of atoms and molecules, and conventional systems for denoting chemical bonding such as Lewis dot structures, chemical equations, and drawings of atomic structures. Even laboratory equipment and the phenomena explored in the lab require reading and interpretation. Each of these texts poses a comprehension problem for the science learner. In this classroom environment, inexperienced academic readers are apprenticed, over time and in multiple ways, to the literacy practices of science and to the reasoning processes that support and sustain science inquiry.

Developing Resilient Literacy Identities

A critical and often unacknowledged part of some adolescents' literacy development involves helping them transform the identities of nonreader and nonlearner—often formed in response to negative experiences in school—into new identities as capable readers and learners (Gee, 1996; Mahiri & Godley, 1998). As adolescents explore, or try on, possible selves, teachers encourage them to try on new reader identities, to explore and expand their visions of who they are and who they can become (Davidson & Koppenhaver, 1993).

This identity work is critical if students are to embrace literacy, reengage as readers, and improve their academic performance.

Lave and Wenger (1991) describe the process of identity formation as a negotiation of the meaning of "participative experiences" and social interpretations of these experiences; through this negotiation, we construct who we are. Feldman (2004) reminds us that "learning not only changes what we know and do, but it changes who we are" (p. 144). When we ask students to learn something new, we are asking them to become someone new. When teachers are able to provide consistent support for students to try on new ways of acting, thinking, and interacting, we have seen evidence of significant shifts in academic identity over the course of an academic year (Litman & Greenleaf, 2008).

Introduction to Chemistry: Developing Resilient Literacy Identities

Key to students' growth as science readers and learners in Will's Introduction to Chemistry class are the many opportunities he offers students to discuss the ideas and texts of chemistry. In Will's classroom, conversational routines include the daily preambles, small groups, and Team Reads already described. These conversational routines generally begin with individual reflection, move to small-group and whole-class discussion, and return to the individual, providing opportunities for students to revisit, revise, and deepen comprehension and content knowledge as well as to practice and refine discipline-based thinking and reading processes. As Will orchestrates these opportunities, he provides students with support for reshaping their conceptions of science, of reading, and of their own capabilities as learners.

But promoting genuine participation in these classroom routines requires patience and tact. Eduardo, a student who recently immigrated from Mexico, appeared, when he first arrived in Will's class, to be an uncooperative and unmotivated student. His participation during the first weeks of class took the form of passive resistance and frequent interruptions and disruptions. He was slow in responding to directions or chose not to follow them at all. When Will asked students to add to their notes what they had learned from their classmates, Eduardo sat with his binder closed. During one lesson, Eduardo kept up a steady stream of negative patter, replying to Will's reminder to work quietly, "We don't have to." In spite of this beginning, and having earned poor marks in the first grading period, Eduardo went on to earn an A for the second semester. Furthermore, he developed a preference for reading science texts over literature, and expressed a desire to become an engineer.

Will observed early on that despite Eduardo's refusal to participate in most classroom activities, he seemed to enjoy being part of class discussions. At first, Eduardo's participation was largely tangential—telling a classmate that he couldn't hear what she said, for example, or piggybacking on another's idea with an offhanded "Sounds good." However, Will consistently demonstrated that he valued students' thinking and participation, including Eduardo's. During one preamble discussion, for example, Eduardo declined to participate, saying his idea was similar to what a classmate had already said. But Will asked him to share his thinking anyway, explaining, "It's important to hear different voices." By mid-October, with Will's mentoring, Eduardo was making more substantive contributions to classroom discussions.

In the ensuing weeks, frequent metacognitive conversations provided ongoing opportunities for the class to explore social, personal, and cognitive aspects of reading and doing science. Will shared strategies he used to make science reading more interesting and comprehensible and had students discuss what was easy, hard, interesting, and confusing for them. Although Eduardo expressed concern that the material was too hard, Will maintained confidence in Eduardo's capabilities, and Eduardo began to realize that reading science requires effort, even for expert readers. Along with Will's modeling and encouragement, the metacognitive reading routines helped Eduardo identify his confusions, supported his problem-solving efforts, and contributed to his growing self-confidence.

Eduardo became increasingly willing to take risks as a reader and learner. In late October, despite complaining that an upcoming lab was "too hard," Eduardo participated and found the lab doable—as Will had predicted. When Eduardo completed his lab report early, Will leveraged Eduardo's increasing resilience, giving him a related reading assignment from the textbook, prefaced by a remedial tutorial on reading logs. Eduardo read his textbook for the duration of the class, making notes in his log. The following week, during group reports on the lab, Eduardo was conspicuous for his engagement. He expressed interest in others' reports, asking one group a sophisticated question about measurement. As he was leaving class, Eduardo asked Will for permission to take home his reading log, despite the fact that there was no assigned reading. "I want to read tonight," he insisted.

As Eduardo gained confidence and expertise as a reader, Will also encouraged him to use disciplinary language to describe his own thinking more precisely. During a lesson on summarizing the "Chemical Reactivity" text, Will asked the class, "What is the important idea that keeps coming up?" When Eduardo responded, "The things about acids and bases," Will prompted, "[Can you use] another word?" Eduardo amended his response: "Properties." During a recap of the lesson, Will highlighted the importance of "finding the word *properties*." About this time, Eduardo also showed increasing interest in chemistry for its own sake. He chatted informally with Will, asking questions about chemistry, and did extra reading for homework.

Although Eduardo's turnaround coincided with exposure to specific reading and science strategies and routines, our data suggest that the change was a result of his broader apprenticeship in the discipline-based literacies in Will's classroom, coupled with Will's constant expectation that he could be successful. Frequent in-class metacognitive conversations that were wide ranging but focused on the thinking processes of reading and science supported Eduardo in rethinking his identity. He came to see himself as having the capability to succeed in class by working at it, and, consequently, experienced the goal Will expressed for all his students—"the joy of figuring things out through science inquiry and science reading."

JOINING A COMMUNITY OF HISTORICAL THINKERS

What Is Specific to Academic Literacy in History?

Since the 1990s, there has been an unprecedented confluence of work among historians, cognitive psychologists, history teachers, professors of history education, multimedia curriculum designers, archivists, and linguists leading to new conceptions and practice in teaching history (Stearns, Seixas, & Wineburg, 2004). As in other areas of research on discipline-specific literacy practices, this work has been influenced by studies on how expert practitioners—historians in this case—carry out literacy practices. At an expert level, the study of history requires the capacity to sift through historical documents with attention to bias and perspective, to construct evidence-based accounts of probable historical events, to place documents and artifacts into larger historical contexts, to evaluate the credibility of different sources of information, and to perceive and have empathy for the experiences of others (Bradley Commission on History in Schools, 1995). This conception of what is involved in historical thinking and literacy has been reflected in the increasing prevalence of document-based questions (DBQs) in some high-stakes assessments such as the College Board advanced placement history exams (Columbia American History On-line, 2007).

Although it is not realistic to imagine that secondary students will develop the level of knowledge and disciplinary sophistication of graduate students or professional historians (Alexander, 2003), a number of promising approaches for apprenticing students to historical thinking have been developed in recent years. For example, based on analysis of differences in the thinking aloud of expert and novice historians, Wineburg and his colleagues have identified explicit cognitive heuristics, or overarching ways of thinking and working, to foster historical thinking. In their framework, students are apprenticed in the practice of "sourcing" documents, that is, looking for, finding, and analyzing the author, intended audience, and purpose of a document in order to evaluate its contents more knowledgeably. In addition, students learn to corroborate evidence and information in documents by relating them to other documents, and to contextualize historical events (Wineburg & Martin, 2004). Rosenzweig and Wineburg's website, Historical Thinking Matters, provides a set of historical cases with carefully scaffolded texts and tasks to support students' active inquiry (*historicalthinkingmatters.org*). Another Internet-based learning environment created to support students' investigation of historical problem solving (*www. pihnet.org*) is based on a design theory that highlights the importance of building inquiries around "a persistent issue with moral and ethical challenges . . . as a means of facilitating motivation and engagement" (Brush & Saye, 2006).

Exploring the problem of helping students learn to read across multiple specialized historical records and make sense of discrepancies as well as similarities, Bain (2005) describes his process of teaching students to "problematize" varied accounts of the same historical event through specific inquiries. Notably, in this approach, he also finds a place for teacher lectures on particular topics—setting out broad contextual information, for example—for those elements of the curriculum in which student inquiry may not be sufficient, given the time and focus of the work. In Bain's work, as in the classroom described below, historical understanding is created through ongoing investigation and conversation within a community of developing expertise.

Honors U.S. History

Students in Gayle Cribbs's honors U.S. History class are being apprenticed into the practices of historical thinking as they work through a set of historical documents relating to World War II. These students live in an agricultural area of California's Central Valley, where many families have immigrated from Mexico. Twenty-five percent of Gayle's students have learned English as a new language, and reading scores in the class range from "basic" to "advanced" on the California Standards Test. Students have been assigned to this honors class with the understanding that although expectations are high, support is available.

In the class session described below, it is late March and students are using a variety of problem-solving strategies as they work together to build understanding of a complex set of texts relating to Japanese internment. Students have just read *Snow Falling on Cedars,* a piece of historical fiction about the internment, and viewed *Something Strong Within,* a documentary about life inside the relocation camps. They are now beginning a weeklong unit focusing on the question of the constitutionality of the Japanese internment. After a close reading of the Articles of the Constitution, described below, they will read the majority and dissenting opinions on *Korematsu v. United States,* a 1944 Supreme Court case challenging the internment.

As students read through the Articles of the Constitution, they think aloud with a partner, stopping to clarify language they do not understand, rephrasing the gist of what they have read, and making notes so they can summarize each article.

In one partnership, Isobel reads aloud, "*Habeas corpus.* Didn't we hear that somewhere else before?" Julio responds, "This is what Abraham Lincoln suspended in the Civil War," "Oh, that's right. Okay," Isobel notes, and continues to read and comment on the text: " 'The privilege of writ of *habeas corpus* shall not be suspended, unless in cases of rebellion, invasion, or if public safety may require it.' So the law would fit the Civil War, you know?" The two work head-to-head over the notes they are making together, starting and finishing each other's thoughts as they work through the meaning of this sentence, literally thinking collaboratively aloud.

Another pair has also come across *habeas corpus* and is working to clarify their understanding of the term. Heather begins hesitantly, "So . . . basically, you can't . . ." and Mary Cruz jumps in, "Suspend *habeas corpus* without extreme cause. So it's really up to them," she continues, "it's not . . ." "It's up to the executive branch," Heather interjects.

"It's up to Congress," Mary Cruz continues. "I think Lincoln got it passed by law. No, he did it by executive order, didn't he? I don't know how he did that. It's probably somewhere in the next article."

In another small group, Anna is reading and thinking aloud, "We didn't go after them before for any specific reason. It was once they bombed Pearl Harbor, we went, 'Ah! Japanese!' " "Yeah," her two partners agree. She continues, "And so we put them in internment camps. And it was after the fact, so it was *ex post facto,* after the fact."

In a group of three girls, who are also working through their understanding of Article I, Section 9, Chanese reads aloud, "No bill of attainder or *ex post facto* law shall be passed." Suze translates this phrase into her own words, "You can't make up new rules in order to jail someone." Immediately Ariel pipes up, "I don't understand that one at all!" Her partners turn to her to explain. Chanese says, "Like, okay, somebody did something and you want to convict that person, so you make up a law specifically to jail that person. You can't do that." The explanation helps: "Oh, okay," Ariel nods. "So it's *ex post facto,* like after the fact." "That's true!" Suze adds. "*Ex post facto.* A law cannot be enforced if created after the crime was committed. . . ." "If created 'post' the crime date," Ariel announces.

As students work, Gayle moves through the room, listening to pairs and stopping to probe student thinking. "What do you make of that dual citizenship thing?" she inquires. After students work for several minutes, Gayle calls the class together to share and solve reading comprehension problems. "I'm hearing lots of good thinking and reading, close reading, which is wonderful. And you are using all you know to make sense of this, which is a somewhat challenging document, yes? What problems are you coming up against, and what are you finding to solve those problems? How are you solving them?"

Sam refers to Article I, Section 9, Number 3, and relates a textbook subhead to the *ex post facto* law. "We were looking at the title of that specific number, 'Unfair Punishments,' " he says, "so we're thinking that that's what it was referring to." In response, Gayle focuses on the reading strategy Sam described, naming it to make it metacognitive and memorable: "So you are using a *text clue* there to understand a little series of words that you don't understand, that you haven't heard before. What other things?"

"Jeannie," Gayle says, "I saw you doing something to solve a problem. I think you were looking at *habeas corpus.*" Jeannie explains, "Oh, we read the footnote at the bottom." Gayle is pleased to reinforce a historical text structure her students are using, "So you found some footnotes. Yay, footnotes!"

She continues to draw from the pairs to enrich the understanding and potential strategic repertoire of the entire class: "In this group, you spent a long time, I believe, on the 'elastic clause,' right? . . . Article I, Section 8, number 18?" Laura describes the problem she and her partner were having and tells how they tackled the reading: "Oh, the wording. The wording was rather odd. And we didn't even know 'the foregoing powers' and it was confusing. We tried to deal with it in sentences. We went up to 'foregoing powers' and tried to figure out what it meant. And then we took the second part." Gayle reframes the strategy for the class, "I'm seeing it's really one long sentence, and you broke it up into phrases and tried to see if you could make sense of phrases and stick it all back together again and see if you could figure it out that way."

Gayle's monitoring of students' reading as they think aloud with partners to surface and solve comprehension problems is strategic. She is helping students build a repertoire of strategies for this kind of rigorous work with text, punctuating students' sustained work with metacognitive conversations (Schoenbach, Greenleaf, Cziko, & Hurwitz, 1999) and discussions of the text. "Shall we move on?" she says. "Back to the text."

Gayle's students continue working their way through the Constitution, thinking aloud and summarizing. Toward the end of the period, Gayle again draws the class together. "I want to pull you back together. Partly I want to say that you're doing really hard work. And the conversations are wonderful that you're having, really trying to understand what this really dense document has to say. . . . As you are going through this—and I know some of you were looking at the Amendments and others haven't gotten that far—what is occurring to you about the relevancy of all of this to the relocation camps? What's come to mind?"

Student responses foreshadow the analysis they will do of the Supreme Court decision. They raise questions about treason by association with blood relatives or nationality. "Doesn't the internment of a whole group of people of the same national origin violate this clause?" someone asks. They note that the Constitution says that you cannot be charged with treason unless there are two testimonies against you or you have confessed, yet the Japanese, they note, were "just taken into the concentration camps." Was there adequate evidence that they were guilty of treason?

The class ends with Gayle asking students to finish summarizing the Articles of the Constitution in preparation for their reading of the arguments in the *Korematsu* Supreme Court case. The homework will be done independently, but Gayle warns students to be ready to share their summaries with a partner the next day. She offers as well a more intrinsically motivating reason for completing the summaries, explaining, "I don't think you're going to follow the arguments really explicitly unless you discipline yourself to do that." In class the next day, students write abstracts of the majority and dissenting opinions in *Korematsu v. United States* to help them analyze which was the stronger argument and why. Following a class discussion of the strength of these two arguments, students write individually to this prompt: "If you had been on the Supreme Court in 1944, which opinion would you have signed, and why? If neither represents your views, you are welcome to write your own opinion."

The engagement of students in making sense of this set of challenging texts is noteworthy. It is clear, as they work, that they not only analyze the implications of the Constitution for decision making in a historically salient case, but that they also care about the complex balance of national security and civil rights and the impact of court decisions on the lives of U.S. citizens. In this class, Gayle has moved students past perfunctory responses to assigned reading into new engaged stances. They are building skills for academic reading: summarizing, paraphrasing, questioning, breaking down complex sentences and paragraphs to clarify meaning, analyzing word parts, and using context to support their understanding of unfamiliar words. Students work collaboratively in what has become for them the routine, ongoing work of making sense of complex texts and ideas.

As the students in this class work through their understanding of the Articles of the Constitution, they are taking responsibility for their own learning rather than taking notes from a teacher's lecture or written blackboard notes. They are learning to read a foundational historical document in U.S. history very closely—they know that not every document will need to be read with this level of attention, but that in order to engage in the coming discussions about the Supreme Court *Korematsu* decision, they will need to know and understand the exact language that the justices will use in making their arguments. As they spend sustained effort and time working through difficult terms, they are also developing the disposition to persist until they have clear enough working understandings to proceed.

At the same time, these students are learning to think historically, examining sources, cross-referencing documents to make intertextual connections, exploring the applicability of documents to specific historical circumstances, analyzing arguments and counterarguments to weigh their strengths and merits, and engaging in critical and evidence-based thinking: What is missing from this account? Whose voice is represented? Whose is missing? What is the specific evidence that the Japanese were engaged in espionage?

Among the dispositions they are developing in reading historical texts, these and other students who practice engaged academic literacy are learning what is perhaps the most important lesson of all: I can think about these things. I can have a voice.

CONCLUSION

In Will Brown's and Gayle Cribbs's classrooms, we see ways in which each teacher brings students' questions and insights into use as a classroomwide resource. In these classrooms, conversation is the central dynamic: Teacher and students discuss the cognitive strategies they use to solve comprehension problems, the structure and language of particular types of texts, and the kinds of knowledge required to make sense of reading materials. Through talk, members of a classroom community naturally make their thinking visible to one another and thereby available for reflection, reappraisal, and appropriation by others.

As we noted in beginning this chapter,

teachers send students messages about the nature of academic literacy and about their role as students through the tasks assigned to them in subject-area classes. These messages and tasks shape students' beliefs about what counts as academic learning, as well as their capacities to do rigorous discipline-based work. Rather than seeing learning chemistry as merely a process of memorizing formulas, Will's students are investigating questions that come from their efforts to make sense of challenging chemistry texts. Rather than calculating around where the answer (to the red square question) should be, as Rosa describes her experience in the beginning of the chapter, Gayle's students are grappling with complex questions across multiple texts. They have internalized the disposition to see themselves as participants in, and contributors to, a discussion of legal and ethical questions in history. With support for their developing dispositions for engaged academic literacy in specific disciplines, these students are consolidating changes in identity, capacity, and knowledge and are stepping into new roles as learners.

REFERENCES

ACT. (2006). *Reading between the lines: What the ACT reveals about college readiness in reading.* Iowa City, IA: Author.

Alexander, P. A. (2003). The development of expertise: The journey from acclimation to proficiency. *Educational Researcher, 32*(8), 10–14.

Alvermann, D. (Ed.). (2002). *Adolescents and literacies in a digital world.* New York: Peter Lang.

Bain, R. (2005). "They thought the world was flat?" Applying the principles of *How People Learn* in teaching high school history. In M. S. Donovan & J. D. Bransford (Eds.), *How students learn: History, mathematics, and science in the classroom* (pp. 179–215). Washington, DC: National Academies Press.

Baker, L. (1991). Metacognition, reading, and science education. In C. Santa & D. Alvermann (Eds.), *Science learning: Processes and applications* (pp. 179–213). Newark, DE: International Reading Association.

Bean, T. (2000). Reading in the content areas: Social constructivist dimensions. In M. L. Kamil, P. B. Mosenthal, P. D. Pearson, & R. Barr (Eds.), *Handbook of reading research* (Vol. 3, pp. 629–644). Mahwah, NJ: Erlbaum.

Berliner, D., & Biddle, B. (1995). *The manufactured*

crisis: Myth, fraud, and the attack on America's public schools. Reading, MA: Addison-Wesley.

Borasi, R., & Seigel, M. (2000). *Reading counts*. New York: Teachers College Press.

Bradley Commission on History in Schools. (1995). *Building a history curriculum: Guidelines for teaching history in schools*. Westlake, OH: National Council for History Education.

Bransford, J. D., Brown, A. L., & Cocking, R. R. (Eds.). (1999). *How people learn: Brain, mind, experience, and school*. Washington, DC: National Academies Press.

Brown, J. S., Collins, A., & Newman, S. (1989). The new cognitive apprenticeship: Teaching the crafts of reading, writing, and mathematics. In L. B. Resnick (Ed.), *Knowing, learning and instruction: Essays in honor of Robert Glaser* (pp. 453–493). Mahwah, NJ: Erlbaum.

Brush, T., & Saye, J. (2006, April). *Scaffolding critical reasoning in history and social studies: Tools to support problem-based historical inquiry*. Paper presented at the annual meeting of the American Educational Research Association, San Francisco.

Columbia American History Online, about document-based questions. Accessed July 21, 2007, at *www.caho.columbia.edu/main/dbq/index.html*.

Cuban, L. (1989). *How teachers taught: Constancy and change in America's classrooms, 1880–1980*. New York: Teachers College Press.

Davidson, J., & Koppenhaver, D. (1993). *Adolescent literacy: What works and why* (2nd ed.). New York: Garland.

Delpit, L. D. (1995). *Other people's children: Cultural conflict in the classroom*. New York: New Press.

Dweck, C., & Molden, D. (2005). Self-theories: Their impact on competence motivation and acquisition. In A. Elliot & C. Dweck (Eds.), *Handbook of competence and motivation* (pp. 122–140). New York: Guilford Press.

Feldman, A. (2004). Knowing and being in science: Expanding the possibilities. In E. W. Saul (Ed.), *Crossing borders in literacy and science instruction: Perspectives on theory and practice* (p. 144). Newark, DE: International Reading Association.

Ford, M. J., & Forman, E. S. (2006). Redefining disciplinary learning in classroom contexts. In J. Green & A. Luke (Eds.), *Rethinking learning: What counts as learning and what learning counts* (pp. 1–32). Washington, DC: American Educational Research Association.

Gee, J. P. (1996). *Social linguistics and literacies: Ideology in discourses* (2nd ed.). New York: Falmer.

Greenleaf, C., Hale, G., Charney-Sirott, I., & Schoenbach, R. (2007). *Reading apprenticeship academic literacy course*. San Francisco: WestEd.

Greenleaf, C., & Schoenbach, R. (2004). Building capacity for the responsive teaching of reading in the academic disciplines: Strategic inquiry designs for middle and high school teachers' professional development. In D. S. Strickland & M. L. Kamil (Eds.), *Improving reading achievement through professional development* (pp. 97–127). Norwood, MA: Christopher-Gordon.

Greenleaf, C., Schoenbach, R., Cziko, C., & Mueller, F. (2001). Apprenticing adolescents to academic literacy. *Harvard Educational Review, 71,* 79–129.

Guthrie, J. (2004). Classroom contexts for engaged reading: An overview. In J. T. Guthrie, A. Wigfield, & K. C. Perencevich (Eds.), *Motivating reading comprehension: Concept-oriented reading instruction* (pp. 1–24). Mahwah, NJ: Erlbaum.

Hillocks, G. (2002). *The testing trap: How state writing assessments control learning*. New York: Teachers College Press.

Holbrook, M. C., & Koenig, A. J. (2000). Literacy skills. In M. C. Holbrook & A. J. Koenig (Eds.), *Foundations of education: Vol. 2. Instructional strategies for teaching children and youths with visual impairments* (2nd ed., pp. 264–312). New York: American Foundation for the Blind.

Langer, J. (2001). Beating the odds: Teaching middle and high school students to read and write well. *American Educational Research Journal, 38,* 837–880.

Lave, J., & Wenger, E. (1991). *Situated learning: Legitimate peripheral participation*. New York: Cambridge University Press.

Lee, C. D. (1995). A culturally based cognitive apprenticeship: Teaching African American high school students skills in literary interpretation. *Reading Research Quarterly, 30,* 608–630.

Lemke, J. L. (1990). *Talking science: Language, learning, and values*. Norwood, NJ: Ablex.

Litman, C., & Greenleaf, C. (2008). Traveling together over difficult ground: Negotiating success with a profoundly inexperienced reader in an introduction to chemistry class. In K. A. Hinchman & H. Sheridan-Thomas (Eds.), *Best practices in adolescent literacy instruction* (pp. 275–296). New York: Guilford Press.

Mahiri, J., & Godley, A. (1998). Rewriting identity: Social meanings of literacy and "re-visions" of self. *Reading Research Quarterly, 33,* 416–433.

McConachie, S., Hall, M., Resnick, L., Ravi, A. K., Bill, V. L., Bintz, J., et al. (2006). Task, text, and talk: Literacy for all subjects. *Educational Leadership, 64,* 8–14.

Moje, E. B., Dillon, D. R., & O'Brien, D. G. (2000). Re-examining the roles of the learner, the text, and the context in secondary literacy. *Journal of Educational Research, 93,* 165–180.

National Institute of Child Health and Human Development. (2000). *Report of the National Reading Panel. Teaching children to read: An evidence-based assessment of the scientific research literature on reading and its implications for reading instruction* (NIH Publication No. 00-4769). Washington, DC: U.S. Government Printing Office.

National Research Council. (2004). The nature and conditions of engagement. *Engaging schools: Fostering high school students' motivation to learn*. Washington, DC: National Academies Press.

Ogle, D. (1986). K-W-L: A teaching model that develops active reading of expository text. *Reading Teacher, 39,* 564–570.

Osborne, J. (2002). Science without literacy: A ship without a sail? *Cambridge Journal of Education, 32,* 203–218.

Palincsar, A. S., & Brown, A. L. (1989). Instruction for self-regulated reading. In L. B. Resnick & L. E. Klopfer (Eds.), *Toward the thinking curriculum: Current cognitive research* (pp. 19–39). Alexandria, VA: Association for Supervision and Curriculum Development.

Pearson, P. D. (1996). Reclaiming the center. In M. Graves, P. van den Broek, & B. M. Taylor (Eds.), *The first R: Every child's right to read* (pp. 259–274). New York: Teachers College Press.

Pressley, M. (1998). *Reading instruction that works: The case for balanced teaching.* New York: Guilford Press.

RAND Reading Study Group. (2002). *Reading for understanding: Toward an R&D program in reading comprehension.* Prepared for the Office of Educational Research and Improvement. Santa Monica, CA: RAND.

Rogoff, B. (1990). *Apprenticeship in thinking: Cognitive development in social context.* New York: Oxford University Press.

Rycik, J., & Irvin, J. (Eds.). (2001). *What adolescents deserve: A commitment to students' literacy learning.* Newark, DE: International Reading Association.

Schoenbach, R., Greenleaf, C., Cziko, C., & Hurwitz, L. (1999). *Reading for understanding: A guide to improving reading in middle and high school classrooms.* San Francisco: Jossey-Bass.

Scribner, S., & Cole, M. (1981). *The psychology of literacy.* Cambridge, MA: Harvard University Press.

Snow, C., & Biancarosa, G. (2005). *Reading Next.* Washington, DC: Alliance for Excellent Education.

Stearns, P., Seixas, P., & Wineburg, S. (2004). Introduction. In P. Stearns, P. Seixas, & S. Wineburg (Eds.), *Knowing, teaching, and learning history: National and international perspectives* (pp. 1–3). New York: New York University Press.

Street, B. (1995). *Social literacies: Critical approaches to literacy in development, ethnography and education.* New York: Longman.

Wineburg, S. S. (1991). Historical problem solving: A study of cognitive processes used in the evaluation of documentary and pictorial evidence. *Journal of Educational Psychology, 83,* 73–87.

Wineburg, S. S. (2001). *Historical thinking and other unnatural acts: Charting the future of teaching the past.* Philadelphia: Temple University Press.

Wineburg, S. S., & Martin, D. (2004). Reading and rewriting history. *Educational Leadership, 62,* 42–45.

Yore, L. D. (2004). Why do future scientists need to study the language arts? In E. W. Saul (Ed.), *Crossing borders in literacy and science instruction: Perspectives on theory and practice* (pp. 71–94). Newark, DE: International Reading Association.

CHAPTER 8

Divided against Ourselves

Standards, Assessments, and Adolescent Literacy

JAMES MARSHALL

The discourse of standards and assessments has become pervasive over the last 25 years or more. In this chapter, I provide an overview of the standards movement as it has developed since *A Nation at Risk* was published in order to explore the ideological tensions that have been part of that movement from its origins. I go on to examine how standards and assessments are reshaping classroom life in contexts where literacy is taught. I conclude by describing the uncomfortable fit that has become visible as uniform standards and standardized assessments have been mapped onto research-based best practices in the teaching of the English language arts.

Standards and mandated assessments have so thoroughly dominated educational discourse for the last quarter century that we may end by labeling this part of our history—with ambivalence, perhaps—as the "standards period" (Hoffman, Paris, Salas, Patterson, & Assaf, 2002) much as we now refer to the common school period (Kaestle, 1983) or to the progressive period (Cremin, 1961; Kliebard, 1987) of American schooling. Stretching roughly from the appearance of *A Nation at Risk* in 1983 to the passage and implementation of the No Child Left Behind Act, the standards movement at this moment is shorter-lived than its predecessors, but it has proved comparably powerful in framing debates about schooling at the national, state, and local levels. Like earlier reform efforts that sought a "one best system" for efficiently building and managing schools (Kaestle, 1983; Tyack, 1974) the standards movement has invested in comprehensive, systemic strategies of educational reform (Clune, 2001; Cross, 2004; Spring, 2005). Proceeding from the belief that there is, in fact, one best system for public schooling, contemporary standards policies have envisioned a model that will work efficiently across different subject areas and local contexts. In so doing, those policies arrogantly ignore assumptions about teaching and learning deeply inscribed within the schools we already have.

Despite calls for evidence-based decision making from some proponents of standards, standards policies themselves are seldom evidence-based; that is, there is little empirical research, scientific or otherwise, that would substantiate the claim that national or state policies framed by standards and their sometimes related mandated assessments will improve student learning (Levin, 1998; Nichols, Glass, & Berliner, 2005). In fact, we have persuasive historical evidence suggesting that such large-scale, policy-driven reforms seldom work in schools as planned (Cuban, 1993; Tyack & Cuban, 1995; Tye, 2000). Rather than drawing on empirical evidence, proponents of standards policies have often rested their arguments on a specific ideological perspective about what education is for (Amrein & Berliner, 2002; Clune, 2001; Cross, 2004; Spring, 2005) and on unexamined assumptions about how students learn (Bransford, Brown, & Cocking, 2000; Bruner, 1996) and why teachers teach (Labaree, 2004; Lortie, 1975). Such assumptions have been especially problematic in the teaching of literacy because, as I argue, they often fit uncomfortably with much of what we have learned about helping students negotiate their increasingly complex literate worlds.

In this chapter, I begin with a brief narrative overview of the national standards movement as it has evolved since *A Nation at Risk*, taking an especially close look at the efforts to develop national standards for the teaching of adolescent literacy. The purpose of this review is less a rehearsal of events than an attempt to make visible the tensions that have informed the standards debate from its beginnings. I then review the research we have on how standards and assessments are affecting students, teachers, and classrooms where adolescents' literacy is the focus of instruction.

TOWARD NATIONAL STANDARDS

The Rhetoric of Crisis

As background I begin with a familiar text:

> Our Nation is at risk. Our once unchallenged preeminence in commerce, industry, science, and technological innovation is being overtaken by competitors throughout the world. This report is concerned with only one of the many causes and dimensions of the problem, but it is the one that undergirds American prosperity, security, and civility. We report to the American people that while we can take justifiable pride in what our schools and colleges have historically accomplished and contributed to the United States and the well-being of its people, the educational foundations of our society are presently being eroded by a rising tide of mediocrity that threatens our very future as a Nation and a people. What was unimaginable a generation ago has begun to oc-

cur—others are matching and surpassing our educational attainments.

> If an unfriendly foreign power had attempted to impose on America the mediocre educational performance that exists today, we might well have viewed it as an act of war. As it stands, we have allowed this to happen to ourselves. We have even squandered the gains in student achievement made in the wake of the Sputnik challenge. Moreover, we have dismantled essential support systems which helped make those gains possible. We have, in effect, been committing an act of unthinking, unilateral educational disarmament. (*A Nation at Risk*, 1983, p. 2)

Though *A Nation at Risk*, released in 1983, was only 36 pages long, it was the language in these opening paragraphs that captured attention (Cross, 2004) and that implicitly provided the rhetorical framework in which standards-based reform efforts would proceed over the next quarter century. The language explicitly makes the long-familiar argument that there is something seriously wrong with American education, but the form in which it makes that argument is worth closer scrutiny.

First, by appropriating the term "at risk" and applying it to "Our nation" instead of "students" or "children," the authors of the report effectively raise the stakes of ongoing debates about the effects of schooling while at the same time trumping any more targeted concern for populations of students who might be more "at risk" than others. As in war, when "our nation" is at risk, we cannot afford politically fractious discussions about the equitable distribution of educational resources. And it is war, and the cost of losing a war, that provides the deep metaphorical power of these paragraphs. "Our once unchallenged preeminence in commerce, industry, science, and technological innovation is being overtaken by competitors throughout the world," we are told. "A rising tide of mediocrity . . . threatens our very future as a Nation." And "If an unfriendly foreign power had attempted to impose on America the mediocre educational performance that exists today, we might well have viewed it as an act of war." As it is, the second paragraph concludes, "We have . . . been committing an act of unthinking, unilateral educational disarmament."

Such rhetorical grandeur might be appropriate for a moment when the country was, in fact, in danger of imminent attack by a foreign power. But the peculiar reality is that the opening language in *A Nation at Risk* was generated in response to some modestly shifting test results that are here linked—without evidence—to a growing economic vulnerability to "competitors throughout the world." The clearly implied argument is that American schooling is somehow to blame for America's economic slippage in comparison to other nations, that this slippage is the equivalent of war, and that the only solution is a serious national recommitment to educational excellence.

It was politically complicated, of course, for the educational community, then as now, to argue against such a recommitment or against the central importance of education to the nation's well-being. But that is precisely the point. The policies that followed from *A Nation at Risk* were from the beginning framed as issues of *national* interest rather than as reforms that would serve the *educational* interests of students and their parents (Labaree, 1997). To interrogate those policies, to marshal research evidence questioning their assumptions or their procedures, would be to stand somehow against educational excellence, against even our national stature in the world. With the debate framed in this way, the educational community often had little choice but to accept the policies' basic terms or retreat somewhat defensively into the role of criticizing high-profile reforms rather than authoring them.

In a bulleted list somewhat later in the main body of the report, the authors of *A Nation at Risk* provided some empirical support for their argument. "About 13 percent of all 17-year-olds in the United States can be considered functionally illiterate," they wrote, "[and] functional illiteracy among minority youth may run as high as 40 percent." "Average achievement of high school students on most standardized tests," they went on, "is now lower than 26 years ago when Sputnik was launched." All the report's other evidence, selectively cited, pointed in the same direction, and even though much of that evidence was later shown to be questionable at best (Berliner & Biddle, 1995), the basic argument—that American schools were failing—had

begun to take root. A crisis had been declared.

Why that crisis became the conventional wisdom and how it led eventually to the standards-based policies of No Child Left Behind requires a narrative that I can only sketch in broad outline here. But at least two significant, intersecting kinds of arguments were made on behalf of those policies—the first based on traditional forms of partisan politics, the second drawing its strength from the cultural politics that played such a large role in educational debate through much of the 1980s and 1990s.

In his history of the federal role in national educational debate, Christopher Cross (2004) documents the ways in which political calculation shaped both *A Nation at Risk* and the policies that followed from it. The *Nation at Risk* report was released near the end of Ronald Reagan's first presidential term, largely through the forceful intervention of then U.S. secretary of education Terrence Bell. Reagan had twice campaigned against the U.S. Department of Education and was especially suspicious of a cabinet-level position that his predecessor, Jimmy Carter, had established. Bell appointed the blue ribbon panel that authored the report on his own authority, largely as an effort "to shore up the department and keep it from being abolished" (Cross, 2004, p. 77). When the report was released to mostly admiring reviews—even American Federation of Teachers president Al Shanker was an initial supporter (Cross, 2004, p. 79)—Reagan embraced its message and used it strategically to disarm Democratic opponents who had traditionally claimed education as one of their core issues. Democrats, meanwhile—especially the moderate "new Democrats" personified by Bill Clinton—saw a commitment to educational excellence with a concomitant endorsement of high standards as a way of reclaiming a political middle ground that had been lost amid charges of liberal "tax-and-spend" educational policies during the presidential elections of 1984 and 1988. By the time George H. W. Bush convened a National Governors Conference on education in 1989, he was able to say that "education is not a Republican or a Democratic issue. And it's not administration versus the Governors. It's an American issue. And everyone in this room . . . is committed to educational excellence" (Cross, 2004, p. 94). Significantly, not a single educator was invited to the conference, but in his closing remarks Bush went out of his way to praise the chair of the National Governors Conference, Governor Bill Clinton of Arkansas: "Bill Clinton took on extra responsibility hammering out a statement upon which there is strong agreement. . . . I agree with Governor Clinton that [an agreement to set national standards in education] is a major step forward in education" (Cross, 2004, p. 94).

But though standards-based policy was advanced in part by conventional forms of partisan politics, it was also enabled by a quickly developing industry in the "cultural politics" documented by Cross (2004), Brock (2002), and Spring (2005). In 1987, two unlikely books appeared on the best seller lists: E. D. Hirsch's *Cultural Literacy* and Allan Bloom's *The Closing of the American Mind*. Both made widely cited arguments that echoed those of the *Nation at Risk* report: whereas American schools and colleges were once strong, rigorous, and free of politics, they have been crippled by low standards and bankrupt theories of educational practice. Also in 1987, U.S. secretary of education William Bennett proclaimed the need for teachers to inculcate a "moral literacy" in their students because those students "need reliable standards for deciding what should be prized and what should be shunned." (Bennett, 1987, p. 9) And in rapid succession other books with comparable themes (Ravitch and Finn's [1987] *What Do Our 17-Year-Olds Know?*; Dinesh D'Souza's [1991] *Illiberal Education*) began to appear, usually with the financial support of policy foundations whose avowed goals included the advancement of deeply conservative approaches to the reform of American schooling (Brock, 2002; Spring, 2005).

By the early 1990s, then, the politically constructed reality of a national educational decline—a crisis—had become the framing assumption in policy debates about schooling, and the ground had been prepared for the development of national standards across school subjects that would address that decline. It is to the story of that development in adolescent literacy education that I now turn.

National Standards for the English Language Arts

Soon after the National Governors Conference on Education, Lamar Alexander, then U.S. secretary of education, in cooperation with Diane Ravitch, then of the Office of Educational Research and Improvement, began to use discretionary funds from the Education Department to support the development of national standards in school subject areas (Cross, 2004). The initial model for those standards was that independently developed by the National Council of Teachers of Mathematics (NCTM) in 1989. As Cross (2004) reports, "For months after he became Secretary, Alexander would invariably take a copy of the NCTM standards with him when he made a speech, to illustrate that it was possible to create good standards" (p. 103).

That national standards for mathematics were the first to appear is significant in several ways. First, because NCTM developed those standards in professional independence from federal funding and oversight, the authors were able to draw from their own research and best practice traditions without specific reference to the political demands of national policymakers. More important, perhaps, the developers of the NCTM standards were working within a subject area that could be relatively well defined by specific academic content. Subject areas that could not be so readily defined—such as English language arts and social studies—would thus have difficulty using the NCTM standards as a model.

In their extraordinarily useful research in this area, Grossman and Stoldosky (1994, 1995) have demonstrated how school subjects differ in their perceived curricular status (science, say, versus music), their perceived sequentiality (foreign language versus social studies), and their coherence and scope (mathematics versus the English language arts). Literacy and social studies education, for example, sample broadly across a range of texts and disciplinary boundaries, whereas mathematics and chemistry are more circumscribed by professional consensus about what counts as content knowledge in the subject. In their research, Grossman and Stoldosky (1995) report that English language arts teachers often spoke of the "permissive" and "negotiable" nature of their subject, affording them a fairly wide latitude in choosing the texts and practices that would compose their teaching. Math teachers, on the other hand, spoke of the "constraints" of the curriculum and of the need for "coverage" (p. 7). Such differences, Grossman and Stoldosky argue, in large measure account for different "conceptual cultures" for teachers across the disciplines—cultures that may reshape and refract comprehensive reform efforts that attempt to cut across those disciplines.

The initiative to develop national standards across the subject areas was, of course, such a comprehensive reform effort, and when the National Council of Teachers of English (NCTE) was granted funds to write national standards in the early 1990s, the organization was almost immediately presented with issues of its own "conceptual culture" and how readily the imperatives of federal policymakers could be mapped onto that culture. The story of how the original, federally funded project in Standards for the English Language Arts proceeded, and of how that project segued into the development of the NCTE/IRA (International Reading Association) standards that we now have, is both complicated and politically charged. John Mayher (1999), in a thoughtfully candid essay, has provided a helpful perspective on how the NCTE/IRA standards evolved after the U.S. Department of Education withdrew funding from the original NCTE project. But I would like to offer a perspective on what happened *before* the federal withdrawal: The earlier part of the story brings into specific relief some of the tensions that continue to inform the debate about standards in the teaching of adolescent literacy.

For the record, I served as executive secretary of the High School Task Force charged with developing secondary-level standards in the English language arts from mid-1993 to the end of 1994. I was delighted to receive the invitation to participate because I believed then, as I still do, that NCTE was the best source of wisdom on how to teach literacy across the grade levels, and that the alternatives—one of the foundations funding the work of Ravitch, Finn, and D'Souza, for example—were unacceptable. Along with Denny Palmer Wolf, who served as executive

secretary of the middle school group, and Bernice Cullinan, who served with the elementary group, I met regularly with the teacher-chairs of the three grade-level task forces, with project leaders Miles Myers and David Pearson, and with a moderately large, but carefully selected group of seasoned teachers and university-based faculty members.

Rather than provide a chronology of events during the project, I focus here on four interrelated themes that informed our discussions throughout the project—recurring questions that were seldom satisfactorily answered although they were often addressed. What follows is based on my papers and notes from the time and on conversations with fellow participants in the years since.

Curricular Sequence

One of the first questions all of the task forces faced was whether our group was organized in ways that would advance the development of meaningful, high-quality standards. Organizing by grade level provided a certain face validity, and given the way schools are structured and the way teaching expertise is distributed, we soon realized that the literacy practices we were most committed to teaching and the pedagogies we were most committed to enact in our classrooms could not be so easily separated. One of our most basic theoretical assumptions as literacy educators was that literacy skills (the development of narrative and argumentative discourse, for example, or the comprehension of written texts) grow and elaborate recursively as students mature and as they are invited into new discursive environments—new "curricular conversations" (Applebee, 1996). It was unclear, given this conceptual frame, whether developing goals or standards for younger students separately from developing goals for adolescent learners made much sense. Moreover, there was significant overlap across grade-level groups in the teaching strategies to which we were most committed—strategies that favored having students read and write for a range of purposes and with a range of choices depending on the classroom context (e.g., Atwell, 1988; Beach & Marshall, 1990; Graves, 1983). When we gathered as a whole group to compare our progress, we were continually struck by the similarities of our efforts, but we were also implicitly aware that the Department of Education was looking for standards that clearly specified a curricular sequence—just as the NCTM standards had done. Our conversations on this issue were complicated by the second theme that emerged.

Curricular Content

The problem of defining a curricular content in the standards was more pronounced for the high school and middle school groups than for the elementary school group because as students enter secondary schools, the curriculum often shifts rather sharply away from the direct teaching of literacy processes and practices to the teaching of specific literary texts and specific modes of writing. Applebee's studies of literature teaching in secondary schools (1993) and his earlier studies of writing in secondary schools (1981, 1984) had documented the relative stability and consistency of teaching practices across secondary literacy classrooms—with 10 novels, for instance, dominating the teaching of literature in high schools and the five-paragraph argumentative essay as the standard mode of extensive writing. But our groups tended to see such sometimes uncritical consistency as a problem to be solved rather than as a model to be embodied in the standards. We were distinctly committed to enlarging the scope of what students read, talked about, and wrote about in their literacy classrooms, and the project of naming specific texts, authors, or even literary genres that secondary students *must* read, or of outlining a scope and sequence chart for writing instruction, seemed an act of both intellectual and political arrogance. Because members of our group were intentionally drawn from different parts of the country and from urban, suburban, and rural contexts, we realized early on that arriving at consensus on specific curricular content was unlikely even if we chose to try—a conclusion that was reinforced in discussions around a third theme.

Diversity

Just as we interrogated the organization of the NCTE project by grade levels, several members of our group also questioned the name given to the project as a whole. By foregrounding the term "English Language Arts" to label our project, these members felt we were implicitly privileging the set of conventional practices associated with "English teaching" while ignoring the other linguistic resources—languages, dialects, modes of expression—that students may bring with them to the classroom (e.g., Lee, 1993). Discussions often returned to the issue of whether mastery of "standard English" or "world English" should be embedded in the literacy standards, and if so how such mastery would be demonstrated by students from highly diverse backgrounds. Here again our conversation was inflected not only by a respect for the rich differences in literacy practices across cultural contexts, but also by our growing sense that we ourselves were separated by very different experiences in schools and by widely varying firsthand knowledge of diverse classrooms. Those of us from the more rural Midwest (I was among this group) had often spent much of our research and teaching time in classrooms where students were mostly English-only speakers and often quite similar in their racial and cultural backgrounds. Those of us from urban settings in California, however, brought to our discussions a keen experiential understanding of what working with diverse student populations means—what it requires and what it provides. It was often difficult to talk around these very different senses of what classrooms "normally" look like and how national standards, no matter how spacious in conception, could accommodate the diversity that was increasingly visible to us.

Opportunities to Learn

Early on in the national push to develop standards across subject areas, there was some discussion at the federal level of tying achievement standards to "opportunity to learn" standards. As Cross (2004) explains, "The logic behind opportunity to learn standards was that neither schools nor students should be held responsible for learning if schools do not have the resources to teach their students the material that would be assessed" (p. 101). Though Cross goes on to argue that this was "a simple, common sense concept," it was not given funding priority and soon disappeared from legislative deliberations because "critics across the political spectrum saw it as something schools would use to avoid accountability" (p. 102). This central, common-sense concept was very much a theme in our task force discussions however. The widely varying material resources available to schools and teachers across the country (Nichols et al., 2005; Snow & Biancarosa, 2003)—conditions that included everything from the number of books available in a teacher workroom to the average number of students in classes to the condition of plumbing fixtures in school buildings—argued strongly for standards that would specify and policies that would enforce the development of equitable learning opportunities for students. But developing such standards was not part of our charge, and we were often halted by a concern that the standards we were developing might be willfully unfair and practically useless to teachers and students working in seriously underfunded conditions.

These themed discussions did not so much hamper the work of the task forces; instead, I think, they taught us what our work was. As a group, we learned together that we could not easily map our subject area onto the sometimes procrustean expectations of policymakers without compromising some important aspects of our professional identity and professional commitments. And in learning that, we also learned that our central commitment—the enhancement of our students' literacy powers from early childhood through adulthood—would not be well served by standards that fit the implied federal profile. Gerald Graff (1987), in his history of literary study in the United States, argues that "theory is what is generated when some aspects of literature, its nature, its history, its place in society, its conditions of production and reception . . . cease to be given and become a question to be argued in a generalized way" (p. 252). If we substitute "literacy teaching" for "literature" in Graff's formulation, I would argue that the NCTE Task Force members charged with developing national standards in literacy were, in fact, theorizing literacy and literacy teaching. The national standards project helped us define who we were by teaching us what we were not.

By the end of 1994, our groups had produced prototype standards that were in many

respects similar to the NCTE/IRA standards we now have. But by that point, it was too late. Because our draft standards were not at all similar to the NCTM standards in their specificity or their sequence, the Department of Education withdrew its funding from the project. Because NCTE and IRA jointly understood that articulating a broad and intellectually generous vision of literacy teaching was important, the work of developing national standards were taken over by the two organizations.

As an ironic coda to the entire process of developing national standards across subject areas, it was recently announced (Lewin, 2006) that the national mathematics standards—the ones meant to demonstrate that "it was possible to develop good standards" (Cross, 2004)—had been significantly revised. The new standards, developed in response to mandated testing, call for elementary math teachers to focus on just three basic skills. Chester Finn, of the conservative Fordham Foundation, observed, "This is definitely a back-to-basics victory . . . moving away from the constructivist approach some educators prefer in which children learn what they want to learn when they're ready to learn it" (Lewin, 2006). It was such a conclusion, I think, that we who served on the NCTE project imagined for our own standards if we had somehow "succeeded" in developing them for federal policymakers.

At the same time that national standards in several school subjects were being developed with support from Washington in the early 1990s, states were developing their own standards and related assessments. I turn now to a discussion of those standards and assessments and of the research we have that examines their effects on adolescents and their teachers.

STATE STANDARDS AND MANDATED ASSESSMENTS

Again as background, I begin with a close reading of a text—this one less familiar than *A Nation at Risk,* but increasingly more common.

ELA9RL1 The student demonstrates comprehension by identifying evidence (e.g., diction, imagery, point of view, figurative language, symbolism, plot events and main ideas) in a variety of texts representative of different genres (e.g., poetry, prose [short story, novel, essay, editorial, biography], and drama) and using this evidence as the basis for interpretation.

The language here is drawn from the Georgia Performance Standards—a state document that seeks to specify what students should know and be able to do in their language arts classes across the grade levels. This particular excerpt, chosen almost at random, is part of the Reading and Composition series for ninth grade. In its syntax, vocabulary, and tone it is nearly identical to other standards in the document.

If the opening paragraphs of *A Nation at Risk* seemed freighted with rhetorical excess, the language of this standard and its counterparts are marked by an almost painful opacity. In its syntactic accumulation of nouns ("diction, imagery, point of view . . . poetry prose, [short story, novel] . . ."), the standard seems less a clearly stated goal for students and their teachers than a compendium of literary terms. Stripped of its parenthetical examples, the basic sentence seems straightforward enough: "The student demonstrates comprehension by identifying evidence . . . in a variety of texts representative of different genres . . . and using this evidence as the basis for interpretation." But its key terms, "comprehension" and "interpretation," are left undefined, and its key assumption—that acts of interpretation provide evidence of comprehension—remains oddly unexamined. Both the comprehension and interpretation of texts are shaped by a wide range of cultural, historical, and autobiographical factors (Fish, 1980; Graff, 1987; Rosenblatt, 1978) as well as by a reader's reasons for reading at any particular moment. But the relationship between the two is neither simple nor linear, which is why the work of literature teachers is so complicated.

It might be argued that texts like this standard should not be put under the kind of interrogative scrutiny I have tried to bring here, but I contend exactly the opposite. Because these standards have a performative power—they are not descriptions but governmental mandates—the language in which they are framed must be clearly and carefully considered. If standards do not examine their own assumptions, if they leave their own key terms undefined, then they model for teachers and students the very kind of low-level literacy practices that the state standards themselves are meant to improve.

Not everyone sees the Georgia Performance Standards in this way, however. Sandra Stotsky, in her 2005 ranking of state standards in English for the Thomas Fordham Foundation, reported that the Georgia standards ranked seventh in the country for their clarity and rigor. Stotsky also commends the Georgia standards because they are "measurable," and it is the measurement of student achievement on state literacy standards, rather than the language of the standards themselves, that has drawn the most widespread research interest.

The Effects of High-Stakes Literacy Assessments

Since 2002, discussions about standards and mandated assessments have usually made reference to the federal No Child Left Behind Act (NCLB). But, as suggested above, the development of standards and high-stakes assessments at the state level was well underway before the federal act became law. Much of the relevant research and policy analysis has focused on these state-level initiatives.

In their examination of the political context in which state assessments have been developed, for example, Hoffman et al. (2002), citing specific data from Texas and Michigan, distinguish between the "illusion" of the tests' positive effects and the evidence that undermines those claims. The illusion, Hoffman et al. argue, is that "students are learning to read and write better" because of high-stakes assessments, whereas the evidence suggests instead that for many students "the consequences of testing are neutral or negative" (p. 626). Likewise, test proponents suggest that "teachers will teach better because they are held directly responsible for student learning," whereas the research suggests that "as the pressure to increase test scores rises, teachers are more likely to employ such practices as teaching to the test, using test preparation materials, and even cheating" (p. 626). Instead of bringing "coherence and order to the reading/language arts curriculum," Hoffman and his colleagues argue, high-stakes tests "fragment" the curriculum, and by removing responsibility for instructional decision making from teachers, diminish teaching effectiveness itself. Ironically, the process of assessment in literacy is itself damaged by high-stakes assessments because such assessments marginalize or even replace more nuanced, complex, and authentic efforts to evaluate student learning (p. 627). Amrein and Berliner (2002) reached similar conclusions in their study of high-stakes testing programs in 18 states. Even when higher scores were reported in these states, Amrein and Berliner argue, the increase was often "the result of test preparation and/or exclusion of students from the testing process" (p. 1).

Part of the problem, as Taylor (1994) suggests, is that states, under pressure to document the success of reform efforts, have encountered an unarticulated tension. Policymakers, Taylor argues, are "demanding assessments that will serve two incompatible purposes: (a) determining whether students are achieving . . . desired standards of performance and (b) providing relative measurements of students, schools, districts, and states on scales of achievement" (p. 232). The National Assessment of Education Progress, for example, does an excellent job of providing normative data on different student populations in different regions of the country across time. But it cannot provide useful information about specific districts, schools, or students because it was never designed for such a project (Applebee, 1999). A valid "standards model" of assessment, Taylor (1994) argues, will require teachers to have strong subject matter knowledge and pedagogical strategies "that help students approach each discipline in appropriate ways" (p. 256). This can happen only if teachers can engage in "ongoing professional development with the disciplines they teach" (p. 256) and if the tests that measure student learning are tied directly to the goals of reform.

A small number of exemplary studies have examined more specifically the effects of high-stakes testing on the teaching of writing, on the teaching of literature, and on teachers themselves. George Hillocks, in *The Testing Trap* (2002), provides the most detailed and comprehensive evidence. Drawing upon his in-depth study of writing assessments in five states, Hillocks argues that most of the state legislation mandating assessments assumes that such assessments "are the only necessary reform" (p. 36). They assume, in other words, that "ineffective teaching and learning is a problem of moral deficiency and that testing will prompt both students and teachers to greater effort" (p. 36). By contrastively studying writing standards, writing prompts, assessment scoring guides, and benchmark papers, Hillocks demonstrates that sample papers offered as "exemplary" in the scoring guides effectively lower the standards that are meant to be measured (p. 74). In this way, the theoretical universe of discourse informing the standards is "substantially reduced to the point where it deals with only a fraction of that universe" (p. 70). Ketter and Pool (2001), in their fine-grained analysis of high-stakes writing assessment in one school, found that the state's tests had privileged psychometric measures of reliability and validity over what they call "consequential validity" (p. 383). The researchers interrogate the belief in the "neutral and universal nature of the [writing prompts]" and argue that the tests "minimize teachers' ability to engage in reflective practice that is sensitive to the needs of individual students" (p. 383). Both Hillocks' and Ketter and Pool's research, in other words, suggests that high-stakes testing, far from motivating or underwriting thoughtful writing instruction, is actually diminishing the possibility that such instruction will occur.

Comparable evidence comes from studies that focus on the effects of high-stakes testing on the teaching of literature to adolescents. Anagnostopoulos (2003, 2005), for example, in a project that closely examined the practices of both an early-career and an experienced teacher of literature found that high-stakes tests "endorse narrow definitions of reading that work against, rather than support, efforts to raise standards and improve students' learning opportunities in urban schools" (2003, p. 205). Like Hillocks (2002), Anagnostopoulos critically observes what happens to the goals represented by standards when they are instantiated in assessment questions and scoring rubrics. In the end, Anagnostopoulos (2003) found that "pressure emanating from the district testing policies led the teachers to take up the definition of reading as text reproduction and to position their students as minimally skilled readers" (p. 191). In an earlier qualitative study, Zancanella (1992) found that changes in literature teachers' practices were dependent on the "fit" between the teachers' conception of literature teaching and the conception embodied in the test, and on the amount of "curricular power" the teachers had to resist the pressures of the test. "To fully understand conflicts between tests and teachers," Zancanella argues, "one must study teachers as well as tests" (p. 293). Rex and Nelson (2004), in their study of two high school English teachers responding to mandated assessments, echo Zancanella's conclusions. Though the teachers were verbally committed to high-stakes test accountability, their own professional identities and the teaching practices associated with those identities led them to "render test preparation to a subordinate position" (p. 1). Rex and Nelson show that, for these teachers, "sustaining the integrity of their professionalism and their personal beliefs" (p. 16) had a greater impact in shaping their teaching than the mandates of the test.

Taken together, these studies of the effects of high-stakes assessment on literacy teaching, like the history of efforts to establish top-down standards for literacy learning, provide a potent reminder of a powerful tension. There is a serious incompatibility between the current standards and assessment movement and our long-established, research-supported best practices in the teaching of literacy. As a field, we do, in fact, face a crisis—though not the kind described in *A Nation at Risk*.

Divided against Ourselves

Current standards and assessment policies have presented literacy educators with several dilemmas at once. As a professional community, we teach the language arts to adolescents, we prepare others for such teaching, and we study the ways adolescents learn and practice literacies in and out of school contexts. Though these projects are often very different in the kinds of work they call for, they have been broadly consonant in their vision of literacy teaching and literacy learning (Applebee, 1999). It is a vision embodied—ironically, under the circumstances—

within the national standards developed by NCTE and IRA about a decade ago.

But that general consensus is being fractured by competing commitments. On one hand, college and university-based teacher preparation programs in adolescent literacy education have largely been informed by research that supports complex, nuanced, and dialogic approaches to teaching practice and that encourages multiple, teacher-designed forms of formative and summative assessment. The pressures of mandated standards and high-stakes assessments, on the other hand, have changed the context in which our teacher candidates will work (Altwerger et al., 2004; Smagorinsky, Lakly, & Johnson, 2002; Valli & Rennert-Ariev, 2002; Zigo, 2001). Though teacher preparation in literacy education has always been challenged by a theory–practice tension, we are now confronted in many schools with assessment policies that directly undermine the teaching and evaluation practices we have long endorsed. The question becomes whether we prepare students to teach comfortably in school cultures that are being reshaped by assessment intensification or attempt to provide them with tools with which they might resist or work around that intensification. The former approach might betray some of our most central professional commitments, whereas the latter would ask young teachers to make difficult, potentially damaging professional decisions near the beginning of their careers.

But we face another important dilemma as well. Theoretical and empirical work exploring new, digital, multimodal literacies across a range of contexts has grown exponentially over the last decade (e.g., Alvermann, 2002; Gee, 2003; Kist, 2005). Such research has expanded our conception of the forms literacies can take, but it has also demonstrated the potential of new media to extend the range and sophistication of our students' literacy practices (Kist, 2005). As I have tried to argue here, however, standards and assessment policies in many school contexts are both narrowing the curriculum and restricting the resources teachers can draw upon in working with students. In other words, at the very moment when a wealth of powerful new literacy tools are being made available—tools that would enlarge and complicate students' own conceptions of literacy—the standards and assessment policies I've overviewed here are implicitly discouraging their exploration in classrooms. Our research in new literacy studies will continue to grow, of course, but we have to ask how such research will become relevant and useful to teachers working in environments where test-driven priorities are increasingly dominant.

SUGGESTED RESEARCH

These dilemmas will not go away soon, but here I suggest three kinds of research that might inform both our understanding of current standards and assessment policies and our ongoing dialogue with those who author those policies.

First, I think we need more local, state, and multistate studies of how standards and assessments are shaping literacy teaching and literacy learning among adolescents. Hillocks (2002) and Anagnostopoulos (2003) provide excellent models for such work, for by tracing how the curricular impact of standards is transformed as standards are instantiated in assessment exercises and then in scoring guides and benchmark performances, Hillocks and Anagostopoulos provide detailed empirical evidence that complicates and deflates the claims made by policymakers about the power of standards to improve student learning. The argument against current policies cannot rest on students' relative achievement on high-stakes assessments because that achievement has significance only when we know in detail how students' performance was prompted and how it was measured.

Second, I think we need more qualitative studies of how standards and high-stakes assessment are shaping the professional lives of teachers. Zancanella (1992) and Rex and Nelson (2004) provide useful models here, but this kind of inquiry can also animate teacher research in local and district contexts (Zigo, 2001). Such research would not be directly concerned with the effects of standards and assessments on student achievement. It would focus, rather, on the way *teachers* are affected by current mandates. How do these mandates affect teachers' understanding of their work? How do they affect their conceptions of their own profes-

sional identities? How are they reshaping their reasons for teaching? To what extent are they contributing to the number of teachers who leave teaching after only a few years?

Finally, I think we need to examine how current standards and assessment policies are affecting the recruitment of those who have chosen to become classroom teachers (Altwerger et al., 2004; Luna, Solsken, & Kutz, 2000; Smagorinsky et al., 2002). If one of the major attractions of teaching literacy to adolescents has been the opportunity such work offers for independence and professional judgment (Grossman & Stodolsky, 1995; Protherough & Atkinson, 1992), then we might expect fewer students or different kinds of students to be recruited as the conditions for such professional autonomy disappear from schools. If the teaching of adolescent literacy is changing in fundamental ways, then we should probably anticipate that the population attracted to our profession will change as well.

The generation-long educational discussion that began with *A Nation at Risk* has resulted in far-reaching policy initiatives that are recasting almost every aspect of schooling, and that are also reshaping how adolescent literacy is taught, how it is measured, and how, in fact, it will be defined in classrooms. The stakes are high not only for our students as they confront newly mandated assessments, they are high for us as we confront a movement that challenges so many dimensions of our professional lives.

REFERENCES

Altwerger, B., Arya, P., Jin, L., Jordan, N. L., Laster, B., Martens, P., et al. (2004). When research and mandates collide: The challenges and dilemmas of teacher education in the era of NCLB. *English Education, 36,* 119–133.

Alvermann, D. (2002). *Adolescents and literacies in a digital world.* New York: Peter Lang.

Amrein, A. L., & Berliner, D. C. (2002). *High-stakes testing, uncertainty, and student learning.* Education Policy Analysis Archives. Retrieved August 13, 2006, from *epaa.asu.edu/epaa/v10n18/.*

Anagnostopoulos, D. (2003). Testing and student engagement with literature in urban classrooms: A multi-layered perspective. *Research in the Teaching of English, 38,* 177–212.

Anagnostopoulos, D. (2005). Testing, tests, and classroom texts. *Journal of Curriculum Studies, 37,* 35–63.

Applebee, A. N. (1981). *Teaching writing in the secondary school: English and the content areas.* Urbana, IL: National Council of Teachers of English.

Applebee, A. N. (1984). *Contexts for learning to write.* Norwood, NJ: Ablex.

Applebee, A. N. (1993). *Literature in the secondary school: Studies of curriculum and instruction in the United States.* Urbana, IL: National Council of Teachers of English.

Applebee, A. N. (1996). *Curriculum as conversation: Transforming traditions of teaching and learning.* Chicago: University of Chicago Press.

Applebee, A. N. (1999). Building a foundation for effective teaching and learning of English. *Research in the Teaching of English, 33,* 352–366.

Atwell, N. (1988). *In the middle: New understandings about writing, reading, and learning.* Portsmouth, NH: Heinemann.

Beach, R., & Marshall, J. (1990). *Teaching literature in the secondary school.* New York: Harcourt, Brace, Jovanovich.

Bennett, W. (1987, February). *Moral literacy.* Speech presented at the annual meeting of the California Association of Teachers of English, San Diego, CA.

Berliner, D. C., & Biddle, B. J. (1995). *The manufactured crisis: Myths, fraud, and the attack on American schools.* Cambridge, MA: Perseus Books.

Bloom, A. (1987). *The closing of the American mind: How higher education has failed democracy and impoverished the souls of today's students.* New York: Simon & Schuster.

Bransford, J. D., Brown, A. L., & Cocking, R. R. (2000). *How people learn: Brain, mind, experience, and school.* Washington, DC: National Academy Press.

Brock, D. (2002). *Blinded by the right.* New York: Three Rivers Press.

Bruner, J. (1996). *The culture of education.* Cambridge, MA: Harvard University Press.

Clune, W. H. (2001). Toward a theory of standards-based reform. In S. H. Fuhrman (Ed.), *From the capital to the classroom: Standards-based reform in the states. The One-Hundredth Yearbook of the National Society for the Study of Education* (pp. 13–38). Chicago: University of Chicago Press.

Cremin, L. A. (1961). *The transformation of the school: Progressivism in American education.* New York: Vintage Books.

Cross, C. T. (2004). *Political education.* New York: Teachers College Press.

Cuban, L. (1993). *How teachers taught: Constancy and change in American classrooms* (2nd ed.). New York: Teachers College Press.

D'Souza, D. (1991). *Illiberal education: The politics of race and sex on campus.* New York: Free Press.

Fish, S. (1980). *Is there a text in this class? The authority of interpretive communities.* Cambridge, MA: Harvard University Press.

Gee, J. (2003). *What video games have to teach us about learning and literacy.* New York: Palgrave Macmillan.

Georgia Performance Standards. Retrieved July 10, 2006, from *www.georgiastandards.org/.*

Graff, G. (1987). *Professing literature.* Chicago: University of Chicago Press.

Graves, D. (1983). *Writing: Teachers and students at work.* Portsmouth, NH: Heinemann.

Grossman, P., & Stodolsky, S. S. (1994). Considerations of content and the circumstances of secondary school teaching. *Review of Research in Education, 20,* 179–221.

Grossman, P., & Stodolsky, S. S. (1995). Content as context: The role of school subjects in secondary school teaching. *Educational Researcher, 24,* 5–11.

Hillocks, G. (2002). *The testing trap: How state writing assessments control learning.* New York. Teachers College Press.

Hirsch, E. D. (1987). *Cultural literacy: What every American needs to know.* Boston: Houghton Mifflin.

Hoffman, J. V., Paris, S. G., Salas, R., Patterson, E., & Assaf, L. (2002). High-stakes assessment in the language arts: The piper plays, the players dance, but who pays the price? In J. Flood, D. Lapp, J. R. Squire, & J. Jensen (Eds.), *Handbook of research on teaching the English language arts* (pp. 619–630). Mahwah, NJ: Erlbaum.

Kaestle, C. F. (1983). *Pillars of the republic: Common schools and American society 1780–1860.* New York: Hill & Wang.

Ketter, J., & Pool, J. (2001). Exploring the impact of a high-stakes direct writing assessment in two high school classrooms. *Research in the Teaching of English, 35,* 344–393.

Kist, W. (2005). *New literacies in action: Learning and teaching in multiple media.* New York: Teachers College Press.

Kliebard, H. M. (1987). *The struggle for the American curriculum 1893–1958.* New York: Routledge.

Labaree, D. F. (1997). Public goods, private goods: The American struggle over educational goals. *American Educational Research Journal, 34,* 39–81.

Labaree, D. F. (2004). *The trouble with ed schools.* New Haven, CT: Yale University Press.

Lee, C. D. (1993). *Signifying as a scaffold for literature interpretation: The pedagogical implications of an African American discourse genre.* Urbana, IL: National Council of Teachers of English.

Levin, H. M. (1998). Educational performance standards and the economy. *Educational Researcher, 27,* 4–10.

Lewin, T. (2006) *Report urges changes in the teaching of math in U.S. schools.* Retrieved September 13, 2006, from *www.nytimes.com.*

Lortie, D. (1975). *Schoolteacher: A sociological study.* Chicago: University of Chicago Press.

Luna, C., Solsken, J., & Kutz, E. (2000). Defining literacy: Lessons from high-stakes teacher testing. *Journal of Teacher Education, 51,* 276–288.

Mayher, J. (1999). Reflections on standards and standard setting: An insider/outsider perspective on the NCTE/IRA standards. *English Education, 31,* 106–121.

A Nation at Risk. (1983). Retrieved July 15, 2007, from *www.goalline.org/goal%20line/natatrisk.html.*

NCTE/IRA standards in the English language arts. Retrieved September 15, 2007, from *www.ncte.org.*

Nichols, S. L., Glass, G. V., & Berliner, D. C. (2005). *High-stakes testing and student achievement: Problems for the No Child Left Behind Act.* Educational Policy Studies Laboratory, Boulder, CO. Retrieved August 2, 2006, from *http://epicpolicy.org.*

Protherough, R., & Atkinson, J. (1992). How English teachers see English teaching. *Research in the Teaching of English, 26,* 385–407.

Ravitch, D., & Finn, C. E. (1987). *What do our 17-year-olds know?* New York: Harper & Row.

Rex, L. A., & Nelson, M. (2004). How teachers' professional identities position high-stakes test preparation in their classrooms. *Teachers College Record, 106,* 1288–1331.

Rosenblatt, L. (1978). *The reader, the text, the poem: The transactional theory of literacy work.* Carbondale, IL: Southern Illinois University Press.

Smagorinsky, P., Lakly, A., & Johnson, T. S. (2002). Acquiescence, accommodation, and resistance in learning to teach within a prescribed curriculum. *English Education, 34,* 187–213.

Snow, C. E., & Biancarosa, G. (2003). *Adolescent literacy and the achievement gap: What do we know and where do we go from here: A report to the Carnegie Corporation of New York.* New York: Carnegie Corporation.

Spring, J. (2005). *Political agendas for education.* Mahwah, NJ: Erlbaum.

Stotsky, S. (2005). *The state of state English standards: A report to the Thomas Fordham Foundation.* Retrieved August 16, 2006, at *www.edexcellence.net/foundation/global.*

Taylor, C. (1994). Assessment for measurement or standards: The peril and promise of large-scale assessment reform. *American Educational Research Journal, 31,* 231–262.

Tyack, D. B. (1974). *The one best system: A history of American urban education.* Cambridge, MA: Harvard University Press.

Tyack, D., & Cuban, L. (1995). *Tinkering toward utopia: A Century of public school reform.* Cambridge, MA: Harvard University Press.

Tye, B. B. (2000). *Hard truths: Uncovering the deep structure of schooling.* New York: Teachers College Press.

Valli, L., & Rennert-Ariev (2002). New standards and assessments? Curriculum transformations in teacher education. *Journal of Curriculum Studies, 32,* 201–225.

Zancanella, D. (1992). The influence of state-mandated assessments on teachers of literature. *Educational Evaluation and Policy Analysis, 14,* 283–295.

Zigo, D. (2001). Constructing firebreaks against high-stakes testing. *English Education, 2,* 214–232.

CHAPTER 9

Adolescent Second-Language Writing

LINDA HARKLAU

RACHEL PINNOW

Second-language writing is a relatively new field drawing from second-language acquisition and composition studies. Most of the work to date has focused on the college level, and research specifically addressing adolescent second- and foreign language writing remains sparse, characterized by isolated studies with few sustained threads of inquiry. This chapter is organized around what we know about three major questions about adolescent second-language writing. We first address whether and how adolescent second-language writing might be different from first-language writing in terms of text and discourse features and composing and editing processes. We then consider what the research tells us about how second-language writing develops in adolescents as a function of age and proficiency. Next we identify major issues in adolescent second-language writing instruction, including the frequency and quality of second-language writing instruction; the role of first-language in second-language writing instruction; the integration of bilingual writers into monolingual writing classrooms; the relationship between second-language writing and content learning; linking second-language writing instruction to adolescents' home and community experiences; implications of Internet and communication technologies for adolescent second-language writing; and assessment. We conclude with an agenda for further research and implications of second-language writing research for adolescent literacy studies.

America's youth today are the most linguistically and culturally diverse in U.S. history. One in five is an immigrant or the child of immigrants. As in other industrialized societies around the world, "Millenial" youth in the United States are increasingly multilingual. They take for granted the digital technologies that have made worldwide communication so immediate and accessible. In an age of globalization, this generation of adolescents is more and more likely to write across languages and cultures. Yet scholarship has barely begun to investigate how adolescence might lend distinctive linguistic, cognitive, developmental, and sociocultural characteristics to second-language (L2) writing. In fact, we believe this may be the first comprehensive review of research specifically on adolescent second-language writing.

The field of second-language writing is a relatively new one, with one foot in applied linguistics and second-language acquisition and the other in composition studies (Matsuda, 1998; Silva & Leki, 2004). The majority of work in this field to date has focused on the college level (see, e.g., Canagarajah,

2002; Ferris & Hedgcock, 2005; Leki, 2007; Schecter & Harklau, 1992). Our review finds that research on adolescent second- and foreign language writing remains sparse (Parks, Huot, Hamers, & Lemonnier, 2005; Roca de Larios, Murphy, & Marín, 2002). Much of the literature consists of essays on curricular approaches that are not included in this review. Only a small proportion of extant work on adolescent L2 writing is based on systematic theoretical or empirical inquiry, and much more work in this vein is needed; we indicate below the directions future inquiry might take. Many studies have featured adolescent L2 writers incidentally, but we have yet to address potentially unique aspects of this age group (see, e.g., Abu-Rabia, 2003; Lee, 2004; Pennington, Brock, & Yue, 1996; Sengupta, 2000; Wong et al., 1994, for studies of writing process; Clachar, 2004; de Courcy, 2002; Dyer & Friederich, 2002; Gamaroff, 2000; Makinen, 1992; Montano-Harmon, 1991; Schoonen et al., 2003; Way, Joiner, & Seaman, 2000, for studies of written texts; and Franken & Haslett, 2002; Ghahremani-Ghajar & Mirhosseini, 2005; Shaw, 1997; Tsang, 1996, for studies of the effects of L2 writing contexts). In addition, even though adolescents in secondary school foreign language classes are perhaps the single largest population of L2 writers both in the United States and internationally (see, e.g., Rijlaarsdam, 2002; Taylor, Lazarus, & Cole, 2005), we need considerably more research on these contexts (O'Brien, 2004). Finally, the second languages examined in studies remain extremely limited. English was the second-language medium in 85% of the studies we reviewed. Ten percent focused on French L2 writing, and only 5% focused on other languages. Work is especially needed on adolescent L2 writing in non-European languages or non-Roman script systems.

Although the notion of "adolescence" itself is rightfully contested (Harklau, 2007; Vadeboncoeur & Stevens, 2005), here we define it as corresponding to middle and high school in the United States, or approximately 12–18 years of age. We also wish to note that although we use the terms *second language* (or L2) and *foreign language* here, in keeping with established usage in the field, the terms are also somewhat limiting, and studies of adolescent L2 writing are in-

creasingly moving to a more complex "multicompetence" perspective on multilingual students' use of language (Cook, 2002; Ortega, 2006). For example, in multilingual contexts such as Hong Kong, English is rarely a first language but is so widely used that it cannot be considered a second or foreign language (Sengupta, 2000). A further example: In the U.S.–Mexico border area, a range of standard and nonstandard dialects of both the first and second languages (Montano-Harmon, 1991) abound, and in the Caribbean, Creole writers may use dialects that vary in distance from the standard (or "acrolect") to the vernacular (or "basilect") (Clachar, 2004).

This review is organized around major questions about adolescent L2 writing that have occupied international researchers, educators, and policymakers: How is adolescent L2 writing different from first-language (L1) writing? How does L2 writing develop in adolescents? And what are the major issues in L2 writing instruction for adolescents?

HOW IS ADOLESCENT L2 WRITING DIFFERENT FROM L1 WRITING?

Differences between first-language and second-language writing and between monolingual and multilingual writers have been investigated from a variety of perspectives.

How Might Text and Discourse Features Differ?

L2 writers are likely to make more errors and different kinds of errors in texts than monolingual students even after protracted learning and instruction (Silva, 1993). For example, Yu and Atkinson (1988) found that Chinese L1 Hong Kong adolescents made errors in English L2 lexical item choices, noun inflections, word classes, spelling, determiners, verb tense/aspect, subject–verb agreement, active/passive voice, and preposition choice even after education in English medium schools. Reynolds (2002) found that English-proficient students were better able to adjust types of causality markers employed in their texts for different composition topics and genres than middle school Spanish L1, English L2 learners. He suggests that L2 learners may favor a narrative mode of development across topics. In a subsequent study, Reynolds (2005) found that the texts of English L2 learners display far less informational density than texts of English-proficient students. L2 writers' texts also evidenced more idiosyncratic use of grammatical features and varied in whether they aligned grammatical usage with the genre elicited by composition prompts (e.g., they might use first person instead of imperative forms or "you" when giving directions or instructions).

Adolescent L2 learners' texts display less lexical diversity (vocabulary variety) than those of proficient bilingual students (Reynolds, 2005). Bilingual students tend to have smaller, more colloquial, less academic vocabularies in L2 than monolingual students of the same age (Hinkel, 2002; Laufer, 1998; Lee, 2003), so augmenting vocabulary is a major concern for adolescent L2 writing. Nevertheless, passive vocabulary size and use in reading has tended to be better studied and understood than active, productive vocabulary use (Laufer, 1998). Gains in adolescents' L2 passive vocabularies may not translate into greater ability to use vocabulary productively in free compositions. In fact, the gap between passive and active vocabulary knowledge may actually increase with language proficiency (Laufer, 1998). Lee (2003) suggests that systematic vocabulary instruction can have positive effects on the variety of vocabulary used by adolescents in compositions as well as on the frequency of sophisticated, infrequent vocabulary items.

Some writing genres, particularly summaries, may be more linguistically demanding for adolescent L2 writers to produce than others (de Courcy, 2002). Moreover, even writers who are quite proficient at the level of syntax and vocabulary may nevertheless apply implicit L1 discourse conventions (Connor, 2002). Studies of adolescent writers show differing L1 and L2 conventions for length of the text, length of sentences, and conjunction use; linear organization or deviations from the main idea; stringing together ideas through adding or explaining, as opposed to enumerating; the extent of writers' responsibility for conveying meaning versus readers' responsibility for text interpretation; the extent to which texts serve as self-actualization for writers; and the extent to which texts focus on sensory description and detail, plot line, or thesis (Dyer & Friederich, 2002; Montano-Harmon, 1991). When such differences exist, it suggests a need for explicit instruction. The uniqueness of cultures' rhetorical forms and the persistence of such forms in L2 writing has been questioned, however (e.g., Atkinson, 2004; Kubota, 1999). Plagiarism and inappropriate use of source materials, whether from lack of linguistic resources or differences in cultural conventions, may be a problem for adolescent L2 writers (de Courcy, 2002). More cross-cultural research is needed to ascertain whether or how genre conventions are taught to adolescent L2 writers. For example, Schleppegrell, Achugar, and Oteíza (2004) describe a project in which secondary school teachers working with English L2 learners were explicitly trained to use functional linguistics to analyze the structure of history texts. While focusing on decoding, the authors note that the method might be a starting point for a writing curriculum.

How Might Composing and Editing Processes Differ?

Work on L2 writing process has proceeded largely under the assumption that L2 detracts from cognitive processing and that writing in an L2 leads to less sophisticated outcomes (see, e.g., Abu-Rabia, 2003). Work has therefore focused on how L1 and L2 enter into adolescents' composing processes and where L2 might "short circuit" composing ability. In recent years Chenoweth and Hayes's (2001) distinction between resource, process, and control levels of the writing process in bilingual students has become influential. Roca de Larios, Marín, and Murphy (2001) and Schoonen et al. (2003) argue that existing models of composing based on monolingual composing processes have not given adequate theoretical or empirical attention to the interaction of L2 fluency or automaticity on metacognition and planning processes. Monolingual models have also presumed that thoughts are separated from their translation into words rather than integrated. Studies in this area suggest that L1 and L2 writing ability are correlated (Schoonen et al., 2003; but see

Wakabayashi, 2002, for contrasting results). However, L2 text formulation is more laborious and generates greater cognitive load than writing in L1, leading adolescent writers to give significantly more of their attention to solving problems with structure and vocabulary than to generating text (Roca de Larios et al., 2001). However, the nature of problem solving varies by age and proficiency level, with older and more proficient L2 writers spending more time on upgrading their linguistic formulations and less on compensating for lack of L2 knowledge than younger or less proficient writers (Roca de Larios, Manchon, & Murphy, 2006). Schoonen et al. (2003) further suggest that there is a linguistic retrieval speed threshold for writing, with L2 writing more dependent on L2 linguistic knowledge and processing speed than L1 writing.

Further work on differences between L1 and L2 composing in adolescents may profitably employ a combination of research techniques, including verbal protocol analysis and interviews to gauge writers' subjective experience. Roca de Larios et al. (2006) note the need to analyze how the transfer of writing skill across languages is socially mediated and reflects old and new cultural values and attitudes about writing (see, e.g., Smagorinsky, 2001). Swain and Lapkin (1995) argue that collaborative dialogue while composing in L2 can provide a unique window into the process. A very different but equally promising approach is Schoonen et al.'s (2003) longitudinal analysis using structural equation modeling with a large sample of writers.

Response and error feedback are especially important issues in L2 composing. Current pedagogical theory advocates selective error marking coordinated with targeted grammar practice and strategy training to develop writers' self-sufficiency as editors (Ferris, 2002). Research indicates, however, that even though such training is effective and improves adolescents' L2 writing and revision processes (see, e.g., Sengupta, 2000; Wong et al., 1994), and even when most teacher corrections are found to be unnecessary and are ignored by students (Lee, 2004), the majority of students nonetheless resist such training (Sengupta, 1998) and prefer teacher editing and comprehensive marking of errors (Lee, 2004). Furthermore,

one study (Franken & Haslett, 2002) found that English L2 adolescents in New Zealand produced more linguistically accurate and complex essays with more information when working alone than when working with peers on topics in which they possessed adequate background knowledge. The effectiveness of peer collaboration also appears to differ with adolescents' L2 proficiency levels (Lapkin & Swain, 2002) and background knowledge (Franken & Haslett, 2002). The ideal peer editor for an adolescent may be another more proficient L2 learner (Fedderholdt, 2001; Strasser, 1995). In all, studies suggest that proficiency, cultural context, and dynamics of social interaction all affect L2 adolescent writers' ability to work as peer collaborators and editors, but more work is needed in this area.

HOW DOES L2 WRITING DEVELOP IN ADOLESCENTS?

Because of the "inherent bias in the research towards university L2 writers" (Reynolds, 2002), L2 writing has thus far been conceptualized as a phenomenon of individuals who have completed literacy development in L1. On the other hand, developmental theories of writing have been based primarily on the experiences of monolingual young children. However, more research is urgently needed on school-age learners, for whom development of second language and literacy coincide (Reynolds, 2002).

A handful of studies have looked at L2 writing development as a function of age. Especially useful are comparative studies of adolescents and L2 writers in other age groups. Some abilities are apparently not age-specific. For example, Wald (1987) finds that the age of Spanish L1 English L2 writers had little effect on ability to differentiate spoken and written language in terms of syntactic complexity. Other aspects of L2 writing development appear to be affected by age. Comparing bilingual Basque-Spanish adolescents who had studied English for the same number of years but at younger and older ages, Cenoz (2002) finds that older learners' compositions were rated more highly, suggesting that adolescence confers some advantages in the pace of L2 writing development. Roca de Larios et al. (2001)

find that when compared to college students, Spanish high school students spent more time on text formulation in both L1 and L2 and significantly less time on planning and revision. High school writers often reinterpreted the task (e.g., from argumentation into personal narrative) and engaged in more off-task commentary. More comparative studies would be useful to gauge if and how differences in cognitive maturity and composing experiences distinguish adolescent L2 writers from better-studied adults and children. Longitudinal studies of the same writers are also necessary to capture development (Reynolds, 2005; Schoonen et al., 2003). Reynolds (2005) argues that adolescent L2 writing development needs to be conceptualized in terms of ability to produce appropriately a widening range of written genres. On a broader level, Welch, Hodges, and Warden (1989) argue that early intervention in elementary school might be crucial to adolescents' long-term development as multilingual writers and scholars.

Other studies have posited stages of adolescent L2 writing development as a function of increasing proficiency. For example, adolescents interviewed by de Courcy (2002) reported that as novice L2 writers, they had depended heavily on composing in L1 and translating, and on bilingual text resources such as articles and dictionaries, to generate L2 text. With increasing proficiency, they began to generate text in L2 but remained dependent on L1 for prewriting and planning processes. Studies of development based on cross-sectional analysis of both highly and poorly rated L2 essays suggest that more proficient adolescent English L2 writers use fewer simple clauses, make fewer errors linking clauses (Leong & Wee, 2005), organize information in more hierarchical fashion, include more elaboration and specific detail, and conclude essays at a higher level of generality than less skillful writers (Makinen, 1992). Studies have also looked at L2 writing proficiency development as a function of instructional interventions. Day and Shapson (2001), for example, tested an experimental curriculum that improved Canadian French immersion students' use of conditional verbs in writing. Evans and Fisher (2005) found that even extremely short (6–11 day) high school study-abroad experiences were associated with gains in British

adolescents' French L2 writing performance in terms of text length and use of expressive language including verbs indicating likes and dislikes and adjectives of evaluation.

Only a handful of studies have offered explicit theoretical frames for examining adolescent L2 writing proficiency development. Some (see, e.g., Cenoz, 2002; Yu & Atkinson, 1988) relate their findings to Cummins's (1981) "threshold hypothesis," suggesting that students must develop a critical level of proficiency in their first language in order to reap cognitive, linguistic, and academic benefits from bilingualism. Swain and Lapkin (1998, 2000) advocate a sociocultural framework that views dialogue as both communication and cognitive tool in improving L2 adolescent writing. Tsang (1996) draws upon Krashen's (1984) input hypothesis, which argues that intensive and extensive reading "input" is the primary determinant of L2 writing development. Tsang found positive effects for an adolescent L2 writing curriculum based on this theory (but see Lightbown, Halter, White, and Horst, 2002, for contrasting results). On the basis of case studies of three Spanish L1 English L2 adolescents in a California middle school, Valdés (1999) proposes a seven-stage model of L2 writing development in adolescents, encompassing communicative tasks performed (e.g., providing personal information, explaining, expressing opinions), syntactic and discourse organization, and mechanics. Valdés also argues for theoretical models to take the writing of fluent bilingual rather than monolingual adolescents as the appropriate target for proficiency development. In all, studies have looked at development in terms of age or L2 proficiency but have rarely addressed both. Developmental research on adolescent L2 writing could also use more diverse and stronger theoretical frames and more longitudinal research (Parks et al., 2005).

WHAT ARE THE MAJOR ISSUES IN ADOLESCENT L2 WRITING INSTRUCTION?

Does L2 Writing Instruction Take Place?

There are surprisingly few studies documenting whether writing even takes place regularly in classrooms where the second language is the explicit object of focus. Those that do suggest that writing instruction is highly variable. This is the case for high school second-language classrooms (Fu, 1995; García, 1999; Harklau, 1994; Valdés, 1999) and foreign language classrooms (Stepp-Greany, 2004) in the United States, as well as foreign language classrooms abroad (Pennington et al., 1996). Whether writing instruction is provided seems to depend in part on teachers' attitudes and teaching approach (Pennington et al., 1996; Stepp-Greany, 2004) as well as students' level of academic achievement (Pennington et al., 1996). We could certainly use much more basic information on whether and how L2 writing is taught across a broad spectrum of secondary classrooms internationally.

What Is the Role of the L1?

Relatively few empirical studies have examined L1 use in adolescent L2 writing instruction, and most have been conducted outside the United States with L1 speakers of the society's dominant language. In Hong Kong, for example, Yu and Atkinson (1988) contend that Chinese L1 adolescents were adversely affected by English L2 medium instruction, based on students' overall poor performance in L2 compositions. However, a subsequent study (Pennington et al., 1996) reported that both Chinese and English were used in varying proportions during writing instruction, depending on whether the classrooms were teacher- or student-centered; individual students' language proficiency, academic achievement, and motivation; and the teacher's immediate objective. In a Canadian French immersion program, Swain and Lapkin (2000) showed that use of L1 in writing activities among adolescents supported the development of the L2. Adolescent L2 writers may use L1 to diminish cognitive demands, manage the L2 writing task, negotiate meaning, and focus on form. Wakabayashi (2002) found that it made little difference whether Japanese L1 students were initially schooled in Japanese or English, but students who transitioned at an early age into programs where English was the classroom medium of instruction performed better on writing tasks than those who did not. However, two other studies of English L2 writers in Japan find that language of instruction is less important than amount of composing instruction and experience (Dyer & Friederich, 2002; Kobayashi & Rinnert, 2002), suggesting that L1 writing instruction can provide a strong basis for L2 writing instruction. Studies of the role of L1 in L2 writing instruction for language minority adolescents are even more rare. Glynn, Berryman, Loader, and Cavanagh (2005) found that students in New Zealand educated in a Maori L1 immersion program with home and school participation and culturally appropriate instruction through middle school could be transitioned into English L2 instruction in high school without impairment of L1 writing skills. García (1999) found that bilingual instruction in itself did not provide a benefit if it was tied to writing tasks that adolescents did not find motivating.

How Do We Integrate Bilingual Students into Monolingual Writing Classrooms?

Many L2 adolescent writers, particularly in Western immigrant-receiving countries, are educated alongside monolingual and proficient bilingual students in "mainstream" classrooms where L2 is the medium of instruction. Although scholars (see, e.g., Meltzer & Hamann, 2004, 2005; Meltzer & Okashige, 2001) have argued that the principles of effective literacy instruction for all adolescents are quite similar to the principles of teaching English learners, empirical reports suggest that English learners in mainstream classrooms may not receive high-quality writing instruction (Duff, 2001; Harklau, 1994, 2001; Valdés, 1999), especially when they are placed in low-track classes where opportunities for extended writing tend to be most limited (Harklau, 1994; Townsend & Fu, 2001). Harklau (1994; 2001) and Fu (1995; Townsend & Fu, 2001) found an implicit deficit orientation in many mainstream writing teachers' attitudes toward English learners, with teachers equating bilingualism with linguistic and even cognitive deficiency. To address such attitudes, O'Bryne (2001) describes a collaborative project by English as a second language (ESL) and mainstream educators in Toronto to develop a curriculum focusing on student writing strengths in content and organization, rather than weaknesses in grammar and usage and a curriculum that provided structured opportunities to develop forms of literary response that were already familiar to L1 monolingual English-speaking students.

What Is the Relationship of L2 Writing and Content Learning?

Although there has been a significant amount of scholarship in recent years on content-based and "sheltered" content instruction for L2 learners (Echevarria, Vogt, & Short, 2000; Stryker & Leaver, 1997), there has nonetheless been little specifically on the role of L2 writing in adolescents' learning of subject matter. Extant studies are concerned primarily with research report writing. These suggest that adolescent L2 writers benefit from training in using libraries and finding appropriate source materials (Villalva, 2006; Werner & Stone, 1993), evaluating the validity and utility of sources (Clankie, 2000), and representing conflicting opinions and information (Villalva, 2006). Welch et al. (1989) further find that explicit training in research and study skills improved L2 learners' self-ratings of writing ability as well as their affiliation with scholarly identity and academic ethos. At a more fundamental level, Valdés (1999) points out that we do not yet know if L2 writing actually facilitates or interferes with learning in bilingual adolescents, and if so, how and under what circumstances.

How Do We Tie L2 Writing Instruction to Adolescents' Home and Community Experiences?

Scholars (e.g., Fu, 1995; Meltzer & Hamann, 2004) argue that linking school-based literacy tasks to adolescent L2 learners' homes and communities is key to maintaining their motivation to learn. Yet several scholars identify a disconnect between home and school literacies for adolescent L2 learners. García (1999), for example, finds that Latino immigrants with little formal schooling in a New York city high school actually wrote a great deal out of school, producing journals and poetry to share with peers. However, school-based writing instruction overlooked these literacy practices in order to teach academic writing and often stymied students' writing production by demanding correct mechanics. Likewise, Fu (1995) shows that Lao L1 adolescents connected with L2 English writing through the exploration of personal experience, but that their experience was largely ignored in their high school classes. Weinstein (2002) examined how bilingual youth used tagging graffiti, poetry, and rap and song lyrics within student enclaves to express their lived home and community realities and to express a sense of belonging. However, once again, these practices were largely overlooked by educators and the school curricula. These studies suggest a need to better prepare educators to link bilingual adolescents' out-of-school literacy practices to in-school academic work.

Efforts along these lines include Landay (2001) "Accelerated Literacy" class in which L2 English high school students worked with photography to capture a visual record of their families and communities, then translated visual images into student poems, letters, and stories and created a performance based on both. Callahan (2002) likewise argues for a broader conceptualization of composition as multimodal design including original narratives produced via audio and video recordings. Glynn et al. (2005) describe and evaluate an English L2 literacy class for Maori L1 students embedded in a program in which the school coordinated with family and community members to provide culturally appropriate instruction. Villalva (2006) found that L1 Spanish students relied on social networks as primary sources for their writing, much as some students might rely on print sources, and argues for an examination of how writers are socialized into different norms for inquiry and language use outside school. Several scholars (Barbieri, 1998; Blair, 1991; Toffoli & Allan, 1992; Vreeland, 1998) advocate autobiographical and family history approaches to connecting language-minority student writing to home and community and to tap students' experiences of acculturation, alienation, and struggle as immigrants. Harklau (2000), however, finds that adolescent immigrants had written autobiographies repeatedly in their school careers and cautions that such approaches can reinforce stereotypes about immigrants and neglect other aspects of multilingual adolescents' experiences and identities.

Kiernan (1991) critiques the lack of civic literacy in commercial high school ESL materials and advocates an L2 writing curriculum that incorporates community service learning. Several studies advocate critical ethnographic (Goldstein, 2002), critical literacy (Ghahremani-Ghajar & Mirhosseini, 2005; Wolfe, 1996), and Freirian problem-posing (Quintero, 2002) approaches to integrate L2 writing instruction in a broader examination of community and societal issues. These approaches aim to move adolescents past descriptive and instrumental uses of writing toward critical self-examination of their educational, social, and political goals and plans for change. However, we found only one study (Ghahremani-Ghajar & Mirhosseini, 2005) that focused on a sociopolitical context outside North America (Iran), indicating that more international perspectives are needed in this area. Goldstein (2002) and Wolfe (1996) suggest that programs are most successful when implemented outside the confines of traditional classrooms in community-based or summer programs. Furthermore, if adolescent L2 writing is assumed to be the product of multiple contexts in and out of school, it will require innovative approaches to research. Villalva (2006), for example, includes three levels of analysis: a focus on language (text) as artifact; a focus on how the roles (e.g., learner, student, researcher, advocate) and types of interactions available to youth affect their L2 writing process; and a focus on how writing is produced in context. Such work is still in development and has looked primarily at language-minority students; virtually none has explored the role of out-of-school literacies in adolescents' learning of heritage or foreign languages.

What Are the Implications of New Technologies for Adolescent L2 Writing Instruction?

An emerging vein of adolescent L2 writing research looks at computer-mediated communication (CMC) and Internet and communication technologies (ICT). Some studies have used computer-mediated communication frameworks to examine the use of computers and word processing programs for traditional modes of writing instruction, such as pen pals and peer editing (Fedderholdt, 2001; High, Hoyer, & Wakefield, 2002; Strasser, 1995). These studies find that even these relatively simple uses of technology increase students' motivation and forge stronger social relationships among peers. They increase student involvement in cross-cultural peer response by making possible the rapid and easy exchange of information (Fedderholdt, 2001; Strasser, 1995). Young (2003), in a study of Taiwanese high school students, found that MOOs, chat rooms, and e-mail provided adolescents with ample time to compose and respond in the L2. Learners were also able to write about controversial topics that cultural norms might not usually allow in face-to-face communication. Young (2003) thus concludes that a CMC environment can lower students' affective filters, allowing them to interact in the L2 freely as well as enhancing critical thinking, problem-solving, and communication skills.

Recent work has focused on how the evolving literate practices of millennial adolescents are prompting redefinitions of the very notions of *literacy* and *text* (Callahan, 2002; New London Group, 1996; Pahl & Roswell, 2006; Kern & Warschauer, 2000). In many nations, the use of ICT is increasing adolescent literacy demands even as adolescent home uses of ICT vastly broaden definitions of what counts as literacy (Moje, Young, Readence, & Moore, 2000). For example, Lam (2000, 2004) suggests that the Internet creates unique opportunities for adolescents to employ L2 writing for the purpose of navigating social identity development through social interactions with other L2 writers. In one study, Lam (2000) found that a Chinese adolescent used English L2 writing in an online international Japanese pop music fan forum to create an online identity and forge social affiliations with peers. Lam (2004) also documented how two Chinese L1 adolescent immigrants were socialized into the language and literacy practices of a bilingual chat room virtual community. Black (2005) likewise found that an online forum—a fanfiction virtual community—provided an adolescent with authentic peer feedback and improved L2 writing. These cases illustrate how ICT-rich environments can afford adolescents access to authentic L2 written interactions and access to peer cultures in ways that are unavailable to them in traditional classrooms.

The application of ICT to adolescent L2 writing instruction is not clear-cut, however. Pinnow (n.d.), for example, finds that schools are often unable to provide L2 writers with relevant and uncontrived interaction on the Internet such that its literacy-building potential can be fully exploited. Moreover, even if schools could provide such access and interaction, popular culture embedded in Internet-based communication can be violent, profane, sexist, racist (Alvermann & Heron, 2001), or commercialized (Zuengler, 2004) and thus not represent values that educators want to endorse or perpetuate. ICT-based communication can also exclude or marginalize, as well as draw in L2 writers (Duff, 2001; van Lier, 2003). Nevertheless, studies suggest that overlooking the potential power of ICT in adolescent L2 writers' lives may result in a school curriculum that is out of step with students' lived experience. For example, Ingram and O'Neill (2002) find that although Australian foreign language teachers rated electronic communication with native speakers as a low priority, their students rated it as a much higher priority.

More research remains to be done on the contrast between adolescents' prolific L2 writing in online forums versus disengagement in school settings. Emerging ecological models of inquiry (Moje et al., 2000; van Lier, 2004) offer a valuable approach to exploring the hybrid, layered identities that bilingual adolescents create for themselves in online forums, highlighting the interplay of L2 writing with sociocultural influences and environmental factors. We could also use more work on how L2 writers deploy multiple modalities to compensate for gaps in language proficiency. Few studies have focused on how technology and multimedia alter adolescents' L2 composing processes (Parks et al., 2005) or how instruction could exploit the scaffolding potential of multimodal composition for novice L2 writers (Pinnow, n.d.). Another gap lies in understanding how L2 writing teachers' conceptualizations of technology affect classroom implementation (Parks, Huot, Hamers, & Lemonnier, 2003).

What Is the Role of Assessment?

In many countries adolescence has become a key time for high-stakes standardized examinations that determine school completion, college entrance, and ultimate life chances. Increasingly these examinations demand proficiency in L2 writing. In the United States, for example, the advent of SAT and ACT timed writing tests, as well as state high school writing graduation tests, will no doubt reshape L2 writing instruction in North American schools. Yet we found virtually no work on the role of assessment in adolescent L2 writing. There is a potential disjunction between L2 writing instruction that emphasizes a protracted process of drafting, redrafting, and feedback, and timed examinations that demand impromptu essays in a short period (Caudery, 1990; Pennington et al., 1996; Sengupta, 1998). The procedures associated with standardized assessments of adolescent L2 writers' texts have also drawn critique. Gamaroff (2000), for example, finds that writing test raters from L1 and L2 English backgrounds differed in their assessments of adolescents' L2 essays in terms of the sources to which they attributed errors, the relative weight they gave to different error types, and how grave they considered errors to be. Way et al. (2000) find that both the elicited genre (e.g., description, expository essay, narrative) and prompt type (simple or "bare" prompt vs. prompt with relevant L2 vocabulary or prompt with prose model) had a significant impact on the quality of French L2 writing produced by English L1 high school students. They note, however, that the proficiency scale used to assess L2 writing in U.S. foreign language classrooms (American Council on the Teaching of Foreign Languages, 2001) does not address genre or prompt type. While limited evidence suggests that time limits do not affect the quality of L2 writers' essays (Caudery, 1990; Kroll, 1990), this finding could use corroboration. The growing importance of assessment in adolescent L2 writing will necessitate more research in coming years.

CONCLUSIONS AND RECOMMENDATIONS

Adolescent second-language writing is a field awaiting further exploration. Although the small amount of extant research makes every contribution valuable, the field has many gaps that limit our ability to draw sound conclusions. Scholarship at present is scattered and could make a much greater impact by developing sustained avenues of inquiry regarding whether and how adolescence lends distinctive characteristics to the writing of L2 learners and multilingual students. Work on pedagogical approaches, at present the bulk of scholarship on adolescent L2 writing instruction, must be better grounded both theoretically and empirically. More research is urgently needed on adolescent L2 writing in languages other than English both in North America and internationally. We also found a notable lack of dialogue between specialists in English L2 and languages other than English regarding research agendas and paradigms. Even though we defined writing broadly in our review, we found that very few researchers define writing outside the narrow parameters of essays and reports. However, as recent work on multimodality makes clear, writing takes many different forms, including note taking, summaries, lists, charts and graphs, diaries and journals, poetry, prayers, blogs, and websites, and these forms all may serve different purposes not only in learning to write in a second language but also in learning a second language through writing (Harklau, 2002). We therefore urge a broadening of the agenda for research on adolescent L2 writing to include varied forms and purposes.

In developing this review, we have found a tendency for adolescent literacy research to use terms that are too broad in discussing linguistically and culturally diverse students. On a practical level, we sometimes found too few details about participants' backgrounds to discern whether they were in fact L2 writers. On a broader level, there is considerable danger that *diverse* becomes a catch-all term that creates a binary between White monolingual students and anybody else who may speak a language or dialect other than standard edited English. We thus believe all literacy researchers, not just second-language specialists, must be more attentive to important distinctions in adolescents' specific linguistic and cultural backgrounds, the community and societal contexts in which they become bilingual, and their proficiency and literacy levels in L1 and L2.

Finally, we are in great need of theories of adolescent literacy that take multilingual students as their norm. Our dependence on monolingual models of teaching and learning literacy leads us to define L2 writing merely as a problem or L2 deficit, rather than considering writers' entire linguistic repertoires and resources. Nevertheless, multilingual students outnumber monolingual students globally, and adolescent second-language writing research would benefit by paralleling the recent move in the field of second-language acquisition toward a model of "multicompetence" (Cook, 2003; Ortega, 2006; Valdés, 1999) that can explore the complex ecology of linguistic and cultural assets that multilingual students bring to composing.

REFERENCES

Abu-Rabia, S. (2003). The influence of working memory on reading and creative writing processes in a second language. *Educational Psychology, 23,* 209–214.

Alvermann, D. E., & Heron, A. H. (2001). Literacy identity work: Playing to learn with popular media. *Journal of Adolescent and Adult Literacy, 45,* 118–122.

American Council on the Teaching of Foreign Languages. (2001). *ACTFL proficiency guidelines—Writing* (Rev. ed.). Retrieved October 26, 2006, from *www.actfl.org/files/public/writingguidelines.pdf.*

Atkinson, D. (2004). Contrasting rhetorics/contrasting cultures: Why contrastive rhetoric needs a better conceptualization of culture. *Journal of English for Academic Purposes, 3,* 277–289.

Barbieri, M. (1998). Holding memories, shaping dreams: Chinese children's writers' notebooks. *Voices from the Middle, 6,* 41–48.

Black, R. (2005). Access and affiliation: The literacy and composition practices of English-language learners in an online fanfiction community. *Journal of Adolescent and Adult Literacy, 49,* 118–128.

Blair, L. (1991). Developing student voices with multicultural literature. *English Journal, 80,* 24–28.

Callahan, M. (2002). Intertextual composition: The power of the digital pen. *English Education, 35,* 46–65.

Canagarajah, A. S. (2002). *Critical academic writing*

and multilingual students. Ann Arbor: University of Michigan Press.

Caudery, T. (1990). The validity of timed essay tests in the assessment of writing skills. *ELT Journal, 44,* 122–131.

Cenoz, J. (2002). Age differences in foreign language learning. *I.T.L. Review of Applied Linguistics, 135–136,* 125–133.

Chenoweth, N. A., & Hayes, J. R. (2001). Fluency in writing: Generating text in L1 and L2. *Written Communication, 18,* 80–98.

Clachar, A. (2004). The construction of Creole-speaking students' linguistic profile and contradictions in ESL literacy programs. *TESOL Quarterly, 38,* 153–165.

Clankie, S. (2000). Teaching students to evaluate Internet source material. *TESOL Journal, 9,* 33–34.

Connor, U. (2002). New directions in contrastive rhetoric. *TESOL Quarterly, 36,* 493–510.

Cook, V. (2002). Background to the L2 user. In V. Cook (Ed.), *Portraits of the L2 user* (pp. 1–28). Buffalo, NY: Multilingual Matters.

Cook, V. (2003). *Effects of the second language on the first.* Buffalo, NY: Multilingual Matters.

Cummins, J. (1981). The role of primary language development in promoting educational success for language minority students. In California State Department of Education Office of Bilingual Bicultural Education (Ed.), *Schooling and language minority students: A theoretical framework* (pp. 3–49). Los Angeles: Evaluation, Dissemination, and Assessment Center, California State University.

Day, E. M., & Shapson, S. M. (2001). Integrating formal and functional approaches to language teaching in French immersion: An experimental study. *Language Learning, 51,* 47–80.

de Courcy, M. (2002). *Learners' experiences of immersion education: Case studies of French and Chinese.* Buffalo: Multilingual Matters.

Duff, P. A. (2001). Language, literacy, content, and (pop) culture: Challenges for ESL students in mainstream courses. *Canadian Modern Language Review, 59,* 103–131.

Dyer, B., & Friederich, L. (2002). The personal narrative as cultural artifact: Teaching autobiography in Japan. *Written Communication, 19,* 265–296.

Echevarria, J., Vogt, M., & Short, D. (2000). *Making content comprehensible for English language learners: The SIOP model.* Boston: Allyn & Bacon.

Evans, M., & Fisher, L. (2005). Measuring gains in pupils' foreign language competence as a result of participation in a school exchange visit: The case of Y9 pupils at three comprehensive schools in the UK. *Language Teaching Research, 9*(2), 173–192.

Fedderholdt, K. (2001). An email exchange project between non-native speakers of English. *ELT Journal, 55,* 273–280.

Ferris, D. (2002). *Treatment of error in second language student writing.* Ann Arbor: University of Michigan Press.

Ferris, D., & Hedgcock, J. (2005). *Teaching ESL composition: Purpose, process, and practice* (2nd ed.). Mahwah, NJ: Erlbaum.

Franken, M., & Haslett, S. (2002). When and why talking can make writing harder. In S. Ransdell & M.-L. Barbier (Eds.), *New directions for research in L2 writing* (pp. 209–229). Boston: Kluwer.

Fu, D. (1995). *My trouble is my English: Asian students and the American dream.* Portsmouth, NH: Heinemann.

Gamaroff, R. (2000). Rater reliability in language assessment: The bug of all bears. *System, 28,* 31–53.

García, O. (1999). Educating Latino high school students with little formal schooling. In C. Faltis & P. Wolfe (Eds.), *So much to say: Adolescents, bilingualism, and ESL in the secondary school* (pp. 61–82). New York: Teachers College Press.

Ghahremani-Ghajar, S., & Mirhosseini, S. A. (2005). English class or speaking about everything class? Dialogue journal writing as a critical EFL literacy practice in an Iranian high school. *Language, Culture, and Curriculum, 18,* 286–299.

Glynn, T., Berryman, M., Loader, K., & Cavanagh, T. (2005). From literacy in Maori to biliteracy in Maori and English: A community and school transition programme. *International Journal of Bilingual Education and Bilingualism, 8,* 433–454.

Goldstein, T. (2002). No pain, no gain: Student playwriting as critical ethnographic language research. *Canadian Modern Language Review, 59,* 53–76.

Harklau, L. (1994). ESL and mainstream classes: Contrasting second language learning contexts. *TESOL Quarterly, 28,* 241–272.

Harklau, L. (2000). From the "good kids" to the "worst": Representations of English language learners across educational settings. *TESOL Quarterly, 34,* 35–67.

Harklau, L. (2001). From high school to college: Student perspectives on literacy practices. *Journal of Literacy Research, 33,* 33–70.

Harklau, L. (2002). The role of writing in classroom second language acquisition. *Journal of Second Language Writing, 10,* 1–22.

Harklau, L. (2007). The adolescent English language learner: Identities lost and found. In J. Cummins & C. Davison (Eds.), *International handbook of English language teaching* (pp. 559–573). Norwell, MA: Springer.

High, J. L., Hoyer, J. M., & Wakefield, R. (2002). Teaching "process editing" skills with computers: From theory to practice on a larger scale. *Unterrischtspraxis/Teaching German, 35,* 153–165.

Hinkel, E. (2002). *Second language writers' text: Linguistic and rhetorical features.* Mahwah, NJ: Erlbaum.

Ingram, D., & O'Neill, S. (2002). The enigma of cross-cultural attitudes in language teaching. Part 2. *Babel, 36,* 17–38.

Kern, R., & Warschauer, M. (2000). Introduction: Theory and practice of network-based language teaching. In M. Warschauer & R. Kern (Eds.), *Network-*

based language teaching: Concepts and practice (pp. 1–19). New York: Cambridge University Press.

Kiernan, H. (1991). Lessons from the new Americans and Dickens. *English Journal, 80,* 67–68.

Kobayashi, H., & Rinnert, C. (2002). High school students' perceptions of first language literacy instruction: Implications for second language writing. *Journal of Second Language Writing, 11,* 91–116.

Krashen, S. D. (1984). *Writing, research, theory, and applications.* New York: Pergamon.

Kroll, B. (1990). What does time buy? ESL student performance on home versus class compositions. In B. Kroll (Ed.), *Second language writing: Research insights for the classroom.* New York: Cambridge University Press.

Kubota, R. (1999). Japanese culture constructed by discourses: Implications for applied linguistics research and ELT. *TESOL Quarterly, 33,* 9–35.

Lam, W. S. E. (2000). L2 literacy and the design of the self: A case study of a teenager writing on the Internet. *TESOL Quarterly, 34,* 457–482.

Lam, W. S. E. (2004). Second language socialization in a bilingual chat room: Global and local considerations. *Language Learning and Technology, 8,* 44–65.

Landay, E. (with Meehan, M. B., Newman, A. L., Wootton, K., & King, D. W.). (2001). "Postcards from America": Linking classroom and community in an ESL class. *English Journal, 90,* 66–74.

Lapkin, S., & Swain, M. (2002). Reformulation and the learning of French pronominal verbs in a Canadian French immersion context. *Modern Language Journal, 86,* 485–507.

Laufer, B. (1998). The development of passive and active vocabulary in a second language: Same or different? *Applied Linguistics, 19,* 255–271.

Lee, I. (2004). Error correction in L2 secondary writing classrooms: The case of Hong Kong. *Journal of Second Language Writing, 13,* 285–312.

Lee, S. H. (2003). ESL learners' vocabulary use in writing and the effects of explicit vocabulary instruction. *System, 31,* 537–561.

Leki, I. (2007). *Undergraduates in a second language: Challenges and complexities of academic literacy development.* Mahwah, NJ: Erlbaum.

Leong, P. A., & Wee, B. G. (2005). Investigating the clause complex: An analysis of exposition-type essays written by secondary school students in Singapore. *ITL, Review of Applied Linguistics, 149–150,* 47–76.

Lightbown, P. M., Halter, R. H., White, J. L., & Horst, M. (2002). Comprehension-based learning: The limits of "do it yourself." *Canadian Modern Language Review, 53,* 427–464.

Makinen, K. (1992). Topical depth and writing quality in student EFL compositions. *Scandinavian Journal of Educational Research, 36,* 237–247.

Matsuda, P. K. (1998). Situating ESL writing in a cross-disciplinary context. *Written Communication, 15,* 99–121.

Meltzer, J., & Hamann, E. T. (2004). *Meeting the literacy development needs of adolescent English language learners through content area learning: I. Focus on motivation and achievement.* Providence, RI: Education Alliance at Brown University, Northeast and Islands Regional Educational Laboratory.

Meltzer, J., & Hamann, E. T. (2005). *Meeting the literacy development needs of adolescent English language learners through content area learning: II. Focus on classroom teaching and learning strategies.* Providence, RI: Education Alliance at Brown University, Northeast and Islands Regional Educational Laboratory.

Meltzer, J., & Okashige, S. (2001). *Supporting adolescent literacy across the content areas: Perspectives on policy and practice* Providence, RI: Education Alliance at Brown University, Northeast and Islands Regional Educational Laboratory. (ERIC Document Reproduction Service No. ED 459 442).

Moje, E. B., Young, J. P., Readence, J. E., & Moore, D. W. (2000). Reinventing adolescent literacy for new times: Perennial and millennial issues. *Journal of Adolescent and Adult Literacy, 43,* 400–410.

Montano-Harmon, M. R. (1991). Discourse features of written Mexican Spanish: Current research in contrastive rhetoric and its implications. *Hispania, 74,* 417–425.

New London Group. (1996). A pedagogy of multiliteracies: Designing social futures. *Harvard Educational Review, 66,* 60–92.

O'Brien, T. (2004). Writing in a foreign language: Teaching and learning. *Language Teaching, 37,* 1–28.

O'Bryne, B. (2001). Needed: A compass to navigate the multilingual English classroom. *Journal of Adolescent and Adult Literacy, 44,* 440–449.

Ortega, L. (2006, May). *Multicompetence, social context, and L2 writing research praxis.* Paper presented at the symposium on Second Language Writing, Purdue University, Lafayette, IN.

Pahl, K., & Roswell, J. (Eds.). (2006). *Travel notes from the New Literacy Studies.* Buffalo, NY: Multilingual Matters.

Parks, S., Huot, D., Hamers, J., & Lemonnier, F. H. (2003). Crossing boundaries: Multimedia technology and pedagogical innovation in a high school class. *Language Learning and Technology, 7,* 28–45.

Parks, S., Huot, D., Hamers, J., & Lemonnier, F. H. (2005). "History of theatre" web sites: A brief history of the writing process in a high school ESL language arts class. *Journal of Second Language Writing, 14,* 223–258.

Pennington, M. C., Brock, M. N., & Yue, F. (1996). Explaining Hong Kong students' response to process writing: An exploration of causes and outcomes. *Journal of Second Language Writing, 5,* 227–252.

Pinnow, R. (n.d.). *On predators, firewalls and Internet inclusion: Assessing middle school ELLs access to ICTs in public school systems.* Unpublished manuscript.

Quintero, E. (2002). A problem-posing approach to using native language writing in English literacy instruction. In S. Ransdell & M.-L. Barbier (Eds.), *New directions for research in L2 writing* (pp. 231–244). Boston: Kluwer.

Reynolds, D. W. (2002). Learning to make things happen in different ways: Causality in the writing of middle-grade English language learners. *Journal of Second Language Writing, 11,* 311–328.

Reynolds, D. W. (2005). Linguistic correlates of second language literacy development: Evidence from middle-grade learner essays. *Journal of Second Language Writing, 14,* 19–45.

Rijlaarsdam, G. (2002). Preface. In S. Ransdell & M.-L. Barbier (Eds.), *New directions for research in L2 writing* (pp. ix–x). Boston: Kluwer.

Roca de Larios, J., Manchon, R. M., & Murphy, L. (2006). Generating text in native and foreign language writing: A temporal analysis of problem solving formulation processes. *Modern Language Journal, 90,* 100–114.

Roca de Larios, J., Marín, J., & Murphy, L. (2001). A temporal analysis of formulation processes in L1 and L2 writing. *Language Learning, 51,* 497–538.

Roca de Larios, J., Murphy, L., & Marín, J. (2002). A critical examination of L2 writing process research. In S. Ransdell & M.-L. Barbier (Eds.), *New directions for research in L2 writing* (pp. 11–47). Boston: Kluwer.

Schecter, S. R., & Harklau, L. A. (1992). *Writing in a non-native language: What we know, what we need to know.* Berkeley, CA: National Center for the Study of Writing and Literacy. (ERIC Document Reproduction Service No. ED 353 825).

Schleppegrell, M. J., Achugar, M., & Oteíza, T. (2004). The grammar of history: Enhancing content-based instruction through a functional focus on language. *TESOL Quarterly, 38,* 67–93.

Schoonen, R., van Gelderen, A., de Glopper, K., Hulstijn, J., Simis, A., Snellings, P., et al. (2003). First language and second language writing: The role of linguistic knowledge, speed of processing, and metacognitive knowledge. *Language Learning, 53,* 165–202.

Sengupta, S. (1998). Peer evaluation: "I am not the teacher." *ELT Journal, 52,* 19–28.

Sengupta, S. (2000). An investigation into the effects of revision strategy instruction on L2 secondary school learners. *System, 28,* 97–113.

Shaw, J. M. (1997). Threats to the validity of science performance assessments for English language learners. *Journal of Research in Science Teaching, 34,* 721–743.

Silva, T. (1993). Towards an understanding of the distinct nature of L2 writing: The ESL research and its implications. *TESOL Quarterly, 27,* 657–678.

Silva, T., & Leki, I. (2004). Family matters: The influence of applied linguistics and composition studies on second language writing studies—past, present, and future. *Modern Language Journal, 88,* 1–13.

Smagorinsky, P. (2001). Rethinking protocol analysis

from a cultural perspective. *Annual Review of Applied Linguistics, 21,* 233–245.

Stepp-Greany, J. (2004). What do communicative foreign language teachers do? Comparing communicative and non-communicative approaches in U.S. middle school classrooms. *Curriculum and Teaching, 19,* 45–55.

Strasser, G. F. (1995). FAX-technology for essay exchanges with German students as an enhancement of a "c"-culture. *Unterrischtspraxis/Teaching German, 28,* 159–164.

Stryker, S. B., & Leaver, B. L. (1997). *Content-based instruction in foreign language education: Models and methods.* Washington, DC: Georgetown University Press.

Swain, M., & Lapkin, S. (1995). Problems in output and the cognitive processes they generate: A step towards second language learning. *Applied Linguistics, 16,* 371–391.

Swain, M., & Lapkin, S. (1998). Interaction and second language learning: Two adolescent French immersion students working together. *Modern Language Journal, 82,* 320–337.

Swain, M., & Lapkin, S. (2000). Task-based second language learning: The uses of the first language. *Language Teaching Research, 4,* 251–274.

Taylor, A., Lazarus, E., & Cole, R. (2005). Putting languages on the (drop down) menu: Innovative writing frames in modern foreign language teaching. *Educational Review, 57,* 435–455.

Toffoli, G., & Allan, J. (1992). Group guidance for English as a second language students. *School Counselor, 40,* 136–145.

Townsend, J. S., & Fu, D. (2001). Paw's story: A Laotian refugee's lonely entry into American literacy. *Journal of Adolescent and Adult Literacy, 45,* 104–115.

Tsang, W. (1996). Comparing the effects of reading and writing on writing performance. *Applied Linguistics, 17,* 210–233.

Vadeboncoeur, J. A., & Stevens, L. P. (Eds.). (2005). *Re/constructing "the adolescent": Sign, symbol, and body.* New York: Peter Lang.

Valdés, G. (1999). Incipient bilingualism and the development of English language writing abilities in the secondary school. In C. Faltis & P. Wolfe (Eds.), *So much to say: Adolescents, bilingualism, and ESL in the secondary school* (pp. 138–175). New York: Teachers College Press.

van Lier, L. (2003). A tale of two computer classrooms: The ecology of project-based learning. In J. Leather & J. van Dam (Eds.), *Ecology of language acquisition* (pp. 53–54). Boston: Kluwer.

van Lier, L. (2004). *The ecology and semiotics of language learning.* Boston: Kluwer.

Villalva, K. E. (2006). Hidden literacies and inquiry approaches of bilingual high school writers. *Written Communication, 23,* 91–129.

Vreeland, P. (1998). The family tree: Nurturing language growth through "All the parts of me." *Voices from the Middle, 6,* 17–25.

Wakabayashi, T. (2002). Bilingualism as a future investment: The case of Japanese high school students at an international school in Japan. *Bilingual Research Journal, 26,* 631–658.

Wald, B. (1987). The development of writing skills among Hispanic high school students. In S. R. Goldman & H. T. Trueba (Eds.), *Becoming literate in English as a second language* (pp. 155–185). Norwood, NJ: Ablex.

Way, D. P., Joiner, E. G., & Seaman, M. A. (2000). Writing in the secondary foreign language classroom: The effects of prompts and tasks on novice learners of French. *Modern Language Journal, 84,* 171–184.

Weinstein, S. (2002). The writing on the wall: Attending to self-motivated student literacies. *English Education, 35,* 21–45.

Welch, O., Hodges, C., & Warden, K. (1989). Developing the scholar's ethos in minority high school students. *Urban Education, 24,* 59–76.

Werner, M. J., & Stone, G. (1993). Library access for all limited English proficient students: One school's approach. *Emergency Librarian, 20*(5), 20–23.

Wolfe, P. M. (1996). Literacy bargains: Toward critical literacy in a multilingual classroom. *TESOL Journal, 5*(4), 22–26.

Wong, B. Y. L., Butler, D. L., Ficzere, S. A., Kuperis, S., Corden, M., & Zelmer, J. (1994). Teaching problem learners revision skills and sensitivity to audience through two instructional modes: Student–teacher versus student–student interactive dialogues. *Learning Disabilities Research and Practice, 9,* 78–90.

Young, S. S. C. (2003). Integrating ICT into second language education in a vocational high school. *Journal of Computer Assisted Learning, 19,* 447–461.

Yu, V. W. S., & Atkinson, P. (1988). An investigation of the language difficulties experienced by Hong Kong secondary school students in English-medium schools: I. The problems. *Journal of Multilingual and Multicultural Development, 9,* 267–284.

Zuengler, J. (2004). Jackie Chan drinks Mountain Dew: Constructing cultural models of citizenship. *Linguistics and Education, 14,* 277–304.

CHAPTER 10

Research on the Literacies of AAVE-Speaking Adolescents

JAMAL COOKS
ARNETHA F. BALL

The language of African American students in the United States has been described using many labels, which include but are not limited to "Ebonics," "African Language Systems," "Pan-African Communication Behaviors," "Black English," and "African American Vernacular English" (AAVE). We begin this chapter by discussing some of the many labels that have been associated with the language of African Americans and then discuss the social and linguistic implications of those labels. In our earlier work together, we concluded that, regardless of how it is labeled, the language of African American students should be viewed as a valued resource that can be tapped by teachers who are generative in their thinking—tapped and used to improve the teaching and learning of all students in general, and of African American students in particular. In this chapter, we examine existing research on AAVE speakers and highlight the literature that emerged as a result of the Oakland, California, schools Ebonics controversy, as well as subsequent studies that can serve to inform classroom pedagogy and curriculum development. Although there are numerous studies that legitimize AAVE as a linguistic system, many practitioners continue to struggle with the successful implementation of instructional strategies that support the literacy learning of AAVE-speaking students in their classrooms. Within this context, we also address concepts of reflective optimism, teacher efficacy, and generativity as tools for addressing the perplexing challenges that many teachers are facing and the critical role of teachers' generative thinking in the establishment of innovative learning environments for AAVE-speaking students. The chapter concludes with a proposal for generativity on the part of teachers in order to advance knowledge concerning the implementation of effective pedagogical practices in classrooms that serve students from culturally and linguistically diverse backgrounds.

In 1997, Ball, Williams, and Cooks (1997) published an article on the educational value of African American Vernacular English (AAVE). In that article, the authors concluded that AAVE must be viewed as an untapped language resource, that teachers must use culturally relevant pedagogical approaches in classrooms that serve AAVE-speaking students, and that educators must continue to consider new and innovative ways to integrate the educationally valuable aspects of AAVE into the curriculum in holistic and nonsimplistic ways to improve the teaching and learning of students who identify this variety of English as their first language or mother tongue (Ball et al., 1997, p. 48). Today, more than 10 years after the publication of that article, researchers continue to come to the same conclusions regarding the need to close the achievement gap between AAVE-speaking adolescents and their non-AAVE-speaking counterparts, the need for more student-centered pedagogy in schools that serve AAVE-speaking adolescents, and the need for more research to find ways to improve the teaching and learning of AAVE-speaking adolescents in classrooms across the country. More than a decade after the publication of the Ball et al. article, this chapter revisits the topic and examines the nature of recent scholarship on the literacy practices of AAVE-speaking adolescents. Our goals in preparing this chapter were to locate empirical research conducted in classrooms and communities that increases our understanding of the nature of the language variety, to illuminate research on effective curriculum and approaches to teaching AAVE-speaking adolescents, and to highlight studies that focus on ways to improve their academic achievement.

In our review of the literature, we noted that the language of African Americans in the United States has been referred to using a wide variety of terms. Language- and literacy-associated organizations have their own perspectives about the language of African Americans. The Linguistics Society of America states that the language varieties known as "Ebonics," "African American Vernacular English," and "Vernacular Black English," and by other names, are systematic and rule-governed like all social speech varieties. The systematic and expressive nature of the grammar and pronunciation patterns of the African American Vernacular has been established by numerous scientific studies over the past 30 years (Linguistics Society of America, 1997).

However, researchers, including Spady, Charles, and Alim (1999), Smitherman (1977), Labov (1997), and Spears (1998), provide a review of the numerous names that have been used and include more than 40 labels and definitions. As they point out, this language variety has been defined by scholars in many different ways over the decades. Smitherman (1977) describes Black

language as Euro-American speech with an Afro-American meaning, nuance, tone, and gesture, which represents Black America's linguistic-cultural African heritage and the conditions of servitude, oppression, and life in America. It has allowed Blacks to create a culture of survival in an alien land, and, as a by-product, has served to enrich the language of all Americans. However, Labov (1997) believes that AAVE shares most of its grammar and vocabulary with other dialects of English. It is not simply slang, or speech with grammatical mistakes, but a well-informed set of rules of pronunciation and grammar that is capable of conveying complex logic and reasoning. Spears (1998) posits that *African American English* (AAE) is a cover term for AAVE and Standard African American Englishes (SAAE) because AAE comprises a number of related standard and nonstandard varieties, and varieties of AAE may have distinctly African American traits while having none of the features widely agreed upon as being nonstandard—for example, the use of *ain't* and multiple negatives within a sentence. Although the definitions may vary, most linguists agree about the systematicity of the language and acknowledge that it is a rule-governed language system that is frequently defined as the most distinctive variety of English in North America.

In this chapter we use the term *African American Vernacular English* (AAVE) to refer to a variety of English spoken primarily by lower- and working-class African Americans. It is a logical and systematic variety of English that has stylistic, phonological, lexical, and grammatical features that distinguish it from academic as well as standard or mainstream American English. For the purposes of this text, we use mainstream American English (MAE) when talking about language in broader societal contexts and Standard American English (SAE) when referring to educational contexts. Although they may appear to be similar, we posit that it is significant to make a distinction between the two terms.

A substantial body of sociolinguistic research has documented the linguistic characteristics of nonmainstream, low-prestige varieties of American English, including AAVE (Ball, 1992; Baugh, 1990, 1992; Edwards, 1992; Fasold, 1972; Labov, 1972a, 1972b;

Kochman, 1981; Poplack & Tagliamonte, 1994; Rickford & Rickford, 2000; Smitherman, 1994, 1999, 2000, 2006; Wolfram, 1969). It is the first language learned by most African Americans throughout the United States and is used primarily in informal settings. Although certain linguistic features appear in AAVE, many of these features also appear in other American English varieties, but they occur in AAVE more frequently, systematically, and consistently than in MAE. We are not proposing that African Americans are a linguistically homogeneous group and recognize that an individual African American's linguistic usage may fall anywhere along a continuum, from using AAVE features almost all the time to using no AAVE features at all (see Ball, 2000).

With the recent perennial debates concerning AAVE as the primary discourse of many low-achieving students and questions about how to build on the language to teach these students more effectively, a host of linguists and educational reformers are concerned about the teaching and learning of students who use this variety of English. They realize that the conceptualization and implementation of a reform vision will require extensive societal and individual learning as well as the unlearning of myths, stereotypes, and misconceptions that surround the teaching and learning of students who speak AAVE. Specifically, owing to social, political, and economic factors, AAVE is still often seen as substandard, stigmatized, and a barrier to the acquisition of literacy. In addition, because the differences in AAVE and academic English are often subtle and thus often overlooked by the "untrained" or uninformed listener or reader, the need to take these differences into serious consideration is often underestimated by educators and policymakers.

Two important events have brought these issues to the attention of educators, researchers, policymakers, and the general public. One occurred in 1979 when a federal court judge in Michigan ruled on behalf of 11 AAVE-speaking students, finding that a school must consider the language practices of a student's home culture to meet federal guidelines for nondiscrimination, even when that language varies from the linguistic system used by most middle-class Americans. Almost 30 years after that seminal ruling,

the challenge remains for teachers who teach AAVE-speaking students to find ways to support their learning and achievement. A long-standing concern has been how to develop classroom cultures and curricula that promote equity in opportunity and accessibility to learning for individuals across boundaries of class and ethnicity. Acting on this concern has been difficult for many teachers who feel overwhelmed when faced with the task of teaching students who come from cultural and linguistic backgrounds that are very different from their own. The Ann Arbor, Michigan, case, however, made it clear that school districts and teachers are responsible for rethinking pedagogy and curriculum in ways that make learning accessible to all students, regardless of their cultural, racial, or ethnic backgrounds.

The second important event occurred during the summer of 1996 when the Oakland Unified School District formed a 37-member task force consisting of parents, community leaders, administrators, and researchers to meet with the school board regarding recommendations to improve the academic standing of the district's students. The task force concluded that the primary deterrent to school success for the predominately African American population of the Oakland Unified School District was *language*. Following the recommendations of the task force, the school board adopted a resolution, which stated:

> Now, therefore, be it resolved that the Board of Education officially recognizes the existence, and the cultural and historic bases of West and Niger-Congo African Language Systems, and each language as the predominantly primary language of African-American students; and that the Superintendent in conjunction with her staff shall immediately devise and implement the best possible academic program for imparting instruction to African-American students in their primary language for the combined purposes of maintaining the legitimacy and richness of such language whether it is known as "Ebonics," "African Language Systems," "Pan-African Communication Behaviors" or other description, and to facilitate their acquisition and mastery of English language skills.

The purpose of the resolution was to acknowledge the district's determination to find a way to recognize and highlight linguistic diversity among its student population. The next step was to develop a program of instruction that would allow teachers to embrace the language and literacy skills students enter the classroom with and build toward students' mastery of Standard American English. However, because of an outcry of resistance from mainstream America concerning this resolution, the need for an expert group to validate the actions of the Oakland school board emerged. On January 10, 1997, a proclamation was issued by the Committee of Linguists of African Descent on language issues related to the education of African American students. It stated:

> We endorse the urgent need for coherent educational policies and practices informed by the current state of knowledge about the variety of language commonly known as Black English, African American English Vernacular (AAVE), Ebonics, and a number of other terms. The Oakland School Board action is a historic landmark which has placed the Black English issue on the public agenda in an unprecedented manner. The lively and heated discussions that have ensued can have desirable consequences insofar as they contribute more enlightened public attitudes toward rich diversity of language varieties spoken in this country and proper respect for the intrinsic worth and dignity of them all.

Since the time of both the Ann Arbor case and the Oakland Unified School District controversy, there has been very little evidence that the attitudes of the general American public or those of most classroom teachers have changed considerably toward AAVE, nor have any major policies been developed to address the issues of language and literacy diversity for African American students (Ball & Muhammad, 2003). In addition, there is little evidence that the language differences of AAVE students have been accommodated in systematic ways in most public or private school systems in the United States. Consequently, a good deal of scholarship has focused on providing information that can serve to change the attitudes of teachers, policymakers, and the general public concerning the legitimacy of AAVE as a coherent language system. Zeigler and Osinubi (2002) point out the uneasy rela-

tionship between Standard American English and AAVE, and they discuss why the relationship remains controversial. These authors note that some varieties of English around the world are more readily recognized as legitimate varieties of English than others. They conclude that the status of AAVE in America reflects the larger postcolonial struggles of its speakers.

Since Ball et al.'s publication in 1997, much research has focused on ways to build on the existing linguistic skills of AAVE-speaking students as they learn to read, write, and speak academic English and on ways to help students communicate effectively in a variety of settings. Our recent search of the Educational Resources Information Center (ERIC) database from 1997 to 2007 used the descriptors *African American vernacular English* to generate 270 entries, and an additional 200 entries using the descriptor *Ebonics*. A review of the entries that emerged revealed that research on the literacies of AAVE-speaking adolescents or Ebonics-speaking adolescents has generally fallen into three categories: (1) the influences of teacher attitudes and classroom and/or community *contexts* on the literacies of AAVE-speaking adolescents; (2) *curriculum*, teaching strategies, and pedagogical approaches used when working with AAVE-speaking adolescents; and (3) *assessment* issues related to students' use of AAVE. Using these three categories—context, curriculum, and assessment—to organize the information, this review focuses on the major findings that have emerged. In the concluding section of this chapter, we discuss some of the implications of this work for teachers who teach AAVE-speaking adolescents and for policymakers. Finally, we propose directions for future research.

CONTEXTS

A primary area of study in the research on literacy practices of AAVE-speaking adolescents focuses on the importance of the context in which teaching and learning occur. This research helps us to understand that the individuals within an environment are but one factor that influences the literacy practices of AAVE-speaking adolescents. Studies confirm that additional factors that influence literacy practices include, but are not limited to, teacher attitudes concerning students' use of AAVE in the classroom, students' identities and self-concept development, and classroom and/or community settings. Each of these factors plays an important role in the literacy practices of AAVE-speaking adolescents and in these students' ultimate achievement. Ball and Lardner (1997) discuss the historical importance of the Ann Arbor case and teachers' dispositions toward the literacy practices of AAVE-speaking students, and Blake and Cutler (2003) focus on AAVE and the variation in teacher attitudes as they relate to the philosophies of the schools students attend. The work of Frederick, Braithwaite, and LaGrange (1998) focuses on the language development of Ebonics-speaking African American youth and contends that school counselors should assume the role of consultants to and collaborators with teachers and students in their efforts to increase and improve students' use of Standard American English without depreciating students' culturally based language use. Looking at issues from the students' perspective, Casteel (1997) investigates the attitudes of African American and European American eighth-grade students concerning praises, awards, and punishments. In addition, Fordham (1999) analyzes the discourse styles of a group of African American high school students and concludes that Ebonics or Black English is the norm against which all other speech practices are evaluated by the students and is used in a form of guerrilla warfare at the research site. Datnow and Cooper's (1997) analysis of African American students' use of AAVE in a predominantly European American elite independent school reveals that formal and informal peer networks and use of language supported these students' academic success, created opportunities for them to reaffirm their racial identities, and facilitated their adjustment to settings that were otherwise difficult for AAVE-speaking adolescents to fit into.

Although the majority of the studies that emerged from our search on the importance of context in the teaching and learning of AAVE-speaking students focused on in-school factors, the work of Mahiri (2000, 2004) and Ball and Lardner (2005) helped us to understand the influences of commu-nity and/or out-of-school contexts on the use of literacies by AAVE-speaking students. Understanding students' engagement with literacy practices that take place outside schools can help us to build bridges between students' home, community, and academic lives. Mahiri (2000) brings classroom and community issues to the forefront as he looks at students struggling for voice through the development of writing skills. In *Shooting for Excellence*, Mahiri describes two teachers, both African American, who teach English in the same inner-city high school. Ms. Parks has astounding success with her students, while Ms. Johnson's students are frequently disruptive and even fall asleep in class. Why the difference? Through a series of vignettes, Mahiri probes the causes and demonstrates how the students' African American and youth culture cannot be ignored if we are to effect change and ensure educational success. He shows how building on African American youth's culture and experiences fosters student ownership and achievement. He recommends that teachers draw on diversity in the curriculum and promote creative social and cultural awareness to address students' historically oppositional nature and that students be encouraged to make viable connections between the streets and schools. Mahiri concludes by imagining new-century schools as building on cultural diversity yet aiming for cultural transformation, teaching students the knowledge, skills, and values that can promote nonoppressive human interactions and benefit students academically and socially.

Ball and Lardner (2005) investigate AAVE in writing and composition classrooms in terms of teacher knowledge and prevailing attitudes and discuss the need to change current pedagogical approaches. The authors acknowledge that many African American students come to writing and composition classrooms with talents that are not appreciated, and they provide practitioners, administrators, teacher-educators, and researchers knowledge and strategies that can help to unleash the potential of African American students in their classrooms. The authors outline 12 changes—referred to as "The Dozens"—that teachers can initiate and monitor as they reflect on, analyze, and transform their classroom practices while they encourage writing program administrators, teacher-educators, and researchers to support needed classroom changes. Drawing on examples from teachers in community-based organizations, the authors advocate the use of oral language to engage students' interest *and* as a precursor to successful writing activities.

CURRICULUM, INSTRUCTIONAL STRATEGIES, AND PEDAGOGICAL APPROACHES

Although most school curricula reflect the values and interests of middle-class European Americans and omit the cultural experiences of racially, ethnically, and linguistically diverse students, some researchers have worked to help us understand the influences of changing curriculum, instructional strategies, and pedagogical approaches on the use of literacies by AAVE-speaking students. Earlier researchers, including Moll (1987, 1990), Means (1991), Ball (1992, 1995), Gutiérrez (1992), Lee (1993), Nieto (1992), Redd (1992), and Au (1980, 1993), have contributed to our appreciation of the language and literacy resources that diverse student populations bring to their classroom life experience and the importance of considering these resources when planning and implementing classroom instruction. Lee (2001) analyzes the quality of intellectual reasoning of a class of low-achieving African American high school students, and she examines a teacher's ability to scaffold a radically different intellectual culture among students, using explicit modeling to align the cultural funds of knowledge of the African American students with the cultural practices of the subject matter. Other more recent researchers who have focused on making connections between home and school when working with AAVE-speaking students include Adger, Christian, and Taylor (1999), who focus on making the connections between home language and academic achievement among African American students; Fisher (2003, 2007), who reports on research that investigates the use of open mics and spoken-word poetry to engage youth in participatory literacy communities; Alim (2004), who discusses the use of style shifting; Cooks (2004) who uses hip-hop as a teaching tool to develop expository writ-

ing skills; Morrell (2004), who explores the use of students as critical ethnographers of their own language and literacy practices; and Alim (2005), who discusses critical awareness pedagogy in working with AAVE-speaking students. Siegel (1999) notes that the public tends to view pidgins, creoles, and minority dialects (such as AAVE) as corrupted or degenerate forms of standardized languages and to fear that their use interferes with students' acquisition of Standard American English. As a consequence, stigmatized varieties are banned from most classrooms. Siegel critically examines this popular view and notes that research on educational programs shows that, contrary to the prevailing viewpoint, using a stigmatized variety in formal education seems to have a positive rather than a negative effect on the acquisition of Standard American English. Marback (2001) focuses on the important issue of changing public attitudes toward literacy, and Gold (2003) examines the pedagogical practices of poet, civil rights activist, and teacher Melvin B. Tolson as a model for teachers to consider. Tolson taught at Wiley College from 1923 to 1947. Gold notes that Tolson's complex classroom style, which mixed elements of classical and African American rhetoric, produced a pedagogy that was at once conservative, progressive, and radical, inspiring his students to academic achievement and social action. Tolson demonstrated that it is possible to instruct students in the norms of the academy without sacrificing the primary discourse that students bring from their home and community environments.

Several researchers have investigated effective pedagogical approaches for working with AAVE-speaking adolescents. Spady et al. (1999) report on four approaches to curriculum articulated by Rickford that can be used when working with AAVE-speaking students. They include (1) the linguistically informed approach, (2) contrastive analysis, (3) dialect readers, and (4) dialect awareness programs. The *linguistically informed approach* is characterized by Labov's (2001) development of Individualized Reading Programs (IRPs) in Philadelphia and California (Labov & Baker, 2003), which begins with one basic and fundamental premise, that teachers should distinguish between mistakes in reading and differences in pronunciation. The *contrastive analysis* approach focuses on making the differences between SAE and AAVE explicit, using strategies such as contrastive analysis along with other second-language acquisition methodology (see Harris-Wright, 1999; LeMoine & Hollie, 2007; Parker & Crist, 1995; Taylor, 1989). *Dialect readers* is an approach that introduces reading in the students' primary discourse and later makes a switch to SAE (Simpkins & Simpkins, 1981). The *dialect awareness* approach seeks to infuse the fundamental principles of linguistic variation into school curricula, and students are encouraged to become ethnographers of their own and their local community's' speech patterns (Wolfram, Adger, & Christian, 1999). In addition, the work of Harris-Wright (1999) and Smitherman (1981) focus on enhancing bidialectalism as an approach for working with urban African American students. However, Ibrahim (1999) investigated the interrelation between identity and learning, using a group of French-speaking immigrant and refugee continental African youth as a case involving students who learned stylized AAVE through hip-hop culture and rap lyrics.

Perlstein (2002) investigated the appeal of progressive pedagogy and the evolution of political and educational ideas among African-American civil rights activists who created alternative schools for Black children in the 1960s and 1970s. He noted that curricular shifts mirrored the broader African American freedom struggle. This author concludes that support for progressive pedagogy depends on the expectation that students will be able to participate fully in the promise of civic life. According to Perlstein, the history of the freedom and liberation schools developed by Black activists suggests that no curricular project can fundamentally transform knowledge and its distribution if it is not part of a process of transforming social relations as well. Liberation schools are a particular type of alternative, sponsored historically by groups like the Black Panther Party, modeled after the program in Oakland, California, during the Civil Rights era.

ASSESSMENT

When looking at issues of assessment and the literacy practices of AAVE-speaking students, Gabrielson, Gordon, and Engelhard's (1995) study of the Georgia High School Writing Test revealed that students' preferences in the type of writing chosen on writing tasks did not have a significant effect on their writing scores. However, when focusing specifically on female students and on African American students, choice seemed to positively impact their assessment scores. Ball (1997) reported on the findings of a study that illustrates the assessment practices of teachers from different cultural groups and highlights the value of including the voices of teachers from diverse backgrounds in discussions on writing assessments. The inclusion of such voices can help not only to inform, but to reshape current assessment practices, research priorities, and policy debates that focus on finding solutions to problems of assessment, particularly as they relate to diverse populations.

In a two-part study, Ball (1997) compared the assessment practices of four European American teachers and four African American teachers and found that European American and African American teachers hold some consistently different views about the assessment of diverse students' written texts. Ball found that European American teachers consistently rated the writing of European American students as superior to African American students, whereas the African American teachers rated African American students' writing as superior to European American students. Ball followed up the holistic writing evaluations with teacher interviews that revealed the concerns of the African American teachers who participated in this study. Through candid and reflective comments, these teachers shared deeply felt concerns and specific suggestions concerning writing assessment. The African American teachers scored the African American students' texts higher than the European American teachers scored the texts. However, the African American teachers were concerned about the level of writing because student scores were still below grade-level expectations. Specifically, the African American teachers stated that they felt the students had the ability to write at a much higher level than was represented in their writing samples. These educators suggested that content and the students' ideas should be emphasized in assessments along with a balanced focus on the conventions and forms of writing, and they called for more research that addresses the teaching of writing to African American students. Ball noted that including the voices of teachers from culturally diverse backgrounds can be useful in broadening debates about the reform of writing assessment for all students, but for culturally and linguistically diverse students in particular.

Ball (1999) also explored issues of assessment with AAVE-speaking adolescents and provided examples of instances in which characteristic features of spoken AAVE appear in a student's written text at the phonological, syntactic, semantic, and discourse levels. Ball's examination of the oral and written discourse preferences of African American adolescents provides teachers with a line-by-line analysis of a student's text and suggests that culture and age are important factors in students' preferred writing patterns. Further, a clearer understanding of students' community-based discourse practices can help to inform teachers' instructional and assessment practices. An understanding of these factors can allow teachers to create curricular bridges that link students' home, community, and school communication practices and demands. As a pedagogical solution, Ball recommends that writing conferences be recognized as a valuable source of communication between student and teacher so that each can better understand and better meet the other's expectations as they relate to writing.

Other researchers have examined the limitations of assessments and propose that assessments and tests need to be adapted and adjusted to the students and should be multifaceted in nature (Ball, 1993). More recent research by McNicol, Reid, and Wisdom (1998) speak to the limitations of language assessment testing. For example, evaluators often view Ebonics usage as reflecting a vocabulary deficiency or impaired auditory functioning (p. 17). Evaluators and researchers propose alternative assessments, including contextualized, ecological, and curriculum-based assessments. In addition, there are a number of researchers who provide insight on how to adapt various assessments. Seymour, Abdulkarim, and Johnson (1999) propose that teachers and speech/language pathologists must understand, accept, and support the dialects their students bring to

school, and adapt and devise educational and clinical strategies that accommodate the language background of their students. In particular, speech/language pathologists who work with AAVE-speaking adolescents are encouraged to seek specialized training so that they are proficient in the evaluation of students from culturally and linguistically diverse backgrounds and become skilled in the administration of multiple assessment tools when investigating the speech and language skills of AAVE-speaking adolescents (Rivers, Rosa-Lugo, & Hedrick, 2004).

CONCLUSIONS AND IMPLICATIONS FOR INSTRUCTION AND FUTURE RESEARCH

Many parents, students, classroom teachers, and policymakers are concerned that too many middle and high school students are not gaining the literacy skills they need to perform at their full potential in school and nonschool settings. This is particularly the case for many African American adolescents. According to the 2002 National Assessment of Educational Progress (NAEP) report, 45% of eighth-grade African American students cannot read at the basic level, whereas only 16% of their eighth-grade European American peers cannot read at the basic level. When we look at the writing abilities of the these students, we find that 26% of eighth-grade African American students cannot write at the basic level and 41% of twelfth-grade African American students cannot write at the basic level, whereas only 10% of their eighth-grade European American peers and only 21% of their twelfth-grade European American peers do not write at the basic level. The number of twelfth-grade African American students who were able to write at a basic level actually declined from 64% in 1998 to 59% in 2002. According to the 2002 NAEP scores, only 9% of twelfth-grade African American students were able to write at a proficient level (see National Center for Education Statistics, 2003).

A long-standing challenge for those charged with the task of educating AAVE-speaking adolescents has been to provide them with the literacy skills they will need to excel in our rapidly changing society. Although new standards for middle and high school achievement require students to be more skilled than ever before, most AAVE-speaking middle and high school students are performing well below their non-AAVE-speaking peers on almost every standardized measure of literacy development.

This review of studies on the literacy practices of AAVE-speaking students over the past decade reveals that much of the research has focused on context, curriculum, instructional strategies, pedagogical approaches, and issues related to assessment. At the center of most of these studies lie issues of social justice, equity, and the need to address the negative undertones of racism. This need is based on the assumption that academic or Standard American English is associated with access, achievement, and privilege, whereas AAVE (like other non-prestigious linguistic systems) is looked upon by many as being inferior. Woodford (1997) explored the democratic aspect of language diversity and concluded that accepting and accommodating the plurality of language patterns, lifestyles, cultural backgrounds, and values of different people are essential for freedom and democracy. According to Woodford, emphasizing the importance of SAE is not contradictory to the democratic idea, for in a democracy, mastery of SAE would help promote equal opportunity and improve the possibility of people to communicate across boundaries and boarders. Ideally, however, we must encourage space for both respect and acceptance of individual differences, as well as simultaneous movement toward the development of tools that allow communication among a wide variety of people in varying contexts. Although much of the research suggests the need to use AAVE as a bridge for teaching academic English and the need for schools to identify strategies that validate the students' home languages and cultures, the scarcity of emerging studies in several other areas warrants mentioning. Although we are confident that some work is being completed in a number of areas (discussed below), our mention of these topics is an appeal for further research. Such research is crucial to the development of literacies for AAVE-speaking adolescents and for accelerating our progress toward closing the achievement gap.

One area of great need is research that distinguishes the differences in the needs of AAVE-speaking students who have learning disabilities, underachieving AAVE-speaking adolescents, and underserved students attending underresourced schools who have been denied access to excellent instruction by fully qualified teachers. Fisher and Frey (2003) looked at writing instruction for struggling adolescent readers and concluded that teachers should focus on both the reading and writing of these students to support their literacy development. Initiatives such as No Child Left Behind pressure teachers to focus on the reading abilities of students in culturally diverse classrooms; however, the writing needs of these students are often neglected. More research is needed on the writing of AAVE-speaking students and the use of writing as a pedagogical tool that facilitates the development of critical and generative thinking skills for these students (see Ball, in press).

In today's technologically advanced global society, it is critically important that a great deal more attention be devoted to research on the use of computer technology in classrooms that serve AAVE-speaking students. It is evident that technology's potential has not been fully explored, realized, maximized, or even made fully accessible to students from culturally diverse backgrounds. Pinkard (2001) is one of few investigators whose research interests focus specifically on the development of computer-based visualizations to support AAVE-speaking students, teacher analysis of these students' literacy practices, and increasing our understanding of how culture influences the design and use of learning environments. The work of Ball-Anthony (2008) investigates the implementation of a laptop program in a midwestern school district and has important implications for policy and practices in implementing technology programs in schools that serve diverse student populations.

A final area in need of further research reflects the realization that teachers are faced with an urgent responsibility to transform their curricula, teaching practices, and approaches to assessment. This area of research should focus on the development of teachers who have the skills, attitudes, dispositions, and desire to become excellent teachers of culturally and linguistically diverse students in general and AAVE-speaking students in particular. Irvine (2003) investigates the education of teachers for diversity and suggests ways for teachers to see their students with a cultural eye. Richardson (2003) provides a compelling account of the language and literacy practices of African American students and suggests new ways for teachers to think about incorporating linguistic diversity into their theories and pedagogical methods when teaching students from AAVE-speaking backgrounds. Thompson (2004) provides teachers with a wealth of knowledge on teaching AAVE-speaking students by discussing "what teachers need to know but are afraid to ask about African American students," and Redd and Webb (2005) provide a teacher's introduction to African American English in which they address "what every writing teacher should know about AAVE and AAVE-speaking students." Ball (2006) reports the results of a cross-national action research study of a teacher education course designed to instill critical thinking and positive attitudes in teachers who teach culturally and linguistically diverse students. Ball's decade-long program of study, based on multiple data sources, documents the effect of a teacher education course on teachers' attitudes, including their journal writing, reflective essays, responses to classroom readings, transcripts of classroom discussions, and observations of their classroom teaching. She reports on the teachers' classroom practices—during and following their participation in the course. In addition to the work of Irvine, Richardson, Thompson, Redd, and Webb, and Ball, more research is needed that can help us to understand those approaches that actually make a significant difference in the literacy lives of African American students and the strategies that are most successful in working with AAVE-speaking adolescents. To facilitate this work, increased funding is needed to support large-scale and longitudinal studies conducted by researchers from culturally and linguistically diverse backgrounds as well as by mainstream researchers. As we develop new paradigms of research to accomplish these goals, we must resist mandates that dictate the types of methodologies that can be used. Rather, researchers should employ methodologies that are most appropriate for addressing these persistent and critically important questions.

In conducting this review of the research, we have not only found the need for further study in unresolved areas, but we have also come to the realization that very little of the current research is breaking new ground. In essence, most of this research concludes that students' home and community language and literacies may be used as a bridge to further develop their academic literacies. In addition, however, we must break new ground in research that (1) builds on sociocultural theory, cultural historical activity theory, and other theoretical approaches that can serve as frameworks for improving teaching and teacher preparation programs that are capable of addressing the complex social, political, and cognitive issues that perplex the educational community; (2) contributes to the development of teachers who are prepared and motivated to use literacies in strategic ways to improve the classroom lives of AAVE-speaking adolescents; and (3) brings innovation to the research on how to use AAVE-speaking adolescents' home language and youth culture as a scaffold for developing academic literacy skills. Numerous studies have focused on the failure and underachievement of AAVE-speaking students. Fewer studies, though, have documented the successful development of AAVE-speaking students' literacy skills in spite of the overwhelming challenges they face. Even fewer studies have provided innovative models to guide the professional development of excellent teachers who are prepared and motivated to teach AAVE-speaking students effectively.

We concluded our 1997 article (Ball, 1997) by encouraging educators to develop and implement a culturally relevant pedagogy that is expanded to focus on students' language practices that can move us toward the desirable consequences of enlightened attitudes and engender a proper respect for the intrinsic worth, dignity, and value of all language varieties. Inasmuch as few educators have actually embraced this challenge, we again issue the call for instructional approaches that incorporate the untapped language resources of AAVE-speaking students as a basis for enriching the learning experiences of all. Only when we begin to rigorously combine effective and innovative approaches to address the educational needs of AAVE-speaking students will we witness transformation in the academic experiences of these students. In a world of changing demographics, it is imperative that educational institutions consider creative, new, and expanded approaches to education that stimulate the intellectual curiosity of, and a sense of agency in, diverse students in authentic ways. AAVE has been a part of the cultural heritage of this country for more than 300 years, and if past trends are an indicator of the future, it will continue to be a vibrant language variety in the coming years. We must, therefore, commit to seriously considering viable approaches that build upon the educationally valuable aspects of AAVE and aid in the process of improving the academic achievement of students who speak this variety of English.

REFERENCES

Adger, C. T., Christian, D., & Taylor, O. (Eds.). (1999). *Making the connection: Language and academic achievement among African American students.* Washington, DC: Center for Applied Linguistics; McHenry, IL: Delta Systems.

Alim, H. S. (2004). You know my steez: An ethnographic and sociolinguistic study of styleshifting in a Black American speech community. *Publications of the American Dialect Society* (No. 89). Durham, NC: Duke University Press.

Alim, H. S. (2005). Critical language awareness in the United States: Revisiting issues and revising pedagogies in a resegregated society. *Educational Researcher, 34,* 24–31.

Au, K. (1980). Participation structures in a reading lesson with Hawaiian children. *Anthropology and Education Quarterly, 11,* 91–115.

Au, K. (1993). *Literacy instruction in multicultural settings.* Fort Worth: Harcourt Brace.

Ball, A. F. (1992). Cultural preference and the expository writing of African-American adolescents. *Written Communication, 9,* 501–532.

Ball, A. F. (1993). Incorporating ethnographic-based techniques to enhance assessments of culturally and linguistically diverse students' written exposition. *Educational Assessment, 1,* 255–281.

Ball, A. F. (1995). Text design patterns in the writing of urban African-American students: Teaching to the strengths of students in multicultural settings. *Urban Education, 30,* 253–289.

Ball, A. F. (1997). Expanding the dialogue on culture as a critical component when assessing writing. *Assessing Writing, 4,* 169–202.

Ball, A. F. (1999). Evaluating the writing of culturally and linguistically diverse students: The case of the African American Vernacular English speaker. In C.

R. Cooper & L. Odell (Eds.), *Evaluating writing: The role of teachers' knowledge about text, learning, and culture* (pp. 225–248). Urbana, IL: National Council of Teachers of English.

Ball, A. F. (2000). Empowering pedagogies that enhance the learning of multicultural students. *Teachers College Record, 102,* 1006–1034.

Ball, A. F. (2006). *Multicultural strategies for education and social change: Carriers of the torch in the US and South Africa.* New York: Teachers College Press.

Ball, A. F. (in press). Toward a theory of generative change in culturally and linguistically complex classrooms. *American Educational Research Journal.*

Ball, A. F., & Lardner, T. (1997). Dispositions toward literacy: Constructs of teacher knowledge and the Ann Arbor Black English case. *College Composition and Communication, 48,* 469–485.

Ball, A. F., & Lardner, T. (2005). *African American literacies unleashed: Vernacular English and the composition classroom.* Carbondale, IL: Southern Illinois University Press.

Ball, A. F., & Muhammad, R. J. (2003). *Language diversity in teacher education and in the classroom.* In G. Smitherman & V. Villanueva (Eds.), *Language diversity in the classroom: From intention to practice* (pp. 76–88). Carbondale, IL: Southern Illinois University Press.

Ball, A. F., Williams, J., & Cooks, J. (1997). An Ebonics-based curriculum: The educational value. *Thought and Action: The NEA Higher Education Journal, 13*(2), 39–50.

Ball-Anthony, A. (2008). *Examining school system influences on teachers' technology integration practices.* Unpublished doctoral dissertation, University of Michigan.

Baugh, J. (1990). A survey of the suffix /-s/ analyses in Black English. In J. A. Edmondson, C. Feagin, & P. Mulhauser (Eds.), *Development and diversity: Language variation across time and space.* Arlington: University of Texas and Summer Institute of Linguistics.

Baugh, J. (1992). Hypercorrection: Mistakes in production of vernacular African American English as a second dialect. *Language and Education, 6,* 47–61.

Blake, R., & Cutler, C. (2003). AAE and variation in teachers' attitudes: A question of school philosophy? *Linguistics and Education, 14,* 163–194.

Casteel, C. (1997). Attitudes of African American and Caucasian eighth grade students about praises, awards, and punishments. *Elementary School Guidance and Counseling, 31,* 262–272.

Cooks, J. (2004). Writing for something: The nexus among raps, essays, and expository organizational patterns of African American adolescents. *English Journal, 94*(1), 72–76.

Datnow, A., & Cooper, R. (1997). Peer networks of African American students in independent schools: Affirming academic success and racial identity. *Journal of Negro Education, 66,* 56–72.

Edwards, W. (1992). Sociolinguistic behavior in a Detroit inner-city black neighborhood. *Language in Society, 21,* 93–116.

Fasold, R. (1972) *Tense and the form "be" in Black English.* Washington, DC: Center for Applied Linguistics.

Fisher, D., & Frey, N. (2003). Finger pointing: Lessons learned from a chronically underperforming high school. *Principal Leadership, 4*(1), 40–46.

Fisher, M. (2003). Open mics and open minds: Spoken word poetry in African diaspora participatory literacy communities. *Harvard Educational Review 73,* 362–389.

Fisher, M. (2007). *Writing in rhythm: Spoken word poetry in urban classrooms.* New York: Teachers College Press.

Fordham, S. (1999). Dissin' "the Standard": Ebonics as guerilla warfare at Capital High. *Anthropology and Education Quarterly, 30,* 272–293.

Frederick, H., Braithwaite, K., & LaGrange, R. (1998). Ebonics and academic achievement: The role of the counselor. *Journal of Negro Education, 67,* 25–34.

Gabrielson, S., Gordon, B., & Engelhard (1995). The effects of task choice on the quality of writing obtained in a statewide assessment. *Applied Measurement in Education, 8,* 273–290.

Gold, D. (2003). "Nothing educates us like a shock": The integrated rhetoric of Melvin B. Tolson. *College Composition and Communication, 55,* 226–253.

Gutiérrez, K. D. (1992). A comparison of instructional contexts in writing process classrooms with Latino children. *Education and Urban Society, 24,* 244–262.

Harris-Wright, K. (1999). Enhancing bidialectalism in urban African American students. In C. Adger, D. Christian, & O. Taylor (Eds.), *Making the connection* (pp. 53–60). Washington, DC: CAL/Delta.

Ibrahim, A. (1999). Becoming Black: Rap and hip-hop, race, gender, identity, and the politics of ESL Learning, *TESOL Quarterly, 33,* 349–369.

Irvine, J. (2003). *Educating teachers for diversity: Seeing with a cultural eye.* New York: Teachers College Press.

Kochman, T. (1981). *Black and White styles in conflict.* Chicago: University of Chicago Press.

Labov, W. (1972a). *Language in the inner city: Studies in the Black English Vernacular.* Philadelphia: University of Pennsylvania Press.

Labov, W. (1972b). *Sociolinguistic patterns.* Philadelphia: University of Pennsylvania Press.

Labov, W. (1997). Sociolinguistic patterns. In C. B. Paulston & G. R. Tucker (Eds.), *The early days of sociolinguistics: Memories and reflections* (pp. 147–150). Dallas, TX: The Summer Institute of Linguistics.

Labov, W. (2001). Applying our knowledge of African American English to the problem of raising reading levels in inner city schools. In S. Lanehart (Ed.), *Sociocultural and historical contexts of African American English* (pp. 299–317). Philadelphia: John Benjamins.

Labov, W., & Baker, B. (2003). *What is a reading error?* Unpublished manuscript. *www.ling.upenn.edu/~wlabov/.*

Lee, C. D. (1993). *Signifying as a scaffold for literary interpretation: The pedagogical implications of an African American discourse genre.* Urbana, IL: National Council of Teachers of English.

Lee, C. D. (2001). Is October Brown Chinese? A cultural modeling activity system for underachieving students. *American Educational Research Journal, 38,* 97–141.

LeMoine, N., & Hollie, S. (2007). The academic English mastery program: Inspiration, Dr. Geneva Smitherman. In H. S. Alim & J. Baugh (Eds.), *Black language, education, and social change* (pp. 23–33). New York: Teachers College Press.

Linguistic Society of America. (1997, January). *Resolution on the Oakland "ebonics" issue.* Drafted by John Rickford.

Mahiri, J. (Ed.). (2000). *Shooting for excellence: African and American youth culture in new century schools.* Urbana, IL: National Council of Teachers of English.

Mahiri, J. (Ed.). (2004). *What they don't learn in school: Literacy in the lives of urban youth.* New York: Peter Lang.

Marback, R. (2001). Ebonics: Theorizing in public our attitudes toward literacy. *College Composition and Communication, 53,* 11–32.

McNicol, S., Reid, G., & Wisdom, C. (1998). The psychoeducational assessment of Ebonics speakers: Issues and challenges. *Journal of Negro Education, 67,* 16–24.

Means, B. (Ed.). (1991). *Teaching advanced skills to at-risk students: Views from research and practice.* San Francisco: Jossey-Bass.

Moll, L. C. (1987). Change as the goal of educational research. *Anthropology and Education Quarterly 18,* 300–311.

Moll, L. C. (Ed.). (1990). *Vygotsky and education: Instructional applications of sociohistorical psychology.* New York: Cambridge University Press.

Morrell, E. (2004). *Becoming critical researchers: Literacy and empowerment for urban youth.* New York: Peter Lang.

National Center for Education Statistics. (2003). *The nation's report card: Writing 2002.* Washington, DC: Author.

Nieto, S. (1992). *Affirming diversity: The sociopolitical context of multicultural education.* New York: Longman.

Parker, H., & Christ, M. (1995). *Teaching minorities to play the corporate language game.* Columbia, SC: National Resource Center for the Freshman Year Experience and Students in Transition, University of South Carolina.

Perlstein, D. (2002). Mind stayed on freedom: Politics and pedagogy in the African American freedom struggle. *American Educational Research Journal, 39,* 249–277.

Pinkard, N. (2001). Rappin Reader *and* Say Say Oh Playmate: Using children's childhood songs as literacy scaffolds in computer-based learning environments. *Journal of Educational Computing Research, 25*, 17–34.

Poplack, S., & Tagliamonte, S. (1994). -S or nothing: Marking the plural in the African-American diaspora. *American Speech, 69*, 227–259.

Redd, T. (1992, April). *Untapped resources: "Styling" in Black students' writing for Black audiences.* Paper presented at the annual meeting of the American Educational Research Association, San Francisco.

Redd, T., & Webb, K. (2005). *A teacher's introduction to African American English: What a writing teacher should know.* Urbana, IL: National Council of Teachers of English.

Richardson, E. (2003). *African American literacies.* New York: Routledge.

Rickford, J., & Rickford, R. (2000). *Spoken soul.* New York: Wiley.

Rivers, K., Rosa-Lugo, L., & Hedrick, D. (2004). Performance of African-American adolescents on a measure of language proficiency. *Negro Educational Review, 55*, 117–127.

Seymour, H., Abdulkarim, L., & Johnson, V. (1999). The Ebonics controversy: An educational and clinical dilemma. *Topics in Language Disorders, 4*, 66–77.

Siegel, J. (1999). Creoles and minority dialects in education: An overview. *Journal of Multilingual and Multicultural Development, 20*, 508–531.

Simpkins, G. A., & Simpkins, C. (1981). Cross cultural approach to curriculum development. In G. Smitherman (Ed.), *Black English and the education of Black children and youth: Proceedings of the national Invitational Symposium on the King decision* (pp. 221–240). Detroit: Center for Black Studies, Wayne State University.

Smitherman, G. (1977). *Talkin' and testifyin': The language of Black America.* Detroit: Wayne State University Press.

Smitherman, G. (Ed.). (1981). *Black English and the education of Black children and youth: Proceedings of the National Invitational Symposium on the King decision.* Detroit: Center for Black Studies, Wayne State University.

Smitherman, G. (1994). *Black talk: Words and phrases from the hood to the Amen corner.* New York: Houghton Mifflin.

Smitherman, G. (1999). CCC's role in the struggle for language rights. *College Composition and Communication, 50*, 349–376.

Smitherman, G. (2000). *Talkin' that talk: Language, culture, and education in African America.* New York: Routledge.

Smitherman, G. (2006). *Word from the mother: Language and African Americans.* New York: Routledge.

Spady, J., Charles G. L., & Alim, H. S. (1999). *Street conscious rap.* Philadelphia: Black History Museum.

Spears, A. (1998). African-American language use: Ideology and so-called obscenity. In S. Mufwene, J. Rickford, G. Bailey, & J. Baugh (Eds.), *African American English: Structure, history, and usage* (pp. 226–250). New York: Routledge.

Taylor, H. (1989). *Standard English, Black English, and bidialectalism.* New York: Peter Lang.

Thompson, G. (2004). *Through ebony eyes: What teachers need to know but are afraid to ask about African American students.* San Francisco: Jossey-Bass.

Wolfram, W. (1969) *A sociolinguistic description of Detroit Negro English.* Washington, DC: Center for Applied Linguistics.

Wolfram, W., Adger, C. T., & Christian, D. (1999). *Dialects in schools and communities.* Mahwah, NJ: Erlbaum.

Woodford, M. (1997). The *Black Scholar* reader's forum: Ebonics. *Black Scholar, 27*, 2–3.

Zeigler, M., & Osinubi, V. (2002). Theorizing the postcoloniality of African American English. *Journal of Black Studies, 32*, 588–609.

CHAPTER 11

Digital Literacies in the Classroom

JOAN A. RHODES

VALERIE J. ROBNOLT

The 21st century is a period of dramatic change in defining literacy. Contemporary students use both traditional text and digital media to communicate and locate information for both in- and out-of-school purposes. This period of change has required researchers, educators, and students themselves to redefine and expand their concept of literacy. This chapter briefly addresses the changing definition of literacy, including a description of digital literacy as it relates to classroom contexts. Multiple perspectives on the emerging definition of digital literacy are presented to encourage further refinement of the construct. In addition, current classroom applications of digital technologies in the areas of oral and written language and two major components of reading, vocabulary development and comprehension are outlined. Extant research related to the use of digital literacy and the study skills adolescents require to become literate in an electronic environment are described. The developing uses of social networking and gaming as a support to classroom instruction are also introduced. The study of the field faces particular challenges: Researchers experience unique problems as they study technology applications that become obsolete before the research results are even published; educators encounter students with a variety of levels of technology skill and reading ability, who are asked to navigate in hypertextual environments using comprehension techniques that differ from those used in linear reading environments; teachers feel a pressing need to increase their own technology skill levels while providing instruction for adolescents who are technologically savvy. This chapter provides instructional approaches and research that address the increasing need for students to read critically, access information efficiently, and overcome the negative impact of the digital divide.

The 21st century has seen profound change in the definition of what it means to be a literate member of society (New Media Consortium, 2005). Today's students are in the midst of a dramatic paradigm shift, similar to the changes experienced during the revolution created by the advent of the printing press (Harnad, 1991; McLuhan, 1962). Contemporary students use both traditional text and digital media to communicate, purchase goods and services, and locate information needed for both in- and out-of-school activities. Web 2.0, a second generation of computer applications that goes "beyond the page metaphor of Web 1.0 to deliver rich user experiences" in online environments, is commonly used and modified by today's students (O'Reilly, 2005). Online applications, like wikis, allow for the remixing of information and individual contributions to collective written work (e.g., Wikipedia). *Time* magazine recognized the profound impact of Web 2.0 on society, including our youth, when it named "You," the public, as *Time*'s 2006 Person of the Year, honoring citizens for "seizing the reins of the global media, for founding and framing the new digital democracy, for working for nothing and beating the pros at their own game" (Grossman, 2006/2007, p. 14).

As recently as 1992, Landow suggested that the shift from paper-based to digital text paralleled the Gutenberg revolution and, like the move to easily accessible printed text, use of digital text forms would take time to become routine. By 2001, findings from the Pew Internet and American Life Project showed that 73% of students ages 12–17 used the Internet regularly (Lenhart, Simon, & Graziano, 2001). This transition was also evident in research on the electronic study skills used by international students, ages 14–25, when 89.9% of participants reported they read from electronic text (Robnolt, Rhodes, & Richardson, 2005). The rate of change to and within digital environments is accelerating at such a rapid pace that print culture cannot keep up with the demands of reporting on digital culture. As Harnad points out:

> Paper has always had one notable drawback. Although it allowed us to encode, preserve and share ideas and findings incomparably more effectively than we could ever have done orally, its tempo was always lamentably slower than the oral interactions to which the speed of thought seems organically adapted. (1992, p. 40)

The use of electronic text eliminates the speed constraint of paper environments and creates the possibility for global, interactive dissemination of information. Therefore, this work, as well as other synoptic views of digital culture, are out of date as soon as they are written.

Although the use of digital text affords many learning opportunities for students, without access to technology, students from economically disadvantaged communities are unable to benefit. Attewell (2001) suggests that there are two digital divides separating the "haves" from the "have nots."

Digital equity should be considered, first, in terms of student access to technology and, second, in terms of student use of technology for educational purposes. DeBell and Chapman (2003) noted several inequities in student access to technology in their analysis of data from the *Computer and Internet Use Supplement* to the *2001 Current Population Survey* (CPS) conducted by the U.S. Census Bureau. DeBell and Chapman found that students ages 5–17 without disabilities were more likely to use the Internet and computer than those with disabilities. Students living outside urban areas and those from two-parent families were also more likely to have computer access. In his study of digital equity in 3,479 schools across 40 states, Becker (2006) reported that African American students and those living in rural areas had less access to educational technology. In addition, findings indicated that when students had access to technology, girls and students in a free or reduced-cost lunch program were most likely to use computers.

The role of schools in bridging the gap for students who lack access to technology at home was clearly evident in the CPS data analysis (DeBell & Chapman, 2003). The researchers found that students from families in poverty and those with parents who had not earned a high school credential reported accessing the Internet only at school. Fifty-two percent of young people from families in poverty access the Internet only at school, as compared with 26% of families living above the poverty level. Moreover, 59% of students whose parents lack a high school credential versus 39% of those who have higher education levels use the Internet only at school. This type of comparison illustrates the importance of ensuring that access to computer technology is equitable in public schools in order to reduce the digital divide and allow youngsters to gain experience working in electronic environments that are essential for economic survival in the 21st century (DeBell & Chapman, 2003).

There have been some improvements in students' access to the Internet since the digital divide began to be viewed as a potentially serious social problem. Krueger (2000) reported that in 1984 Black students were 16% less likely than White students to use a computer in school. This gap was reduced in

1997 to 6% overall, with a complete disappearance of the gap for high school students in the same year, but students in grades 1–8 still experienced a 10% difference.

Further evidence of improvement in access to computers was reported in 2003, when the National Center for Educational Statistics (NCES) noted that public schools in the United States increased access to the Internet from 35% of schools in 1994 to nearly 100% in 2003. Public schools also made progress in providing Internet-accessible computers to 93% of the instructional rooms in 2003, as compared with only 3% of instructional rooms in 1994 (National Center for Educational Statistics, 2005).

THE CHANGING DEFINITION OF LITERACY

Learning in today's literacy environment requires students to have functional skill and knowledge for working in both traditional (i.e., paper-based) and electronic text environments. This continuing transition from a reliance on paper-based material to reading in multimedia, hypertextual environments necessitates the redefinition and expansion of the concept of literacy for both students and educators. Many definitions of literacy have focused on individual competence. For instance, literacy can be defined as a "minimal ability to read and write in a designated language, as well as a mindset or way of thinking about the use of reading and writing in everyday life" (Venezky, 1995, p. 142). Literacy is more than simply reading or writing because it "requires active, autonomous engagement with print and stresses the role of the individual in generating as well as receiving and assigning independent interpretations to messages" (Venezky, 1995, p. 142). Furthermore, this understanding of literacy has evolved into other areas of knowledge (e.g., economic literacy, cultural literacy, and computer literacy) to designate minimal competence required in each field.

Currently, the term *literacy* implies that individual competence interacts with the social demands of the culture. Literacy levels vary across time and cultures on a continuum ranging from illiteracy to high-functioning literacy. For instance, what was considered a more than adequate

level of literacy during the industrial revolution would not be considered sufficient for the literacy demands in current society (Venezky, 1995).

A challenge for those interested in the literacy required for reading in electronic environments is the creation of a label, nomenclature, and definition of each of the literacies involved. Soares (1992, as cited in Harris & Hodges, 1995) indicated that "consensual agreement on a single definition [of literacy] is quite implausible" even for the general term itself (p.140). However, for meaningful discussion of the topic, the field must work toward finding a common understanding of multiple digital literacies.

The challenge of defining literacy in the 21st century is obvious. Researchers, technology gurus, educators, and the public all search for a valid definition of the literacy required for success in new digital environments. In the past, the idea of computer literacy implied acquisition of a skill set needed to function in a computer environment. Students were expected to demonstrate an understanding of the value of computers, knowledge of computer terminology and a computer language, and the ability to use computers to solve problems (Troutner, 1985). Across time technological advances have placed new and varied literacy demands on students. Today students must navigate through hypertext environments where linear movement through text is interrupted with opportunities for linking to other related items with the click of a button. Further, the very relationship of author and reader has become muddied as readers create written work for mass consumption and contribute to the revision of online text. Various researchers have approached defining computer literacy in the midst of this period of extraordinary change.

DEFINITIONS OF LITERACY IN THE NEW MILLENNIUM

Defining literacy in the new millennium is a highly complex task. This section provides a brief overview of several definitions of literacy proposed by contemporary researchers studying the demands of digital environments. Each definition broadens the understanding of literacy, but none appears to have been able to assist in arriving at a fully acceptable construct for future use.

Multiliteracies

In 1994, ten educators met in New London, New Hampshire, to discuss literacy pedagogy (Cope & Kalantzis, 2000). The discussion and resulting article from the New London Group helped broaden the understanding of literacy and literacy teaching to account for the use of multimedia technologies and the multiplicity of available text forms. Focusing on the idea of a multiliteracies approach to pedagogy allowed the New London Group to consider the various ways information is communicated and the expanding relationships between text and other representational forms. *Multiliteracy* implies that meaning making occurs in multimodal settings where written information is part of spatial, audio, and visual patterns of meaning. These individual modes are in dynamic interaction with one another during literacy activities (Cope & Kalantzis, 2000).

To be successful, students are expected to comprehend multimodal materials and deal not only with changes in mass media and technology, but also with cultural and linguistic diversity, multiple languages, and cross-cultural communications that go beyond national boundaries. The New London Group (1996) asserted that multiliteracies approaches would ensure that students were able to deal with modern literacy demands and achieve two literacy learning goals: "creating access to the evolving language of work, power, and community, and fostering the critical engagement necessary for them to design their social futures and achieve success through fulfilling employment" (p. 1).

New Literacies

Leu (2002) has also attempted to define literacy needed by today's students in light of changing technologies. Leu proposes, "The new literacies include the skills, strategies, and insights necessary to successfully exploit the rapidly changing information and communication technologies that continuously emerge in our world" (Leu, 2002, p. 313). Knobel and Lankshear (2006) assert that new literacies are characterized by two changes: first, the incorporation of new "technical stuff" (i.e., digitality) and, second, new "ethos stuff" (i.e., mindset informing literacy practice) (p. 80). The researchers suggest that a new literacy may not have to involve the use of digitality, but it must come from a mindset that espouses a belief that the world is a different place because of the emergence of digital interworked technologies. These definitions of new literacies may be problematic inasmuch as Leu (2000, 2006) suggests that a *specific* definition for new literacies may not be possible because of the deictic, regularly changing nature of emerging technologies. For more on new literacies, see Black and Steinkeuhler (Chapter 18) and Lewis and del Valle (Chapter 20), this volume.

Information Literacy

Information literacy, also deemed necessary by contemporary scholars, requires students to locate and evaluate information for use at the time it is needed. Information literacy crosses disciplinary boundaries and allows students to have greater control over their own learning by enabling them to access needed information, expand investigations, and use information to accomplish specific goals. Information literacy requires individuals to understand the social and ethical issues that surround the use of information (Association of College and Research Libraries, 2000). This definition does not fully capture the variety of ways students use digital environments for self-expression and recreation.

Media Literacy

The National Leadership Conference on Media Literacy, a group of 25 representative leaders of the media literacy movement, met in December 1992 to provide a common vision and objectives for their respective groups. As part of the dialogue, the members settled on a basic definition of media literacy as "the ability of a citizen to access, analyze and produce information for specific outcomes" (Aufderheide, 1993, p. 6). A media-literate person, according to this definition, is able to produce print and electronic media and negotiate meaning in images, words, and sounds. Media literacy also suffers from a multiplicity of definitions based on personal perspective or theoretical framework. Media literacy aims to help students become critical consumers of popular culture and critically reflective about media messages (ReadWriteThink, n.d.). Alvermann and Hagood (2000) indicate that additional perspectives on critical media literacy emphasize the structure of society and politics, how gender and power produce cultural artifacts, and how individuals relate to cultural texts, depending on their interests and positions. For a further discussion of media literacy, see Bruce (Chapter 19), this volume.

Visual Literacy

Students who are visually literate are able to understand information from pictorial or graphic images (Wileman, 1993). In addition, visual literacy requires students to use and create images using conventional and modern media to communicate, make decisions, and learn (North Central Regional Education Laboratory, n.d.). Although there are some universal visual images, visual literacy is culturally specific. Students develop their visual literacy skills by using them as they create visual messages and by learning visual analysis techniques (Stokes, 2001). Visual literacy is important for students when reading in multimedia environments. A further discussion of visual literacy is included in Zoss (Chapter 13), this volume.

Although a clear nomenclature for the changing literacies has not emerged, the possibility of cohesion of thought among visual literacy, media literacy, and information literacy has been suggested. Tyner (1998) indicates that a synthesis where the three fields link their research might result in a unique name for the concept. Although almost a decade has passed since this suggestion, the fields have not arrived at a singular title for the literacy needed in the post-typographic world.

The challenges of multiple definitions of literacy are evident. Meyer and Rose (1999) suggest that the old definitions of literacy are based on an assumption that "print is the primary carrier of information in our culture" (p. 13). However, each new definition of literacy recognizes that electronic formats are increasingly relied upon to carry information and do so using multiple media

for expressing ideas. Owing in part to the challenges of arriving at a clear definition, researchers have shifted focus to the emerging characteristics or skills students will need to be successful in new electronic-based learning environments. Members of the 21st Century Literacy Summit (New Media Consortium, 2005), including representatives from the Massachusetts Institute of Technology (MIT), International Society for Technology in Education (ISTE), and Stanford University, arrived at the following definition of literacy for the new millennium, which demonstrates this focus as they outlined priorities to serve as a literacy road map for the future:

> 21st century literacy is the set of abilities and skills where aural, visual and digital literacy overlap. These include the ability to understand the power of images and sounds, to recognize and use that power, to manipulate and transform digital media, to distribute them pervasively, and to easily adapt them to new forms. (p. 2)

This definition of 21st-century literacy is used synonymously with the term *digital literacy* for the remainder of the chapter. However, the reader should note that in the reporting of research, the nomenclature used by the original author of each work is used.

CHARACTERISTICS OF 21ST-CENTURY LITERACY

Twenty-first century literacy is multimodal, utilizing a variety of levels of meaning, which include the use of sound, visual images including video, and text for communicating (Kress, 2004; New Media Consortium, 2005). Youth must adapt to working in these multilayered environments where messages are received simultaneously in many forms. Literacy for this century implies that students are able to create and interpret meaning within multimodal, digital environments. In addition, students must be able to negotiate hypertext environments that require readers to "transcend the linear, bounded and fixed qualities of written text" (Landow & Delaney, 1991, p. 3). Hypertext allows readers to move through a text nonsequentially, moving from one node to another as interest or need determines. Although hypertext can be described as the computer-based alternative to paper-based texts (Lawless, Brown, Mills, & Mayall, 2003), its unique multilinear characteristics place new demands on readers and authors alike. Many hypertexts are also multimodal and include hypermedia, defined by Jonassen (2006) as "hypertext with multiple representation forms (text, graphics, sounds, videos, etc.)" (p. 185). Multimedia authoring allows students to develop complex representations while working with audio, visual, and text-based material in constructivist learning processes (Liu & Hsiao, 2002).

Twenty-first century literacy is also characterized by the use of interactive, real-time, synchronous communication, which allows students to communicate using text with an immediacy that was not available in traditional print environments. Members of the 21st-Century Literacy Summit highlighted the potential that new forms of language offer for transforming the way students learn by engaging the brain in new ways, communicating more rapidly, and capitalizing on the natural motivation of students for new literacy activities (Liu & Hsiao, 2002; New Media Consortium, 2005).

The quickly and repeatedly changing reading, writing, and communication activities available in modern society require students to critically evaluate information in increasingly social contexts. In addition, the new literacies include strategic knowledge for locating and evaluating extensive resources in networked environments for use in and outside the classroom. The new literacies are especially evident when students work with content information on the Internet. New literacies also provide opportunities for students to explore their own cultural traditions while communicating in social environments with others across the globe (Leu, 2002).

Digital media provide inclusive environments for communication that support students who have had difficulty in the past working in paper-based text environments. Technology provides access to curriculum and increases personal productivity for disabled students (Jackson, 2004). Twenty-first-century literacy offers additional opportunities for students to express themselves in multiple formats and select from a broader range of tools for specific communication tasks in both educational and home environments (Meyer & Rose, 1999).

Digital natives (Prensky, 2001), the youth who have grown up in a digital era, are learning a new grammar for working with literacy through their informal computing activities. This knowledge has applications in the educational environment as classrooms begin to keep pace with the literacy activities occurring outside the classroom.

STUDENT TECHNOLOGY USE IN THE 21ST CENTURY

When focusing on the needs of both teachers and students in the 21st century, one is immediately confronted by the dramatic differences between how adolescents use technology in their home environments and their uses of computers in school environments. Tyner (1998) indicated that "there has been a growing bifurcation between the literacy practices of compulsory schooling and those that occur outside the school house door" (p. 8). Schooling continues to be based on hierarchical access to paper-based literacy instead of practices that allow students to explore and utilize the multimodal, nonlinear literacies available in digital environments. Digital natives (Prensky, 2001) arriving in today's classrooms are working in an environment that does not match their learning needs and/or the changes in the way their minds process information. Prensky (2001) asserts that the greatest problem facing education is the gap between the knowledge and skills digital natives have developed and the instruction provided by their pre-digital-age instructors. Although 95% of teachers are now comfortable using e-mail, their students have moved on to use more specialized tools (e.g., instant messaging) to meet their communication needs (Project Tomorrow, 2006). Students today are becoming less engaged in old-style instruction that ignores the digital skills they bring to the classroom and enraged with teachers who are not re-creating curricula and instruction to meet their needs (Prensky, 2006). Researchers from the American Institutes for Research found that the use of the Internet by public middle and high school students across the United States occurs primarily outside the school day and with no direction from their teachers (Levin & Arafeh, 2002).

The need for educational reform continues to mount as modern students bring the new literacy skills used in their home environments to the classroom. Students are spending increasing amounts of time on the Internet outside school, participating in a variety of activities, including social networking and online gaming. Project Tomorrow-NetDay (Project Tomorrow, 2006), a nonprofit organization that focuses on the development of 21st-century science, math, and technology skills, surveyed students in grades K–12 to determine their use of technology for both in-school and out-of-school purposes. Data collected from 185,000 students from all 50 states, the District of Columbia, Department of Defense schools, Guam, and Puerto Rico show that students are innovative and adopt new technology for personal and educational use. Project Tomorrow (2006) reports that students rate listening to music, playing games, and talking to or e-mailing family and friends as the top three ways they spend time at home. Over a third of 12th-grade students use the Internet to keep informed through news websites and are beginning to use podcasts and weblogs as means of sharing and receiving information (Project Tomorrow, 2006). When they are not in school, much of adolescents' literacy happens online through participation in text messaging, chat rooms, e-mail, and blogs (Williams, 2005).

Modern students show their interest in using technology for communication beginning in sixth grade, where 50% of students report using e-mail or instant messaging (IM) daily. IM is the preferred method for written communication, according to the 65% of students who use e-mail and IM regularly. E-mail is becoming useful as a repository for needed documents and a means of tracking messages rather than being used for pure communication (Project Tomorrow, 2006; Evans, 2007). A student can hold an e-mail in his or her sent box, which includes Microsoft Word document attachments indefinitely. This allows the student to use the sent box as a holding bin for old documents while saving storage space on a hard drive. Students are also able to keep track of their interactions with peers through reviewing the contents of their e-mail files. Through the use of personal websites and social networking sites such as MySpace and Facebook, digital natives share information with friends and connect to others across the globe. These activities provide a broad audience for student sharing of information, writing, and multimedia presentations. Cell phones are becoming the favorite communication tool of youth today and offer increasing potential for educational applications (Project Tomorrow, 2006; Dede, 2007).

Results of the 2006 VNU/Harrison Group Teen Trend survey show that 75% of U.S. teens spend 2–3 hours per day downloading or listening to online music (Olsen, 2006). New computer systems, including the use of MP3 digital audio files, allow students to share music through the Internet with ease (Brown, Sellen, & Geelhoed, 2001). Adolescents discover new musical groups through social networking spaces such as MySpace, where listeners post digital music files and add their favorite bands to their "friend space." The accessibility and use of music and other audio recording is enhancing written text in new multimedia environments. With the recent popularity of Internet sites like YouTube, contemporary students are not only consumers of multimedia, but creators. Students are able to access music and podcasts, create playlists, and record on devices such as iPods with great ease of mobility, allowing them to stay connected to content anywhere and any time.

Today's students are also highly involved in playing video games and increasingly use Internet-based large-scale multiple-user games for entertainment. Video games provide students with an opportunity to apply literacy skills in virtual situations, improve problem solving and strategic thinking, and practice team-building skills. Multiple-user games create environments where students from across the globe engage in online conversations regarding strategy and carry their interest in the game culture into reading and writing activities through fanfiction. Through gaming, millennial students are able to test hypotheses in environments where attempting new challenges without fear of failure and developing creative solutions to problems are valued skills (Glazer, 2006). Increasingly, educators are beginning to see the benefits of multi-use virtual environment

(MUVE) games that simulate real environmental features of geographic areas. Participation in online gaming communities using virtual characters, called avatars, is on the rise, with hundreds of thousands of teens engaging peers in sites such as Second Life (Blaisdell, 2006).

Universities are also beginning to use virtual communication by including Second Life virtual worlds in the academic community (Dede, 2007). Empirical evidence supports adapting the gaming community's use of virtual worlds for educational purposes through programs such as River City, created by a team of researchers from Harvard's Graduate School of Education (Harvard University, 2004–2007). River City uses a problem-based focus to engage middle school students in determining the cause of an epidemic in a 19th-century town. Each student participates in a collaborative team, controls an avatar that lives in the virtual city, and uses the computer to recommend solutions to the simulated health crisis (Dede, 2007; Harvard University and Arizona State University, 2004–2007). Data from the 1,000 students who participated in the project during 2004–2005 indicate that after 20 sessions, students' knowledge of biology improved 32–35% (Blaisdell, 2006). Preliminary results from Ketelhut, Dede, Clarke, and Nelson (2006) indicate that in addition to learning biology content, students' attendance improved, misbehavior decreased, and through this highly engaging activity, students were building virtual communication skills necessary for success in modern society. Use of this type of gaming activity changes classroom instruction from a lecture-based, teacher-driven method of delivery to an interactive delivery whereby students construct knowledge in small group activities through inquiry (Dede, 2007; Ketelhut et al., 2006). See Black and Steinkuehler (Chapter 18, this volume) for more on gaming and virtual spaces.

These observations suggest that educators must begin to find relevant ways to allow students to share their advancing technology skills within classroom settings. Teacher-designed assignments and projects can benefit from the inclusion of the rich multimedia technology present in students' external computing activities. Furthermore, educators can capitalize on student interest by using gaming

scenarios within the classroom and allowing the free flow of information and research through open-access publishing in blogs, wikis, and through social networking sites.

Knowledge of the potential literacy demands of the future workforce is essential as educators develop instructional plans for including technology in their classrooms. Friedman (2006), in *The World Is Flat: A Brief History of the Twenty-First Century*, indicates that the world is becoming an even playing field due to global technological advances. There are four things that one must know to survive in the flat world. Citizens must learn to work well with others and develop a passion and curiosity for learning. In addition, Friedman suggests that successful individuals "need to learn how to learn" so they are able to absorb new information and adapt to a changing, automated, and digitized world (p. 302). Historically, American society values skills such as sequencing and analysis that are used in left-brain activities; whereas in the 21st century, skills such as emotional expression and synthesis will be more useful. Schools typically reward left-brain activities, but in the flat world nurturing only the left brain will be insufficient. Advances in computer technology and the rise in the outsourcing of jobs that use basic computing skills will require American students to be able to think across disciplines and creatively solve problems in order to maintain economic viability. Education itself will need to change to meet the demands of the flat world. For this reason, educators will need to be empowered to develop 21st-century literacy skills and teacher education programs will need revision to ensure that new literacy skills become part of teacher certification programs (New Media Consortium, 2005).

Although the current pace of technology use in the classroom has lagged behind student use outside the school environment, modern students are encouraging, nudging, and pushing educators to move into the 21st century as they bring their experiences and learning into the schoolhouse. The rest of this chapter describes digital literacy practices and instructional strategies for use within classroom settings, including research into areas such as hypertext, instant messaging, and writing in electronic environments. We must acknowledge that research in the area of classroom applications of literacy and technology practices is limited, but expanding rapidly (Dalton & Proctor, 2006). As Landow (1992) expressed, educators and students alike "must abandon conceptual systems founded upon ideas of center, margin, hierarchy, and linearity and replace them with ones of multilinearity, nodes, links and networks" (p. 2). This change profoundly impacts education as reading, writing, and viewing in digital, hypertextual environments become the center of literacy practices.

CLASSROOM APPLICATIONS OF DIGITAL LITERACIES

Many students feel that the literacy they value in their everyday lives is not connected to the literacy valued by their schools, and by teachers in particular (Williams, 2005). Teachers can find many ways to incorporate digital literacy that connects students' outside-school literacy experiences to what they do in school, thus indicating in a powerful way that these experiences are valued. Incorporating new literacy experiences can, in turn, lead to greater engagement by the students. In this section of the chapter, digital literacy and comprehension, reading critically, writing, and the impact on struggling adolescents are addressed.

Digital Literacy and Reading Comprehension

Most instruction and reading in school is done with paper-based texts when, in reality, most people read from a variety of texts, both paper-based and electronic (Gambrell, 2005). Students need instruction that incorporates reading electronic texts so that they are able to comprehend in digital environments as well as they do in traditional text. The methods they use may be similar to those they use in paper-based texts, but there are unique challenges when reading text in electronic environments. Just as Durkin (1993) asserts that "teaching students how to go about constructing meaning of connected text is the essence of comprehension instruction" (p. 36), it is essential now that teachers help students create understanding through digital literacy. Schmar-Dobler

(2003) observed and interviewed adolescent online readers and found that they used the following comprehension strategies similarly when reading paper-based text and the Internet: (1) activating prior knowledge; (2) determining important ideas; (3) synthesizing; and (4) drawing inferences. Because of the volume of text on the Internet, she found the self-monitoring strategy of skimming and scanning was critical for success, as was the ability to ask oneself guiding questions to keep the reading focused. Whereas in print-based texts the reader has to navigate features such as headings and graphics, on the Internet the reader navigates features such as downloading and pop-up ads. To aid students in making adjustments to their comprehension when reading on the Internet, teachers can provide modeling and instruction to "begin to build the bridge connecting literacy and technology" (Schmar-Dobler, 2003, p. 85).

In research conducted by Coiro and Dobler (2007), sixth graders used traditional strategies to comprehend text in an open-ended information system (i.e., the Internet). However, while using prior knowledge, inferential reasoning, and self-monitoring, they were also utilizing skills that were unique to this electronic environment. For example, the participants not only used their prior knowledge of the topic and of informational text structures in paper-based texts, but they also used "their prior knowledge of informational website structures" (p. 230) and of Internet search engines. In terms of inferential reasoning, the participants "appeared to make forward inferences (e.g., predictions) within Internet text each time they were confronted with one or more hyperlinks on a given page" (Coiro & Dobler, 2007, p. 233). They also "engaged in a multilayered inferential reading process that occurred across the three-dimensional spaces of Internet text" (p. 234). One way in which self-monitoring was different when reading on the Internet was that physical actions were necessary in this electronic environment—clicking, typing, and scrolling. In addition, there was a difference in the speed at which the participants made choices when reading various Internet texts. The researchers found that the participants were able to make choices more quickly when reading the results in a search engine than when reading hypertext in an informational website. This research supports the idea that students will use traditional comprehension strategies in electronic environments and that the strategies will also be adapted for that environment.

Just as every classroom includes students with a wide range of literacy abilities and experiences, the reality is that students also come to school with many different abilities and experiences with technology. Evans (2007) of NetDay indicates that the digital natives entering the classroom include students with a range of technological expertise; therefore, it is imperative that teachers spend instructional time interactively demonstrating the use of technology, including software programs and Internet websites (McKenna, Labbo, Reinking, & Zucker, 2007). Projecting an image of the computer screen to the screen in the classroom using an LCD projector is an efficient way to demonstrate how to use particular software for a certain purpose or navigate through the Internet to find information. Although some students may have great facility with various software programs or in using the Internet, when a teacher provides a targeted demonstration for an instructional purpose, the learning takes on new meaning for that particular topic or situation. The students are learning techniques that can be used at that time, as well as skills that can be transferred to other learning situations at a later time. Teachers can help students, as McKenna et al. (2007) note, to "create a rich schema for employing technology in ways that quite naturally involve many literacy-related activities" (p. 346). As teachers are interactively demonstrating the use of technology, they can also use think-alouds (i.e., saying out loud what one is thinking) to help students "think metacognitively about their information-seeking behaviors and processing of information gathered in online environments" (Kymes, 2005, p. 498). The combination of demonstrating interactively and conducting think-alouds can assist students in becoming successful in reading in an electronic environment.

Valmont (2003) asserts that in an electronic environment, students' comprehension is affected by both manipulation of the electronic text and the use they make of the information gained from the electronic text.

He proposes that teachers conduct an electronic version of the traditional Directed Reading–Thinking Activity (DRTA) created by Stauffer (1969). In the traditional DRTA, teachers support students' reading of paper-based texts by encouraging them to set purposes for reading and remain actively engaged while reading, by making and revising predictions before and during reading, and by synthesizing what happened in the text after reading. The same format can be used by teachers and students reading electronic texts, both narrative and expository. When teachers encourage students to use the DRTA while reading texts in an electronic environment, they help students to set a purpose for active engagement in reading, that is, to become independent readers and thinkers.

The use of hypertext is a defining aspect of reading in electronic environments, especially on the Internet, that should be modeled by teachers. When reading hypertext, students must simultaneously navigate through multiple layers to construct their own unique text and monitor their own understanding of the reading. There can be many paths to create a text, where each reading may result in different information or the reader may come to a different understanding or conclusion. Lawless et al. (2003) describe three types of people who navigate hypertext. It is important that teachers understand these three types so that they can target their instruction to support students who fit each profile. "Knowledge seekers" try to find information by selecting links that will forward their goals. The "feature seekers" spend more time clicking on the links to see how the hypertext/hypermedia is organized than they devote to acquiring information. The "apathetic hypertext users" are not interested in gathering information or learning more about the hypertext links. Keeping these profiles in mind, one can clearly understand that students make decisions, while reading hypertext and hypermedia, that have a direct impact on comprehension.

Valmont (2003) states, "Comprehension is affected by the purposes students set for accessing, retrieving, and using information they obtain through electronic media as well as by their navigational and organizational abilities" (p. 93). Because navigating through hypertext and hypermedia is one of the challenges of digital literacy (McKenna et al., 2007), students benefit from teachers' using the LCD projector to model how to maneuver around hypertext and conducting think-aloud sessions to demonstrate the thought processes that readers use when making decisions about what path to take in their reading (Kymes, 2005). The "feature seekers" and "apathetic hypertext users" need more guidance from teachers to learn how to use hypertext and hypermedia to their best advantage. Lawless et al. (2003) found that when readers had greater domain knowledge when reading hypertext, they were able to be more efficient when selecting and sequencing information and had better comprehension of text. Therefore, it is important for teachers to continue to use instructional time to activate, assess, and build background knowledge on a variety of topics. In addition, teachers can help students understand that it is important to independently build their own background knowledge from a variety of sources before they read texts in an electronic environment so they will have more success.

Teachers also support student learning when they demonstrate the use of PowerPoint to create reports or presentations that incorporate a variety of media, such as graphics, video, and hyperlinks. This instruction can directly impact students' use of technology for a project, such as the one described by Kinzer (2005) in which a student used PowerPoint to create a multimedia research presentation on Hinduism. The student used a combination of text and graphics to present her information, including a time line of important dates in the history of Hinduism.

A critical component of comprehension requires students to synthesize and extend their understanding of what they read. In traditional paper-based formats, creating semantic networks or maps, sometimes called concept maps or mind maps, has been a great benefit to students' comprehension (Johnson & Pearson, 1984). Jonassen (2006) describes the construction of Mindtools models that are similar to semantic maps, to help students better learn material that can be presented in class or found in paper-based and electronic-based texts. If a student is trying to understand information found on the Internet, it makes sense for him or her to continue using the computer, instead of using paper, to create a model or representation of that information to enhance understanding. According to Jonassen (2006), "the semantic networks in memory and the maps that represent them are composed of nodes (concepts or ideas) that are connected by links (statements of relationships)" (p. 101). Readers can use the graphic tools found in many word processing programs to create a semantic network by placing the main concept in the middle of the computer screen with lines drawn to other related concepts to show relationships. In electronic environments, the reader can include pictures, such as clip art, and other hypermedia to enhance their understanding of concepts.

An important part of students' connecting to any type of text is for them to respond to it, which in turn, can enhance comprehension. Allowing students to discuss what they are reading can be motivating for them (Guthrie & Wingfield, 2000). Carico and Logan (2004) and Grisham and Wolsey (2006) found positive results when teachers conducted online discussions to facilitate responses to literature. In Carico and Logan's research project, university students partnered with eighth graders to discuss books that both partners had read, providing a unique opportunity to interact. Online discussions afforded anonymity to students who were usually quiet in class so that they and more vocal students had equal opportunities to share. Carico and Logan also found the following positive comprehension outcomes of the online discussions: (1) the participants helped each other by clarifying aspects of the texts that were unclear; (2) they identified both plot elements and relationships; and (3) they made connections between the book they read and other books. Grisham and Wolsey (2006) found that eighth graders involved in an online, threaded book discussion became more engaged as time passed. Owing to the asynchronous nature of the threaded discussions, the students thought "more deeply about their responses to the literature" (p. 656) and were thoughtful in their responses to the postings their peers made. Because the majority of adolescents are online, teachers can take advantage of using online discussions as a mode of communication to enhance comprehension and motivate student reading.

Critical Reading

There is a tremendous amount of information on the Internet. An important part of a teacher's job in the 21st century is to help students become critical readers of the information on the Internet. To be critical readers, individuals need to recognize their own prejudices and beliefs as well as the ways in which people persuade readers to think a particular way or to do something they may not otherwise do (Valmont, 2003). Teachers need to be clear with their students that they should take a stance of skepticism about the information they read, because they will likely find misinformation on the Internet. Part of what a teacher needs to do is help students to be aware of the authors of websites, including their credentials and possible motives. According to Valmont (2003), students can be taught to ask the following questions: What is the purpose of the website? What authority does the author have to present the information? What is the tone of the author's message? To help make these issues clear to students, teachers can show examples of propaganda on websites. For example, there is a website on Martin Luther King Jr., *www.martinlutherking.org*, that might at first seem to be a viable website with information about the civil rights leader's life; however, the website was created by a White supremacist group (Holschuh, 2006). Valmont (2003) also addresses the need for teachers to help students become critical of online advertisements. Students need to understand that there are keywords, attention grabbers, and ways to lure people to do something, which intentionally manipulate readers of online advertisements. In the 21st century, if adolescents do not have guidance to learn to be critical consumers of information and advertisements on the Internet, the consequences are serious. Adolescents can have their identities stolen if they provide their credit card numbers to lurking predators or can commit a violation of academic integrity by cutting and pasting information that is not their own.

Digital Literacy and Writing

When teachers decide to incorporate digital literacy into their teaching, especially their writing instruction, a first step is to provide time for metadiscussions of the students' in-school and out-of-school literacy practices (Lewis & Fabos, 2005). Williams (2005) suggests that teachers can discuss with their students how these literacy practices differ and how and why their out-of-school experiences are more engaging. The discussion can lead to an understanding by students that what they do outside school and how they do it can have a viable application in school. For example, Lewis and Fabos (2005) analyzed the instant messaging practices of adolescents and found that they "used language in complex ways in order to negotiate multiple messages and interweave these conversations into larger, overarching storylines" (p. 482). During the discussions suggested by Williams (2005), students can make connections between the skills they use when they are instant messaging their friends, such as their ability to change their voices, depending on their audience, and transfer the skills to how they create a story in their creative writing class (Lewis & Fabos, 2005).

An efficient way to combine technology and writing is to allow students to move through the writing process (i.e., prewriting, drafting, revising, editing, and publishing) on the computer (McKenna et al., 2007). Russell and Plati (2000) found that 20% more students would pass the state-mandated writing tests if they could use the computer. Goldberg, Russell, and Cook (2003) conducted a meta-analysis of research on the effects of computers on writing. They found the following results, favoring students who wrote on the computer as compared with students who wrote with paper and pencil: (1) students wrote more; (2) students' writing was of a higher quality; (3) students made more changes to their writing; (4) students engaged in more collaboration; (5) the writing process was used in a less linear way and was more integrative; (6) students were more motivated; (7) students improved their literacy skills, attitudes, and higher-level thinking skills.

Publishing is an integral part of the writing process, and technology, especially the Internet, has opened a whole new world of possibilities for getting students' writing published. Whereas in the past, the publishing of students' work was limited to the classroom or school, now students' work can be published on the Internet with the potential of being read by people all over the world (Bruce, 2002). Students then have an integral, real connection to the global community. Bruce further asserts, "As communities develop through shared literacies, they construct technologies that reflect their collective extraction of meaning from experience" (p. 15). Chamberlain (2005) suggests that teachers can create a website in which their students' writing is published; she even goes a step farther to suggest the idea of creating online portfolios in which students have a collection of their writing on their own webpages within the class website. In this model, the teacher needs to establish high expectations for the writing that students include in their online portfolios, especially because their work has the potential to be read by millions of people. Chamberlain (2005) also notes that it is crucial that, for safety's sake, students not use their full names when publishing their work on the Internet.

Incorporating digital literacy into the classroom can have important benefits by providing socially meaningful experiences for students. Because adolescents are already using e-mail and blogs as ways to communicate outside school (Williams, 2005), it makes sense to find instructional uses for them in school. For example, Keypals are Penpals in which the pals communicate through e-mail instead of traditional letters that move through snail mail (Kinzer, 2005). Connecting students to Keypals in other parts of the community, state, country, or even other countries, is a quick, powerful way for students to feel they are part of the global community. There are many ways to use Keypals for students to learn about a variety of topics, such as the customs, traditions, and living conditions in places other than their own communities. Garner and Gillingham (1996) describe messages that were exchanged through the Internet between students in Joliet, Illinois, and students in Tununak, Alaska, in which the students discovered and were able to dispel cultural misunderstandings of stereotypes. For example, the students in Alaska assumed that violent crime was a daily occurrence for people in the mainland United States. Christian (1997) documents another example of students connecting through e-mail to discuss a book. He met with teachers from around the United States who became involved in a project in which their middle school students discussed *Anne Frank: The Diary of a Young Girl*. A great benefit of Keypals over traditional Penpal arrangements is that communication is quick; students can get responses within minutes or hours.

Blogs, short for *weblogs*, can serve similar purposes as Keypals, but the audience is much larger, potentially including millions of people. Keypal relationships can be more personal, whereas blogs can connect students to a larger audience. Huffaker (2005) states, "Any discipline can use blogs to approach a style of *meta-learning*, where concepts or contexts are discussed and articulated in both a personalized and group exchange, and ideas are built on previous educational content" (p. 95). Williams (2005) suggests using transcripts of e-mail and other online communication for instructional purposes in another way. Teachers can have students rewrite their online communication in different genres "to help make them more aware of how genre influences what information we choose to provide and how we choose to provide it" (p. 706). This connects adolescents' outside literacy lives to their school lives.

Multimedia book reviews are similar to the traditional book reports that are completed in thousands of classrooms in thousands of schools. According to Reinking and Watkins (2000), the differences between multimedia book reviews and traditional book reports are that multimedia book reviews (1) allow students to use computers to include graphics and sound to enhance their textual information about a book; and (2) can be shared with more people than the students in a classroom because they can be posted on the Internet, making the reports available to a wider audience. Reinking and Watkins (2000) found that students who were involved in creating multimedia book reviews became more engaged in literacy-related activities and that these projects especially increased independent reading. They also found a secondary benefit to the use of multimedia book reviews: The students and teachers enjoyed learning the technology to create the reviews. This benefit indicates that "various curricular goals can be advanced by embedding relevant content within technologically challenging and engaging tasks" (p. 411).

Digital Literacy and Struggling Adolescents

A key issue in working with adolescents who are struggling with reading and writing (i.e., read and write below grade level) is finding materials that can motivate them to work on the specific skills that need improvement. Anderson-Inman and Horney (1998) describe the ways that technology can be used to support struggling students as they read text that has been electronically changed to support the reader's needs. As a student reads on the computer and comes to a word or phrase that is difficult, the altered version provides sound or graphics to help the student read the text and proceed with greater comprehension. Anderson-Inman and Horney (1998) discuss thoroughly the research that found positive effects when providing struggling readers with supported text. Dalton and Strangman (2006) add to this discussion with a review of the research that indicates how electronically supported text helps struggling readers with decoding and fluency and directly impacts comprehension. This research indicates that struggling adolescents, especially those who are significantly below grade level, can benefit from reading electronically supported text.

CONCLUSION

The use of digital literacies in adolescent life is complex. There are multiple definitions of 21st-century literacy and a variety of ways to view the interaction between literacy and technology. Rapid changes in 21st-century literacies create additional challenges as research reported in print environments tries to keep up with the pace of technological advances. These challenges indicate a crucial need for teachers in the 21st century to merge adolescents' outside-the-classroom use of technology with the literacy practices of the school. This chapter has explored various viewpoints regarding the changing definitions of literacy and the reading and writing instructional activities that support use

of new technologies in the classroom. In any case, it is clear that the importance of digital literacies in the 21st century, as well as the nudging of our adolescents, will continue to expand and impact our classroom instruction for the foreseeable future.

REFERENCES

Alvermann, D. E., & Hagood, M. C. (2000). Critical media literacy: Research, theory and practice in "new times." *Journal of Educational Research, 93,* 193–205.

Anderson-Inman, L., & Horney, M. A. (1998). Transforming text for at-risk readers. In D. Reinking, M. C. McKenna, L. D. Labbo, & R. D. Kieffer (Eds.), *Handbook of literacy and technology: Transformations in a post-typographic world* (pp. 15–43). Mahwah, NJ: Erlbaum.

Association of College and Research Libraries. (2000). *Information literacy: Competency standards for higher education.* Chicago: American Library Association.

Attewell, P. (2001, July). Comment: The first and second digital divides. *Sociology of Education, 74*(3), 252–259. Retrieved July 16, 2007, from *www.jstor.org/view/00380407/di020079/02p0121f/0.*

Aufderheide, P. (1993). *Media literacy: A report of the national leadership conference on media literacy.* Queenstown, MD: Aspen Institute. (ERIC Document Reproduction Service No. 365 294).

Becker, J. D. (2006). Digital equity in education: A multilevel examination of differences in and relationships between computer access, computer use and state-level technology policies. *Education Policy Analysis Archives, 15,* 1–38. Retrieved July 15, 2007, from *epaa.asu.edu/epaa/v15n3/.*

Blaisdell, M. (2006). "All the right muves: The use of computer simulations that appeal to students' love of video games has shown compelling educational benefits (educational gaming)." *Technological Horizons in Education Journal, 33*(14).

Brown, B., Sellen, A. J., & Geelhoed, E. (2001, May). *Music sharing as a computer supported collaborative application.* Proceedings of the European Conference on Computer Supported Cooperative Work 2001. Bonn, Germany: Kluwer Academic. Retrieved January 30, 2007, from *www.equator.ac.uk/var/uploads/Brown,%20B.,%20Geelhoed,%20E.%20and%20Sellen,%20A.%20(2001)%20Music%20sharing.pdf.*

Bruce, B. C. (2002). Diversity and critical social engagement: How changing technologies enable new modes of literacy in changing circumstances. In D. E. Alvermann (Ed.), *Adolescents and literacies in a digital world* (pp. 1–18). New York: Peter Lang.

Carico, K. M., & Logan, D. (2004). A generation in

cyberspace: Engaging readers through online discussions. *Language Arts, 81,* 293–302.

Chamberlain, C. J. (2005). Literacy and technology: A world of ideas. In R. A. Karchmer, M. H. Mallette, J. Kara-Soteriou, & D. J. Leu, Jr. (Eds.), *Innovative approaches to literacy education: Using the Internet to support new literacies* (pp. 44–64). Newark, DE: International Reading Association.

Christian, S. (1997). *Exchanging lives: Middle school writers on-line.* Urbana, IL: National Council of Teachers of English.

Coiro, J., & Dobler, E. (2007). Exploring the online reading comprehension strategies used by sixth-grade skilled readers to search for and locate information on the Internet. *Reading Research Quarterly, 42,* 214–257.

Cope, B., & Kalantzis, M. (2000). Introduction: Multiliteracies: The beginning of an idea. In B. Cope & M. Kalantzis (Eds.), *Multiliteracies: Literacy learning and the design of social futures* (pp. 3–8). New York: Routledge.

Dalton, B., & Proctor, P. (2006, December). *Understanding understanding in a new literacies digital space: Changing the relationship of text, reader, and activity in service of improving diverse learners' comprehension and engagement.* Paper presented at the meeting of the National Reading Conference, Los Angeles.

Dalton, B., & Strangman, N. (2006). Improving struggling readers' comprehension through scaffolded hypertexts and other computer-based literacy programs. In M. C. McKenna, L. D. Labbo, R. D. Kieffer, & D. Reinking (Eds.), *International handbook of literacy and technology* (Vol. 2, pp. 75–92). Mahwah, NJ: Erlbaum.

DeBell, M., & Chapman, C. (2003). *Computer and Internet use by children and adolescents in 2001.* (NCES 2004–014). Retrieved July 13, 2007, from *nces.ed.gov/programs/quarterly/vol_5/5_4/2_1.asp.*

Dede, C. (2007, January). *Emerging educational technologies and neomillennial learning styles.* Presentation at the annual meeting of Educause Learning Initiative, Atlanta.

Durkin, D. (1993). *Teaching them to read* (6th ed.). Boston: Allyn & Bacon.

Evans, J. (2007, January). *The third annual Robert C. Heterick, Jr., lecture. K–12 students speak up about technology and learning: Are we listening?* Presentation at the annual meeting of Educause Learning Initiative, Atlanta.

Friedman, T. L. (2006). *The world is flat: A brief history of the twenty-first century.* New York: Farrar, Straus and Giroux.

Gambrell, L. B. (2005). Reading literature, reading text, reading the Internet: The times they are a'changing. *Reading Teacher, 58,* 588–590.

Garner, R., & Gillingham, M. G. (1996). *Internet communication in six classrooms: Conversations across time, space, and culture.* Mahwah, NJ: Erlbaum.

Glazer. S. (2005, November 10). Video games: Do video games significantly enhance literacy? *CQ Researcher On-line, 16,* 937–960. Retrieved January 30, 2007, from *library.cqpress.com.proxy.library.vcu.edu/cqresearcher/document.php?id=cqresrre2006111000.*

Goldberg, A., Russell, M., & Cook, A. (2003). The effect of computers on student writing: A meta-analysis of studies from 1992 to 2002. *Journal of Technology, Learning, and Assessment, 2*(1), 1–52. Retrieved July 17, 2007, from *www.staff.ucsm.ac.uk/rpotter/ict/research/effects-writing.pdf.*

Grisham, D. L., & Wolsey, T. D. (2006). Recentering the middle school classroom as a vibrant learning community: Students, literacy, and technology intersect. *Journal of Adolescent and Adult Literacy, 49,* 648–660.

Grossman, L. (2006, December 25/2007, January 1). *Time* person of the year: You. *Time,* 38–41.

Guthrie, J. T., & Wigfield, A. (2000). Engagement and motivation in reading. In M. L. Kamil, P. B. Mosenthal, P. D. Pearson, & R. Barr (Eds.), *Handbook of reading research* (Vol. 3, pp. 403–422). Mahwah, NJ: Erlbaum.

Harnad, S. (1991). Post-Gutenberg galaxy: The fourth revolution in the means of production of knowledge. *Public-Access Computer Systems Review, 2,* 39–53. Retrieved July 10, 2007, from *cogprints.org/1580/00/harnad91.postgutenberg.html.*

Harnad, S. (1992, October). *What scholars want and need from electronic journals.* Paper presented at the 55th annual meeting of the American Society for Information Science. Abstract retrieved July 15, 2007, from *scholar.lib.vt.edu/ejournals/vpiej-l/vpiej-l.log9210.html.*

Harris, T. L., & Hodges, R. E. (Eds.). (1995). *The literacy dictionary: The vocabulary of reading and writing.* Newark, DE: International Reading Association.

Harvard University and Arizona State University. (2004–2007). *The River City project: A multi-user virtual environment for learning scientific inquiry and 21st century skills.* Retrieved January 30, 2007, from *muve.gse.harvard.edu/rivercityproject/index.html.*

Holschuh, J. (2006, August). *Teaching students to evaluate Internet information by thinking like a historian.* Paper presented at the 21st World Congress on Reading, Budapest, Hungary.

Huffaker, D. (2005). The educated blogger: Using weblogs to promote literacy in the classroom. *AACE Journal, 13,* 91–98.

Jackson, R. M. (2004). *Technologies supporting curriculum access for students with disabilities.* Wakefield, MA: National Center on Accessing the General Curriculum. Retrieved January 30, 2007, from *www.cast.org/publications/ncac/ncac_techsupport.html.*

Johnson, D., & Pearson, P. D. (1984). *Teaching reading vocabulary* (2nd ed.). New York: Holt, Rinehart and Winston.

Jonassen, D. H. (2006). *Modeling with technology: Mindtools for conceptual change* (3rd ed.). Upper Saddle River, NJ: Pearson Education.

Ketelhut, D. J., Dede, C., Clarke, J., & Nelson, B.

(2006, April). *A multi-user virtual environment for building higher order inquiry skills in science.* Paper presented at the annual meeting of the American Educational Research Association, San Francisco. Retrieved January 30, 2007, from *muve.gse.harvard.edu/ river cityproject/documents/rivercitysympinq1.pdf.*

Kinzer, C. K. (2005). The intersection of schools, communities, and technology: Recognizing children's use of new literacies. In R. A. Karchmer, M. H. Mallette, J. Kara-Soteriou, & D. J. Leu, Jr. (Eds.), *Innovative approaches to literacy education: Using the Internet to support new literacies* (pp. 65–82). Newark, DE: International Reading Association.

Knobel, M., & Lankshear, C. (2006). Discussing new literacies. *Language Arts, 84,* 78–86.

Kreuger, A. B. (2000). *The digital divide in educating African American students and workers.* Working Paper 434, Industrial Relations Section. Princeton, NJ: Princeton University. Retrieved July 14, 2007, from *www.irs.princeton.edu/pubs/working_papers. html.*

Kress, G. (2004). *Reading images: Multimodality, representation and new media.* Retrieved July 17, 2007, from *www.knowledgepresentation.org/BuildingThe Future/Kress2/Kress2.html.*

Kymes, A. (2005). Teaching online comprehension strategies using think-alouds. *Journal of Adolescent and Adult Literacy, 48,* 492–500.

Landow, G. P. (1992). *Hypertext: The convergence of contemporary critical theory and technology.* Baltimore: Johns Hopkins University Press.

Landow. G. P., & Delaney, P. (1991). Hypertext, hypermedia, and literary studies: The state of the art. In P. Delaney & G. P. Landow, (Eds.), *Hypermedia and literacy studies* (pp. 3–50). Cambridge, MA: MIT Press.

Lawless, K. A., Brown, S. W., Mills, R., & Mayall, H. J. (2003). Knowledge, interest, recall and navigation: A look at hypertext processing. *Journal of Literacy Research, 35,* 911–934.

Lenhart, A., Simon, M., & Graziano, M. (2001). *The Internet and education: Findings of the Pew Internet and American Life project.* Retrieved January 15, 2007, from *www.pewinternet.org/pdfs/PIP_Schools_Report.pdf.*

Leu, D. J. (2000). Literacy and technology: Deictic consequences for literacy education in an information age. In M. L. Kamil, P. B. Mosenthal, P. D. Pearson, & R. Barr (Eds.), *Handbook of reading research* (Vol. 3, pp. 743–770). Mahwah, NJ: Erlbaum.

Leu, D. J. (2002). The new literacies: Research on reading instruction with the Internet. In A. E. Farstrup & S. J. Samuels (Eds.), *What research has to say about reading instruction* (3rd ed., pp. 310–336). Newark, DE: International Reading Association.

Leu, D. J. (2006). New literacies, reading research, and the challenges of change: A deictic perspective. In J. V. Hoffman, D. L. Schallert, C. M. Fairbanks, J. Worthy, & B. Maloch (Eds.), *55th Yearbook of the National Reading Conference* (pp. 1–20). Oak Creek, WI: National Reading Conference.

Levin, D., & Arafeh, S. (2002). The digital disconnect: The widening gap between Internet savvy students and their schools. *The Pew Internet and American Life project.* Retrieved January 3, 2007, from *www. pewinternet.org/pdfs/PIP_Schools_Internet_Report.pdf.*

Lewis, C., & Fabos, B. (2005). Instant messaging, literacies, and social identities. *Reading Research Quarterly, 40,* 470–501.

Liu, M., & Hsiao, Y. (2002). Middle school students as multimedia designers: A project-based learning approach. *Journal of Interactive Learning Research 13,* 311–338.

McKenna, M. C., Labbo, L. D., Reinking, D., & Zucker, T. A. (2007). Effective uses of technology in literacy instruction. In L. B. Gambrell, L. M. Morrow, & M. Pressley (Eds.), *Best practices in literacy instruction* (3rd ed., pp. 344–372). New York: Guilford Press.

McLuhan, M. (1962). *The Gutenberg galaxy: The making of typographic man.* Toronto: University of Toronto Press.

Meyer, A., & Rose, D. H. (1999). *Learning to read in the computer age (Reading to practice).* Retrieved January 16, 2007, from *www.cast.org/publications/ books/ltr/chapter5.html.*

National Center for Educational Statistics. (2005, February). *Internet access in US public schools and classrooms: 1994–2003.* (NCES 2005015) Retrieved July 10, 2007, from *nces.ed.gov/surveys/frss/publications/2005015/index.asp?sectionID=1.*

New London Group (1996). A pedagogy of multiliteracies: Designing social futures. *Harvard Educational Review, 66,* 60–92. Retrieved January 17, 2007, from *www.static.kern.org/filer/blogWrite44ManilaWebsite/paul/ articles/A_Pedagogy_of_Multiliteracies_Designing_Social_ Futures.htm.*

New Media Consortium (2005). *A global imperative: The report of the 21st century literacy summit.* Retrieved January 13, 2007, from *www.nmc.net/pdf/ Global_Imperative.pdf.*

North Central Regional Education Laboratory (n.d.). *21st century skills: Visual literacy.* Naperville, IL: Learning Point Associates. Retrieved July 15, 2007, from *www.ncrel.org/engauge/skills/vislit.htm.*

Olsen, S. (2006, December 7). *Teens and media: A full-time job.* Retrieved January 30, 2007, from *news.com. com/2100-1041_3-6141920.html.*

O'Reilly, T. (2005, October 1). Web 2.0: Compact Definition? *O'Reilly radar blog.* Retrieved July 3, 2007, from *radar.oreilly.com/archives/2005/10/web_20_compact_definition.html.*

Prensky, M. (2001). Digital natives digital immigrants. *On the Horizon (NCB University Press),* 9(5), 1–6. Retrieved January 25, 2007, from *www.marc prensky.com/writing/Prensky%20-%20Digital%20 Natives,%20Digital%20Immigrants%20-%20Part1.pdf.*

Prensky, M. (2006). "Engage me or enrage me": What today's learners demand. *Educause Review 40(5),* 60–64. Retrieved January 25, 2007, from *www.edu cause.edu/ir/library/pdf/erm0553.pdf.*

Project Tomorrow. (2006). *Our voices, our future: Student and teacher views on science, technology and education.* National Report on NetDay's 2005 SpeakUp Event. Retrieved January 24, 2007, from *www.netday.org/speakup/pdfs/SpeakUpReport_05.pdf.*

ReadWriteThink (n.d.). *Magazine redux: An exercise in critical literacy.* Newark, DE: International Reading Association/National Council of Teachers of English. Retrieved July 16, 2007, from *www.readwritethink.org/lessons/lesson_view.asp?id=214.*

Reinking, D., & Watkins, J. (2000). A formative experiment investigating the use of multimedia book reviews to increase elementary students' independent reading. *Reading Research Quarterly, 35,* 384–419.

Robnolt, V. J., Rhodes, J. A., & Richardson, J. S. (2005, December). *Study skills for the twenty-first century: Creating a new model.* Paper presented at the meeting of the National Reading Conference, Miami, FL.

Russell, M., & Plati, T. (2000). *Mode of administration effects on MCAS composition performance for grades four, eight, and ten: Executive summary.* A report of findings submitted to the Massachusetts Department of Education. Retrieved February 2, 2007, from *www.bc.edu/research/nbetpp/statements/WE052200.pdf.*

Schmar-Dobler, E. (2003). Reading on the Internet: The link between literacy and technology. *Journal of Adolescent and Adult Literacy, 47,* 80–85.

Stauffer, R. G. (1969). *Teaching reading as a thinking process.* New York: Harper & Row.

Stokes, S. (2001). Visual literacy in teaching and learning: A literature perspective. *Electronic Journal for the Integration of Technology in Education.* Retrieved July 17, 2007, from *ejite.isu.edu/Volume1 No1/Stokes.html.*

Troutner, J. (1985). Toward a definition of computer literacy. *Journal of Computers in Mathematics and Science Teaching, 4*(3), 10–11.

Tyner, K. (1998.) *Literacy in a digital world: Teaching and learning in the age of information.* Mahwah, NJ: Erlbaum.

Valmont, W. J. (2003). *Technology for literacy teaching and learning.* New York: Houghton Mifflin.

Venezky, R. L. (1995). Literacy. In T. L. Harris & R. E. Hodges (Eds.), *Literacy dictionary: The vocabulary of reading and writing* (p. 142). Newark, DE: International Reading Association.

Wileman, R. E. (1993). *Visual communicating.* Englewood Cliffs, NJ: Educational Technology Publications.

Williams, B. T. (2005). Leading double lives: Literacy and technology in and out of school. *Journal of Adolescent and Adult Literacy, 48,* 702–706.

CHAPTER 12

The Secondary English Curriculum and Adolescent Literacy

ROBERT BURROUGHS
PETER SMAGORINSKY

In this chapter we explore the relation between the secondary English curriculum and the ways in which adolescents engage in literacy practices in middle and high schools. We first review a set of key constructs. We define *adolescent literacy* in its plural form, reflecting a literacy that is responsive to the multimedia world in which young people live, and that is concerned with their development of identities, thus involving more than conventional reading and writing. *Curriculum* in our conception includes not just knowledge of facts and concepts, but also the social and educational practices through which literacy is enacted. A curriculum may be viewed as *planned* (e.g., involving standards, scope-and-sequence charts, and lesson plans), *enacted* (i.e., how it is put into action), and *received* (i.e., how students perceive what is presented and enacted); and it serves to socialize students through what is visible, hidden, and excluded. English as an *academic discipline* comprises the specialized ways of knowing, thinking, and doing expected of one's discourse and actions within its community of practice. We next consider issues related to these three foci, including conflicting notions of canonicity, methods of ensuring curricular continuity, the issues that English curricula tend to exclude, and the impact of external (e.g., state and national) curricula on teaching and learning. We conclude with the consideration that curricula are inherently ideological, and that U.S. English curricula tend to be far more conservative than critics believe, socializing students into conventional beliefs about gender, social and economic class, and other aspects of worldview.

In this chapter we explore the relation between the secondary English curriculum design and the ways in which adolescents engage in literacy practices in middle and high schools. We draw on the relatively slim body of research on the English curriculum and therefore review scholarship in curriculum theory and other theories of teaching and learning to inform our understanding of this ubiquitous means of organizing students' learning experiences. We first review the key constructs *adolescent literacy, curriculum,* and *academic disciplines*. We then look more closely at the relations among them. Finally, we review research on the ways in which adolescent literacy is mediated by the construction and implementation of the secondary English curriculum.

ADOLESCENT LITERACY, CURRICULUM, AND ACADEMIC DISCIPLINES

Adolescent Literacy

Street (1995) argues that the term *literacy* is more appropriately used in its plural form because the concept is neither singular nor stable. Rather, it refers to a related set of practices that are employed situationally and selectively. In the secondary English curriculum, attention to *literacies* has largely been confined to knowledge and practices involved in the reading of literature (Applebee, 1974, 1993). The curricular emphasis on the teaching and learning of literature typically comes at the expense of instruction in writing (Tremmel, 2001), although not of the *assignment* of writing and instruction in grammar.

We view literacies from the framework of sociocultural theories of knowledge (e.g., Scribner & Cole, 1981; Street, 1993). According to this perspective, cultural groups value certain ways of knowing and doing that are realized in the texts that they produce and read. *Texts* in this conception refers to *composed artifacts of symbolic systems* (see, e.g., the New London Group, 1996) or *configurations of signs* (Smagorinsky, 2001). Such a view of text includes an array of artifacts including books, films, music, art, clothing, spoken language, architectural designs, landscapes, and other human products imbued with a potential for meaning. These texts may be composed through any symbol system that enables two or more people to communicate with one another, or even for one person to represent ideas for personal use.

The notion of adolescent literacies that we have outlined concerns itself with the texts and textual practices in which adolescents volitionally immerse themselves in or out of school (Moje, Young, Readence, & Moore, 2000). Today's adolescents are part of a digital age that is exploding with new opportunities for communication and commerce. Alvermann (2002) reports findings from Greenfield Online indicating that 73% of 12- to 17-year-olds use the Internet and that the overwhelming majority of them use instant messaging (cf. Lenhart, Rainie, & Lewis, 2001). Moreover, a sizable percentage of the youth surveyed by Greenfield (25%) reported that they take on various identities while instant messaging and playing video games (see Black & Steinkuehler, Chapter 18, this volume; Gee, 2007). The result is that adolescents are engaged in a number of new literacies for "new times," most of which are not widely exercised or even acknowledged in the secondary English curriculum (Luke & Elkins, 1998).

Even as new technologies help to shape adolescents' emerging discourses and literacy practices, older forms of textuality—with or without words—continue to evolve. "Spoken word" poetry, for instance, although available for recording and distribution through compact disks and Internet file sharing, is often performed before live audiences, with little mediation between the speaker and listeners (Meacham, 2000–2001). Other studies have demonstrated that traditional art forms such as conventional poetry (Schultz, 2002), dance (Smagorinsky & Coppock, 1995), art (Whitin, 2005), drama (Wagner, 1999), and other media continue to play powerful roles in the lives of young people.

Just as a notion of literacy that is responsive to emerging conditions includes more than reading and writing words, its companion concept *discourse* involves more than the expression of ideas through texts, no matter how broadly conceived. Gee (1999) argues that discourses serve as *identity kits* that allow groups to understand and be recognized by one another. He gives the example of one motorcyclist asking another for a match in a biker bar. Gee notes that this request most appropriately contains specific vocabulary and specific syntax, along with the body posture, clothing, and movement necessary to communicate that the person making the request is a member of the biker community. Without conveying this identity authentically and convincingly, the person requesting a match might suggest an identity other than that of a biker and end up, at the least, slightly healthier for not having smoked; and unless the person is a T-800 Terminator cyborg, he could end up departing the bar with less than what he entered with.

A person's identity kit "comes complete with the appropriate costume and instruction on how to act, talk, and often write, so as to take on a particular social role others will recognize" (Gee, 1999, p. 127). In the same way, hip-hop artists use accents, dialects, costume, attitude, and stance to communicate "rapper"; or more specifically, "Christian rapper" or "gangsta rapper." Discourse, then, involves a worldview that is fundamentally ideological. Discourse does not simply embody an individual's personal effort to take on a social identity. It simultaneously accounts for the ways in which groups of people attempt to socialize people into their perspectives and practices.

Taking into account the more complex vision of literacy we have sketched and the increasingly varied mediational context in which many youth grow toward adulthood, the notion of adolescent literacy appears to add new wrinkles and dimensions almost daily. Especially if teachers wish to draw on students' prior knowledge about the world to help bridge their worlds with the content of the curriculum, understanding the complex nature of literacy in the 21st century is critical for educators in the new millennium.

Curriculum

Curriculum is customarily conceived as the "what" of instruction: what students will read, what aspects of grammar they should learn, which forms of writing they will produce, and other facets of the substance of students' engagement with the content of their discipline. Such a conception often expresses curriculum in terms of book lists, assignments, skills, and facts to be learned. For example, in the study of *Romeo and Juliet*, a curriculum might include textual knowledge of cultural allusions and extratextual knowledge of Shakespeare's biography and the structure of the Globe Theatre. In addition, the curriculum may include attention to the formal nomenclature of poetic writing: definitions and illustrations of *metaphor, allusion, irony,* and other terms, often accompanied by quizzes and tests that assess students' ability to match terms with definitions. Finally, the curriculum may specify other canonical texts and seek to inculcate habits of valuing certain texts over others according to critical perspectives such as New Criticism (i.e., "close reading" of the text, a focus on the text itself rather than on such extratextual factors as the author's history or presumed intentions, an emphasis on textual ambiguity, an understanding of tech-

nical aspects of form, and other approaches in relation to the text that treat it as a discrete creation that merits careful scrutiny on its own terms).

However, the term *curriculum*, as we use it here, is conceived to include not just "knowledge" (facts and concepts), but "practices" and "preferences" as well (Purves, Li, & Shirk, 1990). Although conventional notions of curriculum foreground "what is taught," our notion of curriculum emphasizes "what is learned." Because classroom learning is dynamic, a learning-oriented curriculum works at several levels. Most explicitly the curriculum may be viewed as *planned, enacted, and received.* The *planned curriculum* is the most familiar level and the most researched. This level includes the requirements of state standards, scope-and-sequence charts, and lesson plans. It is what curriculum planners and teachers intend students to learn within the domains of knowledge, practice, and preferences. The *enacted curriculum* is the plan put into action in the classroom. During instruction, plans may change, so the *enacted* curriculum may differ significantly or not from the *planned.* Finally, the *received curriculum* focuses on how students perceive what is presented and enacted. As with the *planned* and *enacted,* the *received curriculum* interacts with the other levels so that what students take away from class may or may not be what the *planned* and *enacted* intend.

In addition to these formal aspects of curriculum, a set of values is imposed through what are known as the *hidden curriculum* and the *null curriculum.* The hidden curriculum (Jackson, 1968) refers to the social agenda that motivates the explicit instruction in a school. Some believe that "the hidden curriculum is primarily the purview of the teacher ... as teachers communicate their values, expectations and other messages" (McCutcheon, 1988, p. 198). Others argue that "the hidden curriculum is taught by the school, not by any teacher. ... [Students] are picking-up an approach to living and an attitude to learning" (Meighan, 1981, p. 314).

Anyon (1980) found that hidden curricula are likely to vary according to the presumed social futures of the students. Anyon argues that even in elementary schools, children of different economic backgrounds are subject to the reproduction of the social division of labor (Williams, 1977; Willis, 1981); that is, students from working-class backgrounds are rewarded for obedience whereas students from more professional backgrounds are encouraged to show initiative and assertiveness, often in different levels of a tracked curriculum. From this perspective, a hidden curriculum may contribute to social stratification by shepherding students toward futures based on their parents' occupations and income by the ways in which the curriculum structures their experiences in school.

The hidden curriculum is often complemented by what Eisner (1994) calls the *null curriculum*: the content and means of engagement that are *not* taught in school. The null curriculum stands outside what Eisner calls the explicit curriculum, which typically relies on simple explanations that conceal the various interpretive possibilities of literature, history, science, and other areas of inquiry. Yero (2002) argues that the explicit curriculum emphasizes specific bits of information and skills, relegating to the null curriculum what she terms *big ideas*—not just the ideas themselves but the opportunity to approach them as Gordian and contestable (see Loewen, 1994, for the ways in which U.S. history textbooks oversimplify events in order to provide a grand narrative of Western progress). The explicit curriculum's emphasis on atomistic particles of knowledge, then, renders complicated discussions untenable and contested knowledge untestable. This reduction of ideas to their component parts nullifies attention to big questions and big ideas in the curriculum, particularly when multiple perspectives on one topic are viable.

A curriculum thus serves as one of school's most important socializing devices. Like a discourse, a curriculum ultimately poses the question, *"What sort of social group do I intend to apprentice the learner into?"* (Gee, 1999, p. 45; emphasis in the original) through students' engagement with its materials, practices, and other dimensions of its organizing principles. A curriculum is therefore not benign, but a means of mediating students' thinking and identities in particular ways (Apple, 2004), often differentiating students' experiences according to their social class.

Academic Disciplines

In secondary schools, curriculum is tied to *disciplines*. Although disciplines are often regarded as domains of particular subject matters, they can also be conceived as specialized "ways of knowing, thinking, and doing," as Applebee (1996, p. 39) argues, a notion compatible with Gee's concept of discourses. These "ways of knowing, thinking, and doing" form the boundaries of disciplines, as well as the criteria for legitimate participation in a discipline. What counts as an acceptable topic, as a reliable method of inquiry, as compelling evidence, or as a persuasive mode of argument are all examples of features that define aspects of disciplinary knowledge (Bazerman, 1994a; Herrington, 1985; Langer, 1992).

Schwab's (1964) distinction between the substantive and syntactical structures of a discipline is useful for our analysis of research on the curriculum in the discipline of secondary school English. *Substantive structure* is the conceptual structure of a discipline. This structure includes its organization, concepts, propositions, principles, and axioms and the relations among them, with each discipline having its own unique concepts and attendant practices.

Syntactic structure refers to the ways of knowing that are afforded by a discipline or, as Schwab (1964) writes:

> what [the discipline] does by way of discovery and proof, what criteria it uses for measuring the quality of its data, how strictly it can apply canons of evidence, and in general, of determining the route or pathway by which the discipline moves from its raw data through a longer or shorter process of interpretation to its conclusion. (p. 14)

If the substantive structure represents the *substance* of a field, the syntactic structure provides its *methodology*. Taken together, the substantive and syntactic structures of a field result in what Kuhn (1970) calls *paradigms*: the "entire constellation of beliefs, values, techniques, and so on shared by the members of a given community" (p. 175). Schwab (1964) argues that there is no "logical" order of prerequisites or facts with which to present a discipline, but rather "we must look to the capacities of our students, to knowledge of ways in which learning takes place, and to our objectives, what we hope our students will achieve, in order to make our decision" about how to present the scope and sequence of subject matter (p. 21). The ultimate outlook that motivates these decisions is situated in some paradigmatic way of thinking about the discipline: as the embodiment of Western heritage (Hirsch & Wright, 2004), as a vehicle for inquiring into development of a more just society (Fecho, 2004), as a means for students' personal growth (Dixon, 1975), as a structure for taking on the perspectives of multiple cultures (Banks, 2002), or as one of many other lenses available to teachers.

Disciplines, we should emphasize, are not monolithic. The discipline of English, for instance, although broadly oriented to criticism, includes discourse communities whose members perceive and enact the practice of reading in substantially different ways. Applebee (1993) has found that the New Critical approach is institutionalized in U.S. secondary school literature anthologies. The values underlying this perspective are engrained in the sorts of questions and stances that anthology editors inscribe in the questions and assignments included with reading selections. As Appleman (2000) has demonstrated, however, other approaches (in her conception, Marxism, feminism, deconstruction, and reader response) are available to frame the reading of teen readers. The notion of a discipline therefore includes subfields and contending values that often construe the whole project of reading in dramatically different ways, with appropriate stances and classroom practices following from the approach taken.

Relations among Literacy, Curriculum, and Academic Disciplines

A curriculum has implications not only for what students read—is *Robinson Crusoe* out, and *The Color Purple* in?—but for the kinds of activities that students engage in and the stance toward learning that the curriculum suggests. Disciplines (especially at the secondary level) often emphasize the relative stability of content, forms, processes, and conditions. Rather than dealing with multiple discourses (and multiple literacies), school disciplines in general are concerned with *a* discourse, the discourse of chemistry,

math, or history. Accordingly, the concept of "discourse conventions" is one way of describing the norms and shared knowledge that influence reading and writing practices in a discipline. A discipline's discourse conventions are often expressed within various written and spoken genres (Wertsch, 1991). Genres take specific forms—for example, thank-you notes or lab reports on frog dissections—but the form is an embodiment of a way of thinking and being in the world, rather than an end in itself. As Bazerman (1994b) argues, genres persist and develop because they provide responses to recurring social exigencies, so that "eventually the genres sediment into forms so expected that readers are surprised or even uncooperative if a standard perception of the situation is not met by an utterance of the expected form" (p. 82).

Traditions of discourse within disciplines evolve, yet often what one learns in school are the codified notions of disciplinary discourse and the traditions on which they are based (Marshall, Smagorinsky, & Smith, 1995). The five-paragraph essay is an example of a highly codified school genre. Although the five-paragraph form can often solve an academic problem, such as dealing with a state-mandated proficiency test in a timed writing situation, it is a thoroughgoing school form (Hillocks, 2002). It bears almost no resemblance to the texts produced within disciplinary genres; indeed, it bears almost no relationship to genres found anywhere but in secondary school and some first-year college composition programs (Emig, 1971). Whether this form is a help (Dean, 2000) or a hindrance (Rosenwasser & Stephen, 1997) for young writers remains a topic of debate. What seems clear is that it is part of the deep structure of the discipline of secondary school English instruction, supported by state writing test rubrics, traditions of instruction, the self-perpetuating nature of faculty hiring and retention practices, peer pressure among teachers, and other factors of the school environment that contribute to a school's academic culture (Johnson, Smagorinsky, Thompson, & Fry, 2003).

Literacies, then, primarily involve learning to situate texts in a variety of social contexts, whereas *disciplines* primarily involve learning to recognize, reproduce, and modify particular genres within academic domains and their attendant social practices. Research on the secondary English curriculum has largely focused on English as a discipline, rather than English as literacies. We next review more specifically research on the role of curriculum in the literacy development of adolescents in the discipline of secondary school English.

RESEARCH ON ADOLESCENT LITERACY AND THE SECONDARY ENGLISH CURRICULUM

Scope of the Review

Research on adolescent literacy in the secondary English curriculum yields a mixed bag of genres, ideas, and approaches. Further, it is a narrow body of scholarship, consisting largely of status studies and surveys of materials used in schools. A smaller portion of the research concerns case studies of curriculum implementation. An even smaller portion is theoretical in nature, largely based on Applebee's (1994) work, attempting to conceive of ways to structure the literature curriculum. Most of the research concerns the planned curriculum, some the enacted curriculum, and very little the received curriculum. On the whole, adolescent literacy is hardly mentioned as a factor in curriculum planning.

But adolescent literacy is a widely debated topic for discussion among writers on the English curriculum. We thus broaden our view of research to include scholarship on curriculum—that is, publications that draw upon and are situated within the history of ideas, yet are not necessarily data driven. Two genres make up most of the work on this topic. The first is composed of articles written by those advocating that particular kinds of texts or activities be incorporated into the *planned* curriculum. For example, some advocate for more books by women (Lake, 1988) or minorities (Lee, 2000) or more attention to media literacy (Center for Media Literacy, 2006). The second genre is expressed in publications that argue for a particular mix of texts or a particular approach to literacy as a whole (Romano, 2000). These publications focus on the *planned* curriculum as well, but often share vignettes of practice as the curriculum advocated is *enacted*, or samples of student work

to reveal some aspect of the *received* curriculum.

Finally, this review of the research focuses on articles and books published after 1992. Applebee and Purves (1996) provide a comprehensive review of the research on the secondary English curriculum prior to 1992. Their review emphasizes the curriculum as it relates to the teaching of literature and takes a historical approach to the subject, tracing the development of issues in the secondary English curriculum from colonial times to the present (cf. Applebee, 1974; Peel, Patterson, & Gerlach, 2000).

Which Canon(s)?

In the study of the discipline of literature within secondary English classes, teachers have largely looked to the subject matter rather than to their students, focusing on substantive structures of the discipline. The curriculum has overwhelmingly focused on literature study, employing approaches that are either (1) historical, that is, involving the study of a relatively stable collection of texts presented to students in the chronological order of their composition, or (2) "genre" based, that is, organized by short story, poetry, drama, and other forms (note that this meaning of *genre* is quite different from the one we outlined previously) (Applebee, 1993; Squire & Applebee, 1968). Within these types of organizations, the selection of texts relies heavily on "canonical" works; that is, those that teachers, and critics, and often the public—if not all secondary school students—revere as important or essential readings. It appears that secondary English curriculum designers and teachers hope students will achieve a general knowledge of literary history and literary forms through curricula organized in these ways. Yet others have proposed different ways of considering the constitution of a curriculum. We next review several key alternatives for constructing a literature curriculum.

Scholes (1998) endorses a curriculum characterized by a canon of *methods* rather than a canon of texts. Scholes (1985) takes the notion of *textual power* and applies it to the college English curriculum, which Applebee (1974) found often helps to shape the secondary school curriculum. Scholes (1998) bases his view of the English curriculum on the notion that a discipline is a way of knowing, of seeing the world. Disciplines are culturally based, he argues, making the study of English "a part of the cultural equipment" (p. 68) that a student requires to negotiate the world. The animating force of the "cultural equipment" is Scholes's concept of "textuality," the notion that discourses are instantiated in texts: "As disciplines constitute themselves, they institutionalize discourses, regulating not only admission to canonicity but also the right to produce texts with authority, the right to interpret, and in this manner they control the permitted kinds of interpretation as well" (p. 77). Just as Gee's (1999) motorcyclist must employ appropriate dimensions of a suitable identity kit to operate with credibility in a biker bar, members of scholarly disciplines must understand and be fluent with the paradigmatic practices necessary for being taken seriously by their peers, particularly those practices associated with the expectations for discourse.

"We live in a society that is fully and insistently textualized," Scholes (1998, p. 84) argues, and hence the job of English teachers is instructing students in the ways of texts. Such a curriculum would not focus on collections of literature, but on methods for reading not only books but all kinds of texts: "Literacy involves the ability to understand and produce a wide variety of texts that use the English language—including work in the traditional literary forms, in the practical and persuasive forms and in the modern media as well" (p. 130; cf. Pirie, 1997; Semeniuk, 1997; Wolf, 1995).

A different departure from the traditional canonical approach to building a literature curriculum comes through appeals to include a wider range of texts and methods in students' reading. Bancroft (1994) calls for literary theorists to expound upon the pedagogical implications of their theories. Probst (1994) offers such a program, advocating reader-response theory as the center of the secondary literature curriculum. Kazemek (1998) and Davis (1989) call for more literature by and about women, and Evans (2004) calls for more use of popular culture. Others advocate adding multicultural literature to the curriculum (Milner, 2005), and still others counter that multicultural literature falls short of the quality of canonical texts and so fails to either challenge students or improve the academic performance of students of color (Auciello, 2000; Stotsky, 1999). All these educators, regardless of their perspectives, assume that literature has primacy in the English curriculum.

Although many researchers, literary critics, and teachers may advocate teaching a wide range of literature, the general tendency is for teachers to draw upon a narrow range of texts and methods. In a national survey of public, private, and parochial schools, Applebee (1993) found that a relatively limited number of canonical works were taught by teachers across school type, geographical region, and socioeconomic borders. Moreover, the survey found that the titles were remarkably stable over a generation's time; that is, *Romeo and Juliet, The Scarlet Letter,* and *The Great Gatsby,* among others, have been top choices of teachers since the 1960s.

In addition to finding stability in teachers' choices about which literary texts to read, Applebee (1993; cf. Altmann, Johnston, & Mackey, 1998; Stallworth, Gibbons, & Fauber, 2006) found consistency in how they teach these titles. In general, teachers employed both text-centered approaches (such as "careful questioning about content") and reader-centered approaches (such as "focusing on links to everyday experience") in their instruction. At a theoretical level, such approaches offer "incompatible visions of what matters in the teaching of literature" (Applebee, 1993, p. 137) if they are not explicitly linked during instruction.

Scope, Sequence, and Curricular Continuity

Curriculum scholars have tended to focus on the "scope" of the discipline, rather than the "sequence"; that is, the research has focused on *what* texts students should read or what writing assignments they should engage in and not *how* those texts and assignments should be structured or sequenced within a curriculum (yet see Smith & Hillocks, 1988). In a review essay of a number of books on the secondary English curriculum, Kooy (2000) criticizes the authors for failures to articulate scope and sequence, asking, "How are learning experiences [in the curriculum] staged to link this text to other texts and experiences, to locate it in a complex web of textuality?" (p. 483; cf. Beach & Marshall, 1991; Hillocks, McCabe, & McCampbell, 1971; Smagorinsky, 2002, 2008). Burroughs (1999) illustrates the problems that result when scope is emphasized over sequence. In a study of three teachers in the same secondary English department attempting to integrate multicultural literature, Burroughs found that two of the three teachers had difficulty inserting multicultural texts into traditional survey courses in American and British literature. The British literature teacher in particular found that a contemporary novel, *The Family* by Buchi Emecheta, was largely rejected by the students, because they had difficulty "fitting it into the course" and its chronological sequence (p. 144): "Within that thesis, *The Family* was not cohesive; it didn't fit. . . . Though [students] sensed that *The Family* was different from the other canonical texts they'd read, they couldn't clearly articulate their objections" (p. 145). Hence, the "sequence" of texts, experiences, or activities is an important part of how students experience a curriculum. Applebee (1994, 1996, 2002) has argued that paying attention to continuity and coherence in curriculum is essential to thinking about how the secondary English curriculum is organized.

Applebee's (1996) notion of "curriculum as domains for culturally significant conversations" offers a way to think about how curriculum may be organized for continuity and coherence. Applebee argues that by entering culturally significant conversations, students are apprenticed into traditions of discourse that implicitly represent various ways of knowing and doing. That is, knowledge is not only knowing what, but also knowing how: "It is these ways of knowing, thinking, and doing, this knowledge-in-action, that students acquire as they are helped to enter into significant traditions of discourse" (p. 39).

In contrast to a curriculum of "knowledge-in-action," which encourages students to enter into current conversations within living traditions of discourse, many curricula present "knowledge-out-of-context" for students to learn *about*. For example, in the teaching of literature, Williams (1977) has shown how the "lived culture" of a historical record gets distilled into a "selective tradition" (cf. Taxel, 1981). As Applebee (1996) points out, these selective traditions often become "deadly traditions" as students are marched through a list of "classic texts," focusing on "right" answers, with few explicit reasons for why the texts were chosen or what connections there might be among them. Curriculum becomes, as Applebee notes, "specialized content (knowing), ignoring the discourse conventions that govern participation (doing)" (p. 30).

How might this conception of curriculum as domains for conversation play out in classrooms? A study of secondary English teachers over 2 years in 19 classrooms at two sites found that teachers establish a variety of "conventions" for discussing the domain of literature and employ a variety of "structures" to organize those conversations (Applebee, Burroughs, & Stevens, 2000). For example, the study found that conventions for discussion varied in ways of discussing topics of discussion, and the direction of discussion. Similarly, structures ranged from catalogues of relatively unrelated topics to sequences of survey courses to integrations of topics across a range of texts and activities. Students' engagement was highest and their perceived understanding of the domain greatest when domain structure and discussion conventions worked together to support students' entry into significant conversations about interesting issues. For example, in an American Literature survey course, the conversation centered on the nature of the literature canon itself, an issue that is alive and hotly debated both in and out of the academy.

In contrast, that study also found many classrooms in which discussion conventions or domain structures tended to cut students off from live traditions. For example, a British Literature survey course featured a book list composed of largely canonical texts chosen to represent various historical periods. But as the course conversations unfolded, questions of period or history were addressed on an *ad hoc*, book-by-book basis. As a result, students missed much of the historical import; indeed, not all students even recognized that the course had been organized chronologically. Chronology had served as a selection criterion for the teacher, but chronology had not been a significant part of the larger curricular conversation. So it was with other classes studied. Questions of historical continuity, questions of the relation between form and meaning in a text, questions of genre had often lost whatever potency they once had to stimulate debate and interest. Instead they became opportunities to transmit content, "the knowledge-out-of-context" that Applebee (1996) argues is of least lasting value to students.

The Null Curriculum

As we have reviewed, Eisner (1994) has argued that a null curriculum exists alongside a stated curriculum, consisting of those texts, topics, and practices that are avoided in students' education. Generally speaking, the null curriculum removes from students' school experiences any attention to the issues that face them most dramatically in their own lives. Ockerbloom (1993/2005), for instance, details a wide range of books that have been banned in U. S. society and schools. Books have been censored because they include sex, sexual orientation, characters with non-normative mental health profiles, violence, alcohol consumption, experimentation with or addiction to drugs, profanity, offensive language, religion, evolution, sorcery, and other topics. Some (e.g., Vandergrift, 1996) argue that these topics raise issues central to the social growth of young people and that, rather than being banned, should make up the core of the topics that students investigate through their literacy activities (see, e. g., Lancaster & Warren, 2004).

Although some classic texts include sex (*Romeo and Juliet*), violence (*King Lear*), and other taboo topics, for the most part these issues are raised in the genre of young adult literature (YAL). YAL, even though a favorite alternative among many members of the National Council of Teachers of English (see, for instance, *The ALAN Review*, a journal devoted to YAL and its pedagogy), is thought by many to be of insufficient literary rigor for inclusion in the secondary English curriculum (e.g., Finn, Ravitch, & Fancher, 1984). The competing beliefs on the appropriateness of reading YAL help to amplify the effects of the ways in which different paradigms produce different conceptions of the field. From Dixon's (1975) perspective that an education should promote a stu-

dent's personal growth, YAL may seem to be a critical part of the literature curriculum. If, in contrast, one takes Bloom's (1987) cultural heritage position, then one's reading should begin and end with "classic" texts. In any case, the selection of any set of texts often precludes the inclusion of others, thus eliminating potential topics and issues available for young people to read about and respond to in English classes.

District, State, and National Curricula

The primary curriculum that affects teachers and students is the school curriculum, which provides the focus for our review. Yet any school curriculum is nested within district, state, and national curricula that help to shape instruction (and, presumably, learning) at the local level. Research on teachers' experiences within district curricula (e.g., Johnson, Smagorinsky, Thompson, & Fry, 2003; Smagorinsky, Gibson, Moore, Bickmore, & Cook, 2004; Smagorinsky, Lakly, & Johnson, 2002) has demonstrated the ways in which district-level policies can affect a teacher's practice. In these studies, the teachers experienced frustration with the ways in which their agency as teachers was reduced by the strictures of the curriculum, particularly in terms of the ways in which the curriculum required that they follow scripted lessons and prepare students for district assessments.

An implication of these case studies is that teachers who enter the profession with a hope to enliven the pervasively "flat" (Goodlad, 1984, p. 108) atmosphere of schools are often thwarted by curricula that are designed to homogenize instruction across classrooms. Such curricula appear least inviting to teachers who view themselves as change agents or creative thinkers, and most inviting to those who fit comfortably within schools as they have historically been conducted. As Lortie (1975) found, schools tend to attract and retain teachers who enter the profession because they were comfortable with the traditions of schooling when they were students; and as teachers, they then perpetuate those traditions without seeing any need to question or challenge them. A scripted districtwide curriculum thus reinforces the hiring and retention effect by making school a less hospitable work environment for teachers who question the *status quo,* and more inviting to those for whom its historic practices make perfect sense.

At the state level, Hillocks (2002) has shown how a state curriculum and its attendant assessment practices can dictate instruction at the classroom level. This influence is known as the *washback effect:* "the extent to which the introduction and use of a test influences language teachers and learners to do things they would not otherwise do that promote or inhibit language learning" (Messick, 1996, p. 241; cf. Nichols & Berliner, 2007). In particular, Hillocks analyzed writing assessments in five states, finding that when a state instituted a limited yet easily assessable form such as the five-paragraph theme as its means of assessment, teachers directed their writing instruction to meet its reductive requirements.

The effort to link instruction to "standards" appears to employ the definition of standard that refers to its homogenizing effect rather than its elevation of performance. Hillocks found that the writing assessed according to a rubric based on the five-paragraph theme, although uniform across student performances, often fell far short of any qualities that he and many others associated with good writing. Further, the assessments in one state made no distinctions across genres, using a five-paragraph rubric even when students were prompted to produce narratives, thus applying inappropriate criteria for the type of writing they produced in order to suit the assessment's need for uniformity and production-line evaluations of mammoth stacks of student papers. This employment of a single set of rubric criteria for writing involving different qualities in turn affects classroom instruction, leading to teaching and learning that undoubtedly ignore the differentiation required of writers when producing different sorts of texts for different readerships.

As of this writing, secondary schools at this point are not as severely affected by national policy as are elementary schools with their mandated adherence to the dictates of the No Child Left Behind legislation. Yet this policy has begun to affect secondary schools as well, with its accountability requirements and other "measures" of "success" affecting how teachers teach (see the High School Leadership Summit, n. d.). School personnel must file extensive reports documenting students' Adequate Yearly Progress to be in compliance with the mandate. Although research has not yet documented the impact of No Child Left Behind on secondary teaching and learning, we assume from other bureaucratic interventions that in order to do the paperwork required by this mandate, teachers must sacrifice time they might otherwise spend planning instruction, reading student writing, conferring with parents, conferencing with students, discussing students with counselors, conducting action research, meeting with colleagues, reading for professional development, and otherwise meeting their immediate and long-term professional needs and responsibilities.

CONCLUSION

We found relatively few empirical studies on the secondary English curriculum. Most scholarship on curriculum is theoretical, with competing paradigms producing different arguments about what the curriculum should consist of. Some argue for a canonical approach, some for broader reading options that are more oriented to matching reading selections with the cultural backgrounds of students. Yet these theorists tend to talk past each other, largely asserting that their assumptions have greater veracity than those of their antagonists—without demonstrating empirically or convincingly that they produce different and more desirable effects. We see, then, a need for more curriculum studies that analyze the consequences of different curricular contents and organizations for what students do and don't learn in school, on students' affective connection to school, on students' behavior toward one another and other members of their community, and on other effects that curriculum theorists claim follow from their beliefs.

Although Ravitch (2000), Stotsky (1999), and others who believe that a curriculum ought to embody and transmit the nation's cultural heritage have railed against multiculturalists, feminists, French philosophers, and others whose thinking has challenged canonical approaches to curriculum, the secondary English curriculum in fact has remained remarkably stable over time. Rather than serving as some radical, left-wing vehicle for altering young people's consciousness and aligning youth against America, the extant curriculum, in fact, generally reinforces values that have been part of the furniture of schooling for as long as curriculum studies have been conducted. Despite the concerns of traditionalists, most challenges to conventional curricular organizations have been theoretical in nature, at best finding their implications patched onto existing curricula rather than serving to radically reconstruct the organization and content of students' experiences in the domain of English.

Ultimately, our review reveals that a curriculum is not benign. Rather, it suggests to students a worldview that is implied or explicitly taught through the texts, activities, sequences, and other dimensions of learning that are included (and excluded). Empirical studies that document the effects of curricular organizations, we believe, ought to constitute the next generation of curriculum research. Without such investigations, theorists will continue to argue without the benefit of evidence, and the field will be left with many opinions but little data to support why a curriculum is as it is and why it affects students as it does.

REFERENCES

Altmann, A., Johnston, I., & Mackey, M. (1998). Curriculum decisions about literature in contemporary classrooms: A preliminary analysis of a survey of materials used in Edmonton grade 10 English courses. *Alberta Journal of Educational Research, 44*, 208–220.

Alvermann, D. E. (2002). Effective literacy instruction for adolescents. *Journal of Literacy Research, 34*, 189–208.

Anyon, J. (1980). Social class and the hidden curriculum of work. *Journal of Education, 162*(1), 67–92.

Apple, M. W. (2004). *Ideology and curriculum* (3rd ed.). New York: Routledge.

Applebee, A. N. (1974). *Tradition and reform in the teaching of English: A history.* Urbana, IL: National Council of Teachers of English.

Applebee, A. N. (1993). *Literature in the secondary school: Studies of curriculum and instruction in the United States.* Urbana, IL: National Council of Teachers of English.

Applebee, A. N. (1994). Toward thoughtful curriculum: Fostering discipline-based conversation. *English Journal, 83*(3), 45–50.

Applebee, A. N. (1996). *Curriculum as conversation: Transforming traditions of teaching and learning.* Chicago: University of Chicago Press.

Applebee, A. N. (2002). Engaging students in the disciplines of English: What are effective schools doing? *English Journal, 91*(6), 30–36.

Applebee, A. N., Burroughs, R., & Stevens, A. (2000). Shaping conversations: A study of devices that create continuity and coherence in the high school literature curriculum. *Research in the Teaching of English, 34*, 396–429.

Applebee, A. N., & Purves, A. C. (1996). Literature and the English language arts. In P. W. Jackson (Ed.), *Handbook of research on curriculum* (2nd ed., pp. 726–748). New York: Macmillan.

Appleman, D. (2000). *Critical encounters in high school English: Teaching literary theory to adolescents.* New York: Teachers College Press.

Auciello, J. (2000). Chronicle of a battle foretold: Curriculum and social change. *English Journal, 89*(4), 89–96.

Bancroft, M. A. (1994). Why literature in the high school curriculum? *English Journal, 83*(8), 23–25.

Banks, J. (2002). *Introduction to multicultural education* (3rd ed.). Boston: Allyn & Bacon.

Bazerman, C. (1994a). *Constructing experience.* Carbondale: Southern Illinois University Press.

Bazerman, C. (1994b). Systems of genres and enactment of social intentions. In A. Freedman & P. Medway (Eds.), *Genre and the new rhetoric* (pp. 79–104). Bristol, PA: Taylor & Francis.

Beach, R., & Marshall, J. D. (1991). *Teaching literature in the secondary school.* San Diego: Harcourt, Brace, Jovanovich.

Bloom, A. (1987). *The closing of the American mind: How higher education has failed democracy and impoverished the souls of today's students.* New York: Simon & Schuster.

Burroughs, R. S. (1999). From the margins to the center: Integrating multicultural literature into the secondary English curriculum. *Journal of Curriculum and Supervision, 14*(2), 136–155.

Center for Media Literacy. (2006). *Literacy for the 21st century: An overview and orientation guide to media literacy education.* Los Angeles: Author. Retrieved April 26, 2007, from *www.medialit.org/pdf/mlk/01_MLKorientation.pdf.*

Davis, B. M. (1989). Feminizing the English curriculum: An international perspective. *English Journal, 78*(6), 45–49.

Dean, D. M. (2000). Muddying boundaries: Mixing genres with five paragraphs. *English Journal, 90*(1), 53–56.

Dixon, J. (1975). *Growth through English set in the perspective of the seventies* (3rd ed.). Yorkshire, UK: National Association for the Teaching of English.

Eisner, E. (1994). *The educational imagination: On the design and evaluation of school programs* (3rd ed.). New York: Macmillan.

Emig, J. A. (1971). *The composing processes of twelfth*

graders. Urbana, IL: National Council of Teachers of English.

Evans, J. (2004). From Cheryl Crow to Homer Simpson: Literature and composition through pop culture. *English Journal, 93*(3), 32–38.

Fecho, B. (2004). *"Is this English?": Race, language, and culture in the classroom.* New York: Teachers College Press.

Finn, C. E., Ravitch, D., & Fancher, R. T. (1984). *Against mediocrity: The humanities in America's high schools.* New York: Holmes & Meier.

Gee, J. P. (1999). *Social linguistics and literacies: Ideology in discourses* (2nd ed.). New York: Falmer.

Gee, J. P. (2007). *Good video games and good learning: Collected essays on video games, learning, and literacy.* New York: Peter Lang.

Goodlad, J. I. (1984). *A place called school: Prospects for the future.* New York: McGraw-Hill.

Herrington, A. J. (1985). Writing in academic settings: A study of the contexts for writing in two college chemical engineering courses. *Research in the Teaching of English, 19,* 331–361.

The High School Leadership Summit. (n. d.). *No Child Left Behind: Transforming America's high schools.* Washington, DC: U.S. Department of Education. Retrieved April 27, 2007, from *www.ed.gov/about/offices/list/ovae/pi/hsinit/papers/nclb.pdf.*

Hillocks, G. (2002). *The testing trap: How state writing assessments control learning.* New York: Teachers College Press.

Hillocks, G., McCabe, B. J., & McCampbell, J. F. (1971). *The dynamics of English instruction, grades 7–12.* New York: Random House.

Hirsch, E. D., & Wright, S. A. (2004). *Core knowledge.* Charlottesville, VA: Core Knowledge Foundation.

Jackson, P. W. (1968). *Life in classrooms.* New York: Holt, Rinehart, & Winston.

Johnson, T. S., Smagorinsky, P., Thompson, L., & Fry, P. G. (2003). Learning to teach the five-paragraph theme. *Research in the Teaching of English, 38,* 136–176.

Kazemek, F. E. (1998). The things they carried: Vietnam War literature by and about women in the secondary classroom. *Journal of Adolescent and Adult Literacy, 42,* 156–165.

Kooy, M. (2000). Re-imagining the places and landscapes of English education: Conversations from the field. [Review of the books *Why English? The Place and Position of English Studies Circa 2000, Reshaping High School English,* and *The Rise and Fall of English*]. *Curriculum Inquiry, 30,* 473–487.

Kuhn, T. S. (1970). *The structure of scientific revolutions.* Chicago: University of Chicago Press.

Lake, P. (1988). Sexual stereotyping and the English curriculum. *English Journal, 77*(6), 35–38.

Lancaster, E., & Warren, C. (2004). *Mental illness.* Retrieved May 3, 2007, from *www.coe.uga.edu/~smago/virtualLibrary/Lancaster_Warren.pdf.*

Langer, J. A. (1992). Speaking of knowing: Conceptions of understanding in the academic disciplines. In J.

Mangieri & K. Collins (Eds.), *Teaching thinking: An agenda for the twenty-first century* (pp. 69–85). Mahwah, NJ: Erlbaum.

Lee, C. D. (2000). Signifying in the zone of proximal development. In C. D. Lee & P. Smagorinsky (Eds.), *Vygotskian perspectives on literacy research: Constructing meaning through collaborative inquiry* (pp. 191–225). New York: Cambridge University Press.

Lenhart, A., Rainie, L., & Lewis, O. (2001, June 20). *Teenage life online.* Retrieved April 19, 2007, from *www.pewinternet.org/reports/toc.asp?Report=36.*

Loewen, J. W. (1994). *Lies my teacher told me: Everything your American history textbook got wrong.* New York: New Press.

Lortie, D. C. (1975). *Schoolteacher: A sociological study.* Chicago: University of Chicago Press.

Luke, A., & Elkins, J. (1998). Reinventing literacy in "new times." *Journal of Adolescent and Adult Literacy, 42,* 4–7.

Marshall, J. D., Smagorinsky, P., & Smith, M. W. (1995). *The language of interpretation: Patterns of discourse in discussions of literature* (NCTE Research Report No. 27). Urbana, IL: National Council of Teachers of English.

McCutcheon, G. (1988). Curriculum and work of teachers. In L. E. Beyer & M. W. Apple (Eds.), *The curriculum: Problems, politics, and possibilities* (pp. 191–203). Albany, NY: SUNY Press.

Meacham, S. J. (2000–2001). Literacy at the crossroads: Movement, connection, and communication within the research literature on literacy and cultural diversity. *Review of Research in Education, 25,* 181–208.

Meighan, R. (1981). *A sociology of education.* New York: Holt.

Messick, S. (1996). Validity and washback in language testing. *Language Testing, 13,* 241–256.

Milner, H. R. (2005). Developing a multicultural curriculum in a predominately White teaching context: Lessons from an African American teacher in a suburban English classroom. *Curriculum Inquiry, 35,* 391–427.

Moje, E., Young, J. P., Readence, J., & Moore, D. (2000). Reinventing adolescent literacy for new times: Perennial and millennial issues. *Journal of Adolescent and Adult Literacy, 43,* 400–410.

The New London Group. (1996). A pedagogy of multiliteracies: Designing social futures. *Harvard Educational Review, 66,* 60–92.

Nichols, S. L., & Berliner, D. C. (2007). *Collateral damage: How high-stakes testing corrupts America's schools.* Cambridge, MA: Harvard Education Press.

Ockerbloom, J. M. (1993/2005). *Banned books online.* Philadelphia: The Online Books Page. Retrieved April 27, 2007, from *onlinebooks.library.upenn.edu/banned-books.html.*

Peel, R., Patterson, A. H., & Gerlach, J. (2000). *Questions of English: Ethics, aesthetics, rhetoric, and the formation of the subject in England, Australia, and the United States.* New York: Routledge.

Pirie, B. (1997). *Reshaping high school English*. Urbana, IL: National Council of Teachers of English.

Probst, R. E. (1994). Reader-response theory and the English curriculum. *English Journal, 83*(3), 37–44.

Purves, A. C., Li, H., & Shirk, M. (1990). *Comparison of measures of the domain of learning in literature*. Albany, NY: Center on English Learning and Achievement.

Ravitch, D. (2000). *Left back: A century of failed school reforms*. New York: Simon & Schuster.

Romano, T. (2000). *Blending genre, altering style: Writing multigenre papers*. Portsmouth, NH: Heinemann.

Rosenwasser, D., & Stephen, J. (1997). *Writing analytically*. Fort Worth, TX: Harcourt, Brace.

Scholes, R. (1985). *Textual power: Literary theory and the teaching of English*. New Haven, CT: Yale University Press.

Scholes, R. (1998). *The rise and fall of English: Reconstructing English as a discipline*. New Haven, CT: Yale University Press.

Schultz, K. (2002). Looking across space and time: Reconceptualizing literacy learning in and out of school. *Research in the Teaching of English, 36*, 356–390.

Schwab, J. J. (1964). Structure of the disciplines: Meanings and significances. In G. W. Ford & L. Pugno (Eds.), *The structure of knowledge and the curriculum* (pp. 1–31). New York: Rand McNally.

Scribner, S., & Cole, M. (1981). *The psychology of literacy*. Cambridge, MA: Harvard University Press.

Semeniuk, A. (1997). Design for teaching English. In J. L. Aitken & A. Semeniuk (Eds.), *Why English? The place and position of English studies circa 2000* (pp. 6–25). Toronto: University of Toronto Guidance Centre.

Smagorinsky, P. (2001). If meaning is constructed, what is it made from? Toward a cultural theory of reading. *Review of Educational Research, 71*, 133–169.

Smagorinsky, P. (2002). *Teaching English through principled practice*. Upper Saddle River, NJ: Merrill/Prentice-Hall.

Smagorinsky, P. (2008). *Teaching English by design: How to create and carry out instructional units*. Portsmouth, NH: Heinemann.

Smagorinsky, P., & Coppock, J. (1995). The reader, the text, the context: An exploration of a choreographed response to literature. *Journal of Reading Behavior, 27*, 271–298.

Smagorinsky, P., Gibson, N., Moore, C., Bickmore, S., & Cook, L. S. (2004). Praxis shock: Making the transition from a student-centered university program to the corporate climate of schools. *English Education, 36*, 214–245.

Smagorinsky, P., Lakly, A., & Johnson, T. S. (2002). Acquiescence, accommodation, and resistance in learning to teach within a prescribed curriculum. *English Education, 34*, 187–213.

Smith, M. W., & Hillocks, G., Jr. (1988). Sensible sequencing: Developing knowledge about literature text by text. *English Journal, 77*(6), 44–49.

Squire, J. R., & Applebee, R. K. (1968). *High school English instruction today*. New York: Appleton-Century-Crofts.

Stallworth, B. J., Gibbons, L., & Fauber, L. (2006). It's not on the list: An exploration of teachers' perspectives on using multicultural literature. *Journal of Adolescent and Adult Literacy, 49*, 478–489.

Stotsky, S. (1999). *Losing our language: How multicultural classroom instruction is undermining our children's ability to read, write, and reason*. New York: Free Press.

Street, B. V. (1993). *Cross-cultural approaches to literacy*. New York: Cambridge University Press.

Street, B. V. (1995). *Social literacies: Critical approaches to literacy in development, ethnography, and education*. New York: Longman.

Taxel, J. (1981). The outsiders of the American revolution: The selective tradition in children's fiction. *Interchange, 12*, 206–228.

Tremmel, R. (2001). Seeking a balanced discipline: Writing teacher education in first-year composition and English education. *English Education, 34*, 6–30.

Vandergrift, K. E. (Ed.). (1996). *Mosaics of meaning: Enhancing the intellectual life of young adults through story*. Lanham, MD: Scarecrow Press.

Wagner, B. J. (Ed.). (1999). *Building moral communities through drama*. Stamford, CT: Ablex.

Wertsch, J. V. (1991). *Voices of the mind: A sociocultural approach to mediated action*. Cambridge, MA: Harvard University Press.

Whitin, P. (2005). The interplay of text, talk, and visual representation in expanding literary interpretation. *Research in the Teaching of English, 39*, 365–397.

Williams, R. (1977). *Marxism and literature*. New York: Oxford University Press.

Willis, P. E. (1981). *Learning to labor: How working class kids get working class jobs*. New York: Columbia University Press.

Wolf, D. P. (1995). Of courses: The Pacesetter initiative and the need for curriculum-based school reform. *English Journal, 84*(1), 60–68.

Yero, J. L. (2002). *Teaching in mind: How teacher thinking shapes education*. Hamilton, MT: MindFlight.

CHAPTER 13

Visual Arts and Literacy

MICHELLE ZOSS

The use of visual art as a means to communicate is not an unusual tool for teaching children in elementary schools. Once children become adolescents and enter secondary schools, however, the role of visual art in education can become peripheral to literacy development. This chapter explains the integration of visual art within secondary school literacy. It draws on a semiotics model of curriculum in which multiple sign systems for communication are valued. The semiotics model acknowledges that communication and learning occur within language, image, music, and other sign systems. For example, adolescents working within a semiotics-based curriculum that integrates image and language signs can express and represent their ideas in multiple media. In an integrated literacy curriculum, adolescents have the opportunity to explore the affordances and constraints of communicating in complex ways that can develop verbal and visual literacy simultaneously. The first part of the chapter articulates a definition for integrated visual arts and literacy based on the semiotics-based curriculum. The definition for an integrated visual arts and literacy curriculum has four components: (1) Visual art is included as texts for reading and composing alongside literature and other language-based texts; (2) students learn to transmediate their responses from one type of text to another— for example, to respond to literature with a drawing; (3) students use medium-specific analysis to respond to visual texts; and (4) students are offered multiple pathways to make meaning. The second part of the chapter reviews research on integrated visual arts and literacy curricula within secondary school settings. The purpose of the review is to illustrate the complexity of literacy events that occur when visual art is integrated into literacy curricula.

The role of visual arts in a literacy context, such as a literature course in a high school or a language arts course in a middle school, need not simply be decorative. That is, visual art in a literacy context need not be limited to a print of Monet's *Water Lilies* on the wall to be looked at when students need a break from reading and writing. Instead, visual art can be a means for students to learn to communicate ideas and to learn new ways to think about problems and texts.

Certainly, the use of visual art as a means to communicate is not an unusual tool for teaching children in elementary schools (Dyson, 1997). Children in kindergarten through third grade are encouraged to compose texts with both language and image. Curriculum materials marketed for primary grades include paper for children's writing that includes space for writing words and for drawing pictures. Yet, beyond third grade, and especially as adolescents enter secondary schools, the role of images in literacy contexts diminishes and, as a result, composing and attending to images are separated, with communication in images placed in the visual arts class and communication in language placed in the literacy class. In contrast to the separation of image and text within school contexts, adolescents lead rich lives of multimedia communication that sync image and language together. The technology and resources available to adolescents are full of potential to communicate in language, image, or both simultaneously. With the belief that communication for adolescents should be approached from a position that embraces both language and image, in this chapter I argue for the integration of visual art into secondary school literacy contexts.

The idea of using visual art in literacy classes is not new. The role of visual art in secondary school literacy contexts has a historical precedent dating back to the late 19th century. The Committee of Ten (National Education Association of the United States Committee of Ten on Secondary Education, 1892), which included prominent individuals from universities across the country, advocated the use of drawing in English classes as a component of a rigorous curriculum meant to prepare students to enter college. Drawing was recommended as a useful skill for communicating in science and math classes as well. A century-old report, the Committee of Ten document is not proof enough that visual art should be used as a curriculum tool in literacy classes; rather, the document illustrates the idea that using images to teach adolescents about language, literacy, and literature can be a promising endeavor. The Committee of Ten operated in a century without television, radio, computers, the Internet, or cell phones; adolescents in the 21st century have access to a wealth of sophisticated communication tools, and literacy classes are rife with opportunities to teach adolescents about the language and images that can be consumed and composed both in and out of school.

I argue in this chapter for a literacy curriculum based in semiotics (Suhor, 1984), in which multiple means for communication are valued. The chapter is organized in two parts. In the first part, I explore a model for integrated visual arts and literacy based on the semiotics-based curriculum. The integrated curriculum model stems from the rationale that multiple pathways for learning (Eisner, 1998) are important ends for students in secondary settings. The content of an integrated curriculum includes texts of both language and image, and the processes for making meaning within the curriculum include transmediation. In classroom practice, transmediation most often refers to a response composed in a medium other than that of the original text, such as composing a drawing in response to a short story (Siegel, 1995). A discussion of medium-specific analysis, that is, analytic approaches that are particular to a sign system such as language or image, illustrates thinking in different sign systems. In the second part, I review research in which visual art plays a role in literacy classes in secondary school settings. The purpose of the review is to illustrate the complexity of literacy events that can occur when visual art is integrated into literacy curricula. I conclude with a brief discussion of implications regarding the implementation of integrated literacy curricula for adolescents and teachers facing the demands of standardized assessments.

ARTICULATING A LINGUISTIC AND PICTORIAL SEMIOTICS-BASED CURRICULUM

Suhor's Semiotics-Based Curriculum

Suhor (1984, 1992) claims that semiotics provides "a useful framework for conceptualising curriculum" (p. 250). Semiotics is the study of signs (Blonsky, 1985; Eco, 1985); "a sign is something that stands for something else" (Suhor, 1992, p. 228). For example, either a word on a page or a drawing can be a sign for the idea of a water lily. The word and the drawing constitute two different kinds of signs, one linguistic, one pictorial. Signs are not confined to language and image, however. Signs are also constituted in architecture, dance, mathematics, and music. Different kinds of signs are organized into sign systems that people use to convey ideas or meanings. Communicating an idea about a water lily, for instance, can be viewed in terms of the different signs used to convey what water lily means. According to Suhor, human beings draw from a number of sign systems all the time as they communicate with each other in person, in print, in image, and in performance. Semiotics, then, is the study of signs and sign systems.

Suhor (1984) writes that a general model for semiotics-based curricula requires communication via the use of different kinds of signs and sign systems. The assumption is that communication begins with an "experiential store" (p. 251), a repository of all the sensory information a person takes in and from which ideas are then communicated via different sign systems. One has a "range of media theoretically at one's disposal in encoding various experiences" (p. 250). In other words, there is a range of possible signs that one can use to communicate about an experience. The sign systems or media available include linguistic, gestural, pictorial, musical, and constructive, among others (e.g., aromatics, mathematics). Suhor also notes that human expression and communication can be conducted at any time in these media, using multiple sign systems simultaneously. Human expression, then, is not limited to language or image or movement; rather, expression can be achieved through multiple sign systems. For example, a conversation about one of Monet's *Water Lilies* paintings can include verbal language (linguistic) to describe the shape of the flowers and the flow of the water in which they grow, as well as hand and body gestures (gestural) to demonstrate what that language represents, all the while referring to the painting itself (pictorial) as a source for the conversation.

Within his semiotics-based curriculum model, Suhor (1984) notes that the linguistic sign system has a higher priority in schools than the other sign systems. The hierarchy is purposeful, as Suhor (1992) claims that "language is the main arbiter as students learn to use and understand all of the other symbol systems" (p. 229). Suhor's claim assumes that spoken and written language permeates the learning of all students and does not account for students who use sign language as a system to communicate (Ramsey, 1997). Thus, for a semiotics-based curriculum for schools, the role of language is still primary, but the importance of language as the sole means for communication and expression is tempered by an acknowledgement that valuable thinking and learning *also* occur in sign systems that are nonlinguistic. To articulate

a theory that names, describes, and supports literacy curricula that are integrated with the visual arts, I focus on a specific configuration of a semiotics-based curriculum that includes the linguistic and pictorial media.

An Integrated Literacy and Visual Arts Curriculum

To focus specifically on the integration of visual arts in a language arts curriculum, we can narrow the sign systems in Suhor's (1984) general model of six sign systems to include only linguistic and pictorial sign systems. I acknowledge that narrowing the possible media used in an actual classroom to just two media is counter to Suhor's (1984) claim that "in actual human experience many expressions of thought occur simultaneously in more than one medium" (p. 252). Indeed, a lesson that integrates language and visual art is very likely to include gestural, musical, and possibly other sign systems. However, toward the end of defining a specific instance of curriculum, it is useful to limit attention to just the linguistic and pictorial sign systems (cf. Grossman, Valencia, & Hamel, 1997, for a discussion of the challenges in defining the scope of English language arts curricula; also see Burroughs & Smagorinsky, Chapter 12, this volume).

Multiple Pathways for Learning

The rationale for approaching a literacy curriculum from a semiotics perspective generally and from an integrated linguistic/pictorial integration specifically is to produce curricula that provide multiple pathways for learning and expression (Eisner, 2002). The content of an integrated curriculum includes both linguistic and pictorial texts; thus, the texts span a range from literature to painting, to nonfiction, to photography. The process or means for integrating this variety of texts involves learning to read image and language, while also learning to respond with image and language.

To present adolescents with a semiotics-based curriculum that integrates visual art is to present a curriculum that values the variety of ways in which young people express their ideas and learning. The reading and composing processes and products in such a curriculum can yield myriad opportunities for adolescents to explore in language and image the world in which they live and the world they might imagine into being. Integrating visual art into secondary school literacy classrooms thus presents adolescents and teachers with affordances of two sign systems rather than the more traditional exclusive focus on language.

The affordances and constraints of a curriculum are embedded within the materials and activities of which the curriculum is constituted (Eisner, 2002). The activities that a teacher chooses to teach, the materials used to produce those activities, and the responses students compose in relation to the activity and material are both afforded and constrained by the possibilities of the sign system in which the activity, the material, and the response are located. Certainly, linguistic signs are varied: Oral language, written language, literature texts, and informational texts are embedded with different and overlapping affordances and constraints. Adding the pictorial system of signs, which includes two-dimensional images such as photographs, drawings, and paintings, adds a different set of affordances and constraints. The integration of visual art in literacy classes means that the ways students learn are expanded to include "an experientially rich array of resources for understanding some aspect of the human condition" (Eisner, 2002, p. 154).

The expansion of literacy curricula through integration with visual art activities and materials also includes the expansion of potential pathways for learning (Whitin, 2005). Instead of focusing exclusively on language and literature, adolescents learning in an integrated classroom have at minimum two sign systems in which to present their learning and their knowledge. For example, students could learn about internal conflict in a specific piece of literature by reading the original linguistic text, responding to the text by composing a drawing, watching a film version of the text, and then composing a second drawing that is accompanied by an oral presentation to respond to the original text, the first drawing, and the film.

Text

With the affordances and constraints of a curriculum built into the materials and activities that constitute that curriculum, the texts that are included as materials to read and activities to produce become important components. An integrated curriculum meant to teach students the use of linguistic and pictorial signs should include texts primarily of words as well as texts primarily of images. In a typical secondary school literacy class, literature texts, such as anthologies and young adult novels, are the main texts from which teachers and students work (Piro, 2002). The emphasis for reading and composing, then, is on linguistic text (Smagorinsky & Coppock, 1995a; Smagorinsky & O'Donnell-Allen, 1998a; Smagorinsky, Zoss, & O'Donnell-Allen, 2005). Literature anthologies in the recent past have included reproductions of works of art in the student editions, as well as in the teacher edition supplements (e.g., *Literature and the Language Arts: Experiencing Literature*, 1996). Meant to accompany selections of literature in the anthology, these optional materials are provided to support the linguistic learning in literacy classrooms. In an integrated classroom, the images are valued as texts to which questions are posed, into which investigations are launched, and with which relationships are transacted just as scholars describe questioning, investigating, and relational engagements with linguistic texts (Faust, 2000; Rosenblatt, 1995; Sumara, 1996).

The inclusion of images as texts fits with Witte's (1992) argument that a conception of text should be expanded to include the various ways people use and compose texts. Witte criticizes notions of writing that privilege "spoken or written linguistic systems of meaning-making" while ignoring other systems of meaning making, stating that this "can hardly yield a comprehensive or culturally viable understanding of 'writing' or 'text'" (p. 240). Texts for Witte can include signs from any sign system because people use the signs necessary to meet their needs. For adolescents, the available signs within a typical literacy class may be restricted to certain uses of language: writing five-paragraph themes, reading British and American literature, and composing short answers and essays for tests. Smagorinsky and his colleagues have argued that, looking across an entire school experience, it is evident that adolescents use composing processes as diverse as drafting architectural and interior design plans and designing horse ranches, but the school-sponsored composing commensurate with testing practices is the linguistic practice of writing essays in English class (Smagorinsky, Cook, & Reed, 2005; Smagorinsky, Pettis, & Reed, 2004; Smagorinsky, Zoss, & Reed, 2006). Attentive to the rich multimedia composing practices adolescents use in their lives outside school (Heath, 2004), Smagorinsky and his colleagues' work with composing across the curriculum highlights the idea that writing or composing need not be constrained to the signs available in language. The integration of visual art in a literacy course does not negate the value of the work done in language, nor do images provide redundant information (Eisner, 2002). Rather, the use of images supplements and complements the linguistic composition (cf. Howard, 1916, for an early 20th century discussion of images for teachers to use in secondary literacy contexts).

The literacies valued in an integrated curriculum with pictorial and linguistic texts involve both analysis and composition of visual and print texts. Students in literacy classes of this type are not assessed exclusively with tools such as multiple-choice tests and written essays, those found in "heritage traditions" of schooling (Smagorinsky & Taxel, 2005). Rather, performance in an integrated literacy class is assessed through the use of both visual and print media compositions and tests. For example, assessment tools may include portfolios, compositions using language and/or image, and oral performance.

Process

The process for composing and reading image and language texts in an integrated literacy context includes the affordance of *transmediation* (Siegel, 1995; Suhor, 1984, 1992; Whitin, 2005) and the constraint of *medium-specific analysis.* Transmediation is the "translation of content from one sign system into another" (Suhor, 1984, p. 250). In an integrated literacy class, essays can be composed about paintings as well as literature, and drawings and paintings can be composed about literature and, perhaps, other images. For example, a student who composes a drawing as a response to a short story is transmediating the linguistic content of the story into a pictorial set of signs. In this example, the meaning that the student makes of the linguistic story is represented in a pictorial sign. Siegel (1995) explains that students

> must arrive at some understanding and then find some way to cross ("trans") the boundaries between language and art such that their understanding is represented pictorially; it is in this sense that one sign system is explored in terms of (mediation) another. (p. 461)

To do this representation of meaning, it is necessary that the student think in terms of the language of the short story and in terms of the images of the drawing. Through the composition of the drawing, a student represents meanings she constructed that require her to think in both linguistic and pictorial signs.

Smagorinsky (1996) notes that "in translating their thoughts into a material product, learners often develop new ideas about the object of their thinking," and that the product "becomes a symbol that the student can use to promote further reflection (and often reconsideration) of the ideas that produced it" (p. 15). In other words, the drawing that the student produces is a material product of her thinking and is also a text that can be used for further thinking about the short story. Thus, in the composition of a drawn text in response to a literature text, there is a translation of meaning from one medium or sign system (linguistic → print text) to another (pictorial → visual text).

Transmediation in a literacy education context embraces the notion that "*meaning is not limited to what words can express*" (Eisner, 2002, p. 30; emphasis in the original). Eisner's point is that the meaning one makes of something can include more than one form or representation. These forms are not required to have language in order to be meaningful. Eisner goes on to note that when meaning is formed in more than one medium, "these forms enable us to construct meanings that are nonredundant; each form of representation we employ confers its own features upon the meaning we make or interpret" (p. 230). The emphasis in this transmediation component of the integrated literacy curriculum framework is that students are given opportunities to think about, compose, and make meanings of texts that are not limited to language. The opportunities for students to represent the meanings they make are expanded to include the affordances and constraints of both the linguistic and pictorial sign systems.

Medium-specific analysis is a constraint attendant to an integrated literacy curriculum. Suhor (1984), Eisner (2002), and others argue that the analysis of texts in different sign systems requires instances of reasoning specific to the sign system in use. For example, when discussing a short story, it is appropriate to use the elements of a story (i.e., character, conflict, plot, and setting) as analytic tools for making meanings about the short story text. Likewise, when discussing a painting, it is appropriate to use the elements of design (i.e., color, form, line, shape, space, texture, and value) as analytic tools for making meanings about the painting text. Suhor cautions that if students are taught to apply only literary criticism, which includes the elements of story, to nonlinguistic media, the analysis may be flawed. That is, an analysis of a visual medium with analytic tools specific to a linguistic medium does not allow for a full investigation of that visual medium, and, as such, this pedagogical move may be short-sighted. In a literacy context that integrates visual art, then, students learn how to talk and think about both language-based and image-based texts and, potentially, texts based in both language and image (Albers & Murphy, 2000; Kress et al., 2005; Kress & van Leeuwen, 2001).

An affordance for including medium-specific analysis for images is the opportunity to teach adolescents about perceiving the different kinds of texts they encounter in and out of school. Literacy teachers in the past have taught adolescents to be savvy consumers and composers of linguistic texts. To include visual art in a literacy classroom as a text for analyzing and composing is to expand literacy practices to include the multimedia of language and images that adolescents encounter in their everyday lives. A medium-specific analysis for visual art deals with perceiving qualities, also known as *reasoned perception* (Siegesmund, 1999, 2005) or *qualitative reasoning* (Eisner, 2002). Qualities in an image are the colors, forms, lines, shapes, spaces, textures, and values that

constitute the elements of design. When a viewer perceives the relationships among these qualities (e.g., relations of color, of lines, of colors with lines), the viewer begins constructing a meaning of the image. Reasoned perception and qualitative reasoning refer to the process of constructing meaning from the perception of relationships of qualities a viewer encounters in art. Whitin (2005) posits that a semiotics-based curriculum affords opportunities to teach students about how their perceptions of sensory experiences, like that of attending to the visual qualities in art, relate to thinking and "multiple ways of knowing" (p. 366).

For Dewey (1934/1980), the act of perception is also concerned with the perceiver's relationship with the image or work of art. The perceiver's relationship with the image results in a construction of meaning in which the perceiver brings as much of the meaning-making process to the image as the image brings meaning to the perceiver. Eisner (2002) calls this interactive relationship *the work of art,* a reciprocal process in which the art works on the perceiver and the perceiver works on the art. Dewey (1934/1980) posits that work of perception, especially in working with visual art, is a demanding cognitive task: "To think effectively in terms of relations of qualities is as severe a demand upon thought as to think in terms of symbols, verbal and mathematical" (p. 46). The perception of qualities is thus a demanding thought process that can be done before one expresses one's thoughts about this perception in words, image, or other symbol system. Thus, in literacy classes that integrate the visual arts, part of the curriculum is teaching students how to perceive and talk about the qualities in images, a process that Dewey (1934/1980) claims calls for a high degree of intelligent thinking.

Visual art educators (Eisner, 1998, 2002; Siegesmund, 1999, 2005) value the medium-specific analysis of qualitative reasoning and reasoned perception as a fundamental component of art education. Students who use qualitative reasoning in art classrooms think in visual terms and use both language and images to articulate that thinking. In an integrated literacy context, valuing medium-specific tools for thinking and learning in both visual and linguistic media places language and image on a more equal footing. Daniel, Stuhr, and Ballengee-Morris (2006) argue that accomplishing integration that values art in non-art contexts requires that the visual arts be incorporated into the big ideas, key concepts, and essential questions that drive the curriculum. With interconnections of pictorial and linguistic texts at the heart of an integrated literacy curriculum, students can begin to explore the different types of thinking involved in both visual and language arts. Gardner (1993) and Smagorinsky (1995, 1996) have argued that a strong mathematical and linguistic focus in schools has limited the possible sign systems in which students learn and can express their knowledge. Though Gardner's and Smagorinsky's arguments were positioned within discussions of cognition and intelligences, the argument is germane to a discussion of a semiotics-based curriculum that seeks to expand the sign systems available for adolescents to use to perceive, think about, respond to, and compose within schools.

Although transmediation and reasoned perception are processes that students and teachers in integrated literacy classes can use to work with linguistic and pictorial texts toward a goal of multiple pathways for learning, there is an important constraint to note. In the multimedia environment of the 21st century, it is hard to imagine that an integrated literacy classroom would not also take advantage of the music, drama, film, and online media available. The question of how each of these different texts would play out in an integrated curriculum is beyond the scope of this chapter (but see Bruce, Chapter 19, and Black & Steinkuehler, Chapter 18, this volume, for discussions of media and virtual spaces); however, the value of the integrated curriculum lies in the multiple and varied opportunities for students to encounter texts based in language and image, and to think and respond using transmediation and reasoned perception (cf. Walling, 2006, for more ideas for integrating the visual arts with literacy curricula) In the next section, I review a number of studies that have been done with adolescents in secondary school literacy contexts that employ visual art. I discuss these studies in terms of the content and the processes used in the literacy contexts.

RESEARCH IN INTEGRATED LITERACY CONTEXTS

Flood, Heath, and Lapp, the editors of the first edition of the *Handbook of Research on Teaching Literacy through the Visual and Communicative Arts* (1997), argue that the purpose of the *Handbook* is "to bring the visual arts into a central place in literacy and language education . . . to break the trend of literacy educators' exclusive focus on learning as reading and writing" (p. xvi). The resulting collection of 64 articles examines literacy and literacy teaching as practices involving drama, poetry, drawing, television, books, computers, film, video, movement, and play. Among the chapters focusing specifically on the role of visual art in literacy classes in schools, most focus on elementary children, with the exception of articles on adolescent street literacy (Conquergood, 1997), adolescents and youth genre (Daiute, 1997), programs designed to bridge home and school literacies (Lee, 1997), and oral and intergenerational texts (Binstock, 1997; Gadsden, 1997).

Conquergood (1997) examined the embodied literacy practices of adolescents in gangs using images and language to proclaim their affiliations on their bodies and on walls and clothing. The texts the adolescents composed as graffiti used language and image and were meaningful signs that conveyed messages to compatriots and enemies alike. Adolescents in Conquergood's study had to attend to the qualities of line and letters in their texts—for example, two extra points on a star denoted affiliation with a rival gang, and the placement of letters upside down or right side up were indicators of affiliation and respect or disrespect. Although not located in a secondary school literacy class, the literacy practices of the adolescents in this study point to the complex ways in which students encounter and respond to their environments.

Returning to a school-based context, Harste, Short, and Burke (1988) presented drawing as a component of writing for elementary students' emergent writing practices. Whitin (1996a, 1996b, 2005) repurposed the "sketch-to-stretch," originally an activity in which elementary-age students draw their responses to a text they are reading, as an image- and language-composing activity in a seventh-grade context and used sketch-to-stretch as a response to literature. Whitin taught students visual response to literature as a form of composition, as a text that required drafting, editing, and revising, just like the verbal texts they wrote. The sketches were accompanied with written verbal descriptions, and students were provided time in class to confer with peers for suggestions to edit and revise their drawings and accompanying linguistic descriptions. Whitin taught her students how to talk about their drawings in small- and large-group settings, with discussions of the symbols and colors the students used in the drawings as important parts of the curriculum. Students discussed and wrote about the qualities of their drawings and how these qualities functioned as referents to the literature.

The texts used in Whitin's classroom included linguistic and pictorial texts. Students composed drawings and writings about their responses to literature. The drawn responses are examples of transmediation from language to image, and the written responses about the drawings are examples of transmediation from image to language. The students were given multiple opportunities for transmediation with the composing of their drawings and writings as responses to the literature they read. In a subsequent article, Whitin (2005) wrote that the "instances when students composed collaborative sketches best revealed the process of transmediation" (p. 370). The opportunity to compose drawings with other students was accompanied by talk about decisions being made and revised as the students put shapes and lines on paper and negotiated the resulting composition. Reasoned perception was part of this integrated curriculum because the students had to think and talk about the qualities in their drawings—lines, colors, and use of space, for example. Sketch-to-stretch as an activity was further incorporated into the overall literacy curriculum as one possible means for making meaning of literature. Making meaning in Whitin's study was achieved via multiple paths, and sketch-to-stretch was an activity that gave students opportunities to think and respond, using language and image.

An example of an integrated literacy and visual arts curriculum that employs literature and visual art texts, along with rea-

soned perception, transmediation and multiple pathways to meaning, is the work of O'Donnell-Allen and Smagorinsky (1999; Smagorinsky & O'Donnell-Allen, 1998b, 2000). Studying *Hamlet,* students in O'Donnell-Allen's senior English class worked together in small groups to create body biographies (Underwood, 1987) of the main characters in the play. The body biographies were life-sized outlines of a human body that were filled with drawings, quotes, poems, and descriptions of the focal character. O'Donnell-Allen and Smagorinsky argue that the process of composing and negotiating the meaning and rendering of the linguistic and pictorial signs on the body biography was both a mediating and mediated process linked to students' transactions with the text and the social practices of the members of the group. The transmediation in the social and artistic practices informed their reading of *Hamlet,* just as their social and artistic practices and the text of the play informed their reading of the body biography text. Like the students working in Whitin's (1996a; 1996b; 2005) class with the sketch-to-stretch, the students studying *Hamlet* used oral language to mediate their understandings of the play and of their body biographies. These studies illustrate that work in language and in image are complementary in ways that promote variety in student thinking and composing practices.

Another unit in O'Donnell-Allen's class focused on identity and culminated with the composition of identity masks and verbal self-portraits (Smagorinsky, Zoss, & O'Donnell-Allen, 2005). The unit employed a variety of activities, including reading literary texts, viewing artists' self-portraits, and discussing memories of the students' childhoods. The masks were constructed on the students' faces and then painted to represent their identities. The study afforded Peta, the focal student in the study, an opportunity to talk about the meanings he inscribed in his mask. Peta's mask visually represented the nonlinear thinking he preferred, a way of thinking that may have contributed to his dropping out of school. Peta also inscribed emotional meanings in the mask, using colors and shapes to show the intensity of frustration and anger he felt when encountering his classmates as well as some adults in his life.

Eisner (2002) and Siegesmund (1999; Siegesmund & Cahrmann-Taylor, 2008) note that visual arts instruction, especially in terms of teaching and learning about qualities, involves somatic knowledge (knowledge of the body) and connections with emotions. Citing the neuroscience in Damasio's (1999) research, Siegesmund argues that attention to reasoning is intimately connected with the body and emotions. With the mask activity, students had an opportunity to compose pictorial texts that inscribed meaning via visual qualities located on a canvas that not only represented, but was also formed by, the very contours of their faces. The students were expected to compose images that conveyed visually the students' own perceived meanings of their identities. The process of composing the masks was located within reasoned perception because the masks were created using exclusively visual qualities. Peta used language to describe his mask to the researchers, an opportunity for transmediating his understanding of his mask to a linguistic, oral description. As a component within the larger unit on identity, the mask activity was an example of a visual text among many linguistic and pictorial texts that were used to develop meanings about identity and how identity is represented in different media.

In a seventh-grade literacy classroom, Wilhelm (1997) used visual art with struggling and reluctant readers. Wilhelm's integration of visual art was focused on teaching students visualization strategies to help them engage with linguistic texts. The students had difficulties in imagining or visualizing the stories they read for class. Wilhelm claims that "art may provide a means for experiencing what it means for a reader to enter, create, and participate in a story world" (p. 138). Toward the goal of helping his students create visualizations of story worlds, Wilhelm used several different strategies to make concrete and visible for his struggling readers what proficient readers do in their minds while reading. These strategies included (1) symbolic story representation, in which students brought in or made objects to represent characters and themselves as readers and to use as props for recreating scenes of their reading experiences (cf. Enciso, 1992); (2) visual protocols, in which students composed drawings during and after their reading of linguistic texts to help them visualize the text; (3) illustrated books

and graphic novels as entrées into literature (cf. Heath & Bhagat, 1997); (4) illustrations, in which students illustrated print-only stories and later composed their own stories to illustrate; (5) picture mapping, in which students took notes about key details of a story using visual symbols; and (6) collages, in which students used found images to compose a visual response to a poem or a song (pp. 120–124). All of these strategies were shared with peers and Wilhelm, as their teacher, to help the students articulate the meanings they were making of the linguistic texts and to encourage them to continue reading. Wilhelm states, "The creation of artwork provides students with concrete tools and experiences to think with, talk about, and share" (p. 141). Thus, the role of art in this context was a means for representing the experiences the students were having while reading their linguistic texts.

Wilhelm's (1997) visualization practices provided students with opportunities to compose visual art as texts to accompany the literature and other linguistic texts used in the class and allowed students to use transmediation to articulate their responses to reading. Oral language was frequently used for students to talk about their visual compositions and their meanings inscribed in images and in verbal texts they read. The student talk around the visualization strategies was thus important as a sign system for conveying to Wilhelm what students were learning while they read. Wilhelm's use of several different visualization strategies illustrates how visual art can be used in multiple ways to help students develop their literacy practices. The various strategies also take advantage of different types of pictorial texts available for students to use and compose: Students could use found objects and images to compose works that illustrated their reading relationships with texts; students could draw images that showed the relationships among characters, plot, and setting; students could read graphic novels and comic books in which they could learn about sophisticated and professional productions of language and image relations; and students could compose illustrations for both their own writing and that of professional authors. This multiplicity of strategies affords support for literacy practices via explicit instruction and helps students use their experiences in reading and in responding to their reading with images as ways for knowing and understanding linguistic texts.

In another account of attending to the needs of struggling students, Fu (1995) presented the story of a high school student from Laos who began to use English with confidence as a result of talking about his drawings. The student, Cham, brought a drawing of his experiences living in Laos to his English as a Second Language (ESL) class, where Fu was a participant observer. Fu asked the adolescent to tell her about the drawing, and in the subsequent verbal exchange she had with him, he used the most English she had ever heard him use up to that point in the school year. Cham was encouraged by both the ESL teacher and Fu to compose more drawings. The series of drawings that Cham composed became key components in the development of his English oral and written literacy education. Cham knew his reasons for using the qualities of line, shape, and form in his drawings, but he did not have the linguistic skills for articulating those reasons in English until he brought in the first drawing to his ESL class. With time and practice, Cham's language developed quite rapidly, because his language learning was intimately related to what he knew he could talk about with the help of a drawing.

Although not a whole-class curriculum project, Cham's use of drawings as texts in his language development is an example of how visual art can become significant texts in the development of literacy for adolescents. Using his drawings as a starting point, Cham transmediated what he knew in the pictorial sign system into oral and written linguistic signs. Cham's discussion around his drawings revealed how he inscribed meaning in the relationships of color, line, and shape to convey his experiences as a refugee. He seemed to understand the relationships of qualities in his drawing, and he used reasoned perception to explain the relationships and the meanings of those relationships to his ESL teacher and Fu. Furthermore, his pathway to language was different from that of the other students in the ESL class and, as a result of his work in that class, he began to develop his skills in other subject areas. Cham found an alternative

path to learning in school with his drawings that eventually helped him to navigate the linguistic path of the school's instruction and curriculum.

Jacobs (2006) is another educator interested in the learning paths of students who struggle. Her study focuses on male adolescents who have been incarcerated and their reluctance to read. As part of a literacy curriculum in a prison facility, Jacobs held 45-minute classes in which she read aloud a young adult novel that the young men collectively chose. During this reading and listening session, the students composed drawings that conveyed their emotional responses to the text. The drawings were accompanied by oral descriptions. Citing a host of studies about male adolescents in prison and juvenile detention centers as having intense feelings as a result of their experiences, Jacobs reasons that the drawings mediated "an alternative yet socially appropriate method of expression" for the young men (p. 115). Thus, the role of visual art in this alternative secondary context is that of emotional mediator, a role attributed traditionally to the arts (Eisner, 1998), while at the same time promoting a notion of literacy that includes drawing as an appropriate sign system for expressing responses to literature.

Although Jacobs's (2006) study of incarcerated youth draws deeply from literature on male adolescents in prison, it is short on description and explication of the value and role of drawing compositions as a response to literature. In this case, drawings are simply what Jacobs calls a " 'hook' to entice youth" (p. 118) into reading and responding to literature. I include the study here as a recent and not uncommon example of how people are trying to do this commendable work of bringing the visual arts into literacy contexts for adolescents. At the same time, however, this is an example of the visual arts being used only toward specific ends that do not include visual arts education goals of qualitative reasoning. Visual art in this context is used in a supporting role to achieve literacy goals, a scenario that Applebee, Burroughs, and Cruz (2000) and Rényi (2000) find commonplace in schools in which teachers endeavor to bring together multiple disciplines in their curricula. Jacobs has laudable goals in using art as an emotional mediator and a socially constructive means of expression. Other studies with students in alternative school contexts also employ visual and linguistic means for students to compose and express their responses to literature that provide more explicit rationales for and results of integrating visual art with literacy (Smagorinsky & Coppock, 1994, 1995a, 1995b). In literacy contexts located in alternative schools or jails, the integration of art can afford adolescents an alternative, complementary sign system for expressing their thinking. Adolescents gain opportunities for connecting with literature, their teachers, and their own emotions and experiences when given access to explicit teaching and teachers attentive to the role of meaning construction (Whitin, 2005).

IMPLICATIONS FOR INTEGRATING LITERACY WITH VISUAL ARTS

Being able to embrace the idea of multiple points of entry and multiple ends for learning in any classroom requires flexibility on the teacher's part (Eisner, 1994; Huberman, 1993). Eisner (2002) calls this "flexible purposing," a term that is originally Dewey's (1938/1988), to describe "the improvisational side of intelligence as it is employed in the arts ... the ability to shift direction, even to redefine one's aims when better options emerge in the course of one's work" (p. 77). Being able to shift and respond to the needs of students with the flexibility of using language and image, as a teacher in a semiotics-based literacy classroom may do, is a valuable educational end in a world in which the media used to communicate change frequently. A teacher of integrated curriculum uses flexible purposing to choose appropriate texts and activities that students can then transmediate into suitable media for representing their understandings. Furthermore, a teacher who employs flexible purposing can model for students a responsive and inclusive approach to literacy, rather than a dismissive and exclusionary approach to composing and reading texts both in and out of school. In other words, a flexible teacher can model for students the means for attending to their rapidly changing environment in ways that are suitable to their own idiosyncratic needs.

The multiple pathways for learning and meaning making presented in the various studies in this chapter show that the role of visual art in literacy classrooms can vary with the setting, the students, the teacher, and the activity. Compositions using visual art and language in these secondary literacy classes fostered the development of multiple meanings for texts. Unlike literacy classes in which texts are read for one essential meaning (Faust, 2000), the classes in these studies afforded adolescents opportunities to express their ideas in dynamic ways similar to the shifting and fast-paced modes of communication they used outside school. A challenge for teachers embracing the multiple pathways for learning and transmediation approach to students' composing of responses is the nearly singular pathway and lack of opportunities for transmediation included in standardized assessment practices. As teachers face the requirements of accountability systems based on standardized tests, there may be less room for the visual arts in literacy classrooms. Teachers who desire dynamic teaching and learning in their classes may need to strategically use and seek out curriculum tools that will allow them to be responsive to both the needs of their students (Huberman, 1993) and the demands of a culture of testing that posits reading as being at risk in the United States (National Endowment for the Arts, 2004; Smith, Marshall, Spurlin, Alvermann, & Bauerlein, 2004).

Although I present here a model of integrated literacy curricula as stemming from multiple pathways for making meaning, of a content consisting of texts based in language and image, and of a process founded in transmediation and medium-specific analyses, including reasoned perception, I do not seek to make this a prescriptive outline of what such an integrated curriculum should look like. More work can be done to envision literacy activities that also include gestural, musical, and constructive signs in the curriculum. Future research could investigate the potential ramifications for using integrated curricula with high-stakes standardized testing concerns for adolescents while examining the possibilities for fostering excellence in teaching and learning in integrated literacy classrooms.

REFERENCES

Albers, P., & Murphy, S. (2000). *Telling pieces: Art as literacy in middle school classes.* Mahwah, NJ: Erlbaum.

Applebee, A. N., Burroughs, R., & Cruz, G. (2000). Curricular conversations in elementary school classrooms: Case studies of interdisciplinary instruction. In S. Wineberg & P. L. Grossman (Eds.), *Interdisciplinary curriculum: Challenges to implementation* (pp. 93–111). New York: Teachers College Press.

Binstock, E. (1997). Student conversations: Provocative echoes. In J. Flood, S. B. Heath, & D. Lapp (Eds.), *Handbook of research on teaching literacy through the communicative and visual arts* (pp. 346–353). Mahwah, NJ: Erlbaum.

Blonsky, M. (Ed.). (1985). *On signs.* Baltimore: Johns Hopkins University Press.

Conquergood, D. (1997). Street literacy. In J. Flood, S. B. Heath, & D. Lapp (Eds.), *Handbook of research on teaching literacy through the communicative and visual arts* (pp. 354–375). Mahwah, NJ: Erlbaum.

Daiute, C. (1997). Youth genre in the classroom: Can children's and teachers' cultures meet? In J. Flood, S. B. Heath, & D. Lapp (Eds.), *Handbook of research on teaching literacy through the communicative and visual arts* (pp. 323–333). Mahwah, NJ: Erlbaum.

Damasio, A. R. (1999). *The feeling of what happens: Body and emotion in the making of consciousness.* New York: Harcourt Brace.

Daniel, V. A. H., Stuhr, P. L., & Ballengee-Morris, C. (2006). Suggestions for integrating the arts into curriculum. *Art Education, 59,* 6–11.

Dewey, J. (1980). *Art as experience.* New York: Perigree. (Original work published 1934)

Dewey, J. (1988). Experience and education. In J. A. Boydston (Ed.), *John Dewey: The later works, 1925–1953* (Vol. 13, 1938–1939, pp. 1–62). Carbondale, IL: Southern Illinois University Press. (Original work published 1938)

Dyson, A. H. (1997). Children out of bounds: The power of case studies in expanding visions of literacy development. In J. Flood, S. B. Heath, & D. Lapp (Eds.), *Handbook of research on teaching literacy through the communicative and visual arts* (pp. 167–180). Mahwah, NJ: Erlbaum.

Eco, U. (1985). Producing signs. In M. Blonsky (Ed.), *On signs* (pp. 176–183). Baltimore: Johns Hopkins University Press.

Eisner, E. W. (1994). *Cognition and curriculum reconsidered* (2nd ed.). New York: Teachers College Press.

Eisner, E. W. (1998). *The kind of schools we need: Personal essays.* Portsmouth, NH: Heinemann.

Eisner, E. W. (2002). *The arts and the creation of mind.* New Haven, CT: Yale University Press.

Enciso, P. E. (1992). Creating the story world: A case study of a young reader's engagement strategies and stances. In J. Many & C. Cox (Eds.), *Reader stance and literary understanding: Exploring the theories, research, and practice* (pp. 75–102). Norwood, NJ: Ablex.

Faust, M. (2000). Reconstructing familiar metaphors: John Dewey and Louise Rosenblatt on literary art as experience. *Research in the Teaching of English, 35,* 9–34.

Flood, J., Heath, S. B., & Lapp, D. (Eds.). (1997). *Handbook of research on teaching literacy through the communicative and visual arts.* Mahwah, NJ: Erlbaum.

Fu, D. (1995). *My trouble is my English: Asian students and the American dream.* Portsmouth, NH: Heinemann.

Gadsden, V. L. (1997). Intergenerational discourses: Life texts of African-American mothers and daughters. In J. Flood, S. B. Heath, & D. Lapp (Eds.), *Handbook of research on teaching literacy through the communicative and visual arts* (pp. 376–385). Mahwah, NJ: Erlbaum.

Gardner, H. (1993). *Frames of mind: The theory of multiple intelligences* (10th anniversary ed.). New York: Basic Books.

Grossman, P. L., Valencia, S. W., & Hamel, F. L. (1997). Preparing language arts teachers in a time of reform. In J. Flood, S. B. Heath, & D. Lapp (Eds.), *Handbook of research on teaching literacy through the communicative and visual arts* (pp. 407–416). Mahwah, NJ: Erlbaum.

Harste, J. C., Short, K. G., & Burke, C. L. (1988). *Creating classrooms for authors: The reading–writing connection.* Portsmouth, NH: Heinemann.

Heath, S. B. (2004). Learning language and strategic thinking through the arts. *Reading Research Quarterly, 39,* 338–342.

Heath, S. B., & Bhagat, V. (1997). Reading comics, the invisible art. In J. Flood, S. B. Heath, & D. Lapp (Eds.), *Handbook of research on teaching literacy through the communicative and visual arts* (pp. 586–591). Mahwah, NJ: Erlbaum.

Howard, C. (1916). The use of pictures in teaching literature. *English Journal, 5,* 539–543.

Huberman, M. (1993). Teachers' work: Individuals, colleagues, and contexts. In J. W. Little & M. W. McLaughlin (Eds.), *Professional development and practice series* (pp. 11–50). New York: Teachers College Press.

Jacobs, S. (2006). Listening, writing, drawing: The artistic response of incarcerated youth to young-adult literature. *Educational Horizons, 84,* 112–120.

Kress, G. R., Jewitt, C., Bourne, J., Franks, A., Hardcastle, J., Jones, K., et al. (2005). *English in urban classrooms: A multimodal perspective on teaching and learning.* New York: Falmer.

Kress, G. R., & van Leeuwen, T. (2001). *Multimodal discourse: The modes and media of contemporary communication.* London: Arnold.

Lee, C. D. (1997). Bridging home and school literacies: Models for culturally responsive teaching, a case for African-American English. In J. Flood, S. B. Heath, & D. Lapp (Eds.), *Handbook of research on teach-*

ing literacy through the communicative and visual arts (pp. 334–345). Mahwah, NJ: Erlbaum.

Literature and the language arts: Experiencing literature. (1996). St. Paul, MN: EMC Paradigm.

National Education Association of the United States, Committee of Ten on Secondary School Studies. (1892). *Report of the Committee [of Ten] on secondary school studies.* New York: The American Book Company.

National Endowment for the Arts. (2004). *Reading at risk: A survey of literary reading in America* (No. 46). Washington, DC: National Endowment for the Arts.

O'Donnell-Allen, C., & Smagorinsky, P. (1999). Revising Ophelia: Rethinking questions of gender and power in school. *English Journal, 88,* 35–42.

Piro, J. M. (2002). The picture of reading: Deriving meaning in literacy through image. *The Reading Teacher, 56,* 126–134.

Ramsey, C. L. (1997). Deaf children as literacy learners: Tom, Robbie, and Paul. In J. Flood, S. B. Heath, & D. Lapp (Eds.), *Handbook of research on teaching literacy through the communicative and visual arts* (pp. 314–322). Mahwah, NJ: Erlbaum.

Rényi, J. (2000). Hunting the quark: Interdisciplinary curricula in public schools. In S. Wineberg & P. L. Grossman (Eds.), *Interdisciplinary curriculum: Challenges to implementation* (pp. 39–56). New York: Teachers College Press.

Rosenblatt, L. M. (1995). *Literature as exploration* (5th ed.). New York: Modern Language Association.

Siegel, M. (1995). More than words: The generative power of transmediation for learning. *Canadian Journal of Education/Revue canadienne de l'education, 20,* 455–475.

Siegesmund, R. (1999). Reasoned perception: Aesthetic knowing in pedagogy and learning. In L. Bresler & N. C. Ellis (Eds.), *Arts and learning research, 1998–1999: The Journal of the Arts and Learning Special Interest Group of the American Educational Research Association* (Vol. 15, pp. 35–51). Washington, DC: American Educational Research Association.

Siegesmund, R. (2005). Teaching qualitative reasoning: Portraits of practice. *Phi Delta Kappan, 87,* 18–23.

Siegesmund, R., & Cahnmann-Taylor, M. (2008). The tensions of arts-based research in education reconsidered: The promise for practice. In M. Cahnmann-Taylor & R. Siegesmund (Eds.), *Arts-based research in education: Foundations for practice* (pp. 231–246). New York: Routledge.

Smagorinsky, P. (1995). Constructing meaning in the disciplines: Reconceptualizing Writing across the Curriculum as Composing across the Curriculum. *American Journal of Education, 103,* 160–184.

Smagorinsky, P. (1996). Multiple intelligences, multiple means of composing: An alternative way of thinking about learning. *NASSP Bulletin, 80*(583), 11–17.

Smagorinsky, P., Cook, L. S., & Reed, P. M. (2005). The construction of meaning and identity in the composition and reading of an architectural text. *Reading Research Quarterly, 40,* 70–88.

Smagorinsky, P., & Coppock, J. (1994). Cultural tools and the classroom context: An exploration of an artistic response to literature. *Written Communication, 11,* 283–310.

Smagorinsky, P., & Coppock, J. (1995a). The reader, the text, the context: An exploration of a choreographed response to literature. *Journal of Reading Behavior, 27,* 271–298.

Smagorinsky, P., & Coppock, J. (1995b). Reading through the lines: An exploration of drama as a response to literature. *Reading and Writing Quarterly, 11,* 369–391.

Smagorinsky, P., & O'Donnell-Allen, C. (1998a). The depth and dynamics of context: Tracing the sources and channels of engagement and disengagement in students' response to literature. *Journal of Literacy Research, 30,* 515–559.

Smagorinsky, P., & O'Donnell-Allen, C. (1998b). Reading as mediated and mediating action: Composing meaning for literature through multimedia interpretive texts. *Reading Research Quarterly, 33,* 198–226.

Smagorinsky, P., & O'Donnell-Allen, C. (2000). Idiocultural diversity in small groups: The role of the relational framework in collaborative learning. In C. D. Lee & P. Smagorinsky (Eds.), *Vygotskian perspectives on literacy research: Constructing meaning through collaborative inquiry* (pp. 165–190). New York: Cambridge University Press.

Smagorinsky, P., Pettis, V., & Reed, P. M. (2004). High school students' compositions of ranch designs: Implications for academic and personal achievement. *Written Communication, 21,* 386–418.

Smagorinsky, P., & Taxel, J. (2005). *The discourse of character education: Culture wars in the classroom.* Mahwah, NJ: Erlbaum.

Smagorinsky, P., Zoss, M., & O'Donnell-Allen, C. (2005). Mask-making as identity project in a high school English class: A case study. *English in Education, 39,* 60–75.

Smagorinsky, P., Zoss, M., & Reed, P. M. (2006). Residential interior design as complex composition: A case study of a high school senior's composing process. *Written Communication, 23,* 295–330.

Smith, M. W., Marshall, J. D., Spurlin, W. J., Alvermann, D. E., & Bauerlein, M. (2004, November). *Reading at Risk.* Symposium presented at the National Council of Teachers of English annual convention, Indianapolis, IN.

Suhor, C. (1984). Towards a semiotics-based curriculum. *Journal of Curriculum Studies, 16,* 247–257.

Suhor, C. (1992). Semiotics and the English language arts. *Language Arts, 69,* 228–230.

Sumara, D. J. (1996). *Private readings in public: Schooling the literary imagination.* New York: Peter Lang.

Underwood, W. (1987). The body biography: A framework for student writing. *English Journal, 76,* 44–48.

Walling, D. R. (2006). Brainstorming themes that connect art and ideas across the curriculum. *Art Education, 59*(1), 18–23.

Whitin, P. (1996a). Exploring visual response to literature. *Research in the Teaching of English, 30,* 114–140.

Whitin, P. (1996b). *Sketching stories, stretching minds: Responding visually to literature.* Portsmouth, NH: Heinemann.

Whitin, P. (2005). The interplay of text, talk, and visual representation in expanding literary interpretation. *Research in the Teaching of English, 39,* 365–397.

Wilhelm, J. D. (1997). *"You gotta BE the book": Teaching engaged and reflective reading with adolescents.* New York: Teachers College Press.

Witte, S. (1992). Context, text, intertext: Toward a constructivist semiotic of writing. *Written Communication, 9,* 237–308.

CHAPTER 14

Policy and Adolescent Literacy

ALLAN LUKE
ANNETTE WOODS

Literacy education across Western nations continues to contend with the rise of neoliberalism with its expectations for market-based efficiencies. This trend has been accompanied by policy, media, and curriculum initiatives offering simplistic solutions to the latest perceived literacy crisis. Policy matters in important ways. It enables and constrains the responses that systems, schools, and teachers can make in providing equitable access to literacy pedagogy for students, many of whom we know are dealing with the effects of poverty as it plays out with gender, race, indigeneity or First Nation status, and cultural and linguistic diversity. In this chapter we review current education policy and uncover common threads in the assumptions of accountability as testing, standardization, decreased autonomy for schools, and a continued consignment of resources to the early years of schooling. Calling on the example of *Literate Futures*, an evidence-based policy initiative in Queensland, Australia, we consider what large-scale evidence-based policy may look like if the aim is to improve literacy for all students, including those beyond the first 3 years of schooling.

ON THE TEXTS OF LITERACY POLICY

Policy is a symbolic system for the "representing, accounting for and legitimating [of] political decisions" (Ball, 1998, p. 124). Policies are public speech acts, textual bids by bureaucrats, politicians, and governments to shape relations between human subjects, to reorder and distribute material goods, to regulate and govern flows of discourse and the shape of local practices. We can analyze policies in terms of (1) their locutionary content (their truth claims about the world: scientific, ideological, and otherwise); (2) their illocutionary intent (that which they set out to "do" in the world); and (3) their perlocu-

tionary effects (what they effectively "do"). Our aim here is to show how current U.S. literacy education policies turn on a particular logical and epistemological order of "truth claims" that delimits both their intents and effects. We then contrast U.S. policy discourse with an approach to literacy policy we developed for the Australian state of Queensland that has a very different approach to agency and change in literacy education.

Policies are narratives: grand and small *recits* (Lyotard, 1989) about human subjects, orderings (syntaxes) of preferred sequences of events and actions. These narratives are expressions of normative assumptions about how an education system should operate;

197

what its human, material, and representational resources are for doing that work; what the problems and impediments facing the system might be; and, ultimately, who should be doing what, with whom, to what ends, and with what educational and sociocultural consequences. In this regard, policies are necessarily selective narratives that may serve overtly ideological purposes, expressing particular political and economic interests to the exclusion of others (Luke, 1997).

Policies are expository: they state locutionary truth claims about cultural and educational, social and psychological phenomena. U.S. and Australian literacy policy continues to be debated in terms of scientific truth claims: empirical claims about how literacy is currently taught and how it might optimally be taught. If policy rests principally or solely on such claims, they logically lead to particular interventions and assumptions about agency, actors, and effects. In the case of the United States, this foundation amounts to a set of behavioral rewards and punishments for schools adopting those scientific literacy programs that have empirically demonstrated efficacy in generating test score gains. There are comparable claims about educational outcomes (the "perlocutionary"), which tautologically link the logic of policy back to its initial truth claims. Outcomes have been defined in terms of overall system performativity and the efficacy of the institutional practices of teachers and schools in generating gains in test score results for specific communities and cohorts of students. We review these claims here.

At the same time, the effects of policies depend on their mediated uptake in the world. Policies have no hypodermic, empirical effects on individuals, practice, or the world. Through the actions of bureaucrats, administrators, and teachers—in the complex intersubjective ecologies and economies of schools and school systems—policies are translated into local "small stories" about local, everyday teaching and learning practices. So large-scale policy initiatives are as much about the mediating processes and practices of schools and classrooms as policy zones as they are about the documented policy text, its truths, and ideologies. Behind and beneath each grand narrative about the

problems and solutions of literacy education are innumerable *petit recits*: smaller, local stories about teachers' and students' everyday practice (Abedi, 2004; Evans & Hornberger, 2005; Nichols & Berliner, 2007).

The published studies, meta-analyses, and discussions of the current U.S. literacy policy since its inception in 2001 are voluminous and diverse. It is not our intention to go over that literature. Our aim is to contrast two distinctive, contrasting narratives about the definition and constitution of the literate subject, noting indirect and direct narrative approaches to adolescent literacy. To set the context, we begin by examining the general premises of neoliberal educational policy. We then contrast two policies: the U.S. *No Child Left Behind* legislation and Queensland's *Literate Futures* (Luke, Freebody & Land, 2000). Between 1999 and 2003, we were involved in the development and implementation of the latter.

Both of these policies commenced in 2001 and are ongoing. They offer competing narratives about the problems of literacy education in schools, and they define and locate agency in the resolution of these problems in quite distinctive ways. Throughout we note their effects to date. Our discussion concludes with a general appraisal of the efficacy of these two approaches in generating outcomes of improved quality and equity in adolescent literacy. It is neither a simple comparison nor one with clear and definitive outcomes, but it suggests the complexity of definition, scale, and effects in defining and constructing literacy in and through policy. The analysis here reinforces, we argue, the finding that the achievement of literacy is produced by complex social, cultural, and economic forces—of which schooling, curriculum, and pedagogy constitute but one.

NEOLIBERALISM, EARLY INTERVENTION, AND THE DISAPPEARING ADOLESCENT

Literacy policy narratively defines the literate citizen to be constructed by systems for schools and teachers. Policies are state technologies for the shaping of the selective traditions of literacy teaching and learning: "official bids by government to regulate and monitor flows of discourse, human and material resources to schools and classrooms, teachers and students in particular normative directions" (Luke & Grieshaber, 2004, p. 6). As noted above, large-scale state-based policy initiatives themselves do not determine classroom practice. Rather, they attempt to define and delimit what counts as literacy through benchmark statements, objectives, statements of standards, and sanctions and incentives set out as markers for the surveillance of performance.

The current focus on standardization, accountability, and competitive performativity is not a "given." It is not intrinsic to modern educational governance. As the debates over the outcomes of the Program for International Student Assessment (PISA) have shown, there are radical differences in systems of educational governance internationally, with differential effects in terms of the amelioration of social class impacts on school performance. In fact, the 2003 PISA adolescent literacy testing results of 15-year-olds suggest that several educational systems with radically different modes and histories of educational governance have yielded both "high-quality" and "high-equity" outcomes (Organisation for Economic Co-Operation and Development, OECD, 2005). In comparison with countries with systems that have pursued high-stakes testing and accountability policies, such as the United States and the United Kingdom, countries such as Finland, Sweden, Canada, South Korea, and Australia have tended to have smaller standard deviations in overall performance of 15-year-olds across a number of constructs of reading and writing literacy. They also show evidence of lower overall impacts of socioeconomic background on achievement (Schleicher, 2007; cf. Lie, Linnakylä, & Roe, 2003). One of our principal arguments here is that such performance patterns cannot be attributed to curriculum policies per se. If there is a lesson from three decades of ethnographic and linguistic studies of literacy in use, it is that literacy is shaped, selected, and used in schools and everyday life. In this way, local ecologies of literacy are influenced by powerful historical forces of culture and language, population demographics, political economy, and the textual and linguistic practices of everyday life (e.g., Durgunoglu & Verhoeven, 1998).

In the case of Finland and Canada, early literacy results can be attributed to a variety of educational and social conditions that extend beyond pedagogic method per se. These include long-standing government and, indeed, cultural commitments to family support and social welfare, universal free education, child care, universal free health care, and systems of income redistribution and poverty amelioration. Empirically, the impacts of social and economic background can be shown to have variable effects on early and adolescent literacy achievement (e.g., Simons, Bampton, & Bode, 2006). Yet analyses by OECD researchers (Schleicher, 2007) and reanalyses of U.S. national testing data (Lee, 2006) concur that high-stakes, test-driven accountability systems in and of themselves do not have a strong track record in generating equitable spreads of literacy achievement. As it has emerged in the last two decades, neoliberal educational policy has entailed the reorganization of schooling and, indeed, pedagogy as corporate practices. The corporatization of public services and government bureaucracies is part of the privatization of long-standing institutions established by the state for the "public good." It aims, ostensibly, toward the better rationalization of tax dollars and the enlistment of business principles in the governance of public institutions, their employees, and their services. The new socioeconomic contract of free market, globalizing capitalist countries such as the United States, United Kingdom, and Australia has been based on the assumption that elements of public infrastructure, including schooling and education more generally, can be best run following business models, with stresses on increased productivity, quality assurance, and corporate efficiency (Luke, 2004).

Part of the policy dilemma is how school systems more generally are responding to changes in demographic and socioeconomic, cultural, and technological contexts. In the last decade, all Australian state systems have developed better empirical documentation on increasing multilingualism among school-age cohorts, the continuing significant impact of socioeconomic status and location on conventionally measured achievement, declining retention rates, and the emergence of new, complex pathways from school to adult life, work, and civic participation. This accounting is occurring in the context of a globalizing service and information economy where employment mobility and volatility are increasing. In this context, state schooling for print literacy faces major challenges to its operational principles, structures, and practices. Further, emergent work on new youth and work cultures, digital and popular culture, and new systems of representation has called into question long-standing assumptions about the place of new and traditional literacies in childhood, citizenship, and everyday life (e.g., Jewitt, 2008; Lam, 2006; Sefton-Green, 2006).

Yet although literacy education research has expanded its methodological scope and disciplinary purview, educational policy more generally has entailed an economic rationalization of the technologies that historically developed to build modernist, print-based schooling. Literacy education policy in the United States and the United Kingdom is built on a common matrix of premises about accountability as testing, standardization as uniformity of method, competitive marketization of schools, central surveillance of teachers, and an intensified consignment of resources to the early years of schooling. It also has reinforced the status of educational psychology and, specifically, traditional behaviorist psychometrics as the legislated "system of objectification" (Bourdieu, 1990) for defining, constructing, measuring, and assessing what will count as literacy.

The assumptions are (1) that large-scale systems' processes and outcomes can be quantified and (2) that systemic interventions to alter schools and teachers' practice can be calibrated to generate (3) improved levels of literacy (i.e., standardized test scores) and more equitable spreads of student performance. The neoliberal model of governance—based on process and systems engineering models applied to business efficiency—entails steering the work of schools and teachers centrally through monitoring of class, school, and student performance. Large-scale standardized testing data are used to establish an automatic and continual feedback loop, whereby policy that is established on the basis of research claims built from testing data can be validated or altered using ostensive changes in that data base. The view of educational outcomes in terms of yield levels of measurable components of

human capital is not new. The modern sciences of psychometrics and school governance grew hand in hand with the foundation and consolidation of industrial, urban schooling in the past century (Callahan, 1962).

What is distinctive about the current wave of reform is the official sanction of a corporate political economy of pedagogy; a multibillion dollar industry in the production, accreditation, and support of scripted textbook materials for early phonics instruction; and a regime of punishments that, in many states and countries, include marketization strategies based on the concept of parental choice. These options include the issuing of vouchers and the support of transfer of students and resources from the public system to private and semiprivate schools. Literacy is treated as a commodity on an open market (Luke, 2004). In this way—whatever the intentions of their architects—neoliberal policies are not and cannot be about the improvement of student outcomes per se, however measured. By definition, they entail a wholesale reorientation of public policy toward schooling as a corporate, institutional enterprise that can be managed according to principles of corporate efficiency, productivity, and performance.

With an intense ideological, cultural, and political economic focus of resources, policy, and surveillance on early childhood across the United Kingdom, the United States, Australia, and New Zealand (Luke & Luke, 2001), adolescent literacy has been in the background of national policy. Recent claims of declining literacy standards have focused on the failing standards of graduates, workers, and university entrants and, more recently, on the skill shortages facing countries with growing economies and aging workforces (OECD, 2004). Media reports of employer dissatisfaction with the literacy levels of graduating students have become increasingly common. The result is a "beginning groundswell" (Stevens, 2006) of policy discussions in adolescent literacy. This movement has been accelerated in Europe and Commonwealth countries by the OECD's focus on school-to-work pathways and the relationships between school attainment levels, workforce skill levels, and economic growth (OECD, 2005). Studies in Australia and Singapore have begun documenting the new life pathways and providing valuable data on adolescent values, ideologies, and life pathways (cf. Luke & Hogan, 2006).

In Australia, we undertook the first major federally funded study for the federal government on literacy and numeracy programs for adolescent "target groups" (e.g., linguistic and cultural minorities, lower socioeconomic communities). *Beyond the Middle* (Luke et al., 2003) describes state-by-state policies on the middle years of schooling. Local cases of innovative literacy and numeracy policies and programs for the middle years were documented. We identified a lack of data on student achievement in the middle years and inadequate curricular attention to adolescent literacy, especially among linguistic and cultural minorities, Aborigines and Torres Strait Islanders, and students from lower socioeconomic communities.

Although all state policies endorse "middle years" education and recognize the distinctive developmental and sociocultural issues facing adolescents, these concerns pale in extent and scope when compared to the expanding and better-funded policy on early intervention. The Australian Capital Territory's alignment of middle years' philosophies with curriculum and assessment reform and the reorganization of school infrastructure is a notable exception.

In Queensland, more typically, there has been major policy funding for preprimary preparatory education in the last 3 years, but little targeted funding for adolescent literacy or numeracy. *Beyond the Middle* concludes with a call for a national policy and funding commitment to improved adolescent literacy and numeracy. Instead, the federal government endorsed a phonics-based early literacy strategy in 2005 based on its own national reading panel (National Inquiry into the Teaching of Literacy, 2005), whose findings regarding phonics were similar to those of the U.S. National Reading Panel (2000). The Australian panel's conclusions led to an endorsement of early literacy instruction with a strong emphasis on direct instruction in the acquisition of decoding practices. This policy was followed in 2006 by federally mandated and funded inservice for teachers on early reading and phonics.

Whatever its other effects, a policy and funding focus on early literacy teaching and learning has collateral and *de facto* effects on adolescent literacy. The concentration of resources for and attention to the early years is premised on assumptions about the longitudinal developmental and educational effects of coding mastery (cf. Paris, 2005). In the zero-sum politics of state educational policy, it has tended to shift the local concentration of specialist staffing, targeted material, and curricular resources from the upper primary (in the United States, upper elementary) and middle years to early primary programs. *Beyond the Middle* notes that few Australian secondary schools had specialist staff for the teaching of reading. Most lacked whole-school literacy programs and diagnostic and remedial capacity in reading education. In Queensland, there has been no state funding earmarked for literacy coordinators or specialists in secondary school staffing profiles.

To summarize, the No Child Left Behind Act (United States of America, 2001), and similar policies (e.g., the U.K. Literacy Strategy) (United Kingdom, 1997), Australia's Literacy and Numeracy Benchmarks (Department of Education, Training and Youth Affairs, 1997), and National Inquiry into the Teaching of Literacy (2005) lodge a focus on early childhood literacy education within the broader paradigms of neoliberal accountability school reform. The educational assumptions and ideological contexts of these policies have been the object of extensive documentation and critical commentary (e.g., Allen et al., 2007; Enciso, Katz, Kiefer, Price-Dennis, & Wilson, 2007; English, Hardgreaves, & Hislam, 2002; Forrest, 2004; Goodwyn & Findlay, 2003; Lewis & Wrau, 2001; Pennington, 2007; Sloan, 2007; Woods, 2007; Yatvin, Weaver, & Garan, 2003). We now turn to look in more detail at the truth claims and narrative logic of U.S. federal literacy policy.

NO CHILD LEFT BEHIND: THE LOGIC OF SCIENCE AND THE MARKETPLACE

The No Child Left Behind Act (NCLB) began from a focus on improved quality of early literacy acquisition, arguing that the program of teaching and testing is a key strategy for more equitable results and better achievement by cultural and linguistic minority and lower socioeconomic students. It was launched as a bipartisan move for U.S. schooling to address criticisms of lagging literacy standards and a growing achievement gap among students from communities that have historically suffered from socioeconomic disadvantage and cultural marginalization, NCLB is founded on four basic principles: increased accountability, increased flexibility and local control, expanded options for parents, and teaching methods based on a "gold standard evidence base" (*www.ed. gov/programs/readingfirst/legislation.html*). The policy sets the institutional mechanisms of accountability as standardized testing and public reporting. These measures are elaborated through sanctions and incentives for districts, schools, and teachers. Its punitive mode is based on an ideology of parental and school choice: that, given the facts, the market will decide. There is, of course, the assumption that access to the market can be established as a level playing field of parental choice. This premise has led to the publishing of league tables of school test performance and, in some states, voucher and charter school options. The legislation codifies what will count as evidence-based pedagogy by mandating scripted, highly prescriptive reading curriculum programs, approved by the federal government. Here we leave aside for the moment the ongoing controversies about the operational criteria that federal government agencies used to select programs for funding (Gruwald, 2006)—a matter of ongoing contention in current congressional hearings.

What is distinctive about the current debate is the invocation of a "gold standard" of scientific research as the major criterion for adjudicating the validity of truth claims. Beginning with its foundation documents, the reports of the National Reading Panel (2000) and affiliated studies (Snow, Burns, & Griffin, 1998), NCLB is based on a number of propositions, all asserted as empirically warranted truth claims. It begins from what we might term the *phonics hypothesis*: that there is scientific evidence that literacy achievement can be improved through systematic curricular approaches to pedagogy that emphasize "alphabetics." It is important to note that the inverse of this proposition is also taken as axiomatic in the implementation of NCLB: that other methods

that have not been verified by the "gold standard" of randomized field trials contribute to current patterns of early literacy achievement and failure and, specifically, the underperformance of minority and lower socioeconomic groups. The Australian report makes precisely such a claim (National Inquiry into the Teaching of Literacy, 2005). Although the phonics hypothesis is defended in the aforementioned panels and commissions on scientific grounds, none of the studies offer comparable quality evidence that other methods contribute to failure.

There is no conclusive evidence that these other methods—typically affiliated with "whole language," "word recognition," and similar approaches—contribute to failure. The further assumption of NCLB is that the "right method" that will improve minority and at-risk performance can optimally be achieved through what we might term the *standardized curriculum hypothesis*: that standardized curriculum programs that script, monitor, and benchmark teachers' everyday pedagogic practice can be implemented across schools, communities, and student cohorts to achieve a better and more uniform spread of the optimal "method" for teaching literacy.

From these two truth claims—one about the efficacy of a particular approach and another about the efficacy of a long-standing model of teacher skilling and deskilling (Apple, 1990) through "teacher-proofed," standardized packages—a normative story about successful reform is promoted. The grammar of this story reads as follows:

- That current teacher method for early literacy is unscientific and flawed (problem)
- That government identification and selection of a scientifically verified approach to early literacy training that emphasizes phonics (attempt)
- Implemented through an accountability system based on state standardized testing (attempt)
- Will lead to test score gains of children from historically underperforming groups (outcome)

Here we explore the assumptions and the effects of this approach in more detail. What is of interest is how NCLB identifies the problem and where it locates agency in the proposed solution. First, the problem is seen to be teacher failure to implement scientifically verified method. There is little recognition of the host of contributing factors identified in ethnographic, case-based, and quantitative sociodemographic literacy research; these studies include attention to home/school institutional transitions and access; the variable impacts of community cultural and linguistic background; the effects of poverty; the increasing incidence of special needs (e.g., Gregory, 2000); and the impacts of differential school resourcing (OECD, 2005) and internal tracking structures of schools (e.g., Oakes, 1985). Because this corpus of work is multidisciplinary and does not focus principally on pedagogic method as a dependent variable, it was ruled out from the scientific "gold standard" of the national reports as part of the performance variation that cannot be statistically accounted for by pedagogic method and curriculum approach per se.

Second, the agency of NCLB as a policy narrative is located with government. In this story, it is not teachers, students, or communities that act on the world or systematically address the problem. Instead, the focus is on the role of government in selecting, sanctioning, and implementing the proper method. In this regard, the policy is monologic: It centers itself and its institutional location as the sovereign power in identifying truth claims about literacy and implementing the "right" approaches. In terms of adolescent literacy, NCLB offers a further proposition: that adolescent literacy problems and failure will be alleviated or ameliorated by the longitudinal effects of better, more efficient early literacy instruction.

Having established the propositional claims and narrative bases of NCLB, we now turn to briefly review key critiques and evidence of its outcomes. First, key early criticisms of the policy were based on contestation of its truth claims, focusing on the selection of research by the National Reading Panel (2000). The report considered 100,000 instances of research in a 30-year period, with a much smaller sample of research papers meeting the "gold standards" of randomized field trials. The effect of this narrow definition was the omission of much of the conventional educational research base (Yatvin et al., 2003), including correlational studies,

qualitative and discourse-analytic studies, and single case studies. The rigid criteria further led to the exclusion of nonrandomized studies with significant cohorts of English language learners. In consequence, claims about the effectiveness of phonics instruction in early reading were made on the basis of just 38 studies. Further, the panel and policy that has resulted from its findings have been critiqued for discrepancies between the findings of subgroup reports and aggregated findings; the omission of findings related to English language learners and special education cohorts; incomparability of results across different populations; and errors in the predictive validity of early reading achievement assessments (e.g., Allington, 2002; Coles, 2003; Garan, 2002). In a broader critique, Gee (2000) linked the panel's approach to science with its failure to engage with well-documented new cultures, technologies, and practices of literacy.

Second, researchers have questioned the proposition that test-based accountability is an optimal means for literacy gains among minority students and those of lower socioeconomic backgrounds. Amrein and Berliner (2003) found that there were no consistent state-by-state effects in the National Assessment of Educational Progress (NAEP) results. In this large-scale quantitative comparison of state results, there was no evidence to suggest that children's literacy outcomes were improving as a result of new testing regimes. In a reanalysis of state test scores, Rosenshine (2003) also found no consistent effects demonstrated in relation to improved outcomes or standards. Although there is evidence that supports the claim that grade 8 mathematics results have improved as a result of testing (Braun, 2004; Carnoy & Loeb, 2002), there are also claims that the same results are being inflated either by exclusion of lower-achieving students (Amrein & Berliner, 2003) or as a result of rising adolescent dropout rates (Heubert & Hauser, 1999).

Although much of the resourcing and curriculum emphasis of NCLB has been focused on the early years of schooling, the implications of this large-scale policy initiative are important to the field of adolescent literacy. Middle and secondary schools will contend with the students produced by the NCLB initiatives and the affiliated focus on accountability, evidence, and, indeed, literacy over the next 5–10 years. NCLB (2002) sets out four key requirements for middle and secondary schools. These conditions include: the setting of targets for teacher quality and training, graduation rates, testing, and Adequate Yearly Progress, with the ultimate goal being 100% of students at grade-level proficiency by 2014. Critiques of the implications of NCLB for adolescent literacy point to a lack of understanding of adolescent literacy on the part of policy writers (e.g., Stevens, 2006). Our argument is that the focus on early intervention in NCLB is predicated on a "hypodermic model" (Luke & Luke, 2001). The premise underlying NCLB, the U.K. National Literacy program, and, indeed, many early intervention programs, is that early and effective acquisition of "alphabetics" (alphabetic knowledge, phonics, phonemic awareness) has longitudinal consequences for students' literacy development and general academic achievement. Yet the evidence from the reanalyses of state NAEP data suggests that some of the systemic effects of NCLB—the increase of high-stakes testing and stronger punitive consequences for schools not reaching targets—may in fact obstruct an increase in retention and graduation rates (cf. Conley & Hinchman, 2004).

In a major reanalysis of the empirical research bases on early intervention, Paris (2005) makes an empirical and theoretical case that the policy has misconstrued the longitudinal and developmental effects of early achievement of the "constrained skills" of alphabetics. He argues that achievement of the unconstrained skills of comprehension—including vocabulary knowledge, inference, and critical analysis—are much stronger and more robust predictors of later academic achievement. The case is put strongly by Calfee (2002), whose analysis of California state test data noted that lower socioeconomic, linguistic, and cultural minority, and other at-risk students experience significant problems in the transition to secondary school, even where early intervention programs have been put in place. There is a range of plausible explanations for this phenomenon, with traditional comprehension research suggesting the key role of vocabulary knowledge in sustainable upper primary and middle years

reading achievement (for an overview, see Alvermann, 2002). There is, further, a general consensus in the literature on middle years of schooling that at-risk students would benefit from systematic and ongoing instructional foci and school diagnostic and remediation resources in literacy (for a review, see Luke et al., 2003). Our view, in accord with Paris's (2005) analyses, is that the introduction to reading and writing of specialist linguistic registers and discourses of disciplinary knowledge provide a key threshold in the development of adolescent literacy (e.g., Halliday & Martin, 1995; Moje & O'Brien, 2000).

The narrative of NCLB, then, is premised upon the assumption that early intervention and acquisition of alphabetics has longitudinal effects. As Paris (2005) argues, alphabetics are of importance and are necessary, but not sufficient for sustained reading gains. In this regard, the policy focus on early reading has a *proxy effect* on adolescent literacy: it shifts resources and high-stakes accountability to initial literacy programs. Where there are no correlative school and systemic policy and practical focus on reading, writing, and general language development across the curriculum in the upper primary and early secondary years, there is an increased risk of a residualization of gains made in any effective early intervention program. As noted throughout this book, adolescent literacy intervention has not received the same systematic fiscal and political support as early intervention in the United States, Canada, and other English-speaking countries. Finally, to reiterate, any appraisal of the overall collateral impacts of current policy settings on adolescent literacy would have to consider Nichols, Glass, and Berliner's (2007) finding that state-level increases in systemic "pressure" via high-stakes testing has negative effects on secondary school retention and completion rates (for Australian data, see Vickers & Lamb, 2002).

Three years after its inception, the first official results of the policy initiative's effectiveness were published (Center on Education Policy [CEP], 2005). In what are effectively state-by-state self-reports, 73% of states and 72% of districts reported improvement on state tests over the first 3 years of NCLB. Further, 21 states reported a narrowing of the Hispanic achievement gap and 18 states similarly reported a narrowing of the African American achievement gap. These figures suggest improvement, although not of the scale and mass necessary to reach the target of 100% of students at grade proficiency by 2014. Issues related to equitable distribution of trained teachers across all schools, a lack of support for English language learners (ELLs) and special-needs students, a narrowing of the curriculum and issues of content and construct validity, and confidence interval problems with state testing and reporting on some counts, were also reported. In addition, the CEP (2005) raised issues related to the high number of districts absorbing the costs of the policy initiative as first-round funds are expended and grants are frozen or decreased. Although there are significant challenges faced in supporting the many schools that have been identified for improvement, most districts received less federal Title I funding in 2004–05 than in previous years of NCLB, with further cuts for 2006–07 and 2007–08 already a reality or flagged to become so. (See *epsl.asu. edu/epru/articles/EPRU-0504-121-OWI.pdf*, a press release by the Center on Education Policy, March 23, 2005.)

The CEP and other organizations have also noted the problems with state self-reporting. Some states struggle to establish reliable and valid testing and reporting systems, with variable levels of achievement taken as meeting the legislated performance benchmarks, and lack reliable data that would enable meaningful longitudinal comparisons of systemic interventions.

In a major study for the Harvard Civil Rights Project, Lee (2006) used the NAEP national testing data to reanalyze states' performance claims. Lee's findings show no significant positive impacts on NAEP reading or mathematics achievement since the inception of NCLB, with flat or slight declines in reading achievement. Despite some positive transient improvement in grade 4 mathematics after NCLB, these positive effects diminished and achievement returned to pre-NCLB rates. Lee found that there were no signs that the achievement gaps for at-risk groups were diminishing. In itself this finding is troubling, but perhaps of broader concern are the plateau effects that can be seen in the results of those states that moved toward test-based accountability systems in the 1990s (e.g., Texas, North Carolina, and Florida). Lee's (2006) analysis concludes that state achievement tests tend to significantly inflate proficiency levels and underestimate the ongoing racial and social achievement gaps across all states: "The higher the stakes of state assessments, the greater the discrepancies between NAEP and state assessments" (p. 11).

The narrative assumption of policies such as NCLB is that administrative and fiscal incentives and sanctions will have a tonic effect on overall standards and achievement, that teachers and students will increase productivity when faced with incentives and discipline (Nichols et al., 2005). The complex factors that can be shown empirically to mediate student achievement include issues of content and construct validity and test preparation, the overreliance on single-shot assessment, and the dynamics of spatialized poverty and demographic change. Triangulated by extensive qualitative documentation on the unintended effects of NCLB (Nichols & Berliner, 2006), reanalysis of NAEP data suggests that "the relationship between high-stakes testing and its intended impact on achievement is mixed and inconclusive" (Nichols et al., 2005, p. 2).

Nichols et al. (2005) measured and ranked states according to state-level testing pressure through a system of Accountability Pressure Ratings (APR). This rating system was used to query whether "the pressure of high-stakes testing increases achievement" (p. 3). Findings demonstrated that the positive link claimed by many states between the introduction of high-stakes testing through NCLB and improved student achievement is tenuous, with no gains being demonstrable on reading achievement in grades 4 or 8. Like other researchers (e.g., Carnoy & Loeb, 2002) Nichols et al. (2005) did find a positive relationship between the APR and early math achievement of African American students. (However, the same positive relationship was not evident in early reading within the same cohort.) There was a negative correlation between increased accountability pressure and retention to senior and college years.

The foregoing discussion of NCLB is neither exhaustive nor definitive. As this chapter goes to press, there are literally hundreds of academic articles published or in press that provide a complex, mixed, and diverse picture of the perlocutionary effects of the policy. Further, its pending renewal in Congress has generated a series of investigative journalist studies of its implementation (e.g., Grunwald, 2006). Our point here is that NCLB is premised on a narrow set of truth claims about the nature of literacy, literacy teaching, and the performance of students from minority and lower socioeconomic backgrounds. These, in turn, are linked to broadly neoliberal assumptions about educational change and reform, assumptions that place agency specifically in the hands of government and educational markets. These markets entail intraschool and interstate competition, public/private options, and the translation of pedagogic method into standardized curriculum commodities for teacher/school consumers (Luke, 2004). Even among the advocates of scientifically based approaches to pedagogy, there is recognition that the complex social and economic ecologies of school systems do not constitute laboratory settings and may lead to complex, unanticipated, and idiosyncratic effects (e.g., Raudenbush, 2005). The data on the effects and outcomes of this policy aside, literacy educators might ask whether it is indeed possible to develop literacy policies differently, to in effect propose a different narrative about literacy education, reform, and equity.

AN AUSTRALIAN ALTERNATIVE

Policy texts typically entail a process of bricolage: "a matter of borrowing and copying bits and pieces of ideas from elsewhere" (Ball, 1998, p. 126). Australia's recent approach to national literacy policy has entailed a recycling of ideas and initiatives taken from elsewhere, reworked and realigned for a new context. Literacy education policy has been framed by a 2-year neoliberal and neoconservative attack on schools, teachers, and teacher education, led by the coalition government of Prime Minister John Howard and played out in the pages of the national newspaper, *The Australian*, a Newscorp publication. The result is that any evidence-based or principled debate over literacy standards, achievement,

and curriculum has been obscured by a general attack on public schools and teachers as failing to provide "the basics," as walking away from the transmission of canonical literature, history, and disciplinary knowledge, and as mired in a left-wing political correctness (Snyder, 2008). This criticism has occurred despite no definitive state test-score evidence of decline, and PISA findings that Australian 15-year-olds' literacy levels were in the top tier of countries studied (OECD, 2005). In this way, the debates over early and adolescent literacy have been sites for broader conflict concerning federal/state jurisdiction over the curriculum, the federal funding of independent and religious schools, the marketization of the state system, and the regulation of teachers and teacher education (Blackmore & Sachs, 2007).

With continuing federal moves to consistency and normalization in most Australian states, the major policy settings consist of standardized achievement testing in aspects of literacy and numeracy at grades 3, 5, and 7, and more recently grade 9 (although there are some state-based discrepancies in grade-level ages, generally grade 9 students would be 13–14 years of age); the ongoing updating and implementation of curriculum documents, with debates over the technical form and ideological content of the curriculum; and moves toward school-based management, whereby principals can make semiautonomous decisions about school programming, structures, and procedures. There has been a broad increase in the marketization of schools, with state and nonstate sectors in overt competition for federal funding and market share of students.

The resultant bricolage is contradictory. It involves adoption of a narrow approach to evidence-based policy that is explicitly modeled and exemplified in No Child Left Behind. A national reading panel of Australian psychologists and educationists was assembled in 2004 (National Inquiry into the Teaching of Literacy, 2005). It called for a shift toward phonics in early literacy education, school- and system-level targets, standards and outcomes, centrally mandated textbooks and programs, and increased testing. At the same time, merit-based pay, performance-based funding incentives, and the publication of comparative league tables on test performance have been mooted by the federal government. Yet since the release of *Beyond the Middle* (Luke et al., 2003), there has been little focus on adolescent literacy. The result has been a push for basic skills in early literacy teaching, increased accountability through testing initiatives, and a shifting of state funding from school systems toward greater parent choice.

As in the United States, truth claims about literacy and scientific method have been used to rationalize and justify a host of neoliberal structural reforms, many of which bear no direct or logical relationship to the scientific claims. But what if literacy educators were to take an approach that attempted to build literacy strategies from a broader critical realist approach to educational research and evidence—one that is at once both empirical and interpretive and weighs a broad disciplinary range of evidence, quantitative and qualitative, on the nature of the problem and its possible policy solutions? Such an approach would begin from a broad, empirical picture of pedagogical practices, trends, and achievement outcomes. But it would aim for a comprehensive, as opposed to narrow, representation of educational systems at work, locally and systemically.

In 2000, one author (Allan Luke) was part of a team (with Peter Freebody and Ray Land) that was commissioned to review literacy education and develop a policy intervention for the state of Queensland. (*Literate Futures*, implementation materials, periodic reports, and data can be accessed at *education.qld.gov.au/curriculum/learning/literatefutures/*, and national reviews can be found at *cms.curriculum.edu.au/anr2002/ch6_qld. htm*).

Our task was to develop a 5-year literacy strategy for the 1,300 state-run primary, secondary, and middle schools, including 30,000 teachers and three quarters of a million students. We offer here a description of literacy policy that is based on a different set of truth claims than NCLB, and that offers a very different narrative of literacy policy.

The brief from the government for this literacy strategy was twofold. First, we were charged with identifying strengths and weaknesses in current practice with a focus on the improvement of student literacy outcomes. Second, unlike the authors of the NCLB and Australian federal policies, we moved to develop a durable literacy strategy that considered and addressed the impacts of economic globalization on Queensland children and youth: the profound social effects of the unequal spread of capital and declining social infrastructure, the new skill and job demands generated by digital technologies, the shift to service and semiotic information and symbol-based economies, and the new forms of textual practice and identity in play on the Internet and other communications technologies. In this way, *Literate Futures: A Literacy Strategy for Queensland Schools* (Luke et al., 2000) was situated within a broader set of educational, community, and government policies entitled *Education 2010* (Education Queensland, 2000). Its purpose, then, was not to "fix" literacy instruction per se, however construed, but to develop a viable agenda for change and reform geared toward a broad state commitment to equitable educational provision. We began by reviewing the data sets developed for *Education 2010*. Our findings are discussed in the following paragraphs.

Spatialized Poverty

With 20% of families living below the government poverty line—particularly in rural township areas, indigenous communities, and fringe cities where a White underclass has developed over the past 10–20 years—there ensued a gradual but significant movement toward an inequitable division of wealth and resources. This was along with high levels of youth unemployment in areas that were also contending with intergenerational unemployment.

Changing Employment Conditions

With the cumulative effects of two decades of economic restructuring and globalization of the state economy, the casualization, outsourcing, and subcontracting of the workforce had been accompanied by a proliferation of service and information work. This economic restructuring was compounded by an industrial shift from high levels of unionization to less secure and more volatile employment conditions.

The net result was a "delinearization" of life pathways from school to work and further education, employment, underemployment, and unemployment that at the time had not been empirically documented or described on any scale within the government. Despite pathway studies undertaken by all Australian state governments in the late 1990s, systems remained unable to account for where dropouts or even graduates traveled after leaving school systems. At the same time, general retention rates in Queensland and across Australia were in decline, with 74% of the grade 8 cohort completing grade 12 and the percentage of students leaving schools for the (state-subsidized) independent and religious schools at about 30%.

In addition, there was evidence of changing student demographics. Historically, Queensland has had a relatively homogeneous population. By 1999, the population of English language learners had increased to approximately 13–15%, principally migrants. Though well below the national levels of 25%, increased migrant flows were changing the school population. Further, Aboriginal and Torres Strait Islander students, constituting 6% of the school population, consistently performed below the state average on all achievement measures. In two separate major studies undertaken during the implementation of *Literate Futures*, we documented the state conditions and contexts of indigenous underperformance in language and literacy education, proposing a complementary state plan for indigenous literacy (Luke, Woods, Bahr, Land, & McFarland, 2002; Luke, Land, Christie, Kolatsis, & Noblett, 2002).

This "new" evidence provided a baseline for policymaking and further research. Based on two decades of ethnographic work on language and literacy acquisition and use in classrooms and communities, our assumption was that these factors would have direct and indirect impacts on students' performance in schools. These influences would range from improving the difficult transition that many students face when going from home to school, to teachers' capacities to engage with different linguistic and cultural codes, and to more effective strategies for addressing the immediate effects of poverty on families, communities, and early childhood experience.

Our 4-month work program in 2000 involved a reanalysis of student achievement data on grades 3 and 5 reading and writing

from Queensland schools, a review of various other state, national, and regional approaches to literacy policy, and a state-wide public and professional consultation that involved stakeholder consultation with relevant professional organizations, teachers, administrators, teacher educators, and parents in public meetings and school visits. As much as this approach could be taken as a scientific survey of literacy standards, then, it was equally a dialogic exercise in public policy discourse formation among teachers, senior systems bureaucrats, and working literacy researchers and teacher educators. From the consultation, we collected and coded more than 2,000 statements and slightly more than 250 written positions for a discourse analysis of key words and themes.

The general findings of the report are discussed in the following paragraphs.

Writing Instruction

The overall focus of the "text in context" and "genre" approaches to writing over a decade was effective, though there was still some way to go in teacher knowledge of functional grammar. State test scores corroborated the overall success in teaching writing, with about 95% of students reaching state performance benchmarks at grades 3 and 5 in year 2000 test data.

Reading Instruction

Although about a third of all children were identified by a face-to-face reading diagnostic (the Queensland Year Two Diagnostic Net) as struggling in grade 2, according to existing testing systems, in 2000 it was reported that roughly 92% of children were leaving grade 3 having achieved a reading benchmark in functional decoding skills and early comprehension, trending upwards from 85.8% reported in 1999. There was fifth-grade "slump" evidence, with only 78.5% of students by grade 5 achieving the reading benchmark (Ministerial Council on Education, Employment, Training, and Youth Affairs, 2000). At the same time, there appeared to be minimal understanding of reading instruction or assessment at the secondary level, with no available data on reading achievement after grade 5. Our view was that the 1992 introduction of a face-to-face developmental diagnostic assessment in grades 1 and 2 appeared to have led to a consolidation of initial literacy instruction, with no evidence of a "crisis" in early literacy achievement. However, the majority of schools lacked a systematic focus on reading sustained throughout the primary school years. Teachers' eclectic approaches in the middle and upper primary grades reflected a range of training backgrounds and did not appear to be linked, on any systematic basis, to data on achievement and background.

Inclusive Instruction

With an increase in numbers of students from non-English-speaking backgrounds to about 15%, and the mainstreaming of students with learning disabilities and a range of special education needs, teachers reported that they were struggling to provide these students with appropriate or effective intervention. Performance gaps between English language learners and all students were not significant, that is, they were within the range measurement error. Despite reports of emergent problems with boys' literacy, the grades 3 and 5 performance gaps between boys and girls were not statistically significant. In year 2000 state test data, the performance gaps between indigenous and nonindigenous readers were significant: 11.6% in grade 3 (92.6/81) and 24.1% in grade 5 (54.4/78.5) (Ministerial Council on Education, Employment, Training, and Youth Affairs, 2000).

Secondary Literacy Programs

Secondary schools did not have in place diagnostic systems to identify and help nonreaders, programs for increasing comprehension or literacy across the curriculum, or sufficient reading specialists or staff expertise.

Multiliteracies

Despite expanded hardware infrastructure, schools were slow to adapt to new digital literacies, with most teachers sticking to traditional print models and the school-based information technology (IT) expertise prin-cipally concentrated in mathematics and science education.

The schools and students most at risk were those from the aforementioned communities hit hardest by the new patterns of spatialized poverty. The strategy of choice in responding to this new poverty was the proliferation of "pull-out" programs, that is, augmenting specially funded programs for diagnosis and remediation of the bottom quartile of students. These included: learning support programs; Aboriginal and Torres Strait Islander programs; English as a Second Language (ESL) support; reading tutoring especially by volunteers; speech pathology; and school psychology. In many schools, there was no coherent coordination between these programs and there was very little state-wide data about their efficacy. At the school level, performance gains achieved through pull-out programs often were difficult for many schools to sustain. Funding was often on a year-to-year basis, preventing staff continuity, and there was little focus on changing mainstream pedagogical practices.

Literate Futures, then, provided mixed messages. Although there was hardly evidence of an early literacy crisis, it was clear to us as literacy researchers and teacher-educators that schools could improve their overall strategies and approaches to literacy, particularly for those children from lower socioeconomic backgrounds (cf. LoBianco & Freebody, 1997). Our view was that the complexity and diversity of the problem required something other than a "one size fits all" approach. Quite the contrary, in the vast majority of schools, a "back to the basics" or strongly coordinated reemphasis of code and alphabetic knowledge might have been counterproductive. We also considered the more general claims of another major observational study of 900 grades 5 and 8 classroom lessons (Ladwig, 2007; Lingard et al., 2002). That study found that the challenge in the upper primary and lower secondary grades was to provide increased intellectual quality and disciplinary depth, stressing higher-order thinking and connectedness to the world, rather than to focus on basic skills acquisition. Using the design of Newmann & Associates' (1996) Wisconsin observational study of "authentic achievement," we observed more than 600 grades 5 and 8 lessons between 1997 and 2000, coding lessons for indicators of "productive pedagogies" (Ladwig, 2007). The strongest predictors of authentic achievement in the production of quality student artifacts were heightened intellectual demand and connectedness to the world.

Informed by the state test score data, our view was that much of the problem in literacy and general achievement of at-risk groups was not in initial literacy or basic skills acquisition, but rather in sustained levels of overall intellectual demand and connectedness to the world. The result was a suite of policy approaches designed to address these problems, including but not restricted to *Literate Futures*. These included *New Basics* (Luke et al., 2000), the piloting of an alternative project-based curriculum in 52 trial schools, and a wholesale review of secondary school pathways to work and further study. In this regard, our approach was to situate a literacy-in-education policy within a larger suite of educational reforms that aimed for longitudinal effects.

Part of the effort of *Literate Futures* was to capture the complexity of literacy and education in transition. It was a policy that was able to define literacy as constructed, contested, and put to work by individuals across their educational pathways—not as a universally portable, transferable, and applicable set of skills that, once acquired, would automatically generate effects. Making this "policy shift" in current times might allow a subsequent shift to move beyond the view of literacy education as simple pedagogic machinery for the transmission of basic skills, and move to define evidence-based research toward a rich, triangulated, and multiperspectival social science (Luke & Hogan, 2006).

Literate Futures mandated the following policy strategies:

• *Whole-school planning* at a collaborative school level was required, with whole-school plans to be put in place within 18 months. Plans were to be based on local school evaluation of diagnostic evaluation and achievement test data, student demographic data, and school staff and curricular resources.

• *Balanced programs* based on the "four resources model" of literacy (Freebody & Luke, 1990) were required at all schools, with demonstration of collaborative planning, teacher moderation, and reflection on student work. Professional development materials supporting balanced approaches to reading and writing were developed for teachers and inservice centers over the following year.

• *Multiliteracies* (The New London Group, 1996) were targeted as a high priority across the curricula and spanning this and other reform programs.

• *Professional development* was planned for all teachers, with the establishment of 21 regional inservice centers to assist schools in the development of their school plans and to enhance locally based curriculum development and planning.

In addition, in separate reports presented to government during the implementation period, we developed an overall language and literacy education plan for Aboriginal and Torres Strait Islander communities (Luke, Land et al., 2002) and recommendations for the cultural adoption of the Year 2 Diagnostic Net and State Year 3 and 5 tests (Luke, Woods et al., 2002). Neither of these reports was subsequently implemented—with consequences we detail below.

Literate Futures thus set out a different educational and educational policy approach from that underway in many systems: in its refusal to be enticed into the "reading wars" debate, in its focus on school/community analyses and linkages, and in its focus on the capitalization on and development of existing teacher expertise. From what we learned in our consultation process, we concluded that the existing expertise for developing balanced programs was available in the workforce. However, that workforce often was working without a systematic assaying of student and community linguistic and cultural background and resources, and lacked coordinated planning, especially, but not exclusively, at the upper primary level. We viewed the problem of literacy education as a whole-school issue, taking into consideration our ongoing studies of classroom pedagogy and the literature on school renewal, improvement, and reform, as well as studies of literacy education per se. We also considered the host of other variables that can influence literacy achievement, including changing community demographics and general school capacity.

The resultant focus of the strategy was in many ways about reframing the professional development capacity of educational systems as teachers' social capital. The strategy contrasts sharply with a compliance approach that targets short- and medium-term improvement of test scores via the standardization, surveillance, and control of teacher classroom behavior and methods. It was based on the premise that teacher learning and professionalization, rather than de-skilling and centralized control, have the potential for more flexible and sustainable approaches to these problems. Finally, its futures orientation was based on the assumption that an overzealous focus on short-term surface performance gains would fail to engage with the larger educational challenges facing adolescents, schools and systems, governments, and economies: new textual and semiotic economies; blends of oral, print, and technologically mediated language and multiliteracies; the large-scale generational shift in the teacher population; and new pathways for adolescents.

As a policy text, then, it is premised on a very different set of truth claims: Literacy achievement entails the development of early reading *and* writing and that a host of cultural, sociodemographic, school, and curricular factors influence achievement patterns. The major problem facing Queensland schools was not early and initial literacy, but rather the extension of literacy education across the curriculum and into the upper primary and the middle years of schooling.

New technologies and youth and adult cultures present a host of emergent challenges for teachers, schools, and communities.

The resultant narrative structure of *Literate Futures* locates agency with teachers and schools:

- Underachievement in literacy was the result of a host of factors, including the impacts of poverty; changing cultural, linguistic, and demographic conditions; new technologies; and community shift (problem).
- Schools' approaches to reading literacy lacked focus and coordination to address these changes optimally, especially, but

not exclusively, in the upper primary/secondary grades (subproblem).
- Teachers and principals needed to engage in focused and locally relevant whole-school curriculum planning that concentrated on the variable reading problems and literacy needs of specific communities and cohorts of students (attempt).
- These initiatives could be implemented through a mobilization and coordination of existing teacher resources through whole-school curriculum planning and professional development (attempt).
- This comprehensive effort will lead to overall better performance and improved outcomes for underperforming cultural and linguistic groups (outcome).

What is interesting about this story is that it identifies the problem not as one of pedagogic or teacher deficit, but rather in terms of the array of factors that can empirically be demonstrated to have an impact on literacy achievement. First, this approach precludes the simplistic "blame the teacher" argument for failure to generate test score improvement in the face of sociocultural and demographic conditions that are beyond the immediate control of schools. It therefore situates the positive or negative impacts of classroom curriculum and teaching as a key, but not sole, variable in accounting for achievement gains and losses.

Second, it locates agency not with government nor with a high-stakes accountability system. Rather, the policy is predicated on the assumption that it is well-resourced teacher local curriculum development and planning, translated into pedagogic action, that can alter the quality and equity of outcomes. Our assumption is that the generative role of government is not to mandate and enforce a particular method, in the belief that that method will have universal effects. We therefore deliberately promoted a pluralist model of reading (the "four resources" of coding along with semantic, pragmatic, and critical reading; Freebody & Luke, 1990) that argues for a local curricular/pedagogic balance in response to existing capacities and problems of specific student cohorts. We also delegated the matter of selecting methods and materials to schools and teachers. In this narrative, the role of government and policy is to set the conditions in place for increased teacher professionalism and adaptive competence: to establish institutional means and incentives for local and school-level capacity building and planning that is responsive to community problems and local cohort variables.

The results of the implementation of *Literate Futures* are complex and mixed. In the following discussion, we comment on the patterns of test score results during the implementation period from 2001 to 2005. It is worth noting that, unlike U.S. policymakers, we did *not* assume that (1) curriculum approach and teaching method are the principal independent variables influenced by policy and (2) test score trends tell the whole picture. Thus, although we roughly assess the impacts of *Literate Futures* on similar grounds as those outlined in our previous comments on NCLB, we offer explanations for the patterns more in line with the truth claims underpinning *Literate Futures*.

Given the complexity of the causes and concomitants of literacy achievement and failure, it would be misleading to claim that *Literate Futures* "caused" performance improvements in schools. We also acknowledge the inadequacies of this data and the basic assumptions of the testing and benchmarking processes (Woods, 2007). However, the state benchmark testing data for the period following its implementation has trended upward (Ministerial Council on Education, Employment, Training, and Youth Affairs, 2001, 2002, 2003, 2004, 2005). (These data sets are published annually in the *National Report on Schooling* by the Ministerial Council on Education, Employment, Training, and Youth Affairs. Figures cited here can be obtained from *www. mceetya.edu.au/mceetya/anr/*.)

The percentage of grade 3 students meeting the reading benchmark rose from 89% (2001) to 93.8% (2003) and peaked at 97% in (2004). In writing, the percentage of grade 3 students meeting the benchmark rose from 85.4% (2001) to 88% (2003) and 89.3% (2005). Allowing for measurement error, these results appear to indicate some gains in early literacy during and after the policy implementation period as schools developed and implemented whole-school plans. Notably, in both reading and writing at the grade 3 level, the percentage of Aboriginal and Torres Strait Islander students meeting the

reading benchmark increased (from 71.6% in 2001 to 94.6% in 2004), and the overall gaps between indigenous and nonindigenous performance closed substantially, from 17.4% to 2.4% between 2001 and 2004. English language learners' scores moved from 87.4% (2001) to 91.5% (2003) to 94.2% (2004), with no significant statistical difference between English language learners and the state cohort.

Yet performance changes in the upper primary grades were less evident. Comparable grade 5 reading benchmark achievement in reading and writing did not improve substantially. Though the percentage of grade 5 students meeting the reading benchmark trended upward from 78.5% (2000) to 83.4% (2004), these scores remained within standard deviation measurement error and do not indicate significant improvement. Indigenous scores improved from 54.4% to 65%, with the gap closing from 24.1% to 18.4%. Writing scores also remained largely unchanged. Grade 7 state testing was introduced in 2002 and showed steady gains in reading from 2002 to 2004 (from 90.2% to 94.5%) and writing (from 93.9% to 97.3%), with the indigenous performance gap closing only marginally.

By the end of 2002, all schools would have put in place whole-school plans that included analyses of student cohort resources, previous data, audits of staff expertise, and coordinated curriculum approaches. The development and implementation of these plans appeared to correlate with test score gains (especially in grade 3) and a closure in the gap between indigenous and English language learners and the state norms. However, the middle years proved more resistant to any change in overall performance.

There is, however, contrary evidence on the sustainability of the efficacy of *Literate Futures*. In 2005, reading test scores showed a slight downward trend at all levels across the state. At grades 3 and 5 there were marginal drops (from 97% to 93.7% in grade 3; from 83.4% to 79.7% in grade 5), within measurement error. These declines were in part accounted for by a significant drop in Aboriginal and Torres Strait Islander reading performance reported across the board nationally. At the state level, indigenous student performance registered an 11.4% decline at grade 3 and an 8.3% drop in grade

5, and a remarkable 20.6% drop in grade 7 performance. The *National Report on Schooling* for 2005 (Ministerial Council on Education, Employment, Training, and Youth Affairs, 2005) noted this trend, commenting on the overall downward trend of performance in Aboriginal and Torres Strait Islanders after steady incremental performance gains over previous years. Though neither state nor national testing data provide the grounds for a conclusive finding, it appears that there was a significant deterioration of indigenous student achievement after a period of sustained gains in 2005. This dip pulled the overall state performance on benchmark testing down, and it increased the gap between indigenous and nonindigenous performance.

Unlike the architects of NCLB, we began from the position that literacy achievement is the product of a host of variable factors, within and outside schools and classrooms. We therefore offer a series of working hypotheses on the relative performance of *Literate Futures* in terms of achieving its outcomes. The picture is a mixed and necessarily complex one, based on the limited state test data available and our discussions with teachers and senior Ministerial officials during and after the policy implementation. Our view is that *Literate Futures* set the conditions for 3 years of improvements in the overall performance of the system in early literacy, closure of the gaps of indigenous students, and consolidation of achievement across the board in writing.

However, the performance spikes in 2004 and dropoffs in 2005 raise questions about the overall sustainability of improvements. A number of hypotheses are possible about the issues that remain unresolved after the implementation of *Literate Futures*. These include the lack of impact of whole-school planning on the upper primary reading and content instruction, and little evidence of large-scale uptake of secondary school whole-school literacy programs.

Anecdotal evidence from the field is that *Literate Futures* "took" among early primary teachers but did not sufficiently generate a refocus on literacy in the adolescent areas. The implementation was led in 2001–2003 by a Ministry team that had a strong commitment to early literacy. The professional development materials on reading were prepared by a panel of primary experts. No parallel material or advice was prepared for upper primary or secondary schools. Aside from reading programs developed by Christensen (2007) and adopted in several lower socioeconomic secondary schools, no general programmatic advice on diagnostics, remediation, or literacy-across-the curriculum was developed by the Ministry. Secondary school participation in the 21 professional development hubs was not extensive.

In this regard, the reform agenda did not succeed at one of its focal targets: developing systematic approaches to adolescent reading in the upper primary and lower secondary school. There was evidence of policy effects at the early primary level and grade 7 across the implementation period indicating that 90% met the state benchmarks. Further, writing scores remained solid across all levels, evidence of the ongoing effectiveness of a state syllabus based on genre/text-in-context models reported in *Literate Futures*. However, sustained improvement of the grade 5 state reading averages above 80% has proven difficult. At the same time, there is no evidence of a prolonged gap between the performance of English language learners and the state norms. Despite reports of a crisis in boys' literacy performance in *Literate Futures* consultations, the gaps between boys' reading performance and state norms remains within margins of error in grades 3, 5, and 7.

These mixed results aside, the major equity problem of gaps between state averages and the performance of students from lower socioeconomic and indigenous communities persists. In terms of socioeconomic effects, in 2007 the Queensland government undertook its first internal studies of the impacts of socioeconomic background on reading achievement. Regression analyses indicated that socioeconomic background, strongly spatially biased, explained about 20% of grades 3, 5, and 7 test score variance. Following on from PISA's comparative findings about the impacts of socioeconomic background on 15-year-olds' performance, we can ask whether *Literate Futures* has longitudinal effects in diminishing or raising the impacts of class background on performance. Across the period 2003–2005, the impacts of school-based socioeconomic class on reading performance at all levels remained flat, with marginal decreases at grades 3 and 7. It declined slightly in grades 3 and 7 writing but increased marginally at grade 5. Given the system's overall commitment to equity, this means of measurement is a more valid and accurate way of judging policy impacts and the value-adding dimensions of pedagogy than the comparative, unadjusted test score comparisons we and our American counterparts have used here.

In terms of indigenous performance, the radical dropoff in test scores in 2005 following 4 years of consistent gains is anomalous. This may relate to changes in policy or funding arrangements, but any changes to the actual student cohort tested remain unknown and the impact of these changes on scores unclear. Given our view of the complex social, cultural, and economic variables impacting performance, we can offer a series of hypotheses. First, despite Queensland's initiation in 2000 of a new community partnership model, there has been no sustained approach to Aboriginal and Torres Strait Islander language and literacy education in place for several decades. Although *Literate Futures* set the conditions in place for local, community, and regional planning in remote indigenous communities, it did not prescribe what was to be done at a community-school level. That work was undertaken in 2001, while *Literate Futures* was being implemented. *Standard Australian English and Language for Queensland Aboriginal and Torres Strait Islander Students* (Luke, Land et al., 2002) called for a series of "alignments" among community mobilization, school curriculum planning, and local and regional approaches to literacy education, taking into consideration the diverse linguistic and cultural conditions in indigenous communities and the difficult economic, public health, and employment contexts. We subsequently presented an analysis of test bias in state diagnostic and testing instruments, calling for a review and revision of instruments for assessing Aboriginal and Torres Strait Islander students (Luke, Woods, et al., 2002). Though both reports were endorsed by Aboriginal and Torres Strait Islander elders, neither was subsequently adopted or implemented by the Queensland state government.

Since that time, there have been various attempts in Queensland to address indige-

nous performance. These efforts include the successful implementation of *New Basics* (Luke et al., 1999), a systematic school renewal around project-based curriculum, in many Cape York schools, and the mobilization of community resources and school reform by Aboriginal community activist and leader Noel Pearson. In 2007, the federal government declared a crisis in child welfare in indigenous remote communities and, in a politically controversial move, engaged in a large-scale mobilization of child protection authorities. The current overall policy debate continues to date, as this volume goes to press, with the newly elected Labor government promising major coordinated action.

The everyday situation in indigenous communities and schools is difficult, and current policy tends to be reactive and piecemeal. In this regard, the ostensible failure to generate sustained closure of the gap in indigenous–nonindigenous performance recalls Lee's (2006) comments on the impacts of NCLB on minority achievement: that the only significant and sustained NAEP achievement gains for minority and lower socioeconomic students occurred during the large-scale poverty amelioration programs of the 1970s. The intractability of indigenous educational underperformance, it seems, cannot be attributed to literacy education policy per se, but reflects deeper-seated, more profound forms of social, economic, and cultural marginalization.

ON THE POSSIBILITIES AND LIMITS OF LITERACY EDUCATION POLICY

The writing and reading of educational policies is a complex textual practice, an instance of specialized literacies at work: hence, the pun of "reading" policy (Shannon & Edmonston, 2005). Though their authorship is often obscured and concealed, policies are written and read by historical actors working in specific mediating political economies and cultures. We, like the authors of NCLB, were such actors. But the interpretation, uptake, and remediation by governments, schools, teachers, and communities is a more complex and vexing practical matter. Policies, like all texts, have local idiosyncratic effects. That is, regardless of centralized attempts to define and shape the world, and attempts by government and others to determine or centrally fix implementation and outcomes, policies are complex mediations in historically and culturally structured social fields of classrooms, schools, institutional systems, and, indeed, state political economies. Our analyses here are yet another lesson indicating that what policy texts attempt to do, in exposition and narrative, rarely matches the stories told about what they have or might have done.

Narrative analysis enables the "bracketing" of truth claims of policy and a focus on the normatively preferred or targeted chains of events, their sources of agency, and the consequences of that agency. Policy narratives can then be contrasted with the various stories, macro and micro, that data tell about effects. It is not that "truth" and "science" do not matter, for the way that policies declare a particular interpretation of the state of the world counts and can be based on bad science, ideology, and distortions of the world. But if social policy and government more generally consist of a translation of "facts to norms" (Habermas, 1996), then indeed, policy may be queried in terms of the stories it tells, however enticing, and judgments may be made of policy in terms of the stories it had yielded—both micro and macro, local and global.

The stories we have told here are more variegated than they might first appear. Neither is a heroic story with clear successes. It is not simply the case that test-driven accountability-based policy is a failure and teacher-based professional policy succeeds. The questions of social equity and justice in literacy education that both NCLB and *Literate Futures* purported to address have a local empirical and ecological complexity that is overlooked in many policy debates. Our view is that *Literate Futures* succeeded in generating gains where its implementation was concentrated and welcomed by teachers and principals: the early years in primary schools. It has had lesser effects in the upper primary years, unable to turn the "fifth-grade slump," and few effects in the secondary school, where there was reportedly widespread surface compliance, less concentrated professional development and fewer resources, and therefore less substantive up-take. *Literate Futures* shows the possibilities of a policy focus on teacher professionalism and local curriculum development—core elements of successful approaches in Finland, Sweden, and Ontario (Luke, Graham, Weir, Sanderson, & Voncina, 2006). It also raises questions about the contingent factors in sustainable policy effects.

Given its more complex view of the genesis of literacy problems and pedagogic change, *Literate Futures'* successes and failures were and are contingent upon socioeconomic, material, historical, and cultural context. The methods derived from PISA (OECD, 2005) and Simons et al. (2006), furthermore, offer a more effective means for tracking the degree to which social class impact on achievement is sustained or ameliorated by changes in policy and practice. These procedures offer better means, within the limitations of standardized test score data, of tracking "value adding." But although the truth claims and narrative structures of NCLB would lead educators to assess teacher capacity in the adoption of the "right method," their counterpart claims in *Literate Futures* raise equally important questions about the adequacy of sustained governmental will and the concomitant mobilization of educational, social, and economic policy to address a range of factors that influence educational achievement.

In Queensland, will and mobilization have been sporadic. In terms of its effects in closing the gap in indigenous–nonindigenous reading performance, our view is that *Literate Futures* underlines the need for complementary but dedicated literacy policies for specific communities and cohorts that historically have been marginalized. In its implementation of *Literate Futures*, Queensland failed to adopt a systematic, correlative policy for literacy education for indigenous students. The final caveat is that "literacy-in-education policy" necessarily is a component of overarching educational policy that, to be effective with at-risk and marginalized communities, must dovetail with correlative government policies and action in the areas of welfare, health, culture and language, employment, and economic development. Lee's (2006) telling observations about the impacts of social policy on minority literacy achievement in the United States reframes the axiom offered by Bernstein (1972) more

than three decades ago, that "education cannot compensate for society."

But we can sure try. And there are lessons from these two very different policy
narratives. The truth claims and narrative
structures of NCLB attempt to focus on
curriculum/pedagogy as a powerful dependent variable and assume that its influence
can have universal effects. It is indeed the
case that curriculum and classroom pedagogy can lead to performance shifts, accounting for up to 20–30% of performance
variance by many accounts (e.g., Hattie,
1999). What NCLB misestimates is the optimal way of achieving these gains in the
complex industrial ecologies of school systems, schools, staff rooms, and classrooms.
The approach of *Literate Futures* was to
center on teachers and their professional
capacity, stressing the need for local "balanced" curriculum programs tailored to
particular cohort needs. Its impacts on
grade 3 achievement provide evidence that
this sort of approach has the potential to
make a difference at the state level.

The propositional and narrative claims of
NCLB, by contrast, speak to the high risks
related to the use of a narrow evidence base
within systemic policy formation, with documented collateral effects of the narrowing
of the curriculum, teacher de-skilling, misrepresentation of results, and other ill-
conceived ideas. Relying on classical input/
output descriptions, available through standardized test scores-as-evidence, limits the
domains available for policy formation and
action. Paris (2005) claims that "most of the
scientific evidence about reading skills and
reading development, particularly relating to
decoding skills, is based on inadequate theories, measures and interpretations" (p. 201).
Although he encourages a broadening of the
field's understandings of what "valid" reading assessments are, we argue for the need
for more sophisticated triangulation of a
host of systemic data, including sociodemographic data, regression analyses of the impacts of class, qualitative and survey data on
community and school variables, and stronger
local and state models of formative evaluation, particularly in the key area of professional development. This more complex data
corpus would not only provide policy formation and implementation with a richer
picture of the variables at work in reform

and change, it would also reduce the risks of
the host of collateral effects on teachers, students, and schools.

Our argument here is not that systems
tasked with educating adolescents should be
unaccountable or wholly autonomous. Narratives of new adolescent identity and culture do not exempt systems from their educational responsibilities. However, to assess
the effectiveness of an education system does
more than just measure and make "know-
able" the quality or performance of that system. On the contrary, educational researchers, teachers, and policymakers must engage
in dialogue over what will count as "inputs"
and "outputs" of these systems, developing
practical alternatives to simple, fundamentalist answers to complex educational and
social problems. These are not businesses or
corporations, but complex institutions geared
for the social good. Policies such as *Literate
Futures* set out to enable that dialogue at the
state level and at the local school level,
rather than preclude it. Our key aim should
be to produce complex answers and reliable
evidence to questions about how to make
policy differently for new and different
times, how to encourage systematic school
reform with a focus on quality curriculum
and instruction and teacher quality, and how
to address relevant social problems such as
cultural marginalization and spatialized
poverty in communities. These debates must
work to highlight the current issues for adolescent students and their teachers as they
cope with new demands, new technologies,
new texts, and new life pathways (Alvermann, 2001) and not revert to simple pedagogical axioms, however scientific these
might appear to be, about literacies and adolescents past.

Such an approach to policy requires a leap
in faith, a new dialogic contract among
policymakers, teacher educators, researchers, and teachers—one that the ideologically
saturated media and political environments
in both the United States and Australia have
precluded. This step requires more than just
reinstating teachers to their rightful position.
It is a very real problem, given teacher de-
skilling through the overproliferation of
basal-type reading series and highly variable
teacher training in language arts, literacy,
second-language teaching, and reading education within large educational systems.

The challenges for adolescent literacy education policy are to develop new combinations of pedagogic practice that will best serve the growing number of youth presently disengaged with schooling. A policy focus on teacher professionalism, local school autonomy, and capacity in responding to the varied cultural, linguistic, and social characteristics of learners offers a different narrative about the problem of literacy education and about human and institutional agency. Our case, on the basis of evidence to date, is that such a policy narrative has the ongoing potential to change the subject of individual deficit and failure and tell a different story about the educational formation of literacy and its potential consequences for learners and their communities. But, indeed, this is an unfinished story.

REFERENCES

Abedi, J. (2004). The No Child Left Behind Act and English language learners: Assessment and accountability issues. *Educational Researcher, 33,* 4–14.

Allen, J., Altwerger, B., Edelsky, C., Larson, J., Rios-Aguilar, C., Shannon, P., et al. (2007). Taking a stand on NCLB. *Language Arts, 84,* 456–464.

Allington, R. (2002). *Big Brother and the National Reading Curriculum: How ideology trumped evidence.* Portsmouth, NH: Heinemann.

Alvermann, D. E. (Ed.). (2001). *Adolescents and literacies in a digital world.* New York: Peter Lang.

Alvermann, D. E. (2002) Effective literacy instruction for adolescents. *Journal of Literacy Research, 34,* 189–208.

Amrein, A., & Berliner, D. (2003). The effects of high-stakes testing on student motivation and learning. *Educational Leadership, 60,* 32–41.

Apple, M. W. (1990). *Ideology and curriculum* (2nd ed.). New York: Routledge.

Ball, S. J. (1998). Big policies/small world: An introduction to international perspectives in education policy. *Comparative Education, 34,* 119–129.

Bernstein, B. (1972). A critique of the concept of compensatory education. In C. Cazden, V. John, & D. Hymes (Eds.), *Functions of language in the classroom* (pp. 131–151). New York: Teachers College Press.

Blackmore, J., & Sachs, J. (2007). Performing and reforming leaders: Gender, educational restructuring and organizational change. Albany, NY: SUNY Press.

Bourdieu, P. (1990). *The logic of practice* (R. Nice, Trans.). New York: Cambridge University Press.

Braun, H. (2004). Reconsidering the impact of high-stakes testing. *Education Policy Analysis Archives,* 12(1). Retrieved September 11, 2007, from *http://epaa.asu.edu/epaa/v12n1/.*

Calfee, R. (2002, August). *An overview of reading achievement in California.* Paper presented at the Conference of University of California Literacy Educators and Researchers, Berkeley.

Callahan, R. B. (1962). *Education and the cult of efficiency.* Chicago: University of Chicago Press.

Carnoy, M., & Loeb, S. (2002). Does external accountability affect student outcomes? A cross-state analysis. *Educational Evaluation and Policy Analysis, 24,* 305–331.

Center on Education Policy. (CEP). (2005). *From the Capitol to the classroom: Year 3 of the No Child Left Behind Act.* Washington, DC: Author.

Christensen, C. (2007). *The reading link decoding program.* Brisbane: Knowledge Books Software.

Coles, G. (2003). *Reading the naked truth: Literacy, legislation, and lies.* Portsmouth, NH: Heinemann.

Conley, M., & Hinchman, K. (2004). No Child Left Behind: What it means for U.S. adolescents and what we can do about it. *Journal of Adolescent and Adult Literacy, 48,* 42–50.

Department of Education, Training and Youth Affairs. (1997). *National literacy and numeracy benchmarks.* Canberra: Author.

Durgunoglu, A. Y., & Verhoeven, L. (Eds.). (1998). *Literacy development in multicultural context.* Mahwah, NJ: Erlbaum.

Education Queensland. (2000). *Queensland State Education 2010.* Brisbane, Queensland, Australia: Author.

Enciso, P., Katz, L., Kiefer, B., Price-Dennis, D., & Wilson, M. (2007). NCLB day by day. *Language Arts, 84,* 408–409.

English, E., Hardgreaves, L., & Hislam, J. (2002). Pedagogical dilemmas in the National Literacy Strategy: Primary teachers' perceptions, reflections and classroom behaviour. *Cambridge Journal of Education, 32,* 11–25.

Evans, B. A., & Hornberger, N. H. (2005). No Child Left Behind: Repealing and unpeeling federal language education policy in the United States. *Language Policy, 4,* 87–106.

Forrest, S. (2004). Implications of No Child Left Behind on family literacy in multicultural communities. *Clearing House, 78,* 41–45.

Freebody, P., & Luke, A. (1990). Literacies programs: Debates and demands in cultural contexts. *Prospect: An Australian Journal of TESOL, 11,* 7–16.

Garan, E. (2002). *Resisting reading mandates: How to triumph with the truth.* Portsmouth, NH: Heinemann.

Gee, J. P. (2000). The limits of reframing: A response to Professor Snow. *Journal of Literacy Research, 32,* 121–128.

Goodwyn, A., & Findlay, K. (2003). Shaping literacy in the secondary school: Policy, practice and agency in the age of the National Literacy Strategy. *British Journal of Educational Studies, 51,* 20–35.

Gregory, E. (2000). *City literacies*. New York: Routledge.

Grunwald, M. (2006). The education issue. *The Washington Post*. Retrieved October 30, 2007, from *https: // umdrive.memphis.edu/lmcgllvr/public/THE%20ED-UCATION%20ISSUE%20-%20washingtonpost. com.pdf*

Habermas, J. (1996). *Between facts and norms* (W. Rehg, Trans.). Cambridge, MA: MIT Press.

Halliday, M. A. K., & Martin, J. R. (1995). *Writing science*. London: Taylor & Francis.

Hattie, J. (1999, August). *Influences on student learning*. Inaugural professorial lecture presented at the University of Auckland. Retrieved January 8, 2007, from *www.arts.auckland.ac.nz/staff/index.cfm?P=8650*.

Heubert, J. P., & Hauser, R. M. (Eds.). (1999). *High stakes: Testing for tracking, promotion, and graduation*. Washington, DC: National Academy Press.

Jewitt, C. (2008). Multimodality and literacy in school classrooms. *Review of Research in Education, 32*, 241–267.

Ladwig, J. (2007). Modelling pedagogy in Australian school reform. *Pedagogies, 2, 57–76*.

Lam, E. (2006). Culture and learning in the context of globalization. *Review of Research in Education, 30*, 213–237.

Lee, J. (2006). *Tracking achievement gaps and assessing the impact of NCLB on the gaps: An in-depth look into national and state reading and math outcome trends*. Cambridge, MA: Harvard University Civil Rights Project.

Lewis, M., & Wrau, W. (2001). Implementing effective literacy initiatives in the secondary school. *Education Studies, 27, 45–54*.

Lie, S., Linnakylä, P., & Roe, A. (2003). *Northern lights on PISA: Unity and diversity in the Nordic countries in PISA 2000*. Oslo, Norway: University of Oslo.

Lingard, R., Ladwig, J., Mills, M., Hayes, D., Bahr, M., Gore, J., et al. (2002). *Queensland school longitudinal restructuring study*. Brisbane, Australia: Education Queensland.

Lo Bianco, J., & Freebody, P. (1997). *Australian literacies: Informing national policy on literacy education*. Melbourne, Australia: Language Australia.

Luke, A. (1997). The material world: Apologies, stolen children and public discourse. *Discourse, 18, 353–368*.

Luke, A. (2004). Teaching after the market: From commodity to cosmopolitan. *Teachers College Record, 104, 1422–1433*.

Luke, A., Elkins, J., Weir, K., Land, R., Carrington, V., Dole, S., et al. (2003). *Beyond the middle: Research into literacy and numeracy development for target group students in the middle years of schooling*. Canberra, Australia: Department of Education Science and Training.

Luke, A., Freebody, P., & Land, R. (2000). *Literate futures: Report of the literacy review for Queensland state schools*. Brisbane, Australia: Education Queensland. Retrieved September 11, 2007, from *education.qld.gov.au/curriculum/learning/literatefutures*.

Luke, A., Graham, L., Weir, K., Sanderson, D., & Voncina, V. (2006). *Curriculum and equity: An international review*. Adelaide, Australia: Department of Education and Community Services.

Luke, A., & Grieshaber, S. (2004) New adventures in the politics of literacy: An introduction. *Journal of Early Childhood Literacy 4, 5–9*.

Luke, A., & Hogan, D. (2006) Redesigning what counts as evidence in educational policy: The Singapore model. In J. Ozga, T. Seddon, & T. S. Popkewitz (Eds.), *Education policy and research* (pp. 170–184). New York: Routledge.

Luke, A., Land, R., Christie, P., Kolatsis, A., & Noblett, G. (2002). *Standard Australian English and language for Queensland Aboriginal and Torres Strait Islander students*. Brisbane, Australia: Queensland Indigenous Education Consultative Body.

Luke, A., & Luke, C. (2001). Adolescence lost/childhood regained: On early intervention and the emergence of the techno-subject. *Journal of Early Childhood Literacy, 1, 145–180*.

Luke, A., Matters, G., Herschell, P., Grace, N., Barrett, R., & Land, R. (2000). *New Basics Technical papers*. Brisbane, Australia: Education Queensland.

Luke, A., Woods, A., Land, R., Bahr, N., & McFarland, M. (2002). *Accountability: Inclusive assessment, monitoring and reporting*. Brisbane: Queensland Indigenous Education Consultative Body.

Lyotard, J.-F. (1989). *The postmodern condition* (G. Bennington & B. Massumi, Trans.). Minneapolis: University of Minnesota Press.

Ministerial Council on Education, Employment, Training and Youth Affairs. (2000). *National report on schooling*. Canberra, Australia: Author.

Ministerial Council on Education, Employment, Training and Youth Affairs. (2001). *National report on schooling*. Canberra, Australia: Author.

Ministerial Council on Education, Employment, Training and Youth Affairs. (2002). *National report on schooling*. Canberra, Australia: Author.

Ministerial Council on Education, Employment, Training and Youth Affairs. (2003). *National report on schooling*. Canberra, Australia: Author.

Ministerial Council on Education, Employment, Training and Youth Affairs. (2004). *National report on schooling*. Canberra, Australia: Author.

Ministerial Council on Education, Employment, Training and Youth Affairs. (2005). *National report on schooling*. Canberra, Australia: Author.

Moje, E. B., & O'Brien, D. (Eds.). (2000). *Constructions of literacy: Studies of teaching and learning in and out of secondary classrooms*. Mahwah, NJ: Erlbaum.

National Inquiry into the Teaching of Literacy (2005). *Teaching reading*. Canberra, Australia: Department of Education, Science and Training.

National Reading Panel. (2000). *Teaching children to read: An evidence-based assessment of the scientific research literature on reading and its implications for reading instruction.* Washington, DC: National Institute of Child Health and Human Development.

The New London Group. (1996). A pedagogy of multi-literacies. *Harvard Educational Review, 66,* 60–92.

Newmann, F., & Associates. (1996). *Authentic achievement: Restructuring schools for intellectual quality.* San Francisco: Jossey-Bass.

Nichols, S., & Berliner, D. (2007). *Collateral damage.* Cambridge, MA: Harvard University Press.

Nichols, S., Glass, G., & Berliner, D. (2005). *High stakes testing and student achievement: Problems for the No Child Left Behind Act: How high-stakes testing corrupts America's schools.* Tempe, AZ: Educational Policy Research Unit.

Oakes, J. (1985). *Keeping track: How schools structure inequality.* New Haven, CT: Yale University Press.

Organisation for Economic Co-operation and Development. (2004). *Learning for tomorrow's world: First results from PISA 2003.* Paris: Author

Organisation for Economic Co-operation and Development. (2005). *School factors relating to quality and equity: Results form PISA 2000.* Paris: Author. Retrieved September 11, 2007, from *www.pisa.oecd. org/dataoecd/15/20/34668095.pdf.*

Paris, S. (2005). Reinterpreting the development of reading skills. *Reading Research Quarterly, 40,* 184–202.

Pennington, J. (2007). Re-viewing NCLB through the figured worlds of policy and teaching: Creating a space for teacher agency and improvisation. *Language Arts, 84,* 465–474.

Raudenbush, S. W. (2005). Learning from attempts to improve schooling: The contribution of methodological diversity. *Educational Researcher, 34,* 25–31.

Rosenshine, B. (2003). High-stakes testing: Another analysis. *Education Policy Analysis Archives, 11*(24). Retrieved May, 2007, from *epaa.asu.edu/epaa/v11n24/*

Schleicher, A. (2007, August). *Literacy skills in the information age.* Paper presented at the 15th European Conference on Reading, Humboldt University, Berlin.

Sefton-Green, J. (2006) Youth, technology and media literacy. *Review of Educational Research, 30,* 279–306.

Shannon, P., & Edmonston, J. (Eds.). (2005). *Reading education policy.* Newark, DE: International Reading Association.

Simons, R., Bampton, M., & Bode, M. (2006). Socioeconomic position measurement: The devil in the detail. *PMRT Round Table Conference 2005,* Perth, 1–27.

Sloan, K. (2007). High-stakes accountability, minority youth, and ethnography: Assessing the multiple effects. *Anthropology and Education Quarterly, 38,* 24–41.

Snow, C. E., Burns, S., & Griffin, P. (1998). *Preventing reading difficulties in young children.* Washington, DC: National Academy Press.

Snyder, I. (2008). *The literacy wars.* Sydney: Allen & Unwin.

Stevens, L. (2006). Reconceptualizing adolescent literacy policy's role: Productive ambiguity. In D. E. Alvermann, K. A. Hinchman, D. W. Moore, S. F. Phelps, & D. R. Waff (Eds.), *Reconceptualizing the literacies in adolescents' lives* (pp. 184–194). Mahwah, NJ: Erlbaum.

Vickers, M., & Lamb, S. (2002). Why state policies matter: The influence of curriculum policy on participation in post-compulsory education and training. *Australian Journal of Education, 46,* 172–188.

Woods, A. (2007). What's wrong with benchmarks?: Answering the wrong questions with the wrong answers. *Curriculum Perspectives, 27,* 1–9.

Yatvin, J., Weaver, C., & Garan, E. (2003). Reading first: Cautions and recommendations. *Language Arts, 81,* 28–33.

CHAPTER 15

Tracking and Ability Grouping

JO WORTHY
HOLLY HUNGERFORD-KRESSER
ANGELA HAMPTON

Ability grouping or tracking is the practice of sorting students by formal or informal measures of ability or achievement for the purpose of differentiating curriculum and instruction. In this chapter we consider tracking within its historical and social contexts, review past and current research about tracking, discuss tracking reform efforts, and offer implications for practice. Research in the 1970s and 1980s suggested that differences in curriculum and instruction, along with teachers' differential treatment and lowered expectations of students in low groups, had immediate and long-term consequences on students' academic, social, and emotional growth. Tracking was implicated as one of the mechanisms responsible for the achievement gap between poor, minority, and language-minority students and students from backgrounds of privilege. Several decades after hundreds of studies pronounced tracking harmful to students in low tracks and levels, the practice still thrives at all levels of schooling. As in the past, students living in poverty, along with disfavored minority and language groups, continue to be sorted and schooled in ways that engender and perpetuate educational and societal inequities. Detracking, in which students are intentionally placed in heterogeneous groups, has been the most visible effort at reforming tracking, focusing on one or a combination of the following: (1) providing academic support for students; (2) providing information for stakeholders who are resistant to reform or who need help in navigating the system; (3) easing the transition for student teachers who will be working in detracked schools. Yet classes and schools cannot be simply detracked without providing academic and social support for students. Teachers need professional development, along with time and support for planning, in order for untracked education to succeed.

Although few schools track students into vocational and college-bound programs or rigid courses of study, as was common in the early to mid-20th century, most students continue to be sorted and schooled in ways that engender and perpetuate educational and societal inequities. Although debate continues about whether the No Child Left Behind Act (NCLB) has made significant progress in narrowing the achievement gap, we suggest the achievement gap reflects, in part, an opportunity gap created by differences in track placement. Ability grouping by subject is ubiquitous at every level of schooling. The differences in curriculum, instruction, and materials between levels of classes are such that students within the same school can have vastly different educational experiences. For these reasons, we believe it is important to continue the conversation about tracking as it relates to adolescent literacy.

In this chapter, we begin by defining perspectives and terms and then offer a brief history of tracking and descriptions of its characteristics and consequences gathered from research. We follow these sections with discussions of social and cultural issues surrounding tracking, descriptions of tracking reform efforts, resistance to reform, and implications for educational practice.

PERSPECTIVES AND DEFINITIONS

In our view, literacy encompasses a wide-ranging variety of practices and contexts involving language and texts. In preparing to write this chapter, we read abstracts from virtually every study of tracking and ability grouping published in peer-reviewed journals since Esposito's well-cited article in the *Review of Educational Research* (1973) and carefully read all that pertained to tracking or ability grouping in United States schools. We reviewed books that were mentioned by authors of two or more articles. We consulted literature from all grade levels (elementary through university) and all subject areas (including science and mathematics, for example). However, our major focus was research related to language arts (including oral language, reading, and writing) in middle and high school.

Tracking and *ability grouping* have become politically loaded, complex terms, which have been defined in various ways. These terms have been used interchangeably by some writers (Brewer, Rees, & Argys, 1995; Welner, 2001 cited in LeTendre, Hofer, & Shimizu, 2003), as we do in this chapter. Barr and Dreeben (1991) defined ability grouping as "a sorting process begun during the first years of schooling that continues through high school and beyond" (p. 885). They described within-class high, medium, and low reading groups of elementary school and subject-by-subject levels of junior high and high school language arts classes. Lucas's (1999) definition was more restrictive and related to secondary school. He defined it as "the practice of dividing students into programs that rigidly proscribed their course of study and that admitted little opportunity for mobility from program to program" (p. 1). Whatever the structure, the mechanisms for sorting students into groups or levels can include teacher or counselor recommendation, achievement or placement in previous classes, and/or test scores. We consider ability grouping of any kind to be a form of tracking because placement in one group or class typically influences placement in other classes, even across subjects (Lucas, 1999). For example, although it may stand to reason that a student in a low reading group in elementary school is likely to be later placed in basic language arts and reading support classes in middle and high school, a student placed in high-level English in middle school will most likely also be in high-level mathematics classes, both in middle school and, later, in high school. These structures are deeply embedded in schools and have their roots in the history of public education in the United States.

A Brief History of Tracking

This history is based on reviews in Oakes's book, *Keeping Track* (1985/2005) and Lucas's book, *Tracking Inequality* (1999). Prior to the late 1800s, only the children of the wealthy attended secondary schools. Even after the establishment of the first free public schools in New England in the 1860s, only middle- and upper-middle-class Whites attended. As the end of the century neared, the children of the middle class joined the elite in applying to and sometimes enrolling in institutions of higher learning, leading to what Oakes (1985) described as the "first push for schools to help *sort and select* students for higher education as well as to prepare them for it" (p. 18; emphasis in the original). This push came in 1892 when the National Education Association commissioned the Committee of Ten on Secondary Studies, headed by Harvard president Charles Eliot, to provide recommendations for standardizing college admission requirements, as well as secondary and college curriculum and preparation. The Committee recommended that secondary schools offer four different courses of study that would each be acceptable for college admission, rather than offer college preparation to some students and less academic programs to others. These recommendations reflected Eliot's belief that the majority of students were capable of studying and learning academic content, along with his resistance to the differentiation of curriculum to meet individual differences and to the establishment of a single standard college curriculum. The Committee's recommendations fell by the wayside as sociocultural and economic issues forced radical changes in the focuses of educational policy.

Between the late 1800s and the early 1920s, a number of forces led to a drastic increase in the number of students in public schools. As slaves continued making the transition to free status, education was becoming a more realistic goal for African Americans (Donelan, Neal, & Jones, 1994). Northeastern cities were experiencing a population explosion, along with the rise of industrialization, mainly consisting of poor immigrants from eastern and southern Europe along with job-seeking rural youth. Paralleling the enactment of child labor laws and stricter enforcement of compulsory schooling, the rolls in secondary schools swelled with students whose behavior, language, and experiences were vastly different from those of students of the previous century.

In most cities, the eventual response to this relatively sudden need to educate large numbers of diverse students was the formation of comprehensive schools, public schools marked by the separation of students into groups—presumably because of their distinct needs and abilities—for differentiated instruction. Some educators at the time were unapologetic about the clear move away from turn-of-the-century notions of educational equality, advancing the rationale that the new schools would meet the needs of the various social classes in the United States while contributing to the industrialized economy. Others employed rhetoric to redefine the notion of equal educational opportunity as meeting individual needs, abilities, and interests. Those differences, however, were seen as being openly based on race, ethnicity, and socioeconomic background.

In 1905, the French commissioned Simon Binet to develop an IQ test to identify students in need of special education (Neisser et al., 1996). IQ tests were later adapted in the United States for use by the military, schools, and researchers studying the newly arrived immigrants. By the 1920s, a push was made to test every child in America. Educators used scores as a means to sort students into classes that best reflected what was believed at the time to be their proper station in life. Scores were considered a predictor of students' capacity to learn, and teachers were encouraged to adjust their instruction accordingly (Boyer, 1936). Despite Binet's warnings of such misuses, the IQ test became a prominent tool for assessment, placement, and instructional decisions in U.S. schools.

Because the tests were geared toward middle- and upper-class students of eastern European descent and were administered in English, people of other ethnicities and social classes performed poorly on them. Thus, they provided a "scientific" rationale for separating students of color, immigrants, and the poor into programs that would at best prepare them for skilled labor and reserving college preparation programs for those whom the tests showed to be more intellectually able.

In the late 1960s and early 1970s, public school systems in major urban areas, including New York, Chicago, Philadelphia, and Boston, moved away from schoolwide tracking systems, in which track placement determined all courses students took (Lucas, 1999). However, even after the system was dismantled, the same labels previously applied to tracks (e.g., honor, regular, and basic) were applied to individual courses; thus, "the foundational element of tracking, the differentiated curriculum, remained" (p. 6).

During the 1970s and 1980s, academic tracking emerged as a charged issue in educational research, practice, and policy. Several decades after hundreds of research studies pronounced tracking harmful to students in low tracks and levels, the practice appears to again (or *still*) be thriving at all levels of schooling. A recent resurgence of research and academic debate affirms this impression (Blanchett, 2006; LeTendre et al., 2003; Orfield & Lee, 2004a; Watanabe, 2006; Yonezawa & Jones, 2006). Tracking has remained such a fundamental part of the schooling system in part because of the seemingly intuitive logic behind it.

Rationales for Ability Grouping

In the 1970s and 1980s, researchers began to look more closely at the reasoning and practices associated with tracking and other forms of ability grouping, with a focus on what appeared to be its benefits for the efficient and effective delivery of education. The most common justifications were that (1) students would learn better and feel better about themselves when they were grouped with students of similar achievement levels, (2) tracking promoted equality by making it easier to individualize instruction based on students' needs, and (3) teaching and managing students sorted by ability or achievement was easier than teaching students grouped heterogeneously (Esposito, 1973; Oakes, 1985).

Support for these claims was limited at best. In fact, research into ability grouping from elementary through high school (e.g., Alexander, Cook, & McDill, 1978; Brophy & Good, 1970; Esposito, 1973; Oakes, 1985, and scores of other studies and reviews) concluded the opposite: that there were "virtually mountains of evidence indicating that homogeneous grouping doesn't consistently help anyone learn better . . . and that the learning of average and slow students was negatively affected by homogenous placements" (Oakes, 1985, p. 7). The basis for these negative effects can be found in descriptions of the instruction, materials, teacher actions and expectations, and classroom interactions in ability groups and tracks in elementary and secondary schools.

Characteristics of Tracking

Studies of tracking in the 1970s and 1980s consistently found distinct differences between high- and low-track classes on a number of dimensions, including curriculum, classroom interactions, and teacher expectations for students' thinking and behavior (Alexander et al., 1978; Dreeben & Gamoran, 1986; Mehan, 1979a; Oakes, 1985). In high-track classes, students studied and analyzed literature and wrote long, complex expository prose. Critical thinking—including evaluation, synthesis, and problem solving—was a hallmark of high-track classes, and classroom interactions included more discussion, authentic questions, and more student par-

ticipation. Higher-track classes were more likely to be taught by skilled and experienced teachers, whose instruction was more likely to be fast paced, coherent, and engaging.

In contrast, instruction in low-track classes focused on preparation for standardized achievement tests, basic literacy skills within disembodied reading and writing tasks, and simple, low-difficulty-level texts. Students' writing was limited to answering questions in workbooks and writing short paragraphs about teacher-chosen topics. Their academic tasks required mainly rote learning and deductive thinking. The instruction proceeded at a slow pace, and the classroom discourse was characterized by known-answer questions and teacher-dominated talk (Applebee, Burroughs, & Stevens, 2000; Mehan, 1979b). In a study of 25 junior and senior high schools, information from teacher interviews indicated that content in average-level classes was like "watered-down versions of high-tracked classes" (Applebee et al., 2000, p. 77), but distinctly different from low-track classes.

Beyond considering instruction and curriculum, Oakes's (1985) examination of teacher interviews reflected that they had different expectations for students' academic and social behavior. Teachers of higher-track classes expected sophisticated thinking, active participation, independent learning, and creativity. In contrast, teachers' goals for lower-track students focused more on behavior than on learning. They were more likely "to emphasize student conformity: students getting along with one another, working quietly, improving study habits, being punctual, and conforming to classroom rules and expectations" (p. 65). In teachers' descriptions, students came to be defined in terms of the group in which they were placed. Students in low-track classes were openly labeled as having negative learning and behavioral characteristics and were less preferred by teachers. The students, their families, and their socioeconomic circumstances were assumed to be the source of their learning problems.

Consequences of Tracking

Beyond the troubling descriptions of day-to-day instruction, a large body of evidence accrued in the 1970s and 1980s suggesting that the differential treatment and expectations of students in low groups, tracks, and levels had immediate and long-term consequences for students' academic, social, and emotional growth. Students who started out in low groups in elementary school tended to be placed in and to stay in low-level classes in secondary school. The limited content offered in lower levels increasingly constrained students' educational opportunities as well as their mobility between tracks (Meier, Stewart, & England, 1989).

Oakes (1985) found that teachers and other students often looked down on lower-track students and that such students were aware of these attitudes. Researchers have also suggested a connection between students' attitudes and increased misbehavior, social problems, and depressed self-esteem in lower-track students (Marsh, 1984; Parsons, Kaczala, & Meece, 1982). Students' aspirations for and attainment of advanced education were also found to be negatively affected by low-track placement (Alexander et al., 1978; Hallinan & Sorenson, 1987; Oakes, 1985). Limited access to enriched curriculum, along with impoverished discourse and content, severely curtailed aspirations for and attainment of professional employment and advanced education (Vanfossen, Jones, & Spade, 1987). Low-track students learned content and behaviors appropriate for lower-level occupations and were denied academic content and classroom interactions foundational for educational advancement (Meyer, 1977).

The long arm of tracking was shown to reach into higher education as well (Carbonaro & Gamoran, 2002; Letendre et al., 2003; Nieto, 1995; Solórzano & Ornelas, 2002). Students who had advanced placement (AP) classes were more sought after by colleges, had potential for higher grade point averages, and had an opportunity to earn college credit. However, because lower-level classes moved more slowly and covered less material, the same course work covered in a year of higher-level classes was distributed over 2 or more years (Donelan et al., 1994), leaving students no time for AP or other classes needed for college.

Gutiérrez (1995) reached similar conclusions in her study of the content and discourse of minority students' remedial high school and developmental college classes and how the courses prepared the students for traditional college classes. Gutiérrez interviewed the students, collected writing samples, observed in their traditional and remedial college courses, and examined their high school classes. She found that, through these experiences, the students had "appropriated skills that rendered them dysfunctional in traditional and more academic classrooms" (p. 31).

THE ELEPHANT IN THE ROOM: SEGREGATION WITHIN DESEGREGATED SCHOOLS

Perhaps the most disturbing element of tracking is its blatant discrimination against poor and minority students (Meier et al., 1989; Nieto, 1995). Years after the walkouts, protests, and lawsuits that preceded and followed *Brown v. Board of Education*, segregation has found its way back into schools in ways that leave students who are not in the dominant power groups with impoverished schooling.

The achievement gap between poor and minority students and students from backgrounds of privilege and power is a current topic of much concern to educators. Research has identified tracking as one of the mechanisms responsible for the gap (Carbonaro & Gamoran, 2002; Gamoran, Nystrand, Berends, & Lepore, 1995; Rowan & Miracle, 1983). As Wheelock (1992) noted:

> Students at the lower levels move so much more slowly than those at the higher ones that differences that may have been real but not profound in earlier grades become gigantic gaps in terms of achievement, attitudes, and self-esteem. (p. 6)

Theoretically, placement in ability groups is based on measures of achievement and ability. However, many researchers have questioned the accuracy of assessment measures. Using these test scores, which discriminate against students of lower socioeconomic status (SES) and non-White students, "predetermines the placement of a disproportionate number of children of non-white and lower socio-economic status to the lowest homogeneous ability groups" (Esposito,

1973, p. 169). Letendre et al. (2003) contend that ability grouping "has been identified as the major mechanism through which inequality of education opportunity has been transmitted or maintained" (p. 45). Fine et al. (2005) describe this situation in graphic terms:

> In the suburban high schools, diverse bodies pass through the integrated school doors, and then most students funnel into classes largely segregated by race, ethnicity, and social class. Within these buildings, race, ethnicity, and class graft starkly onto academic tracks, overdetermining who has access to academic rigor, and who doesn't. (p. 511)

A number of researchers assert that ability grouping amounts to *de facto* segregation within desegregated schools. Considering the evidence, this assertion is hard to deny.

Immigration in the 1980s and Beyond: Tracking for Language-Minority Students

Tracking is not limited to social class and skin color. Ethnographic researchers in the 1990s began calling attention to the plight of immigrants in public secondary schools with large numbers of immigrants (Olsen, 1997; Valdés, 1998; Valenzuela, 1999).

The United States experienced a new wave of immigration in the 1980s, with the majority of the new immigrants coming from Latin American countries and settling in the West and Southwest. Valenzuela (1999) found that the school she studied segregated students according to the language they spoke as well as by ethnicity. Immigrants in English as a Second Language (ESL) classes spent the majority of their time focused on oral fluency and low-level skills and little time on writing, reading, or developing academic vocabulary. Content-area ESL courses were in short supply, and no ESL courses were offered at the honors level. Just as students who start in the lower tracks or levels tend to stay there, Valenzuela found that the few ESL students who moved out of their ESL classes typically moved horizontally into the non-college-bound track.

Valdés (1998) and Olsen (1997) reached similar conclusions. Valdés (1998) labeled the ESL track "the ESL ghetto" because of the barriers students had to overcome to rise above the system that seemed designed to keep them relegated to one track (p. 12). Valenzuela (1999) and Valdés (1998) recommend that immigrant students be provided with more equitable learning opportunities along with language supports. Olsen (1997) concluded that the poorly supported, highly segregated English-learning programs provided to immigrant students reflected "broader social relations and power relationships in both social and economic systems in our country" (p. 250). When citizens do not learn to speak English proficiently, as is the case in many ESL programs, they will be relegated to menial employment and perhaps poverty.

Classrooms in almost any current high school or middle school with a diverse population reflect patterns of racial segregation shown in earlier studies (Esposito, 1973; Meier et al., 1989). Honors classes are filled with Asian American and European American students, whereas economically disadvantaged and disfavored minorities (mostly African American and Latino American) are disproportionately represented in regular and other lower-level classes. Research affirms what is blatantly visible (Connor & Boskin, 2001; Losen & Orfield, 2002).

Geographic Tracking

Another kind of tracking persists in the educational system, calling up the days prior to *Brown*. Many areas of the country are experiencing a return to neighborhood schools, a change that might at first glance seem positive. However, when these schools are located in areas of concentrated poverty, they experience financial inequities and a "syndrome of inequalities" (Orfield & Lee, 2004b, p. 29) similar to those seen in the days of "separate but equal" schools (Blanchett, 2006; Fine et al., 2005; Kozol, 2005). LeTendre et al. (2003) label this "geographic tracking," the consequences of which are

> differences in curricular offerings, instructional quality, and opportunity to learn associated with the social composition of the neighborhoods in which schools were located, the funding base of the school or district, and the perceived desirability of the school to teachers. (p. 52)

Immigrants experience the additional effect of "linguistic isolation" in such schools, in which there are few fluent English speakers (Orfield & Lee, 2004b, p. 29); thus, they have few models to help them learn the language that is essential for success in U. S. society.

Cultural Foundations of Tracking

It seems inconceivable that anyone could continue to participate in an educational system that allows the inequities described in the previous sections. Letendre et al.'s (2003) study of the cultural bases of tracking provides one possible explanation. In comparing the cultural bases of tracking in Germany, Japan, and the United States, they concluded that in the United States, "the dominant cultural dialogue places the onus on individuals, not groups, and shifts the focus from inequities in the system to questions of individual responsibility or failure to take advantage of the system" (p. 76). As in the case of "enterprising individuals" who rise to the top in a market economy, doing well in school is seen as a matter of choice (Apple, 2001, p. 416). The implication is that students from low-income families and students of color are overrepresented in lower-level classes and in resource and pull-out programs, just as they are disproportionately poor, as a matter of choice and can only blame themselves because they do not take advantage of the opportunities afforded them. Issues of segregation and racial bias within ability grouping can be neatly avoided by focusing on these cultural values.

The teachers Olsen (1997) interviewed professed a commitment to integration and equal opportunity for all students. However, despite the clear inequities of minority student placement in their school, teachers persisted in believing that all students had equal access to a quality education and that achievement differences resulted from choices that students freely made. According to Olsen:

> Most of the educators at Madison believe in integration, fairness, and equal opportunity. They mostly say they enjoy and appreciate living in a diverse community. But the way they perceive the world is that students are all equally positioned and free to participate in school and that matters of achievement are the result of the individual choices students make.

What they collude in not seeing is the active process of exclusion and sorting that goes on in the school's program and practice, a sorting that consigns students by skin color, class, and English fluency into positions of very unequal access to resources, opportunities, and education. (p. 11)

Blaming teachers, many of whom have positive intentions and are sincerely concerned about their students, overlooks the role of the school and "fails to take into account the fact that teachers function within particular structures in society over which they usually have little power" (Nieto, 1995, p. 43). In continuing the tradition of tracking and sorting, school and district policies are following a long history of such practices. However, teachers can be a part of the solution, as we discuss in the "Implications" section.

TRACKING REFORM

Following the negative research findings of the 1970s and 1980s, tracking and ability grouping fell out of favor among most researchers. There were calls for eradication or drastic reforms in tracking practices (Mehan, Villanueva, Hubbard, & Lintz, 1996; Wheelock, 1993), and teachers were being advised to use cooperative learning strategies and to replace ability groups with heterogeneous, flexible, or interest-based formats (Berghoff & Egawa, 1991; Crosby & Owens, 1993; Radencich & McKay, 1995).

In the 1980s and 1990s, the National Governors Association and professional educators organizations, including the National Education Association (NEA) and the National Council of Teachers of English (NCTE), all recommended eliminating tracking on the grounds that the practice was inconsistent with the goals of high-quality learning and equitable education for all students. During the same time period, the National Association for the Advancement of Colored People (NAACP), the American Civil Liberties Union (ACLU), and other civil rights organizations targeted tracking as a second-generation segregation concern (Oakes, 2005).

By the 1990s, judging from activity in the educational research community, the message about the negative effects of tracking appeared to have been received. Research on the topic of ability grouping and tracking began to decrease after the early 1990s, and interest in the topic seemed to be fading. To illustrate: The first and second volumes of the *Handbook of Reading Research* (Pearson, Barr, Kamil, & Mosenthal, 1984; Barr, Kamil, Mosenthal, & Pearson, 1991) each included chapters on tracking and ability grouping and numerous references throughout other chapters. In contrast, the third volume, published in 2000 (Kamil, Mosenthal, Pearson, & Barr, 2000) did not contain such a chapter, and there were only two references to grouping and no references to tracking in the index. The practice of ability grouping was considered by some university educators to be on the way out, as Barr (1995) concluded about elementary grouping: "Although conditions in the early 1990s led to the increased use of ability grouping, current conditions seem to be leading us away from ability grouping to other forms of social organization" (p. 3). Researchers today debate whether elementary ability grouping ever subsided (Baumann, Hoffman, Duffy-Hester, & Ro, 2000; Chorzempa & Graham, 2006). In secondary schools, however, the practice had only changed forms (Lucas, 1999).

Alternative Perspectives about Tracking

Not every educational stakeholder agreed that tracking should be eliminated or even that it was a negative practice. The earliest and most strenuous objections to dismantling tracking came from proponents of appropriate education for gifted and talented students. Like most supporters, their major focus was on preserving the quality in high-track classes rather than on the instruction taking place in low-track classes (Welner & Burris, 2006). Kulik and Kulik (1982), for example, asserted that academically talented students would be held back if classes were not homogeneously grouped. They used England's "highly selective university system" (p. 416) as a positive example of the long-term effects of tracking. More recently, supporters of tracking, such as Loveless (1999) and Kulik (1991), have argued that the research about tracking is inconclusive

or that findings portraying tracking as negative were distorted.

Finally, there are those who do not necessarily *support* tracking but who do not favor dismantling the system altogether. Among these are educators who maintain that the differentiated curriculum of today bears no resemblance to the tracking of yesteryear, making research findings from previous studies of tracking irrelevant. Others are parents whose children benefit from the enriched curriculum, more experienced teachers, extra resources, and academic discourse in higher-level classes and who are reluctant to give up those benefits for their own children, even if they do not necessarily intend to keep other children from having them.

The New Faces of Tracking

Schoolwide tracking systems are now rare; however, in most middle and high schools, subject classes are homogeneously grouped. For example, most middle schools have three or more levels of language arts classes, including academic support, ESL, regular, and, in some schools, honors or pre-AP classes. In high school, there are AP and, in some districts and schools, special academic magnet or international baccalaureate programs. Further, some students are in separate classrooms or pull-out programs for academic or language support or special education, and some schools add other designations, such as advanced or honors, for middle-level students.

In the view of many educators, this current system is a vast improvement over schoolwide tracking because students are not locked into low tracks for the whole school day. Theoretically, students are free to enroll in different levels of classes in different subjects, such as AP English and remedial mathematics. However, in practice this ideal is rarely realized because the classes students take are affected by factors such as peer pressure, scheduling, and historical issues, resulting in a "hidden in-school stratification system" (Lucas, 1999, p. 137).

"Ironically," Lucas asserts, "this dismantling of formal programs has probably increased the information gap" (p. 6) between parents of middle- and upper-middle-class students and parents of low-income and minority students by removing clarity about the system that once existed. Middle-class parents are more likely to have attended college and to know what courses and experiences their children need for college admissions. They are more likely to have access to networks that help them obtain the information about school placements, including teacher and course evaluations and how to override normal placement channels. Navigating the new, hidden system requires cultural capital (Lareau, 1989) that low-income and minority parents are not likely to possess. For example, the parents of ESL students interviewed by Valdés (1998) had difficulty understanding the "subtle labels of the classes" and thought that their children were in "regular" classes (p. 1). Thus, these more subtle and covert practices are potentially more damaging than systems of the past (Lucas, 1999; Worthy, Mejía, Bland-Ho, & Carr, 2004).

Researchers conducting cross-cultural comparisons have formed similar conclusions about the U. S. system of tracking. LeTendre et al. (2003) found that, although it is somewhat controversial, tracking is generally clear-cut in Germany and Japan. It starts at a specific point in both countries, and teachers and parents consider the procedures and criteria to be generally clear. In contrast, tracking in the United States can take so many different forms that parents and students are rarely aware of how placements work, how decisions are made, how grouping can affect their children's current and future schooling and achievement, or even that ability grouping exists. Detailed descriptions of levels and placement criteria are largely unavailable, especially to families who do not have knowledge of the school system. Further, the processes and procedures are idiosyncratic, chaotic, and unclear even to those who make the decisions.

Even though many of the teachers interviewed by LeTendre and colleagues (2003) insisted that tracking was no longer in existence, virtually every teacher mentioned within- and across-class reading and math groups and a range of resource programs for English language learners (ELLs), gifted students, students needing academic support, and students identified as needing early intervention.

Detracking

Detracking has emerged as the most complex and complete alternative to tracking. In detracked schools or classes, "students are placed intentionally in mixed-ability heterogeneous classes, in an attempt to remedy the negative effects of tracking" (Rubin, 2006, p. 4). There have been many attempts at detracking in schools and districts with differing degrees of success.

The Preuss school, a publicly funded secondary school on the University of California San Diego campus, was created as a detracked charter school (Alvarez & Mehan, 2006). All students are from low socioeconomic backgrounds and chosen by lottery. The Preuss school concept is rooted in the belief that students should not be segregated into high and low tracks and that all students, whether entering college or the work world, can benefit from a rigorous curriculum. Alvarez and Mehan (2006) were "attracted to the idea of detracking students due to its commitment to rigorous academic preparation for underrepresented students" (p. 83). Further, the school staff members recognize that home and school share dual responsibility for helping students develop. Small classes help with personalizing and monitoring students' learning, and struggling students are provided support. There is a strong culture of professional learning and research-based practice. The Preuss school continues to be successful in preparing low-income students for college.

The Advancement via Individual Determination (AVID) program (Mehan et al., 1996) does not attempt schoolwide detracking, but focuses on high school students with average to high-average test scores and relatively low grades (primarily from low-income and/or ethnic or linguistic minority backgrounds). The school offers a college preparatory program with a rigorous curriculum, along with social and academic support as needed. As a result of their participation in the program, the AVID students studied by Mehan and colleagues enrolled in college at a higher rate than the national average. The authors argue that, although a complete overhaul of the tracking system may not be palatable to all educational stakeholders, programs such as AVID could be the start of gradual reform.

The detracking efforts discussed so far have focused on providing extra supports for challenged learners or students in low-income areas. These contexts are typically safe from resistance because they do not have an effect on the broader economic and social structures that schooling influences. When middle-class parents are involved, objections to detracking plans are often loud and angry, because their children are typically the ones who benefit from being in higher tracks (Wells & Serna, 1996). Wells and Oakes (1996) studied 10 racially mixed middle and high schools that were in the midst of detracking efforts. All of the schools instituted detracking to provide equitable resources for children, including more balanced appropriation of resources, smaller class sizes, and—where appropriate—in-school support and tutoring. Many also instituted changes in classroom instructional strategies, curricula, and assessment and improved professional development for teachers.

There were many successes among the schools studied by Wells and Oakes (1996), particularly in the achievement of low-tracked students as a result of attending heterogeneous classes. Although there was no evidence that detracking compromised the education of advantaged students, resistance from high-SES parents was still strong in some of the schools and was too great for some of the schools to overcome. Some schools made concessions to these parents in order to continue detracking most of their classes. Some returned to their previous, tracked systems. Oakes (2005) concludes that detracking in these schools often came down to a "struggle between more- and less-privileged families over scarce resources; and it entailed an ideological struggle over the meaning of race and culture as they are enacted in schools" (p. 294).

The Rockville Centre district is a rare example of a diverse suburban school system that successfully detracked classes in its middle and high schools (Oakes, 2005). Over several years, beginning in 1990, the district replaced tracked classes with heterogeneous classes, providing extra support to students who had previously been in low-level classes. The achievement gap between majority and minority students virtually disappeared.

Although the efforts described here are encouraging, they do not appear to have had

an extensive effect on educational reform in the United States, inasmuch as tracking is still pervasive. However, there were many important lessons learned from both successful and less successful efforts. We focus on these lessons and the implications for education and policy in the following sections of the chapter.

IMPLICATIONS: AVENUES FOR SUCCESSFUL TRACKING REFORM

Initiating Detracking Efforts

To make real changes in education, policymakers and reformers must first "become much more aware of how local constituents perceive tracking and its outcomes" (LeTendre et al., 2003, p. 83). Welner and Burris (2006) outlined strategies for analyzing constituents' perceptions about schooling and designing programs that address their concerns, attitudes, and perceptions. The first strategy, "winning them over," is used when a community is willing to engage with reformers. In the school discussed in the article, the experiment started with open enrollment in detracked classes. After students in detracked classes improved in achievement scores, detracking was expanded in phases. An important factor was that parents, community members, and teachers were able to see that achievement improved, curriculum was rigorous, and high-achieving students' performances did not decline. This strategy requires a committed, stable district leadership, elimination of the lower track as a first step, support for learners who struggle, steady progress, collection and dissemination of achievement data, careful selection and continued evaluation of staff, support for heterogeneous classes, response to parental concerns, and "support and praise for, and engagement of, school staff" (Welner & Burris, 2006, pp. 93–94).

It is important to realize that parents of children in upper tracks are often the loudest supporters of tracking (Datnow & Hirschberg, 1996; Oakes, 2005; Wells & Oakes, 1996; Welner & Burris, 2006). They have the most political capital and clout, and schools may be reluctant to lose their support (Lareau, 1989; Oakes, Wells, Jones, & Datnow, 1997; Wells & Serna, 1996; Welner & Burris, 2006). Further, most such parents are college educated, so they understand that detracking will lead to competition for the highest-level classes that are needed for acceptance to high-ranked colleges (Oakes, 2005). When a community is resistant to change, Welner and Burris (2006) recommend a second strategy, "taking them on," which involves confronting the balance of political power while still employing the same phase-in system and careful attention to detracking used in "winning them over" (p. 96). Gently but firmly, beliefs and values grounded in low expectations held by parents, teachers, students, administration, and community members must be challenged for the strategy to succeed.

Developing a College-Going Culture

Even before high school, many children of color and poor students attend schools with inadequate financing and do not have access to enriched curricula. To rectify this situation, LeTendre et al. (2003) recommend that "K–12 institutions must develop a college-going culture" (p. 227), which includes developing school and community norms that support advanced study, advanced academic courses, qualified teachers, and academic support. Establishing such a culture and providing students with the support and preparation necessary for higher education were essential elements of detracking efforts such as those of the Preuss school (Alvarez & Mehan, 2006) and AVID (Mehan et al., 1996).

Parents also need information and support to navigate the school system at all levels. Schools should become transformative rather than reproductive institutions by systematically providing parents of low-achieving students with the support, knowledge, and social capital to support their children in preparation for college. LeTendre et al. (2003) argue that schools should clarify how they are placing students and establish standard classifications, provide clear information about the connection between classes and preparation for college, provide lower-track students with an enriched curriculum, and give parents and students information about the placement process.

Supporting Students and Teachers

Gaining support from the wider community is a necessary step in detracking, but the most important constituents are those who will implement or be affected by the changes—the teachers and students. Yonezawa and Jones (2006) conducted focus groups with students from 12 schools implementing detracking reform to gain their perspectives on how the changes were affecting them and their peers. Students in upper tracks believed that their peers in lower-track classes received a less rigorous and engaging curriculum and argued that all students needed more rigorous instruction along with choices in course offerings. In addition, students believed that detracking required teachers to teach "equitably and fairly" (p. 20) and that detracking required a change in teacher attitudes and a belief in all students. Because of teacher beliefs and student needs, some researchers argue for the inclusion of a structured support class in the school day in order to help students better meet the challenges of rigorous course work—in particular, in English and social studies classes (Mehan et al., 1996; Rubin & Noguera, 2004).

It is difficult to change practices that are entrenched in a system. Ability grouping is such a long-standing, ubiquitous practice in U.S. schools that it has become normalized. Oakes (1985) asserts that "a lot of what we do in schools is done more or less out of habit stemming from traditions in the school's culture. We don't tend to think critically about much of what goes on in schools" (p. 5). In schools where teachers are resistant or do not believe change is needed, part of the solution may be to begin to raise teachers' awareness and for them to confront beliefs, language, and actions through critical reflection. Teachers who participate in an examination of the lowered expectations, lower-level instruction, and limited classroom discourse associated with lower tracks and the effects of these practices on students may become more aware of the existence and harmful effects of tracking.

CHANGES IN CURRICULUM AND INSTRUCTION

Better Curriculum for All Students

It is important to acknowledge that students in high tracks benefit academically from their placements. However, these benefits are largely the result of the enriched curriculum, extra resources, academic discourse, and instructional support provided in those classes, rather than homogeneity (Gamoran, 1992). Thus, one important lesson learned from previous attempts at detracking was that changes in grouping practices must be accompanied by modifications in organization, curriculum, student support, and improved instruction and resources for all students (Donelan et al., 1994; Esposito, 1973).

Rubin and Noguera (2004) discovered that when schools implement detracking plans without advanced planning and teacher education, "some teachers end up 're-tracking' their students in a variety of ways" (p. 95), including requiring less complex work of lower-achieving students, giving more thoughtful feedback to higher achievers, and using instructional strategies that "potentially showcase the academic skills of high achieving students without addressing the specific needs of lower achieving students" (p. 95).

Detracking is easily derailed by wary or unwilling participants, including teachers, administrators, and community members who have had too many reforms thrust upon them in the past. Presumably, aspects of resistance will remain, and teachers will need support in order to feel empowered within a detracked system. Lotan's (2006) perspective of the classroom as a social system is one model to assist teachers as they begin teaching heterogeneous classes. She recommends that "teachers plan for heterogeneity a priori rather than modify post hoc" (p. 33).

Watanabe (2006) explored inquiry groups as forums for teachers to share their thoughts as they began to explore the possibilities of detracking and unpack the meanings of commonly used but often misunderstood terms such as *ability grouping, tracking,* and *detracking*. Watanabe suggested that such structures were able to assist teachers in truly engaging with their own thoughts about ability and intelligence. Involvement in groups led to a sharing of curricular ideas across content areas in a school where such contact was usually limited.

Detracking requires more than declaring open enrollment for all students; it requires teachers to "rethink their approach to teaching and to make it accessible to all students" (Watanabe, 2006, p. 26). For example, Watanabe found that teachers within the same

school had different views about whether their school was actually detracked. Some teachers thought that students had free choice because they could elect to take AP courses. Others believed there were "hidden prerequisites" and other unspoken issues that blocked students' access to AP classes. For example, many teachers did not modify their teaching styles or provide needed support for the newly enrolled students. Thus, removing prerequisites for enrollment did not ultimately result in an increase in student enrollment in AP classes.

Mehan (1979a) argues that *all* students should be provided with more rigorous curricula, along with social and academic supports, and that students' knowledge and expertise should be appropriated for classroom instruction. The move will require much effort from and support for teachers. Donelan et al. (1994) add that

teachers must be prepared to organize and facilitate stimulating experiences for all students. They must see all students as capable and expect their active involvement. School districts must help teachers bring the materials and methods used in enriched and accelerated classes to students and teachers in middle- and low-ability groupings as they abandon these demeaning group designations altogether. (p. 384)

Moving from tracked classes to heterogeneous classes will not be an easy transition for teachers who have taught homogeneous classes for many years. As teacher educators, we understand many teachers' need or desire to learn the ins and outs of teaching in heterogeneous classrooms. However, we are hesitant to offer suggestions that may seem unduly prescriptive. Instead, we offer suggestions of general practices, with some specific examples, to allow for teacher choice in practice.

Strategies and Practices for Detracked Classrooms

Haberman (1991) argued that strong instructional practices involve students in issues that affect their own lives and encourage them to question assumptions and confront uncomfortable issues, such as differences among people and discrimination. The focus of instruction is on major conceptual ideas, and students are involved in planning their education and in applying principles of social justice to their worlds.

As heterogeneous classrooms will necessarily include students from a range of cultures, making use of culturally relevant or responsive pedagogy makes sense (Gay, 2002; Rubin & Noguera, 2004). In describing culturally relevant pedagogy, Ladson-Billings (1995) stressed the themes of academic success, cultural competence, and critical consciousness. Practices that foster community and uphold higher standards for all students, but provide scaffolding and an awareness of students' cultural capital, are highlighted by detracking proponents as well. Even changing seating arrangements can make a difference in initial student interactions in mixed-ability classes (Rubin & Noguera, 2004). Bartolomé (2003) argued that the use of student-centered strategies such as cooperative learning, process writing, reciprocal teaching, and language experience can "help to offset or neutralize our deficit-based failure and recognize subordinated student strengths" (p. 417).

Reading and Writing Workshops, sometimes called Literacy Workshops (Atwell, 1998; Roller, 2002) are based on the premise that students have unique interests and abilities on which they draw for literacy learning. For this reason, choice is a critical component of the practice. Students in Literacy Workshops choose the books they read and the topics they write about when working independently. Through choice, learning becomes more individualized, with students working in materials that provide motivation and appropriate challenge. Assessment is an integral and continual part of Literacy Workshops, allowing students and teachers to participate in an ongoing negotiation of instruction that is shaped by students' changing needs.

Cone (2006) provides a detailed account of how she teaches her heterogeneous English language arts classes. She attended to strategies in great detail and with specific options, offering suggestions for everything from first-day classroom practices to correctness in student work. Cone, an avid proponent of heterogeneous classrooms, argues that detracked classes should involve "low-achieving students working side by side—in effect, apprenticed—with middle and high achievers" (p. 56), thus having an opportunity to see themselves as successful students. In addition to detailing the specifics of her

classroom curriculum, she describes strategies for setting high expectations for behavior and academics, setting the tone and work ethic in the classroom, and teaching the "rules" students need to learn in order to gain access to the culture of power.

Implementing particular approaches will not ensure that heterogeneous classes will work smoothly. Rubin and Noguera (2004) caution that cooperative learning practices, often included in detracked English language arts classrooms "do not guarantee success for all students, and must be implemented thoughtfully" (p. 95); and carefully facilitated approaches or activities such as Reading/Writing Workshop may reinforce inequities that a heterogeneous classroom is intended to alleviate (Bartolomé, 2003). Therefore, teaching practices implemented in heterogeneous classrooms will be most effective when paired with support for teachers.

From her study in predominantly Latino high schools, Nieto (1995) concluded that "student performance is based on subtle and sometimes not so subtle messages from teachers about students' worth, intelligence, and capability" (pp. 42–43). Although few people would openly state that they believe intelligence is a fixed trait, "teachers' notions of ability and intelligence come through their talk about classroom practice, and it is important for teachers to become adept at identifying these perspectives in each other's comments" (Watanabe, 2006, p. 29). Thus, for heterogeneous classrooms to work, educators at all levels of schooling must learn to operate outside deficit notions and develop students' varying strengths, while simultaneously confronting their own biases. Only then will we see all students as capable and able to learn (Bartolomé, 2003). If attitudes about the nature of intelligence are not altered, students dubbed "low achieving" will not have a chance for success in academically challenging classes regardless of the practices used (Lotan, 2006; Watanabe, 2006).

REFERENCES

Alexander, K. L., Cook, M. A., & McDill, E. L. (1978). Curriculum tracking and educational stratification: Some further evidence. *American Sociological Review, 43,* 47–66.

Alvarez, D., & Mehan, H. (2006). Whole-school detracking: A strategy for equity and excellence. *Theory into Practice, 45,* 82–89.

Apple, M. (2001). Comparing neo-liberal projects and inequality in education. *Comparative Education, 37,* 409–423.

Applebee, A. N., Burroughs, R., & Stevens, A. S. (2000). Creating continuity and coherence in high school literature curricula. *Research in the Teaching of English, 34,* 396–429.

Atwell, N. (1998). *In the middle: New understanding about writing, reading, and learning.* Portsmouth, NH: Heinemann.

Barr, R. (1995). What research says about grouping in the past and present and what it suggests about the future. In M. Radencich & L. McKay (Eds.), *Flexible grouping for literacy in the elementary grades* (pp. 1–24). Boston: Allyn & Bacon.

Barr, R., & Dreeben, R. (1991). Grouping students for reading instruction. In R. Barr, M. L. Kamil, P. Mosenthal, & P. D. Pearson (Eds.), *Handbook of reading research* (Vol. 2, pp. 885–910). Mahwah, NJ: Erlbaum.

Barr, R., Kamil, M. L., Mosenthal, P., & Pearson, P. D. (Eds.). (1991). *Handbook of reading research* (Vol. 2). Mahwah, NJ: Erlbaum.

Bartolomé, L. I. (2003). Beyond the methods fetish: Toward a humanizing pedagogy. In A. Darder, M. Baltodano, & R.D. Torres (Eds.), *The critical pedagogy reader* (pp. 408–429). New York: Falmer.

Baumann, J. F., Hoffman, J. V., Duffy-Hester, A. M., & Ro, J. M. (2000). The first R yesterday and today: U. S. elementary reading instruction practices reported by teachers and administrators. *Reading Research Quarterly, 35,* 338–377.

Berghoff, B., & Egawa, K. (1991). No more "rocks": Grouping to give students control of their learning. *The Reading Teacher, 44,* 536–541.

Blanchett, W. J., (2006). Disproportionate representation of African American students in special education: Acknowledging the role of White privilege and racism. *Educational Researcher, 35,* 24–28.

Boyer, P. A. (1936). The administration of learning groups in elementary schools. In G. M. Whipple (Ed.), *Thirty-fifth yearbook of the Society for the Study of Education* (pp. 191–215). Bloomington, IL: Public School Publishing.

Brewer, D., Rees, D., & Argys, L. (1995, November). Detracking America's schools: The reform without cost? *Phi Delta Kappan, 77*(3), 210–215.

Brophy, J. E., & Good, T. L. (1970). Teachers' communication of differential expectations for children's classroom performance: Some behavioral data. *Journal of Educational Psychology, 61,* 365–374.

Carbonaro, W. J., & Gamoran, A. (2002). The production of achievement inequality in high school English. *American Educational Research Journal, 29,* 801–827.

Chorzempa, B. F., & Graham, S. (2006). Primary-grade teachers' use of within-class ability grouping in reading. *Journal of Educational Psychology, 98,* 529–541.

Cone, J. K. (2006). Detracked ninth-grade English: Apprenticeship for the work and world of high school and beyond. *Theory into Practice, 45,* 55–63.

Connor, M. H., & Boskin, J. (2001). Overrepresentation of bilingual and poor children in special education classes. *Journal of Children and Poverty, 7,* 23–32.

Crosby, M. S., & Owens, E. M. (1993). The disadvantages of tracking and ability grouping: A look at cooperative learning as an alternative. *Solutions and Strategies, 5,* 1–9.

Datnow, A., & Hirshberg, D. (1996). A case study of King Middle School: The symbiosis of heterogeneous grouping and multicultural education. *Journal of Education for Students Placed at Risk, 1*(2), 115–134.

Donelan, R. W., Neal, G. A., & Jones, D. L. (1994). The promise of *Brown* and the reality of academic grouping: The tracks of my tears. *Journal of Negro Education, 63,* 376–387.

Dreeben, R., & Gamoran, A. (1986). Race, instruction, and learning. *American Sociological Review, 51,* 660–669.

Esposito, D. (1973). Homogeneous and heterogeneous ability grouping: Principal findings and implications for designing more effective educational environments. *Review of Educational Research, 43,* 163–179.

Fine, M., Bloom, J., Burns, A., Chajet, L., Guishard, M., Payne, Y., et al. (2005). Dear Zora: A letter to Zora Neale Hurston 50 years after *Brown. Teachers College Record, 107,* 496–528.

Gamoran, A. (1992, December). The variable effects of high school tracking. *American Sociological Review, 57,* 812–828.

Gamoran, A., Nystrand, M., Berends, M., & Lepore, P. C. (1995). An organizational analysis of the effects of ability grouping. *American Educational Research Journal, 32,* 687–715.

Gay, G. (2002). Preparing for culturally responsive teaching. *Journal of Teacher Education, 53,* 110–116.

Gutiérrez, K. D. (1995). Unpackaging academic discourse. *Discourse Processes, 19,* 21–37.

Haberman, M. (1991). The pedagogy of poverty versus good teaching. *Phi Delta Kappan, 73,* 290–294.

Hallinan, M. T., & Sorenson, A. B. (1987). Ability grouping and sex differences in mathematics achievement. *Sociology of Education, 60,* 63–72.

Kamil, M. L., Mosenthal, P. B., Pearson, P. D., & Barr, R. (Eds.). (2000). *Handbook of reading research* (Vol. 3). Mahwah, NJ: Erlbaum.

Kozol, J. (2005). *The shame of the nation: The restoration of apartheid schooling in America.* New York: Crown.

Kulik, C. C., & Kulik, J. A. (1982). Research synthesis on ability grouping. *Educational Leadership, 82,* 619–622.

Kulik, J. A. (1991). Findings on grouping are often distorted. *Educational Leadership, 48*(6), 67.

Ladson-Billings, G. (1995). But that's just good teaching! The case for culturally relevant pedagogy. *Theory into Practice, 34,* 159–165.

Lareau, A. (1989). *Home advantage: Social class and parental intervention in elementary education.* New York: Falmer.

LeTendre, G. K., Hofer, B. K., & Shimizu, H. (2003). What is tracking? Cultural expectations in the United States, Germany, and Japan. *American Educational Research Journal, 40,* 43–89.

Losen, D. J., & Orfield, G. (2002). Racial inequity in special education. In D. J. Losen & G. Orfield (Eds.), *Racial inequality in special education* (pp. xv–xxxvii). Cambridge, MA: Harvard University Press.

Lotan, R. (2006). Teaching teachers to build equitable classrooms. *Theory into Practice, 45,* 32–39.

Loveless, T. (1999). *The tracking wars: State reform meets school policy.* Washington, DC: Brookings Institution.

Lucas, S. R. (1999). *Tracking inequality: Stratification and mobility in American high schools.* New York: Teachers College Press.

Marsh, H. W. (1984). Relationships among dimensions of self-attribution, dimensions of self-concept, and academic achievements. *Journal of Educational Psychology, 78,* 190–200.

Mehan, H. (1979a). *Learning lessons: Social organizations in the classrooms.* Cambridge, MA: Harvard University Press.

Mehan, H. (1979b). "What time is it, Denise?" Asking known information questions in classroom discourse. *Theory into Practice, 18,* 285–294.

Mehan, H., Villanueva, L., Hubbard, L., & Lintz, A. (1996). *Constructing school success: The consequences of untracking low-achieving students.* New York: Cambridge University Press.

Meier, K.J., Stewart, J., & England, R.E. (1989). *Race, class, and education: The politics of second-generation discrimination.* Madison: University of Wisconsin Press.

Meyer, J. W. (1977). The effects of education as an institution. *American Journal of Sociology, 83,* 55–77.

Neisser, U., Boodoo, G., Bouchar, T. J., Jr., Boykin, W.A., Brody, N., Ceci, S.J., et al. (1996). Intelligence: Knowns and unknowns. *American Psychologist, 51*(2), 77–101.

Nieto, S. (1995). *Affirming diversity: The sociopolitical context of multicultural education.* White Plains, NY: Longman.

Oakes, J. (1985). *Keeping track: How school systems structure inequality.* New Haven, CT: Yale University Press.

Oakes, J. (2005). *Keeping track: How school systems structure inequality* (2nd ed.). New Haven, CT: Yale University Press.

Oakes, J., Wells, A. S., Jones, M., & Datnow, A. (1997). Detracking: The social construction of ability, cultural politics, and resistance to reform. *Teachers College Record, 98,* 482–510.

Olsen, L. (1997). *Made in America: Immigrant students in our public schools.* New York: Norton.

Orfield, G., & Lee, C. (2004a). *Brown at 50: King's dream or Plessy's nightmare?* Cambridge, MA: The Civil Rights Project at Harvard University.

Orfield, G., & Lee, C. (2004b). *Racial transformation and the changing nature of segregation.* Cambridge, MA: The Civil Rights Project at Harvard University.

Parsons, J. E., Kaczala, C. M., & Meece, J. L. (1982). Socialization of achievement attitudes and beliefs: Classroom influences. *Child Development, 33,* 322–339.

Pearson, P. D., Barr, R., Kamil, M., & Mosenthal, P. (Eds.). (1984). *Handbook of reading research.* New York: Longman.

Radencich, M. C., & McKay, L. J. (1995). *Flexible grouping for literacy in the elementary grades.* Boston: Allyn & Bacon.

Roller, C. M. (2002). Accommodating variability in reading instruction. *Reading and Writing Quarterly, 18,* 17–38.

Rowan, B., & Miracle, A. W. (1983). Systems of ability grouping and the stratification of achievement in elementary schools. *Sociology of Education, 56,* 133–144.

Rubin, B. C. (2006). Tracking and detracking: Debates, evidence, and best practices for a heterogeneous world. *Theory into Practice, 45,* 4–14.

Rubin, B. C., & Noguera, P. A. (2004). Tracking and detracking: Sorting through the dilemmas and possibilities of detracking in practice. *Equity and Excellence in Education, 37,* 92–101.

Solórzano, D. G., & Ornelas, A. (2002). A critical race analysis of advanced placement classes: A case of educational inequality. *Journal of Latinos and Education, 1,* 215–229.

Valdés, G. (1998). The world outside and inside schools: Language and immigrant children. *Educational Researcher, 27*(6), 4–18.

Valenzuela, A. (1999). *Subtractive schooling.* Albany, NY: SUNY Press.

Vanfossen, E. E., Jones, J. D., & Spade, J. Z. (1987). Curriculum tracking and status maintenance. *Sociology of Education, 60,* 104–122.

Watanabe, M. (2006). Some people think this school is tracked and some people don't: Using inquiry groups to unpack teachers' perspectives on detracking. *Theory into Practice, 45*(1), 24–31.

Wells, A. S., & Oakes, J. (1996). Potential pitfalls of systemic reform: Early lessons from research on detracking. *Sociology of Education, 69,* 135–143.

Wells, A. S., & Serna, I. (1996). The politics of culture: Understanding local political resistance to detracking in racially mixed schools. *Harvard Educational Review, 66,* 93–118.

Welner, K., & Burris, C. C. (2006). Alternative approaches to the politics of detracking. *Theory into Practice, 45,* 90–99.

Wheelock, A. (1992). *Crossing the tracks.* New York: New World Press.

Wheelock, A. (1993). From tracking to untracking in the middle grades. *Equity and Choice, 9,* 44–50.

Worthy, J., Mejía, J., Bland-Ho, H., & Carr, N. (2004, November). *Only the names have been changed: Current incarnations of ability grouping.* Paper presented at the annual meeting of the National Reading Conference, San Antonio, TX.

Yonezawa, S., & Jones, M. (2006). Students' perspectives on tracking and detracking. *Theory into Practice, 45,* 15–23.

Part III

LITERACY OUT OF SCHOOL

POLICY MATTERS: Excerpts from *A Test of Leadership*[1]

Unacceptable numbers of college graduates enter the workforce without the skills employers say they need in an economy in which, as the truism holds correctly, knowledge matters more than ever. (p. x)

History is littered with examples of industries that, at their peril, failed to respond to—or even to notice—changes in the world around them, from railroads to steel manufacturers. Without serious self-examination and reform, institutions of higher education risk falling into the same trap, seeing their market share substantially reduced and their services increasingly characterized by obsolescence. (p. xii)

[F]or the country as a whole, future economic growth will depend on our ability to sustain excellence, innovation, and leadership in higher education. But even the economic benefits of a college degree could diminish if students don't acquire the appropriate skills. (p. 1)

Employers report repeatedly that many new graduates they hire are not prepared to work, lacking the critical thinking, writing and problem-solving skills needed in today's workplaces. In addition, business and government leaders have repeatedly and urgently called for workers at all stages of life to continually upgrade their academic and practical skills. (p. 3)

[I]mproved accountability is vital to ensuring the success of all the other reforms we propose . . . . Student achievement, which is inextricably connected to institutional success, must be measured by institutions on a "value-added" basis that takes into account students' academic baseline when assessing their results. This information should be made available to students, and reported publicly in aggregate form to provide consumers and policymakers an accessible, understandable way to measure the relative effectiveness of different colleges and universities. (p. 4)

Finally, we found that numerous barriers to investment in innovation risk hampering the ability of postsecondary institutions to address national workforce needs and compete in the global marketplace. Too many of our colleges and universities have not embraced opportunities to be entrepreneurial, from testing new methods of teaching and content delivery to meeting the increased demand for lifelong learning. (p. 4)

The commission calls on businesses to partner with schools and colleges . . . . Such efforts should include developing students' and parents' knowledge of the economic and social bene-

---

[1]Excerpts from *A test of leadership: Charting the future of U.S. Higher education*. A report of the Commission Appointed by Secretary of Education Margaret Spellings. Available at *www.ed.gov/about/bdscomm/list/hiedfuture/reports/final-report.pdf*.

fits of college through better information, use of role models and extensive career exploration. (pp. 18–19)

To meet the challenges of the 21st century, higher education must change from a system primarily based on reputation to one based on performance. We urge the creation of a robust culture of accountability and transparency throughout higher education. Every one of our goals, from improving access and affordability to enhancing quality and innovation, will be more easily achieved if higher education institutions embrace and implement serious accountability measures. We recommend the creation of a consumer-friendly information database on higher education with useful, reliable information on institutions, coupled with a search engine to enable students, parents, policymakers and others to weigh and rank comparative institutional performance. (p. 21)

COUNTERPOINT

Yancey (Chapter 17, this volume) outlines a complex notion of literacy that enables open-ended thinking about ill-structured problems of the sort found in the "real world" and outlines the generative work in college literacy education that appears well aligned with the Commission's emphasis on innovation.

Schoenbach and Greenleaf (Chapter 7, this volume) suggest that a form of apprenticeship in disciplinary thinking is essential to the development of higher levels of academic literacy. The level of detail in knowledge about teaching and recasting of subject matter demanded in such an approach may suggest that professional development is at least as important to improved learning as is accountability.

A number of contributors to this volume—Alvermann (Chapter 2), Cooks and Ball (Chapter 10), Black and Steinkuehler (Chapter 18), Intrator and Kunzman (Chapter 3), and Lewis and del Valle (Chapter 20)—make a strong case for the importance of identity in adolescent literacy. The notion that students should be tested more often to see what value has been added raises significant questions about how they are positioned in academic institutions.

Beaufort (Chapter 16, this volume) finds that many workplace values and practices are specific to the culture of a particular profession and the corporate values of individual businesses. Because the discourse expectations are often site-specific, students' difficulty in adjusting to them follow more from unfamiliarity with the new conventions than a failure among college professors to teach general literacy practices.

As a group, the authors in this collection view literacy as a tool rather than as a measurable commodity having a direct and immediate application in the workplace.

—L. C., R. B., and P. S.

CHAPTER 16

Preparing Adolescents for the Literacy Demands of the 21st-Century Workplace

ANNE BEAUFORT

On the basis of the research in workplace writing and my experience with high school graduates entering college, I argue that adolescents need an expanded set of literate behaviors, and even more important, the ability to learn independently the new literacy skills required in the varied jobs they will hold. In workplace settings, the higher the level of responsibility, the higher the requirement for strong writing skills. Even those in clerical and sales positions must write frequently. Research also shows that workers must learn a variety of genres, develop flexible processes for getting writing accomplished, and be highly attuned to social dimensions of written communication. The research on transfer of learning suggests that educators can best serve students by teaching them how to be independent learners so that they can continue to develop new writing literacies independent of formal schooling. Analytical thinking and concise, logical prose are the most valued traits in workplace writing. These findings also suggest a need for shifts in heavily literature-based and factual recall-based curricula to a greater emphasis on critical thinking and analysis/writing of nonfiction prose.

Adolescents are already familiar with the workplace: McDonald's, Starbucks, Kmart, and other national chains employ thousands of teenagers, as do hundreds of other retailers and service providers. Though earning minimum wages, students save for college, or support themselves if independent of parents, or make car payments, or pay for the all-important cell phone, or contribute to the family's resources. Well before finishing high school, most adolescents understand some of the realities of being wage earners.

But what adolescents usually don't yet realize is that the higher one wishes to rise on the job ladder, the more written communications skills are required. They probably are not aware that more than half of those who work in clerical and service jobs report that they must often write memos and reports and that more than three-fourths of those in managerial and professional occupations report that they frequently write memos and reports (Kaestle, Campbell, Finn, Johnson, & Mikulecky, 2001). When it comes to writing literacy, what most adolescents are familiar with are the genres that connect them to friends and family: text messaging, e-mail, blogs, MySpace, and as one student told me, "Christmas lists."

There is, of course, nothing wrong with these forms of literacy. What is a problem, though, is the limited amount of sustained abstract thinking and organized analytical writing some adolescents produce, and their inability to figure out how to adapt to new writing situations in school and workplace settings, where the stakes for writing are high. Written literacy is a multifaceted skill. The close reading of texts; the ability to interpret, analyze, and synthesize information; and the ability to use a variety of genres appropriately within a communications context are integral to producing successful written texts.

My contact with adolescents is limited to those 18-year-olds who choose to attend 4-year institutions. On the basis of what I've seen in more than a decade's worth of teaching college freshmen (at three different universities) and what I read about adolescent literacy skills, it appears that most college-bound high school students don't learn the full range of literacy skills in high school that they could to carry over into new areas of either study or work. They learn some skills in decoding literary texts and some skills in writing exam questions and the five-paragraph essay, and they practice thinking and writing analytically, but not nearly enough. When I meet them, barely 3 months out of high school, I find them usually unaware of how college is different from high school in terms of the advanced levels of literacy required to succeed there, and to succeed in the higher-level jobs to which they aspire.

So, from the vantage point of also having been a writer in the business world for 10 years and having done an extensive ethnographic study of workplace writing practices when I transitioned back into academia, I argue that adolescents need an expanded set of literate behaviors, and even more important, the ability to learn independently the new literacy skills required in the varied jobs they will do. Here, for teachers and researchers, I give a snapshot of what's happening in terms of research findings on workplace literacies and some modest suggestions for how adolescents might be better trained to succeed in workplace settings that require advanced literacy skills.

But first, here are a few statistics that may give cause for teacher educators and researchers to attend to workplace contexts for literacy in their work with adolescents. It is well established that educational attainment correlates with both employability and wage earnings. According to the U.S. Census Bureau report in 2004, the unemployment rate among high school dropouts is 21.3%, as compared with 12.9% unemployment for high school graduates. And in terms of the relation between education and earning capacities, those with professional degrees are the highest-paid workers. A college degree will likely double the earned income in comparison to what a high school graduate will earn (U.S. Census Bureau, 2006).

Although these statistics about educational achievement in relation to employment patterns do not demonstrate a direct correlation between writing skills and employment opportunities, studies have shown that workers in Level 2 jobs (no college) scored 17 points below the mean on the National Adult Literacy Survey (NALS), whereas those in Level 4 jobs (college degree) scored 7 points above the mean. As the authors of this study report, "The data strongly suggest that college graduates bring much better literacy skills to their jobs than do high school graduates" (Boesel & Fredland, 1999).

In the late 1970s and early 1980s, researchers in literacy studies and composition studies began to take a particular interest in the writing that is done in workplace and professional contexts. This work has contributed considerably to an enlarged view of literacies in multiple contexts and of a continuum of life-long learning for writers. In particular, research in this aspect of writing literacy has explored five major areas: (1) the importance and pervasiveness of writing in the workplace; (2) the nature of writing processes in the workplace; (3) the effect of changing technologies on workplace writing; (4) the impact of workplace writing on employees, institutions, and society; and (5) socialization processes for writers in school-to-work transitions. These areas overlap, of course, but for the purpose of some orderliness in this review, they appear separate. I conclude the chapter with some of the broad theoretical implications of this body of work and its practical ramifications for teacher-educators.

IMPORTANCE AND PERVASIVENESS OF WRITING IN THE WORKPLACE

Several early survey studies established the value placed on writing by management-level employees in a variety of professions. Faigley and Miller (1982) reported, for example, that white-collar professionals in six occupations wrote an average of 23% of the work week. Another survey (Harwood, 1982) at the same time found that a typical college graduate wrote once or twice a day, and perhaps more important, that as income rose, so did frequency of writing. And, as mentioned above, recent reports on workplace writing practices suggest that not only do managerial and professional workers write frequently, sales and clerical personnel do as well (Kaestle et al., 2001).

Subsequent to early studies, there has been a continuing stream of research on workplace writing activities, looking both at professional writing (in such fields as law, architecture, and nursing) and at blue-collar writing activities. Blue-collar workers' writing skills have become increasingly important as technologies have driven more record keeping and decision making to those who are directly involved in manufacturing, information-processing, and care-giving activities. As Rose (2003) points out, writing is increasingly intertwined in blue-collar jobs with graphic and numeric literacies. A good overview of some of the research on blue-collar writing practices on the job is provided in Hull (1997) and Gowan (1992).

The views of workplace writing in recent research are particularly sensitive to the social and political power (or lack of power) associated with writing activities within institutions. For example, Jolliffe (1997) analyzes rhetorical strategies that upper-management authors evoke in addressing workers in company documents and argues that workers' identities need to be considered in shaping such texts. Hart-Landsberg and Reder (1997) analyze the effect of writing processes on teamwork in a manufacturing firm. All affirm the critical role that literacies play in workers' success in the workplace, and in companies' success as well.

It is hard to communicate convincingly to high school students the important role that writing and decoding texts may have in their future lines of work. Giving them mini-ethnography tasks—to study the literacy practices in a given line of work they are interested in—and showing them studies that correlate writing skills with income potential may be motivational strategies worth exploring.

PROCESSES AND PRACTICES THAT SUPPORT WORKPLACE WRITING

Managing the Writing Process

Managing the writing process can be equated to "getting the job done." Students tend to "get the job done" by starting on their essay the night before it is due. Writing anxiety, studies show (Applebee, Langer, Mullis, Lathan, & Gentile, 1994), increases from grade school to high school. So knowing how to manage the writing process is probably the single most important writing skill that teachers can impress on students. There are a number of studies that discuss how writing gets done in workplace settings that may spark new ideas for teaching this skill.

In the wake of researchers' interest during the late 1970s and early 1980s in the composing processes of writers, a number of researchers of professional writing studied whether the same recursive process of composing identified by Flower and Hayes (1981) is evidenced among seasoned writers in the workplace. A few expanded on the Flower and Hayes model—for example, Doheny-Farina (1986) found that among writers in a small computer firm, "stored writing plans" meant a rich and specific understanding of complex social issues that would affect the writer's decision-making process in composing texts. Hovde (2001) documented the extensive generative nature of the research process that technical writers needed to undertake as part of being able to write software documentation, and Spilka (1988) also found generating content to be an important part of the composing process. In a year-long ethnography following six engineers composing a variety of documents, she found more successful engineers spending more of their energies on content than on arrangement or style.

But several studies convincingly argued that composing processes of writers varied, depending on the nature of the genre and other situational variables found in workplace settings. Broadhead and Freed (1986) documented a very linear composing process of two management consultants who used boilerplate formulas supplied by their company to write proposals to clients. A government proposal, however, could be a daunting genre to tackle. In another study, one writer, after suffering through a laborious, anxiety-ridden round of proposal writing, approached the same task a year later, wiser for her earlier experiences, in her own methodical way: typing out the RFP (request for proposal) in order to internalize what the grantors were requesting, and creating a manila folder for each section of the proposal, where she could place notes, relevant information, and rough drafts of the section for later assemblage into the whole. She wrote sections nonsequentially as well, according to what seemed easiest to tackle first (Beaufort, 1999). In an experiment with journalism students, Schumacher, Scott, Klare, Cronin, and Lambert (1989) found that under one writing condition—composing a news story—the writers needed to spend less time planning, given the preestablished structure of the genre. However, when writing editorials, which have a more open format, the writers spent more time reaching decisions as they wrote.

Couture and Rymer (1993) and Beaufort (1999) documented the influence of situational factors—the amount of time available and whether or not the writing situation was routine—on writers' degree of attention to planning and revising. Beaufort further found that writers in one nonprofit organization varied their writing processes depending not only on the characteristics of the genre being written, but also on the physical realities of the workplace. One writer worked on easy tasks on Mondays and Fridays, when there were a lot of interruptions, and on more difficult projects on Tuesdays, Wednesdays, and Thursdays, when there were greater opportunities for concentrated effort. Even then there were numerous interruptions that themselves became part of the writing process.

Several other variables that influenced the writing processes of workplace writers also demonstrate richly varied composing processes. A number of studies (Beaufort, 1999; Johns, 1989; Selzer, 1993) point to the effect of intertextuality in workplace writing (portions of texts freely borrowed from other texts) on writers' processes. Beaufort describes one writer in a nonprofit agency, for instance, who organized various boilerplate texts for business letters she frequently wrote into file folders on her desktop computer, labeled according to type of letter: rejection letter, request for donation, and so forth. Allen (1993), Dorff and Duin (1989), and Witte and Haas (2001) further complicate conceptions of writing process by observing various forms of collaborative writing that the Flower and Hayes (1981) model cannot account for. For example, Witte and Haas demonstrate the intertwining of different areas of expertise ("distributed cognition") of city workers and engineers in the process of documenting and revising technical documents and reveal the ways in which gestures and diagrams operated in the composing process as "pre-texts."

Collaborative writing (see Jorn, 1993)—sometimes also referred to as document cycling—can also lead writers to feel less ownership of texts and less immediacy in terms of the rhetorical situation. The image of the solo writer as "creator" is often not apropos in workplace writing situations, and the resulting effects on writers' sense of authorship (or lack of it) spawned by social writing practices have been documented. It seems that most writers have to go through a period of psychological adjustment to the loss of control of "their" texts (Anson & Forsberg, 1990; Beaufort, 1999). In one case (Henry, 1995) this loss of sense of ownership of text also affected the writers' abilities to imagine the real audience for the texts, given that internal readers and editors were the most immediate audience. One writer (a public relations writer within an engineering firm) said, "Neither our native tongue nor our professional language is ever entirely our own. We must constitute ourselves in texts that we do not wholly control" (Winsor, 1993, p. 194).

Efficiency with the writing process is a factor in workplace settings as well. One study showed that front-line supervisors who didn't have a good handle on the writing process were losing money for the company with their inefficiencies (Mabrito, 1997). A Silicon Valley company (McIsaac & Aschauer, 1990) formed a Proposal Operations Center to review proposals as part of the writing process in order to improve not only efficiency, but effectiveness of the proposals as well, especially given that as many as 42–100 individuals could be involved in writing of the proposals. The writing process for these documents included storyboarding ("scribble sheets," i.e., early drafts of sections of text) pinned to walls for viewing and a "Red Team" that simulated readers' reactions to early drafts.

Institutional Structures and the Effect on Writing Activity

A number of studies have examined the ways in which organizational culture influences writers' behaviors. Brown and Herndl (1986) found that social hierarchies within an organization influenced writers' sense of what linguistic features and even what genres were appropriate. The authors found that superfluous use of nominalizations was greater among the "average" writers, causing their writing to be "muddy" and "verbose." These traits increased if the writing was for upper management or for powerful people outside the corporation and decreased when the writers composed for those lower in the corporate hierarchy. Nominalizations also increased with a sense of job insecurity: Writers felt such linguistic features conveyed a greater sense of authority. Similarly, Henry (1995) found writers' use of nominalizations, passive voice, and other less direct stylistic choices in a military organization resulted from the layers of approvals (what they referred to as the "chop chain") that removed them from any sense of audience or personal investment in the writing. Others have documented similar stylistic choices made by writers in response to the social milieu in which they wrote (Odell, Goswami, Herrington, & Quick, 1983; Orlikowski & Yates, 1994).

The effects of gender differences on practices in written business communications have, unfortunately, not been a subject of much research. Tebeaux (1990) did one study with technical writing students who had workplace experience and found that both men and women who had worked in jobs requiring interpersonal communications used both "masculine" and "feminine" approaches to communication as specific situa-tions warranted either. On the basis of this study and her review of gender research, Tebeaux argues for business writers to have "androgynous" writing strategies in order to meet a variety of communication situations (cf. Barker & Zifcak, 1999).

In sum, a wide range of social factors influence the ways in which writing must be accomplished in workplace settings. Attention to writing process is, if anything, more important in workplace settings than in school settings. In the workplace, the constraints of time, space, and budgets all become factors in writing. Writers need the metacognitive and creative abilities to use varied approaches to getting writing done. Anything that can be done to educate students to have a robust writing process may help to prepare them for future success with writing in the workplace.

The Effect of Changing Technologies on Workplace Writing

The impact of technology on composing processes has only begun to be investigated and is not exclusive to workplace research. There have been a number of investigations in this arena, generally along two lines: (1) how technologies affect writers' processes (or don't) and (2) how technologies spawn new genres or new communicative patterns (or don't). As technology plays an increasingly important role in both classroom and workplace settings and affects literacy activities significantly, those working with adolescents should keep abreast of this research. Even video games are being scrutinized by researchers for the cognitive skills they may foster (Gee, 2003).

An experimental study of professional and advanced graduate students composing press releases on the computer or with paper and pencil, as well as revising and editing press releases under the same conditions, revealed advantages and disadvantages of composing with computers. On one hand, writers spent less time planning and felt free to write spontaneously and creatively with the computer. They also made five times more changes to the text on the computer than with paper and pencil and more changes at the whole-sentence level. On the other hand, the physical limitations of the computer screen interfered with making whole-text-level structural changes, which were more readily made with the paper-and-pencil version, in which the whole text could be spread out (Lutz, 1987). Haas (1989) also documented the difficulty for writers in reading their texts on computer screens. Follow-up studies can confirm or disconfirm whether newer technologies involve problems of different degrees of severity. Sellen and Harper (2002), looking at writing at the International Monetary Fund, found that managers drafted and did final editing on computers but collaborated on revisions on paper, which accounted for 71% of the writing time. Managers needed to spread papers on tables, mark them, share pages, and otherwise revise them before making changes on the computer. Paper also seems to serve other cognitive functions in critical thinking and composing processes. The authors state:

> Knowledge workers rarely store and file paper documents or refer back to the information they do keep. Rather, it is the process of taking notes that is important in helping them to construct and organize their thoughts. The information that they do keep is arranged around their offices in a temporary holding pattern of paper documents that serves as a way of keeping available the inputs and ideas they might have use for in their current projects. (p. 63)

Gladwell (2002) reports a study by Mackay, a computer scientist, of air traffic controllers making similar use of online technologies and paper. The researcher found that air traffic controllers used little strips of paper to make notes on airplane locations and worked with the slips of paper and the radar images on their computer screens to manage air traffic. It appears that computers aid certain aspects of the writing process and "old-fashioned" paper and pencil aid other aspects of the composing process. On one hand, digital processing of texts facilitates storing and accessing large amounts of information, display of multimedia documents, fast full-text searches, quick links to related materials, and dynamic modifying or updating of content. On the other hand, the use of hard copy of texts facilitates quick, flexible navigation through and around documents, enabling the reader to look across more than one document at once, mark up a document while reading, and interweave reading and writing.

In addition to the influence of technology on reading/writing practices, research has documented the shifting of social roles in relation to written communications in the workplace as a result of technological changes. Dictation has nearly disappeared, as even top executives have turned to desktop computers, and conversely, secretaries have become more than typists, often doing revising and editing of others' documents online (Dautermann, 1996). Other roles, too, have changed as a result of the ready accessibility of digital technologies. Cook-Gumperz and Hanna (1997) found that the social status of nurses in the hospital hierarchy increased when they started using bedside computer terminals to chart patients' conditions and accessing database tools for patient assessment.

More radical perhaps than word processing are several other technical media: personal digital assistants (PDAs), structured document processors (SDPs), instant messaging (IM), and hypertext. PDAs, as exemplified in Geisler's (2001) self-study, may blur the boundaries between personal and work-related writing. Geisler's self-study of a 97-minute composing session also demonstrated the multilayered, multitasking possibilities that Internet technology, computers, and PDAs allow: She was using all three interchangeably as she composed. IM has transformed written communication to nearly match the synchronicity of oral communication and, like PDAs, is a newer technology warranting further research. Adolescents already use multiple computer-based technologies, so the challenge is one of helping them to understand the full rhetorical situation constructed around each technology. E-mail, fax, phone, text messaging, or PDA—each carries with it rhetorical constraints and opportunities.

Researchers also point to the alteration of the concept of "authoring" when writing tools such as these are employed. Reader–writer relationships are affected by the new media. Hypertext enables readers, in a sense, to become "co-authors" with writers (Wenger & Payne, 1994) and presents additional organizational possibilities and problems: Nonlinear organizational patterns such as trees, cycles, grids, and stars can be created that verbal rhetorical devices do not allow (Horton, 1991). In addition, information can be layered for different audiences. Fortune (1989) also presents a case for the use of computer drawing programs as another tool for aiding critical thinking and prewriting in the composing process.

A second line of investigation of technology–writing connections has been an examination of changes in writing styles, genres, and communications patterns as a result of "new" technologies. Yates's (1989) historical study of the rise of business communications reveals a fascinating intertwining of human and material factors that spawned new genres and new communications practices. Her study helps to set current technological changes that affect writing in perspective. Some predicted that the telephone would diminish or eliminate written communication, but other tools—the telegraph, the typewriter, carbon paper, and vertical filing cabinets—all increased the ease and functionality of writing. For example, the genre of the internal memo evolved, gradually, from the more formal business letter: The standard headings of the memo were created for efficiency of referencing documents and allowed dropping unnecessary courtesies such as "Yours very truly." The information in the headings of memos in turn led to adopting the use of vertical files for easy retrieval of documents (p. 96).

E-mail, which took off as a communications medium in the late 1980s, has been examined as a "new" genre. Although early on some researchers raised the question as to whether e-mail was really a genre (Spooner & Yancey, 1996), most of the research suggests that e-mail is a hybrid between oral and written communications and has been developing a set of regularized textual features unique enough to warrant considering it a genre in its own right—for example, more use of incomplete sentences, a preference for coordinated rather than subordinated ideas, and use of specialized vocabulary and graphical symbols to convey emotions (Baron, 2000; Gimenez, 2000; Sims, 1996). Yates, Orlikowski, and Okamura (1999) also found, in an extensive study of organizational culture, a number of e-mail subgenres, for example, the "official announcement genre" and the "dialogue genre."

Changes in organizational structure and patterns of communication as a result of new computer technologies such as e-mail have also been examined. Researchers found that communications with new customers began as standard business letters, but as relationships became established, e-mail became the preferred medium of communication (Murray, 1987). As the memo encouraged more informality than the business letter, likewise, e-mails have increased both the informality and personal nature of business communications (Gimenez, 2000). And yet Yates et al. (1999), studying use of e-mail in two different divisions of a Japanese manufacturing firm, found that corporate cultures in the divisions differed and as a result, "norms" for e-mail communications also differed, suggesting that it is not the medium, but the genre features as shaped by social context that vary the form of communication. The researchers offer this cautionary note: "The migration of existing communication patterns to new media may, however, lead users simply to apply ineffective habits of use from old technologies to new ones" (p. 100). They call for deliberate consideration of genres and genre repertoires in specific contexts for communication.

A final note on technology's influence on writing that has a bearing in particular on workplace environments and business communications: Bernhardt (1993) gives a good overview of the ways in which hypertext is changing acts of reading and writing. Although he does not give empirical evidence of readers' and writers' behaviors with hypertext media, he does a thorough textual analysis, pointing out the features of hypertext that influence the ways writers/readers interact around such texts: Hypertexts are interactive; readers are active rather than passively absorbing information; hypertexts are functionally mapped (text displayed in ways that cues readers to what can be done with it); hypertexts are modular; hypertexts are navigable (reader can move across large pools of information in different directions for different purposes); hypertexts are hierarchically embedded; hypertexts are spacious (unconstrained by physicality); and hypertexts are graphically rich.

As for classroom practices, technology-based genres, such as web pages, blogs, e-portfolios, text messaging, PowerPoint, and e-mail are familiar to most students. Incorporating instruction in and use of these tools—in terms of reading strategies, research strategies, and writing practices—has high appeal to students and can prove useful in developing cognitive and literacy skills if instruction is thoughtfully planned. Further, familiarity with these tools can extend students' skills to technology-rich workplace environments.

INTERRELATIONS OF TEXTS AND VISUALS IN NEW TECHNOLOGIES

As I have mentioned earlier, the physicality of the new genre of hypertext has altered reading and writing processes and meaning making. Others have documented the pervasiveness of visual symbols side by side with written text in home and workplace settings (Hull, 1997; Medway, 2000; Rose, 2003). Witte (1992) even raises the question: What is writing versus nonwriting? Several studies suggest the richness of this area of investigation. Bernhardt (1986) offers an excellent analysis of the interaction of visual and verbal rhetoric in a brochure published by a wetlands agency. Horton (1993) documents research on the culturally specific meanings of graphics, text layouts, and colors. Brumburger (2002), in an experimental study, found that participants consistently assigned personality types to certain typefaces. And Medway (2000) analyzed, in an extensive case study, the use of tools—visual and textual—in an architecture student's critical thinking process as he worked on a building design (cf. Smagorinsky, Cook, & Reed, 2005). Early conceptual thinking was done in words, but later design ideas had to be represented with visual symbols. Other studies of high school students' use of visual and verbal symbol systems for problem solving in home economics (Smagorinsky, Zoss, & Reed, 2006) and in an equine management and production course (Smagorinsky, Pettis, & Reed, 2004) also confirm the importance of considering literacies as multimodal.

Document design has become a subspecialty within rhetoric, drawing on perception studies in psychology, reading studies (how readers process texts), and linguistic anthropology (what symbols mean in context). An example of such research is the study by Zimmerman and Schultz (2000) of two medical questionnaires filled out by cancer patients—one a standard form and the other asking for the same information but employing the principles of information design. Ninety percent of the questions on the designed form elicited better information than the questions on the standard form, demonstrating the efficacy of applying known principles of document design to strategic documents.

Reviews of research on visual design (Albers & Lisberg, 2002) and information design (Redish, 2000; Schriver, 1997) shed light on these areas. Scholars have conducted little empirical research into the effects of other sign systems on writers' processes, on genres themselves, and on the social dynamics of text usage, in spite of calls for such studies (Schriver, 1989). There have been advances, however, in research methods for studying the effects of document design. Instead of relying on abstract readability formulas, for example, researchers now examine readers' actual comprehension and use of documents and have expanded their definition of which aspects of documents to evaluate (Schriver, 1997). Visual literacy is increasingly linked to verbal literacy, such that the two demand equal billing in literacy education.

These reports of research on technology uses in writing production in the workplace do not factor in the new generation of employees entering the workforce in the 21st century. Adolescents have grown up with new media. Often, in this area of literacy, adolescents can teach their elders. They are innovators in communicating in cyberspace. The more our literacy instruction incorporates these media, the higher the probability that students will respond with heightened interest.

The Impact of Workplace Writing on Employees, Institutions, and Society

Writing practices in workplace settings can also have larger-scale effects on employees, institutions, and society. One study in particular exemplifies the interface of technologies, writing practices, and social structures in the workplace. This study found that nurses' use of bedside computers to chart patients' conditions and access data bases for diagnostic purposes (Cook-Gumperz & Hanna, 1997) both depersonalized the writing for the nurses ("I cannot even see my own signature on the chart," Cook-Gumperz & Hanna, 1997, p. 329) *and* raised the visibility of the nurses' observations to the rest of the medical staff. The use of the new technologies even enabled the patients to be more involved in their own medical planning and healing processes.

Cook-Gumperz and Hanna's (1997) study revealed mixed effects of writing technologies in the workplace, and that social factors can also have a negative effect on writers. Paré (2000) documented the ways in which social workers were constrained and influenced by the types of information they could put into case reports on juvenile offenders, even to the point of their attempting to circumvent legal and social constraints when filing reports. Similar studies in the field of psychiatry have documented the ways in which the *Diagnostic and Statistical Manual of Mental Disorders* (DSM-III or DSM-IV) pushes psychiatrists into codifying clients' behaviors for billing and "social accountant" purposes, potentially restricting the actual practice of therapy (Berkenkotter, 2001; McCarthy, 1991; McCarthy & Gerrig, 1994). Schryer (1993) further found similar constraints on social dynamics between veterinarians and pet owners, given the professional standards for forms of documentation.

Stygall (1991) revealed the ways in which jury instructions can interfere with a jury's understanding of the legal process, and Schryer (2000) outlined the ways in which particularly dense boilerplate text (off the charts in readability indexes) in an insurance company's letters turning down clients' disability claims was a major factor in the number of appeals the insurance company received to negative letters (more than 60% were appealed). When the researcher presented her evidence to the company (she was hired as a consultant to help it reduce the number of appeals of negative letters), executives were reluctant to turn dense legal prose into plain English. Even more disconcerting, Sauer (1994) demonstrates that the linear, sequential model of cause-and-effect prose used in accident reports of large government agencies fails to account for the multidimensional nature of accidents. And Herndl, Fennel, and Miller (1991) studied memos that led to both the Three Mile Island nuclear accident and the deaths of eight astronauts aboard the *Challenger* flight. These authors demonstrate, through careful rhetorical analysis of memos and an examination of the social context of the two divisions of the company involved in the *Challenger* decision, that the engineering division was arguing that past performance and some limited data about cold temperatures affecting O-rings warranted canceling the flight, but management discounted the engineers' data. Herndl et al. (1991) say, "The managers reasoned at the level of contracts and programs—successful flights. The warrants of each set of interests, or social groups, were insufficient to the other" (p. 302).

Fortunately, writing practices can also have a positive influence on work activities within organizations. One of the earliest studies (Doheny-Farina, 1986) documents the ways in which the drafting of a business plan in a small start-up computer company, in fact, shaped the direction of the company. More recently, Katz (1998) documented one writer's social agency within an organization through her acumen and self-confidence as a writer.

Another vein of research in workplace writing on the interrelation of social contexts and texts concerns the features of texts themselves as they evolve in relation to their social functions within organizations. Bazerman's (1981) pioneering article comparing the rhetorical approaches of three academic disciplines—sociology, biology, and literature—led to a number of other rich analyses of the ways in which genre conventions arise out of socially constrained or socially motivated situations and enact certain epistemological assumptions—what counts as truth, as evidence, and so on. There is now a substantial body of work on the rhetorical (i.e., nonobjective) nature of science writing (Blakeslee, 2001; Fahnestock, 1986; Myers, 1985; Paul & Charney, 1995). In addition, Fahnestock and Secor (1991) explicate the rhetorical motives and moves of literary scholars, and in business settings, Smart (1993), Orlikowski and Yates (1994), and Devitt (1991) similarly document the interrelations of genre features (evolving, nonstatic, dialogic) and the social purposes to which the texts attend.

Segal (1993), for instance, analyzed more than 200 articles written over a 10-year period in various medical publications to examine the rhetoric of medicine. She found that medical writing was paternalistic and that authority was established through extensive use of citations and nominalizations. She concluded, "Physicians are locked within scientific medicine's frame of reference because of the nature of language itself" (p. 84). Beaufort (1999) found that a single genre, the grant proposal, varied considerably in its features depending on the goals, values, and communications processes of different discourse communities using the genre. Grant proposals for private foundations had different requirements from those for local government agencies, and grant proposals for federal agencies had yet another set of features particular to the communicative context.

Although little in school settings can fully prepare students for the dynamics of social contexts for writing in workplace settings (Freedman & Adam, 2000), nonetheless, teachers would serve students well by introducing the concept of discourse communities and the social nature of written communication. Getting students to articulate the tacit knowledge they have of the social constraints and advantages of writing in school contexts, and how they can apply that "social context" knowledge to other writing situations, may go a long way toward helping them to learn the unspoken values and conventions in other writing situations.

Socialization Processes for Writers and School-to-Work Transitions

Also of interest is how writers learn in workplace settings, where instruction is usually informal, self-motivated, and indirect. Although early research in workplace settings captured what writers were doing or thinking only in a given interview or survey, or in single texts, by the late 1980s researchers began to use ethnographic techniques to take a longer view of workplace scenes for writing. From these studies came increased awareness of the socialization processes of writers making the transition from academic writing to business and professional writing. Doheny-Farina (1989, 1992) followed a student doing a writing internship in a nonprofit organization and documented her process of coming to realize the importance of understanding the political context of the organization in order for her writing to be useful. Anson and Forsberg (1990) also tracked the psychological adjustment of students doing

writing internships, finding such adaptations as coming to see the community's viewpoint, rather than their own, as paramount.

Beaufort (1999) followed for several years the trajectory of four writers at a nonprofit as they gradually adapted their writing behaviors and gleaned knowledge in five areas associated with writing expertise that were crucial to successful written communications both internal and external to the organization. Although there was no formal training program for writers new to the organization, managers were teaching as they worked with the writers, facilitating growth by assigning low-risk tasks (routine business correspondence or small sections of grant proposals), which were gradually replaced by high-risk writing tasks (entire grant applications, etc.), by giving feedback on drafts in face-to-face coaching situations and by treating novices as already part of the professional community they were working in. From the writers' vantage points, learning to write successfully on the job involved constant observation of others' language practices (oral and written), finding out the best grammarian to solicit editing help from, and otherwise being apprenticed into the social practices of the setting. All possible resources for learning on the job were marshaled to accomplish the writing tasks. Though mistakes were made and the learning environment was by no means ideal, many of the features of what Lave and Wenger (1991) term "cognitive apprenticeships" or "legitimate peripheral participation" were present. Dias, Freedman, Medway, and Paré (1999) also document the role of cognitive apprenticeships and distributed cognition in workplace sites for learning.

The more teachers can help students to become independent learners, and to learn what tools and social dynamics can be used to aid learning, the more likely students will be attuned to ways of learning in new environments. Moreover, imparting to students the reality that they need to be lifelong learners of writing practices can aid their learning processes.

THEORETICAL IMPLICATIONS OF WORKPLACE RESEARCH

Theorists in composition studies and literacy studies in the last 20 years have drawn from and expanded their work by looking at the empirical and descriptive research in workplace and professional writing practices reported here. A number of key people come to mind: Bazerman (1994a, 1994b), Berkenkotter and Huckin (1995), Gee (1989, 2000), Russell (1995, 1997), Swales (1990, 1992) and Witte (1988, 1992). The work of Orlinkoski and Yates (Orlikowski & Yates, 1994; Yates & Orlikowski, 1992) in management communications theory has followed a similar trajectory. Drawing from social constructionist theories, literary theory, rhetorical theory, sociolinguistics, and the new literacy studies, and drawing on their own rhetorical analyses of written communications in these contexts, or ethnographic work (their own and others'), these researchers have greatly expanded the understanding of written communication in relation to social contexts for writing. They have added theoretical understanding specifically to matters of writing acquisition and use.

Cope and Kalantzis (2000) employ the term *multiliteracies* to describe the wide variations in "literate" behaviors in out-of-school settings. Here is their definition of the term:

> We decided that the outcomes of our discussions could be encapsulated in one word, Multiliteracies—a word we chose because it describes two important arguments we might have with the emerging cultural, institutional, and global order. The first argument engages with the multiplicity of communications channels and media; the second with the increasing salience of cultural and linguistic diversity. (p. 5)

They argue, as do others (Beaufort, 2000; Hull & Schultz, 2001; Rose, 2003), that there can be no *one* standard for what counts as writing proficiency or expertise. In a similar vein, Gee (1989) states that true literacy in a discourse is possible only outside one's primary (home) discourse because literacy requires the metaknowledge of what the discourse is doing socially, and that is not possible until one has a secondary discourse with which to critique the primary discourse. So, in essence, whether writers are working in a school or workplace setting, they are outside the "home" discourse and immersed in other social, political, cultural contexts that shape the nature of the writing

in multiple ways. What is "correct" or "good" depends on the social context—the activity system, or discourse community, or genre at hand, as determined by its participants (Nystrand, 1986).

In order to conceptualize more specifically how writers and the texts they produce function socially, others have applied activity theory to written communications in workplace and professional contexts (Bazerman, 1988; Bracewell & Witte, 2003; Russell, 1997) and explored the concept of discourse community (Beaufort, 1997; Killingsworth & Gilbertson, 1992; Olsen, 1993; Swales, 1990, 1992), an activity system that focuses specifically on written communication (and the interface with oral and visual communications). Examining the goals, values, communicative patterns, genre sets, and epistemologies that particular discourse communities espouse (for example, nonprofit agencies, government agencies, biologists, stamp collectors, physicists, literary scholars, and other groups) can illuminate what is going on in individual writers' behaviors and in individual texts and groups of texts within discourse communities.

Closely related to theories of activity systems and discourse communities, but not as broad in scope, are the expanded theories of genre, genre systems, and intertextuality that have grown from and been employed in understandings of workplace and professional communication practices. Bazerman's (1982) work in scientific genres, Devitt's (1991) in the genres employed by tax accountants, Berkenkotter's and McCarthy's (Berkenkotter, 2001; McCarthy, 1991; McCarthy & Gerrig, 1994) on the formation of the DSM-III and DSM-IV in psychiatry, Schryer's (1993) on veterinary records, and Yates's (1989) on the rise of the business memo, to name a few studies, have added to conceptions of genres as socially situated and interactive with social forces over time, both influencing and being influenced by those forces.

Devitt (1991) broke new ground theoretically by demonstrating the interrelations of "sets" of genres employed by an accounting firm. She found two types of intertextuality: referential (one text referring to another explicitly) and functional (one text linked by function to another). She states, "In examining the genre set of a community, we are examining the community's situations, its recurring activities and relationships" (p. 340). She also observed that "the stabilizing power of genres, through the interaction of texts within the same genre . . . increases the efficiency of creating the firm's products" (p. 342).

Others likewise have documented the occurrence of interconnected genres that work in concert within given social contexts in the legal system (Bazerman, 1994b), in banking (Smart, 1993), and in interoffice e-mail communications (Orlikowski & Yates, 1994). How texts function in cultures is an ongoing subject of scholarship in business communications, in composition studies, and in linguistic anthropology, in large part as a result of the workplace research from the last 20 years reported here. Arguments for the social construction of knowledge can be supported by the research reported here as well.

Some studies in workplace and professional writing have also taken a cognitive perspective and add to sociocognitive theories of composing and to general understandings of distributed cognition as well. Dias et al. (1999), drawing on theories of situated cognition and situated learning, point to the sociocognitive aspect of collaborative writing processes, common in workplace settings. In banking (Smart, 2000) and in engineering (Witte & Haas, 2001), examples abound of overlapping and specialized knowledge that is shared, leading to "robustness of decision making" in connection with written texts. Knowledge and thinking processes in acts of composing are shared and interactive. Collaborative writing is not just a division of labor; rather, it entails interactive cognitive processes between writers, editors, and managers.

In addition to adding to sociocognitive views of the composing processes of writers, workplace studies have instantiated socially situated views of learning, and in particular, cognitive apprenticeships and legitimate peripheral participation of novice writers in workplace and professional discourse communities (Beaufort, 2000; Freedman & Adam, 2000). Interactive composing sessions, the employment of cultural tools at hand (model texts, visuals, electronic resources, etc.), and tangible results from writing projects are commonplace in workplace and professional settings and suggest an alternative model of learning processes to those typical of formal instructional settings. In fact, the very social underpinnings of much of the writing activity reported here calls for a particular teaching agenda: teaching students how to be self-learners in a variety of social contexts they will encounter that demand writing literacies. Learning how to learn, as literate, communicative future employees, is probably the biggest academic goal educators could aim for with their students.

CONCLUSION

In all, studies of writing in the social contexts of business and the professions has yielded a rich basis for understanding (and theorizing) the social features of language, genres, and acts of composing. Olsen's (1993) review of studies of legal and medical writing illustrates what the impact of this collective body of research has been:

> These studies show that there is indeed an effect—and often a profound effect—of the context and the values of the community of readers and listeners on the content and form of a document. Perhaps more unexpectedly, a few of the studies also suggest that there is sometimes an effect of the content and form of a document on the context, including helping to define the sense of community and to project its set of values and attitudes. (p. 189)

Those in teacher education and adolescent literacy and writing research would do well to heed this field of research as it affects their endeavors. Given the fact that more than half of the workforce today is composed of employees *without* college degrees, what is gained in high school will have a large impact on these individuals' on-the-job performance, which in turn influences the economy and the quality of life for U.S. workers. Literacy education is as important in vocational education as it is in academic and professional programs.

Several decades of research in composition and rhetoric, as well as the literature in cognitive psychology on transfer of learning, have confirmed that most knowledge and skill sets are particular to specific discourse communities and do not readily aid writers when they encounter new contexts for writing. To that end, teaching a narrow set of literacy skills particular to high school literacy tasks or exams does not adequately prepare students to learn and be productive writers in contexts beyond high school So, from what I know of typical curricular initiatives in high school English, the constraints imposed by the literacy skills assessed in state-mandated tests, and the kinds of writing tasks that workers in the 21st century are doing, I urge the following for those responsible for both curriculum design and assessment of writing proficiencies in school:

- Greater emphasis on skills in close reading of nonfiction texts—a range of business, journalistic, scientific genres (this means a less literature-rich curriculum but by no means excludes the teaching of literature).
- More teaching and testing devoted to skills in organizing information into hierarchies on the basis of audience needs or logic (i.e., move beyond reporting or narrating) and addressing varied needs of different audiences.
- Greater emphasis on writing in nonfiction genres, beyond the genres of literary analysis or personal narrative or the information report (for example, emphasis on rhetorical analysis of nonfiction and researched arguments).
- Increased attention to development of independent, critical analysis of sources and information (rather than opinion-based essays or factual recall of material).
- Expanded opportunities to introduce or use new technologies for communications in both academic and vocational classes.
- Greater inclusion of group process skills in the design of collaborative projects where technology, class size, and task warrant group work.

These skills, a departure from those used in a heavily literature-based or fact-based instructional paradigm in English studies, can move students a lot farther across the bridge from school to workplace forms of literate behavior. Students need practice analyzing a range of types of texts and writing in a range of genres and using a range of media. Most important, they need meta-awareness of how writing functions in particular social contexts and how the writing process can be manipulated to meet particular demands of time and place. If they grasp this larger view of writing beyond the English classroom, they will be better equipped to improve their writing skills over the many phases and aspects of their adult lives in the workplace.

REFERENCES

Albers, M. J., & Lisberg, B. C. (2002). Information design: A bibliography. *Technical Communication, 170*–176.

Allen, N. J. (1993). Community, collaboration, and the rhetorical triangle. *Technical Communication Quarterly, 2,* 63–74.

Anson, C. M., & Forsberg, L. L. (1990). Moving beyond the academic community: Transitional stages in professional writing. *Written Communication, 7,* 200–231.

Applebee, A. N., Langer, J. L., Mullis, I. V. S., Lathan, A. S., & Gentile, C. A. (1994). *NAEP 1992 writing report card* (No. 23-W01). Washington, DC: Office of Educational Research and Improvement, U.S. Department of Education.

Barker, R. T., & Zifcak, L. (1999). Communication and gender in workplace 2000: Creating a contextually-based integrated paradigm. *Journal of Technical Writing and Communication, 29,* 335–347.

Baron, N. S. (2000). *Alphabet to email: How written English evolved and where it's headed.* New York: Routledge.

Bazerman, C. (1981). What written knowledge does: Three examples of academic discourse. *Philosophy of the Social Sciences, 2,* 361–387.

Bazerman, C. (1982). Scientific writing as a social act. In P. Anderson (Ed.), *New essays in technical and scientific communication* (pp. 156–184). Farmingdale, NY: Baywood.

Bazerman, C. (1988). *Shaping written knowledge: The genre and activity of the experimental article in science.* Madison, WI: University of Wisconsin Press.

Bazerman, C. (1994a). *Constructing experience.* Carbondale: Southern Illinois University Press.

Bazerman, C. (1994b). Systems of genres and the enactment of social intentions. In A. Freedman & P. Medway (Eds.), *Genre and the new rhetoric* (pp. 79–100). London: Taylor & Francis.

Beaufort, A. (1997). Operationalizing the concept of discourse community: A case study of one institutional site of composing. *Research in the Teaching of English, 31,* 486–529.

Beaufort, A. (1999). *Writing in the real world: Making the transition from school to work.* New York: Teachers College Press.

Beaufort, A. (2000). Learning the trade: A social apprenticeship model for gaining writing expertise. *Written Communication, 17,* 185–223.

Berkenkotter, C. (2001). Genre systems at work: DSM-IV and rhetorical recontextualization in psychotherapy paperwork. *Written Communication, 18,* 326–349.

Berkenkotter, C., & Huckin, T. N. (1995). *Genre knowledge in disciplinary communication: Cognition/culture/power.* Mahwah, NJ: Erlbaum.

Bernhardt, S. A. (1986). Seeing the text. *College Composition and Communication, 37,* 66–78.

Bernhardt, S. A. (1993). The shape of texts to come: The texture of print on screens. *College Composition and Communication, 44,* 151–175.

Blakeslee, A. M. (2001). *Interacting with audiences: Social influences on the production of scientific writing.* Mahwah, NJ: Erlbaum.

Boesel, D., & Fredland, E. (1999). *College for all?: Is there too much emphasis on getting a four-year degree?* Washington, DC: National Library of Education.

Bracewell, R. J., & Witte, S. P. (2003). Tastes, ensembles, and activity: Linkages between text production and situation of use in the workplace. *Written Communication, 20,* 511–559.

Broadhead, G. J., & Freed, R. C. (1986). *The variables of composition: Process and product in a business setting.* Carbondale: Southern Illinois University Press.

Brown, R. L., & Herndl, C. G. (1986). An ethnographic study of corporate writing: Job status as reflected in written text. In B. Couture (Ed.), *Functional approaches to writing: Research perspectives* (pp. 11–28). London: Frances Pinter.

Brumburger, E. R. (2002). The rhetoric of typography: The persona of typeface and text. *Technical Communication, 50,* 224–231.

Cook-Gumperz, J., & Hanna, K. (1997). Nurses' work, women's work: Some recent issues of professional literacy and practice. In G. Hull (Ed.), *Changing work, changing workers: Critical perspectives on language, literacy, and skills* (pp. 316–334). Albany, NY: SUNY Press.

Cope, B., & Kalantzis, M. (Eds.). (2000). *Multiliteracies: Literacy learning and the design of social futures.* New York: Routledge.

Couture, B., & Rymer, J. (1993). Situational exigence: Composing processes on the job by writer's role and task value. In R. Spilka (Ed.), *Writing in the workplace: New research perspectives* (pp. 4–20). Carbondale: Southern Illinois University Press.

Dautermann, J. (1996). Writing with electronic tools in midwestern businesses. In P. Sullivan & J. Dautermann (Eds.), *Electronic literacies in the workplace: Technologies of writing* (pp. 3–22). Urbana, IL: National Council of Teachers of English.

Devitt, A. J. (1991). Intertextuality in tax accounting: Generic, referential, and functional. In C. Bazerman & J. Paradis (Eds.), *Textual dynamics of the professions: Historical and contemporary studies of writing in professional communities* (pp. 336–357). Madison: University of Wisconsin Press.

Dias, P., Freedman, A., Medway, P., & Paré, A. (1999). *Worlds apart: Acting and writing in academic and workplace contexts.* Mahwah, NJ: Erlbaum.

Doheny-Farina, S. (1986). Writing in an emerging organization. *Written Communication, 3,* 158–185.

Doheny-Farina, S. (1989). A case study of one adult writing in academic and nonacademic discourse communities. In C. B. Matalene (Ed.), *Worlds of writing: Teaching and learning in discourse communities of work* (pp. 17–42). New York: Random House.

Doheny-Farina, S. (1992). The individual, the organization, and kairos: Making transitions from college to careers. In S. P. Witte, N. Nakadate, & R. D. Cherry (Eds.), *A rhetoric of doing: Essays on written discourse in honor of James L. Kinneavy* (pp. 293–309). Carbondale: Southern Illinois University Press.

Dorff, D. L., & Duin, A. H. (1989). Applying a cognitive model to document cycling. *Technical Writing Teacher, 16,* 234–249.

Fahnestock, J. (1986). Accommodating science: The rhetorical life of scientific facts. *Written Communication, 3,* 275–296.

Fahnestock, J., & Secor, M. (1991). The rhetoric of literary criticism. In C. Bazerman & J. Paradis (Eds.), *Textual dynamics of the professions: Historical and contemporary studies of writing in professional communities* (pp. 76–96). Madison: University of Wisconsin Press.

Faigley, L., & Miller, T. P. (1982). What we learn from writing on the job. *College English, 44,* 555–569.

Flower, L., & Hayes, J. R. (1981). A cognitive process theory of writing. *College Composition and Communication, 32,* 365–387.

Fortune, R. (1989). Visual and verbal thinking: Drawing and word processing in writing instruction. In G. E. Hawisher & C. L. Selfe (Eds.), *Critical perspectives on computers and composition instruction* (pp. 145–161). New York: Teachers College Press.

Freedman, A., & Adam, C. (2000). Write where you are: Learning to write in university and workplace settings. In P. Dias & A. Paré (Eds.), *Transitions: Writing in academic and workplace settings* (pp. 31–60). Cresskill, NJ: Hampton.

Gee, J. P. (1989). Literacy, discourse, and linguistics: Introduction. *Journal of Education, 171,* 5–17.

Gee, J. P. (2000). The new literacy studies: From "socially situated" to the work of the social. In D. Barton, M. Hamilton, & R. Ivanic (Eds.), *Situated literacies: Reading and writing in context* (pp. 180–196). New York: Routledge.

Gee, J. P. (2003). *What video games have to teach us about learning and literacy.* New York: Palgrave Macmillan.

Geisler, C. (2001). Textual objects: Accounting for the role of texts in the everyday life of complex organizations. *Written Communication, 18,* 296–325.

Gimenez, J. C. (2000). Business e-mail communication: Some emerging tendencies in register. *English for Specific Purposes, 19,* 237–251.

Gladwell, M. (2002, March 25). The social life of paper: Looking for method in the mess. *The New Yorker, 78,* 92–96.

Gowan, S. G. (1992). *The politics of workforce literacy: A case study.* New York: Teachers College Press.

Haas, C. (1989). Seeing it on the screen isn't really seeing it: Computer writers' reading problems. In G. E. Hawisher & C. L. Selfe (Eds.), *Critical perspectives on computers and composition* (pp. 16–29). New York: Teachers College Press.

Hart-Landsberg, S., & Reder, S. (1997). Teamwork and literacy: Teaching and learning at Hardy Industries. In G. Hull (Ed.), *Changing work, changing workers: Critical perspectives on language, literacy, and skills* (pp. 350–382). Albany, NY: SUNY Press.

Harwood, J. T. (1982). Freshman English ten years after: Writing in the world. *College Composition and Communication, 33,* 281–283.

Henry, J. (1995). Workplace ghostwriting. *Journal of Business and Technical Communication, 9,* 425–445.

Herndl, C. C., Fennel, B. A., & Miller, C. R. (1991). Understanding failures in organizational discourse: The accident at Three Mile Island and the shuttle *Challenger* disaster. In C. Bazerman & J. Paradis (Eds.), *Textual dynamics of the professions: Historical and contemporary studies of writing in professional communities* (pp. 279–395). Madison: University of Wisconsin Press.

Horton, W. (1991). Is hypertext the best way to document your product? An assay for designers. *Technical Communication Quarterly, 38,* 20–32.

Horton, W. (1993). The almost universal language: Graphics for international documents. *Technical Communication, 40,* 682–693.

Hovde, M. R. (2001). Research tactics for constructing perceptions of subject matter in organizational contexts: An ethnographic study of technical communicators. *Technical Communication Quarterly, 10,* 59–95.

Hull, G. (Ed.). (1997). *Changing work, changing workers: Critical perspectives on language, literacy, and skills.* Albany, NY: SUNY Press.

Hull, G., & Schultz, K. (2001). Literacy and learning out of school: A review of theory and research. *Review of Educational Research, 71,* 575–611.

Johns, L. C. (1989). The file cabinet has a sex life: Insights of a professional writing consultant. In C. B. Matalene (Ed.), *Worlds of writing: Teaching and learning in discourse communities of work* (pp. 153–187). New York: Random House.

Jolliffe, D. (1997). Finding yourself in the text: Identity formation in the discourse of workplace documents. In G. Hull (Ed.), *Changing work, changing workers: Critical perspectives on language, literacy, and skills* (pp. 335–349). Albany, NY: SUNY Press.

Jorn, L. A. (1993). A selected annotated bibliography on collaboration in technical communication. *Technical Communication Quarterly, 2,* 105–115.

Kaestle, C. F., Campbell, A., Finn, J. D., Johnson, S. T., & Mikulecky, L. J. (2001). *Adult literacy and education in America.* Jessup, MD: U.S. Department of Education, Office of Educational Research and Improvement.

Katz, S. M. (1998). *The dynamics of writing review: Opportunities for growth and change in the workplace* (Vol. 5). Stamford, CT: Ablex.

Killingsworth, M. J., & Gilbertson, M. K. (1992). *Signs, genres, and communities in technical communication.* Amityville, NY: Baywood.

Lave, J., & Wenger, E. (1991). *Situated learning: Legitimate peripheral participation.* New York: Cambridge University Press.

Lutz, J. A. (1987). A study of professional and experienced writers revising and editing at the computer and with pen and paper. *Research in the Teaching of English, 21,* 398–421.

Mabrito, M. (1997). Writing on the front line: A study of workplace writing. *Business Communication Quarterly, 60,* 58–70.

McCarthy, L. (1991). A psychiatrist using DSM-III: The influence of a charter document in psychiatry. In C. Bazerman & J. Paradis (Eds.), *Textual dynamics of the professions: Historical and contemporary studies of writing in professional communities* (pp. 358–377). Madison: University of Wisconsin Press.

McCarthy, L., & Gerrig, J. (1994). Revising psychiatry's charter document, DSM-IV. *Written Communication, 11,* 147–192.

McIsaac, C., & Aschauer, M. A. (1990). Proposal writing at Atherton Jordan, Inc. *Management Communication Quarterly, 3,* 527–560.

Medway, P. (2000). Writing and design in architectural education. In P. Dias & A. Paré (Eds.), *Transitions: Writing in academic and workplace settings* (pp. 89–128). Creskill, NJ: Hampton.

Murray, D. E. (1987). Requests at work: Negotiating the conditions for conversation. *Management Communication Quarterly, 1,* 58–83.

Myers, G. (1985). The social construction of two biologists' proposals. *Written Communication, 2,* 219–245.

Nystrand, M. (1986). *The structure of written communication: Studies in reciprocity between writers and readers.* Orlando, FL: Academic Press.

Odell, L., Goswami, D., Herrington, A., & Quick, D. (1983). Studying writing in non-academic settings. In P. B. Anderson, R. J. Brockman, & C. R. Miller (Eds.), *New essays in technical and scientific communication: Research, theory, practice* (Vol. 2, pp. 17–40). Farmingdale, NY: Baywood.

Olsen, L. A. (1993). Research on discourse communities: An overview. In R. Spilka (Ed.), *Writing in the workplace: New research perspectives* (pp. 181–194). Carbondale: Southern Illinois University Press.

Orlikowski, W. J., & Yates, J. A. (1994). Genre repertoire: The structuring of communicative practices in organizations. *Administrative Science Quarterly, 39,* 541–574.

Paré, A. (2000). Writing as a way into social work: Genre sets, genre. In P. Dias & A. Paré (Eds.), *Tran-*

sitions: Writing in academic and workplace settings (pp. 145–166). Cresskill, NJ: Hampton.

Paul, D., & Charney, D. (1995). Introducing chaos (theory) into science and engineering. *Written Communication, 12,* 396–438.

Redish, J. C. (2000). What is information design? *Technical Communication, 47,* 163–166.

Rose, M. (2003). Words in action: Rethinking workplace literacy. *Research in the Teaching of English, 38,* 125–128.

Russell, D. R. (1995). Activity theory and its implications for writing instruction. In J. Pegralia (Ed.), *Reconceiving writing, rethinking writing instruction* (pp. 51–77). Mahwah, NJ: Erlbaum.

Russell, D. R. (1997). Rethinking genre in school and society: An activity theory analysis. *Written Communication, 14,* 504–554.

Sauer, B. (1994). The dynamics of disaster: A 3 dimensional view of a tightly regulated industry. *Technical Communication Quarterly, 3,* 393–419.

Schriver, K. A. (1989). Document design from 1980 to 1989: Challenges that remain. *Technical Communication Quarterly, 36,* 316–333.

Schriver, K. A. (1997). *Dynamics in document design.* New York: Wiley.

Schryer, C. F. (1993). Records as genre. *Written Communication, 10,* 200–234.

Schryer, C. F. (2000). Walking a fine line: Writing negative letters in an insurance company. *Journal of Business and Technical Communication, 14,* 445–497.

Schumacher, G. M., Scott, B. T., Klare, G. R., Cronin, F. C., & Lambert, D. A. (1989). Cognitive processes in journalistic genres: Extending writing models. *Written Communication, 6,* 390–407.

Segal, J. Z. (1993). Writing and medicine: Text and context. In R. Spilka (Ed.), *Writing in the workplace: New research perspectives* (pp. 84–97). Carbondale: Southern Illinois University Press.

Sellen, A. J., & Harper, R. H. R. (2002). *The myth of the paperless office.* Cambridge, MA: MIT Press.

Selzer, J. (1993). Intertextuality and the writing process: An overview. In R. Spilka (Ed.), *Writing in the workplace: New research perspectives* (pp. 171–180). Carbondale: Southern Illinois University Press.

Sims, B. R. (1996). Electronic mail in two corporate workplaces. In P. Sullivan & J. Dautermann (Eds.), *Electronic literacies in the workplace: Technologies of writing* (pp. 41–64). Urbana, IL: National Council of Teachers of English.

Smagorinsky, P., Cook, L. S., & Reed, P. (2005). The construction of meaning and identity in the composition and reading of an architectural text. *Reading Research Quarterly, 40,* 70–88.

Smagorinsky, P., Pettis, V., & Reed, P. (2004). High school students' compositions of ranch designs: Implications for academic and personal achievement. *Written Communication, 21,* 386–418.

Smagorinsky, P., Zoss, M., & Reed, P. M. (2006). Residential interior design as complex composition: A case study of a high school senior's composing process. *Written Communication, 23,* 295–330.

Smart, G. (1993). Genre as community invention: A central bank's response to its executives' expectations as readers. In R. Spilka (Ed.), *Writing in the workplace: New research perspectives* (pp. 124–140). Carbondale: Southern Illinois University Press.

Smart, G. (2000). Reinventing expertise: Experienced writers in the workplace encounter a new genre. In P. Dias & A. Paré (Eds.), *Transitions: Writing in academic and workplace settings* (pp. 223–252). Cresskill, NJ: Hampton.

Spilka, R. (1988). Studying writer–reader interactions in the workplace. *Technical Writing Teacher, 15,* 208–221.

Spooner, M., & Yancey, K. (1996). Postings on a genre of email. *College Composition and Communication, 47,* 252–278.

Stygall, G. (1991). Texts in oral context: The "transmission" of jury instructions in an Indiana trial. In C. Bazerman & J. Paradis (Eds.), *Textual dynamics in the professions: Historical and contemporary studies of writing in professional communities* (pp. 234–253). Madison: University of Wisconsin Press.

Swales, J. M. (1990). *Genre analysis: English in academic and research settings.* New York: Cambridge University Press.

Swales, J. M. (1992, April). *Re-thinking genre: Another look at discourse community effects.* Paper presented at the Carleton University Conference on Genre, Ottawa, Canada.

Tebeaux, E. (1990). Toward an understanding of gender differences in written business communications: A suggested perspective for future research. *Journal of Business and Technical Communication, 4,* 25–43.

U. S. Census Bureau. (2006). *Statistical abstracts of the United States 2006.* Washington, DC: Author. Retrieved June 12, 2007, from *www.census.gov/prod/www/statistical-abstract.html.*

Wenger, M. J., & Payne, D. G. (1994). Effects of graphical browser on readers' efficiency in reading hypertext. *Technical Communications, 41,* 224–233.

Winsor, D. (1993). Owning corporate texts. *Journal of Business and Technical Communication, 7,* 179–195.

Witte, S. P. (1988, September). *Some contexts for understanding written literacy.* Paper presented at the Right to Literacy Conference presented by the Modern Language Association, Columbus, OH.

Witte, S. P. (1992). Context, text, intertext: Toward a constructivist semiotic of writing. *Written Communication, 9,* 237–308.

Witte, S. P., & Haas, C. (2001). Writing as an embodied practice: The case of engineering standards. *Journal of Business and Technical Communication, 15,* 413–457.

Yates, J. A. (1989). *Control through communication: The rise of system in American management.* Baltimore: Johns Hopkins University Press.

Yates, J. A., & Orlikowski, W. J. (1992). Genres of organizational communication: A structurational approach to studying communication and media. *Academy of Management Review, 17,* 299–326.

Yates, J. A., Orlikowski, W. J., & Okamura, K. (1999). Explicit and implicit structuring of genres in electronic communication: Reinforcement and change of social interaction. *Organization Science, 10,* 83–103.

Zimmerman, B. B., & Schultz, J. R. (2000). A study of the effectiveness of information design principles applied to clinical research questionnaires. *Technical Communication, 47,* 177–194.

CHAPTER 17

The Literacy Demands
of Entering the University

KATHLEEN BLAKE YANCEY

This chapter takes up the two expressions defining the title—"literacy demands" and "entering the university"—to map the currently fluid situation where demands can range from a willingness to earn a GED at a community college to the ability to demonstrate in fluent, well-organized language a knowledge of cultural capital assumed to provide a foundation for collegiate-level reading and writing. Complicating this already complex situation are two additional factors. First, the sites where college literacy is transacted have multiplied so that defining college literacy apart from other literacies is impossible. Second, the preferred version of sites privileged by many postsecondary institutions seems increasingly at odds with the "unschooled" practices of electronic composing. In sum, *literacy* in the postsecondary context is a dynamic term located in very different practices, and in this case the postsecondary world has in general neither acknowledged the value of extracurricular compositions nor incorporated them into the curriculum. At the same time, there still seems to be widespread agreement among college faculty that what entering college students need to be able to do, in David Bartholomae's (1985) terms, is to invent both a university culture and themselves inside that culture. This invention requires the ability to read and use texts, to employ an elaborated writing process in the construction of "academic" texts where argument is a preferred genre, and to reflect on and improve one's writing, often in the company of one's peers. Where students do not participate in a first-year composition course of some kind, they lag behind their peers who do. In conclusion, although college literacy may variously be defined and may be taught at many sites, for it to count as college literacy, it involves a culture of composing, reading, thinking, and revisioning—of writing and of student.

One hundred years ago, as many scholars have documented (Crowley, 1998; Yancey, 2006), the university was a place clearly defined, and the literacies valued in this place were likewise clearly defined. At that moment, postsecondary education—sometimes taking the form of a university, other times a college, but nearly always a four-year school— was the place that 18-year-olds went to complete what was likely to be a liberal arts education. The student population was almost overwhelmingly White and male. Preparation for the students' collegiate experience included healthy doses of canonical literature, especially British literature of the early modern period and before: Chaucer,

Shakespeare, and Milton. The ability of students to write well was assumed, as indicated by a dearth of so-called remedial or basic writing course offerings, which weren't available because they weren't understood to be necessary, and as indicated by writing classes that focused not on writing but on the consumption of literature. The literacy demands in such a world were predictable, narrow, and consistent.

Today the literacy demands of postsecondary education are varied, and tricky to map. More specifically, the task of identifying them is complicated by two fundamental factors: (1) the number and diversity of sites where such postsecondary literacy instruction occurs and (2) the definitions of literacy that obtain in each. The one place of 100 years ago has morphed into a dizzying array of options: the now ubiquitous community college, home to students pursuing one of three tracks (transfer, Associate degree, vocational); historical and recently invented liberal arts colleges (i.e., Century College); the comprehensive university, often regionally based; the leading state public research (R1) university (which in states such as California is a group of institutions, i.e., the University of California campuses); its first cousin the land and/or sea grant institution (although in some states the leading R1 also has this status; e. g., the University of Illinois); and its second cousin, the private research institution, all of which latter institutions are focused on research as much as on teaching; and a relatively new institution, the for-profit college or university, taking both physical and online forms. Moreover, a closer look suggests that postsecondary education is a misnomer. For many high school students, postsecondary education actually occurs *during* high school in state or locally sanctioned dual enrollment programs, in nationally administered Advanced Placement programs, and in internationally governed International Baccalaureate programs. In a neat case of double-dipping, students in such programs can gain college credits for high school work.

Not surprisingly, the site of postsecondary education has everything to do with the literacy demands made on students. Again, the practices map very different notions of literacy. One set of practices obtains within the high school setting, and even there practices vary. At one end of the spectrum, the Advanced Placement testing mechanism offers a kind of uniformity unavailable elsewhere, and at the other end, dual enrollment programs include university-affiliated programs (Farris, 2006), ad hoc programs (Bodmer, 2006), and state-sanctioned programs such as those described by the Missouri Colloquium on Writing Assessment (1995). This colloquium, founded as a network for communication on postsecondary writing assessment issues, responded to concerns about dual-enrollment classes by creating a policy statement to govern such offerings. It begins with the statement, "College faculty should teach all dual-credit composition courses," but moves immediately to identifying the practices recommended for high school offerings that may "count" for college.

A second set of practices operates within the community college context, where literacy demands are tiered according to a readiness for reading and writing. Yet a third set operates within 4-year schools, where students may engage in at least one (and possibly two) of three activities connected to admission and/or placement in appropriate first-year composition courses: (1) composing an application essay, (2) completing a placement exercise for composition course placement, and (3) completing a "Directed Self-Placement" (DSP) activity (which takes different forms at different institutions), allowing students to identify for themselves the appropriate beginning course level for composition. Each of these exercises privileges a different dimension of academic literacy. As a result, for many students, even *before* they have enrolled in a postsecondary institution, postsecondary literacy demands have begun.

Once *in* college, students find a parallel universe of diverse literacy demands, but within competing imperatives, certain themes emerge. Such themes appear in the Writing Program Administrators (WPA) Outcomes Statement for First Year Composition (FYC), for example, adopted by the Council of Writing Program Administrators in 2000. The effort to develop such national outcomes for college writing was the first of its kind, created by faculty from different institutional types working together. As explained in the preliminary remarks, the document's intent is to describe the common knowledge, skills, and attitudes sought by first-year composition programs in American postsecondary education. To some extent, we seek to regularize what can be expected to be taught in first-year composition; to this end the document is not merely a compilation or summary of what currently takes place. Rather, the following statement articulates what composition teachers nationwide have learned from practice, research, and theory. This document intentionally defines only "outcomes," or types of results, and not "standards," or precise levels of achievement. The setting of standards should be left to specific institutions or specific groups of institutions. (*wpacouncil.org/positions/outcomes.html*)

The outcomes are organized into four fields—Rhetorical Knowledge; Critical Thinking, Reading, and Writing; Processes; and Knowledge of Conventions—and as will become evident, the key terms defining these fields are central to postsecondary academic literacy of nearly every definition. At the same time, a review of current research suggests that thinking of academic literacy in terms of themes that are more specific enables educators to speak more conclusively about what they know about such literacy, about the demands made on students, and about the ways the definition of such literacy is undergoing change. These themes include the following:

1. Students need to be able to develop a writing process that is adaptable across occasion, purpose, audience, and time.
2. Students need to be able to access, consume, interpret, and evaluate information, both in print and online.
3. Students need to be able to think critically.
4. Students need to self-assess and reflect on their own performance.
5. Students need to create new texts and, ideally, new knowledge.

Within these five themes, there lurk potential demands and associated issues, often but not always connected to electronic literacy. For example, although a newer electronic literacy related to writing—nearly all college courses in writing and reading require assignments to be word processed, for example, and sometimes submitted online—seems to be assumed; ordinarily it is neither directly taught nor assessed. More recently,

language and cultural theorists have spoken to the home literacy that students bring with them to school, identifying such literacy as both a resource and a strength. Moreover, at the same time that college students—who are both 16-year-old high school honor students and 56-year-old immigrants—are engaged in meeting "official" literacy demands, they are increasingly engaged in a wide range of self-sponsored online literacy activities, such as maintaining MySpace sites, text messaging, instant messaging and others, nearly all of which are typically absent from college curricula, but which are key to a successful education for the 21st century (Prensky, 2005/2006).

POSTSECONDARY LITERACY IN HIGH SCHOOL

If college credits represent college literacy, then college literacy is delivered in high school. Two kinds of course and credit options exemplify different kinds of high-school-delivered postsecondary literacy: Advanced Placement (AP) and dual enrollment. In the case of AP, credits are awarded by the college where the student matriculates, although no college or university participates in the creation of AP exams, and it is the score on the exam that colleges use to award credit or exemption, or not. As is well known, there are two tests associated with AP English, one in literature, the other in language, and it is the latter that is typically used for substitution of first-year composition. The tests are similar in structure and design:

The two AP English examinations are similar in structure, both consisting of an hour's worth of multiple-choice questions and three essay questions, with forty minutes allotted to write each. The AP English Literature and Composition exam's multiple-choice questions test a student's ability to read poetry and fiction closely. Its three essay prompts call for students to write compositions that analyze the style and structure of fiction and poetry and explicate important themes manifest in novels and plays. On the AP English Language and Composition exam, the multiple-choice questions test a student's ability to read non-fiction prose closely. Its three essay prompts call for students to write compositions that analyze the rhetorical structure, technique, and style of prose passages and develop strong, cogent arguments of their own. (Jolliffe & Phelan, 2007, p. 91)

The difference between these exams and what gets taught in FYC is considerable, however, as the research by Hansen et al. (2004) makes clear. These authors documented the progress of students who substituted AP for FYC as compared with those who used AP as a *foundation* for FYC, demonstrating that students who attempt to replace college composition with high school AP scores, particularly those with a score of 3 (or even a 4), find themselves at a distinct disadvantage:

> Our results show that students who score a 3 on the AP exam and do not take a first year writing course are likely to suffer real consequences in sophomore courses that require writing assignments.... At BYU [Brigham Young University], as is likely true of most institutions, FYC provides an introduction to the discourse of the university, to a university library, and to genres of writing students have likely not encountered before. (p. 41)

The BYU study also states, "The students in our sample who performed best overall were those who combined a quality AP experience (as indicated by a 4 or 5 on the exam) with a first year writing course" (p. 40). In sum, what this research documents is that AP preparation assists students in developing a *readiness* to begin tackling the new literacy demands of college—those demands located in a *university discourse*, a *university library*, and *new genres*.

Dual enrollment is often understood as comparable to AP: like AP, it provides college credits to high school students for satisfactory work completed in high school. Moreover, recent research (e.g., Scherff & Piazza, 2005) suggests that the version of academic literacy delivered through dual enrollment more closely duplicates college academic literacy than does AP, at least in its attention to process. According to the 2,000 Florida high school students surveyed by Scherff and Piazza, the *only* students engaged in a full-process approach to writing, including multiple drafts and peer revision, were those enrolled in dual enrollment English classes. From this perspective, dual enrollment begins to sound like a possible facsimile of literacy instruction in postsecondary contexts.

Dual enrollment programs take a variety of forms, however, and often the college awarding credit exercises little or no control in the granting of credits for a course of study over which they have no control and in the design of which they have no input. Still, some programs do build in such a "bridging" feature intended to connect the two sites of education—for instance, the University of North Carolina Greensboro (UNCG) Fast Forward Program (*web.uncg. edu/dcl/web/fastforward/*) and the Indiana University dual enrollment program (Farris, 2006). The Indiana program, for example, brings instructors from the high school to the college so that the faculty members of the cultures can work *together*. In contrast Bodmer (2006) demonstrated how programs isolated from the college awarding credit fail to serve either the college student population or the high school population. Because high school students are required to complete a high school curriculum, whereas college students have already completed this curriculum and need an introduction to college writing, the instructor cannot help but serve the needs of one population at the expense of the other. Without the bridging culture provided in a program such as Indiana's, Bodmer contends, instructors cannot succeed. Data at the University of Arizona (UA) support this claim. Miller (2004) finds that dual enrollment programs at UA cannot substitute for postsecondary academic literacy experiences. He explains:

> We are continuing our research on dual enrollment programs. ... Thomas Kinney, a PhD student here, did a study of several thousand students' performance on our former mid-career writing assessment (a timed writing task). Dual enrollment students failed the assessment at a third higher rate [than did the students who completed composition on campus]. Some administrators did some additional research that they thought would mitigate this striking finding, but [the results] actually [confirmed] it. Their research found that the dual enrollment students also had lower verbal SATs and lower high school GPAs. When these factors were controlled, dual enrollment students still failed the writing assessment at a significantly higher rate. (*lists.asu.edu/cgi-bin/ wa?A2=ind0407&L=wpa-l&D=1&O=D&F= &S=&P=14017*)

Dual enrollment courses and AP exams thus claim to provide postsecondary academic literacy, but the research to date suggests that their more appropriate role is to prepare students to take on such challenges *in* college.

THE DEMANDS OF POSTSECONDARY ACADEMIC LITERACY AS STUDENTS ENTER COLLEGE

Community colleges were created in the early part of the 20th century, but the current *system* of community colleges was initiated after World War II, expanding during the 1960s and 1970s in the age of open admissions. Although many think of the community college mission as singular—that is, providing an opportunity to transfer to a 4-year school (Nash, 2007)—in fact community colleges typically assist students in achieving two other aims: a vocational certificate or an Associate degree. In addition, many community colleges enable students who have not completed high school to gain a GED. Accordingly, the literacy demands students encounter in the community college setting vary dramatically and are rife with contradiction, as Curry (2003) explains: "Basic writing is intended to prepare students to pass tests that certify equivalence to secondary (high school) education, enroll in college transfer courses including freshman composition, or enter vocational training programs" (p. 5).

The one constant in this kind of system is that students, regardless of program, typically take a placement test that determines the appropriate entry course, so community college literacy demands include a test-taking capacity. But more generally, community colleges aim to assist students where they are and help them develop the literacy specified within the particular program—passing the GED exam, for instance, which in theory is a demonstration not of postsecondary literacy, but rather of secondary literacy. Basic writing classes are intended, likewise, to demonstrate readiness for mainstream courses, whose completion is assumed to be equivalent to completion of parallel courses offered in 4-year institutions. That assumption, of course, can mask a good deal of difference.

In cases where students are transferring, however, they are required to meet the same demands as their 4-year-school counterparts, especially in states such as Arizona, where 2- and 4-year schools are governed by an articulation agreement assuring equivalence among such courses. Large institutionally based studies (e.g., Patthey-Chavez, Thomas-Spiegel, & Dillon, 1998) suggest that students who self-identify as transfer students, who at 20% are low in the overall population, are successful at the same rate as native students once they are in a 4-year school. Moreover, in some states (e.g., Washington, Georgia, and Florida), all college graduates are required to pass a test of literacy, which often combines reading and writing. In the case of Florida, 2-year students are required to take the test, which is called the College Level Academic Skills Test (CLAST), although students at 4-year schools can waive the test with a satisfactory grade.

When students apply to and enroll in 4-year schools, they engage in a number of activities that place literacy demands on them; three in particular are connected to postsecondary literacy. The first is completing the college application essay. When students apply to 4-year schools, they typically write a personal essay that accompanies the college application. In addition to completing a well-edited, coherent statement—on topics that range from personal goals to analysis of public issues—students need that text to perform what Paley (1996) calls a "rhetorical paradox," that is, to adopt a rhetorical stance entailing both risk and relaxation. Paley, working with college admissions officers using a read-aloud protocol as they reviewed college application essays, was able to discern differences between successful and unsuccessful writers based *not* on stated criteria, but rather on what she identified as "emotional literacy":

> Applications ask that students engage in a rhetorical paradox: take a risk and disclose some aspect of their personal lives in what becomes a test of "emotional literacy." The institutional request for personal writing for an unknown audience with hidden criteria is one that immediately puts the student in his or her place in the academy. Furthermore, the injunction "to relax" conceals a deep institutional concern about mechanical correctness. Successful es-

sayists are able to compromise with a kind of rhetorical counterparadox that precludes surrender of power and that balances the forces that call for self-exposure and those that "devour" the results. (p. 85)

In other words, with the admonition "to relax" framing the task, it would be easy for students to believe that formal properties such as mechanical correctness didn't matter—when such correctness and formality are both expected and rewarded by admissions officers.

A second activity related to postsecondary literacy occurring before official matriculation is the placement essay used by many institutions to locate entering students in the appropriate composition course. In community colleges, such a test tends to take the form of a multiple-choice measure, but at 4-year schools, locally or systemwide, such a test tends to take the form of a holistically scored impromptu essay. Sometimes the essay prompt asks students to write on a topic deriving from their own experience, and in other situations, students use reading material as the content of the essay. Typical is the exercise staged by the Cal Poly Pomona University Writing Center (n. d.), where the following criteria define the accomplished text:

A 6 essay is superior writing, but may have minor flaws. A typical essay in this category: a. addresses the topic clearly and responds effectively to all aspects of the task; b. demonstrates a thorough critical understanding of the passage in developing an insightful response; c. explores the issues thoughtfully and in depth; d. is coherently organized and developed, with ideas supported by apt reasons and well-chosen examples; e. has an effective, fluent style marked by syntactic variety and a clear command of language [; and] f. is generally free from errors in grammar, usage, and mechanics. (*www.csupomona.edu/~uwc/non_protect/student/CSU-EPTScoringGuide.htm*)

In practice, such an essay, much like the SAT "writing" test (which gains two-thirds of its score from a multiple-choice test of grammar and mechanics: see the National Council of Teachers of English Task Force on SAT and ACT Writing Tests, 2005), is rewarded according to the identified criteria. However, as the Sullivan (1997) study has shown, the "cultural capital" in such an essay accounts for higher scores. In other words, essays that are similar otherwise—in terms of focus, organization, development, and so forth—are awarded different scores, with the essays citing canonical references—"the authors of great literary works, the dates of important historical events, and the authors of famous quotations" (p. 68)—"earning" higher scores. The suggestion thus is that raters aren't scoring texts so much as "evaluating the social identities constructed in student texts" (p. 74). For these students, academic literacy requires a sophisticated identification with an unknown reader expressed through a canonical knowledge not explicitly acknowledged in the scoring guide.

The third and final activity related to postsecondary literacy occurring before matriculation is another version of placement assessment called Directed Self-Placement (DSP), a self-assessment practice by which students decide for themselves which first-year composition course is appropriate after being informed about their options (Royer & Gilles, 2003). Some evidence suggests that such systems can work effectively; Blakesley, Harvey, and Reynolds (2003), for instance, developed a DSP procedure allowing students to choose their own best placements into first-year composition. In terms of both pass rates and retention, students who placed themselves into a longer version of a basic writing course outperformed their nonbasic colleagues who had placed themselves in a standard, shorter course. This research suggests another dimension of academic literacy: a kind of intrapersonal composing knowledge. More specifically, it includes the ability to gauge one's development in writing and to use that benchmark as a means of identifying the next steps in development supported by a specific course.

Taken together, these three activities, typically completed before the first day of the first college course, suggest other dimensions of literacy important for college success: writing to unarticulated demands of a task and assessing accurately one's writerly strengths and weaknesses in a particular institutional context. Once *in* college, students face five major literacy demands, some well documented, others in process.

FIVE THEMES
OF POSTSECONDARY LITERACY

Theme One: Processes
and Novice-ship

Bartholomae (1985) described the literacy task of every entering college student as "inventing" the university "by assembling and mimicking its language" (p. 135). At some level the task has always been so: The *specifics* are what change. When efforts in composition research and theory began in earnest in the 1970s and 1980s, inventing the university meant, in large part, inventing a writing process characterized by multiple drafts and an elaborated revision process in order to write a personal essay. This enthusiasm for process pedagogy, however, had peaked by the late 1980s, as Lindemann (2002) shows. In its place, as Bartholomae (1985) suggests, is the need to do more than create one's own composing process. Such process and the texts it produces are part of a larger discourse, in this case, as noted in the Hansen et al. (2004) research on AP, the discourse of the university. Put differently, Bartholomae observes that a student's first literacy demand is to invent a university culture and (then) to locate him- or herself inside that culture. This invention, in his terms, requires an ability to read and use texts in an elaborated writing process focused on the construction of "academic" texts where argument is a preferred genre. Evidence of three kinds—survey, document and text review, and qualitative longitudinal studies—supports Bartholomae's claim.

Several recent surveys purport to represent the expectations of various stakeholders of both high school and college writing, and often these reports paint a picture of academic literacy as reductive. For example, American College Testing (ACT, 2003) claims that "among six general writing skills categories, grammar and usage skills rank highest in terms of importance at the college level" (*www.act.org/news/releases/2003/4-08-03.html*). It is fair to note, however, that the six categories include redundancies—grammar and usage, sentence structure, writing strategy, organization, punctuation, and style—and do not allow respondents to construct writing in a more capacious way. In other words, given the survey choices, faculty cannot express their valuing of rhetorical matters such as attention to audience or selection of evidence, the processes writers employed, and/or the writer's awareness and understanding of writing, especially as embodied in a particular text.

Other data paint a very different picture. The only large-scale survey detailing the ways that first-year composition is taught by writing teachers and permitting more commodious responses is by Yancey, Fishman, Gresham, Neal, and Taylor (2005). Its intent is to provide an accurate picture of the kinds of literacy demands students in higher education face, at least as understood by the faculty who assist students in understanding and then meeting these demands. The survey included seven areas of inquiry: institutions where faculty teach, the faculty themselves, curriculum, pedagogy, assessment, technology, and changing practices. Distributed nationally, it drew more than 1,800 respondents—at all faculty ranks, including graduate students, and at all institutional types, including tribal colleges—who shared their accounts of curriculum design and teaching practices in all kinds of first-year composition courses, from first-year seminars to single-course offerings to multiple sequenced offerings.

In general, Yancey et al. (2005) found that first-year college academic literacy is embedded in academic argument, composed through a reiterative and reflective multidraft writing process. For example, the first salient question, which pertains to curricular approaches, asked respondents to identify the one or two curricular approaches they employ, from the following list of 10: modes/current traditional, expressivist, academic writing, argument, social epistemic, cultural studies, critical pedagogy, cognitive, "alt" (alternative) discourse, and digital composition/literacy. Overwhelmingly, respondents selected academic writing (57%) and argument (49%).

At the same time, interesting differences obtained between faculty members with different backgrounds. For example, those with an educational background in rhetoric and composition tended to emphasize invention and digital technology, whereas those with other educational backgrounds did not. (It is interesting to note that 15% of the respondents reported no educational background in English of any variety.) Nonetheless, from this perspective, a major literacy demand of college students, even in their first year of college, is the ability to compose academic writing and/or argument.

The second salient question focused on pedagogical practices; respondents were asked to choose the three most important pedagogical practices from a list of 14, including sequenced assignments, collaborative activities, work in invention, and others. Again, there was a consistent response, with faculty overwhelmingly identifying three pedagogical practices as the most important: writing process, revision, and reflection. Reading was also on the list and rated highly but did not appear as one of the top three choices. These results, then, suggest that inventing the university requires a commitment to a certain kind of composing process (elaborated and multidraft) in order to write within a narrow band of genres (argument or academic discourse).

Although taking a different methodological approach, Fulkerson (2005) points to conclusions congruent with Yancey et al.'s (2005) findings. In his study, Fulkerson puts into dialogue two collections of essays intended to prepare teachers of writing, published 20 years apart, as he tried to define the contemporary disciplinary center of rhetoric and composition. What he finds in the current talk of the ways to prepare teachers of writing, compared with that of 20 years ago, is twofold: (1) Composition isn't very unified as a field, and (2) where it is unified, it is focused exclusively on composing processes. All proponents of each of the "schools" Fulkerson identifies—expressivism, cultural/critical studies, and rhetorical approaches (themselves divided into argument, genre analysis, and academic discourse)—locate process at the center of their approach regardless of the priorities they claim. From this perspective, what Fulkerson concludes from scholarly texts focused on preparing faculty to teach writing matches the accounts of the faculty surveyed by Yancey et al. (2005) regarding how they teach writing: through process and assignments privileging a narrow band of genres, notably argument and academic discourse.

As important, however, Fulkerson makes a strong case based on his analysis that the center of composition courses includes more than writing: It includes reading, particularly the version of composition characterized as cultural and critical studies. In his view, such a reading-centered curriculum does not serve students well; attention that previously was given to processes supporting the development of writing, such as invention and peer review, seems increasingly to be given to the analysis of texts in what is almost a reiteration of the early days of freshman English. In other words, although called composition courses, the critical and cultural studies version of composition courses is, rather than a course in writing, a course in textual analysis.

Jolliffe (2007) expresses a different response to the role that reading plays in a college composition class, arguing that postsecondary university literacy demands a kind of "strong" and "complicated" reading of multiple texts and multiple kinds of texts, particularly of nonfiction texts (p. 479). At best, Jolliffe says, students may *begin* developing this ability to read in high school, a point made by Blau (2006) as well, but such literacy, Jolliffe (2007) claims, is fully developed only in college. He observes that the reading of nonfiction texts is central to collegiate academic literacy, with the preferred collegiate textual reading created by "constructive, connective, and active readers of all the material that comes their way" (p. 479), from manuals to biography. In addition, he claims that neither composition theory nor composition classroom practice has addressed this need properly. Jolliffe's response is anecdotal, as is Blau's, but together their views draw on more than 70 years of postsecondary teaching experience and accord well with Bartholomae's (1985) theory and with several longitudinal studies.

Sommers and Saltz (2004) put a face on Jolliffe's (2007) contentions in a longitudinal study investigating the "success" of the writing curriculum at Harvard University. The early writing courses that Harvard students take are rich with scholarly and academic texts and the reading of them. Thus, as part of their study, Sommers and Saltz document and address ways that students seek to make sense of an overwhelming amount of material they must read in order to write. What Sommers and Saltz (2004) also find, however, is that as important as learning how to read in a Jolliffean sense may be, even more important is the student's *disposition* toward the material itself and its uses. This finding has two components. First, the first-year student must willingly adopt the stance of a novice in a new world, one that demands more of his or her writing than was asked in high school, a stance fraught (admittedly) with uncertainty and ambiguity. Second, the student cannot write from a position of expertise, but must write *into* such expertise:

> Students need to immerse themselves in the material, get a sense of the parameters of their subjects, familiarize themselves with the kinds of questions asked of different sets of evidence, and have a stake in the answers before they can articulate analytical theses. (pp. 134–135)

First-year students, in this view, are novices "working on an expert's assignment" (p. 135). Students who were not successful in adopting this novice-as-expert stance, according to the study, did not fare as well as those who did; that is, they may have earned good grades and been graduated from Harvard, but they did not learn to "participate in the world of ideas," or as one student put it, to both "give and get" as a participant in a larger conversation (p. 141).

One objection to these findings might be that Harvard students constitute a very narrow subset of the population of college students, but other studies speak to one or more of Sommers and Saltz's (2004) findings. Carroll's (2002) longitudinal study at Pepperdine, for example, focused on the ways that students navigate the college's writing curriculum, drawing similar conclusions about the need for college students to adopt the stance of a novice, first as they move into college, and then again as they move into their majors. Likewise, Hansen et al.'s (2004) research on the efficacy of Advanced Placement speaks to the need for students to understand college writing, in Moffett's (1968) terms, as a new universe of discourse in which they are novices. From this perspective, university literacy demands require students both to begin as novices in a reiterative process and to understand their novice-ship in three contexts: writing, reading, and the exchange of ideas.

Finally, it is useful to hear from college students themselves as they glance back at what has made a difference to them as they have acquired academic literacy and what they define as literacy demands. Two studies

(Hilgers, Hussey, & Stitt-Bergh, 1999; Jarratt, Mack, & Watson, 2005) are particularly useful here. Conducted at the University of California at Irvine (UCI), Jarratt et al.'s study inquired into what students transferred from FYC into other writing contexts. Perhaps not surprisingly, the most important "take-away" was both the *idea* of writing process and its *practice*. Students reported that in their first-year composition course, they learned about writing as process, about writing as a mode of learning, and about ways to develop their own multidraft composing process, a process *adapted* over time and occasion:

> The UCI undergraduates in our study demonstrated a sophisticated understanding of, or at least familiarity with, their writing processes. The majority reported engaging in pre-writing, drafting, and revision, techniques they learned from their lower-level writing classes. When asked an open-ended question about their approach to writing, students referred to a range of strategies: "cloud and visual diagrams, the use of arrows to organize ideas, brainstorming, and free-writing exercises." Even those who eschewed a formal process and instead preferred "just to start writing" spoke of composing as a process. . . . A cognitive sciences major describes a . . . recursive and process-oriented approach to his writing: "Usually what I do is I will write and I will read through it and then I will write some more and then I will read the whole thing over again, and then if I remember something that I haven't put down, I will work it in. I have never written down an outline, I don't know why. I am writing and revising the whole time." Though these students may not produce discrete drafts for revision, they still view their writings as works-in-progress rather than finished products. (pp. 4–5)

Similar to the UCI study, the Hilgers et al. (1999) Manoa project is interested in the ways that students carry forward what they have learned in earlier contexts. More specifically, Hilgers et al. intend to answer two questions: (1) How does disciplinarity affect students' understanding of writing tasks? and (2)What do students nearing completion of the university's writing-intensive (WI) requirements report that they know about writing? The Manoa research findings correspond with those of both Sommers and Saltz (2004) and Jarratt et al. (2005). Like their counterparts at UCI, Manoa students carried forward what they had learned, adapting processes and approaches to suit the needs of differing rhetorical occasions. Similar to what Sommers and Saltz found at Harvard, what seems surprisingly important is the writer's disposition, in this case a kind of confidence directly related to efficacy in undertaking and completing literacy tasks:

> When we add up the findings from this study, the most prominent term in the sum is confidence—particularly students' confidence that they can deal with the writing requirements of their major and their chosen profession. The range and persistence of this finding quite frankly surprised us. . . . Yet when we look at the aggregate of student experience, we find that the confidence may have a substantial base. First, students have typically had to write in a variety of circumstances and for multiple real and hypothetical audiences. Second, students were either instructed in, or discovered on their own, different ways to go about doing these writing assignments. Third, they knew how to engage a variety of resources to solve writing problems. Fourth, our data also suggest that the students became adept using at least embryonic forms of rhetorical problem solving. [Although] assignment guidelines did not typically prompt students to "think rhetorically," . . . students did construct audiences (most prominently in professional and science courses), set goals, ask questions about arrangement, and, occasionally, select among alternative approaches. Fifth, students on the brink of graduation were engaged in writing assignments that they believed prepared them for future employment or an advanced degree: more than 80% of the students reported preparedness for writing in their chosen fields. (*www.mwp.hawaii.edu/epiphanies.htm*)

Another key factor, then, is the student's ability to project him- or herself into a writing future: to understand current writing assignments functioning as a bridge to future practice.

As interesting, the authors claim, these findings point up the differences between academic literacy as it is practiced in high school and in college:

> This [ability to write for a self-defined and valued purpose] was far more than Hussey et al. (1995) found when studying a parallel group of high-school students nearing graduation, whose sole rhetorical strategy was typically to "find out what the teacher wants and do that."

Also unlike high-school seniors, whose typical "resource" to guide writing was the model five-paragraph theme, students in this study, after multiple WI experiences, were looking to, and accessing, multiple resources. The very fact that they would consult more than one resource suggests that they were operating with rather sophisticated plans for accomplishing both their research and their writing assignments. (*www.mwp.hawaii.edu/epiphanies.htm*)

Considerable evidence, from a variety of data sources, demonstrates that students can expect to begin their college careers as novices in developing elaborate composing processes and in reading texts that will inform their own texts.

Theme Two: Sources and Evaluation of Information

First-year students routinely complete assignments calling for research. The ability to conduct research—sometimes field research but always library research, which is still the gold standard—is a postsecondary literacy demand, although it occurs more often in the second term of a two-term sequence than in the first. This literacy demand is changing, however, as electronic resources become ubiquitous and as plagiarism, given the easy electronic availability of multiple texts for copying and pasting, is constructed as more of a threat. In short, students need to be able to access, consume, interpret, and evaluate information, both in print and online, and the mechanisms for each are somewhat different. Exactly what this will mean in general is not entirely clear to the discipline or to the library supporting such efforts. A small group working on a revision of the WPA Outcomes Statement, for example, is suggesting a change in the kinds of research students should complete. The current outcomes specify research in print; the addition identifies researching electronically as well, through both library databases and informal electronic networks such as blogs.

The libraries supporting such efforts are themselves in the midst of an epistemological shift of seismic proportions. At a recent conference of the American Library Association, for example, George M. Needham, vice president for member services of the Online Computer Library Center, provided this analysis:

The librarian as information priest is as dead as Elvis. ... The whole "gestalt" of the academic library has been set up like a church ... with various parts of a reading room acting like "the stations of the cross," all leading up to the "altar of the reference desk," where "you make supplication and if you are found worthy, you will be helped." Libraries now, he says, need to adapt. (quoted in Jasik, 2007)

Suggestions include scheduling support services on a 24/7/365 basis rather than using schedules "set in 1963," and, interestingly, using the very electronic genres students are assumed to prefer—instant messaging and texting—when communicating with them. Not least, Needham notes the change at the center of this shift, one that has epistemological implications for everyone in the academy, including those specializing in literacy: "Look for ways to involve digital natives in designing library services and even providing them. 'Expertise is more important than credentials,' he said, even credentials such as library science degrees" (quoted in Jasik, 2007). The use of sources, after they have been properly vetted, is a literacy demand for early postsecondary students who increasingly are expected to work with electronic sources as well as those in print.

Theme Three: Critical Thinking

The relation between writing and thinking, much like that between writing and research, has been assumed; critical thinking (CT) is also a postsecondary literacy demand. Although CT appears in institutional programmatic outcomes and is identified as an outcome in the WPA Outcomes Statement, little research in postsecondary English programs has focused in this area, and the topic provokes differing perspectives. Washington State University's CT Project offers one approach with interesting implications (Kelly-Riley, Brown, Condon, & Low, 1999). Working together over several years, faculty at Washington State University (WSU) developed a set of seven criteria defining critical thinking: problem identification; the establishment of a clear perspective on the issue; recognition of alternative perspectives; context identification; evidence identification and evaluation; recognition of fundamental assumptions implicit or stated by the

representation of an issue; and assessment of implications and potential conclusions. Early on in the project, its leaders attempted to see what difference such criteria would make when applied to student work, and one of their first forays involved comparing the scores on "rising-junior" writing portfolios (portfolios submitted at the end of sophomore year) with student work composed later in their careers:

The 1999 Progress Report on the WSU Writing Portfolio showed that 92% of student writers received passing ratings or higher on junior-level Writing Portfolios, indicating that an overwhelming majority of upper-division students demonstrated writing proficiency as defined by WSU faculty. However, a pilot critical thinking evaluation session conducted in the summer of 1999 on papers from three senior-level courses revealed surprisingly low critical thinking abilities (a mean of 2.3 on a 6 point scale). (*wsuctproject.wsu.edu/ph.htm*)

In other words, there appeared to be a disjunction between the critical thinking *assumed* in writing and that identified in the work of senior-level students. At the same time, it's fair to note that the scoring guide for the writing portfolio did not explicitly direct raters' attention toward critical thinking as later defined, nor were the seven dimensions included in the curriculum. On the basis of this work, however, the writing portfolio scoring guide has been revised so that the connection between the "higher-order" values of critical thinking and writing are strengthened. Likewise, some 3 years later, the benchmarks themselves have been altered to include writing as a component of critical thinking:

Communication skills have been added as a new dimension ... even though they are not traditionally considered a construct of critical thinking. While using the Critical Thinking Rubric to assess student work, WSU faculty and others found that skills used in communication impacted their perception of the work and the extent to which critical thinking was effectively expressed. This new dimension captures those criteria. (*wsuctproject.wsu.edu/ph.htm*)

A second perspective is offered by Carter (2007), who (like many others) argues that thinking is grounded in disciplines such that a generalized critical thinking construct or domain is not viable. At the same time, on the basis of his multidisciplinary outcomes-based work at North Carolina State, Carter employs a four-part metadisciplinary classification system including genres and knowledge structures: (1) problem solving, where writing is instrumental, providing a means to a solution; (2) empirical inquiry, where in sciences the writing is important for proving a knowledge claim; (3) research from textual sources, where in humanities the writing is focused on analysis of and is grounded in other documents; (4) performance, where in disciplines such as art and design (and, according to Carter, rhetoric and composition), the writing is a performance that is the end itself. Although one might argue with some of the claims—many disciplines seem to draw on more than one of these metadisciplines—Carter's taxonomy aligns well with the insights of genre theorists and researchers (e.g., Freedman & Medway, 1994) who link the knowledge-making function of genres to disciplinary expertise. In sum, critical thinking is an assumed literacy demand, although how it functions within the first-year course is neither well documented nor understood.

Theme Four: Reflective Practice

Increasingly, students are asked to self-assess and reflect on their own performance, as in DSP, for example. Such practice isn't particularly new, nor is it limited to the college setting. Andrade (1998), for instance, found that scores on middle school students' writing improved at a statistically significant rate when they evaluated their writing with a scoring guide. At the same time, recent interest in reflection—and in what has been learned from studying student development in college—is shaping a new dialogue about collegiate literacy. Several scholars—Beaufort (2007); Downs and Wardle (2007); and Yancey (2007)—argue that reflection combined with a *specific* vocabulary—one new for the field—constitutes the academic literacy needed today and tomorrow. Beaufort's (2007) argument is based on her detailed case study of a single student, as well as on her earlier work with four college graduates making the transition to workplace writing. She identifies five key terms (and knowledge

domains) that define literacy for first-year students: rhetorical knowledge, content knowledge, composing knowledge, genre knowledge, and discourse knowledge.

Similarly, Downs and Wardle (2007) argue that there is no such discourse as academic discourse per Bartholomae (1985), but rather that all discourse is bound by convention. They favor a first-year course-qua-introduction to writing studies, focusing on rhetorical knowledge and awareness and discourse conventions especially. Yancey (2007) argues that a first-year literacy foundation requires the domains identified by Beaufort (2007), the activity theory framework of Downs and Wardle (2007), the knowledge-making, or epistemological, function of genres and tools as part of a larger framework keyed to the university culture, and a more nuanced practice of reflection, informed by Schön's (1983) work especially. In this, they agree with a final conclusion that Hilgers et al. (1999) drew:

> Our interviewees, while confident in their facility with certain genres, seemed unaware that their understanding of genres was limited by the contexts of a specific classroom, a "controlled circumstance." Further, the difficulties interviewees experienced in discovering appropriate inquiry processes and in solving content problems suggested that they had an essentially superficial understanding of genres: they were versed in format and stylistic conventions; they knew that the writing in their major was different from other writing they had done; but they in general lacked an understanding of the underlying values and epistemologies that different genres, or even a particular genre, represented. (*www.mwp.hawaii.edu/epiphanies.htm*)

In other words, to be literate, Yancey argues, there is a bigger picture that is required, what cognitive psychologists call a *mental map,* complete with its own vocabulary and thus available not only to conceptualize the activity, but also to use in self-assessment. Research on the efficacy of this approach is now in process.

Theme Five: New Texts, New Discourses

With the advent of electronic discourse, especially networked computing, new texts have become available, new resources and methods of researching are under construction, and a more spacious sense of the knowledge that students too can create has emerged. Such changes are not limited to the realm of literacy, of course. Revised models of Bloom's (1956) taxonomy of educational objectives add "creation" to the list just after the now-penultimate "evaluation," and undergraduate research initiatives no longer can claim unique status: Nearly every postsecondary institution seems to have at least one such model. Composition in particular is ideally suited to the task of assisting students to create knowledge, however, because of its aim to assist students in communicating and because of its potential connection to the emerging genres of the Web. Trupe (2002) argues:

> Whereas these specialized genres [i.e., genres of academic writing] for students have served as the measure of freshman writing ability for a hundred years, transformation of writing courses by computer technology is a recent phenomenon. Composition instructors first welcomed word processing because it facilitated production of the standard freshman essay. However, the move into electronic environments rapidly began to revolutionize classroom practices and genres. Today the expanding possibilities for writing engendered through desktop publishing, email, Web-based bulletin boards, MOO's, Web page and other hypertext authoring and presentation software show up the limitations the freshman essay imposes on thought and writing. (p. 1)

Others—Sara Robbins at Ball State, for instance—ask their students to take up residence in Second Life and then write about it. In other words, the combination of self-sponsored e-writing experiences, new venues to communicate in, and the interest of academics in incorporating e-writing into literacy courses has the potential to create very new literacy demands for students over time.

A second and related issue, students' knowledge of their own culture and language and the potential that knowledge has for literacy development, is articulated by numerous scholars, including Bizzell (2000) and Mejía (cited in Oldmixon, 2006), and is directly related to postsecondary literacy demands. Historically, the demand has been that students should erase their home culture, evi-denced most dramatically in the removal of Alaskan Native Americans to boarding schools in which the physical removal of the children echoed the erasure of their home language. Very recently, however, home cultures and languages have been identified as linguistic and cultural assets. For example, Bizzell (2000) argues that students' familiarity with and increased use of "mixed forms" should be tapped as a resource rather than penalized or erased. In a similar but stronger claim, Mejía focuses on the "subtractive schooling" that must be reversed. As reported by Oldmixon (2006):

> Mejía acknowledges that first-year college students are in a moment of identity formation in which separation from their parents and communities, their ethnic culture and its elements, plays a pivotal role in their lives. His class incorporated a diverse group of students, one-third of whom were diverse Latinos, including a Spanish-speaking first-generation Mexican immigrant whose parents' first language is Mexican indigenous and second and third-generation Mexican-Americans who may understand, but do not speak or read Spanish. Mejía ascertained that to teach these students effectively, one must not only provide culturally affirming materials—too scarce in supply in popular readers and textbooks—but take into account the "subtractive schooling" that has devalued these students' cultural identity, the psychological and social developmental stage of eighteen-year-old traditional first-year students, and the research that predicts patterns of social and cultural identity formation and community (re)affiliation. (*wac.colostate.edu/atd/reviews/cccc2006/d41.cfm*)

Although not a composition project per se, the LaGuardia Community College electronic portfolio, now in its sixth year, does exactly what Bizzell (2000) and Mejía in Oldmixon (2006) suggest by building in a key structure: a bicultural framework. Each student is expected to bring knowledge of home culture and academic culture to the e-portfolio. Preliminary results suggest that students who engage in the electronic portfolio have higher course pass rates and higher retention rates (Eynon, 2008).

In sum, creating new kinds of texts and venues, as well as developing and tapping new understandings of culture and language, pose yet another kind of literacy demand for postsecondary students, typical in some programs today and increasingly likely tomorrow.

CONCLUSION

The construction of this map of postsecondary literacy, much like the creation of a map of tectonic plates overlaying nation-states, is an exercise in palimpsest, an attempt through multiple arrangements to make a dynamic set of practices stand still. As such, it can only fail. At the same time, it enables a view of each arrangement attempting to foster a kind of literacy, from one oriented to correct answers on a multiple-choice test or the correctness of an impromptu essay to a curriculum rich with writing process, complex texts, new ways of researching, and a sophisticated framework putting all the elements—texts, processes, knowledges, cultures, reflection, and selves—into dialogue. Literacy is always a cultural practice, one that defines a self, and in the plural, a community, for the moment. Literacy changes, as does its instruction; of that we can be sure. Thus, while college literacy is variously defined across very diverse sites, at the beginning of the 21st century in the United States it involves a postsecondary culture of composing, reading, thinking, resourcing, reflecting, creating, and revisioning—of writing and of student.

REFERENCES

American College Testing (ACT). (2003, April 3). *Survey shows writing skills most important to college teachers not always emphasized in high school instruction.* Iowa City: Author. Retrieved July 5, 2007, from *www.act.org/news/releases/2003/4-08-03.html.*

Andrade, H. G. (1998). *Rubrics and self assessment project.* Cambridge, MA: Project Zero at Harvard University. Retrieved December 31, 2004, from *www.pz.harvard.edu/Research/RubricSelf.htm.*

Bartholomae, D. (1985). Inventing the university. In M. Rose (Ed.), *When a writer can't write: Studies in writer's block and other composing-process problems* (pp. 134–165). New York: Guilford Press.

Beaufort, A. (2007). *College writing and beyond: A new framework for university writing instruction.* Logan: Utah State University Press.

Bizzell, P. (2000). Basic writing and the issue of correctness, or, what to do with "mixed" forms of academic discourse. *Journal of Basic Writing, 19,* 4–12.

Blakesley, D., Harvey, E., & Reynolds E. (2003). South-

ern Illinois Carbondale as an institutional model: The English 100/101 Stretch and Directed Self Placement Program. In D. Royer & R. Gilles (Eds.), *Directed Self-Placement: Principles and practices* (pp. 207–243). Cresskill, NJ: Hampton.

Blau, S. (2006). College writing, academic literacy, and the intellectual community: California dreams and cultural oppositions. In P. Sullivan & H. Tinburg (Eds.), *What is "college-level" writing?* (pp. 358–378). Urbana, IL: National Council of Teachers of English.

Bloom, B. S. (1956). *Taxonomy of educational objectives: The classification of educational goals.* New York: Longmans Green.

Bodmer, P. (2006). Is it administrative or pedagogical? Administering distance delivery to high schools. In K. B. Yancey (Ed.), *Delivering college composition: The fifth canon* (pp. 115–127). Portsmouth, NH: Heinemann.

Cal Poly Pomona University Writing Center (n. d.) *CSU English placement test scoring guide.* Pomona, CA: Author. Retrieved July 15, 2007, from *www.Csupomona.edu/~uwc/non_protect/student/CSU-EPT ScoringGuide.htm.*

Carter, M. (2007). Ways of knowing, doing, and writing in the disciplines. *College Composition and Communication 58,* 385–418.

Carroll, L. A. (2002). *Rehearsing new roles: How college students develop as writers.* Carbondale: Southern Illinois University Press.

Crowley, S. (1998). *Composition in the university: Historical and polemical essays.* Pittsburgh: University of Pittsburgh Press.

Council of Writing Program Administrators. (1999). WPA outcomes statement for first year composition. *WPA: Writing Program Administration 23,* 59–66. Retrieved July 5, 2007, from *wpacouncil.org/positions/outcomes.html.*

Curry, M. J. (2003). Skills, access, and "basic writing": A community college case study from the United States. *Studies in the Education of Adults, 35,* 5–18.

Downs, D., & Wardle, E. (2007). Teaching about writing, righting misconceptions: (Re)envisioning "first-year composition" as "introduction to writing studies." *College Composition and Communication, 58,* 552–584.

Eynon, B. (2008). Making connections: The LaGuardia e-portfolio. In D. Cambridge, B. Cambridge, & K. B. Yancey (Eds.), *Electronic portfolios: Emergent findings and shared questions.* Washington, DC: Stylus Publishing.

Farris, C. (2006). The space between: Dual-credit programs as brokering, community-building, and professionalism. In K. B. Yancey (Ed.), *Delivering college composition: The fifth canon* (pp. 104–115). Portsmouth, NH: Heinemann.

Freedman, A., & Medway, P. (Eds.). (1994). *Learning and teaching genre.* Portsmouth, NH: Heinemann.

Fulkerson, R. (2005). Critique and review: Composition at the turn of the twenty-first century. *College Composition and Communication, 56,* 654–687.

Hansen, K., Reeve, S., Sedweeks, R., Hatch, G., Gonzalez, J., Esplin, P., et al. (2004). An argument for changing institutional policy and granting A.P. credit in English: An empirical study of college sophomores' writing. *WPA: Writing Program Administration, 28,* 29–54.

Hilgers, T. L., Hussey, E. L., & Stitt-Bergh, M. (1999). "As you're writing, you have these epiphanies": What college students say about writing and learning in their majors. *Written Communication, 16,* 317–353. Retrieved July 5, 2007, from *www.mwp. hawaii.edu/epiphanies.htm.*

Hussey, E. L., Bayer, A., Hilgers, T. L., & Jones, K. (1995). *Writing in Hawai'i high school senior classes: A glimpse into a few windows* (OFDAS Report #2). Honolulu, HI: University of Hawai'i at Manoa, Office of Faculty Development and Academic Support.

Jarratt, S., Mack, K., & Watson, S. (2005). *Retrospective writing histories.* Paper presented at Writing Research in the Making, University of California Santa Barbara. Retrieved July 5, 2007, from *209.85.165.104/ search?q=cache:oPJgdGoBxBkJ:www.writing.uci.edu/ retrowriting.pdf+retrospective+writing&hl=en&ctclnk &cd=1&gl=us.*

Jasik, S. (2007, June 25). When digital natives go to the library. *Inside Higher Ed.* Retrieved July 5, 2007, from *www.insidehighered.com/news/2007/06/25/games.*

Jolliffe, D. (2007). Learning to read as continuing education. *College Composition and Communication, 58,* 470–495.

Jolliffe, D., & Phelan, B. (2007). Advanced placement, not advanced exemption: Challenges for high schools, colleges, and universities. In K. B. Yancey (Ed.), *Delivering college composition: The fifth canon* (pp. 89–104). Portsmouth, NH: Heinemann.

Kelly-Riley, D., Brown, G., Condon, B., & Law, R. (1999). *Washington State University critical thinking project.* Retrieved July 5, 2007, from *wsuctproject.wsu. edu/ph.htm.*

Lindemann, E. (2002). Early bibliographic work in composition studies. *Profession 2002,* 151–158.

Miller, T. (2004). *Speaking with high schools.* Retrieved July 5, 2007, from *lists.asu.edu/cgi-bin/wa?A2=ind 0407&L=wpa-l&D=1&O=D&F=&S=&P=14017.*

Missouri Colloquium on Writing Assessment. (1995). *Guidelines for the delivery of dual-credit composition courses.* Retrieved July 5, 2007, from *www. missouriwestern.edu/cwa/dualcred.html.*

Moffett, J. (1968). *Teaching the universe of discourse.* Boston: Houghton Mifflin.

Nash, L. C. (2007). *Mind the gap: ESL composition instruction in community colleges in north Florida.* Unpublished master's thesis, Florida State University.

National Council of Teachers of English Task Force on

SAT and ACT Writing Tests. (2005). *The impact of the SAT and ACT writing tests.* Retrieved July 29, 2007, from *www.ncte.org/library/files/About_NCTE/ Press_Center/SAT/SAT-ACT-tf-report.pdf.*

Oldmixon, K. D. (2006). Jaime Armin Mejía, English's "other": The rhetorical uses of Spanish in Chicano/a English classes. In *Interactive review. CCCC 2006 in review.* Retrieved July 5, 2007, from *wac.colostate. edu/atd/reviews/cccc2006/d41.cfm.*

Paley, K. S. (1996). The college application essay: A rhetorical paradox. *Assessing Writing, 3,* 85–107.

Patthey-Chavez, G. G., Thomas-Spiegel, J., & Dillon, P. (1998). *Tracking outcomes for community college students with different writing instruction histories.* (ERIC Document Reproduction Service No. 429-648).

Prensky, M. (2005/2006). Listen to the natives. *Educational Leadership, 63,* 8–13. Retrieved July 7, 2007, from *www.ascd.org/authors/ed_lead/el200512_prensky. html.*

Royer, D. J., & Gilles, R. (Eds.). (2003). *Directed Self-Placement principles and practices.* Cresskill, NJ: Hampton.

Scherff, L., & Piazza, C. (2005). The more things change, the more they stay the same: A survey of high school students' writing experiences. *Research in the Teaching of English, 39,* 271–299.

Schön, D. (1983). *The reflective practitioner: How professionals think in action.* New York: Basic Books.

Sommers, N., & Saltz, L. (2004). The novice as expert: Writing the freshman year. *College Composition and Communication, 55,* 123–146.

Sullivan, F. J. (1997). Calling writers' bluffs: The social production of writing ability in university placement testing. *Assessing Writing, 4,* 53–81.

Trupe, A. (2002). Academic literacy in a wired world: Redefining genres for college writing courses. *Kairos* 7.2. Retrieved July 5, 2007, from *kairos.technorhetoric.net/7.2/binder.html?sectionone/trupeWiredWorld .htm.*

Yancey, K. B. (2006). Delivering college composition: A vocabulary for discussion. In K. B. Yancey (Ed.), *Delivering college composition: The fifth canon* (pp. 1–17). Portsmouth, NH: Heinemann.

Yancey, K. B., with Dowd, E., Francis, T., & Nash, L. C. (2007). "The things they carried": The role of transfer in college composition. Mid-year report to Conference on College Composition and Communication. Urbana, IL: National Council of Teachers of English.

Yancey, K. B., Fishman, T., Gresham, M., Neal, M., & Taylor, S. S. (2005, March). *Portraits of composition: How writing gets taught in the early 21st century.* Paper presented at the annual meeting of the Conference on College Composition and Communication, San Francisco.

CHAPTER 18

Literacy in Virtual Worlds

REBECCA W. BLACK
CONSTANCE STEINKUEHLER

This chapter addresses how the form, nature, and venue of many adolescents' leisure, work, and academic activities have shifted to "virtual" or online spaces in recent years. We review two distinct but complementary lines of research that have implications for language and literacy education: virtual fandoms and online virtual worlds. We address recent investigations into literate and textual practices such as instant messaging, personal websites, online journaling, zining, and gaming that are integral components of youth's social worlds. The chapter describes online fandom and fanfiction sites as virtual arenas for sophisticated literacy practices such as creating unique, hybrid fanfiction texts that require engagement with literary genres; visiting metafandom and fanfiction-specific help sites; conducting research to ensure authenticity of material in fictions; beta-reading and/or peer reviewing; developing texts from diverse linguistic and cultural backgrounds; and performing identities through textual interactions on fan sites. The chapter then discusses the constellation of literacy activities that constitute successful gameplay. Recent empirical and theoretical explorations of massively multiplayer online games highlight the forms of literacy that youth and adults alike engage in during gameplay, including in-game text-based interaction and literacy practices and the literacies found in the out-of-game, online world of fandom. We posit that participation in the virtual worlds of MMOs is no less a literary act than participation in the virtual worlds of fanfiction; in both, adolescent fans actively and enthusiastically engage in reading and writing a wide range of texts. Moreover, many such practices are perfectly within the realm of what various national standards and other policy documents indicate we, as a society, value and ought to foster in our youth.

With ever-increasing access to the Internet and World Wide Web, the form, nature, and venue of many adolescents' leisure, work, and academic activities have shifted to virtual or online spaces. According to a recent report by the Pew Internet and American Life Project (Lenhart, Madden, & Hitlin, 2005), technology has become "a central force that fuels the rhythm of daily life" for American youth. Of the teens surveyed, 87% use the Internet, 81% play online games, 76% retrieve news, and 51% claim to go online on a daily basis. This trend is not unique to the United States, as online spaces have become the preferred sites for many adolescents from across the globe to meet, interact, play, and share their thoughts, perspectives, and languages with one another.

One only needs to log on to a massively multiplayer online game (MMO), a fan-fiction writing site, a social networking site (e.g., MySpace, Facebook), and/or a web log (more commonly known as a blog) to see ample evidence of the complex, multilingual, and conspicuously multimodal nature of adolescents' online literate lives.

To anyone who has spent a great deal of time with teens in such spaces, it is quite clear that the "virtual" or online and "real" or off-line distinction is an artificial one. Youth's online activities are often intertwined with their off-line social worlds. For instance, teens meet at each other's houses to play online games together, maintain relationships with school peers via instant messaging (IM), develop new relationships using social networking software, and fill their blogs with direct references to or stories about off-line friends. There also are multiple points of connection between adolescents' academic endeavors and the activities they engage in out of school. For example, they import genres and forms of writing learned at school into their online publishing and social interactions. Tech-savvy students also rely on the Internet as a tool to facilitate school-based lessons and activities. According to an earlier Pew report exploring students' out-of-school uses of the Internet, "the way students think about the Internet in relation to schooling is closely tied to the daily tasks and activities that make up their young lives" (Levin & Arafeh, 2002, p. ii). The tech-savvy teens interviewed for that Pew study report an array of educational uses of the Internet, such as conducting online research, participating in virtual study groups, corresponding with classmates or tutors about assignments, and visiting content-rich websites that are relevant to their in-school projects and assignments, to name just a few.

However, it is important to note that this particular Pew study documents tech-savvy youth using the Internet *for* rather than *in* school. In fact, schools are one of the few places where students perceive a significant disconnect between their on- and off-line activities. Tech-savvy teens report that their most fruitful uses of the Internet, even for educational purposes, take place outside school walls and that classroom activities in-volving the Internet are either uninspiring, irrelevant to their academic needs, or simply nonexistent (Levin & Arafeh, 2002). Such disparity between students' authentic, out-of-school literate and information-seeking practices and in-school computing activities has been attributed to a range of factors, including administrative policies restricting access to certain sites, mandatory computer classes that focus solely on basic operating skills, lack of computer access due to financial constraints, and teachers' attitudes toward and facility with technology. It is also important to note that this chapter deals only with adolescents who have access to technology in out-of-school spaces, whereas there are still significant numbers of youth who do not enjoy ready access to computers. The issue of access is crucial for broader discussions of adolescents and technology use. Ultimately, such issues must be addressed at the level of policy; yet such reform is unlikely without a clear understanding of students' literacy practices and uses of technology *outside of schools* so we might better grasp their potential for classroom practice within schools.

Toward this goal, this chapter reviews two distinct but complementary lines of research that have both explicit and implicit significance for language and literacy education. In the first section, we contextualize the chapter and define key terms. In the next two sections, we theorize two crucial sites for contemporary out-of-school, technologically mediated literacy in the lives of adolescents—virtual fandoms (Black) and online virtual worlds (Steinkuehler)—exploring how in- and out-of-school and on- and off-line literacy practices of youth both converge and diverge. We conclude with a synthesis of what we see as the import of such findings in the context of the broader national conversation about adolescents, literacy learning, and popular media.

ORIENTATION

Virtual

Our notion of *virtual* is related to the aforementioned publicly perceived distinction between adolescents' on- and off-line lives. Such distinctions are often drawn without ample consideration of the engagement or immersion that youth feel in such online spaces—a sense that often rivals the connection and engagement they feel in many "real-life" settings, such as classrooms. In this chapter, we use the term *virtual* to refer to online settings, whether they be websites, blogs, video games, or writing and publishing environments, where participants either display or profess high levels of commitment and engagement to the literacy, learning, and/or social practices taking place in that particular environment.

Literacy

The term *literacy* is also one that remains highly contested, especially in educational discourse, and debates abound over the best ways to define, teach, and research literacy. Literacy is often conceived of solely as the technical abilities needed to decode and encode print-based forms of standard language. However, considering the varied resources available for making meaning online, such as image, sound, color, space, avatars, video, and movement, it would be difficult to confine research in virtual arenas to such a narrow definition. This difficulty becomes especially evident when one considers the fact that print-based language is often inextricably tied to other modes of communication on the Web. In order to successfully consume and produce messages in online spaces, youth must learn to negotiate or become literate not only in such myriad forms of representation but also in how such multimodal resources can interact with and complement one another. Therefore, this chapter takes a necessarily broader approach to defining literacy. The notions of *literacies* (Alvermann, 2002), *new literacies* (Gee, 1996; Lankshear & Knobel, 2006; Street, 1984), and *multiliteracies* (Cope & Kalantzis, 2000; New London Group, 1996) suggest a research stance or worldview that holds that literacy is not an ever-fixed, standardized mark. Instead, being or becoming literate is an ongoing process that shifts according to participants, context, and the nature of the activity. Such a view recognizes the value in a broad repertoire of meaning-making systems that extends beyond standard national languages in print-based formats.

Adolescence

Adolescence is a nebulous term often used to describe a transitional, "coming of age" phase between childhood and adulthood (Lesko, 2001). Chronologically, most of the studies presented in this chapter deal with youth ranging from about 12 to 20 years of age. Despite the seeming simplicity of the term, however, discussion of "adolescents" in virtual or online spaces can be vexatious. Online technologies facilitate communication across traditional borders of language, geography, and age. So, youth in China, Canada, India, and the United States can meet, collaborate, and participate in the same sort of literate activities in virtual worlds, despite the obvious fact that the experience of being an "adolescent" does not necessarily mean the same thing in these places.

Moreover, the research presented in this chapter deals with youth's participation in what Gee (2004) refers to as online *affinity spaces*—spaces that cohere around a common affinity for a certain topic, passion, or endeavor rather than, say, those features that more traditionally define a given community such as social class, gender, location, or age. Therefore, throughout this chapter, we try not to reify this notion of *the adolescent* in ways more rigid, salient, and enduring than such spaces themselves actually afford. This is not to suggest that features such as ethnicity, gender, and age do not figure into patterns of participation in the kind of online spaces discussed herein; it is to say, however, that the nature of virtual spaces is such that these markers and boundaries do not always carry the same weight or import as they might off-line. For instance, in the fanfiction sites discussed below, traditional expert and novice roles are often reversed as younger members (often adolescents) play the role of "old timers" (Lave & Wenger, 1991) within the community, giving "expert" feedback to adults on various aspects of popular culture. In such contexts, the outward trappings of youth can sometimes disappear, providing adolescents an opportunity to take on and experiment with more adult (or even childlike) roles in a community.

THE LITERATE PRACTICES OF VIRTUAL FANDOMS

In June 2004, the National Endowment for the Arts (NEA) released a report entitled *Reading at Risk: A Survey of Literary Reading in America* that warned of a marked decline in the American public's engagement with "literary" texts and claimed that the young adult population showed the steepest decline for reading in recent years (Bradshaw & Nichols, 2004). The report contrasts books with "electronic media" such as television, radio, video games, and the Internet, claiming that such media "often require no more than passive participation" and "foster shorter attention spans and accelerated gratification" (p. vii). Likewise, the introduction also warns of the cultural impoverishment and lack of civic participation that will likely stem from the American public's continued participation in electronic media.

In clear contrast to the claims of this report, recent empirical investigations into adolescents' uses of electronic media have described an array of literate and textual practices that are integral components of youth's social worlds in both on- and offline spaces. For example, researchers have examined how youth use IM to build on and extend peer relationships from their daily lives (Lewis & Fabos, 2005), how personal websites are emerging as safe spaces for adolescent girls to express and negotiate various social identities (Guzzetti, 2006; Stern, 1999, 2004), how participation in online games fosters exposure to a diversity of worldviews (Steinkuehler & Williams, 2006), and how online journaling (Guzzetti & Gamboa, 2005) and zines (Knobel & Lankshear, 2002) promote social consciousness and political engagement in the lives of youth.

Along such lines, online fandom and fanfiction sites are virtual arenas in which youth's activities center on an array of sophisticated writing and reading practices that extend and often challenge original media productions. These virtual spaces are constituted not only by the archive of fanfiction texts, but also by the social norms, interactions, community artifacts, and collaborative composition-related activities that fans engage in. Thus, this section focuses not only on the genre of fanfiction but also on empirical explorations of the shared social practices that constitute many online fanfiction websites. By one definition, fanfiction is "writing, whether official or unofficial, paid or unpaid, which makes use of an accepted canon of characters, settings, and plots generated by another writer or writers" (Pugh, 2005, p. 25). Thus, when viewed through a "literary" lens, fanfiction can arguably be grouped with forms of derivative or appropriative writing that date back to literature such as Shakespeare's plays, poetic continuations of Geoffrey Chaucer's work, and the many uncommissioned sequels to Jane Austen's novels (Pugh, 2005), to name just a few. In its more modern manifestation, the origins of fanfiction have been located in media fandom and linked to science fiction and Amateur Press Association fan magazines, more commonly known as *fanzines* or *zines,* of the mid-20th century (Coppa, 2006; Jenkins, 1992b).

More recently, the advent of online publishing has brought about changes in fanfiction across several notable fronts (Black, 2008; Hellekson & Busse, 2006). For instance, the fan demographic has shifted from a majority of adults producing hardcopy printed zines and distributing them through mail and at fan conventions to what is now a majority of teens who write and publish their fictions online. Another notable change has been the marked growth in the number of *canons* or original media that fanfictions are based on. These developments may be attributed to the fact that the Internet provides increased opportunity for fans to meet, communicate, and develop fandoms online. As an illustration, a Google search for *fanfiction* and the popular online game World of Warcraft yields about 152,000 hits; the Japanese animation series *Inuyasha* produces 272,000; and the juvenile fiction series *Harry Potter* brings 474,000. As such, the ubiquity and sheer number of fanfiction texts make it a difficult phenomenon to overlook. Moreover, the fact that much of this fiction is being written and read by adolescents makes it a fascinating topic for education and literacy researchers who seek to understand the role of new media and online communication technologies in youth's literate, social, and academic worlds.

Fanfiction Genres

In determining the level of engagement with "literary texts," the aforementioned NEA survey asked respondents if, during the previous 12 months, they had read any plays, novels, poetry, or short stories in their leisure time. Even within the confines of such a narrow definition of literate engagement, there is ample evidence that adolescent fans are actively and enthusiastically engaging with a range of literary as well as popular texts. The vast majority of fanfictions are still narrative in nature—with fan authors introducing unusual plot twists, creating new characters, developing unexpected romantic relationships between established characters, or simply extending the time line of the original series. However, recent inquiry into fan writing communities has also called attention to a range of hybrid genres that are unique to fanfiction such as songfictions (*songfics*), which are fictions based on lyrics of a song; poetry fictions (*poetryfics*), which are based on stanzas of a poem; chatfictions (*chatfics*), which are fictions written as IM or Internet Relay Chat conversations; and fictions based on or written in the format of movies (*moviefics*) and screenplays (Black, 2005a, 2006; Chandler-Olcott & Mahar, 2003b; Lankshear & Knobel, 2006). Furthermore, many fanfiction texts "cross over" or combine the characteristics of different media productions, making intertextual connections among genres such as science fiction, fantasy, angst, comedy, and romance (Black, 2005a; Chandler-Olcott & Mahar, 2003a; Lankshear & Knobel, 2006).

These hybrid textual forms are interesting from a literacy and learning standpoint in several respects. First, in order to create fictions based on poetry, novels, and screenplays, writers must read and engage with works from these various genres. In addition, there is a great deal of effort required for learning to write in these distinct formats. In fact, in order to master such genres, many young authors read other fan texts, plays, and screenplays, as well as different forms of poetry, song lyrics, and fiction. Authors visit metafandom and fanfiction-specific help sites and utilize online writing and style guides to familiarize themselves with the associated techniques and conventions of different genres of writing (Black,

2005a). They also conduct extensive research to ensure the authenticity of material presented in fictions, such as investigating different historical periods or the procedures involved in various professions (Black, 2006).

Fan Writing and Reading Practices

Clearly, the literacy practices that these young fans engage in often bear a striking resemblance to many school-sanctioned composition activities as well as the writing practices that many professional writers rely on. For instance, Jenkins (2006) describes how one home-schooled student developed *The Daily Phoenix*, an online "school newspaper" for the fictional Hogwarts Academy attended by students in the *Harry Potter* juvenile fiction series. The adolescent staff members for the paper meet online to carry out the tasks of writers, reporters, proofreaders, editors, and columnists. Moreover, through their online discussions, the teens are practicing and learning strategies for effective editing and proofreading, improving their own composition skills, and beginning to develop a metavocabulary for talking about writing and revision. Thus, these fannish activities are not unlike those required for work on a school or professional newspaper.

A related shift in fanfiction that has come about with migration to the Internet is the expansion of the reader's role in the author's process. Specifically, collaborative composition, audience feedback, peer review, and mentoring have become prominent features of the online fanfiction writing experience. Popular fanfiction archives facilitate audience response to texts in the form of "review" mechanisms that allow the reader to post instantaneous feedback for the author. Moreover, many fans post their stories to these sites with the expectation of receiving feedback from an audience of peers. Thus, in the Author's Notes (A/N) that precede or follow the story text, it is common to see a request for readers to please R&R, an acronym for "read and review" (Black, 2007). Moreover, the relative ease of reposting or republishing texts online makes it easier for authors to incorporate audience feedback into their texts, thus creating a situation where writers and readers co-construct the writing space through a series of dialogic interactions (Black, 2007, 2006) and/or collaborative writing (Thomas, 2006).

Researchers have also started to take notice of beta-reading, or the practice of handing off a story to another fan for review before publication (Black, 2005a, 2005b; Jenkins, 2006; Karpovich, 2006). In a recent piece exploring the history and development of *beta-reading*, Karpovich (2006) points out that the term "is intimately connected with the Internet age, deriving from the so-called beta testers of computer software" (p. 172). The practice of beta-reading has become an entity in and of itself within the fan community. For example, there are now many online beta-reading sites where fanfiction authors can fill out a form specifying genre (e.g., adventure, comedy, romance) and canon (e.g., *Harry Potter, Star Trek, Card Captor Sakura*) as well as features of writing that they would like help with (e.g., characterization, dialogue, grammar) before submitting their text to the website for review. In this way, authors are matched with beta-readers who are well versed in the media and are able to meet the writers' needs for feedback (Black, 2005b). It is also common practice for fans to establish close and ongoing writer and beta-reader partnerships in which the beta is publicly credited with the production of the text alongside the author (Karpovich, 2006). As such, online fanfiction communities and associated beta-reading and peer review practices provide salient examples of the "heightened modes of coconstruction of texts and meaning" (Bruce, 2002, p. 7) that have been associated with hypertext and online publishing.

Fans and Identity

Another significant area of inquiry into online publishing spaces is the role of identity in virtual fandoms. Empirical investigations have highlighted how fans construct and enact desirable social identities through interactions on fan sites. For example, Lam's (2000, 2007) innovative work has described how English language learners (ELLs) of Asian descent participating in Japanese animation or anime-based fandoms, are often able to display expertise in such media, taking on such roles as anime experts and webmasters. Other studies have also described how the multilingual and multicul-

tural nature of anime-based fanfiction enables some ELLs to act as cultural and linguistic consultants of sorts by helping other fanfiction writers accurately incorporate elements of Asian cultures and languages into their story texts (Black, 2005a) and to represent their identities as multilingual and multicultural youth (Black, 2006). In addition, because anime is the focus of interaction in such spaces, readers are often more interested in content and engaging story lines than in grammatical correctness and form—thus, writers who have not completely mastered English can still create stories that are immensely popular in the community (Black, 2005b). In these ways, ELLs are able to take on powerful roles and meaningfully participate in the writing community even as they learn and develop fluency in different social languages, online registers, and the many global forms of English that are increasingly used for communication in virtual spaces (Lam, 2004).

Other studies have examined how fan writers often fuse their identities with those of the characters in the stories to create autobiographical and/or what are known as "Mary Sue" characters, thus providing a means of expressing issues and concerns from their daily lives. In a long-term ethnographic project, Thomas (2005, 2006), explores such narrative constructions of self in detail, describing how two young focal participants used role playing with fanfiction characters as a route to self-awareness. Specifically, their writing activities helped to create a discursive space for "understanding their pasts and for forging new identities" (Thomas, 2005, p. 30). In another study, one of the first to apply a literacy-related lens to fanfiction, Chandler-Olcott and Mahar (2003a), a teacher/university researcher team, explore how two young women created autobiographical characters and used their fictions as "contributions to an ongoing, intertextual conversation about such issues as friendship, loyalty, power, and sexuality" (p. 583). These young women also used their fanfictions to reconfigure gendered identities by casting female fanfiction characters in many of the "hero" roles that are traditionally occupied by men in popular media.

Chandler-Olcott and Mahar (2003b) also point out that composing and sharing fictions with peers and other fans serves as "social glue" (Beach, quoted in Chandler-Olcott & Mahar, 2003b) or a point of affiliation that helped these teens develop and maintain close social connections with both on- and off-line friends. The social and collaborative nature of participation is a theme that carries across empirical and theoretical conceptualizations of online fandom. Moreover, this conceptualization is in direct contradiction to current negative discourses about electronic media asserting that computers and video games prevent youth from socializing and spending time with friends. Research such as Chandler-Olcott and Mahar's also contradicts claims that electronic media diverts users from activities such as reading, writing, and broader civic participation. Instead, these robust characterizations of virtual spaces serve to reframe a new generation of tech-savvy adolescents and fans as "consumers who also produce, readers who also write, and spectators who also participate" (Jenkins, 1992a, p. 208).

THE LITERATE PRACTICES OF MASSIVELY MULTIPLAYER ONLINE GAMES

The NEA (Bradshaw & Nichols, 2004), however, is not the only constituency that proclaims a contemporary literacy crisis in America due to electronic media; mainstream news reports the same, particularly in response to the increasing popularity of *video games*. Recent publications include books with titles such as *The Collapse of Literacy and the Rise of Violence in an Electronic Age* (Sanders, 1995); survey experts report that video games are now "the fourth most dominant medium, displacing print media" (Mandese, 2004); and news reports quote researchers as stating, "Students will be doing more and more bad things if they are *playing games* and not doing other things like *reading aloud* [emphasis added]" (Wearden, 2001). Yet, all the while, the popularity of gaming has only increased, with half of Americans of all ages playing video games and more that half of those reporting that they expect to play as much, if not more, 10 years from now (Ipsos-Insight, 2005). On the basis of such claims, one might indeed feel cause for alarm.

Such assertions, however, do not fare well empirically. Research into what adolescents actually *do* when they game reveals a very different picture. Massively multiplayer online games (MMOs) are an excellent case in point: Played online in a persistent virtual world allowing individuals to interact with both the game environment and other players via digital characters called "avatars," MMOs represent the fastest growing segment of the videogame market; yet, upon closer inspection, they appear very much aligned with what educators say we want adolescents engaged in. On the basis of data culled from a 2-year online cognitive ethnography of the MMO *Lineage* (both I and II) (Steinkuehler, 2005), it appears more empirically accurate to conclude that successful MMO gameplay is itself a *constellation of literacy activities* rather than something that might displace such practices in the lives of adolescents and young adults. Even with the definition of literacy represented in national standards jointly advocated by the National Council of Teachers of English and the International Reading Association (NCTE/IRA; 1996) that still remains tragically print based and focused on a single national language, it turns out that when adolescents and adults participate in online virtual game worlds, they engage in copious amounts of recognizable literacy work.

The constellation of literacy activities that constitute successful MMO gameplay span three main classes: in-game text-based interaction, in-game literacy practices (largely formed out of those interactions), and the out-of-game, online world of fandom. Figure 18.1 illustrates.

In-game text-based interaction lies at the very heart of gameplay in MMOs (center square of Figure 18.1). A specialized form of writing, hybridized to varying degrees (at its most extreme, called "4337 speak" or "leet-speak," meaning *elite speak*), is used across multiple chat channels simultaneously, each with a defined function and social norms that govern its use. Through such basic interactional resources, participants engage in multiple forms of recognizable literacy practices within the in-game virtual world (center oval of Figure 18.1); for example, letter writing, "orally" delivered narratives and poetry, meeting protocols (e.g., strategy meetings among guild officers), rituals (e.g., weddings), social sports (e.g., games of

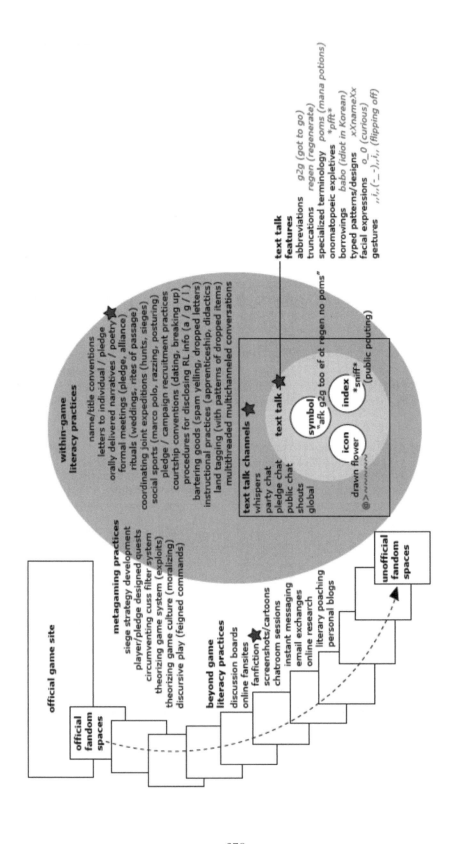

FIGURE 18.1. The constellation of literacy practices that constitute gameplay in the MMO *Lineage I*. Selected practices discussed within this chapter are starred.

"Marco Polo" and "Ritual Insult"; Goodwin, 1990), and instructional practices (e.g., apprenticeship; Steinkuehler, 2004), to name a few. The third class of literacy practices, then, are those that go *beyond* the "magic circle" (Huizinga, 1938) of the game world itself and spill out into world of the online fandom that surrounds it (array of smaller boxes on the left in Figure 18.2); for example, the development and maintenance of fansites, personal game blog writing, argumentation on threaded discussion boards (Steinkuehler & Chmiel, 2006), fan fiction writing and critique, and deliberation about the game both as a designed object and an emergent culture via chat rooms, instant messaging, and in-character e-mails. These three classes of literacy practice are not isolated and autonomous but rather interrelated in complex and mutually defining ways: in-game textual interaction is fodder for both in-game and beyond-game literacy practices, while in-game and beyond-game literacy practices typically "bleed" into one another, with activities in one space moving into the other and back again quite fluidly.

In-Game Text Talk

As Turkle (1995) noted, the specialized linguistic practices that online gamers use to communicate appear to a nongamer much like the "discourse of Dante scholars, 'a closed world of references, cross-references, and code' " (p. 67). It is a sort of *hybrid writing*, "speech momentarily frozen into . . . ephemeral artifact" (p. 183). At first blush, the use of language within such digital worlds appears rather impoverished: Riddled with abbreviations, truncations, typographical and grammatical errors, syntactic erosions, and specialized vocabulary, such typed utterances appear to be a meager substitute for everyday oral and written speech. However, its code-like appearance is misleading: Closer examination of such talk reveals that, in fact, "leetspeak" has the same range and complexity of functions as both oral and written language do in any other context (Steinkuehler, 2006). It is simply forced to accomplish them within the tight constraints of the given medium of communication (58 characters maximum per turn) and the fact that communication typically occurs in tandem with ongoing activities

(e.g., hunts, battles, trades) that require keyboard and mouse commands of their own.

During gameplay, individuals must "use spoken, written, and visual language to accomplish their own purposes" (NCTE/IRA Standard #12), all the while negotiating multiple chat channels, each with its own function and social norms for use. For example, consider the transcript shown in Figure 18.2 (pseudonyms used).

Within roughly 2 minutes of gameplay, at least five overlapping conversational activities occur. In the *public channel*, guild members exchange greetings as they gather in a virtual town. In the *guild channel*, the guild leader (Adeleide) and her members negotiate the addition of a new member (her husband) to their guild and the subsequent self-designated titling of said leader as "Lysanderᵥ"—a form of title (partner's name + a heart represented by a "V") reserved for only those guild members who have undergone an in-game marriage ceremony. Adeleide and Lysander have not; therefore, the guild conversation shifts to debate about the legitimacy of using that title. In the *whisper channel,* Adeleide and Liadon engage in personal banter in private. Meanwhile, in the *yell channel*, a game of "Marco Polo" transpires, followed by a stranger's announcement of equipment for sale. Thus, we see different functions assigned different communication channels, with the community explicitly negotiating the legitimate use of one literacy practice in particular: the titling of one's avatar. Note, too, toward the end of the transcript, that when Adeleide's response to HoHumm's public utterance is delayed, HoHumm presumes *not* that she is unable to keep pace with the multiple chat channels but that *she is ignoring him*. In MMOs, the ability to successfully negotiate multiple threaded conversations across multiple chat channels simultaneously is *presumed,* such that failure to do so successfully is interpreted not as lack of *ability* but lack of *intent*.

In-Game Literacy Practices

Text-based social interaction is the fodder from which virtual world participants create, maintain, and transform in-game literacy practices over time. Using their understanding of game-based dialects of hybridized "lan-

Liadon	Greetings, [Emperor]
BlueReason	ill same some braves fur u next time i hunt ^_^
FireBall	Who is lysander?
Adeleide	my rl bf [real life boyfriend]
Emperor	**how are u this evening?** — Guild Discussion (6 participants)
Liadon	**Very well, and yoruself?**
OriginalSin	Adel's r/l b/f [real life boyfriend]
HoHumm	MARCO
IronFist	eww
Liadon	gah, you told them — Public Social Banter
Emperor	**great ^^**
Adeleide	is that enuf info? — Game of Marco Polo
FireBall	that cant be his name?
HoHumm	there you are
Liadon	of course it's his name — Private Whispered Exchange
IronFist	he play lin [Lineage]?
Emperor	POLO
Adeleide	nope, but its his lineage name
OriginalSin	ive heard that name b'fore
Liadon	you dont' date bob, and then get a tattoo that says 'tom'
Emperor	hohumm i cant see u!!!
FireBall	he plays lineage?
HoHumm	...
Adeleide	lol!!
Stranger	selling sealed forgotten scale mail — In-Town Bartering
IronFist	he dosn't play lineage but its his lineage name?
Adeleide	liadon u too funny!
Liadon	:)
OriginalSin	hehe
Liadon	:)
OriginalSin	hehe
IronFist	Adel u broke the rules for title... we gotta ban u
OriginalSin	haha
HoHumm	yea well be happy u got a title
Liadon	Princess is exempt
OriginalSin	/banished
IronFist	nobody can outgame me sry [sorry]
Adeleide	yall r so funny!
HoHumm	**adel, u still ignorin me?**
Liadon	So when do the wedding notices go out?
Emperor	**we killing cycls?**
HoHumm	**i'll take that as a yes**
Liadon	Sure are

Lin1/07.31.02

FIGURE 18.2. Transcript of roughly 2 minutes of multiple-threaded conversation during a regular evening in *Lineage I*.

guage structure, language conventions . . . media techniques, figurative language, and genre" (NCTE/IRA Standards #5 and #6), gamers not only circulate, discuss, and critique game-related texts (e.g., the open-ended fantasy narratives that structure the virtual world) but also write and rewrite them according to their own needs. One such practice of particular interest is "orally" delivered narratives and poetry. In such performances, individuals adopt and adapt designed-in elements of the game narrative to craft their own "oral" storytelling performances, which often serve some interac-

tional function such as providing explanation of a given group's motivations or sharing game lore as a means for enculturation. Figure 18.3 shows an example of such oral narration. Here, Liadon, a highly skilled gamer within *Lineage*, orally narrates the origins of the fairy creatures that populate the Elven Forest within the virtual world, to Adeliede, a very low-level or "newbie" elf. The episode occurs when the two characters are out hunting together in the Elven Forest in order to give the less-experienced elf practice hunting with a bow.

First, Liadon sets up the motivation for

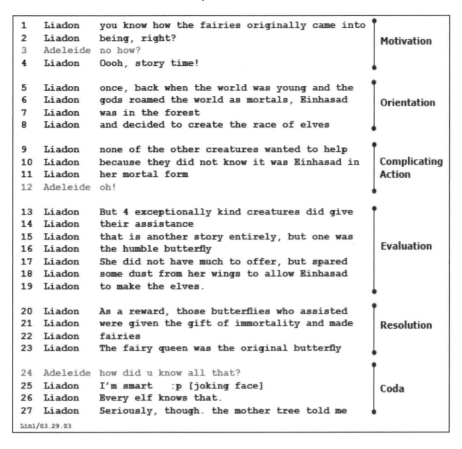

1	Liadon	you know how the fairies originally came into	
2	Liadon	being, right?	Motivation
3	Adeleide	no how?	
4	Liadon	Oooh, story time!	
5	Liadon	once, back when the world was young and the	
6	Liadon	gods roamed the world as mortals, Einhasad	Orientation
7	Liadon	was in the forest	
8	Liadon	and decided to create the race of elves	
9	Liadon	none of the other creatures wanted to help	
10	Liadon	because they did not know it was Einhasad in	Complicating Action
11	Liadon	her mortal form	
12	Adeleide	oh!	
13	Liadon	But 4 exceptionally kind creatures did give	
14	Liadon	their assistance	
15	Liadon	that is another story entirely, but one was	
16	Liadon	the humble butterfly	Evaluation
17	Liadon	She did not have much to offer, but spared	
18	Liadon	some dust from her wings to allow Einhasad	
19	Liadon	to make the elves.	
20	Liadon	As a reward, those butterflies who assisted	
21	Liadon	were given the gift of immortality and made	Resolution
22	Liadon	fairies	
23	Liadon	The fairy queen was the original butterfly	
24	Adeleide	how did u know all that?	
25	Liadon	I'm smart :p [joking face]	Coda
26	Liadon	Every elf knows that.	
27	Liadon	Seriously, though. the mother tree told me	

Lin1/03.29.03

FIGURE 18.3. Transcript of an in-game "orally delivered" narrative explaining the origin of the fairies in the Elven Forest. Stanza breaks and line numbers have been added for ease of reference.

the narration by inquiring about Adeleide's knowledge of fairy origins (lines 1–2), a contextually relevant topic inasmuch as the activity underway is one of elven apprenticeship (cf. Steinkuehler, 2004). He then produces a narrative with all of the classical structural features one might expect (Labov, 1972; Labov & Waletzky, 1967): orientation (lines 5–8), complicating action (lines 9–11), evaluation (lines 13–19), resolution (lines 20–23), and coda (lines 25–27). Although the structural features of the "oral" narrative are not surprising, the way in which Liadon transforms the text originally designed into the game into a situated performance is nontrivial. It is highly abbreviated with all non-elf-related details removed and restructured in a way that reorients the evaluation (lines 13–19) exclusively toward elves and their relationship to fairies rather than the full set of creatures the story was originally about. In this way, Liadon adapts the original narrative to the situated needs of the apprenticeship episode underway: the need to explain what fairies are and, tacitly, why one ought not hunt them as one would other creatures.

In contrast to media claims, here gamers are going one step farther than simply "reading aloud"; they are rewriting the story for situated oral performance, surely a literacy practice no less worthwhile than simply orating another author's text. Such performances within the virtual world are not uncommon, as gamers tend to place a high value on textually produced verbal interaction and, therefore, on storytelling, one of our most important forms of "making sense" (Bruner, 1986, 2003). They play an especially important role in in-game apprenticeship episodes, as this example illustrates, by enculturating newcomers into the game lore that constitutes the community's shared knowledge and history.

Beyond-Game Literacy Practices

MMO gaming is participation in a domain of literacy, one with fuzzy boundaries that expand with continued play: What is at first confined to the game alone soon spills over into the virtual world beyond it (e.g., websites, chat rooms, e-mail) and even life off-screen (e.g., telephone calls, face-to-face meetings). The online fandom that surrounds successful game titles is a rich yet nebulous sphere of multimodal multimedia including websites, blogs, threaded discussion boards, fanfictions, fan art, annotated game screenshots, cartoons, chatrooms, instant messaging, in-character emails, and even voice-over Internet protocol (VoIP). To succeed in the game over time, participants must increasingly engage with the online fandom beyond the virtual world itself in order, for example, to research strategies for success against various in-game challenges (NCTE/IRA Standard #7), or to develop deeper understandings of the type of characters they play not only by using their own in-game experiences to better understand texts about their given class (NCTE/IRA Standard #3), but also by using texts to better understand their own experiences (NCTE/IRA Standard #1).

Like all interpretive communities, MMO gamers take up the symbolic, cultural materials offered them by media to collectively create the form and substance of their own cultural worlds (Squire & Steinkuehler, 2006; Taylor, 2002, 2007). As Jenkins (1998) argues, they are no different from the folk cultures of old, except that now the consumers have increasingly user-friendly tools at their disposal to work with, including online access to sociotechnical networks, such as fan groups and guilds, that enable the easy distribution of cultural, material, and symbolic products.

Consider, for example, the fan fiction excerpt shown in Figure 18.4 that circulated through much of *Lineage* fandom in 2003. In it, the author writes about a pseudo-fictional adventure—partially based on an actual occurrence, partially based on the genre conventions of medieval fantasy stories. The story is written at a grade level appropriate to his age; however, what is most interesting here is the purpose for which he purportedly wrote it. The story is dedicated to the second main character appearing in its pages—a girl gamer roughly the author's age. In one e-mail distribution of the story, the author writes, "I included a new story if you would like to read or post up, its awesome ^^ [raised eyebrows] even though I just used it to hit on this girl."

It is difficult to imagine another cultural space in contemporary American youth culture in which writing a short story might be viewed as a recognizable way to court girls. In the context of MMOs, however, such writing is a central and highly valued practice. Here, adeptness with the pen, so to speak, carries a certain social status such

Blinding Twilight
by ~~Strathington Imposters~~
for ~~Issanka~~

As dawn eclipsed the town of Aden, it seemed that its light would never reach the end of the grand city. Built under the tyrannical rule of Ken Rauhel and the corrupt mage Cereris, it seemed almost impossible that such a beautiful city was grounded in their despotic ideals. I looked across the horizon and nudged at ~~Issanka~~, who had fallen asleep during last night's vigil

FIGURE 18.4. Excerpt of the fan fiction piece written by a *Lineage I* gamer.

that those who show exceptional skill in the creation of content often develop a rather large following. In MMOs, such writing is *not* considered as ancillary to gaming but rather as a central part of participating. The social exchange in Figure 18.5 illustrates.

In this in-game exchange, a beginning high school student who is on summer break discusses the short story he has recently decided to author in commemoration of rejoining the guild and being promoted in rank. When asked whether he likes to write in his spare time, he responds, somewhat baffled, "well na i like to play this in my spare time." In the context of MMOs at least, adolescents appear perfectly willing to engage in long, thoughtful writing projects— "2–3 months" planning, not including the initial work done prior to this exchange—in their own spare time, not as isolated literary "assignments" but as part and parcel of what it means to game online.

CONCLUSION

As these examples illustrate, even when based on a restricted version of what it means to read and write, examination of what gamers actually do during play reveals that *gaming, at least in the context of MMOs, is not re-placing literacy activities but rather* is *a literacy activity*. As such, participation in the virtual worlds of MMOs is no less a literary act than participation in the virtual worlds of fanfiction; in both, adolescent fans actively and enthusiastically engage in reading and writing a wide range of literary (albeit popular) texts. Moreover, many such practices are perfectly within the realm of what various national standards and other policy documents indicate that we, as a society, value and ought to foster in our youth.

But, then, what lies behind these claims of a "literacy crisis"? They are likely rooted in a long-standing fear of technology (Williams, 2003), an equally long-standing fear of youth culture (Jenkins, 1999), and a fear of *what* kids are reading and writing, not *whether* they are engaged in such practices per se. Games, like all new media before them, have roused deeply ambivalent feelings in American culture, often masking deeper societal tensions and problems (consider, for example, the media attention given to the gaming habits of the Columbine High School shooters), an attitude often rooted in societal guilt over the mistreatment of American youth, one that again casts them as the *source* of problems (in this case, violence and crime) rather than the *victims* of those oft-ignored risk factors associated with them (e.g. poverty, neglect, abuse). Without tak-

```
SharpPaw     oh yeah! to celebrate me coming back to pledge &
SharpPaw     being rank ive decided to write another story!
SharpPaw     for site!
Adeleide     omg do it! we need more stories!

SharpPaw     ^^ o'course
SharpPaw     in fact ive planned it
SharpPaw     i got the PERFECT story idea the other day when
. . . . . .

SharpPaw     its called An Old Knight's Tale
SharpPaw     youll see it within the next 2-3months

Adeleide     wow! do u like to write in ur spare time?
SharpPaw     well na i like to play this in my spare time

Lin1/03.01.04
```

FIGURE 18.5. Transcript of an in-game conversation in which a student discusses the short story he has recently decided to author over summer break.

ing a broader historical view, it is easy to re-cycle arguments made again and again in the past claiming that technology and/or popu-lar culture are corrupting our youth, each time simply substituting in the latest "men-ace" (e.g., rock and roll, comic books, televi-sion, telephone, etc.) to all things cultural and good (typically, canonical literature and art and other expensive pastimes of the White, Christian, middle-class majority).

The third likely cause, a fear of *what* kids are reading and writing—not *whether,* has a rich history as well but is perhaps a conver-sation, unlike the other two, worth resur-recting. In today's thoroughly networked, globalized, increasingly "flat" (Friedman, 2005) world, adolescents and adults are en-gaged with copious amounts of reading and writing as part of their everyday lifeworld; they just happen to be doing it in spaces and with content that may not always be sanc-tioned by adults. Perhaps they should be, though. There is much concern expressed about youth culture's seeming engrossment in "merely passive" consumption of corpo-rate-owned and profit-driven content. From that perspective, the virtual worlds of fan-dom described herein look particularly prom-ising, for it is through such affinity spaces that adolescents, through the very act of reading and writing, transform increasingly "corporate owned" culture into the "raw materials for telling [our] own stories and resources for forging [our] own communi-ties" (Jenkins, 1998, p. 32).

REFERENCES

Alvermann, D. E. (Ed.). (2002). *Adolescents and literacies in a digital world.* New York: Peter Lang.

Black, R. W. (2005a). Access and affiliation: The liter-acy and composition practices of English-language learners in an online fanfiction community. *Journal of Adolescent and Adult Literacy, 49,* 118–128.

Black, R. W. (2005b). Online fanfiction: What technol-ogy and popular culture can teach us about writing and literacy instruction [Electronic version]. *New Ho-rizons for Learning, 11.* Retrieved May 3, 2005, from *www.newhorizons.org/strategies/literacy/black.htm.*

Black, R. W. (2006). Language, culture, and identity in online fanfiction. *E-Learning, 3,* 170–184.

Black, R. W. (2007). Digital design: English language learners and reader reviews in online fanfiction. In M. Knobel & C. Lankshear (Eds.), *A new literacies sampler* (pp. 115–136). New York: Peter Lang.

Black, R. W. (2008). Just don't call them cartoons: The new literacy spaces of anime, manga, and fanfiction. In C. Lankshear, M. Knobel, D. Leu, & J. Cairo (Eds.), *The handbook of new literacies research.* Mahwah, NJ: Erlbaum.

Bradshaw, T., & Nichols, B. (2004). *Reading at risk: A survey of literary reading in America* (Research Divi-sion Report No. 46). Washington, DC: National En-dowment for the Arts.

Bruce, B. C. (2002). Diversity and critical social engage-ment: How changing technologies enable new modes of literacy in changing circumstances. In D. E. Alver-mann (Ed.), *Adolescents and literacies in a digital world* (pp. 1–18). New York: Peter Lang.

Bruner, J. (1986). *Actual minds, possible worlds.* Cam-bridge MA: Harvard University Press.

Bruner, J. (2003). *Making stories: Law, literature, life.* Cambridge MA: Harvard University Press.

Chandler-Olcott, K., & Mahar, D. (2003a). Adoles-cents' anime-inspired "fanfictions": An exploration of multiliteracies. *Journal of Adolescent and Adult Literacy, 46,* 556–566.

Chandler-Olcott, K., & Mahar, D. (2003b). "Tech-savviness" meets multiliteracies: Exploring adoles-cent girls' technology-mediated literacy practices. *Reading Research Quarterly, 38,* 356–385.

Cope, B., & Kalantzis, M. (Eds.). (2000). *Multiliter-acies: Literacy learning and the design of social fu-tures.* New York: Routledge.

Coppa, F. (2006). A brief history of media fandom. In K. Hellekson & K. Busse (Eds.), *Fan fiction and fan communities in the age of the Internet* (pp. 41–59). Jefferson, NC: McFarland.

Friedman, T. L. (2005). *The world is flat: A brief his-tory of the twenty-first century.* New York: Farrar, Straus, and Giroux.

Gee, J. P. (1996). *Social linguistics and literacies: Ideol-ogy in discourses.* New York: Taylor & Francis.

Gee, J. P. (2004). *Situated language and learning: A cri-tique of traditional schooling.* New York: Routledge.

Goodwin, M. H. (1990). *He-said-she-said: Talk as so-cial organization among Black children.* Bloomington: Indiana University Press.

Guzzetti, B. J. (2006). Cybergirls: Negotiating social identities on cybersites. *E-Learning, 3,* 158–169.

Guzzetti, B. J., & Gamboa, M. (2005). Online journal-ing: The informal writings of two adolescent girls. *Research in the Teaching of English, 40,* 168–206.

Hellekson, K., & Busse, K. (Eds.). (2006). *Fan fiction and fan communities in the age of the Internet.* Jef-ferson, NC: McFarland.

Huizinga, J. (1938). *Homo ludens: A study in the play-elements in culture* (R.F.C. Hull, trans.) Boston: Bea-con.

Ipsos-Insight. (2005). *Essential facts about the com-puter and video game industry.* Washington, DC: En-tertainment Software Association. Retrieved August 4, 2007, from *www.theesa.com/archives/files/Essen-tial_Facts_2006.pdf.*

Jenkins, H. (1992a). "Strangers no more, we sing":

Filking and the social construction of the science fiction fan community. In L. A. Lewis (Ed.), *The adoring audience: Fan culture and popular media* (pp. 208–236). New York: Routledge.

Jenkins, H. (1992b). *Textual poachers: Studies in culture and communication.* New York: Routledge.

Jenkins, H. (1998, March). *The poachers and the stormtroopers: Popular culture in the digital age.* Paper presented at the Media and Technology Conference, University of Michigan, Ann Arbor.

Jenkins, H. (1999). Professor Jenkins goes to Washington. *Harper's Magazine, 299*(1790), 19.

Jenkins, H. (2006). *Convergence culture: Where old and new media collide.* New York: New York University Press.

Karpovich, A. I. (2006). The audience as editor: The role of beta readers in online fan fiction communities. In K. Hellekson & K. Busse (Eds.), *Fan fiction and fan communities in the age of the Internet* (pp. 171–188). Jefferson, NC: McFarland.

Knobel, M., & Lankshear, C. (2002). Cut, paste, publish: The production and consumption of zines. In D. E. Alvermann (Ed.), *Adolescents and literacies in a digital world* (pp. 164–185). New York: Peter Lang.

Labov, W. (1972). *Language in the inner city: Studies in the Black English vernacular.* Philadelphia: University of Pennsylvania Press.

Labov, W., & Waletzky, J. (1967). Narrative analysis. In J. Helm (Ed.), *Essays on the verbal and visual arts* (pp. 12–44). Seattle: University of Washington Press.

Lam, W. S. E. (2000). Literacy and the design of the self: A case study of a teenager writing on the Internet. *TESOL Quarterly, 34,* 457–482.

Lam, W. S. E. (2004). Second language socialization in a bilingual chat room: Global and local considerations [Electronic version]. *Language Learning and Technology, 8,* 44–65. Retrieved August 16, 2006, from *llt.msu.edu/vol8num3/lam/default.html.*

Lam, W. S. E. (2007). Re-envisioning language, literacy, and the immigrant subject in new mediascapes. *Pedagogies: An International Journal, 1,* 171–195.

Lankshear, C., & Knobel, M. (2006). *New literacies: Changing knowledge and classroom learning* (2nd ed.). Philadelphia: Open University Press.

Lave, J., & Wenger, E. (1991). *Situated learning: Legitimate peripheral participation.* New York: Cambridge University Press.

Lenhart, A., Madden, M., & Hitlin, P. (2005). Teens and technology: Youth are leading the transition to a fully wired and mobile nation [Electronic version]. *Pew Internet and American Life Project.* Retrieved July 15, 2006, from *www.pewinternet.org/report_display.asp?r=162.*

Lesko, N. (2001). *Act your age: Cultural constructions of adolescence.* New York: Falmer.

Levin, D., & Arafeh, S. (2002). The digital disconnect: The widening gap between Internet-savvy students and their schools [Electronic version]. *Pew Internet and American Life Project.* Retrieved July 15, 2006, from *www.pewinternet.org/pdfs/PIP_Schools_Internet_Report.pdf.*

Lewis, C., & Fabos, B. (2005). Instant messaging, literacies, and social identities. *Reading Research Quarterly, 40,* 470–501.

Mandese, J. (2004, April 5). Video games emerge as "No. 4" medium. *Media Daily News.* Retrieved July 8, 2005, from *publications.mediapost.com/index.cfm?fuseaction=Articles.showArticle&art_aid=4814.*

National Council of Teachers of English and the International Reading Association. (1996). *Standards for the English language arts.* Urbana, IL: National Council of Teachers of English; Newark, DE: International Reading Association.

New London Group (1996). A pedagogy of multiliteracies. *Harvard Educational Review, 66,* 60–92.

Pugh, S. (2005). *The democratic genre: Fan fiction in a literary context.* Brigend, Wales: Seren.

Sanders, B. (1995). *A is for ox: The collapse of literacy and the rise of violence in an electronic age.* New York: Random House.

Squire, K. D., & Steinkuehler, C. A. (2006). Generating CyberCulture/s: The case of *Star Wars* galaxies. In D. Gibbs & K. L. Krause (Eds.), *Cyberlines: Languages and cultures of the Internet* (2nd ed., pp. 177–198). Albert Park, Australia: James Nicholas.

Steinkuehler, C. A. (2004). Learning in massively multiplayer online games. In Y. B. Kafai, W. A. Sandoval, N. Enyedy, A. S. Nixon, & F. Herrera (Eds.), *Proceedings of the Sixth International Conference of the Learning Sciences* (pp. 521–528). Mahwah, NJ: Erlbaum.

Steinkuehler, C. A. (2005). *Cognition and learning in massively multiplayer online games: A critical approach.* Unpublished doctoral dissertation, University of Wisconsin-Madison.

Steinkuehler, C. A. (2006). Massively multiplayer online videogaming as participation in a discourse. *Mind, Culture, and Activity, 13,* 38–52.

Steinkuehler, C. A., & Chmiel, M. (2006). Fostering scientific habits of mind in the context of online play. In S.A. Barab, K.E. Hay, N.B. Songer, & D.T. Hickey (Eds.), *Proceedings of the International Conference of the Learning Sciences* (pp. 723–729). Mahwah, NJ: Erlbaum.

Steinkuehler, C. A., & Williams, D. (2006). Where everybody knows your (screen) name: Online games as "third places." *Journal of Computer-Mediated Communication, 11*(4), article 1. Retrieved April 24, 2008, from *http://jcmc.indiana.edu/vol11/issue4/steinkuehler.html.*

Stern, S. R. (1999). Adolescent girls' expression on Web home pages: Spirited, sombre, and self-conscious sites. *Convergence, 5,* 22–41.

Stern, S. R. (2004). Expressions of identity online: Prominent features and gender differences in adolescents' World Wide Web home pages. *Journal of Broadcasting and Electronic Media, 48,* 218–243.

Street, B. (1984). *Literacy in theory and practice.* New York: Cambridge University Press.

Taylor, T. L. (2002). Whose game is this anyway?: Negotiating corporate ownership in a virtual world. In F. Mäyrä (Ed.), *Proceedings of the computer games and digital cultures conference* (pp. 227–242). Tampere, Finland: Tampere University Press.

Taylor, T. L. (2007). Pushing the borders: Player participation and game culture. In J. Karaganis & N. Jeremijenko (Eds.), *Network_netplay: Structures of participation in digital culture.* Durham, NC: Duke University Press.

Thomas, A. (2005). Positioning the reader: The affordances of digital fiction. In J. Clarke (Ed.), *Proceedings of 2005 Queensland Council for Adult Literacy Conference "Reading the Past, Writing the Future: Measuring Progress"* (pp. 24–33). Brisbane, Queensland, Australia.

Thomas, A. (2006). MSN was the next big thing after Beanie Babies: Children's virtual experiences as an interface to their identities and their everyday lives. *E-Learning, 3,* 126–142.

Turkle, S. (1995). *Life on the screen: Identity in the age of the Internet.* New York: Touchstone.

Wearden, G. (2001, August 20). Researchers: Video games hurt brain development. *CNET News.* Retrieved July 6, 2005, from *news.com.com/Researchers+ Video+games+hurt+brain+development/2100-1040_3- 271849.html.*

Williams, D. (2003). The video game lightning rod: Constructions of a new media technology, 1970– 2000. *Information, Communication and Society, 6,* 523–550.

CHAPTER 19

Reading and Writing Video

Media Literacy and Adolescents

DAVID L. BRUCE

This chapter focuses on adolescents reading and writing with various forms of print and nonprint media, which include digital video, movies, the Internet, video games, music, magazines, graphic novels, and text messaging, among others. After providing a guiding definition of media literacy, the chapter explores a vignette of one adolescent's complex video reading and writing about his skateboarding interest. The chapter continues with an exploration of 15 studies—a combination of in-school and out-of-school settings—exploring adolescents' reading and writing with media. The research compiled for this chapter indicates that nonprint media constitute adolescents' dominant form of text. Other themes include the number of complex skills and strategies students used when reading and composing with media texts. Adolescents' use of media also tended to provide positive individual—particularly with identity exploration—and social experiences. Problematic issues with media literacy center on tensions that exist in using adolescents' out-of-school media literacies while studying them within school contexts, as well as logistical problems in using media technologies within school contexts. Several implications arise from this review of literature. One implication is that educators should accept media texts as legitimate in academic curricula, particularly in expanding what it means to read and write. Teacher training for media literacy and funding for equitable access to technology in schools are also areas that need to be addressed. A final implication relates to the funding of promising research in this area. Although qualitative studies (particularly in the form of case studies) continue to be a valuable source of generative findings, funding for research on youth and media has tended to favor quantitative and experimental methods.

Wｅ live in a time of rapid change in the proliferation of media in which adolescents read and compose. The challenges these changes present to educators, however, are not new, inasmuch as scholars have been commenting on them for a half century. Consider, for instance, this 1962 statement from a publication for English teachers:

With respect to the movies and television, I'm afraid many of us have adopted either the defensive maneuvers of the ostrich or the offensive charge of the bull. The ostriches among us seemed to hope that if we hide our heads in our books the enemy will go away; the bulls among us attack the movies and television with insults and derision. Neither attitude is a healthy one; certainly neither has been effective.

Movies and television, the new media of communication, are *new languages*. As teachers, we must realize that they deserve our attention and must prepare our students to live with them intelligently. They are here to stay. To ignore them is impossible; to oppose them is futile. (O'Sullivan, 1962, p. 82; emphasis in original)

Though the media options have multiplied since the preceding statement was written more than 40 years ago, the argument remains the same. Today's *new languages* appear overwhelming: blogs, podcasts, video games, MySpace, graphic novels, camera phones, text messages, and media that will be common 5 years from now but which we do not yet imagine. These various forms, though new, are texts that can be read and studied in a similar manner as books have been read and studied. Moreover, students can not only read these emergent forms, they can create their own texts with them as well.

What are educators and policymakers to make of such a wide array of available and accessible texts in the lives of adolescents? How are students using these various media in their own lives to read, compose, and make meaning? Should these literacies remain outside school contexts or should they be integrated into academic curricula?

A guiding framework through which educators study and examine communications technologies—from the relative simplicity of a photograph to the complexity of computer animation—is that of *media literacy*. In this chapter, I begin with a definition of media literacy and a vignette of one adolescent's reading and composing with media. I then review research done with adolescents and media literacy, highlight some key themes that overlap the various studies, and conclude with implications for adolescents and media usage.

DEFINING MEDIA LITERACY

The most widely cited definition of *media literacy* is Aufderheide's (1993): "to access, analyze, evaluate and communicate messages in a variety of forms" (p. xx). At the heart of this definition is the reading of and writing with various media, which is the guiding definition used in this chapter. Two

media literacy organizations, the Alliance for Media Literate America (2005) and the Center for Media Literacy (Thoman & Jolls, 2005), have taken the core *access, analyze, evaluate,* and *communicate* concepts and added *context* and *purpose* as to why these skills are important. For example, the latter organization defines media literacy as:

> A 21st century approach to education. It provides a framework to access, analyze, evaluate, and create messages in a variety of forms— from print to video to the Internet. Media literacy builds an understanding of the role of media in society as well as essential skills of inquiry and self-expression necessary for citizens of a democracy. (p. 190)

Tyner (1998, pp. 94–95), Kist (2005, pp. 4–16), and the Alliance for a Media Literate America (2005) have also provided extended discussions of the meaning of media literacy.

Media Literacy in an Adolescent (Jonathan)

In this section, I provide a vignette of one student's practices of reading and writing with media. Though I am not suggesting that this individual is representative of all students, I am attempting to portray one example of what media literacy looks like in the life of a particular middle-class adolescent living in the midwest United States, to put a face on this complex topic.

My nephew, Jonathan, is a high school sophomore who is conscientious about his schoolwork, though it is really just something to finish so he can spend time on his real interest: skateboarding. Since getting his first skateboard at the age of 9, he has been consumed with skateboard culture. It influences his taste in clothing (skateboard-themed/ logo pants, T-shirts, sweatshirts, and, especially, shoes), music, friendships, and language. He calls almost everyone "dude."

Jonathan reads skateboard-related texts constantly. He has played and mastered every level of every Tony Hawk video game, which features the famous skateboarder. He owns skateboarding magazines, videos, and DVDs. He searches Google, YouTube, and MySpace for skate videos. He attends professional skateboarding competitions and festivals, which are themselves rich texts of skateboard culture.

Jonathan also composes skateboard videos of himself and his friends, and he has compiled an extensive collection of these videos. After school and on weekends, they skate throughout the community (much of which has posted "No Skateboarding" signs). Jonathan takes his video camera—his second one, because he wore out the internal mechanisms in his first one through extensive use—with them to record their jumps and tricks. After each outing, Jonathan loads the best of that day's footage to a computer hard drive already packed with hours of such video. When he has saved the selected images to the hard drive, he then recycles the videotape to use again for raw footage.

This hard drive serves as a video version of a "writer's notebook" (Bomer, 1995). Just as a notebook provides a space in which to record thoughts, words, and phrases, the hard drive stores images and scenes. Jonathan goes back to archived episodes to find appropriate footage for inclusion in a newer video to fit a theme he is working on. Periodically, he and his friends get together to edit themed videos, such as unsuccessful skateboard landings and wipeouts ("Bails!") or correctly executed stunts ("Beasts!"). As I write this, they have been working on a highlight video for 18 months, and it is already more than an hour long. Though they have included numerous clips with painstaking craft, according to Jonathan, they still have a lot they need to work on. Most recently, Jonathan and his friends have vested their time in posting shorter video clips to their MySpace pages.

Jonathan's reading and writing activities influence one another. He watches professional and/or online videos looking not only for skating tricks that he can imitate, but also for the production techniques, how the camera or editing was used to create a scene. Most recently, Jonathan acquired a "fish-eye lens," a camera accessory that broadens the camera view. This lens is used by many skateboard videographers and Jonathan wanted his productions to have a similar style. He experiments with the camera and his editing software to recreate video techniques. He and his friends also watch themselves on video and critique their performance for improvement in their own skating the next time.

I have invited Jonathan to attend several of my graduate Teaching Video Composition workshops. In addition to having him assist participants with editing software, I have him share his video work with the inservice teachers. This high school student—who has been referred to as a "skate-punk" by educators and community members—speaks to graduate students on broad and complex compositional aspects such as point-of-view, thesis, transitions, and audience. The irony of an adolescent skateboarder helping to teach a workshop for English teachers is not lost on him. After one session when he had been particularly helpful and had gotten encouraging feedback about his work from a number of the participants, he commented to me that maybe he was "not a dumb-ass" after all.

During a period of weeks when he was helping me with a series of such workshops, he created a hybrid music video/skate diary. On Saturday he spoke to the workshop participants about a project he was considering, and the next week he showed them what he had composed. Jonathan spent 18 hours of one day creating a video set to David Bowie's "Fashion" to represent a day in his life. He had been playing this song in the car as we were driving to the workshop and said that it would be the perfect song to use to make a video he had been thinking about. He stated, "When I listen to songs, sometimes I imagine how they could look as a video."

He videotaped the entire video in first person, either showing his face or his perspective as he went from waking up to going to bed. Explaining his filming strategy, he said:

"I took the camera and flipped out the screen, and I would film my facial expressions as I was walking toward the camera. And whenever I was looking down at an object, I would turn the camera to give the illusion that the camera was me looking around. I would turn the camera back around to see what I was seeing and then turn the camera back to my face to see my perspective. I filmed it in real speed and then sped it up two to three times the normal speed on the computer on iMovie."

He did not put the video together through a linear process but instead created the whole piece in a recursive manner:

"I went outside to film and came back in-side to edit it. I didn't film it all at once. I'd film for a little bit, try a bunch of dif-ferent things, go on my computer, edit what I liked and then tape over the rest."

He chose to make the video black and white except for the time he was skating. During the skateboard sequence, the footage changes to color. He explained:

"It seems like whenever you wake up and the things that you go through, you are kind of oblivious. It's just the same thing you do every morning to get ready to go. It gets kind of boring. So whenever I go out to skateboard, it's just all joy and something I like to do, and it's fun. So af-ter that, when you go back inside and fig-ure you have a bunch of other stuff to do, then it goes back to black and white cause it's the same routine you go through every night. The black and white symbolizes the plainness of doing the same thing over and over again. Skateboarding is always changing and new and fun. I guess it's unique to show against the black and white to make the color."

It is noteworthy that Jonathan spent 18 hours in one day to compose this video. I taught high school English and media stud-ies for 11 years prior to working in higher education. Though I remember a number of students postponing writing assignments un-til the last possible moment before cram-ming to get them done, I cannot recall a sin-gle student who *voluntarily* spent 18 hours in a day writing anything with print.

What is also remarkable about Jonathan's work with video is the amount of print-based reading and composition skills he reg-ularly uses. He reads skateboarding texts for information, such as how to perform a skat-ing trick, and for critical analysis, such as figuring out the production techniques in a video in order to imitate them for his own use. In composing his own videos, he has gained a number of complex and recursive composition strategies, including a sustained thesis, point of view, the use of conventions for intended effect, and audience awareness. What surprises me most, though, is not the literacy skills Jonathan has developed on his own. It is that, other than the presentations

he has made in my workshops, he has never had occasion to use his video expertise in any of his classrooms. There is a disconnect between this rich video literacy he has culti-vated on his own and the print literacy that dominates his schoolwork. This year, his English teacher is giving an open-ended as-signment in which students can use their choice of modalities (visual, artistic, and others). Working on that assignment will be the first time Jonathan can connect his video literacy and school.

Jonathan's story highlights a tension be-tween what Hull and Schultz (2002) call "out of school literacies" and the literacies students are expected to demonstrate in aca-demic settings. What happens when those literacies coincide?

REVIEW OF RESEARCH STUDIES ON ADOLESCENTS AND MEDIA LITERACY

Table 19.1 includes 15 studies of adolescents and media literacy. I selected these studies because they investigated the ways adoles-cents read and composed with media. Some of the studies took place in school settings, others in out-of-school contexts, and some in a combination of both. Writings that were primarily theoretical or that mainly offered advice for teachers are not included in this chart.

A finding across all the studies is that ado-lescents were interested in nonprint media texts. The texts varied in modality, but stu-dents responded in positive ways to the re-spective media being examined. I address this especially significant finding separately in the "Discussion" section. Here, I high-light some of the other recurrent findings from these research studies.

Multiple Facets of Reading Media Texts

A number of the studies demonstrated the multiple ways students read media texts. The research suggests that visual and audi-tory texts offer adolescents a rich opportu-nity to demonstrate a wide range of reading skills.

Some studies found that students were able to demonstrate understanding and cri-

TABLE 19.1 Research on Adolescents and Media Literacy

Studies	Questions	In school/ out of school	Research design/context	Data sources	Findings
Alvermann & Hagood (2000)	1. How can literacy educators assist adolescents in developing their literacy practices and affective sensibilities toward the music they appreciate and follow? 2. How can we develop a better understanding of the students we teach?	In school (one student's assignment) Out of school	Case study, 2 students (1 boy, 1 girl)	Interviews, student work, e-mail correspondence	1. Teenagers have varying tastes, desires, interests, and reasons for selecting their music. 2. Reading from different positions (a component of critical media literacy) allows for deeper understanding/meaning making. 3. Parody and imitation help students try on new positions and identities.
Alvermann, Moon, & Hagood (1999)	1. How would students use Cohen's Masquerade strategy to question popular lyrics? 2. What did they discover about their roles as audience members?	In school	Observer-participant Outside researcher in 8th-grade classroom (n = 15 participants, 8 male, 6 female	Observation, student work	1. Students were able to unpack messages of popular media. 2. Modified version of Cohen's (1998) Masquerade was useful for exploration of audience roles.
Beavis (2002)	1. What does it mean to extend the range of texts studied in the English class to include games, consistent with the inclusion of "everyday" and "electronic" texts as deemed appropriate by standards guidelines? 2. What is the nature of computer games as narratives and texts? 3. What are the changing constructions of literacy (reflected in planning, teaching, and evaluation of "computer games as text" unit)?	In school	Observer-participant Outside researchers worked with teachers from 2 Victorian secondary schools (Australia), 1 private and 1 state school	Student work, observation, audiotaped transcriptions of interviews and class discussions, student interviews, teacher interviews	1. Students and teachers embraced inclusion of computer games as "texts." 2. Playing computer games was social and interactive (contrary to popular belief). 3. Students engaged in the games in nonlinear fashion (intuitive play). 4. Technology is an issue (access to, as well as desired function). 5. High level of interest with students (largely with boys, mixed reactions with girls). 6. Students produced thoughtful and high-quality work with print and electronic modes.
Bragg (2002)	1. How does one student's media production work develop (including embedded forms of media literacy, the teachers' responses, and the researcher's understanding)?	In school	Case study, 1 male	Classroom observations, research journal, student work	1. Practical element of production is both richer and more problematic than theoretical critique. 2. Media production can be flexible enough to permit students' pleasure and expertise in classroom settings.

(continued)

TABLE 19.1 (*continued*)

Studies	Questions	In school/ out of school	Research design/context	Data sources	Findings
Bruce (2008)	1. To what extent do lower-achieving students engage with complex composition strategies, particularly when composing a video project in the context of a media-based language arts elective?	In school	Teacher-researcher study Case study, (2 advanced media studies courses) 4 males (1 11th grader, 3 12th graders)	Surveys, think-aloud protocols, classroom observations and videotapes, interviews, student work	1. Students with low print skills were able to demonstrate complex composition skills and recursive composition skills through the medium of video.
Buckingham & Sefton-Green (1994)	1. What is the relationship between students' existing knowledge of the media and the "academic" knowledge we make available in schools? 2. What is the relationship between students' critical analysis of the media and their involvement in practical production?	In school	Participant-observer Collaboration between teacher-researcher and university-based researcher	Classroom observation, interviews (individual and small group), surveys, student work	1. Students made sense of media through a process in which individual and social identities were defined and negotiated. 2. Practical production may offer students the potential for a much more genuinely active and playful relationship with popular culture than can be achieved through analytical critique.
Chandler-Olcott & Mahar (2003)	1. In what ways and for what purposes do adolescent girls use digital technologies in their literacy practices beyond formal academic settings? 2. How does their membership in various online communities of practice influence these technology-mediated practices? 3. How are constructions of gender implicated in the girls' technology-mediated literacy practices within these communities?	In school Out of school	Case study, 2 7th-grade females Partnership of classroom-based teacher and university researcher	Field notes, interviews, observations in home visits and classroom discussions, online artifacts (websites, listservs, e-mail)	1. Adolescent girls employ technological tools in a variety of ways for a variety of purposes. The girls clearly had multiple purposes or objectives for designing in their respective activity systems. 2. Both girls used their membership in online communities to create richer and more satisfying social lives than they had in real time. 3. The girls' membership in their online communities served mentorship and pedagogical functions related to their technology-mediated designing. 4. Gender played a role in their preferred activity systems, primarily as single sex, and provided the girls with a space to explore and express their gender identities.
Fisherkeller (2000)	1. How do young adolescents use, and what do they already know about TV?	In school Out of school	Ethnographic research, participant-observer 60 students, 11–13 years old	Class and home visitations, student work, surveys, interviews	1. Young adolescents understand how the contents of TV programs are crafted as different kinds of stories, using various types of characters and narrative features, and that these TV programs need to have a certain intent. 2. Young adolescents observe the nature and logic of TV programming and scheduling, which characterize the relationship between media industries and audiences. 3. Young adolescents have knowledge of TV as a kind of factory, that TV is an industry.

Study	Research questions	Setting	Design/Participants	Data sources/analysis	Findings
Goodman (2003)	1. How do students' out-of-school experiences learning from the media and their local community shape the kinds of literacies and critical thinking skills they bring with them to school each day? 2. How do oral culture, visual language, and the experience of growing up in economically depressed communities shape the way these kids learn to bring critical literacy to the way they make sense of and act upon the world around them? 3. (In-school questions) What kinds of literacies were developed and what kinds of learning takes place when an out-of-school-based media education program is implemented in a school setting?	Out of school In school	Participant-observer Out of school: Case study, 12 high school male and female participants In school: Case study, $n = 16$ participants (10th–11th graders); 8 female; 8 male	Interviews, student work, observation	**Out-of-school findings:** 1. Students did not use traditional forms of inquiry, research, and exploring possible solutions. Students tended to mistrust printed and media information; rather, they relied heavily on personal and community-based experiences for their information. 2. Students enjoyed exploring their community with a video camera. 3. Watching their interviews allows for the development of critical distance between themselves and their topic. 4. Students exhibited self-reflection through exploring their larger community topic. 5. Students constructed a powerful collection of words, music, and images that represented their own framing of reality and presented it in a public venue. 6. The process of interviewing changed the power relations between the students and the adults they interviewed. **In school findings:** 1. Bringing video into the classroom placed in-school and out-of-school media viewing habits in tension with each other. 2. Students found power in being able to select a topic that was not traditionally in the academic curriculum. 3. Students needed guided practice with production, interviewing, and writing skills. 4. Students' learning progress and problems were made visible through the medium of video. 5. Students worked as interdependent learners on their video projects.
Hobbs (2007)	1. How do students respond to media literacy instruction? 2. Does media literacy improve students' literacy skills? 3. Does media literacy alter students' attitudes about school? 4. Does media literacy affect motivation, confidence, or aspects of identity development? 5. Does media literacy affect quality of relationships between teachers and students? 6. Do media literacy lessons from the classroom transfer to nonschool settings?	In school	Seven-year study of one high school English department Mixed methods: Qualitative Quantitative treatment group: $n = 287$, grade 11 Control group: $n = 89$, grade 11	Qualitative data: observations, interviews, student and teacher classroom artifacts Quantitative design and analysis: quasi-experimental nonequivalent-group design Analysis of covariance (ANCOVA)	Students (treatment group) who received training in media literacy were able to show significant differences from the control group in: 1. Identifying main ideas, purpose, creative construction techniques, point of view, omitted information, and compare/contrast news sources in media texts. 2. Knowledge of advertising production process, including various steps of preproduction, production, and postproduction processes. 3. Reading comprehension, critical reading, and writing skills. Within the treatment group, gender differences arose: 1. Females increased significantly in their ability to understand the complexities of government. 2. Both males and females increased significantly in their sense of empowerment to understand politics but also demonstrated a significant sense of skepticism about politicians and media agents. *(continued)*

TABLE 19.1 (*continued*)

Studies	Questions	In school/ out of school	Research design/context	Data sources	Findings
Moss (2006)	1. How do informal literacies differ from schooled literacies in terms of the knowledge they generate? 2. How do students react to the presence of informal texts in the formal domain? How far are they aware of the different principles at work in each setting?	In school Out of school	4-year study of same group of children 7–11 years of age at the beginning of study; 11–15 years of age at the end of study	Interviews, questionnaires, student work	1. Students demonstrated interest (which shifted over time) in a variety of media texts. Informal literacies developed around present and (horizontal) discourse) contextual interests. 2. Students traveled between and had a clear delineation between their (informal) texts and school (formal) texts. Students did not wish their informal texts, in which they were invested, to be placed in school settings. 3. Students were able to articulate the role of school in their current and future lives: Middle-class students had more visible and inclusive knowledge of school literacies than working-class students.
Niesyto (2001)	1. To what extent is it possible to identify forms of transcultural, audiovisual symbolic language in videotapes produced by groups of young people from different countries and symbolic milieus? 2. What styles of symbolic processing, presentation, and understanding are involved in the process of filming, in the productions themselves, and in the interpretations? To what extent are these styles influenced by factors such as education, gender, ethnic and class background, as well as by the characteristics of the young people's media culture?	In school Out of school	Participant observer Case studies, (international) 14- to 19-year-old males and females	Interviews, surveys, discussion groups, student work (videos)	1. There were transcultural elements of symbolic comprehension, which were situated on the level of "symbolic feeling" rather than "symbolic consciousness." 2. Participants demonstrated various levels of thematic (cognitive), aesthetic (cinematic), and emotional (intuitive) responses to the films. 3. Differences: • Participants tried to make use of "third cultures" to express individual concerns and feelings about life. • There is a relation between types of cultural capital available to young people and their modes of aesthetic production. • Gender-related differences had greater impact on preferences for certain videos and modes of symbolization than differences in education, age, and culture.
Parker (2006)	1. What are the narrative links between print and moving-image media? 2. How do the different conceptual and technological demands of each medium lead to enhanced comprehension of storytelling in general? 3. How can the explicit demands of composition required by the creation of an animated film be used as a scaffold for writing?	In school	Partnership of British Film Institute, King's College, London (School of Education), and public school 2 mixed-ability year 7 classrooms	Observations, student work	1. Students are quicker to come to an overall understanding of a complete story when they have an opportunity to engage with it through more than one medium, especially if moving-image media are involved. 2. Students' compositional skills with regard to structuring a narrative in film were far ahead of their written compositional skills. 3. Reluctant or emergent readers may become more positive about books when they are enabled to talk about and conceptualize one medium in terms of another.

Study		Research questions		Data sources	Findings
Pombo & Bruce (2007)	In school	1. How were students able to demonstrate understanding of key media principles in reflecting how media influenced their self-identities?	Four-month partnership between university researcher and classroom teacher One beginning-level media studies course (9th–12th graders)	Classroom observations, interviews (audio and video), student and teacher work	1. Students demonstrated awareness of media literacy principles and how their identities as teenagers were partially formed by media influences, but also demonstrated little interest in resisting those influences. 2. Students could engage in complex topics (i.e., gender identity) but needed the classroom to be a safe place before sharing. 3. Students' reading and writing of media texts informed each other.
Zaslow & Butler (2002)	Out of school	1. How do young adults understand (videoculture) videos, particularly those not from their culture? 2. How do young adults talk about growing up in a media culture?	Case study, 12 adolescents (8 female, 4 male), 14–17 years old	Observation, research journals, audiotaped student responses	1. Students had a broad conception of adolescence in their own culture as well as a more global experience. 2. The pleasure students experienced watching the videos was linked to their ability to make sense of the video's narrative form, genre, and symbolic representation. They use codes of what they know to help decipher what they did not know. 3. There was a tension between what students heard from parents, teachers, and media and what they knew from their own media experiences.

tique of media texts, skills analogous to print reading comprehension. In comparing the performance of students who received media literacy training (experimental group) with those who had not (control group), Hobbs (2007) found that students in the experimental group showed significant differences in being able to identify main ideas and purpose in a variety of media, including print and video news stories, photographs, advertisements, radio excerpts, and film. In addition to comprehension, students in the experimental group demonstrated a wide variety of critical reading skills using a range of media texts, including identifying creative construction techniques and point of view. Those students also considered what information might have been omitted from a text, compared and contrasted news sources, and inferred the constructed processes of media.

Parker (2006) studied students who adapted a fictional narrative into both poetic and animated form. He found that through multiple versions of the text, the students came to a better overall understanding of a story than through print alone. In addition, reluctant and/or emergent readers better discussed books when comparing them to other media. Both the Hobbs (2007) and Parker (2006) studies suggest that students may better understand commonly assigned reading tasks through media texts (or combining print and media texts) than with print alone.

The following four studies demonstrate that students engaged in a variety of other reading skills as well. Fisherkeller (2000) found that students not only understood the content of TV programs; they identified various character and genre features. Moreover, students explored and understood the audience's complicated relationship with the business aspects of the TV industry. Beavis (2002) discovered that in a classroom where video games were incorporated into the curriculum, students demonstrated a wide range of skill in reading the games through graphics, narrative structure, ratings, packaging and marketing, reviews, and game manuals.

Alvermann, Moon, and Hagood (1999) found that in examining visual messages, music, lyrics, and magazine articles, students could "read and interpret the disparate elements of such messages in a way that signaled their understanding of how things that seem natural and commonsensical on the

surface may be mined for deeper meanings" (p. 106). In studying the ways that adolescents read student-produced videos from other cultures, Niesyto (2001) found that students read the films in several different ways—thematically, aesthetically, and emotionally—though not all students read all the films in all three ways. These four studies suggest that reading media texts allows students to demonstrate a wide range of reading skills.

A common myth of media consumption is that viewers are passive recipients of media messages. These studies suggest that students actively transact with media texts, indicating that media can be read and interpreted as rich texts. In doing so, students exhibit reading skills that are of value in academic settings.

Rich Compositions of Texts

Viewers or listeners of nonprint media perform actions analogous to those of readers, and recent studies have documented how media texts influence students' composition skills. Two studies detailed how classrooms used media texts as prompts to which the students wrote print responses and described how students improved their written skills in the process. In her research regarding an 11th-grade English curriculum, Hobbs (2007) found that students who had formal training with media literacy measurably increased the quality and quantity of their prompted written responses. Beavis (2002) examined a classroom in which the study and playing of videogames were incorporated into the curriculum. Students wrote "reviews, creative and imaginative responses to the games and discussions of issues such as the significance of computer games ('for or against'), and reflection on technology and its place in the community" (p. 58). In both these studies, media were used as prompts to help students increase their print-writing skills.

Studies also detailed how students composed in nonprint modalities as well, using video, music, and images to create in ways that are similar to writers' processes. Several of the selected research studies found that students composed complex and creative media texts. Bruce (2008) studied four male students who engaged in a long-term project of creating a music video through story-boards, original videotaped footage, acting, editing, graphics, and special effects. Like-wise, Goodman (2003) documented how urban youth created representations of their experience through documentary videos. Students planned and made their videos through dialogue, interviews, camerawork, editing, music selection, editing, and graphics. In both of the aforementioned studies, it is important to note that the students demonstrated a higher level of comfort in composing the media texts than they did in composing with print. In their exploration of adolescent females' online communities of practice, Chandler-Olcott and Mahar (2003) detailed how the girls were comfortable composing with technology as a means of expression and communication. They found that the girls in their study employed technological tools for a variety of purposes and/or objectives, including the construction of web pages and using online communities for posting and feedback of anime art.

These studies suggest that media texts can play an important role in the compositional skills of adolescents. Media can both facilitate the print responses of students and serve as a complex and recursive process of composition.

Reading and Writing Connection

In the realm of print literacy, it is widely held that reading and writing are interconnected processes that inform each other. Scholes (1985) asserts that "reading and writing are complementary acts" (p. 20). In addressing the reading and writing connection with media, Tyner (1998) notes that "the analysis–production formula creates a spiral of success: analysis informs production, which in turn informs analysis" (p. 200). Evidence for this assertion can be found in several other studies. Pombo and Bruce (2007) found that students' reading and writing of media texts were symbiotic. As students composed their videos, their reading of media texts became more astute, particularly in noticing production techniques and the constructed form of the media. Reading those media texts, in turn, informed the content and form of their own video compositions.

In a similar manner, when Buckingham and Sefton-Green (1994) examined the writings of one student, they found that his compositions had been influenced by a variety of readings. The researchers found that the student's work was an intertextual composite containing influences—including twists on names, quotes, narrative structures, and character types—from a number of comic books and films. They stated, "'Reading' the media is also a dialogical process, 'writing' media texts brings this dialogue into the open, and thus potentially opens it up for critical reflection and analysis" (p. 82). Through the "written" media product, the normally hidden sources of reading influences were made visible, and thus new opportunities for discussion were made available.

In following the media compositions of one male, Bragg (2002) found that the student was able to express himself better through production than through analysis. The student could not express the media literacy theory presented in the classroom, but "was more articulate with the camera than obviously academically sophisticated students" (p. 47). This study documents other languages in which students can articulate ideas and display their understandings. In cases such as this one, assessment that is limited to print and speech is less accurate than assessment that includes other modalities.

These studies suggest that, as with print literacy, reading and writing with media are interconnected and complementary processes. In examining them together, educators may have a more complete assessment of students' understanding.

Media Texts as Social Events

Another finding from the research studies deals with how media texts served as social events among the adolescents. Several of the studies highlighted the social aspects of contexts in which adolescents have studied media texts. Chandler-Olcott and Mahar (2003) found that the girls in their study had better social support in their online communities than they had in a school's social circles. However, the researchers did not find that the experience of the girls' online communities "made it any easier for them to negotiate their daily lives beyond the Web" (pp. 379–380). Beavis (2002) offers a refutation of a common myth, that video games are isolated experiences for students. In studying video games in a classroom context, she states, "Contrary to popular beliefs, playing games [in school] was intensely social and interactive" (p. 56).

Media productions also served as a means for collaborative group work. Bruce (2008) documented how four students shared the various requirements—guiding ideas, acting, camera, editing, and postproduction decisions—in collaboratively creating a music video. Similarly, Goodman (2003) stated that students' work on their video projects required them to contribute individually and collaboratively. Students functioned as "interdependent learners, at various times collaborating, teaching, and learning from each other" (p. 97). In both studies, the processes of the video projects were highly public (videotaping, watching footage collaboratively, watching each other's work in progress), as was the communal viewing of the final products.

These studies suggest that media texts provide an interactive context within which students build both their out-of-school social lives and their in-school collaborative work.

Tension of Using Media Texts within School Settings

There is an obvious tension between the literacies of students' experiences outside the classroom and those encountered in the print-dominated atmosphere of the traditional school day. The investigations reviewed here that studied academic settings contained a paradox. Although students seemed to enjoy working with media texts, they also felt a tension caused by having media texts brought into academic discourse. A number of the studies (Beavis, 2002; Bragg, 2002; Bruce, 2008; Buckingham & Sefton-Green, 1994; Fisherkeller, 2000; Hobbs, 2007; Parker, 2006) found that students embraced the use of media texts in class and showed a high level of interest in working with media in their classrooms. However, some studies showed that the inclusion of student media texts in academic settings became problematic. Bragg (2002) found that although the male student of her study created a film with many references to his out-of-school film

texts, he had difficulty in articulating his work in academic language. Bragg stated, "By insisting [the student] relate his film to concepts studied in the course . . . we prevent[ed] him from writing about the . . . texts that may have been more relevant for him" (p. 47). In another study, Goodman (2003) found that bringing the modality of video into the classroom put students' in-school and out-of-school viewing habits in tension with each other. Students expressed frustration at the frequent necessity of pausing the video as they watched their compiled video footage, as their out-of-school practice of viewing rarely called for stopping a video.

Pombo and Bruce (2007) also documented the disconnect between the in- and out-of-school literacies of the students in their study. Students who learned academic concepts of media literacy were able to articulate media's formidable impact on their identity formation as teenagers, such as in regard to clothing styles, musical tastes, body art (tattoos and piercings), purchasing habits, and language use. Although students could identify and name those cultural influences through classroom media literacy concepts, they showed little inclination to resist such influences. Moss (2006) found that the students in her study were adamant in their desire to not have their out-of-school texts brought into the classroom for study. Students recognized that the ways schools measure knowledge is much different from the ways in which they measure expertise in an area of interest. Moss (2006) stated, "When informal literacies are transferred to pedagogic settings, they and the texts they are associated with are themselves transformed, and recontextualized" (p. 144).

The studies indicate a paradox between the function and role of in-school and out-of-school literacies. This dilemma is most prominent when students' personal media influences and tastes coincide within an academic context. Yet all the studies found that students have shown an interest in and inclination toward studying media texts in the classroom.

Identity Exploration

Identity is defined as the "presentation of self in a matrix of social relationships" (Davidson, 1996, p. 2). Nowhere is the development and exploration of this presentation of self more evident than during adolescence. Several studies indicated that using media allowed students to explore issues of identity. One area in the research dealing with media influence on identity pertains to the development of students' own interests. Alvermann and Hagood (2000) found that one student played guitar by imitating songs of various artists and incorporating their musical styles into his own compositions. The researchers said that through "safe imitation . . . adolescents may actually be trying on new positions and identities that they had only imagined previously" (p. 444). Through listening to media texts in the form of songs, this student was able to experiment with different sounds and styles and incorporate them into his own instrumental voice.

Buckingham and Sefton-Green (1994) found that students' study of and reflection on media "seemed to have developed their understandings of the ways in which, as individuals, they are constructed by larger social forces" (p. 117). Students realized that although they had individual choices about their own interests, fashions, and so forth, these personal decisions take place within a social network that influences those choices.

Students' exploration of identity in terms of gender also played a role in the results of one study. Chandler-Olcott and Mahar (2003) found that their subjects not only participated in online communities for social support and mentorship in learning to navigate aspects of technology, they also used the space to explore gender identities. The girls in the study almost exclusively sought out female social networks, and the authors concluded that the virtual communities were more satisfying to the girls than the social networks they had at school. The online communities became places for them "to explore the complexities of heterosexuality, develop standards of physical beauty, and explore the relationships between masculinity and femininity" (p. 380).

The research findings on the interaction of media texts and the formation of identity indicate that media not only influence students' taste and interests, they can also serve as a conduit to explore identity (particularly in virtual settings) in ways that are different from those used in face-to-face social networks.

Problematic Issues Surrounding the Use of Technology

Several studies revealed limitations of using technology in academic settings. Because technical knowledge and skill, particularly with expensive equipment, is not evenly or fairly distributed across society, students and teachers encountered some difficulty in implementing its use.

Goodman's (2003) study was conducted with an urban population of adolescents, most of whom had little to no access to video equipment in their homes. Because of their unfamiliarity with the technology, as they had had only sparse access to this sort of technology in their school and community center, his subjects needed explicit guidance in utilizing camera and editing equipment. Such limitations illustrate the "digital divide," which Goodman describes as the "significant inequities emerg[ing] along racial and socio-economic lines . . . [regarding] access to and use of technology in schools" (p. 12).

Even schools face limited access to emergent technologies. Beavis (2002) found, in researching two schools that incorporated video games into the curriculum that the students in the school with less technology tended to be less involved than students in the more technology-rich school. Moreover, even when the technology was available, it did not always work the way it was supposed to. Teachers in both schools found "logistical difficulties" (p. 57) in utilizing the various technologies that they were using with video games. Thus, even when the technologies were available, teachers often lacked the training or technical support to successfully use it.

Integrating technology into an existing curriculum also illustrated the tight time constraints within which teachers work. Parker (2006) found that the animation process teachers included as part of their curriculum was time-consuming. He stated, "In an already overloaded curriculum, we need to carve out the space and time necessary to achieve a greater, more inclusive impact on literacy attainment" (p. 154). Although the teachers found value in the inclusion of technology for the unit, they experienced tension in meeting the existing curriculum requirements.

These studies reveal societal divisions between haves and have-nots, especially because media production requires expensive equipment. The issues of access and training may be exacerbated as we enter an age when technology-related skills are increasingly valued. In addition, meaningful assessments using technology take time. In an era when teachers are being asked to prepare students for high-stakes tests, technology does not often fit within curricular time constraints.

DISCUSSION

The research compiled for this chapter indicates that media texts are adolescents' dominant form of text. A consistent theme throughout all 15 studies was that adolescents took pleasure and interest in their interactions with nonprint media. None of the studies showed students being reluctant to engage with some form of media. The span of media texts included in the survey of research included video, anime, online communities, music, various news sources, advertisements, TV, political ads, film, comic books, video games, and magazines. This range of texts common in adolescents' lives suggests that research, teaching, and policy dealing with adolescents' literacy should take media texts into account.

In recognizing the vast presence of media in adolescents' lives, there needs to be an acceptance of media texts as having legitimacy in academic curricula. Internationally, media literacy—more often referred to as *media education*—is quite common. Canada, Australia, and several European countries all have media literacy as part of their formal schooling curricula (Schwarz, 2005, p. 7). The United States has no national curriculum, and media rarely appears in the national dialogue in regard to schooling, particularly in light of the No Child Left Behind Act, which takes a narrow approach to literacy and curriculum in general. However, in the summer of 2006, the Federal Communications Commission (FCC) commissioner recommended national media literacy standards, stating, "We need a sustained K–12 media literacy program—something to teach kids not only how to use the media but how the media uses them" (Copps, 2006). In addition, the Partnership for 21st Century Skills (2004) advocates media literacy skills as part of its Framework for 21st Century Learning.

Of the major subject areas, the field of English language arts (ELA) has perhaps the most integrated approach to studying media literacy; thus, educators and policymakers can look to ELA for examples of curricular integration, including instruction, classroom application, and assessment with media literacy with adolescents. In the Language Arts Standards adopted in 1996 by the National Council of Teachers of English (NCTE) and the International Reading Association (IRA), 7 of the 12 standards have overt mentions of reading, writing, and/or application of nonprint texts. Two assessment agencies have integrated aspects of media literacy into their English programs as well. The National Board for Professional Teaching Standards (2003) has included a media literacy standard (Standard XI: Viewing and Producing Media Texts) for English teachers. Perhaps of more importance to students, the College Board (2006) has included a visual analysis section for the English Advanced Placement Exam. Students will be asked to conduct rhetorical analyses of verbal and visual aspects of texts that may include cartoons, advertisements, photographs, and graphic representations of data.

Despite these developments, the increasing prevalence of standardized testing is one reason why media literacy is not being systematically included in school, especially because much of the current form of standardized assessment uses pencil-and-paper tests. If media literacy skills—particularly those dealing with nonprint competencies—were legitimized in education systems, stakeholders would have to reconsider what proficiencies should be valued and how they should be assessed.

Hobbs's (2007) study is noteworthy here because her research is the first to demonstrate students' significant gains in print (both reading and writing) skills due to the inclusion of media literacy in the curriculum. Her research should spur further inquiry into tying media literacy to adolescents' print literacy skills. At the same time, attention needs to be paid to nonprint representations of learning as well. In finding that students were better able to demonstrate narrative structure through film than through print composition, Parker (2006) questioned "why the conceptual and compositional skills that can be developed through intelligent use of the new media should not be regarded in themselves as an inherent part of literacy rather than merely playing a subordinate role" (p. 153).

The research indicates that educators need to use broad definitions of reading and composition to guide research and teaching. Thoman and Jolls (2004) assert:

> If our children are to be able to navigate their lives through this multimedia culture, they need to be fluent in "reading" and "writing" the language of images and sounds just as we have always taught them to "read" and "write" the language of printed communications. (p. 19)

Because the research shows that media literacy is so important to adolescents, because it shows that society demands that students be knowledgeable and skillful about emergent technologies, and because research shows that multiple media provide means of expressing and extending knowledge, skill, and ideas, teachers need to know about media literacy. That need for knowledge means that we need teacher development. How should teachers—who have mostly a traditional, print-based background—be invited into a conversation where they are not formally trained, where their students are more literate in emergent media than they? This is an issue for the veteran teaching workforce as well as preservice and early career teachers. Goetze, Brown, and Schwarz (2005) state:

> If media literacy is to become part of the K–12 school experience, enabling transformation in both curriculum and teaching, then teachers need to become literate first. Teachers cannot teach what they have not learned, and learned to value, themselves. (p. 161)

In addition, how can universities provide the technological and pedagogical support that teaching media texts requires? Hobbs (2005) states, "Because even young teachers are often not experienced with how to analyze visual or electronic messages, and do not themselves know how to create messages using media and technology, strengthening young people's media literacy skills in

the 21st century will continue to be an enormous challenge" (p. 95). Educators, researchers, and policymakers must work toward addressing the gap between adolescents' literacies and the necessary teacher training.

One of the most pressing issues to consider is the tension between adolescents' in-school and out-of-school literacies. Are the various forms of media—the dominant forms of adolescent texts, no matter what the modality—better suited for out-of-school learning? Do the findings regarding students who do not wish their vested media texts to be brought into a formal school setting overrule the findings regarding students who were able to achieve a measure of academic success because they were able to use media texts? The research reviewed in this chapter suggests that this may not be an either/or scenario. Goodman (2003) states, "Media education can and should be a natural part of students' language, learning, and work experience in both of these settings" (p. 108).

The studies suggest that the level of student personal interest may account for much of the tension surrounding studying media in school settings. The more vested in media texts the students felt, the less receptive they were to exposing them to academic rigor. If students did not feel a threat to their individual media, then they tended to respond with a high level of interest and enthusiasm.

Media studies have a place both inside and outside academic settings. Of the 15 studies, 8 took place in school settings, 1 took place in an out-of-school environment, and 6 took place in combinations of the two. Adolescents will continue to use new media in their own lives outside the academic realm. However, schools can use those media texts to help invite students into the classroom conversation. Hull and Schultz (2002) observe, "Rather than setting formal and informal education systems and contexts in opposition to each other, we might do well to look for overlap or complementarity or perhaps a respectful division of labor" (p. 3).

I conclude the "Discussion" section of this chapter with implications for research. Fox (2005) offers several suggestions that can provide guidance for further study. He states that researchers need to be versed in print as well as visual media. In addition, they should be deliberate in their selection of critical lenses for data analysis. In addition, Fox advocates continuing case studies while also employing new and hybrid methodologies. Finally, he says that unfettered communication with students is imperative for both research and teaching.

The case study recommendation is noteworthy. Of the 15 studies reviewed for this chapter, only 1 (Hobbs, 2007) used an experimental design, combining quantitative and qualitative methodologies. The remaining studies were much smaller in scale, with 6 of them being conducted in a classroom or series of classrooms. The other 8 were case studies. Despite their small sample size, Fox states,

We especially need case studies that focus on how students negotiate contentious and discrepant events when creating, comprehending, interpreting, and applying media products and events to their own lives. Through case study, we may better understand how young people make sense of media events within their own environments. (p. 258)

The necessity for more case studies may not be obvious, given that it was the dominant research design in the studies reviewed. However, case studies provide the best articulation of adolescents' media literacy processes, especially as much of the emergent forms of their use has not been studied. The more examples we have, the better researchers will be able to theorize how media literacy works, providing hypotheses that can be tested in experimental designs.

Making the case for continued use of case study research does not mean that researchers abandon quantitative methods of study. The latter are important for examining patterns and trends for a number of questions that are better answered through quantitative methods, such as large-scale surveys and comparisons of various data. This scenario is analogous to the in-school/out-of-school literacies tension: Just as the latter is shown in the research not to be either wholly in or out of school contexts, so it is with research paradigms. There is plenty of room for both quantitative and qualitative research and the types of questions being asked should determine the framework used. What is certain is that by using both, we can have a more complete composite of adolescents' learning with media.

Although both paradigms are necessary, funding is unequal. Fox (2005) highlights the general lack of federal funding for research that is not based on quantitative methodology. Policymakers should note the importance and value of qualitative research in providing funds for a broad range of research methodologies that address multiple assessments of students' knowledge about reading and composing in multiple media.

Nonprint media are, and will most likely continue to be, the prominent texts in adolescents' lives. Adolescents will assimilate and use existing and emergent media whether or not those literacies are legitimized in academic settings. For the stakeholders in adolescent literacy, media literacy provides a paradigm through which multiple forms of texts can be researched both in and out of school contexts in teaching adolescents how to broadly read and write.

REFERENCES

Alliance for a Media Literate America. (2005). *What is media literacy?* Retrieved September 15, 2006, from *www.amlainfo.org/home/media-literacy.*

Alvermann, D. E, & Hagood, M. (2000). Fandom and critical media literacy. *Journal of Adolescent and Adult Literacy, 43*, 436–446.

Alvermann, D. E., Moon, J., & Hagood, M. (1999). *Popular culture in the classroom: Teaching and researching critical media literacy.* Newark, DE: International Reading Association; Chicago: National Reading Conference.

Aufderheide, P. (1993). *Media literacy: A report of the National Leadership Conference on Media Literacy.* Aspen, CO: Aspen Institute.

Beavis, C. (2002). Reading, writing and role-playing computer games. In I. Snyder (Ed.), *Silicon literacies: Communication, innovation and education in the electronic age* (pp. 47–61). New York: Routledge.

Bomer, R. (1995). *Time for meaning: Crafting literate lives in middle and high school.* Portsmouth, NH: Heinemann.

Bragg, S. (2002). Wrestling in woolly gloves: Not just being critically media literate. *Journal of Popular Film and Television, 30*, 41–51.

Bruce, D. (2008). Visualizing literacy: Building bridges with media. *Reading and Writing Quarterly, 24*, 264–282.

Buckingham, D., & Sefton-Green, J. (1994). *Cultural*

studies goes to school: Reading and teaching popular media. London: Taylor & Francis.

Chandler-Olcott, K., & Mahar, D. (2003). "Tech-savviness" meets multiliteracies: Exploring adolescent girls' technology-mediated literacy practices. Reading Research Quarterly, 38, 356–385.

The College Board. (2006). English language and composition, English literature and composition: Course description. Retrieved September 15, 2006, from www.collegeboard.com/prod_downloads/ap/students/english/ap-english-0607.pdf.

Copps, M. (2006, June 7). Beyond censorship: Technologies and policies to give parents control over children's media content. Remarks made at Kaiser Family Foundation/New America Foundation Kidvid summit, Washington, DC. Retrieved September 15, 2006, from hraunfoss.fcc.gov/edocs_public/attachmatch/DOC- 265842A1.pdf.

Davidson, A. (1996). Making and molding identity in schools: Student narratives on race, gender and academic engagement. Albany, NY: SUNY Press.

Fisherkeller, J. (2000). "The writers are getting kind of desperate": Young adolescents, television, and literacy. Journal of Adolescent and Adult Literacy, 43, 596–606.

Fox, R. (2005). Researching media literacy: Pitfalls and possibilities. In G. Schwarz & P. Brown (Eds.), Media literacy: Transforming curriculum and teaching. The 104th yearbook of the National Society for the Study of Education, Part I (pp. 251–259). Malden, MA: Blackwell.

Goetze, S., Brown, P., & Schwarz, G. (2005). Teachers need media literacy, too! In G. Schwarz & P. Brown (Eds.), Media literacy: Transforming curriculum and teaching. The 104th yearbook of the National Society for the Study of Education, Part I (pp. 161–179). Malden, MA: Blackwell.

Goodman, S. (2003). Teaching youth media: A critical guide to literacy, video production and social change. New York: Teachers College Press.

Hobbs, R. (2005). Media literacy and the K–12 content areas. In G. Schwarz & P. Brown (Eds.), Media literacy: Transforming curriculum and teaching. The 104th yearbook of the National Society for the Study of Education, Part I (pp. 74–99). Malden, MA: Blackwell.

Hobbs, R. (2007). Reading the media: Media literacy in high school English. New York: Teachers College Press.

Hull, G., & Schultz, K. (2002). Introduction: Negotiating the boundaries between school and non-school literacies. In G. Hull and K. Shultz (Eds.), School's out! Bridging out-of-school literacies with classroom practice (pp. 1–8). New York: Teachers College Press.

Kist, W. (2005). New literacies in action: Teaching and learning in multiple media. New York: Teachers College Press.

Moss, G. (2006). Informal literacies and pedagogic discourse. In J. Marsh & E. Millard (Eds.), Popular literacies, childhood and schooling (pp. 128–149). New York: Routledge.

National Board for Professional Teaching Standards. (2003). Adolescence and young adult English Language Arts Standards (2nd ed.). Retrieved September 15, 2006, from www.nbpts.org/the_standards/standards_by_cert?ID=2&x=51&y=9.

National Council of Teachers of English/International Reading Association. (1996). Standards for the English language arts. Urbana, IL & Newark, DE: Authors.

Niesyto, H. (2001). VideoCulture: Conclusions and key findings. Journal of Educational Media, 26, 217–225.

O'Sullivan, E. (1962). What the English teacher should know about film and television drama. In M. Weiss (Ed.), An English teacher reader: Grades 7–12 (pp. 73–84). New York: Odyssey Press.

Parker, D. (2006). Making it move, making it mean: Animation, print literacy and the metafunctions of language. In J. Marsh & E. Millard (Eds.), Popular literacies, childhood and schooling (pp. 150–159). New York: Routledge.

Partnership for 21st Century Skills. (2004). Framework for 21st Century Learning. Retrieved June 18, 2007, from 21stcenturyskills.org/index.php?option=com_content&task=view&id=254&Itemid=120.

Pombo, M., & Bruce, D. (2007). Media, teens and identity: Critical reading and composing in a video production and media education classroom. In A. Nowak, S. Abel, & K. Ross (Eds.), Rethinking media education: Critical pedagogy and identity politics (pp. 149–166). Cresskill, NJ: Hampton Press.

Scholes, R. (1985). Textual power: Literary theory and the teaching of English. New Haven, CT: Yale University Press.

Schwarz, G. (2005). Overview: What is media literacy, who cares, and why? In G. Schwarz & P. Brown (Eds.), Media literacy: Transforming curriculum and teaching. The 104th yearbook of the National Society for the Study of Education, Part I (pp. 5–17). Malden, MA: Blackwell.

Thoman, E., & Jolls, T. (2004). Media literacy—A national priority for a changing world. American Behavioral Scientist, 48, 18–29.

Thoman, E., & Jolls, T. (2005). Media literacy education: Lessons from the Center for Media Literacy. In G. Schwarz & P. Brown (Eds.), Media literacy: Transforming curriculum and teaching. The 104th yearbook of the National Society for the Study of Education, Part I (pp. 180–205). Malden, MA: Blackwell.

Tyner, K. (1998). Literacy in a digital world: Teaching and learning in the age of information. Mahwah, NJ: Erlbaum.

Zaslow, E., & Butler, A. (2002, Spring). "That it was made by people our age is better": Exploring the role of media literacy in transcultural communication. Journal of Popular Film and Television, 30, 31–40.

Part IV

LITERACY AND CULTURE

POLICY MATTERS: Excerpt from *Ready or Not*[1]

Although high school graduation requirements are established state by state, a high school diploma should represent a common currency nationwide. Families move across state lines, students apply to colleges outside their own state and employers hire people from across the country. States owe it to their students to set expectations for high school graduates that are portable to other states. The ADP benchmarks can help make this portability a reality. States that adopt these benchmarks will have a ready and persuasive answer for students when they ask, "Why do I have to learn these things?"

The ADP benchmarks are ambitious. In mathematics, they reflect content typically taught in Algebra I, Algebra II and Geometry, as well as Data Analysis and Statistics. The English benchmarks demand strong oral and written communication skills because these skills are staples in college classrooms and most 21st century jobs. They also contain analytic and reasoning skills that formerly were associated with advanced or honors courses in high school. Today, however, colleges and employers agree that all high school graduates need these essential skills.

Although most states have worked hard in the last 10 years to raise the quality of academic standards and the rigor of assessments, the ADP benchmarks may seem even more demanding. For example, no state currently requires all students to take Algebra II to graduate, and few high school exit tests measure much of what ADP suggests that students need to know. In some cases, the knowledge and skills in the benchmarks are not sampled at all on state tests.

How important is it for states to put themselves through the tribulations of reworking their graduation standards, rewriting their graduation tests and revisiting their "passing" scores? It is important only if we want our high school diplomas to signify true readiness for successful entry into the adult world—and if we want to ensure that every graduate is really prepared for college or work. States must provide the impetus for restoring value to the diploma, but success will depend upon specific actions taken by leaders from many sectors: governors, legislators, business leaders, state K–12 and postsecondary education officials, employers, trade unions, and non-profit organizations.

COUNTERPOINT

Burroughs and Smagorinsky (Chapter 12) and Marshall (Chapter 18), this volume, discuss what happens to the English curriculum as a result of standardization and accountability systems; they further raise complex questions about this approach to social problems.

---

[1]Excerpt from American Diploma Project. (2004). *Ready or not: Creating a high school diploma that counts.* Washington, DC: Achieve, Inc. Available at *www.achieve.org/node/552.*

Martínez-Roldán and Fránquiz (Chapter 21), Belgarde, Loré, and Meyer (Chapter 27), Fu and Graff (Chapter 26), and Cooks and Ball (Chapter 10), this volume, discuss the ways high school completion is not evenly distributed across all groups in society, and these discussions raise questions about who would benefit and who would suffer from making it more difficult to earn a high school diploma.

Langer (Chapter 4, this volume) discusses the conditions under which standards are raised for students and thereby success is made more likely. Such descriptions may lead readers to wonder about the sorts of large-scale policy that might support schools in creating those conditions.

—L. C., R. B., and P. S.

CHAPTER 20

Literacy and Identity

Implications for Research and Practice

CYNTHIA LEWIS
ANTILLANA DEL VALLE

This chapter examines how research on adolescent literacy is shaped by particular conceptions of identity. We consider three ways that identity has been theorized in sociocultural research on adolescent literacy since the 1970s and provide illustrations of research that has been informed by each conception of identity. These conceptions of identity are roughly aligned to three particular periods of time, or three waves, as discussed in this chapter. In the 1970s–1980s identity was theorized as stable and unified. In the 1990s–2000s identity was theorized as negotiated and performative. As we approach a new decade, the meaning of *identity* is, again, shifting. In recent work on adolescent literacy, identity has been theorized as improvisational, metadiscursive, and hybrid. This chapter argues that, as conceptions of identity change, so does the lens through which researchers view and, ultimately, come to understand adolescent literacy.

Visiting an urban charter high school that emphasizes the recording arts, we were reminded about the central role that identity plays in literacy. The school, with an enrollment mostly of African American males, had received some media attention that the school viewed as positive. A small national magazine had celebrated the school's success in using hip-hop as part of the curriculum with students whom the magazine characterized as dropouts. The article's headline included the words "Hip Hop" and "Dropout" printed in a large, bold font. Noticing the article displayed on a table during an all-school meeting, a soon-to-graduate African American student read the article's headline and quietly remarked that this school was neither a school for dropouts nor one that focused on hip-hop. He did not agree with the broad sweep of these generalizations about the identity of his school and its students. The school's administration, on the other hand, was pleased for the publicity and its positive focus on the school's successes.

This strikes us as a useful anecdote for the start of this chapter because it so clearly demonstrates that texts have little meaning outside the particularly contextualized lives and identities of their readers. Although meanings are produced, in part, through reader–text transactions, both readers and texts are situated within social, cultural, and institutional frameworks that both constrain (close) and destabilize (open) meanings. The article in our anecdote was shaped by the discourse of structural racism that participates in "framing dropouts" (Fine, 1991) as Black and interested in hip-hop. The young man contested those dominant discourses to claim a different identity, one of an accomplished young man who had, in fact, just been awarded a college scholarship. As Duncan (1995) argues, "By critically reading the world, Black teenagers construct their identities through redefining what it is that constitutes respectable thinking and behaving in a racist society" (p. 58). This student redefined respectable thinking and provided a corrective to the way the article framed Black youth identity.

It is entirely possible that some teachers and administrators at the school would have a response to the article similar to this young man's; however, a given text can engender an open set of contradictory interpretations that depend on how and to what effect the text will be read by others. We refer, here, to the text's political economy—how it is consumed and distributed, and with what benefits and losses, within particular structures of power. In this case, the potential for what can be viewed as positive publicity for the school may have resulted in a positive official school response to the article. Given a national climate in which schools are generally the objects of negative media attention and increasingly subject to free-market principles, it is not surprising that the article represented a school identity that could be viewed as strategically desirable. Identity, then, as three decades of work in cultural studies and poststructural theory have taught us, is not just an individual matter. It is social, cultural, historical, institutional, and political, and all of these conditions mean that identity has material effects related to lived realities in the form of resources, goods, and emotional well-being.

Even in this brief example, we can see how identity works in slippery ways not conducive to tidy definitions, and before moving on to describe our categorization of the ways literacy researchers have approached identity, we spend some time here probing the definitional problems surrounding identity. It is a concept that has been copiously covered and variously defined within behavioral, cognitive, and social psychology, psychoanalytic and postmodern/poststructural

philosophy, and feminist, race, postcolonial, critical discourse, and cultural studies. Some of these perspectives (especially those connected to cognitive and early social psychology) represent identity as an essential self that is relatively unified and stable; others represent identity as shifting and contingent, reiterative and reproductive, or oppositional and resistant.

Hagood (2002) argues that it is important to distinguish, as poststructuralists do, between identity and subjectivity. The modernist view of *identity*, as connected to an essential concept of self, saturates the meaning of the term, unlike the concept of *subjectivity*, which theorizes the "self" as socioculturally constructed and discursively positioned but also able to take up positions of agency and resistance. Others view identity in more explicitly political terms. In *The Power of Identity*, the sociologist Manuel Castell (1997) outlines three main forms of identity: legitimizing identity (imposed by dominant institutions), resistance identity (opposition to imposed identities), and project identity (new forms of transformative identities). This tripartite definition defines identity primarily in terms of its relationship to institutions, but underplays the ways in which identities are constructed moment to moment in social and cultural contexts that are shaped by structures of power. This way of conceptualizing identity is most often captured by the phrase "social identity" (Bloome, Carter, Christian, Otto, & Stuart-Faris, 2005; Lewis, 2001; Lewis & Fabos, 2005) or "socially situated identity" (Gee, 2005, p. 141). In considering the use of identity as an analytic lens for educational research, Gee (2000/2001) offers a taxonomy of views on identity ranging from what is usually perceived as the most static (nature or biology) to the most dynamic (affinity groups), with institutional and discursive identities in between. However, as Gee argues, each view of identity can be interpreted differently, depending on who is doing the interpreting. Compare, for example, racist interpretations of the biology of race (e.g., race-based theories of intelligence) versus strategic essentializing of racial identity by those who are members of a racial group. Dichotomous perspectives on identity prevail, particularly between the representation of identity as a core phenomenon and that of identity as fluid. Both have appeal, as McCarthey and Moje (2002) point out in their published e-mail exchange on the topic. They argue that the appeal of viewing identity as unified is that this view serves as a useful story we tell ourselves to get us through our lives in a fragmented, contradictory social world. A view of identity as performative and socially situated has more potential for agency in the moment-to-moment shaping of one's position in the social world. As McCarthey (McCarthey & Moje, 2002) puts it, "It seems that we are trying to work through how identities are coherent, yet hybrid and stabilizing, yet dynamic" (p. 232).

Also in tension with the dynamic conception of identity suggested by the idea of social identities is what Gee (2000/2001) calls "institutional identity" (p. 25). Akin to Castell's (1997) legitimizing identity, this form of identity limits the potential for remaking the self through agentic action. Limited potential is especially evident when one is branded as "other" in relation to an institutional identity, such as when a student who does not fit the middle-class, White institutional identity of a school is identified as a "nonstudent," or "bad student," or "oppositional student." This is a deterministic view of identity, in the sense that identity is determined by social and power relations inscribed in and through institutions.

Some would argue that social identities are no more fluid than institutional identities, but that the former give the illusion of agency and dynamism. Willis's (1981) *Learning to Labor* provides a well-known example in that the working-class "lads" were able to shape their identities as powerful within their own social worlds but not, ultimately, within powerful economic forces that worked to keep them in their place and in industrial jobs. Some cultural theorists argue that popular culture works to undermine traditional relations of power because it allows young people to tactically resist, parody, or alter dominant cultural norms, sometimes forming affinity groups across lines of social class, race, or gender (Fiske, 1990; McRobbie, 1997; Skelton, 1997; Thornton, 1996).

Holland, Lachicotte, Skinner, and Cain (1998) provide an important analysis of identity and the tension between culture and agency. Building on Bakhtin's (1981) sense of the dialogical complexity of social worlds, his sense of productive disequilibrium, Holland et al. (1998) explain that identities are formed in the process of participation in "figured worlds" in which, inevitably, particular acts and outcomes are valued over others but which can be reconfigured by the improvisations of actors. Using the construct of "personhood," Egan-Robertson (1998) suggests something similar, with somewhat less emphasis on the potential for improvisation:

> Although discourses about personhood are dynamic in that they are built and rebuilt as people interact within and across social and institutional contexts, it is also the case that notions of personhood can be viewed as fixatives within discourse practices that constrain and delimit the possibilities for creating identities for oneself and others. (p. 451)

As these nuanced views make clear, identity as a construct has been widely discussed and debated within many disciplines. Not surprisingly, it has also been the focus of much research on adolescent literacy. In the rest of this chapter, we take up Hagood's (2002) call to examine how research on adolescent literacy is shaped by particular conceptions of identity. We consider three ways that identity has been theorized in sociocultural research on adolescent literacy in roughly three periods since the 1970s and provide illustrations of research that has been informed by each conception of identity. We argue that the way that identity is theorized is an important key to understanding the research we highlight in each period. In order to limit the scope of the chapter, we consider adolescents to be young people ages 11–18 and literacy to be the range of practices involved in the coding of socially and culturally relevant signs and symbols (de Castell & Luke, 1986; Kress, 2003; Lewis & Fabos, 2005; Scribner & Cole, 1981; Warschauer, 2002). Because other chapters in this section focus specifically on particular identity groups of adolescents (e.g., male, female, African American, Latino/a, Native, LGBTQ, newcomer), we decided to focus instead on how particular constructs of identity have shaped research on adolescent literacy and, in turn, what we know and can learn about the literacy practices of adolescents.

WHY IDENTITY IS IMPORTANT TO ADOLESCENT LITERACY

In 1996 the cultural theorist Stuart Hall wrote a book introduction titled "Who Needs 'Identity'?" in which he lays out different constructs of identity and the ensuing controversies in the field of cultural studies. For Hall and others, identities are positions that we take up, temporarily, as though they are stable and cohesive. Identity represents ways of being and performing as members of certain groups as well as the way our selfhood is recognized by others (Gee, 2000/2001). Identity is an important construct, Hall argues, precisely because institutions tend to privilege a view of identity as a fixed, stable set of characteristics. When identity is viewed as fixed, then those individuals who do not possess the expected set of characteristics are often marginalized. His ideas apply to the field of education in general and to adolescent literacy in particular. Institutionalized forms of literacy dominate our education system, marginalizing those with identities that don't necessarily fit the dominant mold. For example, literacy has been established in the official curriculum as the ability to decode and code symbols in isolation from any political, social, and cultural context, what Street (1985) refers to as an autonomous view of literacy. Literacy researchers working from a sociocultural perspective, however, have maintained that literacy is socially and culturally situated (Bloome, 1993; Gee, 1996; Heath, 1983). In part, this perspective holds that when the experiences, perceptions, and relationships students value are not acknowledged, they often learn that literacy is an exclusive, limiting activity that diminishes their efforts to construct expanded identities (Enciso & Lewis, 2001). The disparity between the achievement test scores of European American students and those of African Americans, Latinos, Native Americans, and some ethnic minorities of the Asian community is of great concern to committed educators. The burden that autonomous notions of literacy (Street, 1985) have placed on teachers has caused them to look at different ways of understanding literacy that embrace the multiple identities that students bring to the classroom. To counter deficit-oriented perceptions of students as lacking literacy skills,

practitioners and researchers examine the literacy practices that students embrace outside school. Through these literacy practices, students take up identities that position them well within the dominant as well as youth-oriented discourses. Luke (2000) argues that the role of literacy teachers is to enhance students' ability to leverage social, cultural, and economic capital across social fields. We agree that identity work related to literacy is about much more than an individual's sense of self. It is, as Luke (2000) asserts, about "setting the conditions for students to engage in textual relationships of power" (p. 449).

Adolescents confront a world in which the global economy demands constant negotiation of a multiplicity of texts (Moje, Young, Readence, & Moore, 2000). Adolescents of color, in particular, need access to dominant discourses in order to speak and write the language of power (Delpit, 1988) that otherwise threatens to shut them out, but also in order to critically address the way they are positioned in society. The term *culturally relevant pedagogy,* as defined by Ladson-Billings (1995), is informed by a "theoretical model that not only addresses student achievement but also helps students to accept and affirm their cultural identity while developing critical perspectives that challenge inequities that schools (and other institutions) perpetuate" (p. 469). Although this approach has been favored by some, other literacy researchers and practitioners have warned that the model of culturally relevant pedagogy can essentialize cultural practices without accounting for generational changes or individual practices (Gutiérrez & Rogoff, 2003). That does not mean they avoid the examination of adolescent identity from a social and cultural perspective; rather, these scholars emphasize accounting for the complex and often competing identities that each individual must navigate. Using a cultural-historical framework, Gutiérrez and Rogoff (2003) recognize the situated practices of cultural as well as individual ways of learning:

> We argue that it is more useful to consider differences in the children's, their families', and their communities' histories of engaging in particular endeavors organized in contrasting manners. This avoids the implication that the characteristic is "built in" to the individual (or

group) in a stable manner that extends across time and situations, and it recognizes the circumstances relevant to an individual's likelihood of acting in certain ways. (p. 22)

Clearly, identity does matter as it relates to adolescent literacy, but it matters in different ways, depending on how it is conceptualized. We argue that within sociocultural (as opposed to psychosocial) frameworks, identity related to work in literacy research has been conceived in three main ways since the 1970s. Although not strictly chronological, these conceptions of identity are roughly aligned to three particular periods of time, or three waves, as discussed in this chapter. The first wave of identity-related research appeared in the 1970s–1980s when identity was theorized as stable and unified, leading to literacy research that focused on cultural conflict between home and school. The second wave of identity-related research, in the 1990s–2000s, theorized identity as negotiated and performative, leading to literacy research that focused on the positional and resourceful nature of adolescents' literacy practices. Although this view of identity still has a strong shaping influence on adolescent literacy research, as we approach a new decade, the meaning of identity is shifting. In recent work on adolescent literacy—the third wave—identity has been theorized as improvisational, metadiscursive, and hybrid, leading to literacy research that focuses on literacy practices as part of a complex landscape that is both global and local as well as participatory and exclusionary.

Given that *identity* is a key term in the discourse on adolescence, it should come as no surprise that identity plays a key role in research on adolescent literacy. This chapter argues that as conceptions of identity have moved from the first to the second to the third wave, so has the lens through which researchers have viewed and, ultimately, come to understand adolescent literacy. We focus on key studies within each theoretical framework to serve as examples of how theoretical conceptions of identity provide particular lenses that play a role in shaping research questions and findings and, ultimately, in contributing to collective knowledge about literacy practices and literacy instruction.

FIRST WAVE: IDENTITY THROUGH THE LENS OF CULTURAL CONFLICT

Key sociocultural studies of literacy from the 1970s and 1980s theorized identity as constructed through cultural affiliation, with a somewhat stable set of characteristics. The relationship between nondominant groups and the dominant institution of schooling in the research included in this section was represented as one of cultural conflict. This was an important time in the history of literacy research because it marked a move away from the deficit view of cultures that permeated earlier research (see Foley, 1991). In retrospect, the move to essentialize identity—that is, to associate particular social and cultural identities with a stable set of characteristics—was strategic in that it led to research on educational inequality that focused on the mismatch between school and home cultures—the cultural difference between school and home—rather than on deficit in the homes or minds of students from nondominant cultures. Most of the groundbreaking work in this first wave was not about adolescents, but is important to include in this chapter nonetheless because it led the way in underscoring the integral connection between literacy and identity (most often, in these cases, cultural identity).

Sociolinguistic work in educational settings in the 1970s set the stage for cultural conflict studies related to literacy and identity. This work took the form of studies that analyzed the mismatch in language use between home/community and school. For example, McDermott (1977) shows how such linguistic mismatch caused teachers in a first-grade classroom to identify African American children as low-ability readers in need of extensive teacher control of reading behaviors. Likewise, in the early 1980s, Heath's (1983) classic ethnography of a low-income Black and low-income White community in the Piedmont Carolinas shows how the ways of using language in each community conflicted with uses of language (e.g., norms for interaction, question asking) in the school where the children in both communities were enrolled. Heath identifies the particular patterns that characterized language use during literacy events in each community, showing how the patterns were quite stable and tied to the group identity of each culturally bounded community.

The connection between schooled literacy and identity is explicit in Rodríguez's (1982) autobiography describing the cultural conflict he experienced between home and school. The son of Mexican immigrants, Rodríguez argues that there is no place for home and community culture and identity at school. He believes that the only way to succeed in school and achieve the language of power is to separate from one's home language and culture when participating in the public life of schooling. This painful process irrevocably changes one's relationship to home and community, but Rodríguez maintains that in order to succeed, a new identity must be forged. In dramatic fashion, then, identity is essentialized in both sites, home and school. A home identity, with stable and requisite linguistic and cultural characteristics, must be subsumed by a school identity, also assumed to have stable linguistic and cultural characteristics. As Rodríguez (1982) puts it, referring to Hoggart's scholarship boy in the latter's book *The Uses of Literacy* (1957/ 1992): "His story makes clear that education is a long, unglamorous, even demeaning process—*a nurturing never natural to the person one was before entering the classroom*" (p. 68, emphasis in the original).

Cultural conflict between home and school is evident in the work of Delpit (1988) as well, included in this section primarily for her essay, "The Silenced Dialogue: Power and Pedagogy in Educating Other People's Children." Here, Delpit challenges the practices of White middle-class educators who do not provide Black and working-class students with the language of power that they need to succeed in academic and professional life. Her position is based on her view of the Black working class as having a particular set of interaction patterns that conflict with those of White middle-class educators, patterns that disadvantage Black working-class students who do not have access to the unspoken norms and expectations for action and interaction in the classroom. Although not explicitly using the word *identity,* Delpit's argument rests on the assumption that there is a cohesiveness to Black working-class interactions and norms, and that in order to bridge to the White middle-class codes of schooling, students need to "code-switch"

and take up the linguistic codes of power. These codes must be learned, according to Delpit, because they are not the same as those with which Black working-class students identify in their home and community lives.

Hull and Rose also use—and begin to challenge—a cultural conflict framework to push against the construct of remediation (and remedial readers/writers). In the late 1980s and early 1990s, Hull and Rose, sometimes with coauthors, wrote a series of articles (Hull & Rose, 1989; Hull, Rose, Fraser, & Castellano, 1991), the most well known being "'This Wooden Shack Place': The Logic of an Unconventional Reading" (Hull & Rose, 1990), in which they show that textual interpretation is socially and culturally constituted, often in relation to class, cultural affiliation, and personal history. When the social and cultural affiliations are not those associated with academic ways of knowing, the "underprepared" student's ways of reading are assumed to be deficient rather than logical. Hull and Rose make a case for the logic of these students' interpretations.

Although they take pains to complicate the reader as subject—that is, they do not suggest that social class comes with a stable set of characteristics—their work nonetheless marks the difference between vernacular and academic ways of knowing and the need for teachers to rethink their assumptions about deficit thinking by acknowledging but, ultimately, moving beyond social and cultural difference. However, there are ways in which their work gestures toward a new view of identity as performative. Within their framework, the students who are considered "underprepared" or "underachieving" are having trouble understanding how to be a student—they somehow perform the wrong version of what "student" is supposed to mean and therefore the logic of their thinking, related to reading and writing, is underestimated by their teachers.

A key theoretical claim made by all of these groundbreaking scholars is aptly expressed by Ferdman (1990), whose *Harvard Educational Review* article "Literacy and Cultural Identity," has been highly influential on the subject of literacy and identity:

> Since cultures differ in what they consider to be their "texts" and in the values they attach

to these, they will also differ in what they view as literate behavior. An illiterate person is someone who cannot access (or produce) texts that are seen as significant within a given culture. (p. 186)

Readers and writers, then, are constructed through linguistic and social codes that shape their relationships to texts. If for no other reason, this is the crux of why identity matters to the study of literacy.

SECOND WAVE: IDENTITY AS NEGOTIATED AND PERFORMATIVE

In the 1990s and continuing into the present, a good deal of literacy research has focused on the ways in which adolescents employ particular literacy practices to resourcefully mediate their identities in social settings. These negotiated or performed identities shape and are shaped by literacy practices that serve a social function, positioning the individual in relation to peers, family, or institutional authority (in this case, school). In this section, we focus on studies related to literacy and identity in out-of-school and in-school contexts with the caveat that these categories are not neatly delineated. As Finders (1996) explains about her study of middle school girls at home, with peers, and at school, "each context holds certain expectations for how individuals will act and evaluates the worth of individuals in relation to these expectations" (p. 9). To reflect the large body of research that has been shaped by a second-wave perspective on identity, we discuss more studies in this section than we do in the others. Our intention is to provide readers with a sense of the wide range of research that falls into this category and the important shaping influence that this perspective on identity has had.

Out-of-School Contexts

We begin with out-of-school contexts because second-wave identity research turned the lens in that direction, with the result that adolescents were depicted as capable of using literacy for their own powerful purposes and identity representations. In studying adolescents in this way, researchers rejected deficit views and recognized the situated linguistic competence young people often exhibit when they have agency to select, define, and modify their literacy practices. Such research accentuated the contrast between out-of-school and in-school literacy practices, illuminating the resourceful and strategic uses of literacy young people take up when they are invested in their own social practices outside school (Guzzetti & Gamboa, 2004) even as they continue to be labeled as "struggling" or "at-risk" students in school contexts (Alvermann, 2001; Alvermann & Heron, 2001; Knobel, 2001; O'Brien, 2001; Rubinstein-Ávila, 2003/2004). An edited volume by Hull and Schultz (2002) that we locate within this framework examines adolescents' out-of-school literacies in order to bridge the gap between in-school and out-of-school practices so that teachers can build on the competence and investment that youth bring to their peer and community literacies. This research direction has been taken up internationally, especially in response to the current passion for manga (Japanese graphic novels) that youth exhibit worldwide. As Allen and Ingulsrud (2005) argue, on the basis of their study of manga readers in Japan, it would behoove educators to understand the reading practices involved in successfully navigating the social, aesthetic, and economic world of manga that students regularly enjoy and consume on their own time. Their pleasure in this out-of-school literacy practice is tied up in the network of readers with whom they perform their identities. Moreover, as Ito (2007) has shown, manga readers not only read but creatively remix manga characters in other genres (i.e., machima and fanfiction).

The findings of research on adolescents' out-of-school literacies have contributed to knowledge about young people's strategic uses of literacy, thus legitimizing their practices and broadening what counts as literacy. This research has also served to critique, resist, and illuminate the ways youth are positioned differently, in terms of skill capacity, agency, and power, in different contexts. In her study of two groups of early adolescents, Finders (1996, 1997) reveals how literacy practices shape social roles and relations among peers. The "popular" girls used their social capital to claim insider status and patrol the boundaries of their group. The performance of identity among these girls was a part of the social literacy of purchasing, reading, and displaying zines. The relationship between literacy and social identity was mutually constituted, with literacy functioning as a resource for enhancing social identity and, at the same time, the performance of social identity enhancing the literacy practice.

In recent years, digital tools and virtual social worlds have been central features of out-of-school literacy practices. A chapter in this volume addresses literacy in virtual communities (Black & Steinkuehler, Chapter 18), so we limit this discussion to a few representative studies that make a point of connecting digital literacy to a second-wave identity construct. Internet communication lends itself to using multimodal literacy practices to perform and negotiate identities. Features that allow for photos, video, profiles and "away" messages, and immediate feedback allow users to playfully create multiple identities that they adjust and transform, depending on the purpose and audience for the communication. For example, one of the digitally savvy young people in Thomas's (2004) study reported making conscious linguistic choices to perform alternative identities online and playfully trick her friends. Instead of gender swapping in their role playing, however, most of these young women chose avatars that represented idealized notions of being female through their talk about appearance and the body. Similarly, in a study of young people's uses of instant messaging (Lewis & Fabos, 2005), one of the participants chose to pose as blonde-haired and blue-eyed in keeping with her vision of what it meant to be the idealized female. As Thomas (2004) pointed out: "In the online context . . . to write is to exist. . . . writing is an essential component for performing identity" (p. 366).

Because Internet communication, in particular, is overtly social in nature, it offers an environment in which young people create identities that allow them to enter the textual worlds of groups they want to join. In the process of creating identities, participants demonstrate numerous literacy skills, including adjusting the tone and content of their writing to address a variety of audiences and purposes. They analyze rhetorical context (Lewis & Fabos, 2005) and assert

agency regarding peer relationships (Stern, 2007). Enacting identities, in these studies, involved performing multivocal textual repertoires with speed and flexibility, all within the boundaries of normative structures of gender and power. In spite of these boundaries, participants in these studies manipulated texts in new ways, reconfiguring messages, cutting and pasting, parodying, and creating textual forms to fit their social and self-representational needs. Not always centered on peer relationships, other studies reveal that adolescents turn to the Internet to express their political activism as well, choosing language to affiliate with the common goals of a particular political community (Humphrey, 2006) and reading online journals to learn about the activities of an interest group or organization (Guzzetti & Gamboar, 2005).

A study of two African American adolescents as "voluntary writers" (Mahiri & Sablo, 1996) shows that family as well as peers can drive the connection between social identity and literacy. The act of writing and the recognition by others, including family members, were important aspects of these young people's identity construction. Through their writing they addressed issues of race, drugs, violence, and poverty, which are not usually incorporated into the official curriculum. Similarly, a study by Noll (1998) addresses the importance of community recognition in the literacy lives of Lakota and Dakota adolescents. Performing and visual arts were part of the literacy practices of these adolescents, as acknowledged by their American Indian communities. Nonschool literacy practices provided status and important social roles in relation to peers and family, but in school they were subject to different, culturally incongruent expectations. Their out-of-school practices also offered an outlet for self-expression and creativity that set them apart in their community.

This kind of agency, although powerful in particular contexts, can maintain marginalized identities in others, as is the case in Moje's (2000) analysis of the transformative aspects of adolescent gang members' literacy practices. She focuses on the written, oral, and body discourses used to construct an identity in relation to peer gang members and rivals. These adolescents learned from their peers to generate codes and symbols that established membership and affiliations as they claimed space, a creative process not acknowledged in the classroom for any purpose, either to challenge mainstream literacy practices or to extend the knowledge of literacy that students bring to the classroom. Because gang literacy practices are loaded with values viewed negatively by dominant groups in society, claiming an empowering identity in relation to peers marginalizes these adolescents in the eyes of institutional authorities and potentially limits their social and academic futures. In general terms, the primary implication of second-wave identity research is that classrooms should offer a space to build on out-of-school literacy practices to negotiate and critically examine systems and structures that students deal with in their everyday lives but that too often serve to marginalize students at school and in other institutional contexts.

School Contexts

The negotiated or performed identities that are evident in second-wave research serve a social role that sometimes functions to contest institutionalized authority at school. At times, writers and readers perform identities that resist, appropriate, or transform particular values and ascribed ways of being in the world, in relation to gender, class, and race, for instance. Tatum (2000) argues that students are often required to take up dominant cultural identities, a particular problem for African American students for whom dominant identities have served to erase their own. His work, focusing primarily on African American boys, suggests that other identity constructions are possible through multiple forms of literature that critique dominant identities and open new possibilities. For the African and Caribbean adolescents in Fecho's (2000) action research, the classroom provided a space for critiquing dominant identities. In his classroom, students questioned the way code-switching positioned them and acknowledged "the pervasiveness of standard English" (p. 386). Students had more control over their language use and challenged the deficit view often imposed on them. They began to see language as a social act of claiming power and representing their

identities in relation to institutionalized authority as well as to peers and family.

The Black adolescent girls in Sutherland's (2005) study discovered new possibilities for critiquing dominant identities in their discussions of Toni Morrison's The Bluest Eye (1994), which allowed them to not only validate the personal and group identities they embraced but to also critique those that have been imposed upon them. The African American young women in Carter's study (2006) established bonds through nonverbal communication (e.g., eye gaze) to assert their gendered, raced, and cultural identities in the face of dominant identities valued in the British literature classroom—those that were male, upper-class, and Eurocentric. This bond enabled the young women to withstand frequent assaults to their racial, gendered, and cultural identities and to accomplish the academic work necessary for the class. Lee (2006) points to the necessary but difficult task of creating classrooms that teach academic literacy without dismissing students' cultural identities and, in her research, has worked to build this connection through a cultural modeling framework that links African American cultural resources with literary interpretation (Lee, 1995).

The performative and negotiated nature of identity is underscored in a number of studies that focus on the triad of text, reader, and context in school or school-like (e.g., after-school book clubs) settings. Lewis (2001) relies on the field of performance studies (Bauman & Briggs, 1990; Conquergood, 1989) to reveal the performative nature of literature discussions:

> Speakers and writers take up positions in relation to the expectations of others and the social and discursive codes available within a given context. . . . Individual and group identities are defined through repeated performances (ways of talking, listening, writing, using one's body) as participants "perform the self," which is always in relation to the group. (p. x)

Her work shows how performances of identity can be both fluid (shaped through moment-to-moment interaction) and reified through repeated performances that resist or embrace the social and interpretive norms of a community of practice. These identity performances shaped how texts could be read and discussed among boys choosing to read horror stories together in a classroom setting (Lewis, 1998), in the literary culture of a classroom (Lewis, 2001), and in a professional learning community of teachers grappling with race (Lewis, Ketter, & Fabos, 2001), demonstrating in all these contexts that interpretation is not just a transaction with text but also a socially coded and negotiated transaction.

Discursive codes and expectations shaped the literacy experiences and constructions of identity of adolescent girls in a multiyear case study of three girls' literacy experiences in school (Fairbanks & Ariail, 2006). The researchers found that the girls both accepted and negotiated positions in relation to school literacy with varying degrees of success, depending on resources and dispositions that shaped their interactions with texts, tasks, and teachers. These students' identities in their classrooms were integrally related to literacy learning and academic status.

The fluid yet reified nature of identity is evident as well in studies on book clubs in school (Broughton, 2002) and after school (Enciso, 1998). Broughton's (2002) participants were Mexican immigrants whose subjectivities related to texts were constructed through dominant cultural and masculinist discourses (e.g., identifying a character as a "slut"; p. 22). However, the acts of reading and discussion sometimes made these constructions visible for reexamination and possible transformation. In Enciso's (1998) study of early adolescent working-class girls positioning themselves in relation to books in the *Sweet Valley High* series, the girls positioned themselves primarily as "good" and "bad" girls according to the dominant cultural discourses that were available to them. Nonetheless, at "carnivalesque" (p. 57) moments, the girls enacted bad girl positions that challenged authoritative—both school-based and masculinist—expectations. Reader identities in an after-school book club for Asian high school students (Vyas, 2004) were more fluid, as the young women navigated their bicultural Asian and American identities by connecting to and resisting representations of Asian identity and intergenerational relationships in the books they read. A study by Athanases (1998) also complicates essentialized views of reader identification. Focused on the ways two ethnically diverse classes of adolescents responded to the implementation of more inclusive multi-ethnic literature, Athanases found that in some cases readers identified with cultural experiences or characters of ethnic backgrounds similar to their own, but in other cases, students reported identifying with characters and authors not of their own race or ethnicity.

Signaling a New Direction in Identity and Adolescent Literacy

In the preface to their 1998 edition of *Reconceptualizing the Literacies in Adolescents' Lives,* Alvermann, Hinchman, Moore, and Phelps tell readers that their "aim has been to capture adolescents' know-how and evolving expertise in an array of literacy contexts" (p. xvii). True to these words, the book chapters reveal insights into adolescents' identities as agentic knowers, whose literacy practices are "multilayered" (p. xvii). Hearing from the adolescents themselves, the preface suggests, would lead to a more authentic view of adolescents' literacies. The second edition of the book (2006) retains the value placed on the importance of adolescent voices, but with a difference. In this new edition, identity is mediated by discourse:

> First, a substantially greater number of students' voices are included in the second edition, primarily to make visible their identity-making practices, that is, the things they tell others and themselves about who they are as literate beings and the actions such tellings induce. (p. xxii)

In this new edition, then, youth do more than perform their identities; they are discursively engaged in a process that brings identity into being. This process is intertextual, relying on story lines that intermingle, overlap, and sometimes conflict, gesturing toward a "third wave" of identity-related sociocultural research on literacy, a new direction we take up in the next section.

THIRD WAVE: IDENTITY AS HYBRID, METADISCURSIVE, AND SPATIAL

A number of recent studies on the relationship between literacy and identity have theorized identity as hybrid, metadiscursive, and spatial. Particularly salient in research conducted in digital and transnational spaces, literacy practices related to third-wave theories of identity are understood to be networked within local and global flows of activity (Brandt & Clinton, 2002; Leander & Lovvorn, 2006). Digital media, in particular, hold the potential for a more "participatory culture" (Jenkins, 2006, p. 3) for literacy and learning. At the same time, however, digital media can limit participation (i.e., through the digital divide) and control capital through commercial content. Although youth may not be tuned in to the commercial content of digital media (Fabos, 2004), in terms of social identity and power relations, youth often are quite aware of the discursive fields that position them in particular ways, and they comment, at times with irony, on elements of this positioning (Knobel & Lankshear, 2004).

These paradoxes are resonant in adolescent literacy research related to third-wave identity. As Bean and Moni (2003) put it, "Identity is now a matter of self-construction amidst unstable times, mores, and global consumerism" (p. 642), with media and digital flows connecting macro- and microcultures in a postmodern landscape. In this landscape, institutions are viewed as "fragmented and unreliable" (Wyn, 2005, p. 45), causing adolescents to forge their own futures in risky and uncertain new economies. "Shape-shifting portfolio people" is the phrase Gee (2002, p. 62) has used to describe millennial adolescents, arguing that it is not only affluent White youth but also working-class immigrant and ethnic minority youth who manage their identities by assembling skills and experiences to achieve goals in the face of uncertain futures. The literacy practices of these youth are highlighted in research reported in recent edited volumes, in which contributors turned to third-wave identity constructs as analytic tools, including *Adolescents and Literacies in a Digital World* (Alvermann, 2002), *Spatializing Literacy Research and Practice* (Leander & Sheehy, 2004), *What They Don't Learn in School: Literacy in the Lives of Urban Youth* (Mahiri, 2004), *Re/constructing "the Adolescent": Sign, Symbol, and Body* (Vadeboncoeur & Stevens, 2005), and *Reframing Sociocultural Research on Literacy: Identity, Agency, and Power* (Lewis,

Enciso, & Moje, 2007). In the rest of this section, we briefly discuss some examples of research on literacy and identity that falls within the paradigm we have described.

Beach, Thein, and Parks (2007) and Thein (2006) focus on the identity construction of working-class high school students as they read and discuss literature. The researchers show how students mediate their identities through competing discourses related to the multiple social worlds they must negotiate and the textual world that is the object of discussion. Although this basic description of the work is in line with second-wave identity research, we found that its emphasis on the hybrid identities that students improvise as they embrace, resist, and critique literature in relation to each other and to societal discourses of economics, race, and gender has been informed by third-wave notions of identity as described in this section. Moreover, the transcripts of literature discussions throughout the book show students engaging in metadiscursive talk about the ways in which they have been positioned within their various social worlds and how this impacts their ways of reading and interpreting the texts.

Improvisation and metadiscursivity are key in Blackburn's (2003, 2005) studies of the literacy performances of lesbian, gay, bisexual, transgendered, and queer (LGBTQ) youth. In her participatory action research at a youth-run center for LGBTQ youth, Blackburn documents the ways in which the youth's literacy performances resulted in power struggles that subsequent literacy performances interrupted and commented upon. In other words, in response to difficult tensions that arose, youth responded by performing new acts of literacy that inevitably repeated some acts of privilege and power but identified and interrupted others.

A number of researchers who study the literacy practices of immigrant youth employ what we are calling third-wave identity as an analytic tool. For example, adolescents' hybrid identities are foregrounded in Sarroub's (2002) ethnography of Yemini girls in a Michigan high school. Sarroub attributes this hybridity to the girls' "in-betweenness," as they embodied several locations at once in relation to texts and culture. The challenge of traversing different geopolitical and psychosocial locations is the subject of Guerra's (2007) recent work on what he calls "transcultural repositioning" (p. 138). He uses this phrase to refer to the postmodern experience of living on the border, geographically, at times, but always in terms of the social imagination. In order to navigate new cultural and linguistic situations, Guerra explains, young people must "establish new hybrid identities as they move from one social site to another" (p. 139). He describes this as "rhetorical work" (p. 139) in the sense that it involves careful discernment of audience and strategic understandings of self in relation to other.

A similar strategic awareness is evident in the words of one of Moje's research participants (Moje & Lewis, 2007), a Latina student who responded to the young adult novel *The Outsiders* (Hinton, 1967). Pilar first enacted the "good student" identity by meeting the goals of the activity and addressing the themes of the novel. As the discussion ensued, she continued in "good student" form to relate the book to her experiences and analyze the experiences she brought to the discussion. The exchange was complicated, however, because the topic she initiated was about gangs, and her comments strategically deconstructed facile media and public representations of gangs. Given what she knew about her audience's negative views on gangs, she found ways to state her opinions within the conventions of typical school literature discussions, while at the same time hedging and qualifying her remarks about gang behavior in ways that allowed her to be seen as credible and as a "good person" (p. 37) in the eyes of her teacher and classmates. Moje's analysis shows how a "critical sociocultural" (p. 31) approach combines features of activity theory and critical discourse analysis to arrive at a fully contextualized understanding of the local play and distal effects of power and identity evident in Pilar's strategic moves.

Combining research related to immigrant youth with research on global media, Lam (2004, 2006a, 2006b) found that Asian immigrant youth used literacy in digital contexts to mobilize transnational identities and create affinity spaces across geopolitical borders. Lam also points out, as have others (e.g., Lankshear & Knobel, 2007) that new forms of adolescent literacy using digital media merge the producer and consumer roles, situating youth as agents who create, critique, rearticulate, and juxtapose as they consume popular forms of transmediated global culture. As Hull and Katz (2006) argue in their article on agency in digital storytelling, "individuals and groups can define and redefine themselves, voicing agentic selves through the creation of multimodal texts" (p. 71).

In several of the studies discussed in this section, identity was both enacted (in time) and placed (in space). We see this most obviously in research such as Sarroub's (2002) and Guerra's (2007) about adolescents whose lives can be said to be lived in border spaces, as already discussed. However, there is a movement in recent research on literacy that draws from Bakhtin (1981) and Lefebvre (1991) to place space–time chronotopes and trialectics (perceived, conceived, and lived space, in Lefebvre's schematic) at the center of theories of identity and literacy. Of those who focus on spatial theories in adolescent literacy research, Leander (2002, 2004) offers research that is most connected to the production of identities. Leander (2004) shows how tensions around race in a high school English class discussing offensive language existed in relationship to perceived (routine) and conceived (ideological) space in the classroom and in the school—through the history of school artifacts, activities, and design. The histories of the teachers were key as well, so that one teacher's previous position at an alternative school accustomed to such lessons influenced her decision to introduce the activity in this quite different context (lived space). These spatial and temporal histories were coordinated in particular ways and rearticulated in the classroom as the production and instantiation of group and individual identities. Leander (2004) argues that examining the production of identity in moment-to-moment interaction is not sufficient, but that what is needed is "to move outward from focal data to practices stretched out over broader expanses of space and time" (p. 117).

IDENTITY AS A LENS FOR RESEARCH ON ADOLESCENT LITERACY

It is important that the taxonomy of first-, second-, and third-wave identity research developed in this chapter be viewed as an analytic rather than evaluative tool for understanding the relationship between identity and literacy and the kinds of research used to examine this relationship. Our goal has been to understand overarching movements and their shaping effects on research and practice as well as the ways these theoretical constructs of identity have been shaped by larger social and cultural forces. We do not view the theoretical constructs as having evolved in any evaluative or developmental sense (e.g., from simple to more complex). In fact, we gravitated toward the term *wave* because it is a moving entity that ebbs and flows. The movement of waves is, at once, forward and back, hence metaphorically representing an eye toward the future and a serious respect for previous contributions. The fact that this movement is not unidirectional is important as well. The identity constructs we have described are not bounded by precise time periods but have been loosely chronological and recursive. Even in present times, specific educational problems may call for identity constructs related to cultural conflict. For example, charter schools for specific populations often are created to address issues related to the cultural conflict that exists between mainstream schools and a particular ethnic or racial group. Notwithstanding reasonable philosophical debates about whether strategic segregation of this sort is beneficial to the system or the individuals, these schools clearly serve a perceived need for addressing issues of cultural conflict and a view of within-group identity as relatively stable and unified.

Second- and third-wave identity constructs both inform different kinds of present-day research. Consider the example with which we began this chapter—the hip-hop magazine headline about the project-based charter high school that emphasized the recording arts. If we were to conduct research on students' literacy practices at that site, we could adopt a second-wave identity stance and examine how students use reading and writing in the course of project-based learning in the recording studio. We could then examine the creative and skill-based resources they marshal to complete this work and the ways they perform their identities as they apprentice as recording artists and technicians. We might also want to study students' identity negotiations as they engage in literacy practices, with the goal of understanding more about how they navigate the shift from self-identification and institutional positioning as unsuccessful students to enacting a different sort of student as defined by this project-based, apprenticeship-oriented context. If, however, we are working from a third-wave theoretical construct of identity, we might be interested in how the language and circulation of artifacts and documents construct the school as a particular kind of space—serving adolescents who are articulated as deviant in widely circulated documents; offering an innovative curriculum and cutting-edge design for open community spaces and private work spaces. We would want to think about students' literacy practices as related to these circulated articulations of space, mapped onto ideologies of project-based schools versus traditional schools and the history of the school's formation as a space for saving kids from deviance. Taking another tack, we might examine how it is that the student who was offended by the magazine headline came to this metadiscursive awareness of how the school and his peers were positioned. Finally, we might want to explore the political economy of hip-hop as it relates to these students' social futures, their relationship to global media, and the school's media representation.

Our intent with these examples has been to offer a brief array of research possibilities that could reasonably emerge from each construct of identity in order to show how particular identity constructions can shape research on literacy and what we understand about the impact of identity on literacy practices. As previously noted, the larger social and cultural spheres determine, to some degree, the identity constructs that are most needed and most often taken up at a given time. Identity as an analytic tool in adolescent literacy research typically has served to challenge limited, one-dimensional definitions of literacy and highlight the complex contextual factors that enhance or restrict adolescents' literacy practices and capacities.

REFERENCES

Allen, K., & Ingulsrud, J. E. (2005). Reading manga: Patterns of personal literacies among adolescents. *Language and Education, 19*, 265–280.

Alvermann, D. E. (2001). Reading adolescents' reading identities: Looking back to see ahead. *Journal of Adolescent and Adult Literacy, 44*, 676–690.

Alvermann, D. E. (2002). *Adolescents and literacies in a digital world*. New York: Peter Lang.

Alvermann, D. E., & Heron, A. H. (2001). Literacy identity work: Playing to learn with popular media. *Journal of Adolescent and Adult Literacy, 45,* 118–122.

Alvermann, D. E., Hinchman, K. A., Moore, D. W., & Phelps, S. F. (1998/2006). *Reconceptualizing the literacies in adolescents' lives*. Mahwah, NJ: Erlbaum.

Athanases, S. Z. (1998). Diverse learners, diverse texts: Exploring identity and difference through literacy encounters. *Journal of Literacy Research, 30,* 273–296.

Bakhtin, M. M. (1981). *The dialogic imagination* (C. Emerson & M. Holquist, Trans.). Austin: University of Texas Press.

Bauman, R., & Briggs, C. (1990). Poetics and performance as critical perspectives on language and social life. *Annual Review of Anthropology, 19,* 59–88.

Beach, R., Thein, A. H., & Parks, D. L. (2007). *High school students' competing social worlds: Negotiating identities and allegiances in response to multicultural literature*. Mahwah, NJ: Erlbaum.

Bean, T. W., & Moni, K. (2003). Developing students' critical literacy: Exploring identity construction in young adult fiction. *Journal of Adolescent and Adult Literacy, 46,* 638–648.

Blackburn, M. V. (2003). Exploring literacy performances and power dynamics at the Loft: Queer youth reading the world and the word. *Research in the Teaching of English, 37,* 467–490.

Blackburn, M. V. (2005). Talking together for change: Examining positioning between teachers and queer youth. In J. A. Vadeboncoeur & L. P. Stevens (Eds.), *Re/constructing "the adolescent": Sign, symbol, and body* (pp. 249–270). New York: Peter Lang.

Bloome, D. (1993). The social construction of intertextuality in classroom reading and writing lessons. *Reading Research Quarterly, 28,* 305–333.

Bloome, D., Carter, S. P., Christian, B. M., Otto, S., & Stuart-Faris, N. (2005). *Discourse analysis and the study of classroom language and literacy events: A microethnographic perspective*. Mahwah, NJ: Erlbaum.

Brandt, D., & Clinton, K. (2002). Limits of the local: Expanding perspectives on literacy as a social practice. *Journal of Literacy Research, 34,* 337–356.

Broughton, M. A. (2002). The performance and construction of subjectivities of early adolescent girls in book club discussion groups. *Journal of Literacy Research, 34,* 1–38.

Carter, S. P. (2006). "She would have still made that face expression": The use of multiple literacies by two African American young women. *Theory into Practice, 45,* 352–358.

Castell, M. (1997). *The power of identity*. Cambridge, MA: Blackwell.

Conquergood, D. (1989). Poetics, play, process, and power: The performative turn in anthropology. *Text and Performance Quarterly, 1,* 82–95.

de Castell, S., & Luke, A. (1986). Models of literacy in North American schools: Social and historical conditions and consequences. In S. de Castell, A. Luke, & K. Egan (Eds.), *Literacy, society, and schooling* (pp. 87–109). New York: Cambridge University Press.

Delpit, L. D. (1988). The silenced dialogue: Power and pedagogy in educating other people's children. *Harvard Educational Review, 58,* 280–298.

Duncan, G. A. (1995). What is Africa to me?: A discursive approach to literacy and the construction of texts in the Black adolescent imagination. In P. H. Dreyer (Ed.), *Toward multiple perspectives on literacy: Fifty-ninth yearbook of the Claremont Reading Conference* (pp. 46–62). Claremont, CA: Claremont Reading Conference.

Egan-Robertson, A. (1998). Learning about culture, language, and power: Understanding relationships among personhood, literacy practices, and intertextuality. *Journal of Literacy Research, 30,* 449–487.

Enciso, P. E. (1998). Good/bad girls read together: Young girls' coauthorship of subject positions during a shared reading event. *English Education, 30,* 44–62.

Enciso, P. E., & Lewis C. (2001). Introduction: Already reading: Children, texts, and contexts. *Theory into Practice, 40,* 175–183.

Fabos, B. (2004). *Wrong turn on the information superhighway: Education and the commercialization of the Internet*. New York: Teachers College Press.

Fairbanks, C. M., & Ariail, M. (2006). The role of social and cultural resources in literacy and schooling: Three contrasting cases. *Research in the Teaching of English, 40,* 310–354.

Fecho, B. (2000). Critical inquiries into language in an urban classroom. *Research in the Teaching of English, 34,* 368–395.

Ferdman, M. B. (1990). Literacy and cultural identity. *Harvard Educational Review, 60,* 181–204.

Finders, M. J. (1996). Queens and teen zines: Early adolescent females reading their way toward adulthood. *Anthropology and Education Quarterly, 27,* 71–89.

Finders, M. J. (1997). *Just girls: Hidden literacies and life in junior high*. New York: Teachers College Press.

Fine, M. (1991). *Framing dropouts: Notes on the politics of an urban high school*. Albany, NY: SUNY Press.

Fiske, J. (1990). *Understanding popular culture*. New York: Routledge.

Foley, D. E. (1991). Reconsidering anthropological explanations of ethnic school failure. *Anthropology and Education Quarterly, 22,* 60–86.

Gee, J. P. (1996). *Social linguistics and literacies: Ideology in discourse*. New York: Falmer.

Gee, J. P. (2000/2001). Identity as an analytic lens for research in education. *Review of Research in Education, 25,* 99–125.

Gee, J. P. (2002). Millennials and bobos, *Blue's Clues* and *Sesame Street:* A story for our times. In D. E.

Alvermann (Ed.), *Adolescents and literacies in a digital world* (pp. 51–67). New York: Peter Lang.

Gee, J. P. (2005). *An introduction to discourse analysis: Theory and method* (2nd ed.). New York: Routledge.

Guerra, J. C. (2007). Out of the valley: Transcultural repositioning as a rhetorical practice in ethnographic research and other aspects of everyday life. In C. Lewis, P. Enciso, & E. B. Moje (Eds.), *Reframing sociocultural research on literacy: Identity, agency, and power* (pp. 137–162). Mahwah, NJ: Erlbaum.

Gutiérrez, K., & Rogoff, B. (2003). Cultural ways of learning: Individual traits or repertoires of practice. *Educational Researcher, 32,* 19–25.

Guzzetti, B. J., & Gamboa, M. (2004). Zines for social justice: Adolescent girls writing on their own. *Reading Research Quarterly, 39,* 408–436.

Guzzetti, B. J., & Gamboa, M. (2005). Online journaling: The informal writings of two adolescent girls. *Research in the Teaching of English, 40,* 168–206.

Hagood, M. C. (2002). Critical literacy for whom? *Reading Research and Instruction, 4,* 229–246.

Hall, S. (1996). Introduction: Who needs "identity"? In S. Hall & P. du Gay (Eds.), *Questions of cultural identity* (pp. 1–17). London: Sage.

Heath, S. B. (1983). *Ways with words: Language, life, and work in communities and classrooms.* New York: Cambridge University Press.

Hinton, S. E. (1967). *The outsiders.* New York: Viking.

Hoggart, R. (1957/1992). *The uses of literacy.* New Brunswick, NJ: Transaction.

Holland, D., Lachicotte, W., Jr., Skinner, D., & Cain, C. (1998). *Identity and agency in cultural worlds.* Cambridge, MA: Harvard University Press.

Hull, G. A., & Katz, M. (2006). Crafting an agentive self: Case studies of digital storytelling. *Research in the Teaching of English, 41,* 43–81.

Hull, G. A., & Rose, M. (1989). Rethinking remediation: Toward a social-cognitive understanding of problematic reading and writing. *Written Communication, 6,* 139–154.

Hull, G. A., & Rose, M. (1990). "This wooden shack place": The logic of an unconventional reading. *College Composition and Communication, 41,* 287–298.

Hull, G. A., Rose, M., Fraser, M. K., & Castellano, M. (1991). Remediation as social construct: Perspectives from an analysis of classroom discourse. *College Composition and Communication, 42,* 299–329.

Hull, G. A., & Schultz, K. (Eds.). (2002). *School's out: Bridging out-of-school literacies with classroom practice.* New York: Teachers College Press.

Humphrey, S. (2006). "Getting the reader on side": Exploring adolescent online political discourse. *E-learning, 3,* 143–157.

Ito, M. (2007, February). *Amateur, mashed up, and derivative: New media literacies and Otaku culture.* Paper presented at the National Council of Teachers

of English Assembly for Research mid-winter conference, Nashville, TN.

Jenkins, H. (2006). *Confronting the challenges of participatory culture: Media education for the 21st century.* Chicago: MacArthur Foundation. Retrieved August 5, 2007, from *www.digitallearning.macfound.org/site/c.enJLKQNlFiG/b.2108773/apps/nl/content2.asp?content_id=%7BCD911571-0240-4714-A93B-1D0C07C7B6C1%7D&notoc=1.*

Knobel, M. (2001). "I'm not a pencil man": How one student challenges our notions of literacy "failure" in school. *Journal of Adolescent and Adult Literacy, 44,* 404–414.

Knobel, M., & Lankshear, C. (2004). Critical cyber-literacies: What young people can teach us about reading and writing the world. *Desencuentros, 4,* 49–72.

Kress, G. (2003). *Literacy in the new media age.* New York: Routledge.

Ladson-Billings, G. (1995). Toward a theory of culturally relevant pedagogy. *American Educational Research Journal, 32,* 465–469.

Lam, W. S. E. (2004). Border discourses and identities in transnational youth culture. In J. Mahiri (Ed.), *What they don't learn in school: Literacy in the lives of urban youth* (pp. 79–98). New York: Peter Lang.

Lam, W. S. E. (2006a). Culture and learning in the context of globalization: Research directions. *Review of Research in Education, 30,* 213–237.

Lam, W. S. E. (2006b). Re-envisioning language, literacy, and the immigrant subject in new mediascapes. *Pedagogies: An International Journal, 1,* 171–195.

Lankshear, C., & Knobel, M. (2007). *A new literacies sampler.* New York: Peter Lang.

Leander, K. M. (2002). Locating Latanya: The situated production of identity artifacts in classroom interaction. *Research in the Teaching of English, 37,* 198–250.

Leander, K. M. (2004). Reading the spatial histories of positioning in a classroom literacy event. In K. M. Leander & M. Sheehy (Eds.), *Spatializing literacy research and practice* (pp. 115–142). New York: Peter Lang.

Leander, K. M., & Lovvorn, J. F. (2006). Literacy networks: Following the circulation of texts, bodies and objects in the schooling and online gaming of one youth. *Cognition and Instruction, 24,* 291–340.

Leander, K. M., & Sheehy, M. (Eds.). (2004). *Spatializing literacy research and practice.* New York: Peter Lang.

Lefebvre, H. (1991). *The production of space* (D. Nicholson-Smith, Trans.). Cambridge, MA: Blackwell.

Lee, C. D. (1995). A culturally based cognitive apprenticeship: Teaching African-American high school students' skills in literary interpretation. *Reading Research Quarterly, 30,* 608–631.

Lee, C. D. (2006). "Every good-bye ain't gone": Analyzing the cultural underpinnings of classroom talk. *International Journal of Qualitative Studies in Education, 19,* 305–327.

Lewis, C. (1998). Rock 'n' roll and horror stories: Students, teachers, and popular culture. *Journal of Adolescent and Adult Literacy, 42,* 116–120.

Lewis, C. (2001). *Literary practices as social acts: Power, status, and cultural norms in the classroom.* Mahwah, NJ: Erlbaum.

Lewis, C., Enciso, P. E., & Moje, E. B. (Eds.). (2007). *Reframing sociocultural research on literacy: Identity, agency, and power.* Mahwah, NJ: Erlbaum.

Lewis, C., & Fabos, B. (2005). Instant messaging, literacies, and social identities. *Reading Research Quarterly, 40,* 470–501.

Lewis, C., Ketter, J., & Fabos, B. (2001). Reading race in a rural context. *International Journal of Qualitative Studies in Education, 4,* 107–129.

Luke, A. (2000). Critical literacy in Australia: A matter of context and standpoint. *Journal of Adolescent and Adult Literacy, 43,* 448–461.

Mahiri, J. (2004). *What they don't learn in school: Literacy in the lives of urban youth.* New York: Peter Lang.

Mahiri, J., & Sablo, S. (1996). Writing for their lives: The non-school literacy of California's urban African American youth. *Journal of Negro Education, 65,* 164–180.

McCarthey, S. J., & Moje, E. B. (2002). Identity matters. *Reading Research Quarterly, 37,* 228–238.

McDermott, R. P. (1977). The ethnography of speaking and reading. In R. W. Shuy (Ed.), *Linguistic theory: What can it say about reading?* (pp. 153–185). Newark, DE: International Reading Association.

McRobbie, A. (Ed.). (1997). *Back to reality: Social experience and cultural studies.* London: Manchester University Press.

Moje, E. B. (2000). "To be part of the story": The literacy practices of gangsta adolescents. *Teachers College Record, 102,* 651–690.

Moje, E. B., & Lewis, C. (2007). Examining opportunities to learn literacy: The role of critical sociocultural literacy research. In C. Lewis, P. Enciso, & E. B. Moje (Eds.), *Reframing sociocultural research in literacy: Identity, agency, and power* (pp. 15–48). Mahwah, NJ: Erlbaum.

Moje, E. B., Young, J. P., Readence, J. E., & Moore, D. W. (2000). Reinventing adolescent literacy for new times: Perennial and millennial issues. *Journal of Adolescent and Adult Literacy, 43,* 400–410.

Morrison, T. (1994). *The bluest eye.* New York: Plume.

Noll, E. (1998). Experiencing literacy in and out of school: Case studies of two American Indian youths. *Journal of Literacy Research, 30,* 205–232.

O'Brien, D. (2001). "At-risk" adolescents: Redefining competence through the multiliteracies of intermediality, visual arts, and representation. *Reading Online, 4.* Retrieved August 5, 2007, from *www.reading on-line.org/newliteracies/lit_index.asp?HREF=/new literacies/obrien/index.html.*

Rodríguez, R. (1982). *Hunger of memory: The education of Richard Rodríguez: An autobiography.* New York: Bantam.

Rubinstein-Ávila, E. (2003/2004). Conversing with Miguel: An adolescent English language learner struggling with later literacy development. *Journal of Adolescent and Adult Literacy, 47,* 290–301.

Sarroub, L. K. (2002). In-betweenness: Religion and conflicting visions of literacy. *Reading Research Quarterly, 37,* 130–148.

Scribner, S., & Cole, M. (1981). *The psychology of literacy.* Cambridge, MA: Harvard University Press.

Skelton, T. (1997). *Cool places: Geographies of youth culture.* New York: Routledge.

Stern, S. T. (2007). *Instant identity: Adolescent girls and the world of instant messaging.* New York: Peter Lang.

Street, B. (1985). *Literacy in theory and practice.* New York: Cambridge University Press.

Sutherland, L. M. (2005). Black adolescent girls' use of literacy practices to negotiate boundaries of ascribed identity. *Journal of Literacy Research, 37,* 365–406.

Tatum, A. (2000). Against marginalization and criminal reading curriculum standards for African American adolescents in low-level tracks: A retrospective of Baldwin's essay. *Journal of Adolescent and Adult Literacy, 43,* 570–572.

Thein, A. H. (2006, November). *Working-class girls' improvising flexible interpretive practices in negotiating lived and text worlds.* Paper presented at the 96th annual convention of the National Council of Teachers of English, Nashville, TN.

Thomas, A. (2004). Digital literacies of the cybergirl. *E-Learning, 1,* 358–382.

Thornton, S. (1996). *Club cultures: Music, media, and subcultural capital.* Hanover, NH: University of New England Press.

Vadeboncoeur, J. A., & Stevens, L. P. (Eds.). (2005). *Re/constructing "the adolescent": Sign, symbol, and body.* New York: Peter Lang.

Vyas, S. (2004). Exploring bicultural identities of Asian high school students through the analytic window of a literature club. *Journal of Adolescent and Adult Literacy, 48,* 12–23.

Warschauer, M. (2002). Languages.com: The Internet and linguistic pluralism. In I. Snyder (Ed.), *Silicon literacies* (pp. 62–74). New York: Routledge.

Willis, P. (1981). *Learning to labor: How working class kids get working class jobs.* New York: Columbia University Press.

Wyn, J. (2005). What is happening to "adolescence"? Growing up in changing times. In J. A. Vadeboncoeur & L. P. Stevens (Eds.), *Re/constructing "the adolescent": Sign, symbol, and body* (pp. 249–270). New York: Peter Lang.

CHAPTER 21

Latina/o Youth Literacies

Hidden Funds of Knowledge

CARMEN M. MARTÍNEZ-ROLDÁN
MARÍA E. FRÁNQUIZ

In the recent past, policymakers, curriculum planners, school administrators, and teacher-educators have provided marginal attention to literacy instruction for students in middle and high schools. In an era of high-stakes testing, the public at large has focused on the literacy learning of young children. Researchers Vacca and Alvermann have argued that limited policy initiatives and lack of schoolwide commitment for the ongoing literacy development of older students have resulted in a national crisis. They further contend that the crisis lies in misconceptions about the literacy development of youth and the important role hidden literacies play in their lives. This chapter focuses on the literacy resources of Latina/o youth, which more often than not remain unrecognized by teachers and educators. From a sociocultural perspective on literacy and a critical review of the literature on Latina/o adolescent literacy, we show how the languages and multiple texts that Latina/o students encounter in their lives are resources for learning. Because schools often attempt to develop academic language and literacy in English to the exclusion of the powerful hidden literacies of adolescents, we argue for the recognition and incorporation of out-of-school literacies and students' funds of knowledge in middle and high schools in order to boost Latina/o youth's interest in furthering their schooling.

This chapter offers a review of research regarding the literacy practices of Latina/o youth in and out of school in the United States. Our use of *Latina/o* attempts to be inclusive of males and females of U.S.-born Spanish-speaking origin or descent as well as recent immigrants. Because Spanish grammar historically privileges the masculine form, we deliberately use the feminine ending first in the identity descriptor *Latina/o*. We use the term *Latina/o* to refer broadly to youth of North, Central, South American or Caribbean heritage with roots in 21 Spanish-speaking nations (Zentella, 2005), acknowledging the great intragroup differences among Latinas/os, including language. The many dialects of Spanish and English spoken by this population reflect the great linguistic repertoires that can be found within these communities, a linguistic situation that may be better understood along a continuum (Hornberger, 1989; Zentella, 2005). At one end of the continuum, states Zentella (2005), "less than 10% of all Latinas/os in the U.S. are monolingual in one or more dialects of Spanish and at the other, 20% are monolingual in one or more dialects of English. All the gradations of Spanish- or English-dominant bilingualism exist in between those two poles" (p. 22).

Our review of the research literature is grounded in and interpreted from our personal and professional experiences as Puerto Rican/DiaspoRican scholars. The term *DiaspoRican* was popularized by Nuyorican poet Mariposa and refers to the increasingly diverse and dynamically evolving nature of Puerto Rican identity within the United States (Antrop-González & DeJesús, 2006; Valldejuli & Flores, 2000). We share combined experiences teaching and researching in diverse settings from preschool through university, and we align ourselves with sociocultural theorists and critically caring (Antrop-González & De Jesús, 2006) feminist theorists. Noddings (1992) proposed that caring theorists value an ethos of caring and are concerned when the curriculum and school are not actively promoting a search for meaningful connections between teacher and student, between student and family, and among students themselves. These interpersonal connections are the ones that have profound consequences for how students' identities develop and how their academic resiliency is influenced (Fránquiz & Salazar, 2004).

It is our premise that when interpersonal relationships, curricula, and institutional structures do not place value on the native languages, histories, and cultures of students, literacy resources for learning are subtracted (Nieto, 2002; Valenzuela, 1999) and academic resiliency suffers (Salazar, 2004). This has been one of the most consistent findings in research on Latinas/os' education and, as a result, in relation to writing, Nieto (2002) suggests:

> Using students' *words* and *worlds* (Freire, 1970) that is, their experiences, how they express those experiences (in whatever language they happen to use), and the social and cultural action embedded in their lives, can result in far richer and more "real" writing than does a focus on only academic deficiencies, social problems, or limited proficiency in English. (p. 165)

Nieto's words are aligned with an ethic of care. As Thompson (1998) explains, educators working from this position, as we do, do not equate caring with emotionally laden practices of feeling pity for Latina/o students' circumstances and lowering academic expectations. Critical researchers Bartolomé and Balderrama (2001) and Berzins and López (2001) poignantly explain that this critical caring is not motivated by *ay bendito* or *pobrecito* ("poor little one") (García, 2001) forms of teacher caring. Instead, communities of color understand caring within their own sociocultural context. Our goal is to build on sociocultural and educational caring scholarship (Antrop-González & DeJesús, 2006; McKamey, 2004; Thompson, 1998; Valenzuela, 1999) by seeking to uncover the existing knowledge base of culturally marginalized youth that all too often is not academically validated in schools. We offer our research literature review as a counter story to formulas such as given in Payne's aha! Process, Inc. (*www.ahaprocess.com*), which positions socioeconomically and culturally marginalized students as deficient and relegates their teachers to an uncritical color-blind form of caring. As scholars of color ourselves, we do not offer monolithic views of Latinas/os nor advocate "best practices" for them in schools—no matter where they are on the language and literacy continuum. Instead, our counter story highlights social science frameworks that identify and document the promising, rather than deficient, funds of knowledge (Moll, Amanti, Neff, & González, 1992; Vélez-Ibáñez & Greenberg, 1992) in students' homes, kinship networks (real and fictive), and communities.

The purpose of this chapter, then, is to synthesize research that makes visible some of the multiple literacy practices of Latina/o youth. We pay particular attention to how the uses of languages and literacy practices among Latina/o students demonstrate potential for academic success but have remained neglected and misunderstood hidden literacies (Villalva, 2006). We begin with a discussion of the changing demographic context and a review of the main theoretical perspectives orienting the research included in this chapter. We then identify ways the research literature discusses funds of hidden literacies and recommendations for mobilizing these literacies with the mediation of critically caring adults. Finally, we highlight programs that are effectively meeting the social and academic needs of Latina/o youth.

THE DEMOGRAPHIC CONTEXT

According to one of the latest reports from the Pew Hispanic Center (2005), the U.S. Latina/o population in 2004 was 40.4 million, a jump of more than 14% in 4 years. U.S. Latina/o youth include both recent immigrants and U.S-born citizens, youth from different social classes and with different literacy experiences. According to the 2000 U.S. Census, Latinas/os can be found in all states (Klein, Bugarin, Beltranena, & McArthur, 2004). Not only are they living in New Mexico, California, and Texas, states that traditionally have had the largest Latina/o population, but also in Maine, West Virginia, Vermont, Iowa, Georgia, Nebraska, and Washington, where the growing number of Latinas/os keeps increasing. Unfortunately, the rate of poverty is high in this population. Latina/o households own less than 10 cents for every dollar in wealth owned by Anglo households, with 22.5% of Latinas/os living below poverty lines, as compared with only 8.2% of Whites (Pew Hispanic Center, 2005). These numbers are significant because, as Moll and Ruiz (2002) propose, social class is the factor, more than any other, that determines the nature of schooling for Latina/o students.

Many researchers have expressed concerns about how Latina/o youth's local literacy practices are overwhelmingly ignored in classroom instruction precisely because they do not align with mainstream middle-class literacy practices valued at school. Mercado (2005a) asserts, "Because of their lower social value, local literacies (in contrast to official, institutional, or colonial literacies . . .) often go unrecognized in dominant discourses about literacies" (p. 238). One problem, then, is the inability of some policymakers and educators to view students from working-class families as emerging from households rich in intellectual and social resources (González et al., 2005).

As demographic shifts impact sociocultural contexts, teachers and policymakers must address another pervasive view: Children from Latina/o, African American, and Native American homes need to be deculturalized of beliefs from their primary cultures and forced to accept middle-class, Anglo-Protestant beliefs (Macedo, 1994; Spring, 1994). Rather than deculturalization, researchers studying families' funds of knowledge or community cultural wealth (Yosso, 2005) propose that family literacies be used as resources for learning in schools. Because family and "nonacademic" literacies are most likely to motivate students' interests in further schooling (Vacca & Alvermann, 1998), it is imperative to study the actions, interactions, and language used by Latina/o youth to describe their lived experience both in and out of school contexts.

SOCIOCULTURAL AND CRITICAL LITERACY PERSPECTIVES

As we reviewed the research on Latina/o youth literacy, we found that most researchers drew on sociocultural and critical perspectives whereby literacy was embedded in sociocultural practices and issues of power. Research informed by sociocultural and critical perspectives on literacy draw on constructs and methods from an interdisciplinary body of work that includes anthropology, sociology, sociolinguistics, cultural psychology, and education, among others (Gee, 1999; Heath, 1983; McCarty, 2005; Moll, 1990; Pérez, 2004; Street, 1995; Vygotsky, 1978). When examining literacy as a social practice, researchers focus on studying reading, writing, and other aspects of literacy not as linear processes or as mastery of neutral skills but as situated practices within specific contexts and situations. As McCarty (2005) puts it, adopting a sociocultural perspective does not imply we ignore the psycholinguistic, cognitive, or technical aspects of literacy; rather, a sociocultural perspective "embeds them [those different aspects] within sociocultural settings and the discursive practice and power relations of every day life" (p. xviii). This broader conception of literacy emphasizes the social, cultural, and historical experiences of youth and the literacy approaches associated with the groups to which they belong. It emphasizes the presence of multiple literacies (Lankshear & Knobel, 2006). Villalva (2006) explains:

Multiple literacies tend to be described within the following categories: school or academic (Gallego & Hollingsworth, 2000), community or social (Barton, 1994; Barton & Hamilton, 2000; Barton, Hamilton, & Ivanic, 2000; Gee,

1997), and personal or critical (Gee, 2000; Maybin, 2000; Muspratt, Luke, & Freebody, 1997). Multiple literacies approaches highlight that the literacy demands of classrooms are complex and that a learner's use of school literacies will be influenced by his or her experience with a unique repertoire of personal and community literacies. . . . In other words, multiple literacies have the potential to reveal "hidden literacies" that are often neglected or misunderstood. (p. 94)

Researchers working from a sociocultural perspective often refer to language and literacy practices as "Discourse" (Gee, 1990). To talk about language—oral and written—as Discourse (with a big "D") is to talk about language as conditioned by other, nonlinguistic parts of society. Discourses, as defined by Gee (1990), are "ways of being in the world, or forms of life which integrate words, acts, values, beliefs, attitudes, social identities" (p. 142). They are ways of displaying membership—however fluid that membership may be—in particular social groups. The literacy practices youth use in each social group become an important part of their identity work. The different texts they use become meaningful for those members who participate in the same literacy practices, in the same Discourse communities (Gee, 1990, 1999; Lankshear, 2007). These literacy and discursive practices and the factors that mediate their learning across contexts are not only highly complex but merit uncovering. Sociocultural and critical theories provide us with insights into the multiple memberships and Discourses Latina/o youth share in and out of school and the kinds of literacy and language practices that these memberships and relationships entail. An important dimension of these practices is Latina/o youth's linguistic repertoire.

LINGUISTIC REPERTOIRE OF LATINA/O YOUTH

Twenty years ago Anzaldúa (1987) wrote in her preface to *Borderlands/La Frontera*, "It's not a comfortable territory to live in, this place of contradictions." This is still true for many Latina/o youth today who live between family language and school language, family culture and popular culture. On the other hand, Anzaldúa theorized about building tolerance for ambiguity, the placing of one's feet in the spaces where worlds, languages, identities, and cultures overlap, the in-between space that is more a synthesis than contradiction, dispositions that are hybrid rather than assimilative, a confluence that is creative in anticipation of liberating possibilities (Fránquiz & Reyes, 1998).

When teachers and students consider the in-between space as a resource for liberating possibilities, then their sociocultural and linguistic experiences account for their different positionings in relation to the locations they occupy on the continuum of bilingualism. In some states with sufficient numbers of Latina/o immigrant children, such as Texas, families have options for the enrollment of their progeny. If a child has low literacy skills, a newcomer program is suggested so that sufficient English can be acquired for transfer to mainstream classes (typical duration is 6–12 months). In states such as California, Arizona, and Massachusetts where legislation prevents bilingual instruction, enrollment is limited to newcomer programs or English immersion programs (typical duration is 1–2 years). If the parents in an immigrant family are interested in their children's adding English while maintaining Spanish literacy, they enroll the children in bilingual instruction—in states that do not have antibilingual education restrictions. Students are typically enrolled in bilingual instruction until sufficient academic English is acquired (typically within 3 years). They may remain in bilingual programs, but the percentage of native language instruction is reduced in the upper elementary grades. Unlike immigrant students, children of Mexican descent who are born in the United States and acquire sufficient English before kindergarten do not have the option to enroll in bilingual programs unless a two-way immersion or dual-language model of bilingual education is available in the local school district. This specific model, though, which is not as typical across the states, is highly successful and requires a commitment from parents and staff to help each child become literate in two languages (Lindholm-Leary, 2001; Thomas & Collier, 2003). It is important for teachers to understand language learning, not only as a linguistic transitional process (from Spanish to English or vice versa) but also as an identity-formation process. This understanding will assist them and their students in retheorizing how the multiple language and knowledge systems available in the world outside the classroom can be integrated into the "reading [and writing] of the word" (Freire & Macedo, 1987) in the classroom in ways that affirm the range of linguistic diversity represented in the class community.

This range of language diversity can be better understood within Hornberger's (1989, 2003) *continua model of biliteracy*. The continua model offers a framework that describes the complex interrelationships between bilingualism and literacy and the importance of contexts, media, and contents as critical dimensions for biliteracy development. The idea embraced by the framework is that a bilingual person does not have two separate sets of linguistic resources. Instead of being a "double-monolingual" person, a bilingual person has special linguistic resources beyond what a monolingual person in either of the languages has. Becoming bilingual, then, requires the ability to employ language resources from two codes strategically and with great sensitivity to contextual factors.

An important consideration in examining the biliteracy continua are the ways in which some end points of the continua tend to be privileged in society, and others tend to be marginalized. For instance, English-only legislation makes it clear which end point of the monolingual–bilingual continuum is valued in U.S. society and education. In fact, Hornberger and Skilton-Sylvester (2003) argue the necessity for "paying attention to and granting agency and voice to actors and practices at what have traditionally been the less powerful ends of the continua" (p. 38).

Because middle and high schools make "foreign" languages available as course options, Latina/o students can enroll and begin to reclaim the study of their native language in order to move along the continua framework. Unfortunately, some of these same students experience forced linguistic border crossing from the native language, in this case Spanish, to English-only instruction during their initial years of schooling. Such crossings have the power to homogenize more than linguistic identities and require strong doses of critical caring. It is not that

children are passive victims of linguistic and cultural hegemony, but that the subordination of their primary socialization from the home delimited social and academic identity choices along the continuum. In so many ways youth must construct selves within multiple contexts of domination and resist persistent oppressive forces in their struggle for recognition and liberation.

For Latina/o students who do take the opportunity to reclaim their heritage language, it is common to find the presence of loan words, calques, and codeswitching in their speech, which has sometimes been described by sociolinguists as *Spanglish* (Poplack, 1981; Timm, 1993; Zentella, 1997). Lay people, recent immigrants, and even educators have tended to interpret the use of Spanglish as a reflection of poor language abilities and laziness. However, the old deficit paradigm has been replaced by theoretical positions that view codeswitching as an inclusionary, meaningful, and available strategy for communication in academic and social contexts and part of students' cultural resources and funds of knowledge (Fránquiz & Reyes, 1998; Martínez-Roldán & Sayer, 2006; Mercado, 2003; Zentella, 1997). Given the important presence Spanish has in the lives of Latina/o adolescents, and that their location on the biliteracy continua may influence not only how students speak but also how they write, some researchers suggest that educators learn what students can do in their native language and provide opportunities to build on that expertise (García, 2001), which has been identified as part of students' funds of knowledge (Mercado, 2005a).

HOME AND COMMUNITY LITERACY PRACTICES OF LATINA/O YOUTH

We now turn to research that has offered and keeps offering important insights regarding the hidden funds of knowledge and literacy practices of Latina/o youth, their families, and their communities. After reviewing some of the seminal research related to funds of knowledge, we present various studies that address caring literacy practices facilitated by adults, as well as studies focusing on youth-initiated literacy practices. Both lines of studies bring community funds of knowledge and cultural wealth to the forefront. We begin with examples of home and community literacy practices. We then focus on in- and out-of-school literacy practices by describing specific studies (e.g., It's About YOUth! in northern Colorado, the Social Justice Education Project in southern Arizona) and how students use popular culture to engage with literacy on their own terms. This section is followed by a discussion of studies that address how to support teachers in learning about their students' linguistic and cultural resources so they can be better used as resources for literacy instruction. Finally, we present two programs that have been successful in supporting literacy development of Latina/o youth and helping those youth plan for postsecondary education.

Because the two largest Latina/o communities in the United States are of Mexican and Puerto Rican ancestry, these are the communities whose literacy practices have been broadly documented. Given the intragroup differences within the Puerto Rican diasporic history and the binational persistence of Mexican communities, researchers studying those communities make it clear, as we also do in this chapter, that there are no typical Puerto Rican, Mexican, or Latina/o households (Mercado, 2005b; Nieto, 2004; Valdés, 2001; Zentella, 2005). Even within a single family, youth with different language and literacy development, ideologies, and practices may be found (Fránquiz & Brochin, 2006). Nevertheless, these studies inform us about literacy practices and identities that have been historically hidden in Latina/o homes (González, 2001), churches (Baquedano-López, 1997; Ek, 2005), or community-based organizations (Heath & McLaughlin, 1991, 1994).

For several decades, Farr (1989, 2004) has studied language and literacy practices within Mexicano communities in Chicago. Findings indicate that some texts and literacy artifacts are actually hidden, in the material sense of the word (e.g., documents about the participants' legal status concealed in the household). However, through their prolonged involvement in these communities, Farr and Guerra (1995) document how families manage a variety of literacy practices that serve their specific literacy needs. The researchers also identified various domains essential for Mexicanos' survival and prosperity in newcomer settings, including religion, home, education, commerce, and law/state, which involve the use of language and literacy to different extents. In the domain of religion, literacy texts included bulletins for religious services, documents for *quinceañeras,* books describing appropriate traditions for *doctrina* (catechism) and other religious traditions, such as *las Posadas.* Most of the literacy practices associated within this textually infused domain took place in Spanish. In the state/law domain most of the literacy practices were in English and required English comprehension and knowledge of bureaucratic and legal processes from the families. The commercial domain involved the use of Spanish language and literacy through advertisements in grocery stores and on radio and TV stations. In the education domain, the authors documented how schools and classrooms varied widely in receptiveness to the Spanish language and to Mexican culture, which led the authors to advocate that whatever programs are developed, it is of prime importance that they be based on respect for the knowledge—both oral and literate—that individuals of this culture bring with them.

Other important research that addresses the hidden literacies of Latina/o families is Moll et al.'s (1992) work on funds of knowledge, in which the scholars applied what they learned from the anthropological study of Mexican households in Arizona to the schooling of Latina/o students. Research on funds of knowledge uses constructs and methods from anthropology to document the accumulated bodies of knowledge and skills essential for household and individual functioning (Moll et al., 1992; Vélez-Ibáñez & Greenberg, 1992). This approach has been useful for examining family literacy practices (Mercado, 2005b) and community literacy practices (Moje et al., 2004). By involving teachers in some of these studies, the researchers aimed at impacting teachers' attitudes toward the linguistic and cultural resources their students bring from home and community literacies. They also aimed at influencing the kinds of learning experiences Latina/o students are offered at school by supporting innovations in teaching that draw on the knowledge and skills found in local households (Moll et al., 1992). These funds of knowledge include activities and knowledge related to agriculture and mining (e.g., soil and irrigation systems), economics (e.g., accounting and sales), household management (e.g., creating and managing budgets), medicine (e.g., knowledge of contemporary as well as folk medicine), and religion (e.g., Bible studies), among others. Often these activities involve uses of literacy in Spanish and English.

Working collaboratively with a variety of teachers, Mercado has also documented the funds of knowledge and hidden uses of literacy of Puerto Rican households in New York City (Mercado, 2003, 2005a, 2005b; Mercado & Moll, 1997). She describes local literacies of Puerto Rican households as hybrid practices, in the sense that families draw on a range of literacy practices from different domains and are influenced by the media, official literacies (school and government literacies), and the household's social networks. Among the many functions that reading and writing have in these households, Mercado highlights the ways these families used reading and writing for the following broad purposes:

a) for sensemaking of lived experiences and understanding of everyday issues related to: health and nutrition, legal issues affecting household members, the upbringing of children, one's identity and the identities of those who are new to the community, and the need for spiritual comfort and guidance;

b) for social participation in different groups such as church, parents' association, etc., in which the different activities carried out by each group make different literacy demands on its members;

c) for private leisure, reading about the lives of music, film, and TV personalities, reading love stories, newspapers, and magazines in English as well as Spanish;

d) for documenting life through photos, party souvenirs, and mementos. (2005a, pp. 242–244)

As in previous studies of household funds of knowledge in Arizona (Moll et al., 1992) and in New York (Mercado & Moll, 1997), Moje et al. (2004) found that funds of knowledge in Latina/o households in Detroit were related to the parents' work in and out of their homes. For instance, fathers' work as landscapers, farmers, dry cleaners, construction workers, and auto mechanics (all industries with direct connections to the issue of community air and water quality) had the potential for providing Latina/o students with an important foundation for understanding air and water quality when they studied these scientific topics at school. For fathers working, for example, as landscapers, the availability and quality of water was a topic they discussed often because it affected their work. Similarly, some students talked about the farms that their parents owned in Mexico and the products cultivated in them. The researchers proposed that the students' familiarity with these processes is part of their homes' funds of knowledge, with potential for considering the cultural, historical, economic, and scientific connections among them and school curricula. Moje and colleagues found, however, that as these youth were reading and writing classroom texts about water cycles and molecular structures of pollutants, their parents' work lives—and the economic and scientific conditions of their work—were absent from the classroom conversations.

Other valuable funds of knowledge identified in the Moje et al. (2004) study came from community members who valued the development of three areas: a strong ethnic identity, achieving educational and economic success, and a responsibility to become active agents of change. The mobilization of these values occurred when community members developed a two-way bilingual immersion public school of choice to provide children and youth with access to English language and literacy learning while maintaining and developing Spanish language and literacy. This mobilization involved community organizations, such as libraries and churches, which organized after-school and summer enrichment programs for the youth. The community's social activism provided robust funds of knowledge for scientific literacy learning at school. The mobilization of organizations engaged parents and students alike in various literacy activities, such as writing letters against environmental infractions. For example, the community was involved in protesting the building of an elementary school on a toxic waste site. Its members not only wrote letters to city leaders, but published editorials speaking out against the use of the site. Rather than transmitting messages delegitimizing the literacies used in Latina/o households and communities, this study documented how a not-so-hidden curriculum was enacted and integrated across home and school contexts in the community-initiated educational program.

In the Moje et al. (2004) study, all the students interviewed identified additional funds of knowledge, family relationships, and work practices that crossed state and national boundaries. The adolescents talked about traveling within and across countries. These experiences raised awareness of a number of social issues, which became the foundation for the production of narratives that were indeed related to the scientific topics discussed in school, such as the pollution along the Mississippi and the Rio Grande rivers. The authors found that such connections between students' knowledge, based on their experiences, and the school curriculum were not explicitly made in the classroom. Building on students' knowledge, acquired from their contact and experiences with transnationalism, provides a way to capitalize on that knowledge and validate students' ever changing bicultural identities (Browning-Aiken, 2005). We now focus on studies of situations in which those connections were indeed made and placed at the center of learning and teaching experiences for Latina/o students.

IN- AND OUT-OF-SCHOOL LITERACY PRACTICES: WORKING THE HYPHENS

Although "few books have focused on the richness of the cultural, linguistic, and experiential resources that Latina/o students bring to school, and what teachers need to know and do to tap into these resources" (Nieto, 2001, p. ix), there are studies describing caring adults who assist Latina/o students with the literacy work required in piecing together fragments of buried personal and social histories. These acts of cultural recovery, which are omitted from the typical history textbook and state standards (Campano, 2007), make visible how literacy can be used to create possibilities for personal liberation, rather than standardization or domestication (Freire, 1970; Shor & Freire, 1987). They are deliberate paths with alternative vi-

sions that redress the pervasive dropout/push-out rate (Olsen & Jaramillo, 1999) of Latina/o youth from middle and high schools.

Instead of "flipping the binary" between in-school and out-of-school learning, there are teachers who provide their students plenty of language arts opportunities to learn about the structures and dynamics that deepen inequality, seek to ground literacy activities in an ethic of compassion and care (Fránquiz, 2002; Noddings, 1992; Valenzuela, 1999), and engage themselves, their students, and whenever possible, their families with literacy aimed at social justice outcomes (Edelsky, 2006). These are teachers who are sociocultural mediators (Díaz & Flores, 2001) between and across in-school and out-of-school learning, which has been described as "working the hyphen" between these two contexts (Fine, 1994). The importance of working the hyphen aligns with the research findings of Gándara (1995), who showed that high-achieving Latina/os moved successfully and fluidly between the culture of the *barrio* or the fields and the culture of high-achieving Anglos in spite of the literacy levels of their parents. Unfortunately, using Anderson's (1983) metaphor of "imagined community," most Latina/o students are prevented from imagining membership in a bilingual, bicultural, and biliterate community. A program with caring adult mentors that has been successful is It's About YOUth!, in which Latina/o youth were invited to learn about, claim, and use their community funds of knowledge.

This after-school group in Colorado, It's About YOUth!, sought to assist Latina/o youth at risk of not completing high school, with opportunities to imagine membership in their own ethnic community (see Fránquiz, 2001, for a more detailed account). An important opportunity taken by the group, made up of adult mentors and Latina/o youth, was to engage in actions that effectively linked historical knowledge derived from home, peer culture, community, and school. For example, the youth learned about decades of contributions members of their ethnic community (Mexican) had made to the local economy through the beet industry. They also learned about many discriminatory acts against their families that were recorded in a collection of oral histories, *We, Too, Came to Stay* (Longmont Hispanic

Study, 1988). The realities of past racism toward relatives included the erection of an 8-foot cross by the Ku Klux Klan to remind Mexicans to be off the street by sundown, refusal to serve Mexican American World War II veterans in local bars, posting of "White Trade Only" signs on restaurant and shop windows, and the murder of two unarmed brothers-in-law by rookie police officers in 1980.

Access to the oral histories and newspaper articles was used to scaffold the development of a critical consciousness. In addition, *testimonios* of parents and grandparents were used. *Testimonios* are narratives that aim to bring immediate and emotive attention to a lived experience in an effort to raise consciousness (Jara & Vidal, 1986). They bear witness (Beverly, 2000) to persistent challenges and draw on knowledge of and from everyday life. *Testimonios* also become "the basis for theorizing and constructing an evolving political praxis" (The Latina Feminist Group, 2001, p. ix). Thus, testimonies are important resources that document the material conditions of many Latina/o students' authentic lives (Fránquiz, 2003).

The idea was for adult mentors in the after-school program to work with students to understand, critique, and take a position regarding the inequities that local institutions perpetuated from one generation to the next. The purpose of learning about discrimination was twofold: (1) to examine the place of contradictions in the local community, and (2) to reconsider the purpose of literacy in the lives of youth through participation in culturally relevant projects. In the case of It's About YOUth!, students examined local and often hidden facts of their community's history and as a result decided to participate in projects such as making a film for public access television that showcased the importance of lowrider bikes and cars in their lives.

The literacy practices associated with lowrider bikes and lowrider cars provide an opportunity for discussions regarding technical vocabulary such as *bondo,* a material applied to the frame of an older Schwinn bike in order to create a canvas for color, patina, and visual art, as well as for discussions about detailing the bikes with bajita wheels, crushed velvet seats, brass spokes, and shocks. Deeper discussions involve the use of semiotic symbols that represent religious icons, historical figures, and deceased loved ones. Such dialogue does not leave hidden that women are too often treated as sexual objects in lowrider magazines, alcohol and drugs interrupt learning, and gang affiliations limit life in and out of school. Through critical discussion students in this or any other such group are more apt "to build culturally grounded self respect" (Heath & McLaughlin, 1994, p. 13) and to make informed choices for the visual art represented on their bikes, cars, and other canvases (e.g., class assignments, notebook covers, clothing, tattoos). This is the type of discussion that adult mentors in It's About YOUth! and critical educators encourage in the official and unofficial spaces for learning both in and out of schools. One such critical educator is Julio Cammarota.

Cammarota (2007) developed the Social Justice Education Project (SJEP), an innovative curriculum that serves the cultural, social, and intellectual needs of working-class Latina/o adolescents in Tucson, Arizona. The intention of the program is for students to learn the requirements necessary for graduation as well as to experience consciousness-raising materials. They also learn research skills and are allowed to use their research to address inequities that students of color experience in public schools (Harwood, 2007). The SJEP provides Latina/o students with content in American History, U.S. government, Chicano studies, critical race theory, and critical pedagogy while they learn to conduct and report sophisticated critical analyses of their own social contexts. Students meet every day for one period for four semesters; they work on applied research projects on issues that matter to them and then present them to district, city, and state officials: "Self-advocacy granted the students the opportunity to see themselves as knowledgeable, intellectual, capable, and empowered" (Cammarota, 2007, p. 90).

While the students' voices are brought to the forefront of their learning experiences, they also engage in an analysis of their schools and their local communities for their applied projects. As part of this inquiry process the students integrate various practices associated with the kinds of academic literacies and literary writing that may support future college work. The Latina/o youth participating in this program write their observations of a number of sites on campus (including other classrooms, main office, and cafeteria) and/or in their communities in weekly field notes, document them through photographs, and conduct taped interviews. Students select research topics by creating poems about the problems they face in their social worlds. Before writing their own, the students read and discuss "social justice-minded poems" presented by the instructors. They learn to identify generative themes through their poems (e.g., border and immigration policies affecting family members who may have died crossing the desert). Using Chicano studies concepts and critical race theory as their analytical lenses, they analyze poems, notes, photos, and interviews, and their analyses become the basis of written reports, presentations, and video documentation.

The students' reflections about their learning experience in the SJEP illustrate how they felt empowered by the program and how it had an impact on not only their academic learning but their identities as Chicanos. For instance, one student commented:

> Before this class [SJEP] I didn't know who I was, I didn't know where my family came from. I just was thinking about Christopher Columbus. And it just made me realize what everything is and who I am. You know, be proud. . . . It just, like, gives you power to do better for yourself—to keep learning. (Cammarota, 2007, p. 92)

POPULAR CULTURE AND LATINA/O YOUTH LEARNING ON THEIR OWN TERMS

In their community ethnography Moje and colleagues (2004) documented out-of-school literacy practices in which Latina/o students engaged on their own, that is, without organized participation of adults. These literacy practices were described as belonging to the youth's peer funds of knowledge and popular culture funds. The researchers pointed to the need for strategic integration of the various knowledges and literacies that youth bring to and experience in school. They proposed the need to create experiences and spaces that integrate students' texts, framed

by everyday discourses and knowledges, with disciplinary learning to construct new texts and new literacy practices. This integration, they acknowledged, may work to challenge, destabilize, and, ultimately, expand the literacy practices that are typically valued both in school and in students' communities. In pursuing this integration of students' knowledge and literacies, however, some educators worry about the risk of co-opting youth practices for schooling purposes (Gustavson, 2007), as discussed next.

As a former seventh-grade teacher, Gustavson (2007) traced the out-of-school creative practices of three high school youth. In his work he promotes the nurturing of "youthspaces" in schools where such work can flourish. He contends that when youth work "on their own terms" without adult supervision, their work ought not be co-opted as subject matter or units of study. Rather, the ways youth work within art forms such as:

> zine writing, graffiti, and turntablism—all types of work that youth pursue on their own terms and often outside officially sanctioned adult spaces of learning—offer rich insights into the ways youth work and learn when they ask questions they want to pursue, develop projects that they want to complete, and perform products of this work to communities of peers and mentors. (p. 7)

Accordingly, Gustavson (2007) states, "Most young people are engaged in some kind of creative practice . . . whether it is blogging, video gaming, shopping, TV watching, clubbing, collecting and burning music. . . . Most youth are involved in some kind of practice of their own making that involves a community of practice (actual and imagined), rituals, materials, skills, and tacit knowledge" (p. 8). Gustavson also points out that youth dedicate a considerable part of their everyday lives to keep this work going even at the expense of schoolwork.

Gustavson (2007) traced the authentic practices his students cultivated in out-of-school communities. Doing ethnographic case studies of three 15-year-old males, he learned that Ian, as an affluent European American teen, had the resources of time and space to mobilize when he wanted to work on his zine writing or spoken word pieces, and that Gil, an African American turntablist, could count on using his DJing earnings for equipment to support his creative practice. However, Miguel, a working-class Puerto Rican, was constrained by his overcrowded home and consequently moved to the spaces in the streets to develop the creative practice of graffiti as a public art form. In barrio streets he found mentors who brought materials for collaborating artists to share. When he was arrested, "the negative reception of his graffiti as well as the difficulty to find space and time to write encouraged him to move to a 'canvas' that was his property and could not be evaluated in the same way by the dominant society" (Gustavson, 2007, p. 90). Miguel took up the practice of tattooing his body. Although this art form is not exclusively a practice among Latinas/os, Miguel and his brother tattooed their bodies in order to best express their creative ideals. Because school did not value the art of graffiti or tattooing, he dropped out of high school to find a job and take better care of his family, whereas Ian and Gil graduated and went to college. Gustavson (2007) concludes that the goal is not to turn students into graffiti artists or turntablists or zine writers, but to look at "the common rituals, routines, and skills that youth within these and other practices employ in order to do the work of literacy" (p. 136). The literacy practices identified by Gustavson in the out-of-school youthspaces involved experimentation, collaboration, performance, evaluation, and reflection.

Along these lines, Aguilar (2000) analyzed more than 100 samples of graffiti from eight Los Angeles barrios and found that creative literacy practices, such as graffiti, involve writers' control of genre, forms, symbols, and audience. That is, practitioners acquire "a structured and rule-governed practice, which they can use purposefully toward signification that is meaningful to both the individual and the group" (p. 25). Although Aguilar (2000) acknowledges that Chicano gang graffiti further marginalizes their practitioners (Moje, 1998), she agrees with Fine (1991) that the low-quality literacy that is often offered to urban youth at schools has the same effect (Valdés, 2001).

In the Moje et al. (2004) study, music was the strongest category of popular culture these researchers observed among the youth,

specifically pop Latino, gangster rap, and traditional Mexican folk music. Interestingly, the females in their study engaged in the literacy practice of writing and sharing quotes from the lyrics they liked. These quotes and the information about the songs and artists the girls read in magazines served as catalysts for interaction and socialization into a specific music genre. The hip-hop element of rap is worth mentioning here because it expresses youth voices on their own terms and is readily available to youth on CDs, radio, television, and the Internet. This increased availability of media creates not only "new and unpredictable forms of connection, identification, and cultural affinity, but also dislocation and disjuncture between people, places and cultures" (Gillespie, 1995, p. 7). An influential Latino rap artist of Mexican descent, Jae-P (Juan Pablo Huerta), has used the lyrics of his songs to describe the tactical strategies he uses to communicate about the borderlands where many Latina/o youth live and where they must make choices. The text of his own lived experience is embedded in the chorus of his Latin Gold Album signature award-winning 2003 rap song, "Ni de aquí, ni de allá." In the rap song he says, "Porque no soy de aquí ni soy de allá, con dos acentos en la lengua llegaré a triunfar" (translation: "Because I'm not from here and I'm not from there, with two accents I will still triumph").

This counter narrative is produced to increase understanding of and within the Latina/o youth culture. It personifies the struggle of a Mexican American caught between two worlds, a fusion of two languages and cultures, a clash of two languages and cultures, a marginalized space. Jae-P's story challenges nationalistic discourse about nationality and language. Jae-P's story claims and creates a dynamic new space of representation that Anzaldúa (1987) referred to as *nepantla*—a space where one places his or her feet among worlds, identities, and cultures. This phenomenon of living in *nepantla* invites overlaps and hybridity in anticipation of liberating possibilities. It is where linguistic and cultural borders are crossed and old identities are transformed (Fránquiz, 1999; Fránquiz & Reyes, 1998). Although Jae-P represents only one voice of the Mexican American experience, Spanish and Spanglish rap are increasingly conceived by Latina/o youth as a means of constructing and expressing their authentic selves (Fránquiz & Salazar, 2007).

COLLABORATING WITH TEACHERS IN SUPPORTING LATINA/O YOUTH'S LANGUAGE AND LITERACY LEARNING

Schools of education prepare teachers for working with Latina/o youth and thus have a responsibility for providing a coherent approach to educating culturally responsive instructors (Villegas & Lucas, 2002). One way to better prepare preservice and in-service teachers is to create spaces for discussing research literature regarding authentic challenges faced by teachers with Latina/o students in their classrooms. Mercado (2003) collaborated with a middle school teacher in a low-performing school to address students' lack of exposure to academic literacies. Together researcher and teacher created inquiry-oriented learning experiences. The participants included first- and second-generation children of Spanish-speaking immigrants from different countries and second- and third-generation Americans of Puerto Rican background. They were described as circumstantial/functional Spanish/English bilingual persons, that is, "members of a group of individuals who as a group must become bilingual in order to participate in the society that surrounds them" (Valdés, 1992, p. 95).

The students in this mainstream (nonbilingual) classroom experienced a range of literacy practices "associated with the work of social scientists . . . and they applied these practices to locate, document, and legitimize local knowledge on social issues that were of concern to them" (Mercado, 2003, p. 171). As in Cammarota's (2007) Social Justice Education Project, the process of documenting local knowledge from their communities in English or Spanish with tools that social scientists use created a context where students' social worlds were redefined as sources of knowledge and sources of emotional support.

Moreover, the students used their multidialectal repertoire in their writing to represent themselves within the various social networks to which they belonged. Mercado (2003) documented how Spanish in the students' multidialectal repertoire was evident in many ways. Sometimes the content dictated their choice of language and code-switching. At other times, the influence of their bilingualism was evident in the rhetorical strategies they used (e.g., conversational tone, giving advice, using humor) and in the genres and modalities they preferred to frame their ideas (e.g., an oral performance such as a speech or rap, storytelling, a letter). Mercado's (2003) and the teacher's analyses of students' writings illustrated that literacy knowledge and skills in Spanish did not impede but aided the learning of knowledge and skills in English. In fact, the study showed that the writing of these Spanish/English bilingual students was "qualitatively different from the written language of non-bilinguals as it reveals evidence for the continued influence of Spanish . . . long after students have entered mainstream instructional settings" (p. 176).

Demystifying the belief that the native language is a problem for Spanish speakers, Mercado's study corroborates substantial research showing how Latina/o youth are capable of accessing multiple social, cultural, and literate worlds as resources for their thinking and literacy development (Fránquiz & Reyes, 1998; Pérez & Torres-Guzmán, 2002; Zentella, 1997). Deep dialogue among educators of Latina/o youth regarding linguistic and cultural assets from home and community helps them understand why the vital connections among language, community, and identity must not go underground and become a stockpile of hidden literacies. When educators, administrators, and "teacher education programs emphasize the role of language in learning from purely linguistic, psycholinguistic or psychological models, teachers are not being prepared to understand the important role that language plays in the formation of self. This, in turn, has dangerous consequences for perpetuating existing social and educational inequalities" (Mercado, 2003, p. 184).

A concrete and effective means of mediating a dialogue among teachers regarding linguistic and cultural assets of Latina/o youth is the use of Latina/o literature in teacher education and graduate programs in education. For the last 3 years, Martínez-Roldán (2008) has been conducting research on teachers' responses to Latina/o literature in a graduate course on Latino literature for children and adolescents, offered every year. Through the reading and analysis of literature written by authors such as Julia Alvarez, Viola Canales, Judith Ortiz Cofer, Francisco Jiménez, and Pam Muñoz Ryan, among many others, the teachers become familiar not only with quality literature, but with themes related to Latinas/os' experiences in the United States, such as issues of borderland, language, identity, and immigration (Ada, 2003; Martínez-Roldán & Ratliff, 2008; Medina & Enciso, 2002). They also learn to evaluate literary quality and cultural authenticity and explore ways to bring this literature into their curricula—regardless of how prescriptive their curricula may be.

In spring 2007, one of the teachers, Angelic, whose students were mostly of Latino background and English language learners, chose for her inquiry project to interview Alberto Ríos, a Latino poet from the Southwest, who after having being punished as a child for speaking Spanish at school recovered his lost Spanish language and used his bilingualism as an asset in his poetry. Angelic organized literature discussions and asked her students to respond to Ríos's poems. She found that her students engaged more with Ríos's poetry than with the work of the canonical poets they had been studying, which suggests that in this class, Latina/o literature may have been a better starting point for the study of literature. She wrote:

> "As we traveled along side Alberto Ríos and his Nani, who did not speak a word of English . . . my students began to write poems about people they held close: lost fathers, an uncle who passed, mothers who had come to the states without knowing a word of English. . . . Since we returned from winter break, this was the first writing assignment that I had about 90% turn in rate. . . . Never had writing come so easily for this class."

As in the SJEP (Cammarota, 2007), Angelic's students wrote poems about problems they faced in their social worlds. However, they also wrote about simple everyday life events, using some of Ríos's poems as mentor texts. Inspired by Ríos's poem *Nani*, Francisco, one of the students, drew on his bilingualism and experiences to create a literary piece:

At the Park
Sitting in the park con mi familia
enjoying a carne asada
reunited once again
me and my familia talking to each other
disfrutando del calor that comes up high
cooling down with some bebida
enjoying los corridos that come from a guitar.
The time has come for us to leave
the sun is setting down
the family says adiós until next time.
　　　　　—by Francisco Olivo, seventh grader

As part of the same Latina/o literature course described above (Martínez-Roldán & Ratliff, 2008), some teachers chose to write their own pieces of literature for their final inquiry projects. A Latino teacher, Thom, who chose this option, commented:

> "My development as a Latino writer and teacher over the past semester has been one of the most rewarding experiences of my life. It has shown me that my strengths as a reader and writer originated at home. Not until I began exploring Latino literature for youth did I truly understand the profound impact living near the border had on my family, spirituality, language, and literacy development. . . . Encountering these themes in books by authors who share my heritage has set me on a new course as a teacher and children's writer."

The teachers' responses in this Latina/o literature class point to the potential of using Latina/o literature to support teachers as they reevaluate and uncover their own and their students' untapped cultural resources and histories, especially the value of their linguistic repertoire in an antibilingual state that through English-only legislation (Proposition 203, Arizona) has virtually eliminated the use of Spanish language and texts from public schools' classrooms.

MEETING CHALLENGES OF SECONDARY SCHOOLS IN THE 21ST CENTURY

In one of the first efforts to bring together research on youth, bilingualism, and English as a Second Language (ESL) in secondary schools, Faltis and Wolfe (1999) edited a volume in which they took a stance in favor of improving education for immigrant and bilingual secondary students through research and action. The editors brought together various authors who recognized the necessity of making changes in secondary schools to address the needs of English language learners and bilingual students, and who contributed to this agenda through their chapters. Faltis and Wolfe highlighted the social and political obstacles operating at that time—anti-immigrant, antibilingualism, and antipluralism movements and actions. Nearly a decade later, those obstacles are still some of the strongest challenges facing educators and researchers committed to improving the education of linguistically and culturally diverse secondary students. Having said that, we have shown that there are some successful programs, documented in the research literature, designed to build on Latina/o students' linguistic and cultural backgrounds and prior experiences. Now we present two examples of programs supporting literacy education in secondary schools that not only build on Latina/o students' funds of knowledge but also prepare them for postsecondary education. Both programs, the Puente High School English Program (Cazden, 2002; Duffy, 2001; Pradl, 2002) and the nationally acclaimed Advancement Via Individual Determination (AVID) program (Minato, 2007), were developed in California.

The Puente High School English Program is a curricular subject, English (literature and composition), and a *familia* (teachers, counselors, community mentor liaisons, parents, and mentors). All members of the Puente *familia* are expected to work together, "creating social bonds and social capital to support the students and their learning" (Cazden, 2002, p. 515). The three-part Puente design includes teaching, counseling, and mentoring. Mentors must be Latina/os, and when the mentees are in college and beyond they are expected to return support to the program. The Puente High School English Program has been a documented success in California. Since 1993 it has linked curriculum intervention and professional development for Latina/o youth academic success. It was estimated that in 2001, 80 secondary English teachers taught a Puente class at 33 sites (Pradl, 2002). Puente curriculum materials

and pedagogical approaches are designed to anticipate the range of literacy practices that Latina/o students will need for successful navigation in higher education. There are also community college Puente programs.

Puente's meaning-making approach to high school English integrates Mexican American literature with texts from the traditional literary canon. Selections by Latina/o and Chicana/o authors include *Bless Me, Ultima, Rain of Gold, House of the Spirits, Like Water for Chocolate, House on Mango Street, Living up the Street,* and *Zoot Suit.* Other classical texts include *Coffee Will Make You Black, Romeo and Juliet, Of Mice and Men, The Pearl, Julius Caesar, Antigone,* and *A Midsummer Night's Dream.* Students taking Puente High School English (*Puentistas*) create writing portfolios where they include autobiographical narratives, family legends, issue commentaries (persuasive writing), analysis of literature, community-based reports, poetry, and creative writing such as *calacas* for *Día de los Muertos* (Days of the Dead, November 1–2). Puente classes use the Bay Area Writing Project principles for writing. This approach encourages students to talk about their writing and receive responses in small groups. Students are guided by their teachers through editing revisions of drafts toward completion of papers. Because the Puente High School program is based on the idea that youth will flourish if they are taught strong writing skills in a supportive environment that validates their cultural assets, *Puentistas* attend 4-year colleges and universities at nearly twice the rate (43% vs. 24%) of matched controls (Gándara, 1998).

Like *Puentistas,* the participants in the AVID program work in collaborative groups in which the curriculum focus is on writing and inquiry. This program targets underachieving students with high academic potential (demonstrated by above-average test scores) who show promise to complete college preparatory courses in high school. Typically, Latina/o students who are underachieving or academically in the middle are placed in general tracks of education during high school. AVID places these low-achieving youth in the same academic programs as high-achieving students. At the same time, AVID provides a system of supports such as small-group tutoring, a variety of writing-to-learn activities, instruction in test-taking strategies, field trips, guest speakers, heterogeneous cooperative grouping practices, and peer support groups to assist youth in taking on the challenge of competing with their more economically and academically advantaged peers. The idea is to make the hidden curriculum of secondary schools visible and to provide students with the "cultural and social capital" valued at school that is not usually available to students of color and poverty. The success of the AVID program has reached well beyond San Diego, California, where an English teacher, Mary Catherine Swanson, introduced the idea in 1980 at Clairemont High School. As founder of *avid online*, Ms. Swanson was CNN's and *Time* magazine's 2001 America's Best Teacher.

Participants in the program are tutored by college students who are usually AVID graduates. In this way, aspirations for postsecondary education are kept alive among today's youth by mentors who had dealt with similar social and academic challenges in the not-too-distant past. AVID continues to grow by tremendous proportions and offers its website (*www.avidonline.org*) with research-based information and professional development opportunities for students, teachers, and administrators. Remarkably, AVID began with one high school and 32 students, and in 2007 was serving nearly 200,000 students in more than 2,700 middle and high schools in 39 states and the District of Columbia. For example, in 1997 the San Antonio Independent School District became the first Texas district to implement AVID. In 2006–2007 a total of 303 Texas secondary schools implemented AVID and enrolled 23,000 students, largely in response to demands for the narrowing of the achievement gap between children of color and poverty and more advantaged groups. The growth of AVID as a reform effort is paralleled with impressive results; the percentage of AVID graduates applying to and being accepted by 4-year colleges in 2006 was 75%. Given that the majority of AVID students are Latinas/os and African Americans who may lack a college-going tradition in their families, these results are indeed stellar.

AVID is summed up by a communications specialist of the nonprofit organization in its summer 2007 publication of *ACCESS*, AVID's educational journal:

Growth takes place inside an individual AVID student. But it is the support of others that kindles the growth within every student. By learning together side-by-side and day-by-day, AVID students instill their school environment with a college-going culture. Like branches of a tree, AVID students grow and flourish into confident, successful individuals while their roots remain firmly planted. (Minato, 2007, p. 3)

FINAL THOUGHTS

The studies presented in this chapter challenge deficit perspectives about Latina/o youth and document some of the practices that constitute the remarkable repertoire of language, literacy resources, and funds of knowledge Latina/o adolescents have access to out of school. These funds of knowledge and multiple uses of languages and literacy practices among Latina/o students and their families are resources for learning and have great potential to support academic success but have remained neglected and misunderstood hidden literacies. As some of the studies show, connections between students' knowledge based on their experiences and the school curriculum are not explicitly made in classrooms as often as they could be.

It takes time, planning, listening, observation, and care on the part of teachers to uncover and use those literacies to support students' acquisition of the academic literacies that schools aim to offer. We argue that in classrooms where the three B's are valued (students' *bilingual, bicultural,* and *biliterate* identities), students experience linguistic and cultural affirmation because they are invited to use all linguistic and cultural resources from family and community to reach their highest academic and social potential. These language and literacy practices, described as belonging to youth's peer funds of knowledge and popular culture funds, offer rich insights into the ways youth work and learn when they are engaged in meaningful inquiry and learning for their own purposes. However, to acknowledge Latina/o youth's linguistic and literacy resources is not enough. As several studies suggested, it is also necessary to make the hidden curriculum of secondary schools visible to students.

In this chapter we reviewed studies that instead of "flipping the binary" between in-school and out-of-school learning, described teachers who "work the hyphen." One of the ways to work the hyphens is through curricula that engage students in writing and inquiry using both students' multidialectal repertoires and the schools' literacies. Some of the studies pointed to the effectiveness of supporting students to learn literacies specific to different disciplines, for example, thinking and writing as scientists, writers, and ethnographers, while using those literacies to read, question, and write their worlds. Bringing students' social worlds, the resources as well as the problems they identify within their communities, into the curriculum enables students to examine the influence of multiple discourses in their lives and to set them on a new path toward the development and affirmation of their academic and social identities. As part of this inquiry process students can integrate various practices associated with the kinds of academic literacies and literary writing that can support future college work. With this approach, academic tasks are no longer inaccessible, and students' academic and social identities are also redefined. Such was the curriculum described as part of the Social Justice Education Project. In commenting on the impact of the project for the University of Arizona College of Behavioral Science newsletter (Harwood, 2007), the director of the school reported that of the approximately 100 students who had completed the project, 100% graduated from high school and more than 80% had gone on to college.

The studies also point to the importance of providing students with access to multiple kinds of texts and genres, including texts the youth want to contribute from their out-of-school literacies. However, the research presented in this chapter advances the perspective that more than trying to co-opt youth's popular culture and out-of-school literacies— such as hip-hop culture (rap, break dancing, turntablism, graffiti)—it is the complexity of the creative work and the habits of mind and body employed within them that ought to be translated to middle and high school classrooms (Gustavson, 2007). Also noteworthy as teachers work the hyphen is the use of texts written by Latina/o authors, as several of the studies highlight. The use of Latina/o literature provides teachers with knowledge of culturally relevant aspects of the multidimensional experiences of Latinas/os. It also supports students' learning and identities as they learn from the writing craft, the *testimonios,* experiences, and knowledge of Latina/o authors. The use of both Latina/o literature and the traditional literary canon was a component of a successful program aimed at preparing students for postsecondary education, the Puente program.

We end this chapter highlighting the importance of supporting Latina/o students to think of postsecondary education, as the Puente and AVID programs do. These programs include not only culturally relevant teaching, but also involvement of the community, counseling, and mentoring. Latina/o students need to be offered not only the alternative but the tools to continue postsecondary education, and this is not always the case. Two years after their high school graduation, *Puentistas,* for example, have been 20% more likely to be enrolled in a postsecondary educational institution than non-*Puente* students (72% vs. 52%) (Moreno, 2002). These two successful programs are an invitation to educators, policymakers, and researchers to be creative and rethink the educational experiences offered to Latina/o youth. We cannot afford to keep hidden all the multilingual talents and intellectual resources that Latina/o youth have to offer.

REFERENCES

Ada, A. F. (2003). *A magical encounter: Latino children's literature in the classroom* (2nd ed). Boston: Allyn & Bacon.

Aguilar, J. A. (2000, April). *The Chicano street signs: Graffiti as a public literacy practice.* Paper presented at the annual meeting of the American Educational Research Association, New Orleans.

Anderson, B. (1983). *Imagined communities: Reflections on the origin and spread of nationalism.* London: Verso.

Antrop-González, R., & De Jesús, A. (2006). Toward a theory of critical care in urban small school reform: Examining structures and pedagogies of caring in two Latino community-based schools. *International Journal of Qualitative Studies in Education, 19,* 409–433.

Anzaldúa, G. (1987). *Borderlands/La frontera: The New Mestiza.* San Francisco: Spinsters/Aunt Luke.

Baquedano-López, S. P. (1997). Creating social identities through doctrina narratives. *Issues in Applied Linguistics, 8,* 27–43.

Bartolomé, L., & Balderrama, M. V. (2001). The need for educators with political and ideological clarity. In M. de la Luz Reyes & J. J. Halcón (Eds.), *The best for our children: Critical perspectives on literacy for Latino students* (pp. 48–64). New York: Teachers College Press.

Berzins, M. E., & López, A. E. (2001). Starting off right: Planting the seeds for biliteracy. In M. de la Luz Reyes & J. J. Halcón (Eds.), *The best for our children: Critical perspectives on literacy for Latino students* (pp. 81–95). New York: Teachers College Press.

Beverly, J. (2000). Testimonio, subalternity, and narrative authority. In N. K. Denzin & Y. S. Lincoln (Eds.), *Handbook of qualitative research* (pp. 555–565). Thousand Oaks, CA: Sage.

Browning-Aiken, A. (2005). Border crossings: Funds of knowledge within an immigrant household. In N. González, L. C. Moll, & C. Amanti (Eds.), *Funds of knowledge: Theorizing practices in households, communities, and classrooms* (pp. 167–181). Mahwah, NJ: Erlbaum.

Cammarota, J. (2007). A social justice approach to achievement: Guiding Latina/o students toward educational attainment with a challenging, socially relevant curriculum [Electronic version]. *Equity and Excellence in Education, 40*(1), 87–96.

Campano, G. (2007). *Immigrant students and literacy: Reading, writing, and remembering.* New York: Teachers College Press.

Cazden, C. (2002). A descriptive study of six high school Puente classrooms. *Educational Policy, 6,* 496–521.

Díaz, E., & Flores, B. (2001). Teacher as sociocultural, sociohistorical mediator: Teaching to the potential. In M. de la Luz Reyes & J.J. Halcón (Eds.), *The best for our children: Critical perspectives on literacy for Latino students* (pp. 29–47). New York: Teachers College Press.

Duffy, H. (2001). Taking an anthropological stance: Implications for supervising new teachers. *English Education, 33,* 136–145.

Edelsky, C. (2006). *With literacy and justice for all: Rethinking the social in language and education* (3rd ed.). Mahwah, NJ: Erlbaum.

Ek, L. (2005). Staying on God's path: Socializing Latino immigrant youth to a Christian Pentecostal identity. In A. C. Zentella (Ed.), *Building on strengths: Language and literacy in Latino families and communities* (pp. 77–92). New York: Teachers College Press.

Faltis, C., & Wolfe, P. (Eds.). (1999). *So much to say: Adolescents, bilingualism, and ESL in the secondary school.* New York: Teachers College Press.

Farr, M. (1989, November). *Learning literacy lyrically: Informal education among Mexicanos in Chicago.* Paper presented at the annual meeting of the American Anthropological Association, Washington, DC.

Farr, M. (Ed.). (2004). *Ethnolinguistic Chicago: Language and literacy in the city's neighborhoods.* Mahwah, NJ: Erlbaum.

Farr, M., & Guerra, J. C. (1995). Literacy in the community: A study of Mexicano families in Chicago. *Discourse Processes, 19,* 7–19.

Fine, M. (1991). *Framing dropouts: Notes on the politics of an urban public high school.* Albany, NY: SUNY Press.

Fine, M. (1994). Working the hyphens: Reinventing self and other in qualitative research: In N. Denzin & Y. Lincoln (Eds.), *Handbook of qualitative research* (pp. 70–82). Thousand Oaks, CA: Sage.

Fránquiz, M. (1999). Learning in the transformational space: Struggling with powerful ideas. *Journal of Classroom Interaction, 34*(2), 30–44.

Fránquiz, M. E. (2001). It's About YOUth!: Chicano high school students revisioning their academic identity. In M. de la Luz Reyes & J. J. Halcón (Eds.), *The best for our children: Critical perspectives on literacy for Latino students* (pp. 213–228). New York: Teachers College Press.

Fránquiz, M. E. (2002). Caring literacy and identity struggles: The transformation of a Chicano student. In L. D. Soto (Ed.), *Making a difference in the lives of bilingual/bicultural children* (pp. 185–194). New York: Peter Lang.

Fránquiz, M. E. (2003). Essay book review: Literacy reform for Latina/o students. *Reading Research Quarterly, 38,* 418–430.

Fránquiz, M. E., & Brochin, C. (2006). Cultural citizenship and visual literacy: U.S.–Mexican children constructing cultural identities along the U.S.–Mexico border. *Multicultural Perspectives, 8*(1), 5–12.

Fránquiz, M., & Reyes, M. de la Luz. (1998). Creating inclusive learning communities through English language arts: From chanclas to canicas. *Language Arts, 75,* 211–220.

Fránquiz, M. E., & Salazar, M. (2004). The transformative potential of humanizing pedagogy: Addressing the diverse needs of Chicano/Mexicano students. *High School Journal, 87*(4), 36–53.

Fránquiz, M. E., & Salazar-Jerez, M. (2007). Ni de aquí, ni de allá: Latin@youth crossing linguistic and cultural borders. *Journal of Border Educational Research, 6,* 101–117.

Freire, P. (1970). *Pedagogía del oprimido.* DF, Mexico: Siglo Veintiuno Editores.

Freire, P., & Macedo, D. (1987). *Literacy: Reading the word and the world.* New York: Bergin & Harvey.

Gándara, P. (1995). *Over the ivy walls: The educational mobility of low income Chicanas.* Albany, NY: SUNY Press.

Gándara, P. (1998). *Final report of the evaluation of high school Puente, 1993–1998.* New York: Carnegie Corporation.

García, E. E. (2001). *Hispanic education in the United States: Raíces y alas.* New York: Rowman & Littlefield.

Gee, J. P. (1990). *Social linguistics and literacies: Ideology in discourses.* New York: Falmer.

Gee, J. P. (1999). *An introduction to discourse analysis: Theory and method.* New York: Routledge.

Gillespie, M. (1995). *Television, ethnicity and cultural change.* New York: Routledge.

González, N. (2001). *I am my language: Discourses of women and children in the borderlands.* Tucson: University of Arizona Press.

González, N., Moll, L., Floyd Tenery, M., Rivera, A., Rendón, P., Gonzales, R., et al. (2005). Funds of knowledge for teaching in Latino households. In N. González, L. C. Moll, & C. Amanti (Eds.), *Funds of knowledge: Theorizing practices in households and classrooms* (pp. 89–111). Mahwah, NJ: Erlbaum.

Gustavson, L. (2007). *Youth learning on their own terms: Creative practices and classroom teaching.* New York: Routledge.

Harwood, L. (2007, Winter). Great expectations: The Social Justice Education Project (Electronic ed.). *SBS Developments.* Retrieved June 18, 2007, from *sbs.arizona.edu/development/index.html.*

Heath, S. B. (1983). *Ways with words: Language, life, and work in communities and classrooms.* New York: Cambridge University Press.

Heath, S. B., & McLaughlin, M. W. (1991). Community organizations as family: Endeavors that engage and support adolescents. *Phi Delta Kappan, 72,* 623–627.

Heath, S. B., & McLaughlin, M. W. (1994). The best of both worlds: Connecting schools and community youth organizations for all-day, all-year learning. *Educational Administration Quarterly, 30,* 278–300.

Hornberger, N. H. (1989). Continua of biliteracy. *Review of Educational Research, 59,* 271–296.

Hornberger, N. H. (Ed.). (2003). *Continua of biliteracy: An ecological framework for educational policy, research, and practice in multilingual settings.* Buffalo, NY: Multilingual Matters.

Hornberger, N. H., & Skilton-Sylvester, E. (2003). Revisiting the continua of biliteracy: International and critical perspectives. In N. H. Hornberger (Ed.), *Continua of biliteracy: An ecological framework for educational policy, research, and practice in multilingual settings* (pp. 35–67). Buffalo, NY: Multilingual Matters.

Jara, R., & Vidal, H. (Eds.). (1986). *Testimonio y literatura.* Minneapolis: University of Minnesota, Institute for the Study of Ideologies and Literatures.

Klein, S., Bugarin, R., Beltranena, R., & McArthur, E. (2004). *Language minorities and their educational and labor market indicators: Recent trends.* (NCES Report No. 2004-009). Washington, DC: U.S. Department of Education, National Center for Education Statistics. Retrieved February 4, 2007, from *nces.ed.gov/pubs2004/2004009.pdf.*

Lankshear, C. (2007, April). *The "stuff" of New Literacies.* Paper presented at the Mary Lou Fulton College of Education symposium, Arizona State University, Tempe. Retrieved May 29, 2007, from *www.geocities.com/c.lankshear/stuff.pdf.*

Lankshear, C., & Knobel, M. (2006). *New literacies. Everyday practices and classroom learning* (2nd ed.). New York: Open University Press.

Latina Feminist Group. (2001). *Telling to live: Latina feminist testimonios.* Durham, NC: Duke University Press.

Lindholm-Leary, K. J. (2001). *Dual language education.* Buffalo, NY: Multilingual Matters.

Longmont Hispanic Study. (1988). *We, too, came to stay: A history of the Longmont Hispanic community.* Longmont, CO: Longmont Hispanic Study and El Comité.

Macedo, D. (1994). *Literacies of power: What Americans are not allowed to know.* Boulder, CO: Westview Press.

Martínez-Roldán, C. M. (2008). *Teachers' critical reading of texts in a Latino/a literature class.* Manuscript in preparation.

Martínez-Roldán, C. M., & Ratliff, J. (2008). *Sociopolitical themes in Latino/a literature and teachers' responses.* Manuscript in preparation.

Martínez-Roldán, C. M., & Sayer, P. (2006). Reading through linguistic borderlands: Latino students' transactions with narrative texts [Electronic version]. *Journal of Early Childhood Literacy, 6,* 293–322.

McCarty, T. (Ed.). (2005). *Language, literacy, and power in schooling.* Mahwah, NJ: Erlbaum.

McKamey, C. (2004, April). *Competing theories of care in education: A critical review and analysis of the literature.* Paper presented at the annual meeting of the American Educational Research Association, San Diego.

Medina, C., & Enciso, P. (2002). "Some words are messengers/*Hay palabras mensajeras*": Interpreting sociopolitical themes in Latino/a children's literature. *New Advocate, 15*(1), 35–47. (ERIC Document Reproduction Service No. EJ638885)

Mercado, C. (2003). Biliteracy development among Latino youth in New York City communities: An unexploited potential. In N. Hornberger (Ed.), *Continua of biliteracy: An ecological framework for educational policy, research, and practice in multilingual settings* (pp. 166–186). Buffalo, NY: Multilingual Matters.

Mercado, C. (2005a). Reflections on the study of households in New York City and Long Island: A different route, a common destination. In N. González, L. C. Moll, & C. Amanti (Eds.), *Funds of knowledge: Theorizing practice in households, communities, and classrooms* (pp. 233–255). Mahwah, NJ: Erlbaum.

Mercado, C. (2005b). Seeing what's there: Language and literacy funds of knowledge in New York Puerto Rican homes. In A. C. Zentella (Ed.), *Building on strength: Language and literacy in Latino families and communities* (pp. 134–147). New York: Teachers College Press.

Mercado, C. I., & Moll, L. C. (1997). The study of funds of knowledge: Collaborative research in Latino homes. *CENTRO, Journal of the Center for Puerto Rican Studies, 9,* 26–42.

Minato, N. (2007). AVID Summer Institute 2007 preview. *ACCESS, AVID's Educational Journal, 13,* 3.

Retrieved June 1, 2007, from *www.avidonline.org/content/pdf/2838.pdf*.

Moje, E. B. (1998, October). *"To be part of the story": A study of urban adolescents' literacy practices in and out of school*. Paper presented at the fall forum of the National Academy of Education/Spencer Post-Doctoral Fellows meeting, Palo Alto, CA.

Moje, E. B., Ciechanowski, K. M., Kramer, K., Ellis, L., Carrillo, R., & Collazo, T. (2004). Working toward third space in content area literacy: An examination of everyday funds of knowledge and discourse. *Reading Research Quarterly, 39*, 38–70.

Moll, L. C. (Ed.). (1990). *Vygotsky and education: Instructional implications and applications of sociohistorical psychology*. New York: Cambridge University Press.

Moll, L. C., Amanti, C., Neff, D., & González, N. (1992). Funds of knowledge for teaching: Using a qualitative approach to connect homes and classrooms. *Theory into Practice, 31*, 132–141.

Moll, L. C., & Ruiz, R. (2002). The schooling of Latino children. In M. M. Suarez-Orozco & M. M. Páez (Eds.), *Latinos: Remaking America* (pp. 362–374). Berkeley, CA: University of California Press.

Moreno, J. F. (2002). The long-term outcomes of Puente. *Educational Policy, 16*, 572–587.

Nieto, S. (2001). Foreword. In M. de la Luz Reyes & J. J. Halcón (Eds.), *The best for our children: Critical perspectives on literacy for Latino students* (pp. ix–xi). New York: Teachers College Press.

Nieto, S. (2002). *Language, culture, and teaching: Critical perspectives for a new century*. Mahwah, NJ: Erlbaum.

Nieto, S. (2004). *Affirming diversity: The sociopolitical context of multicultural education* (4th ed.). Boston: Pearson.

Noddings, N. (1992). *The challenge to care in schools: An alternative approach to education*. New York: Teachers College Press.

Olsen, L., & Jaramillo, A. (1999). *Turning the tides of exclusion: A guide for educators and advocates for immigrant students*. Oakland, CA: California Tomorrow.

Pérez, B. (Ed.). (2004). *Sociocultural contexts of language and literacy* (2nd ed.). Mahwah, NJ: Erlbaum.

Pérez, B., & Torres-Guzmán, M. (2002). *Learning in two worlds: An integrated Spanish/English biliteracy approach*. Boston: Allyn & Bacon.

Pew Hispanic Center. (2005). Hispanics: A people in motion. *Trends 2005* (pp. 71–89). Retrieved February 26, 2007, from *pewhispanic.org/reports/report.php?ReportID=40*.

Poplack, S. (1981). Syntactic structure and social function in code-switching. In R. Durán (Ed.), *Latino language and communicative behavior* (pp. 169–184). Norwood, NJ: Ablex.

Pradl, G. M. (2002). Linking instructional intervention and professional development: Using the ideas be-

hind Puente High School English to inform educational policy. *Educational Policy, 16*, 522–546.

Salazar, M. (2004). *Echándole ganas: The elements that support or constrain the academic resiliency of Mexican immigrant students in a high school ESL program*. Unpublished doctoral dissertation, University of Colorado, Boulder.

Shor, I., & Freire, P. (1987). *A pedagogy for liberation: Dialogues on transforming education*. South Hadley, MA: Bergin and Garvey.

Spring, J. (1994). *Deculturalization and the struggle for equality: A brief history of the education of dominated cultures in the United States*. New York: McGraw-Hill.

Street, B. (1995). *Social literacies: Critical approaches to literacy in development, ethnography and education*. New York: Longman.

Thomas, W. P., & Collier, V. P. (2003). The multiple benefits of dual language. *Educational Leadership, 61*(2), 61–64.

Thompson, A. (1998). Not the color purple: Black feminist lessons for educational caring. *Harvard Educational Review, 68*, 522–554.

Timm, L. (1993). Bilingual code-switching: An overview of research. In B. Merino, H. Trueba, & F. Samaniego (Eds.), *Language and culture in learning: Teaching Spanish to native speakers* (pp. 94–112). New York: Falmer.

Vacca, R. T., & Alvermann, D. E. (1998). The crisis in adolescent literacy: Is it real or imagined? *NASSP Bulletin, 82*, 4–9.

Valdés, G. (1992). Bilingual minorities and language issues in writing: Toward professionwide responses to a new challenge. *Written Communication, 9*, 85–136.

Valdés, G. (2001). *Learning and not learning English: Latino students in American schools*. New York: Teachers College Press.

Valenzuela, A. (1999). *Subtractive schooling: U.S.-Mexican youth and the politics of caring*. Albany, NY: SUNY Press.

Valldejuli, J. M., & Flores, J. (2000). New Rican voices: Un muestraria/o sampler at the millennium. *Journal of the Center for Puerto Rican Studies, 12*(1), 49–96.

Vélez-Ibáñez, C., & Greenberg, J. (1992). Formation and transformation of funds of knowledge. *Anthropology and Education Quarterly, 23*, 313–335.

Villalva, K. E. (2006). Hidden literacies and inquiry approaches of bilingual high school writers. *Written Communication, 23*, 91–129.

Villegas, A. M., & Lucas, T. (2002). *Educating culturally responsive teachers: A coherent approach*. Albany, NY: SUNY Press.

Vygotsky, L. S. (1978). *Mind in society: The development of higher psychological processes*. (M. Cole, V. John-Steiner, S. Scribner, & E. Souberman, Eds.). Cambridge, MA: Harvard University Press.

Yosso, T. (2005). Whose culture has capital? A critical

race theory discussion of community cultural wealth. *Race, Ethnicity, and Education, 9*(1), 69–91.

Zentella, A. C. (1997). *Growing up bilingual.* Malden, MA: Blackwell.

Zentella, A. C. (2005). Premises, promises, and pitfalls of language socialization research in Latino families and communities. In A. C. Zentella (Ed.), *Building on strength: Language and literacy in Latino families and communities* (pp. 13–30). New York: Teachers College Press.

CHAPTER 22

Beyond Hip-Hop

A Cultural Context View of Literacy

YOLANDA J. MAJORS
JUNG KIM
SANA ANSARI

In this chapter we argue for a cultural context view of literacy. We argue that, when leveraged within a classroom, literacy from this perspective can provide an alternative space that structures opportunities for all students to sort through their real-life dilemmas as well as work through the academic tasks they are expected to take up. Research that acknowledges students' literate problem-solving and problem-posing processes as culturally situated underscores and challenges the dominant theme in education that either (1) views students' cultural practices (e.g., ways of speaking, communicating, listening, responding) as deficits rather than as resources or (2) tends to link popular culture practices, such as rap and hip-hop music, to classroom practices without making explicit how and where such links occur. In framing the activities of students in this way, we are attempting to account for the mediational role of literacy practices in community contexts. We are also attempting to account for the role of participating members of these communities not just as active participants who are viewed as resistant to literate practices, but as active teachers and learners who use such practices in culturally responsive, authentic ways.

Classroom discourse events are a kind of community of practice (Lave, 1996)—hybrid in nature—in which students and teachers collaborate to build on culturally and socially constructed academic knowledge toward the goal of dealing with problems within literary texts. This hybrid space is polycontextual, multivoiced, and multiscripted, a space within which students become expert learners as they wrestle with themes in text as both local (near to) and distal (far from), but always meaningful to their lives.

The kinds of practices found in most classroom communities of practice, particularly those in secondary language arts, center on the reading of literary texts (Booth, 1974; Lee, 1993; Rabinowitz, 1987; Rosenblatt, 1978). In its functional form, reading is viewed as a practice taking up certain ideas and value systems in regard to written texts. Omitted from this view, however, is how similar ideas and value systems operate in other kinds of readings of oral texts and the skills involved in such readings. Social readings, readings that involve an appropriation of cultural norms, can provide situated context for engaging youth, not only in traditional academic literacies, but in broader problem-posing and problem- solving strategies that extend beyond the classroom. A consideration of social readings thus enables those interested in the social and academic development of all students and those who are drawn particularly to the experiences of African American students to better account for the interplay between culture and context in learning. Social readings also account for the role of cultural community processes for reasoning through texts and the ways a classroom can be a critical site for engaging in and utilizing cultural literacies in academic tasks.

Here we call attention to work that acknowledges students' readings of social texts as productive responses to *word* and *world* (Fisher, 2003; Foucault, 1980; Freire & Macedo, 1987; Mahiri, 2003; Majors & Ansari, 2008; Majors & Orellana, 2003; Morrell & Duncan-Andrade, 2004). Through secondary language arts instruction, one goal of the work presented is to provide secondary language arts students with the opportunity to unpack both *processes* and *practices* in reading and writing texts, both oral and written, in order that they may participate in the problem solving and decision making of their community and world. The perspective guiding this work holds with Moje (2007) that "it is not enough to talk about developing literacy as usable knowledge" in the world. Rather, "producing and assessing knowledge in the disciplines and in everyday life relies heavily on one's ability to access, interpret, critique, and produce texts, both oral and written, on both paper and electronic media" (p. 33). Our belief is that this empirical research illuminates useful ways in which to leverage the fundamental out-of-school practices of students of color—practices that mediate the production of knowledge—for in-school disciplinary literacy learning. As noted in the chapter abstract, such research underscores and challenges the dominant theme in education, which either (1) views students' cultural practices (e.g., ways of speaking, communicating, listening, responding) as deficits rather than as resources or (2) tends to link popular culture practices, such as rap and hip-hop music, to classroom practices without making explicit how and where such links occur.

This chapter is organized in three sections. In the first section, "Toward a Cultural-Context-Based Perspective," we explore three dominant paradigms of literacy teaching and learning: literacy as social/cultural practice, literacy as power, and literacy as identity. We synthesize these paradigms and argue for a cultural context view of literacy. We believe that, when leveraged within a classroom, literacy from this perspective can provide an alternative space that structures opportunities for all students to sort through the real-life dilemmas that they face as well as to work through the academic tasks they are expected to complete.

As members of the African American cultural community, many high school students develop with and through the kinds of routine, problem-solving strategies that characterize theirs as a community of practice. Such practices, like ways of speaking, have affordances for the kinds of things that many English teachers want all students to do—understand what texts mean and how texts mean.

The second section of this chapter, "A Cultural Community View of Literacy," introduces the community-based discourse practice of *Shoptalk*. Shoptalk grounds the consideration of culturally shared strategies for problem solving and coping in order to clarify what constitutes *community-based* and *culturally relevant* literacy practices. In this section we look closely at the cultural community practice of social reading within Shoptalk as an aspect of community and classroom literacy practices. We view Shoptalk as a possible framework useful for understanding the social and cultural tools that many African American students have access to and use for grappling with complex themes in text and life.

In the third section, we present a brief description of a particular unit of instruction taught within an urban secondary language arts classroom. This unit centers on our perspective of literacy as culturally situated, goal-oriented practice. We argue that many students enter the classroom already equipped with skills for engaging critically with texts. Our task is to draw upon these as sites for engagement that is both culturally responsive and academically purposeful.

TOWARD A CULTURAL-CONTEXT-BASED PERSPECTIVE

Literacy as Social Practice

Literacy is a complex activity, a way of thinking and being in the world, that goes beyond the ability just to read and write, as it takes place in complex relationships with others. Rather than how literacy has traditionally been viewed in academic settings such as schools—as an isolated activity consisting of a discrete set of skills—literacy is being redefined as a multifaceted and complex social activity that occurs across a variety of contexts (Barton & Hamilton, 1998; Gutiérrez, Baquedano-Lopez, Alvarez, & Chiu, 1999). It is "the ability to think and to reason like a literate person" (Langer, 1987, p. 3) and encompasses not just the skills used in reading and writing but the ability to utilize those skills across a variety of text- and non-text-based situations to communicate with others. Meaning thus can be constructed across media and across individuals. As a result, literacy encompasses the skills used in interpreting the most recent Blockbuster rental or television movie (e.g., *Crash, High School Musical*) with friends as much as those used in the interpretation of canonical literature (*The Scarlet Letter, The Odyssey*) within a classroom.

This view of literacy incorporates social practices, conceptions of reading and writing, as a way of thinking. It requires an individual's awareness of both his or her own understandings and interpretations of the world and those of others. In this way, literacy skills are used to create, think, and rethink adolescent worlds. This perspective shifts the focus away from the functional aspects of literacy, derived from most definitions, and enables us to consider how literacy, language, and culture are intimately connected.

Reading, as one aspect of literate practice, requires more than making sense of what is on a page. It requires attending to what is embedded beneath it, the often hidden nuances of written and social texts that humans create in our interactions with texts (Booth, 1974; Rabinowitz, 1987). Characterizations of literate ability imply certain specialized skills, and these skills lend themselves to specialized ways of thinking and reasoning through written texts—or in the case of illiteracy, the absence thereof. Although a great deal of attention is often directed toward a certain set of specialized skills, what tends to get lost in this perspective is an account of modes of thinking and reasoning as aspects of an individual's repertoire of practice and what these modes do and do not account for (Rogoff, 2003). Even less frequently considered are the constraints that this very popular, albeit very narrow, view of literacy places on interpersonal relationships, cultural identity, and problem solving beyond the immediate context (Bennett, 1983).

Literate thinking evolves through the socialization of learners in a culture (Bruner, 1990; Rogoff, 2003; Scribner & Cole, 1981). Literacy activities become mediating behaviors of higher mental thought, which are rooted in social interaction (Cole, 1996; Engeström, 1996b; Engeström, Miettinen, & Punamaki, 1999; Wertsch, 1985). Of interest is the process by which learners become socialized into the literacy practices of their community and eventually become independent members themselves. Adults in a community initiate learners into cultural activities through modeling and scaffolding practices. In a socially cooperative environment, learners practice and master the skills needed to accomplish a variety of activities in socially and culturally accepted ways and to evaluate the successful completion of said activities using the parameters of that community. As learners negotiate their world and internalize these processes, the mediational tools of literacy affect the ways in which they view and make sense of that world and the very ways in which they think about it (Cole, 1996; Gee, 1997). Simultaneously, learners master both their world and the skills needed to be successful in their world. Thus, ultimately, "how people think and reason depends upon the uses for literacy in the culture and the ways in which those activities are transmitted to younger generations" (Langer, 1987, p. 5; see also Rogoff, 2003).

Texts are a crucial part of literacy events, and the study of literacy is partly a study of texts and how they are produced and used. These three components—practices, events, and texts—constitute the first proposition of a social theory of literacy, that is, that literacy is best understood as a set of social practices and that these are observable in events that are mediated by written texts. This work complements other studies, primarily in linguistics, that focus on the analysis of texts. The study of everyday literacy practices directs attention to the texts of everyday life, the texts of personal life; these are distinct from other texts, mass media texts and other published texts. (This study also brings to bear the question, What constitutes a text?) Work in the field of literacy studies adds the perspective of practices to studies of texts, encompassing what people do with texts and what these activities mean to them. In our work, practices remain central and we focus on how texts fit into the practices of people's lives, rather than the other way around.

Literacy as Power

With the understanding that literacy occurs across various media and sites, it becomes clear that literacy is not the same in all contexts, nor, as is explored further, are all literacies seen as equal. These literacies are situational and can often be seen within specific, identifiable discourse practices of particular communities or domains (such as home or school). "These communities are groups of people held together by their characteristic ways of talking, acting, valuing, interpreting and using written language" (Barton & Hamilton, 1998, p. 3). Hence, discourses from this perspective are viewed as "ways of behaving, interacting, valuing, thinking, believing, speaking, writing and 'reading' that are accepted instantiations of particular roles by specific groups of people" (Hull & Schultz, 2002, p. 22). Taking a critical view of discourse enables us to consider the very complex roles, social identities, or social perspectives from which people are invited/summoned to speak, listen, act, read, write, think, feel, and value in certain characteristic, historically recognizable ways in combination with their own individual styles and creativity (Bourdieu, 1997; Foucault, 1980; Gee, Hull, & Lankshear, 1996).

Domains and the discourse communities associated with them are not clear-cut, however. There are questions of permeability of boundaries, of leakages and movement between boundaries, and of overlap among domains. Domains are structured, patterned contexts within which literacy is used and learned. Activities within these domains are not accidental or randomly varying. There are particular configurations of literacy practices, and there are regular roles in which people act in many literacy events in particular contexts. Various institutions support and structure activities in particular domains of life. These include family, religion, and education, which are all social institutions. Some of these institutions are more formally structured than others, with explicit rules for procedures, documentation, and legal penalties, whereas others are regulated by the pressure of social conventions and attitudes. Particular literacies have been created, structured, and sustained by these institutions. Hence, literacy practices are patterned by social institutions and power relationships, and some literacies are more dominant, visible, and influential than others (Bennett, 1983).

Furthering this consideration of discourse, Goffman's (1969, 1974, 1981) construct of participation framework allows an understanding of the social phenomena of practice, in particular the role of identities and power relations in workplace learning contexts. Goffman's (1969, 1974, 1981) participation framework identifies the roles that participants play in an act of communication. These roles include animator (one who gives voice to the message), author (one who crafts the words of the message), and principal (the source that provides authority to the message). The distribution of these roles across participants allows ideas to be put forth, amended, elaborated, extended, and contested (Lee & Majors, 2003). Furthermore, the distribution of these roles affects relations of power within the group, and also invites dialogic relationships with other discourses, ideas, and persons who may not be present in the communicative act (Majors, 2007). These roles are constituted not only by the creative and idiosyncratic intentions of individuals, but also socially constituted through the historical traditions of discourses. Thus, as people learn over time to participate in various discourse communities, they also learn to take on particular kinds of roles in talk (Lee & Majors, 2003).

As learners traverse domains, such as home and school, they encounter differentiated levels of appreciation (or rejection) of formerly accepted literacy practices. Because meaning is socially constructed in these views of literacy, the practices must change according to the context. Those who are unable to adapt, however, can suffer consequences. For example, there has been a great deal of writing about sharing time and the privileging of certain kinds of discourses in the elementary school classroom (Cazden, 2001). As young schoolchildren are encouraged to share stories about themselves, it becomes evident that certain discourse patterns, those most in alignment with European American middle-class patterns, are encouraged and rewarded over others, such as working-class African American patterns. Ultimately, then, what begins in grade school as an innocuous activity snowballs. Older learners understand who is considered literate or intelligent and who is not. This understanding manifests in discrepancies in grades, standardized test scores, attendance rates, self-confidence, and so on, as certain groups become stigmatized and certain groups are privileged. Consequently, as power relationships are implicated in the social functionings of individuals within a group, they are an integral part of identity formation. The following discussion outlines the ways in which identity development is a function of literate practices within a group, culture, community, or other such entity.

Literacy as Identity Formation

Barton (Barton & Hamilton, 1998) argues that "literacy practices are the general cultural ways of utilizing written language which people draw upon in their lives. In the simplest sense literacy practices are what people do with literacy" (p. 5). In presenting their case for a practice view of literacy, however, Barton and Hamilton argue that practices are not always observable. Being social in nature, literacy also involves values, relationships, perceptions, understandings, and attitudes. Although embodied in the individual, these psychological, cultural, and communal tools are constructed and enacted among community members—negotiated by the social rules and practices agreed upon by members.

A number of theorists have suggested that language and literacy are ideological in nature (Graff, 1987; Hull & Schultz, 2002; Street, 1994) and that uses of literacy have implications for identity construction and representation. Who people are, who they are allowed to be, is shaped in part by the ways they use literacy (Gee, 1996; Luke, 1995, 1996; Moje, 2000; Street 1994). For example, in her investigations within the African American community of Trackton (in the Piedmont region of the Carolinas), Heath (1983) has argued that literacy is best understood when viewed as a matter of social and ideological practices implicated in power relations and embedded in specific cultural meanings and norms. Heath supports this claim through a consideration of community literacy events among rural African Americans. Within literacy events in the African American community of Trackton, there is use of a tool kit, whose contents include systems of language and discourse structures and modes of reasoning. According to Heath, there are rules for the occurrence of literacy events, just as there are rules for speech events and participation in discourses. These may describe, repeat, reinforce, expand, frame, or contradict written materials, and participants must learn whether the oral or written mode takes precedence in literacy events.

Lee (1993) pushes this argument, illuminating the fact that literacies within the African American community include not only rules, but attitudes toward language use:

> Whether the text is an oral sermon, political oratory, autobiographical narrative, or simply a good story, language use must demonstrate flair and style, rhythm through selective repetition, and indirection articulated through the use of figurative language. (p. 9)

Lee's (1993, 1995, 2007) work with cultural modeling locates spaces within the discipline to link students' everyday discourses and practices specifically for the purpose of enhancing academic discourse and literate development (Moje, 2007). Lee draws upon the identities and community literacy practices of African American students and uses those resources as strengths in the mainstream language arts classroom. Recognizing how students were participants in and producers of African American English (AAE), and working to incorporate their understandings into the curriculum, allowed students to extend their community literacy practices into the classroom and to have greater success (Lee, 1993, 2007). Both the production and interpretation of the rules and attitudes inherent in literate practices (and as a consequence the modes of thinking and reasoning associated with them) involve participants' choices of what to attend to linguistically and otherwise. It is when researchers consider such choices that they can then consider how linguistic difference, "ways with words" as Heath (1983) calls it, plays a part in the construction of the literate practices that young people bring to school.

Whereas literacy is a function of social practices and is embedded within cultural norms and values, literacy practices provide a particular context for identity formation. However, these ways of thinking are part of the larger context of power structures within society.

A CULTURAL COMMUNITY VIEW OF LITERACY

Research into community discourse has implications for culturally relevant practices in the classroom. Such research has considered the kinds of cultural funds of knowledge—the networked expertise woven through community practices (Moll, 1992), particularly language forms and discourse structures to which students have access (Heath, 1983; Lee, 2007; Mahiri, 2003). In recent years, a number of researchers across the disciplines have made strong cases for the importance of understanding the nature of skilled reasoning embedded in localized social discourses (Engeström, 1996a; Hutchins, 1996; Lave, 1996; Lave & Wenger, 1991; Rose, 2004; Scribner, 1997). The ethnographic investigations of Majors (2001, 2003, 2004, 2007), for example, research into the processes of teaching and learning in African American hair salons contribute to our understanding of literacy as medi-

ated practice. Earlier research employed ethnography to explore constructions of self among African American women in midwestern hair salons. However, Majors examines the women's conversations—or *Shoptalk*—to illuminate how members of that community provide to one another access to culturally shared and situated knowledge and practices. Within this context members have opportunity to learn—to question, challenge, and reconstruct knowledge—as well as transmit their understandings of the world through such verbal strategies as participation, collaboration, and negotiation (Banks, 2000; Jacobs-Huey, 2006; Majors, 2003, 2004, 2007).

In the African American community, the hair salon has several functions. One is that it serves as a safe space where members of the community come to "skillfully deflect the psychological attacks" that come with being human in an othered body (Hill-Collins, 2000). These attacks are encountered each day on their personhood, their adulthood, and their dignity, and attempt to lure individuals into accepting definitions of themselves as inferior (p. 97). As a safe space, the hair salon functions as a site where, through and beyond the sorrows and the joy, members of that community can collectively come to terms with "the contradictions separating one's own internally defined images of self as African American men and women with one's objectification as the Other" (Hill-Collins, 2000, p. 99). According to Hill-Collins (2000), "this struggle of living two lives, one for a dominant white society and one for ourselves creates a peculiar tension to construct independent self-definitions within a context where African American personhood remains routinely derogated" (p. 100). This coming to terms is a process of knowing (and coming to know) within a discourse that is culturally and socially situated, nested within a space where, as a part of its function, members resist objectification as the Other and do the things that everyday African Americans do. As Hill-Collins (2000) states:

> These spaces are not only safe . . . [members] observe the images of the larger culture, realize that these models are at best not suitable and at worst destructive to them, and go about the

business of fashioning themselves after the role models of their own community. (p. 101)

In addition to being a safe space, another function of the hair salon is that it is a distinct "ritual setting" (discourse being a part of that ritual) where valuable cultural and economic resources, as well as knowledge and information, are available to members of that community to be created, recreated, and shared. An important aspect of this ritual is the routine, dialogic act of members making public to an audience how they think, particularly in regard to the everyday, how they access others' thinking, and how that thinking shapes present and future actions that affect the individual as well as other members of the group.

Hence, the African American hair salon offers to its members possibilities for transformation, not only of the novice, young adult learner, or adult learner, but of the context in which such learning and social action takes place. These cultural and socially defined spaces allow participants to construct independent self-definitions while deflecting, resisting, and deconstructing oppressive and dominant ideologies (Lacewell-Harris, 2004; Majors 2004).

To further explore teaching and learning in the context of the classroom, we relied on a conceptual framework of Shoptalk to view talk as a mediational tool in *community*- and *classroom*-based activity systems (Majors, 2007). The concept of Shoptalk becomes useful when researchers want to examine the role of thinking and speech in goal-directed activities, not just in one cultural community's practices, but within and across culturally situated activity systems. In community-based systems, for example, Shoptalk enables us to view (1) how members of that community provide to one another access to culturally shared and situated knowledge and practices, (2) the processes of deflecting (coping with) the everyday within which members reason about what is meaningful to them, and (3) the interplay of thought and language within social problem solving as well as occupational work tasks. Likewise, in the classroom, Shoptalk makes it possible to extend this view of safe space, language, and thought as instruments of practice in a context where robust, hybrid spaces for disciplinary problem solving are created through the community-derived routines with which students are familiar.

Black hair salons for women, like barbershops for men, are often places where co-constructed, community forms of talk—stories, personal narratives, jokes, folklore, and folktales—can be found. The popularity, success, and controversy surrounding the comedic movie *Barbershop* (and, more recently, *Beautyshop* and MTV's *The Shop*), were due in part to the fact that each show or movie "peels back the curtain" of this tradition of talk and allows both insiders and outsiders to eavesdrop on the discourse of Black folks, when White folks aren't around (Mitchell, 2002). Like barbershops, many Black hair salons are also sites where cultural traditions of talk, which include AAE, are used as resources for critical reasoning and the construction of arguments.

In these spaces, participants make use of particular skills and tools, such as language use, in order to collaboratively construct knowledge, distribute, and cope with task completion for success, and manage the everyday nuances of maneuvering within a culturally shared and situated site of academic learning (Majors, 2001, 2003, 2004). In addition, the skills and tools associated with literary-based problem-solving tasks are not just bound to one site, but are mediational tools that correspond across contexts, continuing to affect discourse practices and individual development.

In earlier findings, narrative, for example, played a tremendous role in the process of problem posing and problem solving in the hair salon (Majors, 2007). This process involved both coherence and an appropriation of cultural norms for talk and teller-ship; temporal, logical, and referential continuity; inferencing; and narrative composing and telling skills, as a way of fathoming the social and moral meanings of life and everyday events (Ochs & Capps, 2001). In the hair salon, the process of problem solving, as a kind of reading of events, involved both collaborative sense making and performance. Readers of narrative texts "may dialogically probe alternate, sometimes conflicting, versions of what (could have) transpired in an event and attempt to piece together moral perspectives on events" (Ochs & Capps,

2001, p. 62). Readings of narrative texts call for openness to contingency, improvisation, and revision. In the context of everyday discourse, such narratives also require skillful collaboration with interlocutors "who may desire soothing coherence, but may yield to the quest for experiential complexities and alternative possibilities" (p. 111). Participating members in Shoptalk, with its dialogic nature, offer that coherence.

By examining the processes through which students take up, resist, and extend readings of written and oral texts, we are able to unpack the role of thinking and speech in the acquisition and appropriation of literate skill. Thus, Shoptalk as a cultural community-based tool and conceptual frame enables us to consider talk within problem-solving task performances, in which:

- Talk functions as a tool that allows participants to meet developmental and cognitive needs.
- Speakers evoke certain images and assume roles before an audience.
- The most engaged forms of talk are communicated through AAE discourse norms.
- Oral narratives of personal experience and storytelling are produced and interpreted through "acting" participants, generally for the purpose of providing resources, problem solving, and/or building knowledge.

Previous work with Shoptalk suggested that participants' discourse practices in the hair salon were enacted through particular kinds of skills. These include:

- An understanding of the positioning of the speaker/author as it shapes authorial intent.
- The identification of implied audience.
- The appreciation of the underlying meaning or intent of a text.
- An understanding of coherence within inference generation.
- The generation of response to claim within a narrative.
- The taking on of roles (and the ability to step in and out of them within the discourse) through the appropriation of contextualized terms to construct an expert knowledge and enact an epistemic stance.

Such skills are akin to what some have called literary schemas within domain-based, literary reasoning and thus may be used as a scaffold for reasoning in complex problem-solving tasks in other contexts, such as the language arts classroom (Lee, 2005). In particular, the kinds of skills often generated within narrative production and interpretation as an aspect of Shoptalk are highly informative and akin to tools of literacy that call on skills of revision, improvisation, recounting, inferencing, and making and fathoming the social and moral meanings of events (Ochs & Capps, 2001). They are part of the psychological (Wertsch, 1985), communal (Bruner, 1990), cultural (Swindler, 2001) and linguistic (Moll, 2000) tool kits that all individuals draw upon to reason through problem-solving activities.

Our consideration of literacy as culturally mediated practice begins by examining the process of *social reading* of oral narrative texts within an African American hair salon (Majors, 2004). Recent studies, for example, call attention to the "difference in the social and academic prestige of written" texts in the home and school lives of English language learners (Guerra & Farr, 2002; Skilton-Sylvester, 2003). It is important to be aware of such differences, in value and practice, of home and school literacy across contexts. Bringing attention to the range in students' literacy practices across contexts, however, "does not translate into an intentional building of bridges" between them (Resnick, 2003, p. 93). Nor does it translate into an acceptance of the home and community practices, which shape and frame the literacy skills the students bring into the classrooms, or the ability of teachers to harness these in important and productive ways. Unfortunately, few empirical studies exist that investigate the socially and academically relevant literacy skills cultivated within and across communities and culturally responsive classrooms (Ladson-Billings, 1994; Lee & Majors, 2003).

In recent years, researchers have contributed valuable empirical evidence as to how these funds of knowledge are taken up in classrooms, in particular by those who are labeled "underachieving" (Gutiérrez, Baquedano-Lopez, & Tejeda, 1999; Lee, 2004). These contributions are important, particularly given the tendency to posit overgeneralized questions regarding the inequities in student achievement and performance, and assumptions about the identities, values, skills, and reasoning abilities of students who underperform, the languages they speak, and the communities they come from seemingly embody the same deficit models and thus limit our responses.

The Skill of Social Reading

Social reading is an active evaluation of some action in events by protagonists (texts), whose actions, thoughts, and feelings are collaboratively and publicly interpreted by local group members in light of local notions of what is right, wrong, and just. The skill of social reading involves both coherence and an appropriation of cultural norms for talk and teller-ship; temporal, logical, and referential continuity; and inferencing, as well as narrative composing and telling skills, as a way of fathoming the social and moral meanings of life and everyday events. In social reading both collaborative sense making and performance are critical. As stated earlier, readers of narrative texts "may dialogically probe alternate, sometimes conflicting, versions of what (could have) transpired in an event and attempt to piece together moral perspectives on events" (Ochs & Capps, 2001, p. 62). Readings of narrative texts call for openness to contingency, improvisation, and revision. In the context of everyday discourses, such narratives also require skillful collaboration with interlocutors "who may desire soothing coherence, but may yield to the quest for experiential complexities and alternative possibilities" (p. 111).

The skill of reading the social relations and intentionality embedded within socially constructed oral narrative texts—instances of oral or written language in use within specific social group discourses—are rehearsed and developed within specific discourse communities, such as the African American hair salon. Arguably, cultural border crossers—people who actively move across the socially constructed and imposed divides that help to distinguish cultural groups/discourse communities, one from another—develop the skills of social reading through their participation within such communities, as well as through their movement *between* different kinds of communities (Majors & Orellana, 2003).

Certainly all people (not just those who frequent hair salons) engage in this kind of reading social texts and of performing roles. However, the skill of reading the social relations and roles embedded within these oral display texts may be heightened for many African Americans who have simultaneously and historically been denied societal power, yet must navigate across institutions and interface daily with groups who hold and exercise such power (Majors, 2007; Majors & Orellana, 2003). The skill of reading social relations within events that are socially reconstructed as oral narrative texts (Fairclough, 2003; Ochs & Capps, 2001) is one that is harnessable and should be acknowledged and cultivated by teachers of linguistic and cultural minority students in general, African American and Latino students in particular. Why?

Although members of these historically oppressed and marginalized groups may be skillful readers of social relations and sophisticated problem solvers in community-based contexts, too often they do not experience success at navigating the processes of problem solving in school. When their linguistic, social, and cultural tool kits are recognized, they are too often viewed as localized, impermeable, and harnessable only *within* contexts rather than *across* them. The argument we make in this chapter is meant to challenge the tendency in research that assumes that bringing attention to the range in students' literacy practices will generate success. It also challenges the current practice of ignoring how students' out-of-school skills can be incorporated into successful problem-solving strategies.

In preceding sections, we have attempted to (1) lay the foundations for a view of literacy as cultural community practice, (2) characterize *the skill of social reading* as it relates to this conceptualization of literacy, and (3) illustrate how individuals draw on a repertoire of literate practices that includes social reading to think, reason, and problem solve within and across contexts. In the following section we detail how African American adolescents narrate their readings of culture, class, and other social relations in an urban midwestern classroom. Such reading, we think, is a literacy skill that these students rehearse and develop through their participation within specific, socially contingent discourses and/or through their movement *across* different kinds of discourse communities such as families, peer groups, workplaces, and schools.

READING AT THE INTERSECTION OF COMMUNITY AND CLASSROOM

Shoptalk provides a lens through which to view the classroom not only as a potential safe space, but as a place where students grapple with how knowledge is produced, consumed, and reproduced for future use. As in the hair salon, the engagement of participants (in this case, students) with texts and text images can be viewed as a dialogic process of understanding and making public to an audience how they think, particularly in regard to the everyday, how they access an author's thinking, and how that thinking shapes present and future actions. When viewed this way, as in an educational context, discourse in community settings that frame cultural practices offers us a way to externalize the internal thinking strategies that youth engage in and many classroom teachers would like to foster with their students. "This externalization serves not only the research objective of analysis, but also the practical objective of facilitation" (Kuhn, 1991, p. 23). In seeking to understand problem-solving events and practices involving urban youth, and the sites they traverse as they engage in those practices, we turn our attention to the secondary language arts classroom where the first author is the instructor. Our starting point is the transformation of the traditional classroom into a safe space; students come there and view themselves as participating in a discourse of doing the things that expert members of the African American community do when faced with a dilemma instantiated in text and/or world. The enactment of a safe space as classroom involves attending to situated dilemmas (presented as claims within an oral or written text) as social and cultural practices and as literacy events. We view those events and practices as the actions through which critical engagement, ideologi-

cal stances, and counter narratives are enacted in the classroom, a safe space that has social, political, ideological, historical, cultural, and literate dimensions.

Participants in these events were African American adolescents between the ages of 15 and 17. The site is a language arts classroom in a small (< 500 students) secondary high school in a midwestern city. Major's work as a secondary language arts instructor in an urban high school has shown that students take up similar discourse patterns that involve social reading while engaging in problem-solving strategies. The example that we present is drawn from a 3-week writing unit discussion about understanding structures of argumentation. The students are 10th to 12th graders engaged in a process of social reading while attempting to discuss alternative perspectives in written texts. The written text was a downloaded news release from *CNN.com* that referred to William Bennett's statement that aborting "every black baby in this country" would reduce the crime rate as a sound argument ("Bennett Under Fire," 2005; see below for full quote). However, it seemed that before students could address this written text, there was some heavy discussion in which the students had to spend time representing their own perspectives across three contexts: their own lives, the broader social community, and the textual context in which Bennett's comments were made. In doing so, students were able to use discursive practices familiar to them and similar to those identified within the Shoptalk discourse in order to engage in strategies for determining what the text was, who was meant to be the reader, and how best to respond to a text that could be disempowering. These discursive practices involved both social reading strategies and norms for talk that were similar to those found within the discourse in the hair salon.

The selection of texts and writing activities in the Shoptalk language arts classroom are intended to help students interrogate the word and the world. In the context of discussing complex literary and life texts, both the structure and content of talk plays a significant role in framing and creating context and unveiling the positionings and thinking of speakers (narrators, authors) as social actors, while simultaneously unveiling the ideologies and institutional assumptions inherent in those positionings. Students bring familiarity and various levels of expertise and understanding of this "talk" to generate and unpack complicated readings of texts.

In this unit, called "Understanding Structures of Academic Argumentation," instruction began by spending 2 weeks as a class unfolding what it meant to construct well-framed, strategic responses to what students were reading, in the form of traditional argument. This unit was designed to provide students with practice in considering alternative points of view, how texts are constructed and read by various audiences, and the implications of those readings. For one exercise, students spent time during the early part of the unit learning to identify the various parts of an argument (claims, grounds, warrants, and backing) based on brief written excerpts from mainstream canonical texts.

As the unit progressed, students were invited to consider viewpoints that were arguably relevant to their lives as African American youth. Shoptalk contributed to the nature of classroom discourse, as here we returned to the creation of safe space, that is, a class where participants can talk about/write about what is meaningful to their lived lives. For example, students were asked to identify the claim presented by William Bennett in his radio show, in which he stated:

> If you wanted to reduce crime, you could—if that were your sole purpose—you could abort every black baby in this country and your crime rate would go down. That would be an impossibly ridiculous and morally reprehensible thing to do, but your crime rate would go down. ("Bennett Under Fire," 2005)

The instructional goal was that by the end of this unit (introducing students to canonical structures of argumentation) students should have a better understanding of the nature of argument and the routine strategies that are involved in justifying claims and generating counterclaims. In addressing Bennett's argument, it was necessary for students to face the contradictions experienced by many other African Americans in regard to self and socially defined images and to call forth the processes necessary for grappling with them. Although the instructional goal was to teach students to identify how

authors might construct arguments concerning everyday matters that go beyond traditional text models, ultimately and collectively the process for getting there called for making explicit how others think, what constitutes the subject of thought, and how to respond for future action. As in the hair salon, this process also involved a coming to terms with the contradictions—separating one's own thinking and self from those of others.

In regard to enacting a safe space, we view this classroom as a site of culture, negotiation, and constructed knowledge where students were allowed initial responses that were emotional and visceral (i.e., sorrows and joy) to a text that they deemed threatening to their lives and insulting to their experiences. The literacy aspect of this event addresses two questions: First, how do instructors make explicit the "expert" process of determining what the problem is that the students, as readers of texts, are being called upon to address? Second, what are the literary devices, techniques, and mechanisms available to students that can enable them to respond intellectually to that text? This event mirrors what happens in many mainstream classrooms when students are asked to respond to a text. What is often absent from this process of engaging readers is a push back or, rather, a space where perspectives can be interrogated through cultural meanings and norms.

Hence, to propel this interrogation, students grappled (for the duration of the unit) with the dilemma of facing the claim as an instance of narrative retelling. The main instructional goal was to propel students into (1) laying claim to and telling their own counter (argument) narrative responses and (2) recognizing how points of view can be framed and can themselves frame others. Second, students interrogated the arguments as oral texts, Bennett's and those created by the students in response, enabling the students to begin to draw from their own cultural understandings of language, participation, and power in order to lay the foundations of responding beyond the affective. By taking a political issue and situating it within a hybrid context combing the social and academic through the use of narrative, the instructor attempted to allow students the space to make connections between the claim made by Bennett and how it speaks to their experience in particular ways as members of a particular community. The following are students' written examples in which they conveyed their initial reactions in their journals during the second week of the unit.

Example 1:

"This passage is appalling. How could someone be so selfish? The comment that this man says is very ignorant. He is saying that our ethnic background is the main reason why the crime rate is so high."

Example 2:

"I feel that this man was wrong and that the comment was full of bigotry. He should be ashamed of himself and offer his apology to all African Americans."

Example 3:

"The comments made by Bennett are clearly the result of an ignorant mind reluctant to release his prejudices and misconceptions on another."

Example 4:

"I believe that Bennett is terribly ignorant and insensitive. Bennett's remarks are very hurtful and helps my belief that there is still racism in the world."

In these examples, students present emotive reactions to what we call a kind of social narrative text. In each of the examples, the student expresses horror in addition to making a judgment about Bennett's character. However, none appears to address the argument Bennett is making. Such responses illuminate what researchers have contended (Cazden, 2001; Mehan, Cazden, Coles, Fisher, & Maroules, 1974), that for many students there is only one kind of participation structure within which to engage and one way to address texts. The traditional participation structure of I-R-E, (initiate, respond, evaluate), for example, is one in which the teacher, in initiating the text, evaluates students' responses as either appropriate or inappropriate. In this structure the process ends with the evaluation, from which the students take away the *correct,* yet uninter-rogated and unapplied answer. We argue that it is in the aftermath of the text where instruction can move beyond the traditional structure into a deeper engagement that is safe space, where I-R-E is transformed to I-R-A (initiate, respond, apply). In this format, the student, after making the initial response, is pushed to justify his or her response and to reevaluate it against the text. In addition, participation is not teacher-directed but, rather, student-driven.

In Example 4, the student appears to find Bennett's comment to be symptomatic of society's racism. As a result, there is an interaction here between audience and speaker, undergirded by a self-awareness of belief systems and values. Through shared understandings students were able to see how statements or text, by default, position them as readers and, as in this case, subjects of this text. They are able to see how power operates through language, specifically, how they are labeled and represented to a larger audience.

However, through the process of socially working through the text, enacting it, and carrying out their readings of it, students were able to reposition themselves in relation to that text and to reposition how they responded to it in socially and academically productive ways. This structure allowed students to enact roles, as opposed to being positioned within them, with narrative telling acting as a literacy tool, which in turn helped them cope with this experience of being forcefully and succinctly positioned by one statement.

Following the journal assignment, the instructor revisited and specified the routine strategies and skills it takes to identify claims within traditional structures of argument, the kind framing Bennett's claim, by reading the various texts surrounding it and taking an inquiry approach to problem solving. In taking this approach, students confronted their derived understanding of the meaning in Bennett's statement and held it as a claim that must, in order to be a true argument, have certain warrants that could establish it as truth. This process meant examining various transcripts of the radio broadcast and the ensuing media coverage.

The implications of this exercise, we believe, are that (1) it enabled students to identify a point of view and how that point of view is embedded in a belief system; (2) it forced students to go beyond the literal meanings of the text; and (3) it pushed their thinking away from their initial response, toward a process of interpreting and unpacking the issues implicit within the text.

In the example that follows, the student has appropriated the academic language of argument to address particular points. However, she does not directly respond to Bennett. Rather, she problematizes Bennett's claim by addressing larger issues of media sources, power, and representation:

"Based on what I have collaborated [researched], Bennett's argument is based upon factual evidence from the media when he stated that the crime rate in America will go down if more black babies will be (should be) aborted. Bennett is influenced by the facts that the media sends out. For example, the media, such as the news, depict images that only make light of the poverty level and crime in America and how African Americans are the major contributions [contributors]. He thinks that if more black babies are aborted the crime rate would go down."

Our focus was not on the reading of the text, but on interrogating how that text positioned the author, the reader, and the student specifically as African American. Hence, the argument embedded within various texts in this unit becomes our tool for laying claim to issues concerning what gets read, who is the reader, and how to talk back to disempowering texts. This groundwork begins the process of helping students to move beyond the routine acceptance of a claim toward identifying alternatives, generating counterclaims, and weighing reasons for and against the claim.

As a third exercise in taking alternative perspectives, students were told to consider the positioning of Bennett and locate potential justifications for his claim, if indeed they could. To foster this perspective taking, students were grouped in pairs and given the task of gathering data to support the hypothesis presented by Bennett. This exercise encouraged students to take an alternative position. We believe that this allows for (1) an engagement in culturally familiar problemsolving strategies, (2) the sharing of multiple

points of view, (3) the exploration of epistemological roles within the discourse, (4) generation of readings of texts (both socially constructed oral texts and written texts) that account for alternative perspectives, (5) generation of proactive "coping" responses (as opposed to reactive, but sometimes in addition to) to socially and academically threatening mechanisms, and (6) extension beyond the intended participation structure within the classroom.

In addition, these participation structures are enacted through the discourse of shoptalk that accounts for students' readings of events *and* modes of learning through pedagogical practices that attempt to be culturally responsive, not assumptive. This means that what is encouraged through Shoptalk is the availability of a problem-solving process that anticipates students' contributions of their worldviews, in relation to what they experience and what they understand, as a part of that problemsolving equation. One aspect of this equation is the overlap between culturally situated strategies and those that are specific to domainbased problem solving.

In an excerpt from one student's final writing exercise (a personal letter to Bennett), he points out attitudes that are reflected in the statement Bennett made. He reads the statement not just for what Bennett is literally saying, but the attitudes, values, and ideas instantiated by that claim. Thus, he is attempting to access the nonliteral meanings of the text:

"Dear Bennett,

. . . To me your statement was a philosophically insensitive remark made with ignorance of the sensitivity towards a minority ethnic group. What leaves me still skeptical about your statement is your emphasis on the fact that such an inhuman action such as this would work. If you already mentioned that this act would be morally reprehensible why reiterate that it would work? Were you trying to make a quiet stab at African Americans and enlighten racist individuals (not you of course) with your notion? What also infuriated me was your direct correlation between African Americans and crime. Though you meant no harm in your comment your hypothesis does not directly reflect your opinion towards minorities. The timing in which to make this remark was off as well as your decision in expressing this barbaric, thoughtless act."

CONCLUSION

In order to maintain that the reading of social texts is a literate process, it is essential to first take to task traditional notions of literacy (e.g., power, identity, social practices) and their often embedded meanings and tie these notions into discourse communities. For example, a theory of literacy as social practice emphasizes a view of literacies as multiple and situated within cultural practices (Barton & Hamilton, 1998). However, such a view, we argue, privileges the use of written tools and culturally neutral positionings over linguistic and cultural tools as instruments for "changing thought and experience" (Barton & Hamilton, 1998, p. 8) through oral representations of canonical and noncanonical relationships and values. We argue for a view that extends the theoretical claim of a social practices view of literacy in order to challenge what constitutes literacy and texts as the gatekeeper of literate practice and includes in this view *the oral production and transformation of literate social texts.*

In framing the actions of African American participants of discourse in this way, we are attempting to account for the *mediational role of literacy practices in community contexts.* We are also attempting to account for the role of participating members of these communities not just as active participants who are viewed as being in resistance to literate practices, but as active teachers and learners who use such practices in culturally responsive, authentic ways. Such an account disrupts deficit models and provides insight into alternative spaces for harnessing valuable skills for teaching and learning. As such, there are various conceptualizations of literacy that are extended through our work in the language arts classroom, particularly in urban communities.

To our knowledge, there has been little qualitative and empirical evidence documenting such meaning-making experiences outside the family unit. Such research is needed, and across contexts, to externalize these meaning-making processes for practical and empirical purposes. Shoptalk in the classroom moves beyond an explication of discourse analysis and recognizes the importance of making use of that which is produced within cultures and to which students have access and bring into the classroom. However, it also recognizes and argues for the understanding of the knowledge produced within that culture and knowing how to produce and therefore critique that knowledge (Moje, 2007). This knowledge is a part of a dual consciousness generated within the student as a member of his or her community, one in which the student is socialized into familiarity with the language and manners of a larger dominant society, while developing a self-defined standpoint from which to respond.

Educational reformers concerned with leveraging the out-of-school practices of students of color for in-school literacy learning have frequently argued that students should be empowered to bring their personal (cultural) ways of knowing to the fore of classroom learning (Lee, 2004; Rosenblatt, 1978). According to this view, cultural practices are akin to music and entertainment and not problem-solving processes.

Most recent literacy reform efforts, particularly at the secondary school level where literacy is typically dealt with within the domain of responses to literature, have focused on making use of the cognitive research on reading to enhance curriculum on teaching those reading comprehension strategies that characterize good readers of literary texts (Lee, 2007). One problem that we see with this approach, however, is that struggling adolescent readers, Black and White, often do not understand what good, expert readers of literature do (Rabinowitz, 1987). Little if any of the cognitive research on reading in classrooms, and in regard to harnessing students' cultural funds of knowledge (Moll, 2000), is aimed at making transparent the processes of becoming a good reader by making use of one's cultural ways of knowing. Rather, students understand whether they are good readers or bad readers and that the ultimate goal of good reading is one to be desired. In the classroom, where the stated challenge is to unpack the themes presented before them (e.g., What are the characteristics of the protagonist? What are the roles of males and females presented in the literature? What are the characteristics of the folk hero?), such themes too often tend to reflect the beliefs, experiences, and values of the dominant culture. Particularly for many African American students, many literacy reforms, especially those that do not address the changing world and values, have generated and maintained ethnocentric and often assumptive representations of multiculturalism. By *ethnocentric* we mean a lens that leads to viewing others against our own experiences, assumptions, and expectations. In research, ethnocentrism tends to force one to see difference as deficit (Rogoff, 2003). Research situated in this perspective is only a superficial consideration of students' responses to themes in a work and offers little empirical representation of how those responses are situated in the beliefs, value systems, and practices of the cultures to which the student belongs.

REFERENCES

Banks, I. (2000). *Hair matters: Beauty, power, and black women's consciousness*. New York: New York University Press.

Barton, D., & Hamilton, M. (1998). *Local literacies: A study of reading and writing in one community*. London: Routledge.

Bennett, A. (1983). Discourses of power and dialects of understanding. *Journal of Education, 165*, 53–74.

Bennett, A. (2005, September). Bennett under fire for remarks on blacks, crime. Retrieved November 10, 2005, from *http:///www.cnn.com/2005/POLITICS/09/30/bennett.comments/*

Booth, W. (1974). *A rhetoric of irony*. Chicago: University of Chicago Press.

Bourdieu, P. (1997). *Education: Culture, economy, society*. New York: Oxford University Press.

Bruner, J. (1990). *Acts of meaning: Four lectures on mind and culture*. Cambridge, MA: Harvard University Press.

Cazden, C. (2001). *Classroom discourse: The language of teaching and learning* (2nd ed.). Portsmouth, NH: Heinemann.

Cole, M. (1996). *Cultural psychology: A once and future discipline*. Cambridge, MA: Harvard University Press.

Engeström, Y. (1996a). Developmental studies of work as a testbench of activity theory: The case of primary care practice. In S. Chaiklin & J. Lave (Eds.), *Understanding practice: Perspectives on activity and context* (pp. 64–103). New York: Cambridge University Press.

Engeström, Y. (1996b). Interobjectivity, ideality, and dialectics. *Mind, Culture, and Activity, 3*, 259–265.

Engeström, Y., Miettinen, R., & Punamaki, R. L. (Eds.). (1999). *Perspectives on activity theory*. New York: Cambridge University Press.

Fairclough, N. (2003). *Analyzing discourse: Textual analysis for social research*. New York: Routledge.

Fisher, M. (2003). Open mics and open minds: Spoken word poetry in African diaspora participatory literacy communities. *Harvard Educational Review, 73*, 362–389.

Foucault, M. (1980). *Power/knowledge: Selected interviews and other writings, 1972–1977* (C. Gordeon, Ed.). Brighton, UK: Harvester.

Freire, P., & Macedo, D. (1987). *Literacy: Reading the word and the world*. New York: Bergin & Garvey.

Gee, J. P. (1996). *Social linguistics and literacies: Ideology in discourses*. Bristol, PA: Taylor & Francis.

Gee, J. P. (1997). *The social mind: Language, ideology, and social practice*. New York: Bergin & Garvey.

Gee, J. P., Hull, G., & Lankshear, C. (1996). *The new work order: Behind the language of the new capitalism*. Boulder, CO: Westview Press.

Goffman, E. (1969). *Strategic interaction*. Philadelphia: University of Pennsylvania Press.

Goffman, E. (1974). *Frame analysis*. New York: HarperCollins.

Goffman, E. (1981). *Forms of talk*. Philadelphia: University of Pennsylvania Press.

Graff, G. (1987). *Professing literature*. Chicago: University of Chicago Press.

Guerra, J., & Farr, M. (2002). Writing on the margins: Spiritual and autobiographic discourse among Mexicans in Chicago. In G. Hull & K. Schultz (Eds.), *School's out!: Bridging out of school literacies with classroom practices* (pp. 96–123). New York: Teachers College Press.

Gutiérrez, K., Baquedano-Lopez, P., Alvarez, H., & Chiu, M. M. (1999). Building a culture of collaboration through hybrid language practices. *Theory into Practice, 38*, 87–93.

Gutiérrez, K., Baquedano-Lopez, P., & Tejaeda, C. (1999). Rethinking diversity: Hybridity and hybrid language practices in the third space. *Mind, Culture, and Activity, 64*, 286–303.

Heath, S. (1983). *Ways with words: Language, life, and work in communities and classrooms*. New York: Cambridge University Press.

Hill-Collins, P. (2000). *Black feminist thought*. New York: Routledge.

Hull, G., & Schultz, K. (Eds.). (2002). *School's out!: Bridging out of school literacies with classroom practices*. New York: Teachers College Press.

Hutchins, E. (1996). Learning to navigate. In S. Chaiklin & J. Lave (Eds.), *Understanding practice: Perspectives on activity and context* (pp. 35–63). New York: Cambridge University Press.

Jacobs-Huey, L. (2006). *From the kitchen to the parlor: Language and becoming in African American women's hair care*. New York: Oxford University Press.

Kuhn, D. (1991). *The skills of argument*. New York: Cambridge University Press.

Lacewell-Harris, M. (2004). *Barbershops, Bibles and BET: Everyday talk and Black political thought*. Princeton, NJ: Princeton University Press.

Ladson-Billings, G. (1994). *The dream keepers: Successful teachers of African American children*. San Francisco: Jossey-Bass.

Langer, J. (1987). A sociocognitive perspective on literacy. In J. Langer (Ed.), *Language, literacy, and culture: Issues in society and schooling* (pp. 1–20). Norwood, NJ: Ablex.

Lave, J. (1996). The practice of learning. In S. Chaiklin & J. Lave (Eds.), *Understanding practice: Perspectives on activity and context* (pp. 3–32). New York: Cambridge University Press.

Lave, J., & Wenger, E. (1991). *Situated learning: Legitimate peripheral participation*. New York: Cambridge University Press.

Lee, C. D. (1993). *Signifying as a scaffold for literary interpretation: The pedagogical implications of an African-American discourse genre*. Urbana, IL: National Council of Teachers of English.

Lee, C. D. (1995). A culturally based cognitive apprenticeship: Teaching African-American high school students' skills in literary interpretation. *Reading Research Quarterly, 30*, 608–631.

Lee, C. D. (2004). Double voiced discourse: African-American vernacular English as resource in cultural modeling classrooms. In A. Ball & S. W. Freedman (Eds.), *Bahktinian perspectives on language, literacy, and learning* (pp. 129–147). New York: Cambridge University Press.

Lee, C. D. (2005). Intervention research based on current views of cognition and learning. In J. King (Ed.), *Black education: A transformative research and action agenda for the new century* (pp. 73–114). Mahwah, NJ: Erlbaum.

Lee, C. D. (2007). *Culture, literacy, and learning: Taking bloom in the midst of the whirlwind*. New York: Teachers College Press.

Lee, C. D., & Majors, Y. (2003). Heading up the street: Localized opportunities for shared constructions of knowledge. *Pedagogy, Culture and Society, 11*, 49–67.

Luke, A. (1995). Text and discourse in education: An introduction to critical discourse analysis. In M. Apple (Ed.), *Review of research in education* (pp. 3–48). Washington, DC: American Educational Research Association.

Luke, A. (1996). Genres of power? Literacy education and the production of capital. In R. Hasan & G. Williams (Eds.), *Literacy in society* (pp. 308–338). New York: Longman.

Mahiri, J. (Ed.). (2003). *What they don't learn in school: Literacy in the lives of urban youth*. New York: Peter Lang.

Majors, Y. (2001). Passing mirrors: Subjectivity in a midwestern hair salon. *Anthropology and Education Quarterly, 32*, 116–130.

Majors, Y. (2003). Shoptalk: Teaching and learning in an African-American hair salon. *Mind, Culture and Activity, 10*, 289–310.

Majors, Y. (2004). "I wasn't scared of them, they were scared of me": Constructions of self/other in a midwestern hair salon. *Anthropology and Education Quarterly, 35*, 167–188.

Majors, Y. (2007). Narrations of cross-cultural encounters as interpretative frames for reading word and world. *Discourse and Society, 18*, 479–505.

Majors, Y., & Ansari, S. (2008). Cultural community practices as urban classroom resources. In L. Tillman (Ed.), *Handbook of African American education*. New York: Sage.

Majors, Y., & Orellana, M. (2003, April). *Envisioning texts, or reading the other*. Paper presented at the annual conference of the American Educational Research Association, Chicago.

Mehan, H., Cazden, C. B., Coles, L., Fisher, S., & Maroules, N. (1974). *The social organization of classroom lessons* (Center for Human Information Processing Report No. 67). La Jolla, CA: University of California-San Diego Press.

Mitchell, M. (2002, September 17). "Barbershop" shows blacks—warts and all. *Chicago Sun Times*.

Moje, E. (2000). "To be part of the story": The literacy practices of gangsta adolescents. *Teachers College Record, 102*, 651–690.

Moje, E. (2007). Developing socially just subject-matter instruction: A review of the literature on disciplinary literacy teaching. *Review of Research in Education, 31*, 1–44.

Moll, L. C. (1992). Literacy research in community and classrooms: A sociocultural approach. In R. Beach, J. L. Green, M. L. Kamil, & T. Shanahan (Eds.), *Multidisciplinary perspective in literacy research* (pp. 211–244). Urbana, IL: National Conference on Research in English and National Council of Teachers of English.

Moll, L. C. (2000). Inspired by Vygotsky: Ethnographic experiments in education. In C. Lee & P. Smagorinsky (Eds.), *Vygotskian perspectives on literacy research: Constructing meaning through collaborative inquiry* (pp. 236–268). New York: Cambridge University Press.

Morrell, E., & Duncan-Andrade, J. (2004). What they do learn in school: Hip-hop as a bridge to canonical poetry. In J. Mahiri (Ed.), *What they don't learn in school: Literacy in the lives of urban youth* (pp. 247–268). New York: Peter Lang.

Ochs, E., & Capps, L. (2001). *Living narrative: Creating lives in everyday storytelling*. Cambridge, MA: Harvard University Press.

Rabinowitz, P. (1987). *Before reading: Narrative conventions and the politics of interpretation*. Ithaca, NY: Cornell University Press.

Resnick, M. (2003). Marci Resnick responds. In G. Hull & K. Schultz (Eds.), *School's out: Bridging out of school literacies with classroom practice* (pp. 93–95). New York: Teachers College Press.

Rogoff, B. (2003). *The cultural nature of human development*. New York: Oxford University Press.

Rose, M. (2004). *The mind at work*. New York: Viking.

Rosenblatt, L. (1978). *The reader, the text, the poem: The transactional theory of the literary work*. Carbondale: Southern Illinois University Press.

Scribner, S. (1997). A sociocultural approach to the study of mind. In E. Tobach, R. J. Falmagne, M. Brown-Parlee, L. Martin, & A. S. Scribner Kapelman (Eds.), *Mind and social practice: The select writings of Sylvia Scribner*. New York: Cambridge University Press.

Scribner, S., & Cole, M. (1981). *The psychology of literacy*. New York: Cambridge University Press.

Skilton-Sylvester, E. (2003). Literate at home but not at school: A Cambodian girl's journey from playwright to struggling writer. In G. Hull & K. Schultz (Eds.), *School's out: Bridging out of school literacies with classroom practice* (pp. 61–90). New York: Teachers College Press.

Street, B. (1994). Struggles over the meaning(s) of literacy. In M. Hamilton, D. Barton, & R. Ivanic (Eds.), *Worlds of literacy*. Buffalo, NY: Multilingual Matters.

Swindler, A. (2001). *Talk of love: How culture matters*. Chicago: University of Chicago Press.

Wertsch, J. (1985). *Vygotsky and the social formation of mind*. Cambridge, MA: Harvard University Press.

CHAPTER 23

Boys and Literacy

Complexity and Multiplicity

MICHAEL W. SMITH
JEFFREY D. WILHELM

In this chapter we provide reviews both of research that documents the fact that boys underperform girls on measures of reading and writing and of critiques of that research that question its significance. We go on to consider two fundamentally different explanations for the difference in boys' and girls' test scores, one rooted in biology and the other in social constructivism. We also examine two kinds of responses to the disparity: those that focus on individual interest and those that focus on situational interest. We provide evidence that boys have a wide range of diverse interests and consequently argue that attempts to reform curricula rooted in providing texts that boys like may miss the mark by assuming that educators can know in advance what books will attract all male students. Consequently, we contend that approaches focusing on developing instructional contexts that are characterized by ample instruction, appropriate challenges, clear goals and feedback, demonstrated utility in the here and now, and social connections are more promising. We conclude with a consideration of research on how young men read and talk about texts and argue that stereotyped views of masculinity are problematic in thinking about curriculum or classroom interactions.

Recent years have witnessed an unprecedented attention to what many see as a surprising achievement gap: Girls are outperforming boys on a variety of measures of educational attainment. This surprise has manifested itself in unprecedented attention to young men and literacy, both in educational research and in the popular press. The purpose of this chapter is to take a close look at what we see as the major strands of research on young men and literacy. Our goal is to identify the major issues in this area of research rather than to provide a comprehensive review of every study that has been done. Our analysis has led us to the following conclusion: *When it comes to boys and literacy, things are more complicated than you think.*

THE PROBLEM

A variety of research has demonstrated that boys underperform girls on standardized measures of reading and writing achievement. In fact, a large international study found that in all 32 countries studied, boys significantly underperformed relative to girls on all the literacy skills tested, with the sole exception of workplace literacies in 18 of the 32 countries (Elley, 1992). The International Association for the Evaluation of Educational Achievement investigated achievement in composition across 14 countries and found that "gender by itself or in combination with certain home variables was the most powerful predictor of performance, particularly with academic tasks" (Purves, 1992, p. 201). More recently, Newkirk (2000) pointed out that the difference between boys' and girls' literate achievement is "comparable to the difference between whites and racial/ethnic groups that have suffered systematic social and economic discrimination in this country" (p. 295). Clearly, the data offer a challenge to all trying to understand and address issues of underachievement.

In the United States, the Educational Testing Service reported that boys in grade 8 are six times farther behind girls in literacy than girls are behind boys in math (Cole, 1997). The National Assessment of Educational Progress (NAEP), known as the nation's report card, has long documented gender differences on literacy tests. In 1996 girls outperformed boys in reading by a significant margin at all three age levels tested. In the 1998 NAEP, boys' scores improved slightly in grades 4 and 8 and remained constant at grade 12. In 2005, females in grade 8 scored higher, on average, in reading than their male counterparts, despite the fact that males in grade 8 had a higher average reading score in 2005 than in 1992. The one exception to this pattern of boys' underperformance is the SAT critical reading test, on which boys outscored girls by 3 points in 2005 (Snyder, 2006). But this gap has been narrowing, and more girls take the test than boys do, which typically leads to lower average scores.

The gap in writing is especially large. In the NAEP writing assessment for 2002, its most recent administration, 21% of eighth-grade boys scored at or above proficient, whereas twice as many girls (42%) scored at the same level. Results for twelfth graders were similar, but the gap was greater: 14% of boys scored at the proficient or advanced level, as compared with 33% of girls. The *Philadelphia Inquirer* (Snyder, 2006) reported that girls outscored boys by 11 points on the SAT writing test. This gap isn't new. Hedges and Nowell (1995) studied gender differences in mental test scores, their variability, and the numbers of high-scoring individuals. They "performed secondary analyses on six large data sets collected between 1960 and 1992," each of which "used a nationally stratified probability sample of adolescents" (p. 42). One of the data sets was from the NAEP for those years. Across the areas of reading, mathematics, science, and writing, they examined the difference between boys' and girls' scores as effect sizes (the difference divided by the standard deviation of the population). They comment, "Average sex differences were small except for writing, in which females performed substantially better than males in every year. Although average sex differences in mathematics and science have narrowed over time, differences in reading and writing scores have not" (p. 44). They view this situation with apprehension: "The large sex differences in writing ability suggested by the NAEP trend data are alarming. The data imply that males are, on average, at a rather profound disadvantage in the performance of this basic skill" (p. 45).

THREE IMPORTANT CAVEATS

Boys' Absolute Performance Has Been Improving

We have noted that a wealth of research establishes that boys underperform girls on literacy tasks, but these findings are more complex than they initially appear. In the first place, some question whether a crisis in boys' literacy achievement exists at all. Mead (2006) argues that research findings that boys are falling behind fail to acknowledge that boys' performance on many academic measures is actually improving, though girls' performances are improving more rapidly. The gender gap, therefore, may be more a function of good news about girls than bad news about boys. If boys' performances are improving, she contends, the language of crisis isn't justified. What she terms the "hysteria" (p. 3) surrounding discussions of boys' achievement relative to girls' may have arisen because "the idea that women might actually surpass men in some areas (even as they remain behind in others) is hard for many people to swallow" (p. 3).

Gender Might Not Be the Most Important Variable

Mead (2006) offers another caution that may be more important. Although she rejects the notion that boys in general are in crisis, she does argue that there are subgroups of boys "for whom 'crisis' is not too strong a word. When racial and economic gaps combine with gender achievement gaps in reading, the result is disturbingly low achievement for poor, black, and Hispanic boys" (p. 9).

Indeed, the NAEP Reading Report Card for 2002 (Grigg, Daane, Jin, & Campbell, 2002) indicates that Blacks and Hispanics score well below their White peers. As Table 23.1 indicates, at eighth and twelfth grades, two to three times as many Blacks score "below basic" than do Whites, and the proportion for Hispanics in comparison to Whites is nearly the same. At the other end of the scale, two to three times as many Whites score at proficient or above than do Blacks and Hispanics.

The Differences in Achievement May Be a Function of Measurement Bias

There is also some evidence that the underperformance of boys may be in part a function of the way achievement is measured. For example, Peterson (1999) investigated large-scale provincial writing assessment and found that girls' narrative writing was privileged during the assessments. For instance, if boys tend to write more action stories than do girls and if that genre is not rewarded on large-scale assessments, boys' poor scores may be a function of evaluation bias and not actual performance. Barrs (1993) makes a similar argument with regard to reading. She contends that girls' generally higher levels of achievement in reading may reflect the nature of the reading demands made of them, and may in fact mask substantial underachievement in some areas of reading, which, for a complex of reasons, are less carefully monitored in schools, such as the reading of informational texts (p. 3). Researchers have clearly established that some assessment practices discriminate (consciously or unconsciously) against various groups, for example, because their home communication styles are not understood by teachers (see, e.g., Gee, 1989). The same may hold true for boys.

THE CAUSE

Though the gender achievement gap may be due at least in part to girls' increased achievement rather than boys' decreased achievement or to biases in assessments, and though working-class and minority boys are at greater risk than are their middle- and upper-class majority counterparts, it is undeniable that a gap exists. Writers in the popular press as well as educational researchers have offered various explanations for why this is so.

Kimmel (1999), a gender historian, provides one way to understand the different approaches to answering this crucially important question. He explains that some see the achievement gap to be largely a function of biology, whereas others see it as primarily socially constructed, views that we explore in turn.

TABLE 23.1. 2002 Percentages of Students by Race/Ethnicity and Reading Achievement Level

	% below basic	% at basic	% at or above proficient
Grade 8			
White	16	43	41
Black	45	42	13
Hispanic	43	42	15
Grade 12			
White	21	37	42
Black	46	38	16
Hispanic	39	39	22

The View from Biological Determinism

Perhaps the most influential author articulating the argument that boys' difficulties in school are a function of biology is Michael Gurian. Gurian has written a number of popular books, including *The Wonder of Boys* (1997), *A Fine Young Man* (1999), *Boys and Girls Learn Differently!* (2001), and *The Minds of Boys* (Gurian & Stevens, 2005). Gurian explains that the foundation of his work is neurobiology. He argues that evolution explains why men's and women's brains are hardwired differently and argues that these brain differences explain differences in achievement. For example, Gurian and Stevens (2004) argue that girls have, in general, stronger neural connectors in their temporal lobes than boys have. These connectors lead to more sensory detailed memory storage, better listening skills, and better discrimination among the various tones of voice. The stronger neural connections lead, among other things, to greater use of detail in writing assignments.

On the other hand, they argue that the male brain is set to renew, recharge, and reorient itself by entering what neurologists call a *rest state*. The more words a teacher uses, the more likely boys are to "zone out," or go into rest state. The male brain is better suited for symbols, abstractions, diagrams, pictures, and objects moving through space than for the monotony of words.

The View from Social Constructivism

Critics of the biological determinism position, such as Mead (2006), argue that although brain research has identified differences in the structure of brains, that research does not provide any kind of causal links to behavior. Others posit that gender is a social rather than a biological construction. West and Zimmerman (1991) provide a succinct statement of this position: "Rather than as a property of individuals, we conceive of gender as an emergent feature of social situations: as both an outcome of and a rationale for various social arrangements and as a means of legitimating one of the most fundamental divisions of society" (p. 14).

Interestingly, those advocating social constructivism come from both the political right and the political left. Perhaps the most famous and vitriolic of the arguments from the right is Sommers's (2000) *The War against Boys*. She argues that boys are so oppressed by the feminist ideology that is typically expressed through schools that they have in fact become "victims" and "the second sex." Sommers calls into question the research of influential feminist scholars and calls efforts to feminize boys misguided. Sommers contends that boys have become marginalized in schools and that this state of affairs is leading to frustration, depression, and a host of other difficulties.

In contrast, the argument from the political left has it that boys' difficulties with literacy in school are a function of hegemonic masculinities, that is, definitions of masculinity that constrain what young men see as acceptable masculine behavior. Some of the most provocative such research comes from Wayne Martino, an Australian scholar. Martino (1994a, 1994b, 1995, 1998, Chapter 25, this volume) argues that hegemonic versions of masculinity are not consistent with being literate, and in fact militate against and undermine literacy and literate behavior. He contends that boys see literacy as feminized, and because boys see masculinity and femininity as "diametrically opposed" (1994a, p. 29), they reject literacy.

Martino's work builds on that of Walkerdine (1990), one of the first to argue that boys are pushed by culture toward conceptions of masculinity that are incompatible with literate activity. His work resonates with other research as well. Cherland (1994), for example, studied the way various media portray literacy and found that the images were almost entirely of females reading in private situations or with other females. Osmont (1987) found that what children observed adults reading out of school had a far-ranging effect on their conceptions of reading as a gendered act.

If modeling is indeed crucial, it would make sense that having male teachers to serve as models for young men would have positive effects on their literate engagements and achievement (Bradley, 1999; Carrington & Skelton, 2003; Coulter & McNay, 1993; Gamble & Wilkins, 1997; Mancus, 1992; Martin, 2005; Mulholland & Hansen, 2003). However, despite theoretical and anecdotal support for the provision of male reading models, the data supporting this contention are sporadic and unclear. Numerous large-scale and international studies have shown that the performance of boys for male teachers is not significantly different from their performance for female teachers (see Butler & Christianson, 2003; Carrington & Skelton 2003; Carrington, Tymms, & Merrell, 2005; Froude, 2002; Martin, 2003; Sokal et al., 2005).

Dee (2006) offers a more optimistic assessment of the impact of same-sex teachers. He found that 13-year-old boys (and girls) did perform better when working with same-sex teachers. In a reanalysis of existing data for more than 24,000 eighth-grade students, Dee found that 1 year with a male teacher of language arts could eliminate, on average, one-third of the 1.5-year reading gap between female and male students. The data used for the analysis also suggest that students are often consciously assigned to specific teachers for reasons that include gender. For example, troublesome male students or those with low literacy achievement tend to be assigned to male teachers. This assignment, according to Dee, does tend to have positive effects.

A Third Possibility

Our own research (Smith & Wilhelm, 2002, 2006) suggests a third possible explanation for boys' underperformance on measures of literacy. They choose not to engage in the kinds of literate activity privileged in schools. We spent several months following each of 49 boys from four different schools in three different states who also differed in their backgrounds, ethnicities, social classes, and levels of academic achievement and literate engagement. We gathered four different kinds of data: an interview on the boys' favorite activities; an interview on their responses to a series of short profiles that highlight different ways of being literate; three monthly interviews on the literacy logs that the boys kept in which they tracked all of the reading, writing, listening, and viewing they did in and out of school; and think-aloud protocols on four stories that differed in the sex of the main character and the relative emphasis on action versus character.

Our findings surprised us. Instead of rejecting literacy, we found that every single boy in our study enthusiastically engaged in a host of literacy practices outside school.

Although only 7 of the boys identified themselves as readers of books, all of the young men in our study detailed their engagement with newspapers, magazines, and a variety of electronic texts. Some were poets, others rappers, and still others writers of stories.

Indeed, the boys in our study did not dismiss literacy as feminized, even when they were invited to do so. For example, we crafted one of the profiles to invite the boys to discuss the belief that school literacy is not appropriately masculine. The description of the young man in the profile includes a number of details that might mark him as feminine, or at least unconventionally masculine. We made him a reader and a churchgoer. We said he was interested in being a teacher or a librarian, two occupations that have traditionally been dominated by women. We tried to make him appear sensitive and emotional. As a consequence, we fully expected that some of the boys would reject him and in so doing express disdain for his unmasculine behavior. However, only one of our participants did. Instead, the majority of the boys applauded his accomplishments. One of the young men, for example, said, "I admire that he likes to read so he is going to be able to go somewhere in life because most people that read a lot are smarter."

Although the boys didn't reject literacy because they saw it as feminized, they did reject the forms of literacy they saw as schoolish. Many of our informants regarded all schoolwork as busywork that has nothing to do with life. One took such an extreme stand that he refused to do homework for an entire year, choosing to be grounded rather than allowing school to invade home. Even successful readers tended to draw this line. One of our informants was a highly successful student who talked about how much he enjoyed his English classes, yet he refused to read on vacations, citing his need to "get away" from school.

Our work resonates with that of other researchers. For example, the importance of choice and of connecting school literacy to home and world literacies has been found to be important. Love and Hamston (2004) studied how reading was taken up by the families of committed and reluctant readers. They found that the committed readers saw themselves in control of their reading, whereas the resistant readers saw it as something to be done for school. The parents who were more successful in fostering their sons' literacy "took their lead from their sons' emerging identities" (p. 368) by nurturing reading and reading-based communication around their boys' emerging interests and through the use of popular culture materials. Successful parents often transformed earlier routines such as bedtime reading into mutually satisfying, dialogic routines based on multimodal and digital texts that their sons saw used in the world. Cavazos-Kottke (2005) reflects on contexts of language arts instruction that alienate boys from active engagement with academic literacy practices. He argues that most language arts curricula are too divorced from and impervious to students' home literacies, a state of affairs that leads to a disconnect and a rejection of academic literacies.

SO WHAT TO DO?

If young men tend to reject the school literacy (for whatever reason), it seems crucially important to do something to encourage them to embrace it. Scholars have made a variety of recommendations to do just that. Hidi and Harackiewicz (2000) provide one way to understand those recommendations. In their review of research on motivation, they make a critically important distinction between individual and situational interest. They explain that researchers have focused both on the "origins and effects of *individual interest*" (emphasis in original) and on "the environmental . . . and contextual factors that elicit . . . interest across individuals" (p. 152). We believe that this distinction is also manifest in research on boys and reading.

Fostering Individual Interest

One problem young men encounter in schools is, according to Millard (1997), that they read fewer books and that their preferred "genres are less in harmony with the English curriculum and the choices made for them in class by their teachers" (pp. 75–76). Although Worthy, Moorman, and Turner (1999) found that that the gap between what kids like and what schools offer exists for both boys and girls, a number of scholars have worked to identify the kind of books young men tend to enjoy. If we understand what books boys might choose to

read, the argument goes, we have a better chance of encouraging their reading. Brozo (2002), for example, draws on Jungian analysis to identify 10 archetypes that might appeal to male readers—the Pilgrim, the Patriarch, the King, the Warrior, the Magician, the Wildman, the Healer, the Prophet, the Trickster, and the Lover—and identifies books that are informed by these archetypes. Tatum (2005) suggests a list of "must-read" books that can be used as "cultural hooks" to engage Black male students (pp. 58–59). His list includes such titles as Walter Dean Myers's *The Beast* (2003) and James Baldwin's *Letter to My Nephew* (originally published in Baldwin's *The Fire Next Time*, 1963).

Other scholars have taken a different tack and have looked beyond conventional literacies to document the range of literacies in which young men engage, especially outside school. Alvermann (2006), for example, argues that schools provide a far too narrow definition of what counts as literacy and so are "*making* struggling readers out of some youth, especially the ones who have turned their backs on a version of reading and writing commonly referred to as academic literacy" (p. 95, emphasis in the original). In their review of research on family and community literacy, Cushman, Barbier, Mazak, and Petrone (2006) argue that recent research in those areas debunks the myth of inferiority that plagues urban and language-minority students. They cite Hull and Schultz (2002) to argue that research on out-of-school literacies has the capacity to help educators to see students "as capable of learn[ing] and do[ing] in the world" (p. 1; quoted in Cushman et al., 2006, p. 204). Such research, according to Mahiri (2004), presents a "more comprehensive view of urban youth and young adults than is usually presented in the media, in politics, and in schooling" (p. 14).

A wealth of research considers young men's engagement with technological literacies. In his review of research, Sutton (1991) found that boys identify computers and computer use as masculine. This effect is even stronger for minority youth. Millard (1997) argues that boys' greater interest and engagement in technology is part of what makes them "differently literate." Lewis and Fabos (1999) found sophisticated literacies were expressed and developed through the use of IM (instant messaging), as did Alvermann (2001) and Mahiri (1994, 1998) in the playing of computer and video games as well as activities associated with or surrounding such games. Likewise, adolescents have been found to be willing to undertake tremendous amounts of work over sustained time periods to create complex compositions (Knobel & Lankshear, 2001; Moje, 2000; Morrill, Yalda, Adelman, Musheno, & Bejarano, 2000).

Technology has also been shown to assist in increasing boys' achievement in school, particularly that of low-achieving boys (Bangert-Drowns, Kulik, & Kulik, 1985; Niemiec & Walberg, 1985). Comprehension has been shown to improve when males read e-books versus traditional print sources (Doty, Popplewell, & Byers, 2001; Pearman, 2003).

Fostering Situational Interest

The problem with attempting to foster individual interest is that such interests are just that: individual. For example, although it may be true that many, perhaps even the vast majority of young men enjoy using the computer, it is certainly not true of all young men, as one of the informants in our study (Smith & Wilhelm, 2004) explained:

> "I don't know, something about computers, I'm really not all that, I mean, I like the communication aspect of computers, but I'm really not, I don't know, something about them that I'm not—first of all I'm not all that computer literate and second of all there's just something about them that I'd rather—they're too complicated for me I guess."

As teachers work with students to develop individual interests, one danger of treating boys as a monolithic group is that teachers can miss seeing boys as specific human beings. Another danger is that teachers may reinforce stereotypes or the hegemonic masculinities that Martino (1994a, 1994b, 1995, 1998, Chapter 25, this volume) and other scholars critique.

Building on Situational Interests

Because of the difficulty of catering to a wide range of individual interests, Hidi and Harackiewicz (2000) encourage teachers to focus on situational interest as a way to "promote learning for all students, regardless of their idiosyncratic interests" (p. 157). That is, they encourage teachers to identify those features of a learning context that motivate learners who may have different individual interests.

In our research (Smith & Wilhelm, 2002), we found that our participants had a wide variety of interests. Some liked to play sports; others didn't. Many loved video games, but some did not. Some were artists, others mechanics. Despite the great variety of interests and the many ways in which the informants differed from each other, the contextual features that motivated their interests were remarkably similar.

Drawing on the work of Csikszentmihalyi (1990), we identified five characteristics of contexts that motivated young men's achievement and engagement with any activity, including literacy:

- A sense of competence and control
- A challenge that requires an appropriate level of skill
- Clear goals and feedback
- A focus on the immediate experience
- The possibility of social relationships

Virtually every boy talked about how feeling competent and being able to exercise some kind of control kept him involved in an activity. The boys talked about how the tasks they enjoyed had to be appropriately challenging, that is, neither too difficult nor too easy, and how the teachers they liked helped them meet the challenges set before them. Most of the boys gravitated toward activities in which their competence or developing competence was readily manifest—for example, video games, sports, and the arts. They valued activities for what those activities brought them in the here and now, not in some far-off imagined future. They valued activities that let them connect with others.

In fact, one of the most striking findings of our work was that all of the boys in the study reported having a small close–knit group of male friends. The adolescent boys in our study did not resemble the alienated loners that are sometimes portrayed in the popular press. Indeed, their literate engagements were motivated by the relationships they developed with friends and family, with classmates, with authors and characters, and with their teachers. One of the most hopeful findings of our research was just how important relationships with teachers are for boys. The young men in our study had what we came to think of as an implied social contract with their teachers. That is, if a teacher cared about them as individuals, addressed their interests in some way (inside or outside class), actively assisted them to learn, and displayed passion for the content and the doing of the subject being taught, the boys would, in return, be motivated to try to reach that teacher's academic goals.

Once again, our research resonates with the work of others. Taylor (2005), in a study on boys' reading interests, reports that allowing wider reading choices and expanding the availability and privileging of text types (what we call *control*), allowing more time for individual development (that is, providing an *appropriate challenge*), and engaging in a wider variety of hands-on, activity-oriented, multimodal teaching (which all provide *clear goals and feedback*) resulted in greater engagement and achievement for a case study student.

Triplett (2004) did a case study of a struggling middle school reader's emotions in the context of a tutoring relationship. Through cognitive explanations of emotions, aspects of tutoring that influenced the student's feelings of enjoyment, pride, and success were identified. Especially important was the opportunity to make choices, to engage in interesting activities that were immediately functional and personally relevant. Also important to these positive emotions was working with texts and tasks that were at the student's instructional level, which in turn allowed him to achieve visible, verifiable, and significant successes. The tutoring situation strongly contrasted with other school experiences in which this learner struggled with tasks at the frustration level, suffered from social comparisons, and was alienated from teachers.

Strommen and Mates (2004) also identified the importance of social relationships in fostering achievement. In their study of 14 engaged readers and 14 reluctant readers, family culture was found to be important in promoting reading. Engaged readers were cognizant of and motivated by how their reading helped them forge memberships in a community of readers and with family members who shared their reading interest. Modeling pleasure in reading and providing time and situations for familial reading and sharing were found to be important ways to promote literate identities and practices.

One reason we find the argument for situational interest powerful is that it does not reduce teachers' efforts to engage boys in literacy to a zero-sum game. In other words, if differences are solely biological, then what we do for boys would be an exclusive privileging of boys because it would not work as well for girls and their different biology. But if Csikszentmihalyi (1990) is correct about the situational conditions that motivate all human beings, then we can address the needs of most boys and most girls at the same time. Because Csikszentmihalyi developed his theory of flow after years of research with boys and girls, men and women, and because his work so clearly resonates with our own findings and that of other researchers cited here, we are convinced that we can motivate most students' engagement in literacy by developing instructional contexts that feature the conditions he identifies. However, recognizing that young women might also benefit from attention to the characteristics of activities that foster situational interest does not mean that that it isn't especially important for young men. As Newkirk (2000) and Millard (1997) point out, the kinds of literacies embraced by many young men are squarely at odds with those sanctioned by schools. And as we found (Smith & Wilhelm, 2002), boys in turn tend to reject schoolish literacies. If that rejection is to end, something must be done.

HOW YOUNG MEN RESPOND TO DISCUSSION AND TEXT

The research that we have reviewed relates to issues surrounding the achievement gap. But there is another kind of gap that researchers have investigated: differences in the classroom performances of young men and women. And here too the lesson seems to be that things are more complicated than you think.

The extremely influential American Association of University Women (AAUW) report *How Schools Shortchange Girls: A Study of*

Major Findings on Girls and Education (1992) popularized the contention that men dominate classroom discussion at all levels of education. The AAUW makes this dramatic statement:

> Whether one looks at preschool classrooms or university lecture halls, at female teachers or male teachers, research spanning the past twenty years consistently reveals that males receive more teacher attention than do females. (p. 68)

One critic of this report, however, offers a variety of critiques of this contention (Kleinfeld, 1998). The most germane to our review is that the AAUW claim is informed by research in math and science classrooms, and even then the disparity in participation rates is more a function of the performance of a few focal students rather than the class as a whole.

Moore (1997) took up the question of how gender might affect classroom performance through an in-depth analysis of the performance of two 12th-grade case study students in their advanced placement (AP) classroom. He concludes that "thinking about gender as a deterministic external force is problematic" (p. 524) and that "multiplicity and fluidity" (p. 524) characterized his case study students' roles in discussion. He goes on to argue that "thinking about gendered classroom interaction is problematic if it fosters a stereotyped dichotomous view of male and female actions" (p. 525).

Another potential gap that researchers have examined is in how young men and young women respond to issues of gender in texts. Rice (2000), for example, looked at sixth-grade boys' and girls' responses to a folktale that had characters of both sexes who displayed both traditional and nontraditional traits. She found that the responses of both groups indicate a "traditional frame of reference" (p. 229), though there was some movement away from traditional gender positioning by the girls. However, it is important to note that the similarities between the groups outweighed the differences.

Young's (2000) research suggests that the traditional frame of reference may be amenable to change. She examined the changes in four young adolescent boys' awareness of how masculinity constructs and is constructed through and by various kinds of perma-

nently coded texts and ephemeral oral texts. The researcher pursued the question of how critical literacy activities within a home-schooling setting might sustain or transform the boys' awareness of gendered identities and inequities in texts. The researcher (the mother of two of the boys) and the four case study students pursued a variety of critical literacy activities that focused specifically on the topic of masculinity. She found that the direct engagement and exploration of various perspectives around the topic developed explicit awareness of masculine portrayals, definitions, and practices in a variety of texts. As a result, the boys became more critical and questioning both of masculinity as a social construct and of practices and expressions of the masculine. These capacities, however, were unstable and sometimes disconcerting to the boys. Two themes were highlighted by the analysis: "(a) the instability and uncertainty of the boys' awareness of gendered identities, and (b) the impact of power relations within and among the local, institutional, and societal contexts on the boys' participation in the critical literacy activities" (p. 312). The study indicates that the use of both critical literacy activities and pointed, direct inquiry into cultural issues affecting young men seems to hold some promise. But given the instability Young documents and the uniqueness of the instructional situation, it is unclear whether her research suggests that teachers in conventional classrooms would be able to foster transformative understandings of gendered identities.

CONCLUSION

So where does the research on boys and literacy leave us? It is clear that a gap exists between the performance of boys and girls, especially in regard to writing, and that minority and working-class boys seem especially at risk. It seems equally clear that the scholarship in this area offers no easy answers for how to address this gap.

Rather than providing easy answers, the major implication of the research we have reviewed is that researchers, teachers, and the general public need to be more attentive to multiplicity and difference. Possibilities abound if we begin to see literacies as multiple, literacy practices as diverse, and varied texts as valuable. Even gender and masculinity can be usefully seen as multifarious. Indeed, our own research causes us to wonder about the extent to which *boys* is a useful category to think with, given the wide variety of interests and achievement we discovered in the lives of our young men. In fact we found that the young men in our study were certainly much more different than they were alike.

Unfortunately, although the research seems to be calling for more nuanced understandings and interventions, the policy environment seems to be looking for easy answers. Conley and Hinchmann (2004) explore the connection between what we know about adolescent literacy and the mandates and initiatives of the No Child Left Behind Act (NCLB) in the United States. They argue that NCLB ignores the all-important issues of meaningful and motivating contexts for literacy, the need for teachers to understand the developmental needs of adolescent boys, and what can be done to meet diverse developmental and learner needs. Kozol (2006b) more emphatically condemns NCLB and the practices engendered by it (particularly the mania for standardized measures) as undermining the literacies of the marginalized populations it was supposed to help. He argues that standardized testing pervades everything teachers do each day, and that this keeps educators from focusing on the lived experiences of the specific human beings, "incandescent and essentially various" (Kozol, 2006a), whom we are charged with teaching each day.

By being open to different ways of being a boy, different ways of being literate, different notions of text, different ways of teaching and assisting students, and by promoting a connection between school activity and literacies from outside the school walls, we will enrich our research and deepen student engagement with literacy. In so doing we will surely benefit not only the boys in our classrooms, but also the girls.

REFERENCES

Alvermann, D. E. (2001). Reading adolescents' reading identities: Looking back to see ahead. *Journal of Adolescent and Adult Literacy, 44,* 676–690.

Alvermann, D. E. (2006). Struggling adolescent readers: A cultural construction. In A. McKeough, L. M. Phillips, V. Timmons, & J. L. Lupart (Eds.), *Understanding literacy development: A global view* (pp. 95–111). Mahwah, NJ: Erlbaum.

American Association of University Women. (1992). *How schools shortchange girls: A study of major findings on girls and education.* Washington, DC: AAUW Education Foundation and National Education Association.

Baldwin, J. (1963). *The fire next time.* New York: Dial.

Bangert-Drowns, R. L., Kulik, J. A., & Kulik, C. C. (1985). Effectiveness of computer-based education in secondary schools. *Journal of Computer-based Instruction, 12,* 59–68.

Barrs, M. (1993). Introduction: Reading the difference. In M. Barrs & S. Pidgeon (Eds.), *Reading the difference* (pp. i–xx). London: Centre for Language in Primary Education.

Bradley, H. (1999). *Gender and power in the workplace: Analyzing the impact of economic change.* London: Macmillan.

Brozo, W. (2002). *To be a boy, to be a reader: Engaging teen and preteen boys in active literacy.* Newark, DE: International Reading Association.

Butler, D., & Christianson, R. (2003). Mixing and matching: The effect on student performance of teaching assistants of the same gender. *Political Science and Politics, 36,* 781–786.

Carrington, B., & Skelton, C. (2003). Re-thinking role models: Equal opportunities in teacher recruitment in England and Wales. *Journal of Educational Policy, 12,* 253–265.

Carrington, B., Tymms, P., & Merrell, C. (2005, August). *Role models, school improvement and the "gender gap"—Do men bring out the best in boys and women the best in girls?* Paper presented at the European Association for Research on Learning and Instruction conference, University of Nicosia, Cyprus.

Cavazos-Kottke, S. (2005). Tuned out but turned on: Boys' (dis)engaged reading in and out of school. *Journal of Adolescent and Adult Literacy, 49,* 180–184.

Cherland, M. (1994). *Private practices: Girls reading fiction and constructing identity.* Bristol, PA: Taylor & Francis.

Cole, N. (1997). *The ETS gender study: How females and males perform in educational settings.* Princeton, NJ: Educational Testing Service.

Conley, M. W., & Hinchman, K. A. (2004). No Child Left Behind: What it means for U.S. adolescents and what we can do about it. *Journal of Adolescent and Adult Literacy, 48,* 42–50.

Coulter, R., & McNay, M. (1993). Exploring men's experiences as elementary school teachers. *Canadian Journal of Education, 18,* 398–413.

Csikszentmihalyi, M. (1990). *Flow: The psychology of optimal experience.* New York: Harper & Row.

Cushman, E., Barbier, S., Mazak, C., & Petrone, R.

(2006). Family and community literacies. In P. Sma-gorinsky (Ed.), *Research on composition: Multiple perspectives on two decades of change* (pp. 187–217). New York: Teachers College Press.

Dee, T. (2006). *Teachers and the gender gaps in student achievement* (National Bureau of Economic Research Working Paper # 11660). Retrieved November 13, 2006, from *www.swarthmore.edu/SocSci/tdee1/Research/w11660revised.pdf*.

Doty, D. E., Popplewell, S. R., & Byers, G. O. (2001). Interactive CD-ROM storybooks and young readers' reading comprehension. *Journal of Research on Computing in Education, 33,* 374–384.

Elley, W. B. (1992). *How in the world do students read?* The Hague, Netherlands: International Association for the Evaluation of Educational Achievement.

Froude, L. (2002). Study defies the "boys need men" credo. *Times Educational Supplement, 4471,* 3–9.

Gamble, R., & Wilkins, J. (1997). Beyond tradition: Where are the men in elementary education? *Contemporary Education, 68,* 187–194.

Gee, J. P. (1989). What is literacy? *Journal of Education 171,* 18–25.

Grigg, W. S., Daane, M. C., Jin, Y., & Campbell, J. R. (2002). *The nation's report card: Reading 2002.* Washington, DC: U.S. Department of Education, Institute of Education Sciences.

Gurian, M. (1997). *The wonder of boys: What parents, mentors and educators can do to shape boys into exceptional men.* New York: Tarcher.

Gurian, M. (1999). *A fine young man: What parents, mentors and educators can do to shape adolescent boys into exceptional men.* New York: Tarcher.

Gurian, M. (2001). *Boys and girls learn differently!: A guide for parents and teachers.* San Francisco: Jossey-Bass.

Gurian, M., & Stevens, K. (2004). With boys and girls in mind. *Educational Leadership, 62,* 21–26.

Gurian, M., & Stevens, K. (2005). *The minds of boys: Saving our sons from falling behind in school and life.* San Francisco: Jossey-Bass.

Hedges, L. V., & Nowell, A. (1995). Sex differences in mental test scores, variability, and numbers of high-scoring individuals. *Science, 269,* 41–45.

Hidi, S., & Harackiewicz, J. M. (2000). Motivating the academically unmotivated: A critical issue for the 21st century. *Review of Educational Research, 70,* 151–180.

Hull, G., & Schultz, K. (Eds.). (2002). *School's out: Bridging out-of-school literacies with classroom practice.* New York: Teachers College Press.

Kimmel, M. (1999). "What are little boys made of?" *Ms., 9*(6), 88–91.

Kleinfeld, J. (1998). *The myth that schools shortchange girls: Social science in the service of deception.* Retrieved November 13, 2006, from *www.uaf.edu/northern/schools/download.html*.

Knobel, M., & Lankshear, C. (2001). Cut, paste and publish. The production and consumption of zines.

In D. E. Alvermann (Ed.), *Youth's multiliteracies in a digital world* (pp. 164–185). New York: Peter Lang.

Kozol, J. (2006a, October). *Shame of the nation.* Paper presented at Boise State University, Boise, ID.

Kozol, J. (2006b). *Shame of the nation: The restoration of apartheid schooling in America.* New York: Basic Books.

Lewis, C., & Fabos, B. (1999, December). *Chatting online: Uses of instant message communication among adolescent girls.* Paper presented at the National Reading Conference, Orlando, FL.

Love, K., & Hamston, J. (2004). Committed and reluctant male teenage readers: Beyond bedtime stories. *Journal of Literacy Research, 36,* 335–400.

Mahiri, J. (1994). Reading rites and sports. Motivation for adaptive literacy of young African American males. In B. J. Moss (Ed.), *Literacy across communities* (pp. 121–146). Cresskill, NJ: Hampton.

Mahiri, J. (1998). *Shooting for excellence: African American and youth culture in new century schools.* Urbana, IL: National Council of Teachers of English.

Mahiri, J. (2004). New literacies in a new century. In J. Mahiri (Ed.), *What they don't learn in school: Literacy in the lives of urban youth* (pp. 1–19). New York: Peter Lang.

Mancus, D. (1992). Influence of male school teachers on children's stereotyping of teacher competence. *Sex Roles, 26,* 109–128.

Martin, A. (2003). Primary school boys' identity formation and the male role model: An exploration of sexual identity and gender identity in the UK through attachment theory. *Sex Education, 3,* 257–271.

Martin, A. (2005, November 6). Wanted: Male teachers for young students. *Chicago Tribune.* Retrieved November 5, 2006, from *pqasb.pqarchiver.com/chicago tribune/access/922362281.html?dids=922362281:92 2362281&FMT=ABS&FMTS=ABS:FT&type=current &date=Nov+6%2C+2005&author=Ann+R+Martin% 2C+Special+to+the+Tribune&pub=Chicago+Tribune &edition=&startpage=1&desc=Wanted%3A+Male+ teachers+for+young+students*.

Martino, W. (1994a). The gender bind and subject English: Exploring questions of masculinity in developing interventionist strategies in the English classroom. *English in Australia, 107,* 29–44.

Martino, W. (1994b). Masculinity and learning: Exploring boys' underachievement and under-representation in subject English. *Interpretations, 27,* 22–57.

Martino, W. (1995). Deconstructing masculinity in the English classroom: A site for reconstituting gendered subjectivity. *Gender and Education, 7,* 205–220.

Martino, W. (1998). "Dickheads," "poofs," "try hards," and "losers": Critical literacy for boys in the English classroom. *English in Aotearoa, 25,* 31–57.

Mead, S. (2006). The truth about boys and girls. *Education Sector.* Retrieved November 2, 2006, from *www.educationsector.org/usr_doc/ESO_BoysAndGirls. pdf*.

Millard, E. (1997). *Differently literate.* New York: Falmer.

Moje, E. B. (2000). To be part of the story: The literacy practices of gangsta adolescents. *Teachers College Record, 102,* 652–690.

Moore, D. (1997). Some complexities of gendered talk about texts. *Journal of Literacy Research, 29,* 507–530.

Morrill, C., Yalda, C., Adelman, M., Musheno, M., & Bejarano, C. (2000). Telling tales in school: Youth culture and conflict narratives. *Law and Society Review, 34,* 561–565.

Mulholland, J., & Hansen, P. (2003). Men who become primary teachers: An early portrait. *Asia-Pacific Journal of Teacher Education, 31,* 213–224.

Myers, W. D. (2003). *The beast.* New York: Scholastic.

Newkirk, T. (2000). Misreading masculinity: Speculations on the great gender gap in writing. *Language Arts, 77,* 294–300.

Niemiec, R. P., & Walberg, H. J. (1985). Computers and achievement in the elementary schools. *Journal of Educational Computing Research, 1,* 435–440.

Osmont, P. (1987). Teaching inquiry in the classroom, reading and gender set. *Language Arts, 64,* 758–761.

Pearman, C. (2003). Effects of CR-ROM story books on the independent reading comprehension of second grade students. *Dissertation Abstracts International, 64* (07a) 2427.

Peterson, S. (1998). Evaluation and teachers' perception of gender in sixth grade student writing. *Research in the Teaching of English, 33,* 181–206.

Purves, A. (Ed.). (1992). *The IEA study of written composition: II. Education and performance in fourteen countries.* Oxford, UK: Pergamon Press.

Rice, P. (2000). Gendered readings of a traditional "feminist" folktale by sixth-grade boys and girls. *Journal of Literacy Research, 32,* 211–236.

Smith, M. W., & Wilhelm, J. (2002). *"Reading don't fix no Chevys": Literacy in the lives of young men.* Portsmouth, NH: Heinemann.

Smith, M. W., & Wilhelm, J. (2004). "I just like being good at it": The importance of competence in the literate lives of young men. *Journal of Adolescent and Adult Literacy, 47,* 454–461.

Smith, M. W., & Wilhelm, J. (2006). *Going with the flow: How to engage boys (and girls) in their literacy learning.* Portsmouth, NH: Heinemann.

Snyder, S. (2006, August 30). Girls outdo boys on SAT writing test. *Philadelphia Inquirer.* Retrieved November 10, 2006, from *www.philly.com/mld/philly/living/education/15393121.htm.*

Sokal, L., Katz, H., Adkins, M., Grills, T., Stewart, C., Priddle, G., et al. (2005). Factors affecting inner-city boys' reading: Are male teachers the answer? *Canadian Journal of Urban Research, 14,* 107–130.

Sommers, C. H. (2000). *The war against boys: How misguided feminism is harming our young men.* New York: Simon & Schuster.

Strommen, L., & Mates, B. (2004). Learning to love reading: Interviews with older children and teens. *Journal of Adolescent and Adult Literacy, 48,* 188–200.

Sutton, R. (1991). Equity and computers in the schools: A decade of research. *Review of Educational Research, 61,* 475–503.

Tatum, A. (2005). *Teaching reading to Black adolescent males.* Portland, ME: Stenhouse.

Taylor, D. L. (2005). Not just boring stories: Reconsidering the gender gap for boys. *Journal of Adolescent and Adult Literacy, 48,* 290–298.

Triplett, C. (2004). Looking for a struggle: Exploring the emotions of a middle school reader. *Journal of Adolescent and Adult Literacy, 48,* 214–222.

Walkerdine, V. (1990). *Schoolgirl fictions.* London: Verso.

West, C., & Zimmerman, D. (1991). Doing gender. In J. Lorber & S. Farrell (Eds.), *The social construction of gender* (pp. 13–37). London: Sage.

Worthy, J., Moorman, M., & Turner, M. (1999). What Johnny likes to read is hard to find in school. *Reading Research Quarterly, 34,* 12–27.

Young, J. (2000). Boy talk: Critical literacy and masculinities. *Reading Research Quarterly, 35,* 312–337.

CHAPTER 24

Lessons on Literacy Learning and Teaching

Listening to Adolescent Girls

BARBARA J. GUZZETTI

Adolescent girls report feeling disconnected from the teaching and learning process; often, literacy activities inside classrooms have little connection to girls' out-of-school explorations with literacy. In addition, preteen and teenage girls feel discouraged rather than encouraged in their classroom performance. They perceive that they are marginalized by their lack of representation in texts and disenfranchised in class discussions of those texts when males dominate discussions. Their writing, like the texts they read and discuss, is often gendered and reflects stereotypical topics and ideas.

In this chapter, I present both an overview of the concerns of adolescent girls and the perspectives and strategies that encourage adolescent girls in their interactions with literacy. These ideas are drawn from research conducted during the past decade that focused on girls in middle school, junior high school, and high school both in the context of classrooms and in out-of-school settings. This research represents my own studies as well as the investigations of my colleagues and is intended to be an acknowledgment and a synthesis of the unique issues and conditions that empower as well as trouble adolescent girls in their literacy development and practice.

This chapter is divided into three sections. The first section reviews gender issues and concerns of adolescent girls and summarizes recent research that identified the conditions in classrooms that prevent or limit females from full participation in literate activity. This section concludes with studies that provided recommendations for addressing these issues.

The second part of this chapter reviews the research conducted with teenage girls regarding their informal or out-of-school literacy practices and describes adolescent girls' consumption of popular culture texts, such commercial magazines and media, and their production and consumption of alternative texts and independent or "indie" media. This section focuses on appropriate implications of these inquiries for classroom instruction and assignments.

The final section of the chapter synthesizes the recent research that focuses on views of or stances toward adolescents. This part of the chapter presents insights from researchers and from students on the ways in which adolescent girls can be acknowledged and encouraged in literate activity. These recommendations have implications for adults' interactions with adolescent girls in their literacy activities both in and out of school.

As noted in the chapter abstract, I present both an overview of the concerns of adolescent girls and the perspectives and strategies that encourage adolescent girls in their interactions with literacy. These ideas are drawn from research that focuses on girls in middle school, junior high school, high school, and their early years of college both in the context of classrooms and in out-of-school settings. In summarizing the findings of these inquiries, I respond to the call to listen to the voices of adolescent girls (DeBlase, 2003a; Gilligan, 1993) by highlighting their concerns and insights through drawing attention to their collective voices. Thus, this chapter is intended to be an acknowledgement and a synthesis of the unique issues and conditions that empower as well as trouble adolescent girls in their literacy development and practice.

Adolescent girls report feeling disconnected from the teaching and learning process. Young women that my colleagues and I interview typically confide that instructional activities and materials have little or no relevance to their everyday lives (e.g., Guzzetti, 2008; Guzzetti & Gamboa, 2005; Guzzetti & Yang, 2005). Often, literacy activities inside classrooms have little connection to these adolescent girls' out-of-school explorations with literacy.

Too often, preteen and teenage girls feel discouraged rather than encouraged in their classroom performance. They perceive that they are marginalized by their lack of representation in texts. Young women feel disenfranchised in class discussions of those texts when young men dominate discussions. Their writing, like the texts they read and discuss, is often gendered and reflects stereotypical topics and ideas, as their perceptions of themselves and their roles as young women are influenced by these texts (Blair, 1998). Because of this sense of disfranchisement and a fear of ridicule or embarrassment by their male peers, females are likely to be hesitant to share their ideas either orally or in writing (Blair, 1998; Guzzetti, 2001; Guzzetti & Williams, 1996).

Researchers have lent insight into effective ways to address these problems. Young women have not only identified to researchers the limiting and dismissive conditions in classroom activity, texts, and talk about that activity, they have also voiced their ideas about or participated in interventions to address their concerns. Using this information, researchers explored the types of in-school activity that adolescent girls find motivating and empowering.

In addition, researchers conducting recent investigations describe the out-of-school literacy practices in which teenage girls engage and find intriguing and relevant in their everyday lives, ameliorating the disenfranchisement they perceive in school settings. Researchers examine how these literacy activities have both powerful social and academic functions. In some instances, young women revealed how they naturally and independently make connections between their out-of-school practices and their in-school instruction (Guzzetti & Gamboa, 2004, 2005). In other studies, researchers identify implications for incorporating the motivating and intriguing elements of these practices into classroom instruction. Although classrooms are not comfortable places for all girls, these literacy practices provide young women with a sense of empowerment and competency that helps to compensate for their marginalization in school literacy activities.

Researchers conducting studies with preteen and teen girls also lend insights into ways to draw adolescent girls into literacy and instructional activities for literate development and expression (e.g., Chandler-Olcott & Mahar, 2003b; Finders, 1996; Guzzetti & Gamboa, 2005). These ideas are based on their own successes in gaining access to adolescents' and young women's participation in literacy practices that are unsanctioned or unrecognized by schools. Researchers adopt or recommend stances toward their female adolescent informants that can inform the positions of other adults to make them more cognizant of the perceptions and abilities of teenage girls. Teachers, parents, and others can view and interact with adolescents, particularly girls, in new ways to encourage their interest and participation in literate activity.

To explore these topics, this chapter is divided into three sections that address common questions that I often hear from my graduate students who are former, aspiring or practicing teachers. The first section characterizes the research on adolescent girls and literacy and reviews studies that identified the gender issues and concerns of adolescent girls in classrooms. This section summarizes the extant research that identified the conditions in classrooms that prevent or limit females from their full participation in literate activities. These activities include reading, writing, and discussing texts in classrooms in both off-line and online instructional settings. This section concludes with recommendations for addressing these issues.

The second part of this chapter reviews the research conducted with preteen and teenage girls regarding their informal, out-of-school literacy practices both off-line and online. It describes adolescent girls' consumption of popular culture texts, such as commercial magazines and media, and their production and consumption of alternative texts and indie media (independent media). This section also details adolescent girls' facilities with and uses for digital texts, such as instant messaging, online journaling, and zining (producing self-publications as alternatives to commercial ones). Thus, I summarize the current research conducted in various nations to demonstrate "glocality," or the global nature of these new literacies. Finally, the section focuses on appropriate and inappropriate implications of these inquiries for classroom instruction and assignments. These recommendations are drawn from my conversations with and observations of adolescent females in their interactions with others in both social and academic settings (e.g., Guzzetti, Campbell, Duke, & Irving, 2003).

The final section of this chapter synthesizes recent theory and research that focuses on views of or stances toward adolescents. In this part of the chapter, I present theories from youth culture. In doing so, I also provide insights, from researchers and from the young people whose literacy practices they investigated, on the ways in which adolescent girls can be acknowledged and encouraged in literate activity. These recommendations have implications for adults' interactions with adolescent girls in their literacy activities both in and out of school.

WHAT DOES RESEARCH ON GENDER ISSUES AND CONCERNS OF ADOLESCENT GIRLS LOOK LIKE?

For more than a decade, researchers have been observing adolescent girls in their content-area classrooms. Although some of these studies were conducted more than a decade ago and there is more awareness of gender issues today, more recent studies elaborate on and confirm findings from earlier investigations that described how girls are often marginalized in literacy activities in a variety of content classrooms. Researchers have directly observed the ways in which young women are disempowered in literate instructional activity and have talked with adolescent girls about the conditions that marginalize their participation in literacy events in classrooms.

There is, however, one caveat. In general, the research on gender and literacy in content classrooms was conducted in classrooms with Caucasians or European American students of middle-class backgrounds, as is typical of most literacy research (Alvermann, 1993). Only a relatively few researchers have investigated gender and literacy issues in middle, junior high, and secondary schools with students from upper socioeconomic backgrounds (e.g., Cherland, 1994; Guzzetti & Gamboa, 2004) or students of color from working-class and poor families (e.g., DeBlase, 2003b, 2002; Henry, 1998; Schultz, 1996; Sutherland, 2005).

Thus, less is known about how gender issues play out in classrooms that predominantly consist of students of low or high socioeconomic status or students with varying ethnic and cultural backgrounds. Studies that describe gender issues are important because there is some evidence that norms of gender behavior in classrooms that are mainly composed of students of various ethnic, cultural, and socioeconomic backgrounds may be different from those in classrooms composed chiefly of middle-class and European American students. For example, in one study (Kyle, 1996), females dominated class discussions and served as instructional assistants or tutors for their less confident male classmates in middle school classes that were chiefly composed of African American students. DeBlase (2003c) noted that an African American female in a class may very likely negotiate and interpret a particular literacy event in a way that might be quite different from that of her European American female classmate. Thus, the findings from studies on gender and literacy with adolescent girls are limited by and speak only to the ethnic and cultural groups and social classes in which those investigations were situated.

HOW ARE ADOLESCENT GIRLS MARGINALIZED IN LITERACY ACTIVITIES INSIDE CLASSROOMS?

Despite these limitations of the extant research, a plethora of studies on gender issues in literate activity has produced a picture of how adolescent girls are typically disenfranchised in their classroom literacy instruction. These studies have relied both on researchers' observations of students in their instructional activity and on students' self-reports of their own experiences. These studies provide insight into the nuances of gendered performances and behaviors displayed by students and teachers.

In these studies, females in secondary schools typically report being disenfranchised in a variety of content-area classrooms. These classes are typically male dominated and male oriented, such as physical science, computer science, and mathematics. Perhaps surprisingly, however, females also report and researchers observe (e.g., Phelps & Weaver, 1999) that males dominate discussions in English language arts classes, in subject matter that is often considered to be more appealing to females.

The biological sex of the teacher does not seem to make a difference in promoting gender-equitable instructional activity or discussions, either. Researchers note that both male and female teachers pay more attention to adolescent boys (Guzzetti, 2001). Both male and female teachers call on males more than females for answers to their queries, provide males with more feedback (whether positive or negative), and value and elaborate more on boys' responses to their questions than on girls' answers during discussions of concepts in texts.

Although gender bias may originate from teachers who marginalize females, there are other sources as well. In particular, textbooks often discourage females from participation by their inordinate inclusion of males in their photographs, illustrations, and chapter questions and problems. In some instances, when females are portrayed in content textbooks, they are pictured in subservient roles or as passive observers, and not as active participants engaging in or con-

tributing to content activity, such as scientific inquiry and experimentation. Girls in science classes report that their underrepresentation or misrepresentation in science textbooks discourages them from choosing careers in science (Guzzetti & Williams, 1996).

Female students also complain about required readings, particularly the novels that they must read in their English language arts classes. Females find few role models in the authors, the characters, or the content of these texts. Too often, required reading lists contain only books with male authors. In addition, girls report that these texts portray women as weak, subservient, incompetent, or insane (Guzzetti & Gamboa, 2004; Guzzetti, 2008).

Although teachers and texts contribute to gender bias in the classroom, patterns across studies by various researchers show that the greatest source of gender bias in the classroom is actually students' interactions with each other. Those who have the most social power in classrooms—usually males—typically dominate classroom activity and talk about that activity. They do so by taking over instructional activities, such as science labs, by setting up the equipment for the experiments, actually conducting the experiments, and making the observations. Females typically serve as passive "scribes" and simply record the observations (Guzzetti & Williams, 1996). Girls' voices are often silenced by fear of ridicule and criticism by adolescent boys; girls hesitate to share their writing in whole-class or heterogeneous groupings for fear of those repercussions (Blair, 1998).

Females are also marginalized in discussion of concepts by males' domination. Young men dominate instructional conversations by calling out, interrupting, taking up each other's comments and ignoring females' responses, increasing their vocal pitch and tone, making their voices louder, and by gaze aversion or not looking at or acknowledging girls who speak out. These patterns were observed in both whole-class and small-group discussions and in both middle school language arts classes (Cherland, 1994) and high school physical science classes (Guzzetti, 2001; Guzzetti & Williams, 1996). These patterns of domination prevailed even when there was only one male in the group. In these studies of both language arts classes and science classes, male students dominated the discussions by speaking longer and more often.

There have been some exceptions to these patterns, however. One study portrayed an adolescent male who gave tentative responses, and a female who occasionally dominated discussions in high school language arts classes (Moore, 1997). Another study showed that other subjectivities or layers such as race/ ethnicity and culture affect gender in discussion; females in a middle school language arts classroom composed predominantly of African Americans dominated instructional talk and activity and served as aides or tutors for the males in the class (Kyle, 1996). Yet another study demonstrated that social power that allows for domination of instructional conversations is variable and shifts over the course of the academic year (Alvermann, 1995/1996). These instances point to the problematic thinking of gender performance in discussion as a dichotomy of stereotypical male and female behaviors, or the dangers of essentializing or stereotyping images of what males' and females' participation in discussion should look like in classrooms.

The studies described above offer encouragement for teachers' and students' acceptance of nongendered performance. Nongendered classrooms are safe spaces in which females are valued for their ability to debate and young men are enabled and encouraged to voice their questions and tentative ideas. Instructional discussion that is nongendered enables females' participation by allowing for ways to include rather than exclude girls' elaborations on their classmates' remarks and encourages boys' queries.

Nevertheless, the problem of girls being marginalized in classroom discussions is a common occurrence and a widespread concern. To address this issue, one researcher attempted to conduct electronic discussions instead of oral discussions with young men and women in high school and college classrooms (Fey, 1998). This study was conducted to determine if online discussions would be more gender-fair and symmetrically balanced than those conducted face-to-face and orally in the classroom. Even these online discussions were dominated by a male, however, and the same patterns of gendered discussion identified in oral discussions in classrooms were evidenced in electronic forums.

Why is this problem of gender bias in literacy activity in content-area classrooms so widespread? Often, teachers do not notice that females are being marginalized in classroom activity and the talk about that activity. In fact, researchers find that teachers are typically unaware of gender bias in their instructional activities, materials, and discussions. Teachers are not deliberately and actively looking for behaviors among students that might marginalize others; therefore, they do not find them. Another reason that marginalizing behaviors prevail in classrooms is that teachers do not recognize them as disenfranchising because they are so commonplace. These conditions become perpetuated over time.

In some cases, however, teachers are aware of these behaviors and their impact on females' participation but accept the situation as the norm. The old adage, "Boys will be boys" is often used to excuse males' domineering behavior. Girls may complain about particular instances or general conditions that prevent their full participation, but, unfortunately, educators do not always respond to girls' complaints even when these conditions are pointed out to them. Too often, classrooms remain sites where young women's voices are silenced and their participation is devalued.

WHAT CAN BE DONE TO PROMOTE GENDER-FAIR LITERACY ACTIVITIES?

Past research demonstrated that gendered power relations among students are resistant to change even in cases in which both the teacher and the students are well aware of them and their impact on learning (e.g., Guzzetti & Williams, 1996). Females do not appear to be able to disrupt power inequities displayed by and among males even in instances where some allegiance exists between male and female peers or when males profess to be sympathetic to females' disempowerment (Guzzetti, 2008). These attitudes and behaviors displayed in school position them as less competent than their male counterparts and reflect messages in the media and society that indoctrinate young women into stereotypical ways of performing gender (DeBlase, 2003b; Heilman, 1998).

There are, nevertheless, some stances and strategies that have been tested in classrooms and shown to be effective in changing these inequities. First, the agenda of interrupting gendered practices must become the agenda of teachers. In cases in which teachers did not actively set that agenda, there was resistance to disrupting marginalizing practices when other adults tried to intervene (Alvermann, Commeyras, Young, Randall & Hinson, 1997). Teachers resisted such interventions and did not actively and consistently correct their students' gendered or marginalizing behaviors when researchers' intentions did not match their own priorities.

In instances in which the teacher was an active participant, however, and set the plan for interventions, created the methods to intervene, and involved the students in acknowledging and addressing the problem, those interventions were successful in empowering females in content learning. For example, in physics classes, having same-sex groups for instructional activity and discussion empowered adolescent girls. Young women reported becoming actively involved in their own learning by being enabled to set up their own lab equipment, conduct the experiments, and voice their ideas to help form and represent scientific concepts (Guzzetti & Williams, 1996). Clearly, the stance and the actions of the teacher are important in disrupting behaviors that marginalize girls.

Second, girls can help each other participate when enabled to do so. In language arts classes, all-girl writing groups enabled females to share and discuss their writing without fear of ridicule (Luce-Kapler, 1999). Small groups formed by gender created safe spaces for adolescent girls to participate in the writing process and share and appreciate each other's writing. Females reported that they were encouraged and motivated to write without fear of intimidation or scorn.

Girls can also be taught to deconstruct texts and to critically analyze and respond to literature. Some researchers (DeBlase, 2003b, 2003c; Sutherland, 2005) found that adolescent girls, including young women of color, make connections between literature and their own experiences that reflect the identities they have constructed for themselves as females. Those identities are based on society's assumptions of who they are and who they are capable of becoming (DeBlase, 2003b) and on Eurocentric models of what a woman should like or be like (Sutherland, 2005). These are often limiting visions that are reinforced by textual portrayals of women and are taken up in the content of girls' writing (Blair, 1998) and their discussion of and reactions to texts (DeBlase, 2003a). Therefore, teaching girls the perspective of critical literacy—teaching young women to understand how literature positions them in certain ways of performing gender, and teaching them to resist those messages—can be empowering.

Finally, teachers and students working together to create solutions is a productive way to address language behaviors that promote domination and to correct inequities. One effective strategy is metacommunication. Teachers and students talking together about the talk in classrooms can be a productive way of recognizing and addressing the problem of power imbalances that can create inequities among students. When students openly discuss their instructional discussions and their conversational styles, they can also become actively involved in creating solutions to the problem of domination. In some classrooms, these student-generated solutions included putting time limits on speakers, limiting the number of times a student can speak, keeping participation records, and self-monitoring participation. Other effective strategies for addressing gender disparity in literacy activity, such as asking students to suggest solutions, can be found in a review of the intervention research (Guzzetti, Young, Gritsavage, Fyfe, & Hardenbrook, 2002).

One caution is that such attempts to intervene may be dangerous to students when disrupting the status quo. Those who have power (typically adolescent boys) may not wish to surrender that power. Adolescent girls may hesitate to discuss their concerns openly in the presence of their male peers for fear of damage to their reputations—for example, becoming known as "whiny," as reported in one study (Guzzetti & Williams, 1996)—or harm to their popularity among boys. For these reasons, interrupting gendered discursive practices may be difficult to do, as Alvermann and her colleagues (1997) pointed out, and such attempts may create a different set of problems and stressors for girls.

HOW ARE ADOLESCENT GIRLS' NEW LITERACY PRACTICES EMPOWERING OR DELIMITING?

Although young women may often be marginalized in literacy activity inside classrooms, they frequently find empowerment in their informal literacy practices, chiefly conducted outside school, both off-line and online. Researchers describe how adolescent girls are using informal literacy practices, such as the new literacies of technoliteracies (e.g., instant messaging, blogging, online journaling, etc.) and indie media (such as zines and e-zines) to express their voices and represent their identities (Lankshear & Knobel, 2003). These studies explore how adolescent girls' consumption of electronic and popular culture media texts can both enhance and limit their ways of being and conceiving their futures. In doing so, these studies also describe how young women may be marginalized by new textual practices and communities.

Researchers detailed how adolescent girls engage in new literacies, including digital literacies and technologies. In doing so, they described how these new literacies and technoliteracies are used by young women in various beneficial ways. Although their expertise with new technologies enhances girls' participation in literacy activity that might subvert gendered norms, these practices, in some cases, also led to detriments to girls' images among their peers as they used these new literacy practices for identity exploration, negotiation, and representation.

Adolescent girls have shown how they turn to new literacies when their writing in classrooms appears to be irrelevant to their lives and the messages conveyed by both academic and popular culture print texts alienate them. For example, three adolescent girls demonstrated how they created alternative texts to discuss topics unsanctioned by the school, and not often addressed in commercial magazines, through indie media by publishing three issues of a zine (Guzzetti & Gamboa, 2004). These zinesters (those who write zines) published articles that they, their

classmates, and their relatives authored about social issues, such as self-injurious behavior, gay rights, bulimia, anorexia, rape, the importance of bilingual education, and border and immigration issues. They wrote articles using a feminist frame, writing against sexism, racism, and classism. In doing so, these young women used zines as "sites of resistance" (Schilt, 2003) by creating safe spaces to examine and oppose the cultural devaluation of women.

Certain characteristics set adolescent girls as zinesters apart from other writers. In an analysis of zines created by young women, Sinor (2002) points out that zinesters put themselves in opposition to mainstream culture in both the form and content of their writing, and they usually write for a likeminded audience. Although some alternative bookstores and record stores may carry zines, for the most part, readers must be inside the zine community to have access to their writing through online distribution centers or "distros." Zinesters are careful to keep their writings hidden from authority figures such as teachers or adults who may wish to censor their writing or make it "school appropriate." By their nature, zines are underground publications that represent the tendency of adolescents toward creative subversion and, therefore, do not belong in school as classroom writing assignments.

In fact, zines have been used as texts that empower females and serve as a contrast to the classical texts of the canon that perpetuate gendered power relations (Guzzetti, 2008). Zining provides young women with an opportunity to have a public voice, a voice that is often lost or suppressed in classrooms. Zines offer young women a safe space to illuminate women's issues of personal importance and express aspects of their identities as activists and feminists that are ignored or unrecognized in their classrooms.

Another recent study (Guzzetti & Yang, 2005) described how two adolescent girls were inspired by indie music to create a zine centered on entertainment and punk rock. These girls made intertextual connections between concepts that they learned in school and the political and feminist messages of punk songs. Their consumption and production of lyrical texts was inspired by the information they learned through listening to and co-creating music. Their writings reflected their feminist and political beliefs and served as a vehicle to experiment with and rebel against gendered sexual representations and deconstruct sexist messages about women found in pornography.

Perhaps one reason that these girls found refuge in creating their own indie media was that, as Schultz (2002) noted, adolescents write to make sense of their lives and the world around them at critical moments. Her own study (Schultz, 2002) described how an adolescent girl used journaling to write about issues of importance to her, issues not asked about or solicited in school writing assignments. These writings included the young woman's emotions, her thoughts about and plans for her future, and her self-reflections on her personal qualities that would contribute to her future.

Another example of journaling empowering adolescent girls was evidenced by young women who used online journals for this purpose. In a study of two adolescent girls, one in high school and the other in college, online and interactive journaling through *LiveJournal.com* (Guzzetti & Gamboa, 2005) assisted these young women in forming and representing their identities, in making connections to school literacies, and in fostering their social relationships. They used interactive and online journaling in diverse and empowering ways. The older girl used online journaling to write against gender stereotypes. Although in doing so she met with some sarcasm and resistance from a male reader of her journal, online journaling provided her with feedback on her story from her peers to improve her writing and give her support. The younger girl used online journaling more frequently to post events in her life on a moment-by-moment basis and to seek and receive emotional support from her friends. In addition, she used the e-journal for more traditional school activities, that is, to practice German with her boyfriend and to record her notes from her social studies class.

Other researchers described how adolescent girls use technologies and the language of technology to create themselves by using a hybridized language that they could change according to their shifting purposes (Cammack, 2002; Merchant, 2001). Adolescent girls used cyberspeak, such as using single letters or numbers to stand for whole words, changing punctuation, and using all lowercase letters, as are used in instant messaging (IM). In these studies, researchers noted that girls learned to communicate gestures, emotions, and expressions through the use of color, emoticons, and capital letters.

Still other researchers have reported additional benefits of technology practices for adolescent girls. Thomas (2006) found that an Australian adolescent girl's facile abilities with technology and technoliteracies enhanced her ability to multitask. Her online role playing supported her interests in other forms of media, such as movies, books, games, music, and text messaging. In this study, girls collaborated with boys in writing novels and posted them online and supported each other's writing attempts on message boards and blogs.

In another study of adolescent girls' explorations with new technoliteracies, Lewis and Fabos (2006) described how middle school girls used IMing (instant messaging) to keep them aware socially, to gain some degree of control in their social relationships, to make connections among their peers, and to enhance their social status. These girls used IMing to experiment with play, parody, and performance in language and to disguise their gender. At times, they were enabled by having their physical presence hidden from view to observe, monitor, and engage in dialogue with boys and exchange their thoughts and words. In some cases, however, even these girls' acts of agency reproduced gendered social structures, such as when one of the girls self-selected descriptors that that would signal her to others as a desirable female.

Other studies showed both the benefits and the limits of gender performance with technology. For example, Chandler-Olcott and Mahar (2003a) described how two middle-school girls used technology to enact their fandom of Japanese animation, or anime. One girl composed fanfictions (stories that drew on characters from popular culture texts) and constructed personal web pages; the other girl drew fan art and participated in an electronic mailing list for aspiring artists (see Black and Steinkuehler, Chapter 18, this volume. Collectively, their online literacy practices were characterized by expertise in technological tools that represented breaking down gender boundaries; in fact, one of the girls identified herself as the only female "techie" in the school. Although she took satisfaction in breaking down these boundaries and entering into a male-dominated domain, she also perceived that her abilities would label her as a "geek" among her peers and make her less desirable as a friend or romantic partner.

In a similar study, Thomas (2004) described how adolescent girls in Australia used chatting and the digital language of cyberspeak for empowerment. These new technologies and language forms allowed the young women to explore new types of femininities and experiment with gender swapping. At times, however, when enacting their femininity, they did so in exaggerated ways, such as giggling incessantly by typing "*giggles*" or "<laughs coyly>" and by making flirtatious remarks, such as "flutters her eyelashes and winks at you" (n.p.). Nevertheless, these girls demonstrated that young women who gain an expertise and power in online worlds are those who display competency with language by using and manipulating words, images, and technology. The girls in this study valued articulate and entertaining words that created positive and deep interactions with others and illustrated that ability to use language well is essential to girls' identity construction in virtual worlds.

Kelly, Pomerantz, and Currie (2006) explored Canadian teenage girls' online learning about femininity through chat rooms, instant messaging, and role-playing games. Girls reported that these online activities allowed them to rehearse different ways of performing gender before trying them out off-line. The girls enjoyed playing with gender by masking their gender identity or posing as the opposite sex, and being gender rebellious by creating mockingly ultrafeminine online names and taking on masculine or gay personas. Some of these adolescent girls also fought back in cyberspace against sexual harassment by confronting males about their sexist online and off-line behaviors, including annoying requests for cyber sex and teasing. These initial attempts at alternative representations of gender and altered gender identities did not necessary result in the transformation of unequal gender relations, however. Online interactions remained just as gendered as off-line interactions.

Merchant (2001) described changes in the communication landscape as evidenced by six teenage girls in England in their use of digital technologies, including chatting, e-mailing, and participating in an electronic discussion list. Like the girls in Lewis and Fabos's (2006) study, these girls used digital literacies to form social relationships. In a typically gendered way, most of their online communications were interactions between the sexes that served to explore or consolidate their personal relationships. In one instance, a girl provided online advice to a teenage boy on negotiating a difficult social situation with another teenage girl. Nevertheless, their online interactive conversations and their exchange of additional digital information, such as image files and web addresses, enabled these girls to develop sophisticated and marketable skills.

These technoliteracies and electronic literacy practices are considered to be so central to adolescents' identities that cyberspace has been touted as an ideal site for their identity formation and exploration inasmuch as it is socially mediated (Holloway & Valentine, 2003). Yet two of my own studies (Guzzetti, 2006a; Guzzetti, 2008) suggest conflicting messages about the utility of cyberspace as ideal space for adolescent girls' formations and representations of self. In my earlier study (Guzzetti, 2006b), two adolescent girls made use of electronic message boards, "distros," and sites for Internet resources, such as BYOFL, a site for touring underground rock bands, for finding crash pads or places to stay when visiting new locations, and for finding online publications, journals, venues, or bands. These girls used these cybersites for affirmation, reflection, reinforcement, and negotiation in the process of making claims about themselves, such as their punk or DIY (do-it-yourself) orientation. These websites allowed them to develop their technoliteracies and to engage in various identities, to position themselves as learners and teachers, to affirm their identities through others' feedback, and to reflect on their enactment of identity. These girls' online interactions through their choice of topic and use of language enabled them as competent contributors who found a social structure online that permeated the domain of White males in cyberspace (Valentine & Holloway, 2002). Their use of websites demonstrated how the online environment can provide safe spaces for girls that are not found off-line.

Conversely, my later study (Guzzetti, 2008) of the experiences of one of the adolescent girls from the earlier study showed how cyberspace may be a hostile place for young women when attempting to use cybersites for identity formation and representation. In this research, a young woman was marginalized in her attempts to post to an electronic message board for punk rock fans. Other members ignored her posts, did not elaborate on or take up her posts, and posted misogynist messages that repelled her participation. This discrepant case runs contrary to the findings of my past research (Guzzetti, 2006b) and the research of my colleagues (e.g., Cammack, 2002; Thomas, 2004) that demonstrated websites as safe sites for adolescent girls' identity formation and representation.

How do I account for this disparity? Perhaps this later study had conflicting findings because I asked the question of how cybercommunity and cyberculture might be limiting to young women and went looking for an answer. Another possibility is that I traced this young woman's participation on cybersites over a period of years from the time she was 17 years old and in high school until the time she was 21 and in college. Yet another explanation is that I specifically explored her use of cybersites and cybercultures that were dominated by young men—in sheer numbers of site members, by their frequency of posts, and by their patriarchal language and sexist displays. Young men on these sites used the language behaviors typically associated with males—offending, asserting, positioning, flaming, and debating (Jackson, 1990), thereby interrupting and silencing females' voices. Regardless, this case demonstrated how cyberculture can reflect off-line culture in the taking up of dominant culture gender roles and interfere with young women's attempts to represent their identities through technoliteracies.

HOW DO POPULAR CULTURE TEXTS POSITION YOUNG WOMEN?

Gendered roles and role relations are often perpetuated by the messages that young women receive from their readings of commercial magazines and the importance that young women assign to those publications. Finders (1998), in her study of junior high school girls, described how those who subscribed to popular culture magazines were "social queens" who used magazines such as *YM* as a marker of their progression into womanhood. They considered the messages in these magazines as instructional manuals for desired experiences and appearances. They identified with a traditional notion of womanhood portrayed in the magazines and attributed authority to teen magazines to define their emerging roles in society.

Other researchers showed how adolescent girls take up gendered messages and genres in media such as popular novels (Christian-Smith, 1993) or teen magazines (Willinsky & Hunniford, 1993) Adolescent girls in these studies saw romance novels as a guide for interacting with boys and commercial magazines as offering ways to pattern themselves in appearance as "girly" (Guzzetti & Gamboa, 2004) and to establish their social relationships (Cherland, 1994). The novels provided what the girls thought was valuable information about romantic relationships, particularly those whose parents forbade them to date (Christian-Smith, 1993).

HOW CAN POPULAR CULTURE TEXTS AND NEW LITERACIES BE INTEGRATED APPROPRIATELY INTO CLASSROOM INSTRUCTION?

There has been resistance in educational settings to the notion of incorporating the out-of-school literacy practices of adolescents into classroom instruction. Recent research has shown that teachers are often unwilling to bring popular culture into the literacy curriculum (Marsh, 2006). Often, teachers are unfamiliar with the popular culture and media texts with which adolescent girls engage. In addition, adolescent girls themselves caution against appropriating their out-of-school literacy practices, such as zining, into classroom instruction and rebel against possible misappropriations, such as making zines writing assignments (Guzzetti & Gamboa, 2004). Researchers caution that teachers' attempts to incorporate electronic texts often consist simply of "old wine in new bottles" (Lankshear & Knobel, 2003) or traditional uses for new technology and technoliteracies, such as using computers for keeping students' grades or using word processing programs for writing classroom assignments.

What, then, do adolescent girls themselves recommend? My conversations with young women have focused on their suggestions for appropriate ways to include appealing aspects of their hidden literacies into literacy instruction and assignments. Their recommendations are based on their own experiences and are consistent with the values they place on both social and academic settings.

Rather than making blogs, online journals, or zines school assignments, the adolescent girls in my studies suggested that teachers allow students to talk about their blogging and zining in school as a literacy practice. They suggested that students be acknowledged for their literacy efforts outside school by permitting them to inform others and making them aware of the new technoliteracies and literacies available to them. In keeping with the DIY ethos of zines, the girls suggested that teachers might invite guest speakers to discuss indie media with students.

Another suggestion that these young women made was for teachers to allow creative subversion in their writing assignments. This instructional flexibility may take the form of allowing students to draw on their unique prior knowledge, such as choosing a punk rocker as a subject for a required historical essay on a famous deceased person. Other ideas included using hybrid texts, computer texts with hypertext links to websites, and other related texts and textual forms to capitalize on the appeal of the pastiche of zining and blogging.

A key idea these girls offer echoes those of researchers (e.g., Blake, 1997; Edelsky, 1999): to include topics of importance to adolescents as writing assignments and allow young people, especially girls, to write about their concerns and take up in their writing the social issues and problems that impact young women. These girls also suggest allowing adolescents to incorporate their outside interests into school assignments. They perceive that teachers could make writing assignments more motivating and relevant to their daily lives in these ways.

These girls realized that reading popular culture magazines and romance novels in school was not school appropriate (although girls often bring these texts to school and share them with each other secretively in class). They did suggest, however, that teaching girls to deconstruct the gendered messages in these texts through promoting a critical stance would be an effective way to counteract gendered messages in the texts. They posited that encouraging alternative representations of gender inside schools would also be appropriate and advocated for after-school clubs to be sanctioned by the school, such as the Gay–Straight Alliance or clubs for social justice.

As a caveat, Hull and Schultz (2002) note that the boundaries between in-school and out-of-school are becoming blurred. At times, girls have been observed to be privately performing their typical out-of-school literacies in classrooms, such as text messaging, reading teen magazines, distributing and reading zines, and checking e-mail or online journals (Guzzetti & Gamboa, 2005). These young women also illustrate that females are learning and mastering the new skills required by the technologies that they embrace, skills that will be important to them as they prepare for the world of work in a changing and global economy, such as multitasking and commanding various forms of technology simultaneously. The girls in these studies serve as perennial reminders that learning takes place outside the confines of the classroom, as out-of-school and virtual worlds expand classroom walls.

HOW CAN ADOLESCENT GIRLS BE MOTIVATED AND ENCOURAGED IN LITERATE ACTIVITY?

The key to motivating and encouraging adolescent girls in their literacy practices and development appears not to rest merely with a change in literacy activities or assignments in classrooms, but with a shift in stance toward adolescents and adolescence. Researchers challenged the "not-yet-adult" culture model or the view of adolescents as less than adults (e.g., Alvermann, 2006; Guzzetti & Gamboa, 2004). Literacy researchers who have been successful in getting young women to confide in them and let them into their private or virtual worlds have adopted a stance toward adolescents that recognizes them for their ability to articulately inform research or researchers. Often, this stance has been evidenced by the researcher assuming the role of "least adult" by reducing authoritarian power relations between the researcher and the researched.

Accordingly, the study of youth culture is experiencing "a paradigm shift from a conceptualization of young people as objects of adult practices to a model in which they are active participants in the processes of interpreting and framing their own social realities" (Durham, 1998, p. 194). Hence, popular culture theorists have called for new conceptualizations of childhood (Buckingham, 2000). At the same time, adolescents are experiencing online communities that empower them through opportunities to become active and participatory citizens with full social, cultural, and political rights (Thomas, 2006).

For teachers, this change in stance toward adolescents may imply allowing identities to shift from student to teacher by permitting young people, particularly adolescent girls, who are often subordinated, to assume roles of authority and competency that compensate for marginalization by their male peers. Sharing their out-of-school literacies with others may position girls as competent beings who display facility with social literacies, if not academic literacies. By recognizing the literacy pursuits and practices that adolescent girls engage in for their own purposes, teachers can acknowledge and support adolescent girls as capable, articulate, and interesting young women.

REFERENCES

Alvermann, D. E. (1993). Researching the literal: Of muted voices, second texts, and cultural representations. In C. K. Kinzer & D. Leu (Eds.), *Examining central issues in literacy research, theory and practice: Forty-second yearbook of the National Reading Conference* (pp. 1–10). Chicago: National Reading Conference.

Alvermann, D. E. (1995/1996). Peer-led discussions: Whose interests are served? *Journal of Adolescent and Adult Literacy, 39,* 282–289.

Alvermann, D. E. (2006). Ned and Kevin: An online discussion that challenges the "not-yet-adult" cultural model. In K. Pahl & J. Rowsell (Eds.), *From the local to the global: Multimodal literacies at home and at school* (pp. 39–56). Buffalo, NY: Multilingual Matters.

Alvermann, D. E., Commeyras, M., Young, J. P., Randall, S., & Hinson, D. (1997). Interrupting gendered discursive practices in classroom talk about texts: Easy to think about, difficult to do. *Journal of Literacy Research, 29,* 73–104.

Blair, H. (1998). They left their gender prints: The voice of girls in text. *Language Arts, 75,* 11–18.

Blake, B. E. (1997). *She say, he say! Urban girls write their lives.* Albany, NY: SUNY Press.

Buckingham, D. (2000). *After the death of childhood: Growing up in the age of electronic media.* Cambridge, UK: Polity Press.

Cammack, D. W. (2002). Literacy, technology, and a room of her own: Analyzing adolescent girls' online conversations from historical and technological literacy perspectives. In D. Schallert, C. Fairbanks, J. Worthy, B. Maloch, & J. Hoffman (Eds.), *Fifty-first yearbook of the National Reading Conference* (pp. 129–141). Chicago: National Reading Conference.

Chandler-Olcott, K., & Mahar, D. (2003a). Adolescents' anime-inspired "fanfictions": An exploration of multiliteracies. *Journal of Adolescent and Adult Literacy, 46,* 1081–3004.

Chandler-Olcott, K., & Mahar, D. (2003b). "Techsavviness" meets multiliteracies: Exploring adolescent girls' technology mediated literacy practices. *Reading Research Quarterly, 38,* 356–385.

Cherland, M. R. (1994). *Private practices: Girls reading fiction and constructing identity.* Bristol, PA: Taylor & Francis.

Christian-Smith, L. K. (1993). *Texts of desire: Essays on fiction, femininity and schooling.* New York: Falmer.

DeBlase, G. (2002). Striving for success: The impact of high stakes testing on urban adolescent girls' engagement with literacy. *Ohio Journal of the English/Language Arts, 35,* 16–23.

DeBlase, G. (2003a). Acknowledging agency while accommodating romance: Girls negotiating meaning in literacy transactions. *Journal of Adolescent and Adult Literacy, 46,* 624–635.

DeBlase, G. (2003b). Tracing texts of desire: Assisting adolescent girls to (re)envision the male gaze. *WILLA, 12,* 4–9.

DeBlase, G. (2003c). Missing stories, missing lives: Urban girls (re)constructing race and gender in the literacy classroom. *Urban Education, 38,* 279–329.

Durham, M. G. (1998). Girls, media, and the negotiation of sexuality: A study of race, class and gender in adolescent peer groups. *J&MC Quarterly, 76,* 193–216.

Edelsky, C. (1999). *Making justice our project: Teachers working toward critical whole language practice.* Urbana, IL: National Council of Teachers of English.

Fey, M. (1998). Critical literacy in a school–college collaboration through computer networking. *Journal of Literacy Research, 30,* 85–115.

Finders, M. (1996). *"Just girls": Literacy and allegiance in junior high school.* New York: Teachers College Press.

Finders, M. (1998). Queens and teen zines: Early adolescents reading their way toward adulthood. *Anthropology and Education Quarterly, 27,* 71–89.

Gilligan, C. (1993). Joining the resistance: Psychology, politics, girls and women. In L. Weis & M. Fine (Eds.), *Beyond silenced voices: Class, race and gender in the United States schools* (pp. 253–285). Albany, NY: SUNY Press.

Guzzetti, B. J. (2001). Texts and talk: The role of gender in learning physics. In E. Moje & D. O'Brien (Eds.), *Constructions of literacy: Studies of teaching and learning literacy in secondary classrooms* (pp. 125–146). Mahwah, NJ: Erlbaum.

Guzzetti, B. J. (2006a). Cybergirls: Negotiating social identities on cybersites. *E-Learning, 3,* 158–168.

Guzzetti, B. J. (2006b, November). *Identities and cyber-communities: A young woman's critique of cyber-culture on cybersites.* Paper presented at the annual meeting of the National Reading Conference, Los Angeles.

Guzzetti, B. J. (2008). Adolescent girls performing gender through literacies: Marginalized or resistant youth? In K. Sanford & R. Hammett (Eds.), *Boys, girls and the myths of literacy* (pp. 219–233). Toronto: Canadian Scholars Press.

Guzzetti, B. J., Campbell, S., Duke, C., & Irving, J. (2003). Understanding adolescent literacies: A conversation with three zinesters. *Reading Online.* Retrieved April 26, 2008, from *http://www.readingonline.org/newliteracies/guzzetti3/*.

Guzzetti, B. J., & Gamboa, M. (2004). Zines for social justice: Adolescent girls writing on their own. *Reading Research Quarterly, 39,* 408–436.

Guzzetti, B. J., & Gamboa, M. (2005). Online journaling: The informal writings of two adolescent girls. *Research in the Teaching of English, 40,* 168–206.

Guzzetti, B. J., & Williams, W. O. (1996). Gender, text and discussion: Examining intellectual safety in the science classroom. *Journal of Research in Science Teaching, 33,* 5–20.

Guzzetti, B. J., & Yang, Y. (2005). Adolescents' punk rock fandom: Production and construction of lyrical texts. In B. Maloch, J. V. Hoffman, D. L. Schallert, C. M. Fairbanks, & J. Worthy (Eds.), *54th yearbook of the National Reading Conference* (pp. 198–210). Oak Creek, WI: National Reading Conference.

Guzzetti, B. J., Young, J., Gritsavage, M., Fyfe, L., & Hardenbrook, M. (2002). *Reading, writing, and talking gender in literacy learning.* Newark, DE: International Reading Association and National Reading Conference.

Heilman, E. E. (1998). The struggle for self: Power and identity in adolescent girls. *Youth and Society, 30,* 182–208.

Henry, A. (1998). "Speaking up" and "speaking out": Examining "voice" in a reading/writing program with adolescent African Caribbean girls. *Journal of Literacy Research, 30,* 233–252.

Holloway, S. L., & Valentine, G. (2003). *Cyberkids: Children in the information age.* New York: Routledge.

Hull, G., & Schultz, K. (2002). *School's out: Bridging out of school literacies with classroom practice.* New York: Teachers College Press.

Jackson, D. (1990). Patriarch, class and language: A critical autobiography. *English in Education, 23,* 8–19.

Kelly, D., Pomerantz, S., & Currie, D. H. (2006). "No boundaries"? Girls' interactive, online learning about femininities. *Youth and Society, 38,* 3–28.

Kyle, S. (1996). *Discussion patterns of African American students in classroom discourse.* Unpublished manuscript, Arizona State University, Tempe.

Lankshear, C., & Knobel, M. (2003). *New literacies: Changing knowledge and classroom learning.* New York: Open University Press.

Lewis, C., & Fabos, B. (2006). Instant messaging, literacies, and social identities. *Reading Research Quarterly, 40,* 470–501.

Luce-Kapler, R. (1999). As if women writing. *Journal of Literacy Research, 31,* 267–291.

Marsh, J. (2006). Popular culture in the literacy curriculum: A Bourdieuan analysis. *Reading Research Quarterly, 41,* 160–174.

Merchant, G. (2001). Teenagers in cyberspace: An investigation of language use and language change in Internet chatrooms. *Journal of Research in Reading, 24,* 293–306.

Moore, D. (1997). Some complexities of gendered talk about texts. *Journal of Literacy Research, 29,* 507–530.

Phelps, S., & Weaver, D. (1999). Public and personal voice in adolescents' classroom talk. *Journal of Literacy Research, 31,* 321–354.

Schilt, K. (2003). "I'll resist with every inch and every breath": Girls and zine making as a form of resistance. *Youth and Society, 35,* 71–97.

Schultz, K. (1996). Between school and work: The literacies of urban adolescent females. *Anthropology and Education Quarterly, 27,* 517–544.

Schultz, K. (2002). "Looking across space and time": Reconceptualizing literacy learning in and out of school. *Research in the Teaching of English, 36,* 356–390.

Sinor, J. (2002, March). *Adolescent girls' zines: Uncommon pages and practices.* (ERIC Document Reproduction Service ED 462 707). Paper presented at the meeting of the Conference on College Composition and Communication, Chicago.

Sutherland, L. M. (2005). Black adolescent girls' use of

literacy practices to negotiate boundaries of ascribed identity. *Journal of Literacy Research, 37,* 365–406.

Thomas, A. (2004). Digital literacies of the cybergirl. *E-Learning, 1,* 358–382.

Thomas, A. (2006). "MSN was the next big thing after Beanie Babies": Children's virtual experiences as an interface to their identities and their everyday lives. *E-Learning, 3,* 126–142.

Valentine, G., & Holloway, S. L. (2002). Cyberkids? Exploring children's identities and social networks in on-line and off-line worlds. *Annals of the Association of American Geographers, 92,* 302–319.

Willinsky, J., & Hunniford, M. R. (1993). Reading the romance younger: The mirrors and fears of a preparatory literature. In L. Smith (Ed.), *Texts of desire: Essays on fiction, femininity and schooling* (pp. 87–105). New York: Falmer.

CHAPTER 25

Literacy Issues and GLBTQ Youth

Queer Interventions in English Education

WAYNE MARTINO

This chapter investigates the significance of queer interventions in English education and the implications for gay, lesbian, bisexual, transgender, and questioning adolescents. I ague for the need to develop reading practices that move beyond a focus on including texts which deal with sexual minorities, to examine how heterosexuality becomes normalized. The emphasis is on promoting reading practices in the English classroom which require reflection on the structures of intelligibility that inform identificatory practices governed by the impulse to normalize and the idea that gay, lesbian, bisexual, transgender, and queer (GLBTQ) students are alike as a group or just human like everybody else. This focus involves interrogation of the tendency to resort to the familiar identity management strategy that relies on an expulsion of otherness as a basis for relating to the self and others. Kumashiro argues for the need to exceed pedagogical interventions which focus on education *for* and education *about* "the other" in order to embrace analytic frameworks that address institutionally embedded practices of *privileging* and *othering*. I link these frameworks to the ideas of teacher threshold knowledge and authentic pedagogies. In this sense, queer interventions in the English classroom are located more broadly within a research-based literature on effective pedagogy that acknowledges the need to embrace a politics of difference. This approach enables educators to imagine possibilities of thinking beyond what is conceived of as normal.

In this chapter I draw on theoretical positions and standpoints adopted by Britzman (1995, 1998) and Kumashiro (2000, 2002), as well as literature in the field, to investigate the significance of queer interventions in English education. I also refer to one drama presentation—performed in seven high schools as part of a broader school board initiative in Ontario to address violence, sex-based harassment, and homophobia—to illustrate the significance of the need to embrace analytic frameworks and reading practices in the English classroom that foreground the tendency to normalize (Britzman, 1998). Merely introducing texts that include gay characters as a basis for increasing students' tolerance of homosexuality is not the solution. What is needed, as Yescavage and Alexander (1997) argue, is pedagogy that "umasks heteronormativity" in its attempt to encourage all students to think critically about "how their own sexuality is socially constructed" (p. 3). Sumara (2001) defines the term *heteronormativity* as "represent[ing] the way in which 'heterosexual' has become a normative category against which all other subject positions are identified and judged" (p. 2). This approach requires an examination of how sexual orientation is marked or categorized and involves engaging students in an analysis of the power to name and classify through addressing the social construction of sexual identity.

In addition, it requires raising awareness about the taken-for-grantedness of heterosexuality and involves sensitizing students to the ways in which sexuality is often an unacknowledged part of the fabric of their everyday lives at school. For example, Yescavage and Alexander (1997) talk about how simply providing an opportunity for students to get to know one another during the first week of classes, by arranging them in small groups, provides numerous examples of students "casually" or "innocuously" *outing* themselves as heterosexual. By just listening to students talk about themselves, they argue, data can be gathered for later discussions about the *flaunting* of heterosexuality as a naturalized everyday occurrence. Such a focus on the marking of heterosexuality is consistent with Kumashiro's (2002) approach to embracing reading practices that are critical of *privileging* and *othering* (p. 44). As I illustrate in this chapter, this perspective forms a necessary basis for moving beyond assimilationist approaches to addressing gay, lesbian, bisexual, transgender, and queer (GLBTQ) issues in the English classroom, which are driven by the assumption or imperative to demonstrate that queers are really not that different from straight people (see Britzman, 1995).

LITERACY AND SEXUAL IDENTITY IN THE ENGLISH LANGUAGE ARTS CLASSROOM: A REVIEW OF THE LITERATURE

Moje and MuQaribu (2003) claim that there has been limited research conducted into the relationship between literacy and sexual identity. For example, they assert that "there is a dearth of research or models of practice that address the question of how sexual identity and literacy are intertwined and even less attention to preparing teachers to engage with students in classroom interactions as sexed

identities are brought out in discussion about texts" (p. 207). This problem has been identified in a study undertaken by Sumara, Davis, and Iftody (2006), which investigated English language arts student teachers' reading of a young adult novel that challenged stereotypes surrounding normative sexuality. These scholars challenge the view that reading literature can create the conditions for broadening our understanding of social and cultural diversity without attending to the norms governing the teaching of literary texts (Mellor & Patterson, 2001).

Although engagement with literary texts that require students to develop some form of identification with characters has the potential to interrupt heteronormativity, Sumara et al. (2006) argue for a deliberate pedagogical imperative committed to interrogating systemic forms of homophobia and heterosexism as they are depicted in literary texts. They discuss students' responses to the novel by Huser (2003), *Stitches*, for example, that deals with a gay character and his best friend, who is physically disabled. Rather than targeting the homophobic abuse experienced by the gay character as a consequence of his gender nonconformity, the discussion tended to revolve around the depoliticized notion of bullying, with no attempt to make available understandings about the consequences of and policing associated with enforcing rigid gender expectations (see Martino & Pallotta-Chiarolli, 2003; Morris, 2005).

In fact, Sumara et al.'s (2006) study revealed that many student teachers actually came away from this novel study with their stereotypes about homosexuality simply being reaffirmed. Furthermore, some student teachers felt that they were unable to present their opinions or what they really thought about the gay character, particularly those who identified themselves as queer or nonheterosexual. Thus, although the possibility existed for creating conditions for identifying with the literary character which enable productive discussion about "the complex ways in which personal experiences of self-consciousness emerge from nested layers of situated cognition" (p. 62), the pedagogical norms governing the use of the novel, as well as an absence of queer analytic frameworks, foreclosed such opportunities. For instance, the instructor failed to address the character's gay sexuality directly, which meant that specific issues of homophobia and heterosexism became subsumed under the generalized phenomenon of bullying.

There was potential to deploy the literary text as a site for enabling discussion about the limits of heteronormativity, and hence the emergence of new subjects and forms of subjectivity, governed by a commitment to facilitating the range of individual reader responses to literary texts. However, the fact that this expression of divergent views did not eventuate is attributed to already institutionally sanctioned pedagogical practices that determine what is to count as a legitimate response to a literary text. This absence of a broader range of literary responses and identifications resulted, according to Sumara et al. (2006), in "normalized narratives of sexual youth and identity" (p. 65) being reinforced. Their conclusion in this study is that the teacher needs to be able to create the conditions for alternative responses or readings to become represented and used in meaningful ways. In this sense, they argue that "literary experiences are to be used as opportunities for cultural transformation" (p. 65), as opposed to being mobilized to maintain heteronormative constructions of sexual identity. However, in order for this shift to be achieved, Sumara et al. (2006) argue that "deliberate attention must be given to providing students with opportunities both to represent and to analyze the diversity of personal readings within a safe and intellectually supportive context" (p. 65). Not securing such pedagogical conditions, they claim, is likely to lead "prevailing normalizing discourses to dominate the perceptual awareness of students" (p. 65).

The call for teaching queer-inclusive English language arts, therefore, needs to be framed in terms that move beyond merely importing texts into the classroom that include GLBTQ characters (see Blackburn & Buckley, 2005; Britzman, 1995; Spurlin, 2000). For example, representing GLBTQ characters needs to be deconstructed in terms of the heteronormative limits imposed for understanding sexual identity (see Blackburn, 2002). Blackburn and Buckley (2005), in fact, argue for the need to interrogate and disrupt notions of the *normal* as they relate specifically to sexual identity labels and categories. For instance, they raise questions about literary texts that perpetuate stereotypes of lesbians as either masculine (butch) or feminine (femme). Linne (2000) also cautions against problematic representations of gay characters in fiction who are often compelled to conform to strict stereotypical gender roles that are consistent with culturally desirable or acceptable versions of hegemonic masculinity (see Martino, 2006). For some authors, he claims, this heteronormative gravitation translates into gay male characters being cast as avid hockey players or as embracing stereotypical masculine interests, such as auto repair. The problem with such representations in young adult novels, he argues, is that they "limit the range of experiences and characterizations of gay people to a few tired clichés . . . and may in fact simply reproduce old stereotypes and fears" (p. 205). Moreover, such representations appear to be driven by both assimilationalist logic and an impulse to normalize that is organized around proving that gay males can be masculine, just like *normal* boys!

Although integrating GLBTQ literature into the English language arts curriculum is important, Blackburn and Buckley (2005) caution that teachers cannot rely on the mere inclusion of such texts as a means by which to counteract stereotypes (see Athanases, 1996). What is needed, as illustrated throughout the rest of this chapter, are pedagogical strategies that engage with queer analytic perspectives as a basis for promoting reading practices that throw into question oppressive "sedimented, rigid gender/sexuality categories" (Morris, 2005, p. 12; see also Loutzenheiser & MacIntosh, 2004; Sumara, 2001; Sumara & Davis, 1999).

USING TEXTS TO ADDRESS VIOLENCE AND HOMOPHOBIA IN SCHOOLS

The problems outlined by many of the aforementioned scholars in the field, regarding both the inclusion of GLBTQ content in the English curriculum and the reading practices that need to be fostered through specific sorts of pedagogical interventions, were driven home for me recently when I attended a special drama performance designed to address violence and homophobia in schools. This performance was initiated and driven by a school board in Ontario under an overarching and officially endorsed safe schools policy. By focusing on this drama presentation involving interactive or forum theater within the context of an instituted program of violence intervention, I want to raise important and troubling questions about the limits of reading practices and pedagogical interventions that foreclose the potential for examining "how heterosexuality becomes normalized as natural" (Britzman, 1995, p. 153; Sumara, 2001). Interactive theater is derived from the work of Boal (1985), who developed the theater of the oppressed as a site for political action and intervention. It involves presenting a play for a second time to allow the audience to stop the action and to intervene to address the polemic involved in the particular situation being acted out.

I illustrate the extent to which this dramatic performance, particularly in its attempt to imagine sexual difference through the inclusion of a gay character, supports reading practices that are governed by "the impulse to normalize." In this sense, I draw attention to how such reading practices actually support heteronormativity rather than challenge homophobia and heterosexism. Moreover, I show that deliberately inserting a gay character into the play, although well intentioned, in the absence of queer-informed and critical theoretical frameworks, actually contributed to disenfranchising and disempowering GLBTQ students. Ultimately, the problem is one that is related not so much to the text in itself (Hunter, 1984), but to the failure to provide analytic frameworks and pedagogical conditions capable of engaging with the "unthinkability of normalcy" (Britzman, 1998, p. 87). The absence of such frameworks, I argue, ultimately supports reading practices and literacy performances that are committed to identity work that relies on reinforcing rather than interrogating notions of normal or the imperatives of normalcy (see Blackburn, 2002).

One of the key players in organizing the forum theater event was Katrina (a pseudonym), a drama teacher *on special assignment*, seconded by the school board to support its work in building and developing safe school communities. Katrina, given her wealth of experience as a classroom teacher and her skills in managing teenage audiences

participating in interactive theater, was in a key position to use this forum as a site for engaging adolescents in issues related to homophobia, dating violence, and what was termed "bullying" in schools. She worked closely with a drama teacher at another high school, and together they coached a group of drama students who had both the dramatic skills and willingness to perform in interactive theater. They became the cast. The play, however, was written by Katrina in collaboration with a senior drama student. Having heard of this project, I contacted Katrina, and she invited me to attend one of the performances, advertised as dealing with and addressing conflict resolution in schools. I was able to attend one of the performances delivered to a large audience of more than two hundred year-12 students, ages 16–17, in their school auditorium. The audience comprised mainly White students with a small number of identifiable visible minorities.

The play revolves around the friendship between two popular boys, Mathew and Steven, age 17. Mathew is constructed as the stereotypical masculine jock who is the key perpetrator of violence and harassment in the play, and Steven is the typical bystander who is complicit in supporting such an abusive dynamic through his silence and, hence, failure to intervene. As already highlighted, drawing on stereotypical representations of characters in texts is one of the problematic issues identified in the field vis-à-vis addressing GLBTQ issues in the English language arts classroom (see Blackburn, 2002; Linne, 2000; Sumara et al., 2006). This dynamic of the complicity of the bystander and his or her failure to intervene are constantly invoked throughout the play, highlighting the norms that govern its production and drive its stated aims: to raise awareness about violence and bullying and to encourage, as I understood it, intervention by bystanders. In fact, the whole play appeared to be underscored by a logic that was driven by an imperative to recuperate the bystander as a failed moral subject, an issue that I take up further in the following section.

The play begins with scenes involving the two friends talking about their girlfriends, Roxanna and Julie, respectively, and is suffused with some of the typical male sexist banter in terms of how the boys refer to the girls in their absence. For example, Mathew boasts about having sex with his girlfriend and starts prodding Steven about his sexual experiences. Although Steven is clearly uncomfortable, he tries to play along, but the audience can sense his embarrassment and his feeling of entrapment. Sensing his discomfort, Matthew interjects, "Hey, what are you, a fag or something?" The scenes sometimes end abruptly, but build to certain climaxes, such as the one involving Mathew putting pressure on his girlfriend to have sex with him. Roxanna becomes upset because she believes Matthew is not respecting her, and she tells him how she is feeling. This scene culminates in an outburst of anger, resulting in Mathew violently grabbing Roxanna's arm. She sobs, screaming, "You're hurting me!" and the scene ends. This shift in temperament contrasts with the male bravado of the previous scene and exposes it for the farce that it is.

The following scene involves Steven talking with his girlfriend. They have a very different relationship. Steven is sensitive and caring, and mutual respect is evident in his relationship with his girlfriend, Julie. He cares deeply for her, but as the scene builds, so too does the tension. This aspect of the relationship is portrayed well as he stumbles and becomes increasingly ill at ease in attempting to end the lie that he is living in his relationship with her. He finally musters up the courage to tell her that he is gay. Although this is an important scene in the play, particularly in terms of the reaction it elicits from the audience, it is by no means developed to the extent that it could have been because the focus is clearly on the abusive straight White male who occupies center stage.

There are, however, other scenes that take us into Roxanna's family life, where there are tensions in the relationship between her parents with intimations of potential domestic violence. In addition, there is a scene with Mathew and his father at a parent–teacher night, which presents the latter as a top executive who is rude, obnoxious, and prone to being abusive. The relationship between father and son is used to help the audience understand the connection between the son's abusive behavior and that of his father. These scenes are purportedly included to raise the whole issue of the cycle of violence and how

patterns of oppression are enacted in families and affect or are internalized by children—one becomes like his father, an abuser, the other like her mother, a victim. Throughout the play there are also a number of scenes involving peer group dynamics of perpetrator, victim, and bystander, in which we witness Mathew being verbally abusive to his girlfriend, while Steven and his friends, as onlookers, fail to intervene or question such behavior.

REAFFIRMING TAKEN-FOR-GRANTED NOTIONS OF *NORMAL*

Although the play provides food for thought and is deliberate in its attempt to address homophobia by including Steven as a closeted gay male character, it is plagued by serious limitations that are only in part exacerbated by the form of its delivery as interventionist theater. The play was constructed to deliberately represent stereotypical characters and, as I understood it, was not informed by a knowledge of queer frameworks for addressing heteronormativity in the classroom (see Blackburn, 2002; Sumara & Davis, 1999).

As I attempt to illustrate in this section, the play requires only limited forms of participation that are driven by the imperative to recuperate the bystander as a failed moral agent. As a result, it unwittingly dismisses the full significance of the role that broader sociocultural systems, institutions, and structures of feeling play in the motivations, desires, behavior, and conduct of the characters who are meant to represent *real* people. A pedagogical context is established that appears to be governed by an imperative to fix the problem of violence in relationships, and this motive gets rendered too simplistically in terms of the individual bystander or witness being required to take action. This is not to say that bystanders should not be morally incited to take action or that their failure to do so cannot be explained in terms of their fear. Rather, what is needed are pedagogical conditions which are able to engage with the complex dynamics and structures of feeling at play that are involved for participants in such situations without the risk of diminishing or eliding their significance (see Sumara et al., 2006).

I believe a lot remains to be learned about

the pedagogical requirements or demands that are placed on teachers committed to addressing heteronormativity in the English classroom by reflecting on this experience of interactive theater and by focusing on the way many of the adolescent students inserted themselves into this text. For example, what do the students' responses to the play reveal about their capacity or willingness to resist the impulse to normalize? To what extent are their reading practices implicated in the production of normalcy and linked to particular forms of identity work? What are the limits of inclusive pedagogies which are grounded in the imperatives of educating for and about the *other* that appear to be informing the production of such a text (Kumashiro, 2000)? What are the necessary pedagogical conditions for addressing heteronormativity in the English classroom?

The critique of this particular school board initiative is not designed to detract from the performance or from many of the scenes that were powerful in their capacity to evoke deep emotion and to involve the audience. For example, when Steven actually *comes out* to his girlfriend in a scene that captures the fear, pain, and anguish wrought through a misplaced sense of betrayal, the audience is given a glimpse into the specter of guilt that hangs over him as he grapples with the system of heteronormativity and compulsory heterosexuality that mark the limits of normalcy (Britzman, 1998; Rich, 1980). However, it is during the second performance, when individual students are invited to interrupt the play and insert themselves into its dynamic of shifting relationships, that concerns arise which lead me to reflect more deeply on the significance of this experience for addressing heteronormativity in the English classroom. The focus on this performance, with its pedagogical imperatives and context of production, provides a platform for raising concerns about the limits of the reception regimes it authorizes and what I consider to be the implications for addressing GLBTQ issues in the English classroom.

In this way, I draw attention to the necessity of considering broader sociopolitical, cultural, and historically specific institutionalized contexts in which texts are produced, performed, and interpreted. For example, failure to attend to the connection between these macrodimensions of literacy practices and the micropolitics implicated in how individuals actually make and negotiate meaning (Luke & Freebody, 1997) may lead unreflectively and unwittingly to support the conditions for limiting people's understanding of sexual difference. As illustrated in further discussion, the effect is to authorize either/or positions that are determined by the individual's capacity for a certain form of moral agency in the absence of providing a deeper understanding of the sexed, raced, classed, and gendered dimensions of identity (see Kendall & Martino, 2006; Kumashiro, 2000, 2002; McCreedy, 2004; McNinch & Cronin, 2004; Morris, 2005; Sears, 1997).

In short, what is invoked is the liberal subject who must be compelled to act, but under the guise of the freedom to choose (Rose, 1999). This ambiguity is reflected in one of the central tenets of this special safe schools program, which appears to be governed too simplistically in its enactment by the imperative for the individual to intervene, as opposed to taking the position of bystander. Moreover, in talking with Katrina, the person who actually wrote and facilitated students' engagement with the play, I learned that the play was simply performed as a "one-off" in each school. There did not appear to be any concerted follow-up in the form of facilitating critical dialogue about peer group hierarchical relationships and the role that homophobia and compulsory heterosexuality play in imposing severe limits on young people's lives in schools. In this sense, it represented a piecemeal approach that fits nicely under the umbrella of the district school board's overarching violence prevention policy framework.

For instance, during the second performance, individual students were invited and chose to participate under the careful and skillful facilitation provided by Katrina, who ensured that explosive or silly situations were contained. If a student made an inappropriate comment, Katrina was quick to intervene and to guide the student to respond to the enacted situation in what she considered to be an appropriate manner. Thus, in her capacity as facilitator of forum theater, as I grew to understand it, she was compelled to assume the burden of either protecting or containing the individual student who had volunteered to participate, given the sort of surveillance and policing of the latter under the riveted eyes of the adolescent audience. This observation does not detract from the fact that Katrina was highly skilled and adept at managing such situations. For example, at times she was firm in ensuring that the participating student was prevented from playing to the audience, as was a tendency for many of the male students who used the intervention as an opportunity to score a cheap laugh. There were countless incidents of boys strutting to the stage to perform, or rather parade, their heterosexuality for all to see. Katrina realized the capacity of such a performative space for amplifying a certain dynamic—acting cool/performing a certain culturally validated masculinity (Martino, 1999, 2001)—that detracted from the issues of violence and sex-based harassment that the play was urging students to address. In these situations she would intervene by verbally prompting the students or by giving them cues. She often resorted to merely telling them what to say and appeared to be anxious to cut the performance short, given the sort of banter erupting in the audience.

I remember one boy swaggering up to the stage to intervene in a particular scene, incited by the wolf whistling and laughter of his peers. Katrina handled the situation well as the student assumed the character of one of the bystanders early in the play. He intervened in an abusive situational dynamic between Matthew and Roxanna. But, by citing paternalistic discourses, he actively took up the position of rescuing "the damsel in distress" (see Coulter, 2003). For example, one of the first statements he uttered to Matthew was, "Hey, you shouldn't treat a beautiful girl like that!" which incited the audience to erupt in an outburst of laughter. The charade continued under the careful facilitation of Katrina, who cut the performance short, but not before the student had the opportunity to ask the beautiful blond girl out on a date. Meanwhile, the whole issue of Steven's "coming out" was forgotten and was continually undermined as individual students continued to hijack and recuperate the heteronormative limits of sexual and gender identity already at play in this institutional context of surveillance. Ultimately, as I understand it, Katrina's role appeared to be

one that necessitated continually reframing the situation, while simultaneously directing the participating subjects to an acceptable outcome, whether they had any intention of arriving at that place or not.

The effect of such a pedagogical program, supposedly designed to raise awareness of abusive power dynamics, while simultaneously working to inculcate conflict resolution skills, is to lay responsibility for intervention with the individual bystander as a failed moral subject. In this sense, it is driven by a therapeutic and recuperative logic that centers on addressing moral passivity, or rather deficiency, through treating interactive theater as a skill-building exercise. This imperative fails to provide the necessary conditions for promoting deep understanding about the psychic and cultural forces that structure the ways in which feelings inform identifications and modes of address or action. It also forecloses the possibility of entertaining other modes of intervention grounded in restorative approaches to dealing with conflict resolution (see Morrison, 2006). Restorative approaches involve creating conditions for building communities of healing and support through dialogue and public acknowledgement by the perpetrator of the pain and suffering inflicted on victims. This recognition involves what has been termed a process of "reintegrative shaming" whereby the perpetrator comes to a realization of the impact of his or her actions and the full significance of the consequent social disapproval.

The point is that to invoke such a voluntary rationalist subject is to deny the significance of complex identificatory processes and structures of feeling at play in students' responses through authorizing reading practices that rely on simplistic notions of intentionality and individual responsibility. As Britzman (1998) asserts, "Feelings are symptomatic of more than the individual's intentionality":

In the context of a queer pedagogy, a more useful way to think about feelings requires attention to what it is that structures ways in which feelings are imagined and read. This means constituting feelings for another as a curious reading practice, as a problem of ethical conduct, and as a symptom of identificatory engagement. (p. 84)

Thus, the focus needs to be on developing an understanding of knowledge/power relations and how they structure the ways in which people learn to relate to themselves as particular sorts of sexual subjects (see Foucault, 1980). This analytic focus on the relationships to the self and encounters with the *other* points to the limits of using forum theater as a pedagogical intervention for addressing homophobia and violence prevention in the absence of mobilizing knowledge about the production of normalcy. Failure to draw on such knowledge forecloses the pedagogical possibilities for examining the psychic investment and structures of feeling/motivation informing certain identity management practices and strategies that are driven by the impulse to normalize. In this sense, an understanding of oneself and of others as sexual subjects is inextricably tied to knowledge/power relations that rely on historically contingent explanatory frameworks (Foucault, 1978). Desire is therefore inscribed and supported by structures of feeling and forms of thought that depend on what Britzman (1998) terms "historically specific spheres" (p. 84).

Thus, reading practices need to address the limits imposed by normalcy in terms of interrogating a conceptual order that refuses to entertain the possibility of the *other* outside a structure of binary hierarchical identity categories or labels (see Blackburn, 2002; Sumara & Davis, 1999; Yescavage & Alexander, 1997). Accordingly, for Britzman (1995), what is needed are pedagogical conditions and interventions that are conducive to interrupting heteronormativity. For example, she emphasizes that reading practices that evoke empathy as a basis for instituting a pedagogical commitment to including the voices of GLBTQ youth in the English language arts curriculum are not the answer. This necessity for inclusion, she argues, is often based on the liberal imperative to recover the authentic voice of the other as a basis for humanizing GLBTQ subjects through a recognition that *they* really are just like *us* (see Britzman, 1995). Moreover, such reading practices fail to encourage reflection on processes of identification for individual readers and their impact on their engagement with texts (see Sumara & Davis, 1999; Sumara et al., 2006). What is required, then, is the need to shift the analytic

gaze to a focus on heterosexuality as a system of power relations and, hence, as a conceptual order that regulates and polices how it is possible to think about sexual identity in terms that are circumscribed by a binary logic. In this sense, queer theory is best thought of as an analytic tool which enables a critical focus on deconstructing sexual categories and identities that are often circumscribed by a logic determined by defining heterosexuality in opposition to homosexuality.

One of the central tenets of queer theory, therefore, is the need to focus on the heteronormative system that organizes and authorizes the homo–hetero distinction. The focus is not on claiming a particular sexual identity, but rather on developing a deeper understanding about the regimes of normalization that operate to establish certain identifications and truths about the nature of sexuality and desire in the first place (Morris, 2005; Sumara, 2001). The effect of this conceptual shift is to make the limits of heterosexuality as a system of power relations the object of analysis. There needs to be a shift in focus by directing attention to the impact and effects of compulsory heterosexuality—the requirement to present oneself as appropriately heterosexual—which produces homophobia in the first place:

> Queer theory is suggesting that the study of homosexuality should not be a study of a minority—the making of the lesbian/gay/bi-sexual subject—but a study of those knowledges and social practices that organize society as a whole by sexualizing-heterosexualizing or homosexualizing bodies, desires, acts, identities, social relations, knowledges, culture, and social institutions. (Seidman, 1996, pp. 12–13; quoted in Gamson, 2000, p. 355)

Hence, Britzman (1995) argues for a pedagogy that calls into question "the conceptual geography of normalization" (p. 152).

The assumption, therefore, that merely including the voices and perspectives of the "other" in the curriculum will bring about attitudinal change is questioned. There is a sense that a politics of inclusion risks slipping into reclaiming and reframing representations of gay and lesbian people in the spirit of presenting more authentic images as a means by which to remedy attributions of deviancy and perversion ascribed by the dominant culture. Britzman (1998) emphasizes interrogating the structures of feeling and analytic frameworks which support the production of social selves that are driven by "the confinement of sameness and the seduction of affirmation" (p. 85). Such reading practices reinforce rather than disrupt taken-for-granted notions of normal (Blackburn, 2002).

THE CONSEQUENCES OF ENABLING HETERONORMATIVITY

The limits of such a liberal pedagogical program, with its focus on recuperating the responsible individual as a potential moral agent capable of exercising judgment, are further highlighted when taking into consideration the audience's response to and subsequent erasure of the gay character in the play. In fact, the impulse to reproduce heteronormativity through exclusion and repudiation of the sexualized *other* arises in ways that are unruly and unable to be contained in this context. This tendency raises important questions, not so much about the text in itself (Hunter, 1984), but rather about the reading practices that are authorized by the audience participants in such a context which provides a site for amplifying, celebrating, and confirming hegemonic masculinity and heteronormative systems of thought (Martino, 2001). Rather than confronting the limits of normalcy, many of the male students who chose to intervene in the second performance of the play engaged in ways that reinforced such limits. The constitution of the conceptual order of normalcy emerges through the capacity of the play, given the context (and other factors that I elaborate on later) to activate or mobilize certain interpretive practices that amplify and celebrate forms of identity management work. Such interventions are not ruptures, but involve reinscribing the limits of normalcy. In fact, interactive theater provides some students with an opportunity to reassert their heterosexuality and also incites homophobia.

This problem was highlighted for me when loud bursts of laughter and snickering emanated from the audience in response to the scene where Steven comes out to his girlfriend. It was also reflected in the way that many of the students consciously performed for their peers in a manner that trivialized the violence. Furthermore, although most of the students who participated in previous scenes willingly insert themselves as an active moral agent and savior, no one is game enough to intervene in the situation involving Steven's coming out or when his so-called friend actually called him a "faggot." This erasure or silencing of the homophobia directed at the gay character was probably the only safe position for the students to adopt, given the public exposure and policing of heteronormativity afforded by such a context with its capacity to amplify, objectify, and marginalize queer students through homophobic surveillance and compulsory heterosexuality. In fact, the absent presence of the gay subject, as Butler (1993) points out, is at the basis of sustaining the force of heteronormativity: "The subject is constituted through the force of exclusion and abjection, one that produces a constitutive outside of the subject, an abjected outside, that is, after all, 'inside' the subject as its own founding repudiation" (p. 3).

What this positioning highlights is the ever haunting presence of the constitutive "outside" of the subject that can never be erased within a sex-gender system supported by the regulatory apparatus of compulsory heterosexuality (see Fuss, 1991). Hence, the whole system of compulsory heterosexuality is built on rigidly defining sexual difference in binary oppositional terms through a form of gender cleansing that involves expelling the faggot from consciousness (Bersani, 1995; Kendall & Martino, 2006; Yallop, 2004). But if securing straight identity is built on the force of rejecting an *other* outside itself and despised, the heterosexual subject can never erase what it actually despises and needs in order to assert itself in the first place.

As Britzman (1998) highlights, the benefit of queer theory lies in its capacity to conceptualize "normalcy as negation": "It constitutes normalcy as a conceptual order that refuses to imagine the very possibility of the other precisely because of the production of otherness as an outside is central to its own self-recognition" (p. 82). In this sense, the much needed gay character emerges as a despised figure of abjection and is simply dismissed and erased through an act of denial that is manifested in students' engagement with this play, culminating in an amplification of compulsory heterosexuality. Moreover, the fact that the audience burst into derisory laughter when Steven came out raises the question about the limits of the pedagogical imperatives driving this liberal program in the first place, with its authorization of reading practices governed by the therapeutic recuperation of the bystander as a transformative moral agent. By not alerting the teacher to address or anticipate this audience response, the program's analytic frameworks set limits for thinking about potential reading practices and student engagement with the text. The ultimate effect of this limitation is to erase full consideration of the potential impact of homophobia, compulsory heterosexuality, and regimes of normalization on the GLBTQ students in the audience, and hence represents another instance of reinforcing their invisible presence. In this sense, such a pedagogical regime and the reading practices it authorizes set limits to thinking about normalcy. What is highlighted, as a result of this experience, is the need to rethink reading practices beyond the heteronormative impulse to rely on pernicious binaries such as self/other, inside/outside as a basis for structuring the intelligibility for imagining sexual difference and addressing homophobia (see Britzman, 1998).

FURTHER IMPLICATIONS

This experience has highlighted for me the need, as Spurlin (2005) argues, "to widen the interrogatory lens through which [we] read and analyze sexual difference" in the English classroom (p. xxxi). This critical literacy agenda can be realized through acquiring a deeper understanding about the impulse to normalize at both the level of the production of the text and the context of its reception (see Blackburn, 2002; Sumara et al., 2006). It requires a conceptual framework that explicitly acknowledges the socially performative dimensions of reading practices and the accompanying realization that the production of normalcy may well be integral to such meaning-making processes (see Britzman, 1998). Thus, what is required are analytical frameworks that draw attention to the ways in which feelings and performative practices are symptoms of identifi-

catory engagement that either avow or disavow hegemonic forms of sociality. As I have illustrated, under the guise of skill building and raising awareness about violence and the need to address homophobia in schools, this special project initiated by an Ontario district school board did not address the question of reading practices and how they are linked to specific forms of identity work that incite compulsory heterosexuality. What was foreclosed was any possibility of examining what Britzman (1995) refers to as the *identity labor* that is invested in being recognized as *normal*. Thus, the play that I discuss in this chapter exemplifies Britzman's (1995) concern that

> arguments for inclusion produce the very exclusions they are meant to cure. ... But in thinking beyond the limits of curriculum, more is required than simply a plea to add marginalized voices to an already overpopulated site. Inclusion, or the belief that one discourse can make room for those it must exclude, can only produce, as Butler puts it, "that theoretical gesture of pathos in which exclusions are simply affirmed as sad necessities of signification." (p. 158).

In this sense, simply including a gay character is not sufficient to remedy homophobia or to incite attitudinal change. Such inclusion actually resulted in inciting forms of identity work and interpretive practices that erased the *other*, proliferating and intensifying further the very exclusion that the play was hoping to address in the first place—the absence of gay- or queer-identifying students in school communities. This play and the broader context of its production and performance then raise some very important questions about reading practices and the need to address the very structures of intelligibility that govern forms of identity labor symptomatic of the limits imposed by normalcy. The answer, then, is not simply to include more texts about GLBTQ subjects or texts which include a GLBTQ subject in an attempt to recover some authentic representation or humanization of sexual difference that merely confirms the presumption that gays and lesbians are just like us! As Britzman (1998) argues:

> Reading practices might well perform something interesting, and this has to do with the

production of social selves whose thinking about their own structures of intelligibility recognizes and refuses the confinement of sameness and the seduction of affirmation that has as its cost the expulsion of otherness. Reading practices might be educated to attend to the proliferation of one's own indentifcatory possibilities and to make allowance for the unruly terms of undecidablity and unknowability. (p. 85)

Kumashiro's (2000, 2002) work provides further justification for alternative reading practices that exceed both the desire to correct prior knowledge about gays and lesbians as deviant subjects and the impulse to assimilate them into the dominant heteronormative culture through invoking the realization that they too are human beings. For example, Kumashiro (2000) provides an analytic framework for anti-oppressive education, which cites the need to move beyond teaching *about* and *for the other* to embracing reading practices that are critical of *privileging* and *othering*. This analytic approach involves, in relation to addressing GLBTQ issues in the English classroom, promoting reading practices that support "a critique and transformation of hegemonic structures and ideologies" as a basis for examining and *unlearning* the processes by which subjects are normalized and heterosexualized or incited to relate to themselves as *normal* subjects (p. 36). The ways in which heterosexuality is privileged as normalcy and morality and how this positioning in turn relates to avowing and disavowing certain forms of sociality and modes of identification for limiting self-understanding become the focus in using texts to investigate investments in such systems of thought (see Hagen, 2004; Mitchell, 2005; Reese, 2005; Sears, 1997; Spurlin, 2005; Sumara & Davis, 1999; Wells, 2004).

Lorenz (2005) argues, for example, that it is the "job" of the English teacher to "empower students with the tools of resistant reading, that is, to help them achieve cultural literacy by recognizing, and perhaps sabotaging, the representational mirror of the surrounding heterosexual imperative" (p. 39). Kumashiro (2002), however, highlights the need to deploy an interpretive and analytic framework that attends to hierarchical power relations and how they are informed by classed, racialized, sexualized, and gendered forms of identification (see

also Kendall & Martino, 2006; Kumashiro, 2001; McCready, 2004). For example, he writes about a racialized form of heterosexism in Asian American communities, where queer sexuality is defined as a "white disease" (p. 52). In addition, he refers to a "queered racism" in gay communities where the feminized Asian American gay male is often perceived to be sexually undesirable, on one hand, or exotic and highly desirable, on the other.

Thus, Kumashiro (2000) advocates knowledge about "the way in which oppression is multiple, interconnected, and situated" (p. 41). In this sense, he advocates pedagogical practices that call into question the limits of a self-knowledge that is driven by the "impulse to normalize" and the "anxious repetition of sameness" (Britzman, 1998, p. 92). As Kumashiro points out, such an approach exceeds merely a recognition of the harmfulness of stereotypes and their citation; it rather, involves supplanting and investing them with new meanings or associations. This pedagogical intervention may involve examining narrative representations of transgression in terms of making available readings that refuse to cite deviancy as an explanatory basis for making sense of those individuals who defy dominant cultural norms for self-presentation. For example, students may be encouraged to resist reading the boy who transgresses normative masculinity as deviant. Rather, he is presented as brave in his willingness to embrace and imagine difference that is not built on a disavowal of culturally defined associations of the feminine (see Martino & Mellor, 2000).

Such reading practices, however, cannot be implemented outside a consideration for attending to the pedagogical conditions necessary for facilitating effective classroom learning (see Athanases, 1996; Sumara et al., 2006). In building on the work of Darling-Hammond (1997) and Newman & Associates (1996), Hayes, Mills, Christie, and Lingard (2006) outline what they consider to be the necessary conditions for supporting student learning and the principles of equity and social justice. They indicate that four dimensions—intellectual quality, connectedness, supportive classroom learning environment, and valuing difference—are key elements in any commitment to pedagogical reform in schools. Embracing this approach must entail developing tasks that support higher-order thinking and require students to manipulate information and ideas in ways that involve them in synthesizing, hypothesizing, and generalizing in developing their understanding of concepts. It also requires helping students to develop their understanding about the nature of knowledge as constructed and problematic through engaging in substantive conversation involving teacher–student and student–student interaction.

In addition, the curriculum needs to be connected to the everyday world beyond the classroom and to develop student knowledge and skills within the context of solving real-life issues and problems. A supportive classroom learning environment is also necessary and must involve providing appropriate scaffolds for students to take risks in their learning without feeling afraid to make mistakes. Moreover, educators need to ensure that the potential for amplifying the policing and surveillance of hierarchical peer group relations is minimized. Minimizing the potential for this sort of surveillance requires providing both academic and social support, where teachers have high expectations and are attuned to the production and valorization of normalcy within the context of the social dynamics of peer groups as a site for legitimating hegemonic social relations and identifications. Valuing difference pertains to integrating diverse cultural knowledges into the curriculum, as well as the need to acquire a literacy about the formation of cultural identity in terms of the intersecting influences of gender, sexuality, race, ethnicity, religion, and economic status (see Athanases, 1996).

These dimensions combined help to provide an understanding of the pedagogical conditions that are necessary for promoting the sort of reading practices which exceed the limits of normalcy outlined in this chapter. For example, expecting forum theater to teach important lessons about homophobia and the gender-based dimensions of violence, while failing to create the necessary pedagogical conditions that are informed by analytical frameworks about the politics of difference and the production of normalcy, is misguided. In fact, as I have argued, the absence of reflection on such pedagogical conditions can lead to reinforcing rather than transgressing notions of sexual identity

that rely on hierarchical binary classifications of the divided self. Such reading practices—those committed to troubling oppressive systems of thought and relations of violence—cannot be grounded in decontextualized notions of skill building that attempt to rehabilitate the bystander as a failed moral agent without considering the structures of feeling and relations of power driving particular forms of social identification. Moreover, to attempt to address such relations of power through awareness-raising strategies in the absence of employing analytic frameworks that attend to the performative and heteronormative dimensions of identity formation is to overlook the possibilities of inciting homophobia and supporting the impulse to normalize. Furthermore, importing such a performance into a context as a one-off production does not consider the labor required to build and nurture the necessary pedagogical conditions for ensuring that students feel safe when addressing sensitive issues such as bullying and sexual difference.

CONCLUSION

In this chapter I have highlighted the danger of embracing pedagogical conditions and promoting critical awareness outside the need to engage with analytic frameworks that attend to the politics of normalization and, hence, a knowledge about the processes of *othering* and *privileging*. As Blackburn and Buckley (2005) contend, the English language arts classroom is a productive site for examining the limits of normalcy through promoting reading practices that open up possibilities for interrogating heteronormativity. By targeting such systems of thought that are governed by regimes of compulsory heterosexuality or, as Lorenz (2005) terms it, "the heterosexual imperative" (p. 39), a space is created for thinking beyond what is tolerated as *normal* with the view to troubling representations of the self that cannot be thought outside of binary oppositional frameworks. It is imagining sexual difference outside such conceptual frameworks that needs to inform pedagogical interventions committed to promoting reading practices in the English language arts classroom which challenge heteronormativity.

REFERENCES

Athanases, S. (1996). A gay-themed lesson in an ethnic literature curriculum: Tenth graders responses to "Dear Anita." *Harvard Educational Review, 66,* 231–256.

Bersani, L. (1995). *Homos.* Cambridge, MA: Harvard University Press.

Blackburn, M. (2002). Disrupting the (hetero)normative: Exploring literacy performances and identity work with queer youth. *Journal of Adolescent and Adult Literacy, 46,* 312–324.

Blackburn, M., & Buckley, J. F. (2005). Teaching queer-inclusive English language arts. *Journal of Adolescent and Adult Literacy, 49,* 202–212.

Boal, A. (1985). *Theatre of the oppressed.* New York: Theatre Communications Group.

Britzman, D. (1995). Is there a queer pedagogy? Or stop thinking straight. *Educational Theory, 45,* 151–165.

Britzman, D. (1998). *Lost subjects, contested objects.* Albany, NY: SUNY Press.

Butler, J. (1993). *Bodies that matter: On the discursive limits of sex.* New York: Routledge.

Coulter, R. (2003). Boys doing good: Young men and gender equity. *Educational Review, 55,* 135–145.

Darling-Hammond, L. (1997). *The right to learn: A blueprint for creating schools that work.* San Francisco: Jossey-Bass.

Foucault, M. (1978). *The history of sexuality* (Vol. 1). (R. Hurley, Trans.). New York: Vintage.

Foucault, M. (1980). *Michel Foucault: Power/knowledge: Selected interviews and other writings 1972–1977* (C. Gordon, Ed. & Trans.). Sussex, UK: Harvester Wheatsheaf.

Fuss, D. (1991). *Inside/out: Lesbian theories, gay theories.* New York: Routledge.

Gamson, J. (2000). Sexualities, queer theory and qualitative research. In N. Denzin & Y. Lincoln (Eds.), *Handbook of qualitative research* (pp. 347–365). Thousand Oaks, CA: Sage.

Hagen, D. (2004). Growing up outside the gender construct. In J. McNinch & M. Cronin (Eds.), *I could not speak my heart: Education and social justice for gay and lesbian youth* (pp. 19–28). Regina: Canadian Plains Research Center, University of Regina.

Hayes, D., Mills, M., Christie, P., & Lingard, B. (2006). *Teachers and schooling making a difference.* Sydney: Allen & Unwin.

Hunter, I. (1984). The "text in itself": A symposium. *Southern Review, 17,* 129–134.

Huser, G. (2003). *Stiches.* Toronto: Douglas & MacIntyre.

Kendall, C., & Martino, W. (2006). *Gendered outcasts and sexual outlaws.* New York: Haworth Press.

Kumashiro, K. (2000). Toward a theory of anti-oppressive education. *Review of Educational Research, 70,* 25–53.

Kumashiro, K. (Ed.). (2001). *Troubling intersections of race and sexuality.* Lanham, MD: Rowman & Littlefield.

Kumashiro, K. (2002). *Troubling education: Queer activism and antioppressive pedagogy.* New York: Routledge.

Linne, R. (2000). Choosing alternatives to the well of loneliness. In S. Talburt & S. Steinberg (Eds.), *Thinking queer: Sexuality, culture, and education* (pp. 201–214). New York: Peter Lang.

Lorenz, J. (2005). Blame it on the weatherman: Popular culture and pedagogical praxis in the lesbian and gay studies classroom. In W. Spurlin (Ed.), *Lesbian and gay studies and the teaching of English: Positions, pedagogies and cultural politics* (pp. 36–53). Urbana, IL: National Council of Teachers of English.

Loutzenheiser, L., & MacIntosh, L. (2004). Citizenships, sexualities, and education. *Theory into Practice, 43,* 151–158.

Luke, A., & Freebody, P. (1997). The social practices of reading. In S. Muspratt, A. Luke, & P. Freebody (Eds.), *Constructing critical literacies: Teaching and learning textual practice* (pp. 185–226). Sydney: Allen & Unwin.

Martino, W. (1999). Cool boys, party animals, squids and poofters: Interrogating the dynamics and politics of adolescent masculinities in school. *British Journal of the Sociology of Education, 20,* 239–263.

Martino, W. (2001). "Dickheads, wuses, and faggots": Addressing issues of masculinity and homophobia in the critical literacy classroom. In B. Comber & A. Simpson (Eds.), *Negotiating critical literacies in classrooms* (pp. 171–187). Mahwah, NJ: Erlbaum.

Martino, W. (2006). Straight-acting masculinities: Normalization and gender hierarchies in gay men's lives. In C. Kendall & W. Martino (Eds.), *Gendered outcasts and sexual outlaws: Sexual oppression and gender hierarchies in queer men's lives* (pp. 35–60). New York: Haworth Press.

Martino, W., & Mellor, B. (2000). *Gendered fictions.* Urbana, IL: National Council of Teachers of English.

Martino, W., & Pallotta-Chiarolli, M. (2003). *So what's a boy? Addressing issues of masculinity and schooling.* New York: Open University Press.

McCready, L. (2004). Understanding the marginalization of gay and gender nonconforming black male students. *Theory into Practice, 43,* 136–143.

McNinch, J., & Cronin, M. (Eds.). (2004). *I could not speak my heart: Education and social justice for gay and lesbian youth.* Regina: Canadian Plains Research Center, University of Regina.

Mellor, B., & Patterson, A. (2001). Teaching readings? In B. Comber & A. Simpson (Eds.), *Negotiating critical literacies in classrooms* (pp. 119–134). Mahwah, NJ: Erlbaum.

Mitchell, C. (2005). "What's out there?" Gay and lesbian literature for children and young adults. In W. Spurlin (Ed.), *Lesbian and gay studies and the teaching of English: Positions, pedagogies and cultural politics* (pp. 112–130). Urbana, IL: National Council of Teachers of English.

Moje, E. B., & MuQaribu, M. (2003). Literacy and sexual identity. *Journal of Adolescent and Adult Literacy, 47,* 204–208.

Morris, M. (2005). Queer life and school culture: Troubling genders. *Multicultural Education, 12,* 8–13.

Morrison, B. (2006). School bullying and restorative justice: Toward a theoretical understanding of the role of respect, pride and shame. *Journal of Social Issues, 62,* 371.

Newman, F., & Associates. (1996). *Authentic achievement: Restructuring schools for intellectual quality.* San Francisco: Jossey-Bass.

Reese, J. (2005). Creating a place for lesbian and gay readings in secondary English classrooms. In W. Spurlin (Ed.), *Lesbian and gay studies and the teaching of English: Positions, pedagogies and cultural politics* (pp. 131–146). Urbana, IL: National Council of Teachers of English.

Rich, R. (1980). Compulsory heterosexuality and lesbian existence. *Signs: Journal of Women in Culture and Society, 5,* 631–660.

Rose, N. (1999). *Powers of freedom: Reframing political thought.* New York: Cambridge University Press.

Sears, J. T. (1997). Centering culture: Teaching for critical sexual literacy using sexual diversity wheel. *Journal of Moral Education, 26,* 273–283.

Spurlin, W. (Ed.). (2005). *Lesbian and gay studies and the teaching of English: Positions, pedagogies and cultural politics.* Urbana, IL: National Council of Teachers of English.

Sumara, D. (2001). Queer theory and literacy education. *English Quarterly, 33,* 1–5.

Sumara, D., & Davis, B. (1999). Interrupting heteronormativity: Toward a queer curriculum theory. *Curriculum Inquiry, 29,* 191–208.

Sumara, D., Davis, B., & Iftody, T. (2006). Normalizing literary responses in the teacher education classroom. *Changing English, 13,* 55–67.

Wells, K. (2004). Safe in my heart: Found poetry as narrative inquiry. In J. McNinch & M. Cronin (Eds.), *I could not speak my heart: Education and social justice for gay and lesbian youth* (pp. 7–18). Regina: Canadian Plains Research Center, University of Regina.

Yallop, J. G. (2004). Gay and out in secondary school: One youth's story. In J. McNinch & M. Cronin (Eds.), *I could not speak my heart: Education and social justice for gay and lesbian youth* (pp. 29–42). Regina: Canadian Plains Research Center, University of Regina.

Yescavage, K., & Alexander, J. (1997). The pedagogy of marking: Addressing sexual orientation in the classroom. *Feminist Teacher, 11,* 113–123.

CHAPTER 26

The Literacies of New Immigrant Youth

DANLING FU
JENNIFER M. GRAFF

During the 1990s, the U.S. population included more than 14 million new immigrants, with new immigrant youth constituting approximately 20% of school-age children. The first section of this chapter illuminates the strengths new immigrant youth possess, strengths often overshadowed by deficit models of thought: their bilingual and biliterate capacities, resilience, hardworking spirit, and passionate commitment to succeed in unfamiliar cultural landscapes. It also discusses how new immigrant youth, although very similar to mainstream adolescents, are often caught in the crossroads of physical, mental, emotional, and cultural transformations as they traverse periods of disconnection, uncertainty, hope, and resilience. Low self-esteem, social segregation, issues of conflict, and high dropout rates often temper these sociocultural and sociolinguistic strengths. A general awareness of new immigrant youth's complex psychological and social negotiations seems to be constantly eclipsed by their immediate need for English language instruction. The second section of this chapter highlights some of the institutional obstacles currently in place that limit the academic success of new immigrant youth. In addition to a lack of available cultural and educational resources, current education policy, which sets virtually unattainable time lines for new immigrant youth to pass mandated achievement and language proficiency tests, places them in precarious positions. This chapter concludes with an argument for culturally responsive professional development that begins with teacher preparation and administration programs and continues with ongoing inservice professional development. It is evident that a more concerted effort to reach and research new immigrant youth is requisite if educators wish to fulfill their democratic promise for social and educational equity.

School-age immigrant children, as one of the fastest-growing populations in the United States, possess a rich array of linguistic, religious, cultural, and educational identities. These children, most of whom are English language learners (ELLs), constitute approximately 20% of the U.S. school-age population (Suárez-Orozco & Suárez-Orozco, 2001; U.S. Census Bureau, 2003). By 2030 immigrant children should account for 40% of the school-age population. Their fortitude, dexterity, and passionate commitment to succeed in unfamiliar cultural landscapes are often belied by the oversimplified and reductive depictions of immigrant youth by mainstream media. Immigrant youth's lived experiences, determination, hardworking spirit, and funds of knowledge (Moll, 2001)—that is, their communities of interaction and in formation—are replete with insight into their multiple and transformative literacies. Yet these literacies remain largely untapped in educational research (Genesse, Lindholm-Leary, Saunders, & Christian, 2005). Therefore, it is imperative that educators become more knowledgeable about the literate lives of new immigrant youth. The lived experiences of these youth, often nuanced and multifaceted, can help educators transform their perceptions and approaches to providing new immigrant youth with the academic education they deserve.

ELLs, many of whom are immigrant children, are often considered by education researchers as members of one of four groups: (1) newly arrived children with adequate formal schooling, (2) newly arrived children with limited formal schooling, (3) children with simultaneous exposure to two languages, and (4) children who are long-term ELLs (Lenski, Ehlers-Zavala, Daniel, & Sun-Irminger, 2006). Likewise, social science researchers delineate U.S. immigrant youth as (1) children who were born to immigrant parents or arrived prior to elementary school (*second generation*), (2) children who arrive before secondary school and "straddle" their old and new lives (*1.5 generation*), and (3) teenagers who arrive and more readily identify with first-generation immigrant adults (*newcomers*). Given the accelerating presence of and limited scholarly discussion about newly arrived teenagers, we have concentrated on research including new immigrants in grades 6–12 for this chapter. This population encounters the most challenges due, in part, to their late entrance into the United States, their critical age in life, high academic demands, and limited time for graduation.

NEW IMMIGRANT YOUTH'S LITERACIES AND IDENTITIES

The educational portrait of immigrant learners has unwittingly omitted the broad spectrum of new adolescent immigrants. Genesse et al. (2005) confirm the predominant focus on the Latino/a population in their review of more than 200 publications of language and literacy research with immigrants. A surge of research concerning adolescent Latino/a immigrants is noteworthy and crucial, given the substantial presence of Latino/a immigrant students in schools and given that approximately 40% of Mexican-heritage teens, who are a part of the Latino/a population, leave school (Godina, 2004; Ruiz-de-Velasco & Fix, 2000). However, it is dangerous to extrapolate Latino/a immigrant needs to the needs of other immigrants. A concerted focus on other immigrant groups' literacy experiences and activities is needed for a more comprehensive understanding of their expertise and their needs (Genesse et al., 2005).

Contingency Factors of New Immigrant Youth's Literacies

When viewing adolescent newcomers in society, one is often unable to distinguish them from other U.S. adolescents. Like many teenagers in the United States, they play sports, join clubs, date, and talk about their future aspirations while negotiating the psychosocial angst commonly associated with maturation. In addition, some of them experience academic and social difficulties due to their differential educational and social experiences. They either struggle or feel constrained by their grade level or program placements in school. Yet they also feel as though they are competent global citizens. Fu's (2003) observations and interviews with new immigrant teens indicate their strong literary, historical, and geographical knowledge of their home country and their consistent search for contemporary sociopolitical news of both the United States and their home culture. They are committed to reading newspapers, watching televised news, and visiting local libraries in their spare time. These activities suggest their strong dedication to civic duty and their need for transnational understanding. Inter- and intrapersonal written communications via diaries, e-mails, and blogs serve as their expressive outlets, especially if they feel uncomfortable with their spoken English.

However, when one deepens the "gaze," one sees newcomers encountering particular circumstances that illustrate how different their needs and talents are from those of many teenagers who have grown up in the

United States. Newcomers often assume familial responsibilities and become "cultural and linguistic brokers" (Rubinstein-Ávila, 2006, p. 40). Approximately 80% of new immigrant youth live in families where parents have limited English proficiency (Fix & Passel, 2003). Thus, the youth translate and explain various legal documents to their families; search for employment, affordable housing, and social service programs; or work in their families' take-out restaurants or street kiosks late at night and on weekends. Rather than finding role models to help them navigate their social terrains (Gibson, 1997), they become role models and surrogate parents for other young children in the community and their families. They care for their young siblings or cousins, take them to see doctors, and attend parent conferences. Although these responsibilities help ensure familial and societal sustainability and reflect their linguistic, cultural, and social competencies, the consequences can include absences from school, low academic performance, and increased dropout rates (Perreira, Harris, & Lee, 2006).

In addition to the overwhelming responsibilities forced upon these youth, society's increasing immersion into the digital age compels them to become highly proficient individuals in media literacy, rather than just traditional print literacy. The computer, music, and dance are critical cultural resources for new immigrant teens as they forge new identities in the United States (Vargas, 2006). The textual richness in this country, whether physical, visual, or virtual, assists them in their search for independence. It provides them with a sense of being a "modern American." Like their U.S.-born peers, these youth consider computer-based gaming and chat room conversations to be both entertainment and extensions of their friendship circles (Fu, 2007). Popular culture acts as a critical determinant in their development as literate citizens. More research on popular culture and literacy identities for newcomers would illuminate their resilience and adroitness, thereby dispelling the current and questionable conceptions of them as illiterate individuals in need of saving.

Educators' approaches to literacy instruction play a pivotal role in these youth's successes. Most newcomers have little difficulty with comprehension in bilingual programs in which they are using their first language to study content areas; it is expressing their comprehension in English that proves difficult. Fu (2003) observed many newcomer youth in New York City actively questioning, engaging in group discussions, and conducting critically based presentations in class. Displays of the newcomers' work in their native languages adorned classroom walls and hallways, honoring their competency as writers and thinkers. In addition, the newcomers outperformed their peers in both academics and school attendance. Upon entrance into U.S. society, although mired in psychosocial upheaval due to unfamiliar circumstances, cultural differences, and linguistic barriers, newcomers are often successful and surpass the experiences of second- or even third-generation immigrant children (Rumbaut, 1994; Suárez-Orozco, 1991; Wilkinson, Gonzalez, & Rumbaut, 1993).

Identity Formation: Living at the Crossroads

Growing up in the United States can be a difficult and confusing process for immigrant youth. Upon arriving in the United States, new immigrant youth begin their lives situated between two worlds. They are frequently caught between the pressures to assimilate into American society and pressures to preserve their own cultural origins. This process becomes complicated when these youth constantly have to negotiate and transform their identities through their experiences in school, at home, and among their peers.

At the critical stage of establishing their social identities, immigrant youth are struggling to fit into frameworks espoused by their U.S.-born peers, television, and other forms of mass media. These young people see and compare themselves with those around them, with those reference groups directly affecting their experiences. Comparative studies of first-generation and second-generation immigrants (Rumbaut, 1994; Suárez-Orozco, 1991) found that first-generation immigrant youth tend to hold onto their family traditions and demonstrate a particular outlook of "immigrant ethics." They stress working hard, getting an education, and striving for upward social mobility. Rather than focusing on the negative aspects of American social structures, they, like their parents, tend to persevere because they see greater opportunities in the United States in comparison to their homelands.

In contrast, second-generation immigrants may take fragmented paths to identity formation and resolution because of differences in gender, class, social context, and geographic settlements. Rumbaut (1994) and Zhou (1997) report that children of well-educated and/or wealthy immigrant parents, regardless of their ethnicity, tend to make a relatively smooth transition into American mainstream society. Yet this population is a fraction of the overall immigrant population in the United States. Many individuals, arriving as refugees or seeking economic sustenance, settle in inner-city neighborhoods and have a tendency to assimilate into ghettoized youth subcultures in terms of dialects, dress, music, and attitudes. This absorption of the behaviors and ideas of marginalized American groups is further facilitated by an intense dislike and distrust of a system that keeps them and their parents from realizing the "American dream." Their adaptation to this environment and their identity formation based on U.S. social categories may either result in downward mobility or trap them at the bottom of society.

Immigrant youth, especially Mexican American high school students, are significantly affected by television, adolescent–adult interactions, and cultural mores. When comparing the self-reported survey data of 5,000 Mexican and Mexican American high school students in five similar cities across the U.S.–Mexican border, Pumariega, Swanson, Holzer, Linskey, and Wuintero-Salinas (1992) found that adolescents in Mexico had lower incidences of substance use and abuse than that of their peers in the United States. Increased solitude, TV viewing, and peer–peer interactions, coupled with fewer adult and adult mentor interactions, greatly contributed to high levels of substance use and abuse by Mexicans living in the United States. Further, cultural clashes concerning respect and culturally defined gender roles contributed to substance abuse owing to increased levels of confusion of appropriate

behaviors. The downward spiral of poverty, lack of role models, and limited economic opportunities are exacerbated by the inferior education offered at many overcrowded urban schools (Orfield & Yun, 1999).

Conflicting gender roles also seem instrumental in new immigrant youth's development in the United States. Suárez-Orozco and Suárez-Orozco (2001) found that some immigrant Latina women's entrance into the workforce had an impact on traditional child-rearing practices and gender roles in the home. These changes resulted in their husbands' increased feelings of emasculation as well as diminished parent–child interactions and familial support of the immigrant youth. For some Latino/a youth, as exhibited in Suárez-Orozco and Todorova's (2003) case study, the "street" provided some adolescent males ample opportunities to construct an identity of a competent, masculine, and empowered leader, as opposed to the frustrated, incompetent individual encased by four scholastic walls. It was on the streets that they appeared adjusted, yet felt as if any day they could unravel.

Adaptation in the United States may be largely dependent on how immigrant youth fit into their own ethnic communities and how these communities fit into the larger society. Zhou and Bankston's (1994) study of Vietnamese adolescents' social relationships within their ethnic community in a poor, urban area of New Orleans revealed that these Vietnamese youth were guided to live, behave, and make decisions on the basis of adults' ethnic values. Being a part of a Vietnamese network resulted in upward mobility and academic success more than becoming "Americanized" into a local disadvantaged native-born youth subculture. This study suggests that young immigrants may benefit from cultivating their ethnic ties in their ethnic communities, thereby breaking the "cycle of disadvantage" and fostering "upward mobility" (Zhou, 1997, p. 91). In alignment with Zhou's findings, Gibson (1997) argues that the best course for immigrant youth appears to be one that "encourages them to remain securely anchored in their ethnic communities while pursuing a strategy of paced, selected acculturation" into the U.S. society (p. 440).

Indeed, immigrant youth are rapidly becoming acculturated through public media and popular culture; however, this "Americanization" is not unilateral. It is often referred to as incremental hybridization (Violand-Sánchez & Hainer-Violand, 2006). Immigrant youth engage in multilayered interactions, or "Remix-tino" (Hernandez, cited in Violand-Sánchez & Hainer-Violand, 2006, p. 37). They compose identities by adopting and discarding a mixture of variables from the United States and their homeland. This hybridization, when reframed to exclude a deficit model of thinking, explicates the fortitude and finesse new immigrant youth possess. Further investigation is warranted in order to shift and broaden pedagogical perceptions of new immigrant youth.

Becoming Bilingual and Biliterate

As soon as new immigrant youth arrive in the United States, they begin living in a dual-language environment. As their stay in the United States lengthens, codeswitching, or speaking one language mixed with foreign words or phrases, such as integrating the English term "yard sale" when speaking in Chinese, becomes "a natural consequence of a situation of intense daily contact" (Callahan, 2004, p. 121). For new immigrant students, codeswitching (linguistic borrowing) may be a strategy for communicative convenience. For proficient bilingual speakers, this can be a deliberate choice in order to add a certain cultural flavor to the communication or to make connections with audiences who share the speaker's cultural roots. Regardless of the purpose, this practice not only reflects an individual's understanding of each language but also provides insight concerning the importance of word choice and the distinct voice of a particular culture. When new immigrant youth begin to codeswitch, they indicate the onset of a hybridization identity process mediated by language (Zentella, 2002).

Viewing codeswitching as an important linguistic resource, Berzins and Lopez (2001) encouraged their new immigrant students to codeswitch in class discussion and discovered that allowing their students to codeswitch fostered greater participation. Codeswitching enabled immigrant youth to practice their emerging second language in a learning community, thus constructing new meanings and communicating their developing knowledge. Their students indicated pleasure in being acknowledged and complimented on their efforts and abilities. The use of codeswitching practices is also a necessary stage in their new immigrant students' development of English language skills and their development as bilingual writers (Fu, 2003). In their English as a Second Language (ESL) and bilingual classrooms, students were encouraged to codeswitch because it broke their willful silence in class, facilitated more expressive writing, and helped accelerate their literacy development. Rather than seeing codeswitching as a deficit, the teachers viewed it as a beneficial linguistic resource, and the students, realizing this, excelled academically.

Codeswitching can also be used for informal assessment as it indicates what teachers need to teach their students and what the students have already mastered. Fu (2003) found that 11- to 13-year-old new Chinese immigrants un-self-consciously codeswitched in oral and written communication as soon as they acquired some English vocabulary. They found it easy to use high-frequency English words and concepts that were often difficult to translate into Chinese, such as *have a party, uncle,* or *aunt*. Codeswitching, commonly conceptualized as a marker of limited English proficiency, actually signifies linguistic savvy and sophistication as young people become bilingual and biliterate (Fu & Matoush, 2006).

Social science research currently views immigrants as an asset to the United States. The homeland culture, ethnic language, and immigrant ethics that the newcomers bring with them are valuable resources that enrich and empower American society. Similarly, advocates of multiculturalism and bilingualism who support and encourage the preservation of immigrant native languages and cultures have drawn great attention from education researchers in the past two decades. A growing body of empirical evidence indicates that cognitive abilities and scholastic achievement are positively associated with bilingualism. Fernandez and Nielsen (1986) provided evidence from national longitudinal data that proficiency in both English and parental native languages was positively related to Latino/a and European American high school students' academic achievement.

Matute-Bianchi's (1986) ethnographic study of Mexican American children determined that advanced bilingual skills were related to a strong Mexican identity and that young fully bilingual Mexican Americans tended to perform better in school than those who lacked proficient bilingual skills. She concluded that proficiency in their native languages allowed young people to gain greater access to the emotional and normative supports of the ethnic group. Sung (1987) found that bilingual Chinese immigrant students in New York City's Chinatown had higher student retention rates, higher graduation rates, and higher self-esteem than their native-born peers.

Other researchers have found that language-maintenance bilingual programs, as opposed to transitional bilingual programs, helped students learn the language of the dominant society effectively (Cazden & Snow, 1990). Tse (2001) posited that bilingual students of Latino/a heritage were better readers in English and had higher academic aspirations than those Latino/as who were monolingual in either English or Spanish. Tse's (2001) study indicates that those who develop their heritage language and know English will do better in school than those who leave the heritage language behind. Thus, bilingual individuals have an advantage because they have more than one way of thinking about a given concept, making them more "divergent" thinkers and more effective problem solvers.

Bilingual youth are at the forefront of global competency but are currently undervalued in the United States. Rather than viewing their bilingual and biliterate capabilities as versatile strengths, mainstream U.S. society focuses on their "imperfect" or "nonstandard English." This perspective propels "English-only" initiatives and the dissolution of bilingual services in many U.S. states, which has minimized newcomers' opportunities for educational success, economic advancement, and self-worth as "Americans." It has also reduced lines of communication with immigrants' immediate or extended families, neighbors, and cultural affiliates. Such counterproductive measures affect most new immigrants personally and academically. They place them at a distinct linguistic and cultural disadvantage by determining the nature of the educational programs that serve their children in American schools across the nation (Fu & Matoush, 2006).

Socioeconomic status also influences students' bilingual status, as the majority of immigrant children are members of low-income families. Most have little choice but to adopt English as their preferred language if they hope to flourish in this country. Although some might herald this "choice," Tse (2001) points out that these students are not afforded additional opportunities to further develop their native language skills beyond those required by domestic situations, so they must shift to monolingual English within the first three generations. This loss of native language abilities reduces one's capacity to entertain multiple perspectives and signifies a potential loss of culture. The current demand for new immigrant students to pass the same standardized tests as their native-English-speaking peers augments the pressure to become monolingual. Some have argued that these losses are simply the price immigrant families must pay for choosing to live in the United States. However, many believe this high price is not paid by immigrants alone. The negative consequences of language loss and the benefits of preserving heritage language have far-reaching implications for the individual and larger U.S. society alike (Tse, 2001).

SCHOOL LITERACIES: SENSES OF DISLOCATION

Social research on new immigrant youth tends to emphasize the difficulties and sacrifices these individuals make after arriving in the United States. In discussing this research, we acknowledge the risk of perpetuating a deficit model of thinking; however, we recognize the need to complement newcomers' resilience with the hardships many encounter. This balance is necessary to better understand new immigrant youth's uniqueness and meaning-making processes.

Although many immigrant youth are members of Latin American or Asian families (Landale & Oropresa, 1995), their familial structures are quite diverse. Some newcomers are members of formally educated and economically prospering families, and others are members of families with less experience of academic literacy situated in economically stagnant employment. Some arrive with the intention of staying permanently, whereas others embody a transnational approach, arriving and departing multiple times owing to their guardians' employment status. Regardless of their situations, all of these youth are of "exile status" (Grinberg & Grinberg, 1989). They were omitted from the decision to move to the United States, were uprooted from their peer and cultural communities, and may have lacked opportunities to say good-bye to friends and family, which resulted in feelings of fear, chaos, and dislocation (Fu, 2003).

These feelings of dislocation and discrimination reverberate throughout the new immigrant youth's experiences before they even enter school. The stressors encountered as they build new lives include: familial and community separation, discrimination by other immigrant ethnic communities and American minority groups, and their immersion into a culturally and linguistically disorienting environment with little social support (Lucas, 1997; Rothe, 2004; Zhou & Bankston, 1994). When arriving in the United States, new immigrant youth and their families often leave behind everything familiar and enter foreign terrain both inside and outside their new homes, reuniting with other members of their families only after many years of separation. According to the Harvard Graduate School of Education's longitudinal study of 400 new immigrant youth between the ages of 9 and14, more than 85% of youth from China, Central America, the Dominican Republic, Haiti, and Mexico were separated from either one or both of their parents for a period ranging from 6 months to more than 10 years (Suárez-Orozco & Todorova, 2003). Upon reuniting with their parents, they had to minimize or dissolve their relationships with their caretakers and encounter new familial structures that often involved stepparents and unknown siblings or relatives. These youth's relocation resulted in feelings of loss, confusion, and resistance, which were exacerbated by their feelings of loneliness due to their loss of emotional connection to or physical interactions with one or both of their parents.

Yet within these tumultuous times, immigrant youth have bonded through shared linguistic and cultural/community identities (Tienda & Mitchell, 2006). They are able to develop their identities as they attempt to balance their positions within their cultural communities and the U.S. dominant culture, and are sometimes able to succeed academically. These newly created bicultural identities are positively associated with students' growth as academic, cognitive, and linguistically adept individuals (Cummins, 2000).

Newcomers' School-Based English Language Learning

Almost all new immigrant youth are placed in separate ESL or bilingual programs at school for an extended period of time. Although research has indicated the academic benefits of bilingual and ESL programs, the personal and social ramifications of such experiences for newcomers have received limited press. Research on newcomer ELLs (Cummins, 2003; Genesse et al., 2005) reveals their confusion about new vocabulary and instructional management styles that conflict with their native country's instructional styles. Oral communication is named by newcomers as the most difficult mode of participation. Extremely self-conscious because of their position as adolescent immigrants, these teens are afraid of being laughed at and afraid to draw any attention to their inability to speak in an age-appropriate way (Fu, 1995). These feelings might be attributed to most adolescents, regardless of their citizenship and linguistic competency. However, the situation appears more tenuous for newcomers, in part, because of the disparity between their knowledge and their ability to express it, especially from the perspective of their teachers. Their "resistant" behaviors, such as pretending not to care about learning or refusing to participate in any activities that require presentations in English, overshadow their strong desire to learn English. Many wish they could learn more efficiently and be able to speak, read, and write like their English proficient peers, yet their impatience and low self-esteem hinder their progress (Fu, 1995).

In addition, although most newcomers enjoy and believe they benefit greatly from studying in ESL and bilingual programs, they lament the social stigma of participating in such programs (McKay & Wong, 1996). Their peers consider them unintelligent because ESL and bilingual programs are "remedial programs." This diminished status among their peers fuels their desire to transfer to "mainstream" classrooms for social acceptance, sometimes before they are ready, resulting in a cycle of further humiliation, diminished self-efficacy, and low self-esteem.

These school-based tensions of academic dedication and frustration evaporate once they leave school. Outside their academic environments, newcomer youth are perceived as highly competent and literate individuals. The street, where they are viewed as competent leaders in their communities, provides them with a sense of comfort and empowerment (Suárez-Orozco & Todorova, 2003). Thus, continuing to probe how to effectively practice out-of-school literacy in the development of school-based literacy competencies for new immigrant youth might help alleviate feelings of frustration by both newcomers and educators.

Educational Determinants for Academic Achievement or Departure

Most new immigrant youth and their families express a strong desire to achieve in school (Fu, 1995, 2003). Formal education in the United States seems sometimes more accessible, economical, and rigorous than in their native country's schools (Gibson, 1997). In addition, learning English and graduating from high school are often equated with ensuring the realization of the American dream. New immigrant youth tend to fare better than their native-born peers in terms of attendance, school aspirations, and assignments, which results in rapid academic improvement (Wilkinson et al., 1993). However, almost one-quarter of new immigrant youth are dropping out, despite their aspirations (Fry, 2005). Even "academically successful" immigrant groups have increasing numbers of dropouts or incarcerated individuals. In New York City, 11.1% of Asian immigrant youth, often portrayed as the "model minority," have not completed high school (New York City Board of Education, 2000), and the number of felons among Asian immigrant youth has increased by 38% between 1993 and 1996

(Coalition for Asian American Children and Families, 1999). Many factors contribute to the ever-increasing rate of dropouts among immigrant teens, including poverty, absentee parents because of extended work hours, teachers' and guidance counselors' negative attitudes, low expectations, and preconceived notions of immigrant students (Godina, 2004; Lew, 2003).

School placement is also a determinant of new immigrant youth's scholastic success. Immigrant adolescents receive ESL or bilingual instruction less often than elementary school children, despite the ever increasing number of immigrant adolescents attending secondary school (Van Hook & Fix, 2000). In addition, more than half of the 3.9 million ELL students attend schools with more than 30% ELL enrollment, and in six major immigration states, California, New York, Texas, Florida, Illinois, and New Jersey, 60% of ELL students attend schools where more than 30% are designated ELL (Fix & Passell, 2003). Although a strong ethnic identity is positively correlated with literacy and academic success (Matute-Bianchi, 1986; Obgu, 1991; Zhou & Bankston, 1994), linguistic and cultural segregation diminishes the potential for academic success among immigrant youth because they are denied easy access to practicing and learning English or familiarizing themselves with mainstream culture. Because new immigrants often reside in communities with similar sociolinguistic characteristics, schools may be the primary venues to engage in consistent English language and cultural learning. Therefore, realization of limited opportunity for success may result in increased resistance toward mainstream society by culturally segregated youth (Gibson, 1991; Ogbu, 1991).

Another factor to consider is the previous school experiences of new immigrants. Approximately 32% of the secondary school ELL immigrant youth have missed 2 or more years of formal education since they were 6 years old, and others possess limited proficiency in their native language and English (Ruiz-de-Velasco & Fix, 2000). Moreover, they often come from cultures whose definitions of youth and school-age children differ from those of the United States. Considering that the school performance of first-generation immigrant students is influenced by their age upon arrival, length of residence, previous school experience, and school support (Gibson, 1991; Macias, 1990), it seems educationally counterproductive to have an abbreviated understanding of and to provide minimal resources for secondary school immigrants, which force them to remain within their own linguistic and cultural communities in school. While educators actively seek out diverse instructional methods, if U.S. society is truly committed to this fast-growing population, equal dedication is required to understand and capitalize on the multifarious cultural and linguistic dynamics of new immigrant youth.

THE CHALLENGES AND SUCCESSES OF EDUCATING NEW IMMIGRANT YOUTH

Literacy Program Placements and Academic Expectations

Secondary schools in the United States are severely underequipped to assist immigrant youth in middle and high schools (Rubenstein-Ávila, 2006; Ruiz-de-Velasco & Fix, 2000). Schools lack resources, teacher preparation, curriculum requirements, and a structure that can help ensure that new immigrant youth remain in school and receive quality education. A 2002 National Public Radio report on Latino/a students stated, "The window of opportunity for academic success begins to close for most students by the time they leave middle school" (Rubinstein-Ávila, 2006, p. 40). This situation can be extended to all immigrant students. School placement, adequate time for learning, and teachers' pedagogical and cultural preparation can help widen the windows of opportunity for new immigrant youth.

Many new immigrant youth are placed in U.S. schools according to their age, without consideration of their previous school experiences or levels of literacy. This determinant typically places many in grades that are 2–3 years above their literacy capabilities, intensifying the academic struggle of those already experiencing pressure outside the classroom. ESL services in these schools are also heavily dependent on resource availability. Some schools provide self-contained ESL classes where ELLs learn English language skills integrated with the content-area subjects. Others are able to provide ELLs with pull-out

ESL service for only 1 or 2 hours a day, with the rest of the day spent in content-area classes designed for fluent speakers of English, with teachers who lack expertise in instructing ELLs. In fact, only 2.5% of teachers nationwide have received appropriate professional development for instructing ELLs (Ruiz-de-Velasco & Fix, 2000).

New immigrant youth not only have to develop their functional and academic English proficiency, they also need to obtain the content knowledge required by the secondary curriculum. It typically takes ELLs 2–3 years to develop communicative language proficiency, and 5–7 years or longer to develop academic (cognitive) language proficiency (Cummins, 2000; Thomas & Collier, 2002). Immigrant youth who are ELLs simultaneously have to develop communicative and academic English while studying content subjects. Despite the variance in time in ESL classes, immigrant youth, regardless of their level of English proficiency, have virtually the same number of semesters to meet their graduation requirements and pass mandated achievement and proficiency tests, in accordance with current education legislation. This policy is unequivocally unfair and demoralizing and serves as a catalyst for high school immigrants to drop out. New immigrant youth, despite their motivations and aspirations, find themselves stuck in a Catch-22. They need to learn English in order to succeed in and out of school, yet limited school instruction and an unattainable time line for proficiency make success virtually impossible.

Expert Personnel

Personnel shortages for ESL and bilingual classrooms are ongoing (Schneider, Martinez, & Owens, 2006). The ESL and bilingual programs of schools are dependent on enrollment, with ESL teachers responsible for 30–80 students of various abilities and grade levels, or ESL teachers who serve multiple schools in a district, visiting each school only once a month (Li & Zhang, 2004). Each of the aforementioned scenarios contributes to sporadic, rushed, and potentially incongruent instruction. While focusing on functional English skills and academic vocabulary, ESL teachers at the secondary level often serve as counselors, coordinators, and translators between school administrators, regular classroom teachers, and parents. Cancellation of ESL instruction happens frequently, resulting in higher probabilities of extended ELL classifications of 6 years or more (Ruiz-de-Velasco & Fix, 2000). The shortage of bilingual teachers is even more severe. Many schools find it difficult to fill their positions with qualified bilingual teachers who have content knowledge, understand effective teaching methodology, and are proficient in two languages (Ruiz-de-Velasco & Fix, 2000). Bilingual teachers are often hired solely because they know two languages. Thus, they must learn both content material and sound pedagogical practices while teaching, which minimizes their effectiveness in the classroom.

Minimal support, resource shortages, and the linguistic diversity of school staffs result in overcrowded classes with limited effective instruction and individual assistance. When Fu (2007) asked new immigrant teens how much of their textbooks they understood, they indicated 30% at most. Their teachers claimed that some could barely understand 10%; however, they were unaware of and unable to find any supplementary material that their ELLs could read and understand, thus leaving everyone frustrated. The inflexible, fragmented, and specialized nature of 50-minute secondary school classes further complicated the teachers' desires to meet the educational needs of immigrant youth, especially those with limited English proficiency and low native language literacy. Eventually the teachers admitted ignoring the problems as their new immigrant students increasingly withdrew, acted out, or failed to come to class. When the newcomers realized they had no chance of graduating, they said they would just drop out of school.

Bilingual programs also have limited language options. Many are available only for Spanish- or Chinese-speaking students. Therefore, new immigrant youth from geographical areas such as Southeast Asia, the Middle East, or Africa are either placed in Spanish-speaking or Chinese-speaking bilingual classes or are simply mainstreamed in the regular classes. Numerous universities, such as the University of California at Los Angeles (UCLA), the University of Wisconsin-Madison, and the University of Maryland have garnered federal grants to create programs and re-

sources to help K–12 bilingual and foreign language teachers learn contemporary content and pedagogical skills for teaching non-European languages such as Urdu, Swahili, or Arabic, or teaching English to speakers of these languages. However, their programs are still under development.

Much research has documented that bilingual education is necessary, especially at the secondary level, to help new immigrant ELLs build content knowledge while developing their English skills (Cummins, 1986, 2000; Freeman & Freeman, 1998). However, without qualified bilingual teachers and sufficient monetary and personnel resources, researchers' findings cannot translate into academic success. Both policymakers and some immigrant parents choose to eliminate bilingual education in many states, especially in California and Arizona, because they do not view it, as it exists in the school system, as a viable option (see Martínez-Roldán & Fránquiz, Chapter 21, this volume).

Culturally Responsive Professional Development

Educators have recognized the need for culturally responsive pedagogy and linguistic training for secondary school teachers, yet it is far from being actualized. New immigrants of Mexican heritage have said that although their motivation to succeed remained high, they felt that the school had much lower standards for them (Giacchino-Baker, 1997). Their motivation continued to decline because of a lack of successful language experiences and teachers' stereotypical assumptions. They felt "locked" into particular classes, experienced disconnected personal and academic lives, and experienced many comprehension problems. Although well intentioned, teachers correcting their work for them and minimizing their opportunities for collaborative learning elicited frustration from these teens. They were placed in classes where critical thought was unnecessary, and they often felt isolated (Giacchino-Baker, 1997). Other newcomers have indicated that they desire relationships with teachers that transcend classroom walls and offer social and academic "refuges" for them (Lucas, 1997, p. 109). They feel that these relationships with their teachers would minimize stereotypical thought and increase their opportunities to succeed.

Students who feel they are members of the school community and perceive their teachers as secure sources for information fare better academically (Finn, 1989). However, teachers' stereotypes and negative attitudes toward minority students diminish newcomers' capacity for learning (Valenzuela, 1999). When minority students are aware of their teachers' negative stereotypes, they become defensive and underperform (Martinez, 2003), to the extent of feeling happier and more competent if they are not with their teachers (Csikszentmihalyi & Schneider, 2000). Immigrant youth's testimonies regarding teacher perceptions, actions, and daily scholastic activities remind us that teachers' unconscious behaviors, although seemingly inconsequential and sometimes well intentioned, are potentially debilitating for new immigrants.

Professional development in second language acquisition is also a targeted area for improvement. Available ESL training tends to relay the misconception that English language learning occurs merely via exposure and interactions or that there is a uniform rate of learning for all ELLs (Harper & de Jong, 2004). Teachers, especially content-area teachers, are placed in a precarious situation. They are ill prepared to help new immigrant ELLs develop English proficiency and build content knowledge, yet are given an extremely short time to cover the grade curriculum for tests and graduation. This tremendous pressure typically results in resignation about the immigrant ELLs' learning outcomes and performances. The teachers' obligations to mandates and their responsibilities to the individual students clash, with mandates unfortunately becoming the priority at the cost of the youth.

Other instructional gaps exist in the education of new immigrants and ELLs at the secondary level. Content-area teachers are rarely educated to teach language skills (for functional or academic literacy), and the ESL teachers are not specialized in content instruction. There is also an erroneous assumption of language as a homogenous entity. Godina's (2004) study of Mexican newcomers revealed how the well-intentioned placement of newcomers in a Castilian Spanish class curtailed the newcomers' literacy acquisition and elevated their levels of frustration because of the distinct differences between Castilian and Mexican Spanish. Leading literacy researchers such as Alvermann, Phelps, and Ridgeway (2002) and Nieto (2002) recommend that literacy instruction should be framed within culturally responsive contexts and that educators should seek to tap into the students' "funds of knowledge" (Moll, Amanti, Neff, & Gonzalez, 1992). Further, teachers need to remember that "tests in English are also tests of English" (Lenski et al., 2006, p. 29). Alternative assessments that involve computer technology and nonthreatening participatory activities may provide additional opportunities for newcomer youth to think critically and use technology, something to which many immigrants may not have consistent access.

Blaming teachers for these educational shortcomings erroneously simplifies a complex dilemma and is an injustice to educators' convictions and aptitudes for teaching. Many teacher education programs in the United States are just beginning to infuse ESL components at every level and subject area, due to teacher requests and demonstrated need. However, these courses fall short of matching the needs of such a rapidly growing and extremely diverse population. Moreover, ongoing political disputes involving immigrants, languages, and education have affected education policy. Legislated standardized tests for all students have not only left many new immigrant youth behind, but forced them out of school. Many policymakers operating under a "factory production" mentality demand immediate results from their "investments," whereas many educators and education researchers prefer a process-oriented model that includes long-term benefits for human growth and societal improvement. Because of this fundamental philosophical difference, an educational impasse, with underlying tensions vacillating between product and process, can occur. It is hoped that cutting-edge research involving new immigrant youth will help end the impasse and incite change.

Model Programs

There have been successful programs for new immigrants, such as at the Liberty High School Academy and the Manhattan International High School in New York City.

These transitional schools help hundreds of newcomers from more than 40 countries adjust to life in the United States. Counselors are available to help with coping processes, dual-literacy programs help students become biliterate while learning valuable content knowledge, and teachers arrange field trips to local health clinics for medical and dental checkups. In addition, Dr. Sun Yat Sen Middle School in New York City's Chinatown redesigned the curricula in its ESL and bilingual programs to include integrated and interdisciplinary classes to meet the needs of its newcomer population, almost half the student body. Within 3 years the school changed from being one of the worst "gangster" schools with the lowest performance rate in the city to one of the best city middle schools (Fu, 2003). These scholastic models identify and address the distinct needs of newcomer youth. They allow them to become immersed in U.S. life and help ensure their success in their new home while retaining their own culture (Merchant, 1999; Schnaur, 1999).

As exemplified by the aforementioned schools, new immigrant youth need reliable support beyond their families and ethnic communities in order to make smoother transitions within U.S. culture and become engaged citizens. These youth and our society expect U.S. schools to prepare them linguistically, culturally, socially, and academically to succeed. For many newcomers, school is the first and probably the only place where they have contact with the mainstream culture, English language, and formal education. They and their families all know education is the key to realizing the American dream. As people who had few chances in their own homelands, they trust the U.S. education system to give them and their children hope and skills to become like the majority of Americans and climb the ladder of success. This hope makes their current hardship tolerable and makes them feel that any sacrifice they have made is worthy. The consequences of U.S. secondary schools failing to meet the needs of these youth are far-reaching (Perreira et al., 2006; Portes & Stepick, 1993). If the new immigrant youth continue to straddle the border, our nation will have more youth and families on welfare and this country will be more socially, economically, and racially segregated.

Forging Ahead

Despite the increasing number of new immigrant youth entering the United States and its schools, we know alarmingly little about them and their literacy practices. What we do know indicates that their linguistic and cultural expertise is not often honored or used within the current education community. New immigrant youth are marginalized in mainstream society as individuals of low socioeconomic status, initially unaware of unspoken cultural rules and behaviors. They are also marginalized as ELLs, whose English proficiency is erroneously considered to be a marker of their intellect in school. Their evolving capabilities as bilingual and biliterate persons, attributes actively solicited in the corporate world, are quashed in many educational settings owing to fear, ignorance, and Eurocentric nationalism.

Despite their socioeconomic, sociocultural, and educational obstacles, new immigrant youth exhibit high levels of multiliteracy within their ethnic communities. Outside their communities they strive to quickly determine how to successfully "fit in," juggle two cultures, and seek prosperity. Their journeys require the guidance of schools and teachers. However, available institutional resources such as basic teacher preparation, quality ESL and bilingual teacher programs, psychologists and other health care workers, and physical resources such as texts suitable for ELLs are minimal at best. Compounding the scarcity of resources are the secondary schools' departmentalized organizations, which are incompatible with newcomers' needs (Schneider et al., 2006). When polled about what they needed, new immigrants cited classes longer than 50 minutes, information on careers, future training opportunities, sex health information, drug information, knowledge of how to improve family relationships, and strategies for how to stay in school and get ahead (Wilkinson et al., 1993). These needs are often not met in schools, and the informal settings quickly become the role model and mentor for many newcomers. Choosing the streets, some newcomers may become immersed in static and dangerous lifestyles.

A more concentrated effort to reach and research new immigrant youth is requisite if our nation is to honor its democratic ideals.

Researchers should make it a priority to include new immigrant youth in their studies and emphasize the need to continually reimagine what literacies encompass and recontextualize instructional practice in alignment with those literacies. New immigrants are a visible and valuable presence in schools and society, and their presence in all its richness should be mirrored in education research. New immigrant youth are caught in the crossroads of physical, mental, emotional, and cultural transformations as they traverse periods of disconnection, uncertainty, hope, and resilience beyond what is typically experienced by mainstream adolescents. They begin these journeys with unwavering trust and dedication and can become successful global citizens with the necessary support and understanding. All we need to do is meet them halfway.

REFERENCES

Alvermann, D., Phelps, S., & Ridgeway, V. (Eds.). (2002). *Content reading and literacy: Succeeding in today's diverse classrooms*. Boston: Allyn & Bacon.

Berzins, M., & Lopez, A. (2001). Starting off right: Planting the seeds for biliteracy. In M. Reyes & J. Halcon (Eds.), *The best for our children: Critical perspectives on literacy for Latino/a students* (pp. 81–95). New York: Teachers College Press.

Callahan, R. (2004). Tracking and high school English learners: Limiting opportunity to learn. *American Education Research Journal, 42,* 305–328.

Cazden, C., & Snow, C. E. (1990). Preface: English plus: Issues in bilingual education. *Annals of the American Academy of Political and Social Science, 508,* 9–11.

Coalition for Asian American Children and Families. (1999). *Half full or half empty? Health care, child care, and youth programs for Asian American children in New York City*. New York: Author.

Csikszentmihalyi, M., & Schneider, R. (2000). *Becoming adult: How teenagers prepare for the world of work*. New York: Basic Books.

Cummins, J. (1986). Empowering minority students: A framework for intervention. *Harvard Educational Review, 56,* 18–36.

Cummins, J. (2000). Academic language learning, transformative pedagogy, and information technology: Towards a critical balance. *TESOL Quarterly, 34,* 537–547.

Cummins, J. (2003). Reading and the bilingual student: Fact and friction. In G. Garcia (Ed.), *English learners: Reading the highest level of English literacy* (pp.

2–33). Newark, DE: International Reading Association.

Fernandez, R. M., & Nielsen, F. (1986). Bilingualism and Hispanic scholastic achievement: Some baseline results. *Social Science Review, 15,* 43–70.

Finn, D. J. (1989). Withdrawing from school. *Review of Educational Research, 59,* 117–142.

Fix, M., & Passel, J. (2003, January). *U.S. immigration: Trends and implications for schools*. Paper presented at the National Association for Bilingual Education's No Child Left Behind Implementation, New Orleans.

Freeman, D., & Freeman, Y. (1998). *ESL/EFL teaching: Principles for success*. Portsmouth, NH: Heinemann.

Fry, R. (2005). *The higher drop-out rate of foreign born teens* (Report of Pew Hispanic Center). Retrieved September 5, 2006, from *pewhispanic.org/files/reports/55.pdf*.

Fu, D. (1995). *My trouble is my English: Asian students and American dreams*. Portsmouth, NH: Heinemann.

Fu, D. (2003). *An island of English: Teaching ESL in Chinatown*. Portsmouth, NH: Heinemann.

Fu, D. (2007). Teaching writing to English language learners. In T. Newkirk & R. Kent (Eds.), *Teaching the neglected "R": Rethinking writing instruction in secondary classrooms* (pp. 225–242). Portsmouth, NH: Heinemann.

Fu, D., & Matoush, M. (2006). Writing development and biliteracy. In P. Matsuda, C. Ortmeier-Hooper, & X. You (Eds.), *The politics of second language writing* (pp. 5–29). West Lafayette, IN: Parlor Press.

Genesse, F., Lindholm-Leary, K., Saunders, W., & Christian, D. (2005). English language learners in U.S. schools: An overview of research finding. *Journal of Education for Students Placed at Risk, 10,* 363–385.

Giacchino-Baker, R. (1997). Recent Mexican immigrants: Forgotten voices in the high school restructuring process. In T. E. Jennings (Ed.), *Restructuring for integrative education: Multiple perspectives, multiple contexts* (pp. 109–126). Westport, CT: Bergin & Garvey.

Gibson, M. (1991). *Accommodation without assimilation: Sikh immigrants in an American high school*. Ithaca, NY: Cornell University Press.

Gibson, M. (1997). Complicating the immigrant/involuntary minority typology. *Anthropology and Education Quarterly, 28,* 431–454.

Godina, H. (2004). Contradictory literacy practices of Mexican-background students: An ethnography from the rural Midwest. *Bilingual Research Journal, 28,* 153–180.

Grinberg, L., & Grinberg, R. (1989). *Psychoanalytic perspectives on migration and exile*. New Haven, CT: Yale University Press.

Harper, C., & de Jong, E. (2004). Misconceptions about teaching English-language learners. *Journal of Adolescent and Adult Literacy, 48,* 152–162.

Landale, N. S., & Oropresa, R. S. (1995). *Immigrant children and the children of immigrants: Inter- and intro-ethnic group differences in the United States* (Population Research Group [PRG] research paper). East Lansing, MI: Institute for Public Policy and Social Research.

Lenski, S. D., Ehlers-Zavala, F., Daniel, M. C., & Sun-Irminger, X. (2006). Assessing English-language learners in mainstream classrooms. *Reading Teacher, 60,* 24–34.

Lew, J. (2003). Korean American high school dropouts: A case study of their experiences and negotiations of schooling, family, and communities. In S. Books (Ed.), *Invisible children in the society and its schools* (2nd ed., pp. 53–66). Mahwah, NJ: Erlbaum.

Li, X., & Zhang, M. (2004). Why Mei still cannot read and what can be done. *Journal of Adolescent and Adult Literacy, 48,* 92–101.

Lucas, T. (1997). *Into, through, and beyond secondary schools: Critical transitions for immigrant youths.* McHenry, IL: Center for Applied Linguistics and Delta Systems.

Macias, J. (1990). Scholastic antecedents of immigrant students: Schooling in a Mexican immigrant-sending community. *Anthropology and Education Quarterly, 21,* 291–318.

Martinez, S. (2003). *Explaining patterns of disengagement of Mexican Americans in high school.* Unpublished doctoral dissertation, University of Chicago.

Matute-Bianchi, M. E. (1986). Ethnic and assimilation patterns of school success and failure among Mexican-descent and Japanese-American students in a California high school: An ethnographic analysis. *American Journal of Education, 95,* 233–255.

McKay, S. L., & Wong, S. C. (1996). Multiple discourses, multiple identities: Investment and agency in second-language learning among Chinese adolescent immigrant students. *Harvard Educational Review, 66,* 577–608.

Merchant, B. (1999). Now you see it, now you don't: A district's short-lived commitment to an alternative high school for newly arrived immigrants. *Urban Education, 34,* 26–51.

Moll, L. C. (2001). The diversity of schooling: A cultural-historical approach. In M. Reyes & J. H. Halcon (Eds.), *The best for our children: Critical perspectives on literacy for Latino/a students* (pp. 13–28). New York: Teachers College Press.

Moll, L. C., Amanti, C., Neff, D., & Gonzalez, N. (1992). Funds of knowledge for teaching: Using a qualitative approach to connect homes and classrooms. *Theory into Practice, 31,* 132–141.

New York City Board of Education. (2000). *Class of 2000 four-year longitudinal report and event drop out rates.* New York: Author.

Nieto, S. (2002). *Language, culture, and teaching: Critical perspectives for a new century.* Mahwah, NJ: Erlbaum.

Ogbu, J. U. (1991). Immigrant and involuntary minorities in comparative perspectives. In M. A. Gibson & J. U. Ogbu (Eds.), *Minority status and schooling: A*

comparative study of immigrant and involuntary minorities (pp. 3–33). New York: Garland.

Orfield, G., & Yun, J. T. (1999). *Resegregation in American schools* (Civil Rights Project report). Cambridge, MA: Harvard University Press. Retrieved August 6, 2006, from *www.civilrightsproject.harvard. Edu/research/deseg/Resegregation_American_Schools 99.pdf.*

Perreira, K. M., Harris, K. M., & Lee, D. (2006). Making it in America: High school completion by immigrant and native youth. *Demography, 43,* 511–536.

Portes, A., & Stepick, A. (1993). *City on the edge: The transformation of Miami.* Berkeley: University of California Press.

Pumariega, A., Swanson, J. W., Holzer, C., Linskey, A. O., & Wuintero-Salinas, R. (1992). Cultural context and substance abuse in Hispanic adolescents. *Journal of Child and Family Studies, 1,* 75–92.

Rothe, E. M. (2004). Hispanic adolescents and their families: Sociocultural factors and treatment considerations. *Adolescent Psychiatry, 28,* 251–278.

Rubinstein-Ávila, E. (2006). Connecting with Latino/a learners. *Educational Leadership, 63,* 38–43.

Ruiz-de-Velasco, J., & Fix, M. (2000). *Overlooked and underserved immigrant students in U.S. secondary schools.* Washington, DC: Urban Institute.

Rumbaut, R. (1994). The crucible within: Ethnic, identity, self-esteem, and segmented assimilation among children of immigrants. *International Migration Review, 28,* 748–794.

Schnaur, B. (1999). A newcomer's high school. *Educational Leadership, 56,* 50–52.

Schneider, B., Martinez, S., & Owens, A. (2006). Barriers to educational opportunities for Hispanics in the United States. In M. Tienda & F. Mitchell (Eds.), *Hispanics and the future of America* (pp. 179–227). Washington, DC: National Academies Press.

Suárez-Orozco, C., & Suárez-Orozco, M. (2001). *Children of immigration.* Cambridge, MA: Harvard University Press.

Suárez-Orozco, C., & Todorova, I. (2003). The social worlds of immigrant youth. In C. Suárez-Orozco (Ed.), *New directions for youth development* (pp. 1–24). New York: Wiley.

Suárez-Orozco, M. (1991). Immigrant adaptation to schooling: A Hispanic case. In M. Gibson & J. U. Ogbu (Eds.), *Minority status and schooling: A comparative study of immigrant and involuntary minorities* (pp. 37–61). New York: Garland.

Sung, B. (1987). *The adjustment experience of Chinese immigrant children in New York City.* Staten Island, NY: Center of Migration Studies.

Thomas, W., & Collier, V. (2002). *A national study of school effectiveness for language minority students' long-term academic achievement.* Santa Cruz, CA: Center for Research on Education, Diversity and Excellence.

Tienda, M., & Mitchell, F. (Eds.). (2006). *Hispanics*

and the future of America. Washington, DC: National Academies Press.

Tse, L. (2001). *Why don't they learn English? Separating fact from fallacy in the U.S. language debate.* New York: Teachers College Press.

U.S. Census Bureau. (2003). *Population reports.* Washington, DC: U.S. Census Bureau, Population Division. Retrieved August 19, 2006, from *www.census.gov/prod/2003pubs/02statab/pop.pdf.*

Valenzuela, A. (1999). *Subtractive schooling: U.S.-Mexican youth and the politics of caring.* Albany, NY: SUNY Press.

Van Hook, J., & Fix, M. (2000). A profile of the immigrant student population. In J. Ruiz-de-Velasco & M. Fix. (Eds.), *Overlooked and underserved: Immigrant children in U.S. secondary schools* (pp. 9–33). Washington, DC: Urban Institute.

Vargas, L. (2006). Transnational media literacy: Analytic reflections on a program with Latina teens. *Hispanic Journal of Behavioral Sciences, 38,* 267–285.

Violand-Sánchez, E., & Hainer-Violand, J. (2006). The power of positive identity. *Educational Leadership, 64,* 36–40.

Wilkinson, D. L., Gonzalez, R. M., & Rumbaut, M. H. (1993, January). *Newcomers: Different language, different culture, big challenge.* Paper presented at the annual meeting of the Southwest Educational Research Association, Austin, TX.

Zentella, A. C. (2002). Latino/a languages and identities. In M. Páez & M. Suárez-Orozco (Eds.), *Latino/as: Remaking America* (pp. 321–338). Berkeley: University of California Press.

Zhou, M. (1997). Growing up American: The challenge confronting immigrant children and children of immigrants. *Annual Reviews in Sociology, 23,* 63–95.

Zhou, M., & Bankston, C. L., III. (1994). Social capital and the adaptation of the second generation: The case of Vietnamese youth in New Orleans. *International Migration Review, 28,* 775–799.

CHAPTER 27

American Indian Adolescent Literacy

MARY JIRON BELGARDE
RICHARD K. LORÉ
RICHARD MEYER

This chapter opens with a review of the very limited research findings on Indigenous adolescent students' literacy. It then presents a historical review of Native American students' experiences in school, finding that they have been treated according to a deficit model of literacy; that is, they are viewed not in terms of their own cultural experiences, but in terms of what they lack relative to expectations for mainstream White students. This perception that they are intellectually underdeveloped has led to disproportionate placements in remedial and special education classes and high dropout rates; and yet the problem is more likely grounded in culturally insensitive instruction than deficient academic performances. We next outline a Native American epistemology, one characterized by a close and respectful relationship with the earth and all its creatures and phenomena. Individuals must take into account their physical, mental, emotional, and environmental health, all of which are interconnected and must be understood in relation to the greater whole. These dispositions are often not valued in school, where the individual student competes against others, students' funds of knowledge are excluded from what counts in the classroom, and other aspects of Native American epistemology are degraded and dismissed. The chapter concludes with implications for teaching and research. Teachers need to be better educated about culturally sensitive instruction in order to provide more flexible and responsive learning environments, and researchers need to be more inclusive in their samples and investigate such issues as biliteracy and how biliterate students' resources may better be drawn on to serve all students' education.

> *Our children cannot relate to the story about George Washington chopping down a cherry tree. Such stories may be told to teach certain values—in this case, not to tell a lie. But they are not teaching our most important values. To us, young George's parents should have told him that cherry trees, like all living things, should be treated with respect.*
>
> —Tall Bull (2007, p. 192)

Tall Bull's explanation suggests the differences between the dominant majority and Indigenous experiences in school. From the moment that many Indigenous children enter school, they face stories, uses of language, worldviews, and ways of knowing that differ vastly from those in their home settings. The ways of the home and community are often ignored, marginalized, or actively devalued in the school setting, imparting to the children the idea that school is more valuable, important, and relevant than home. As all children grow into the Western definition of adolescence, they face crises of identity (Moje, 2002) that may be resolved in a myriad of ways: dropping out of school, becoming extremely successful academically, joining clubs and athletic teams, joining gangs, participating in religious and spiritual activities, engaging in drug/alcohol use, initiating sexual activity and promiscuity, and forming allegiances and friendships along with enmities and hatreds. They make decisions about school, learning, and literacy that are rooted in their tentative and emerging understandings of who they are, the options they have available, and the possibilities that are open to them.

The need to know more about adolescent literacy pervades this book; the dearth of information about Indigenous adolescent students' literacy borders on embarrassing. As we began work on this chapter, we initiated a search of the extant research literature on the teaching and learning of adolescent literacy among Indigenous students and confirmed what we suspected at the outset. We examined nearly 1,400 articles published in four peer-reviewed literacy journals during the last 11 years (1996–2006): *Journal of Adolescent and Adult Literacy* (447 articles), *Journal of Reading Behavior/Journal of Literacy Research* (320 articles), *Reading Research Quarterly* (310 articles), and *English Education* (314 articles). In the literacy journals, we found only 8 articles addressing Native populations and 2 articles that included Native adolescents. Three addressed literacy among the Aborigines of Australia (Doherty, 2002; Dunn, 2001; Kapitzke et al., 2000/2001), 1 addressed a Native population in Canada (Hulan & Warley, 1999), 1 addressed the Indigenous people of Altai (Calhoun & Annett, 2003), 1 addressed vocabulary learning among the Northern Cheyenne (Hopkins, Bean, & Thomas, 1998/1999), and 1 article (Noll, 1998) was a case study of two Indian youth attending White-dominant schools. The 3 articles that included Native adolescents were case studies that described the use of dance and mask making as literacy practices among adolescents in alternative school (Smagorinsky & Coppock, 1995) and mainstream English class (Smagorinsky, Zoss, O'Donnell-Allen,

2005; Zoss, Smagorinsky, & O'Donnell-Allen, 2007) settings.

We also examined the *Journal of American Indian Education* (120 articles), *Anthropology and Education Quarterly* (406 articles), and one issue of the *Phi Delta Kappan* (Vol. 88, No. 3, 2006) devoted to Native education. We found 1 article claiming to focus on children 3–18 years old, but the research review was actually about early childhood literacy (August, Goldenberg, & Rueda, 2006). Buly (2005) focused on fourth graders' needs for specific reading strategy instruction. Hawkins (2006) claims to have integrated "native tradition and culture" (p. 74) into a teacher development program aimed at improving reading instruction, but we found that the demand to teach "scientifically based reading research" (research employing experimental or quasi-experimental designs) trumped the importance of a culturally responsive reading curriculum. Further, it was not possible to determine the number of teachers who dealt with Indigenous adolescent students.

One of the more encouraging studies (Costantino & Hurtado, 2006) reviewed and developed curriculum from a larger document (Bergeson, Griffin, & Hurtado, 2000). Costantino and Hurtado focused on kindergarten through second grade, but Bergeson et al. focused on schooling and reading instruction across all grade levels. Both pieces discussed the importance of culturally responsive teaching that included multiple voices (school, community, students, and families), Indigenous epistemologies, and a sense of the past and present in reading instruction. The inclusion of Native authors, storytellers, events, spirituality, and community activities as integral parts of a reading curriculum seems to offer promise, yet there is little discussion of the implementation or any systematic study of the curriculum. It remains, then, something that needs to be studied.

Further, we considered recent work under the heading of "neurophysiology." Under this umbrella, neuroimaging is an emerging area of study (Pugh, Sandak, Frost, Moore, & Menci, 2006) that is extremely contentious (Strauss, 2005). Pugh et al. (2006) believe they will eventually be able to determine which reading disabilities are environmental and which are "a gene-linked syndrome" (p. 61). They also suggest that neuroimaging will be helpful in determining "the efficacy of different approaches to the teaching of reading in *these* children" (p. 61; emphasis added). Strauss, a neurologist and a PhD in linguistics, points out the absurdity of claims such as this, arguing that the imaging techniques being used are so primitive that researchers cannot determine much more than which part of the brain is active when the reader focuses on a word. Our concern is that the search for organic reasons for reading problems will marginalize the cultural, linguistic, socioeconomic, and political issues that are much more pressing and determinable.

Unable to provide a review of literacy literature when almost none exists, we offer a brief history of adolescent Natives in school. Against this backdrop, we examine Indigenous adolescent epistemologies, specifically considering how Indigenous adolescents know what they know, make meaning, and learn to view the world. We then consider the ways in which the epistemologies influence learning in school and the implications of that work for literacy instruction. We conclude with specific implications for further research.

A BRIEF HISTORY OF INDIGENOUS ADOLESCENTS IN SCHOOL

Throughout history and in much of the literature, many different terms have been used to describe Native American people as a group: American Indians, Native Americans, Natives, First Nations People, and Indigenous populations, for example. In this chapter we use the terms *Native American, American Indian, Indigenous,* and *First Nations People* interchangeably to reflect the research authors' application of the terms. In addition, we capitalize these terms and the term *Nature* to honor Native ontology and reflect the reverence that Natives give them.

Consistently throughout the history of adolescent Indigenous students attending public schools, the students have been "minoritized" (McCarty, 2002). The word *minoritized* intentionally suggests the active stripping away of Indigenous students' language and culture and grounding this diminishment in the assumptions that Indigenous students are less than other students. Their language is less, their culture is less, their homes are less, their ways with words are less, and their achievement is less. Pittman and Leckie (1989) present the story of a clergyman who used the metaphor "taming wild roses" to reflect the prevalent philosophy in educating Native students of Canada. The clergyman described the taking of a rose bush from the wild (Native children from their communities), stripping away its original soil (Native language and culture), and then giving it new soil in which to grow (a strict European style of education). He explained that weeding it (taking away any new or intervening Native experiences) can enable the rose bush to adapt readily to its new environment (assimilate into the White world). The clergyman perceived himself as saving the Indians from the terrible burden of living their traditions and maintaining their "heathen ways." In reality, missionaries feared that if children returned home, they would resume their old ways of thinking and believing. For more than 150 years, and primarily through the process of formal education in American schools, Native students have been subjected to the most severe forms of oppression, subjugation, and forced assimilation policies sponsored by any government, particularly in the colonized areas of the world (Connell-Szasz, 1999; Deloria & Wildcat, 2001; Meriam, 1928).

Connell-Szasz's (1999) discussion of American Indian education is worthy of summary here. American Indians have been formally educated through religious missions, the United States government, and state public institutions since the mid-17th century. A study conducted by the Brookings Institution in the 1920s revealed that Indian children attending the U.S. federal and mission boarding schools were living under horrid conditions (starving, being used for child labor, dying from diseases, or running away). In all of these schools, Indian children experienced a deficit approach to assessment, were punished for speaking their Native tongue, and were taught rote memorization, simple cognitive skills, and vocational skills that kept them in low-paying and subservient occupations and ultimately financially dependent on others. Furthermore, until the late 20th century, most teachers and administrators knew little about the students' culture and assumed that *everyone* had to learn English and adapt to Western institutional norms. It became the students' responsibility to learn what was expected of them; and if they wanted to progress to the next level, they had to follow formalistic rules. Native children remained illiterate; learned to feel inferior, denigrated, and unchallenged; and became torn between their own culture and that of the dominant society. On the whole, and throughout history, when Native students are compared to their non-Native counterparts, Native children have lower achievement scores (Belgarde, 1992; Connell-Szasz, 1999). More recent research that accounts for levels of traditionality (understanding of cultural traditions and exposure to Native languages in nonacademic settings), types of schooling (public/private/government sponsored), and geographic location (urban/rural) shows that more traditional students raised in rural and reservation communities are at a disadvantage when contrasted with their more urban and assimilated Native counterparts (Belgarde, 1992).

Today, many Native children are often misdiagnosed as needing special education, and adolescent Indigenous students are overrepresented in special education (McCarty & Watahomigie, 2004). They are forced into programs in which they are given substandard education (Deyhle & Swisher, 1997). Many of these children rebel at the treatment they receive, leading to an overrepresentation in the number of Indigenous dropouts. Contentious experiences in school are value laden against the essence of their culture and traditions and the deep and abiding respect they hold for Nature (Jacobs & Jacobs-Spencer, 2001; Romero, 1994). They struggle with being forced away from a holistic, intuitive, and community-based integrative thinking process to which they are accustomed (Belgarde & LoRé, 2007; Benally, 1994; Cajete, 1994; Cowell, 2002; Deyhle & Swisher, 1997; Hulan & Warley, 1999; Kapitzke et al., 2000/2001). Unfortunately, most are taught to believe that they have to forfeit or feign forfeiture of their Native values and proclivities and embrace those values that are antithetical to the essence of who they are as individuals and Native people (Deyhle & Swisher, 1997; National Indian Education Association, 2005).

Administrators believe that they have little choice and succumb to the flawed organizational structures they inherit (Deyhle &

Swisher, 1997; National Indian Education Association, 2005). As a result, very little real change has occurred. The reality is that most Indigenous adolescents realize that they must learn to survive in two very different worlds: the one within the school itself and the one beyond. They know or intuit that school is a place where learning is acceptable only as being linear and committed to written forms, contradicting the oral culture in which stories change to accommodate contexts and individuals. Written language is viewed as the creation of the White society, one that has historically rejected them and used literacy against them in the form of treaties and other documents that cost them dearly.

Agreeing to learn to be literate in the White way in a school setting entails learning the individualistic ways in which students from the dominant White culture learn. In Montana, after a series of legislative acts and lawsuits demanding that those acts be respected, the state is working toward integrating an Indigenous perspective across the curriculum (Juneau & Broaddus, 2006). The state is working to acknowledge the complexity of the histories, disrupted lives, and vulnerable identities that must be addressed when written language assumes great prestige and serves as a gatekeeper to many definitions of success. Understanding that Indigenous adolescents must live in two worlds, educators in Montana are working to find ways in which the local and historical can be honored and central to teaching and learning, while concomitantly being attentive to the power and possibilities that written language in the Anglo world offers.

McCarty (2002) tells the poignant and powerful story of a similar effort at Rough Rock on the Navajo Reservation. Yet, in the strict standard-driven environment of public schools, McCarty's work to put Navajo spirituality and thinking at the center of a curriculum was not as successful as she and others hoped. She quotes one teacher as saying, "We don't have time for Navajo; we've been told to teach to the standards" (p. 198). Ultimately, White ways of thinking, teaching, learning, and assessing trumped the culturally responsive work at hand. The ways in which Native people learn to learn and come to know is the epistemological issue to which we now turn, because it is the differences between these (across cultures) that create images of and realities for Indigenous adolescents in the literacy classroom.

INDIGENOUS ADOLESCENT EPISTEMOLOGIES

Epistemology is the study of the ways in which people come to know, understand, make meaning, and develop systems of beliefs about their world. Adolescence is often portrayed as a time of upheaval, during which children-becoming-adults make decisions about who they are and how they will be in the world. These decisions take place within the social contexts and the cultural worlds in which the adolescent lives. Learning about self within and across contexts in agreement with or opposition to others involves "shifting the analytic focus from the individual as learner to learning as participation in the social world, and from the concept of cognitive process to the more-encompassing view of social practice" (Lave & Wenger, 1991, p. 43). Learning how to learn is, then, a social practice. Indigenous adolescents learn about language, beliefs, and ways of learning within their home cultures; Gee (2002) refers to this language and cultural space as their primary discourse. The primary discourse is the forum in which the episteme (the ways of knowing) is composed. The more similar that primary discourse is to school discourse (secondary discourse), the easier it is to be successful. We do not reiterate mainstream dominant discourse here, but provide some generalized ideas from various Indigenous discourses, leaving the comparison between Indigenous and non-Indigenous to the reader, except where we believe specific points may not be clearly comparative or contrastive.

A noteworthy difference between the dominant majority and Native epistemologies, for example, is that Navajos believe that they are endowed with mind, spirit, physical bodies, and emotions and that these endowments help relate the individual to the natural laws and order of the physical world (Benally, 1994). Along with most Native worldviews, they must learn skills and knowledge that will enable them to survive and understand their relation to all other phenomena, because they are responsible for the next four and seven generations, respectively, that will live on earth. They must develop the mind and skills for survival, learn to appreciate positive relationships, and understand and relate to their environment. This form of collective understanding is similar to many Native American ideologies (Belgarde & LoRé, 2007; Cajete, 2000; Cowell, 2002; Deloria & Wildcat, 2001; LoRé, 1998).

Cajete (1994), a Pueblo scholar and philosopher, explains that there is a direct relation between Nature and learning. One learns by studying and observing Nature and then relating that understanding to the human experience, an informal association that is often at variance with the effective, formal experience of Western thinking. Benally (1994) posits that when a person is firmly grounded in spiritual teachings and traditional wisdom, he or she finds strength and stability; together these form the basis for learning and living. He calls this grounding the "first basic principle of learning," which is built on the belief that individuals are better able to make decisions once traditional values are understood. Benally (1994) refers to this process as "that which gives direction to life." Cajete (1994) defines this first basic lesson as "finding face" or finding ways to happiness. Kapitzke et al. (2000/2001), Hulan and Warley (1999), and Cowell (2002) emphasize these characteristics as well when referencing First Nation, Aboriginal, and Arapaho values. Learning is recognized as a spiritual experience, and it serves to help adolescents understand their responsibilities to the community.

The Western model of learning as a school-based activity has its roots in the Enlightenment, where separating the individual from the environment (and the collective) helped to objectify Nature and therefore reinforce the Christian perspective of having to control it (Cajete, 1994, 2000; LoRé, 1998). Indigenous perspectives look to Nature as a living entity that is to be revered and from which understanding and wisdom emanate; it is not something that one can own or control. Doctrines and beliefs such as *Manifest Destiny* that presuppose Westerners' right to own and use the planet solely for their own good are therefore antithetical to Indigenous epistemology. In American Indigenous thought, life is seen as a process that is guided by principles whereby "knowledge, learning, and life itself are sacred and are interwoven parts of a whole" (Benally, 1994, p. 23). This holistic tendency is in direct conflict with the Western belief in having to segment the world into many parts and then to analyze them as unrelated elements of a whole (Belgarde & LoRé, 2007). The idea of "essence" then is understood in the Western view as a microcosm rather than the "Gaia" of the whole—that the earth is a living, breathing organism where all things rely on other things in order to survive (Campbell, 1991). Native adolescents, particularly among the Pueblo Indians of New Mexico, struggle with reconciling these divergent views. They exercise their intuitive and insightful capacities through culture and ceremony and understand that reality is based on these types of holistic relationships. Schools, however, are forcing them into a nonrelational dichotomized process of thinking and learning and relating to the world (Belgarde & LoRé, 2007; Cajete, 2000; LoRé, 1998).

In Navajo culture, as one matures the guiding principle called "sustenance" comes into play. It means that the individual must take into account his or her physical, mental, emotional, and environmental health. All of these parts are seen as being interconnected and must be understood in relation to the greater whole. The Blessing Way Ceremony, for example, is prescribed for just such a purpose: to clear one's spiritual, mental, physical, and emotional system of any deterrent to physical health, vigor, and vitality. In order to care for one's health, one must satisfy the mental, physical, emotional, and spiritual process of becoming an environmentally sound human being. "All of these parts of health are inter-connected and must therefore be understood as a whole. The mind must be kept strong, pure, and in alignment with the principle of harmony" (Benally, 1994 p. 27). Navajo children are forced to prioritize mental growth in school, and their spiritual, physical, and emotional growth is marginalized to out-of-school settings. For the Arapahoe adolescents (and other Natives in the United States, the Aboriginals of Australia, and First Nations of Canada), schools and their organizational structure, particularly in their insistence on written literacy as a mechanism for learning,

are antithetical to the tribe's traditional ways of knowing (Basso, 1996; Cajete, 2000; Cowell, 2002; Hopkins & Bean 1998/1999; Hulan & Warley, 1999; Kapitzke et al., 2000/2001; LoRé 1998; Romero, 1994).

Teaching and learning have been a part of everyday life among Indigenous groups. Romero (1994) describes traditional Pueblo education as the accepted practice by the community to help develop the personal qualities of the child with an emphasis on compassion and the strengthening of the willingness of the learner to "give back" for the good of the whole (giving back is the process of helping the community with one's talents and gifts). Traditionally, Pueblo education is tied to the environment; it provides for reflection, ingenuity, and the ability to create, thereby initiating an intimate relationship with Mother Earth. Developing skills such as perceptual organization, spatial reasoning, visualization, insight, and visual–motor coordination are looked upon as meaningful and necessary for growth and development (LoRé, 1998).

Romero (1994) maintains that "it is through such things as verbal proficiency, high abstract thinking, visual reasoning, and extreme creativity that traditional [Pueblo] approaches to education are best reflected" (p.41). LoRé (n.d.) writes that in the past, learning was accomplished through holistic associations that came from traditional forms of speech, traditional forms of advisement, and song and dance composition. The role of memory within the Pueblo context then is demonstrated most notably through the remembering of songs, inspirational speeches, traditions of various kinds, dance and choreography, legends, and the recounting of personal histories. These experiences and reflections therefore "become the grist for wisdom"; they carry with them the spiritual and practical food for nourishing future generations (LoRé, 1998).

In Aboriginal, First Nations, and American Indian cultures, moderation is encouraged in almost every endeavor; humility is expected to be shown in thought, speech, and behavior, including the school environment. Adolescents hesitate to participate in class discussions because they have learned not to bring attention to themselves in a way that makes them appear smarter or superior to another (Belgarde, 1992; Belgarde & LoRé,

2007; Cajete, 2000). In one study, Philips (1972) observed Warm Springs, Oregon, children talking a lot on the playground but rarely in the classroom. However, consistent with the idea of not being singled out, when these particular Native students were encouraged to work in groups, participation in the classroom increased. Nevertheless, in most instances, Native students are often seen as "slow learners" and shy (Cowell, 2002; Hulan & Warley, 1999; Kapitzke et al., 2000/2001, Romero, 1994). Native students are taught to contribute to the community as a whole without setting themselves apart from others (Belgarde, 1992; Belgarde & LoRé, 2007). Aboriginal, First Nations, and Arapaho cultures expect their children to observe and listen and, when appropriate and serving the good of all, demonstrate what they have learned (Cowell, 2002; Hulan & Warley, 1999; Kapitzke et al., 2000/2001).

INDIGENOUS EPISTEMOLOGIES AND LEARNING IN SCHOOL

Epistemology can not be separated from the language in which people come to know; the relation between language and culture is well known (Sapir, 1958). Approximately two million American Indians and Alaska Natives reside in the United States, speaking 150–200 languages among 560 federally recognized tribes and another 60 tribes that lack federal recognition. Nearly one quarter of this population are school-age children who attend federal (Bureau of Indian Affairs, tribally operated grant or contract schools), public (including charter), and mission/parochial schools. Many of these schools are located on or near reservation lands; 56%, or more than 250,000 students, attend public schools with less than 25% Native enrollment (Belgarde, Mitchell, & Moquino-Arquero, 2002; McCarty & Watahomigie, 2004). Mass media, technology, and the influence of dominant societal values diminish the use of Native languages as well (Krauss, 1996). Some believe that the community is the place for learning the Indigenous language. Others support the idea that schools may offer opportunities for respected elders in the tribe to share their linguistic, cultural, and historical knowledge in the curriculum—to

have voice in the community and to communicate directly to the children of the community (Cowell, 2002; McCarty & Watahomigie, 2004). McCarty (2002) argues that "bilingual/bicultural education was cultural reclamation, the unseating of historical relations of authority and control" (p. 121). Language is only one facet of the complexity of Indigenous adolescents' learning in school.

Adolescent Indigenous education was, historically, a holistic, sensual, kinesthetic, and social activity that reinforced the importance of each individual as a contributing member of the social group. LoRé (1998) points out, "The cultivation of all of one's senses through learning how to listen, observe, and experience holistically through creative exploration is a highly valued philosophical approach to Native American education. In addition, the ability to use language through storytelling, oratory and song is highly regarded by most tribes as a primary tool for teaching and learning" (p. 199). For Cajete (1994), the purpose of education and learning for Indigenous people then is to increase awareness and develop one's innate human potential: "One learns through experiential learning (learning by doing or seeing); storytelling (learning by listening and imaging); ritual/ceremony (learning through initiation); dreaming (learning through unconscious imagery); tutoring (learning through apprenticeship); and artistic creation (learning through creative synthesis)" (p. 34). Schools that have sought to develop curricula consistent with these beliefs were and are places in which Indigenous adolescents can succeed (McCarty, 2002).

The sense of community and responsibility to others that Indigenous adolescents bring to school is reflected in their desire to help others. Helping in a non-self-aggrandizing way is viewed as a form of giving, a value found in many Indigenous cultures (Benally, 1994, p. 27). When students mentor one another, they are giving knowledge, which is believed to return to them when they need help. The Indigenous adolescent comes to school with a deep reverence for the interconnected relation between the home and environment. Respect for Nature is returned with favors, and disrespect is reciprocated in a negative way; the relationship is circular. The Navajo approach this relation consciously, desiring to keep themselves in harmony. They believe that a person's heart becomes hard when he or she loses respect and reverence for Nature. "How one treats animals and [N]ature directly relates to how one treats other people" (Benally, 1994, p. 27). In many schools, biology classes insist that students learn how to dissect animals. This teaching method contradicts the Navajo respect for Nature (LoRé, 1998) and is seen as well by the Aborigine and First Nations students as an affront to their belief systems and their reverence for the natural world (Hulan & Worley, 1999; Kapitzke et al., 2000/2001). Even during a "nature walk," an Indigenous adolescent may refuse to pick up or move rocks or engage in other activities that seem quite ordinary and sensible from a Western perspective. Thus, knowledge from the home culture may not always serve the adolescent well in school (a point to which we return later).

Indigenous adolescents are extremely careful about their use of language, believing that thoughts and words are sacred. For example, Aboriginal children are raised to "feel strong" by a reinforced and continuing sense of responsibility to family and the community; they are linked to a sense of place and the significance of the land (Kapitzke et al., 2000/2001). Basso (1996) refers to the connections among thought, words, and the community in his writings about the White Mountain Apaches. Because of these oral traditions, grounded as they are within the sense of place, it is easy for the words and thoughts to come alive so that adolescents, as they become active community members, must carefully think before they speak. Their words, then, have the power to honor, heal, degrade, and curse. Within the school setting, this care about language is often misunderstood as slowness, shyness, or lack of cognitive facility.

The extant view within many communities is that the purpose of education is to help students "find face, heart, and foundation." Finding face is seen as a process by which students discover who they are as persons. They discover their innate characteristics and then find ways to express those potentialities. Finding heart occurs when students search the self for those inner passions that motivate and inspire them to perform good

acts. And in finding "foundation" is where the students discover their vocations, which in turn gives them the opportunity to express their truths and serve their community (Cajete, 1994, p. 33–38). The passionate pursuit of one's interests to serve the common good may seem consistent with the altruistic goals of Western education, but in reality it is not. Indigenous adolescents know that their goals are inextricably derived from the community and, as such, lie both within and beyond themselves. Most dominant mainstream students' goals, reflective of the individualistic-entrepreneurial epistemologies that drive their learning, are more inclined toward seeking personal wealth and security. The less competitive, seemingly complacent and hesitant Indigenous adolescent is, again, often misunderstood.

In traditional Indian cultures, stories are the medium through which theories of the world are constructed (Hulan & Warley, 1999). American Indian adolescents think abstractly through story and metaphor, but the abstraction is not traditionally expressed in abstract words. For example, Chief Seattle said, "Man did not weave the web of life; he is merely a strand in it. Whatever he does to the web, he does to himself." There is an abstract metaphoric lesson in that quote, but the lesson does not depend on abstract words. Successful teachers of Indigenous adolescents depend on visual and experiential learning activities because they find the oral/aural language in instruction less effective unless the language is in the form of stories. They have learned to give explicit lessons to help students learn and use mainstream language and discourse structures (Cleary & Peacock, 1998). Belgarde (n.d.) asserts that many Indigenous adolescents coming from oral societies can see multiple relationships in everything they learn and in many of the activities in which they participate. Because of their ability to imagine and associate relationships through an intuitive process, many students extrapolate information and ideas and then associate them with experience and relationships that have greater meaning or connectivity to the larger whole (Cajete, 2000; LoRé, 1998).

It is difficult for these same students within the Western context of emphasizing vocabulary, subjects, and nouns to sort through all the detail and make sense of it in the linear way often required in the writing of compositions: Their emphasis is on the context—the whole, rather than the specific subject. Communicating to people in a language or a written form that is heavily weighted in subject and noun idioms and then interpreting its literary content can be very vexing and frustrating. The idea of "living in two different worlds" is therefore an appropriate metaphor in expressing the dynamics within which most Indigenous students find themselves while trying to balance the need to succeed in school with their cultural traditions, customs, and worldviews (Cajete, 1994, 2000; LoRé, 1998).

As suggested in the "Brief History of Indigenous Adolescents in School" section and the statistics at the beginning of this section, adolescent Indigenous students in schools are representatives of cultures and languages that have been decimated. They may have not learned their Native languages because their parents were conditioned to believe that they would be severely punished or disadvantaged for speaking their Native languages while in school (Cleary & Peacock, 1998). In the histories passed down from those parents and grandparents forced into "relocation" and placed in boarding schools that worked to eliminate their culture, many returned home having lost not only their language, but their culture as well. When the young men and women returned home they saw themselves and were recognized as being outsiders. The heartbreak for the families was devastating, their children sensing that they were part of a diaspora—separated from their foundations—and boarding at school with a growing sense of disconnectedness. Yet they bring with them deeply rooted ways with words and cultural practices that reveal themselves in classroom interactions, conflicts with calendars and scheduling, attitudes toward the isolative and cellular nature of schooling, and responses to curriculum. Others arrive at school well connected to their histories, languages, and cultural practices. They are active participants and have learned that they have responsibilities in two worlds, worlds that may be in conflict or resonance with each other. Within this complicated and multifaceted backdrop, literacy instruction occurs for the adolescent Indigenous student.

IMPLICATIONS FOR LITERACY INSTRUCTION

Literacy instruction for adolescent Indigenous students is a sociocultural and sociopolitical activity. The lack of texts that accurately portray historical and contemporary Indigenous people and events may be interpreted by students as disenfranchisement, marginalization, racism, and exclusion. The use of existing texts is often carried out in a way that is inconsistent with Indigenous ways. The traditional initiate-respond-evaluate (Mehan, 1982) classroom recitation script singles out individuals and demands that they rise above others in the class. The focus on individual performance and quick responses to what some Indigenous students interpret as complex questions leaves them out of conversations even when they may have read and understood the material at hand. Reyhner et al. (2001) argue that schools are highly dependent on commercially driven textbooks that are irrelevant to the students' home background. The scripted nature of many reading and phonics programs also limits their usefulness for Indigenous learners. As a result, elders and other Native educators are incorporating background knowledge (community-based instruction) in reservation-based communities in the states of South Dakota and Washington (Bergeson, Griffin, & Hurtado, 2000; Costantino & Hurtado, 2006; Hawkins, 2006).

The practice of turn taking in a lesson explored at the Warm Springs Reservation (Philips, 1972) was reviewed by Au (2006) in relation to Indigenous Hawaiian children. Both found that when traditional Western turn-taking behaviors were replaced with interactions more consistent with cultural practices outside school, student participation increased. Au's work was with young children, but may be applicable to adolescents as well. The use of culturally familiar structures of participation (the ways in which they were allowed to interact), typically controlled by the teacher, may make it possible for more adolescent Indigenous students to participate more actively in lessons. Levitt (2007) found that Socratic seminars in which students prepare questions before meeting in class are effective in encouraging discussions of readings in her high school class on the Navajo Reservation in Arizona.

Levitt physically sits outside the circle, and students bring to the floor questions about the text that are thought out well in advance of the class session. The questions become a common quest for all members of the class as they work together to make sense of the text with each other.

Reyhner (2001) argues that changing the curriculum to reflect the culture taught in the home helps create meaning for students, whose learning is facilitated when current information is associated with their prior knowledge and experiences. In Levitt's (2007) classroom the ways that the students use language are consistent with how they use it outside school. Levitt is teaching the children to find ways to use their language and culture as strengths, while dealing with texts that they may confront in a college situation. Theoretically, Levitt's work and the work of teachers that are thinking like her, is a conscious effort to help students understand and engage in literacy activity in ways that honor their *funds of knowledge* (Moll, Amanti, Neff, & González, 2005). Funds of knowledge are the talents, resources, and skills that are shared within the community, but these may not be apparent to teachers. In striving to compose classroom-based literacy strategies that make sense to Indigenous adolescents, these funds are valued and incorporated into the regular classroom activity. The wisdom of Levitt's students became increasingly apparent as she withdrew and as she learned to have the classes see the "problem" within a text as a group endeavor.

Gee's (2002) idea of primary and secondary discourse may better be explained in terms of "spaces" in the scenario in Levitt's (2007) classroom. The first cultural and linguistic space in which her students lived was their home community. The second space was a formal high school English curriculum that demanded that a certain canon be studied in a certain way. Levitt, with her students, composed a "third space" (Gutiérrez & Larson, 1994) in which the students' culture and linguistic practices were honored, other texts were studied, and all groups were represented. In the classroom, Levitt gave attention to curriculum and the talents, skills, resources, and cultural perspectives that students brought with them.

When there is no third space in the literacy classroom, students' funds of knowledge are marginalized or bracketed. Stuckey (1991) argues that such an act of marginalization is an act of violence against adolescent Indigenous youth. We acknowledge that written text is a non-Indigenous invention, and imposing such texts on Indigenous adolescents is somewhat precarious. That precariousness becomes an act of violence when it undermines students' social, cultural, and linguistic identities. The ways in which schools tend to reproduce the knowledge and power structures of the greater society (Bourdieu & Passeron, 2000) are acts that systematically reduce the cultural and linguistic capital that Indigenous adolescents bring to school. Holland, Skinner, Lachicotte, and Cain (1998) argue that viewing someone else's capital as a deficit or defect is an act of symbolic violence. When cultural and linguistic capital are not accepted so that they can be used for cultural profit (e.g., success in school) (Lareau, 2000), an act of violence has been committed. We know that these are very strong, perhaps even upsetting words, but we are faced with the reality that when adolescent Indigenous students do not receive the culturally relevant curricula and literature that they can relate to, they are the most at-risk group for dropping out, abusing themselves with alcohol and drugs, and/or committing acts of violence toward themselves and others, whether living within the boundaries of a reservation or beyond.

There are instances, however, demonstrating that there has been a movement to include many Native-based and culturally relevant art, dance, literature, and narrative courses and programs in schools and colleges to help students find meaning and educational relevancy in their lives (Scully, 1975; Smagorinsky & Coppock, 1995; Wright, 1976). In one case study, a high school English teacher incorporated the process of mask making as one activity in a broader thematic literature unit on Identity that incorporated multimodal opportunities for learning and personal reflection (Smagorinsky et al., 2005; Zoss et al., 2007). Her instruction provided a Native American student with one of his few opportunities to engage with schoolwork before he dropped out of school because of his inability to connect with his studies across the curriculum. We have also witnessed Native American and Native Hawaiian charter schools that honor Native pedagogy and community-based, culturally relevant curricula (including Native literacy-based practices), providing cultural sensitivity training and Native teachers and mentors, to mitigate against the negative affects of mainstream schooling and forced assimilation practices (Belgarde, 2004).

Freire's (Freire & Macedo, 1987) idea of reading the word and reading the world forms the substance of critical literacy. In critical literacy classrooms, students and teachers work together to identify and even challenge power structures that undermine their success. In such classrooms, students consider the critical issues that confront their lives locally and more broadly as a vehicle for understanding and acting upon their worlds (Bomer & Bomer, 2001). Luke and Freebody (1999) point out that in such classrooms, students need to learn the skills and strategies necessary for using literacy for the greater democratic good. Of course, students need to learn phonics, vocabulary, grammar, and other facets of the language. But they must always learn these within a meaningful and meaning-driven setting (Meyer, 2001). Without such a setting, they learn other lessons that are neither consistent with Indigenous epistemologies nor useful for the broader democracy in which they may eventually participate. Meyer found that many of the Pueblo students of New Mexico were learning compliance, above any other literacy lesson, when they were forced to engage in year-long lessons in which they were taught to say nonwords (e.g., *supermand*).

Critical literacy lessons build on what the students bring to school; these lessons honor the culture and language at hand and also look beyond the local to question, research, inquire, reflect, and, ultimately, act. Singer's (2006) adolescent students dealt with critical issues such as peace, bullying, homosexuality, and more. They were encouraged, as high school students, to take a position and understand and act upon it. When these actions are carried out from perspectives consistent with Indigenous epistemologies, we anticipate a high degree of engagement. Further, once that level of engagement exists, along with trust, students and teachers may consider issues such as the skills needed to succeed in college or the needs of the local community and what groups have to do to respond to those needs effectively.

But in the present climate of the No Child Left Behind law in which progressive traditions in education have been marginalized, teachers are not finding windows of time in which to engage in such important pedagogy. Rather, they are reduced to dealing with standards and assessments (the latter of which typically cause the former to dissipate) that ignore the local. Au (2006) reconsiders the "achievement gap," which we put in quotes here to suggest its artificial nature. The perception of the gap is based on tests that are officially accepted (by the government) as accurate measures of what they claim to measure. Yet the achievement gap is a sociocultural and sociopolitical construction that favors some and hurts others because of the reliance on those assessments. The achievement gap is based on a Western view of learning and the demonstration of learning (assessment). There is no achievement gap. There is, more accurately, a pedagogical gap that does not make the leap between how some learners learn and what actually occurs during literacy lessons. There is a participation gap that does not consider culturally responsive strategies for engagement in literacy lessons and leaves some learners with the impression that they are defective. And there is a definition gap that limits the definition of learning and performance to what has been happening for hundreds of years in Europe but does not serve the Indigenous adolescent literacy learner (National Indian Education Association, 2005). Ultimately, then, there is a justice gap, one that is not paying attention to "the effects of prejudice, cultural alienation, discouragement, and differential aspirations" (Stedman & Kaestle, 1991, p. 126). When these gaps are not addressed, Au (2006) argues, what occurs is *reciprocal distancing*, "a discourse process in which teacher and students invoke existing sociohistorical and political distances between their communities in classroom interactions" (Au, 2006, p. 26, cited in Larson & Irvine, 2006, p. 396).

Goodman (1996) explains the reading process as a sociopsycholinguistic process that involves (among other things) initiating, predicting, confirming, and meaning making. Readers always bring their prior experiences with them to any literacy event, experience that may consist of success or failure, familiarity with the stuff of the text or lack of it, and knowledge of how words can make meaning. Those words, Goodman asserts, have meaning rooted in the individual, the individual's culture, and the relationships that the individual has in the context in which the reading takes place. Reading is social, cultural, political, and relational (Luke & Freebody, 1999). And the very act itself has a history that matters, particularly when an Indigenous adolescent takes written text in hand. It would serve educators well to honor this complexity and to understand their complicity with the West when they work to teach Indigenous students to be literate. Teachers need to understand that they are taking part in an act, at the very least, of biculturality and thus need to consider how they might go about it, whose blessings they need to do so, where the lines between home and community are, their position with respect to those lines, the community's position with respect to them, and the ways in which they are to act as teachers. Of course, teaching reading is different for every teacher, family, and community. Consistent with Indigenous epistemologies, teaching and learning are local and must be thought out and enacted with the nature of that locale very much in mind.

IMPLICATIONS FOR FURTHER RESEARCH

More than 30 years ago, Rich (1973) suggested that teachers learn Indigenous epistemology in order to apply that knowledge to classroom literacy activities. All of our suggestions in the previous sections are in need of further study because they remain, at this point in time, just that: suggestions. We have worked to compose them in a way consistent with more generalized notions of Indigenous epistemologies, but the specificities are deeply important to the success of Indigenous adolescents in school. One area in need of increased study is biliteracy. There are many issues attached to biliteracy (the place of Indigenous language in school; who may teach it; the roles it plays in learning English) that need to be addressed. Access to engaging in such a study is also an issue worthy of further investigation. Some Indigenous groups may not want outsiders involved in such a study, whereas others may welcome the support. A history of language abuse has certainly contributed to the ambiguity about such cooperation.

Our interest in critical literacy reflects some of the current thinking about the importance of such an approach (Lewison, Flint, & Van Sluys, 2002). Critical literacy should not be confused with older notions of "critical thinking" or "higher-order thinking"; rather, critical literacy engages students in issues important to them—issues of power, access, and position (Bomer & Bomer, 2001; Lewison et al., 2002). We wonder how teachers might work with students to compose an agenda for study in which the adolescents truly engage with heart, mind, and an Indigenous perspective. Perhaps students would gain a sense of agency if they, as a collective, were involved with their community in a study and subsequent actions based on the results of the study. For example, how might students become instrumental in studying poverty, attitudes about poverty, and possibilities for action in response to issues rooted in poverty? Students can write their own texts after interviewing elders and tribal community members in their own language, much as Aboriginal students did in their web page texts (Doherty, 2002). The interviewing and reporting process could be used to help create social studies texts about the community while developing reading and writing skills in the tribal language and in English.

Freire (Freire & Macedo, 1987) knew that such work involved much more than reading words; Street (1995) argues that simply learning to read is not sufficient and that the belief that improved literacy rates will improve the economy is simply wrongheaded and reversed. Rather, enhanced economic conditions pave the way for increased literacy. Yet, in regard to Indigenous students, history complicates achievement in literacy further. The research that is urgent appears to be on the "hows" of working with students and communities to develop and act on agendas that they see as important and to include the necessary literacy learning that will provide access to sustained change while including the community as much as possible. Such studies are based on the idea that Indigenous adolescents live in two worlds and that they can thrive in both. With their help, literacy researchers and educators can determine the accuracy of this supposition.

REFERENCES

Au, K. (2006). *Multicultural issues and literacy achievement*. Mahwah, NJ: Erlbaum.

August, D., Goldenberg, C., & Rueda, R. (2006). Native American children and youth: Culture, language, and literacy. *Journal of American Indian Education, 45*, 24–37.

Basso, K. (1996). *Wisdom sits in places*. Albuquerque: University of New Mexico Press.

Belgarde, M. (1992). *The performance and persistence of American Indian undergraduate students at Stanford University*. Unpublished doctoral dissertation, Stanford University.

Belgarde, M. J. (2004). Native American charter schools: Culture, language, and self-determination. In E. Rofes & L. M. Stulberg (Eds.), *Towards a progressive politics of school choice* (pp. 107–124). Albany, NY: SUNY Press.

Belgarde, M. (n.d.). *Responding to Native American language and culture issues in the Southwest: A Native American professor's story*. Unpublished manuscript.

Belgarde, M. J., & LoRé, R. K. (2007). The retention/intervention study of Native American undergraduates at the University of New Mexico. In A. Seidman (Ed.), *Minority student retention* (pp. 167–194). Amityville, NY: Baywood.

Belgarde, M. J., Mitchell, R., & Moquino-Arquero, A. (2002). What do we have to do to create culturally-responsive programs?: A story about American Indian teacher education [Special issue]. *Action in Teacher Education, 24*, 42–54.

Benally, H. (1994). Navajo philosophy of learning and pedagogy. *Journal of American Indian Education, 12*, 23–31.

Bergeson, T., Griffin, A., & Hurtado, D. (2000). *Reading and the Native American learner research report*. Evergreen, WA: Evergreen Center for Educational Improvement. Retrieved May 30, 2007, from *www.evergreen.edu/ecei/docs/RdgNAlrner.pdf*.

Buly, M. R. (2005). Leaving no American Indian/Alaska Native behind: Identifying reading strengths and needs. *Journal of American Indian Education, 44*, 28–52.

Bomer, R., & Bomer, K. (2001). *For a better world: Reading and writing for social action*. Portsmouth, NH: Heinemann.

Bourdieu, P., & Passeron, J.-C. (2000). *Reproduction in education, society, and culture* (2nd ed.). Thousand Oaks, CA: Sage.

Cajete, G. (1994). *Look to the mountain: An ecology of Indigenous education*. Durango, CO: Kvaki' Press.

Cajete, G. (2000). *Native science*. Santa Fe: Clear Light.

Calhoun, J. A., & Annett, C. (2003). American Indian and Indigenous Altai literacies. *International Journal of Learning, 10*, 2113–2124.

Campbell, J. (1991). *The power of myth*. New York: Anchor Books.

Cleary, L. M., & Peacock, T. D. (1998). *Collected wisdom*. Needham Heights, MA: Allyn & Bacon.

Connell-Szasz, M. (1999). *Education and the American Indian: The road to self-determination since 1928*. Albuquerque: University of New Mexico Press.

Costantino, M., & Hurtado, D. S. (2006). Northwest Native American reading curriculum, *Journal of American Indian Education, 45*, 45–49.

Cowell, A. (2002). Bilingual curriculum among the Northern Arapaho: Oral tradition, literacy, and performance. *American Indian Quarterly, 26*, 24–43.

Deloria, V., & Wildcat, D. (2001). *Power and place: Indian education in America*. Golden, CO: Fulcrum Resources.

Deyhle, D., & Swisher, K. (1997). Research in American Indian and Alaska Native education: From assimilation to self-determination. In M. W. Apple (Ed.), *Review of research in education* (Vol. 20, pp. 113–194). Washington, DC: American Educational Research Association.

Doherty, C. (2002). Extending horizons: Critical technological literacy for urban Aboriginal students. *Journal of Adolescent and Adult Literacy, 46*, 50–59.

Dunn, M. (2001). Aboriginal literacy: Reading the tracks. *The Reading Teacher, 54*, 676–687.

Freire, P., & Macedo, D. (1987). *Literacy: Reading the word and reading the world*. South Hadley, MA: Bergin & Garvey.

Gee, J. P. (2002). Identity as an analytic lens for research in education. In W. Secada (Ed.), *Review of research in education* (Vol. 25, pp. 99–125). Washington, DC: American Educational Research Association.

Goodman, K. (1996). *On reading*. Portsmouth, NH: Heinemann.

Gutiérrez, K., & Larson, J. (1994). Language borders: Recitation as hegemonic discourse. *International Journal of Education Reform, 3*, 22–36.

Hawkins, D. (2006). The impact of the Reading First teacher education network on increasing the reading proficiency of American Indian children: How a summer reading institute brought together educators, parents, and community. *Journal of American Indian Education, 45*, 72–76.

Holland, D., Skinner, D., Lachicotte, W., Jr., & Cain, C. (1998). *Identity and agency in cultural worlds*. Cambridge, MA: Harvard University Press.

Hopkins, G., & Bean, T. (1998/1999). Vocabulary learning with the verbal–visual word association strategy in a Native American community. *Journal of Adolescent and Adult Literacy, 42*, 274–284.

Hulan, R., & Warley, L. (1999). Cultural literacy, First Nations and the future of Canadian literacy studies. *Journal of Canadian Studies, 34*, 59–86.

Jacobs, D. T., & Jacobs-Spencer, J. (2001). *Teaching

virtues: Building character across the curriculum. Lanham, MD: Scarecrow Press.

Juneau, D., & Broaddus, M. S. (2006). And still the waters flow: The legacy of Indian education in Montana. *Phi Delta Kappan, 88,* 193–197.

Kapitzke, C., Bogaitini, S., Min, C., MacNeill, G., Mayer, D., Murihead, B., et al. (2000/2001). Weaving words with the dreamweaver: Literacy, indigeneity, and technology. *Journal of Adolescent and Adult Literacy, 44,* 336–348.

Krauss, M. (1996). Status of Native American language endangerment. In B. Cantoni (Ed.), *Stabilizing indigenous languages* (pp. 16–21). Flagstaff: Northern Arizona University Press.

Lareau, A. (2000). *Home advantage: Social class and parental intervention in elementary education.* Lanham, MD: Rowan & Littlefield.

Lave, J., & Wenger, E. (1991). *Situated learning: Legitimate peripheral participation.* New York: Cambridge University Press.

Levitt, J. (2007). *Socratic seminar in a Navajo classroom.* Manuscript submitted for publication.

Lewison, M., Flint, A. S., & Van Sluys, K. (2002). Taking on critical literacy: The journey of newcomers and novices. *Language Arts, 79,* 382–392.

LoRé, R. K. (1998). *Art as development theory: The spiritual ecology of learning and the influence of traditional Native American education.* Unpublished doctoral dissertation, University of New Mexico, Albuquerque.

LoRé, R. (n. d.). *Aesthetic values, culture and transcendence: East Asian and "Traditional Pueblo" thinking.* Unpublished manuscript.

Luke, A., & Freebody, P. (1999). Further notes on the four resources model. *Reading Online, 4*(2). Retrieved April 2, 2006, from *www.readingonline.org/research/lukefreebody.html.*

McCarty, T. (2002). *A place to be Navajo: Rough Rock and the struggle for self-determination in Indigenous schooling.* Mahwah, NJ: Erlbaum.

McCarty, T., & Watahomigie, L. J. (2004). Language and literacy in American Indian and Alaska Native communities. In B. Pérez (Ed.), *Sociocultural contexts of language and literacy* (pp. 79–110). Mahwah, NJ: Erlbaum.

Mehan, H. (1982). The structure of classroom events and their consequences for student performance. In P. Gilmore & A. Glatthorn (Eds.), *Children in and out of school: Ethnography and education* (pp. 59–87). Washington, DC: Center for Applied Linguistics.

Meriam, L. B. (1928). *The problem with Indian administration.* Baltimore, MD: Johns Hopkins University Press.

Meyer, R. (2001). *Phonics exposed: Understanding and resisting systematic direct intense phonics instruction.* Mahwah, NJ: Erlbaum.

Moje, E. (2002). Re-framing adolescent literacy research for new times: Studying youth as resource. *Reading Research and Instruction, 41,* 211–227.

Moll, L., Amanti, C., Neff, D., & González, N. (2005). Funds of knowledge for teaching: Using a qualitative approach to connect homes and classrooms. In N. González, L. Moll, & C. Amanti (Eds.), *Funds of knowledge: Theorizing practices in households, communities, and schools* (pp. 71–87). Mahwah, NJ: Erlbaum.

National Indian Education Association. (2005). *Preliminary report on No Child Left Behind in Indian Country.* Washington, DC: National Indian Education Association.

Noll, B. (1998). Experiencing literacy in and out of school: Case studies of two American Indian youths. *Journal of Literacy Research, 30,* 205–232.

Philips, S. (1972). Participant structures and communicative competence: Warm Springs children in community and classroom. In C. Cazden, V. John, & D. Hymes (Eds.), *Functions of language in the classroom* (pp. 370–394). New York: Teachers College Press.

Pittman, B. (Director), & Leckie, K. R. (Writer). (1989). *Where the spirit lives* [Film]. Toronto, Ontario, Canada: Canadian Broadcasting Company.

Pugh, K. R., Sandak, R., Frost, S. J., Moore, D., & Menci, W. E. (2006). Examining reading development and reading disability in diverse languages and cultures: Potential contributions from functional neuroimaging. *Journal of American Indian Education, 45,* 60–76.

Reyhner, J. (2001). *Teaching reading to American Indian/Alaska Native students.* Charleston, WV (ERIC Document Reproduction Service No. ED 459 972). Retrieved June 9, 2007, from *www.ericdigests.org/2002-3/reading.htm.*

Rich, G. (1973). *Teaching reading to the American Indian.* Berkeley: University of California Press.

Romero, M. E. (1994). Identifying giftedness among Keresan Pueblo Indians: The Keres study. *Journal of American Indian Education, 34,* 35–58.

Sapir, E. (1958). The status of linguistics as a science. In D. G. Mandelbaum (Ed.), *Culture, language and personality* (pp. 129–165). Berkeley: University of California Press.

Scully, V. (1975). *Pueblo mountain village dance.* New York: Viking.

Singer, J. (2006). *Stirring up justice: Reading and writing to change the world.* Portsmouth, NH: Heinemann.

Smagorinsky, P., & Coppock, J. (1995). The reader, the text, the context: An exploration of a choreographed response to literature. *Journal of Reading Behavior, 27,* 271–298.

Smagorinsky, P., Zoss, M., & O'Donnell-Allen, C. (2005). Mask-making as identity project in a high school English class: A case study. *English in Education, 39,* 60–75.

Stedman, L. C., & Kaestle, C. F. (1991). Literacy and reading performance in the United States from 1880 to the present. In C. F. Kaestle, H. Damon-Moore, L. C. Stedman, K. Tinsley, & W. V. Trollinger (Eds.), *Literacy in the United States: Readers and reading since 1880* (pp. 75–128). New Haven, CT: Yale University Press.

Strauss, S. (2005). *The linguistics, neurology, and politics of phonics: Silent "E" speaks out.* Mahwah, NJ: Erlbaum.

Street, B. (1995). *Social literacies: Critical approaches to literacy in development, ethnography and education.* New York: Longman.

Stuckey, J. E. (1991). *The violence of literacy.* Portsmouth, NH: Heinemann.

Tall Bull, L. (2007). Preserving our histories for those yet to be born. *Phi Delta Kappan, 88,* 192.

Wright, B. (1976). *Pueblo shields.* Phoenix, AZ: Northland.

Zoss, M., Smagorinsky, P., & O'Donnell-Allen, C. (2007). Mask-making as representational process: The situated composition of an identity project in a senior English class. *International Journal of Education and the Arts, 8*(10). Retrieved from *http://www.Ijea.org/v8n10.pdf*

Author Index

Subject Index